States, Nations, and the Great Powers

Why are some regions prone to war while others remain at peace? What conditions cause regions to move from peace to war and vice versa? This book offers a novel theoretical explanation for the differences in levels of and transitions between war and peace. The author distinguishes between "hot" and "cold" outcomes, depending on intensity of the war or the peace, and then uses three key concepts (state, nation, and the international system) to argue that it is the specific balance between states and nations in different regions that determines the hot or warm outcomes: the lower the balance, the higher the war proneness of the region, while the higher the balance, the warmer the peace. The international systemic factors, for their part, affect only the cold outcomes of cold war and cold peace.

The theory of regional war and peace developed in this book is examined through case studies of the post-1945 Middle East, the Balkans and South America in the nineteenth and twentieth centuries, and post-1945 Western Europe. It uses comparative data from all regions and concludes by proposing ideas on how to promote peace in war-torn regions.

BENJAMIN MILLER is a professor in the School of Political Sciences at the University of Haifa, Israel. He is the author of *When Opponents Cooperate: Great Power Conflict and Collaboration in World Politics* (1995).

CAMBRIDGE STUDIES IN INTERNATIONAL RELATIONS: 104

States, Nations, and the Great Powers

Cambridge Studies in International Relations is a joint initiative of Cambridge University Press and the British International Studies Association (BISA). The series will include a wide range of material, from undergraduate textbooks and surveys to research-based monographs and collaborative volumes. The aim of the series is to publish the best new scholarship in International Studies from Europe, North America, and the rest of the world.

CAMBRIDGE STUDIES IN INTERNATIONAL RELATIONS

103 *Beate Jahn (ed.)*
Classical theory in international relations

102 *Andrew Linklater and Hidemi Suganami*
The English School of international relations
A contemporary reassessment

101 *Colin Wight*
Agents, structures and international relations
Politics as ontology

100 *Michael C. Williams*
The realist tradition and the limits of international relations

99 *Ivan Arreguín-Toft*
How the weak win wars
A theory of asymmetric conflict

98 *Michael Barnett and Raymond Duvall*
Power in global governance

97 *Yale H. Ferguson and Richard W. Mansbach*
Remapping global politics
History's revenge and future shock

96 *Christian Reus-Smit*
The politics of international law

95 *Barry Buzan*
From international to world society?
English School theory and the social structure of globalisation

94 *K. J. Holsti*
Taming the sovereigns
Institutional change in international politics

93 *Bruce Cronin*
Institutions for the common good
International protection regimes in international security

Series list continues after index

States, Nations, and the Great Powers

The Sources of Regional War and Peace

Benjamin Miller

CAMBRIDGE UNIVERSITY PRESS
Cambridge, New York, Melbourne, Madrid, Cape Town, Singapore, São Paulo

Cambridge University Press
The Edinburgh Building, Cambridge CB2 8RU, UK

Published in the United States of America by Cambridge University Press, New York

www.cambridge.org
Information on this title: www.cambridge.org/9780521691611

First published 2007

Printed in the United Kingdom at the University Press, Cambridge

A catalogue record for this book is available from the British Library

ISBN 978-0-521-87122-8 hardback

ISBN 978-0-521-69161-1 paperback

Contents

Figures

Tables

Preface and acknowledgments

This book investigates the origins of regional war and peace. My interest in this subject can be traced back to the first day of a major regional war in which I actively took part as a very young soldier – the 1973 Yom Kippur War. On the first day of that war I found myself engaged in tank battles with Syrian forces and in the early morning of the day after I – together with a few other Israeli soldiers – was surrounded by a major Syrian armored force in a very small bunker in the southern part of the Golan Heights.

I will not go here into the details of the very frightening experience in that bunker and following experiences later in the war. But such traumatic events have left me with a strong desire to look for an explanation for the occurrence of armed conflicts, notably those which escalate to large-scale violence, and how to manage, reduce, or overcome such conflicts and to move from war to peace.

As a student of Kenneth Waltz at the University of California, Berkeley, I fully realized the importance of the international system, and specifically the great powers and their influence on a great variety of events in world politics. Thus, my first book focused on the sources of conflict and cooperation among the great powers. Even though the great powers exercise important effects on regional affairs as well, as this book fully acknowledges, I have felt that they do not provide the only answer to the great differences among different regions with regard to their level of war and peace. Thus, I faced two major challenges:

1. To define the general type of effects the great powers have on regional war and peace as compared to the effects of the regional and domestic factors. Here came the idea – developed in this book – that rather than just a dichotomy between war and peace, we may have "cold" and

"hot/warm" war and peace situations: the great powers affect the cold outcomes, while the regional/domestic factors affect the more intense hot outcomes.

2. Which are the key regional/domestic factors that provide the most powerful explanation of the variations in war and peace among regions and of the transitions of regions from war to peace and vice versa? My thinking and research have led me to the idea that the concepts of "state" and "nation," and especially the balance between them, as explained in this book, while overlooked in the mainstream international relations theorizing on war and peace, deserve a closer look. Indeed, they are especially crucial for understanding the phenomenon of regional war and peace – both civil and interstate wars and a significant number of "mixed" domestic and transborder violent incidents.

This process of a search for an explanation of the regional war and peace puzzle has been a long one, sometimes enjoyable and at times frustrating. At least one big advantage of such a protracted process is that it enabled me to benefit from the wise advice of many wonderful people. Thus, I have accumulated a lot of debts to numerous colleagues and students even if, unfortunately, I may have forgotten to acknowledge some of them here. While the comments improved the manuscript quite a bit, I remain, of course, fully responsible for the book's content.

The initial stages of thinking about these issues started in an exciting fellowship year at the Center for International Studies at Princeton University. I would like to thank Professor Aaron Friedberg for giving me the opportunity to spend the year in such a stimulating environment and to benefit also from the many insights of George Downs, Michael Doyle, Robert Gilpin, and Bill Wohlforth, as well as Ilene Cohen, among other engaging people at the Princeton Center. My conversations and exchanges with Jack Levy, Ed Rhodes, Matthew Randall, and Jeffrey Taliaferro were also helpful in shaping my theoretical thinking on war and peace issues.

When I came back to teach at the Hebrew University, a group of colleagues helped to develop the initial ideas I brought from my stay at Princeton – particularly Hillel Frisch, Avraham Sela, Norrin Ripsman, Galia Press Bar-Nathan, and Elie Podeh, as well as Yitzhak Brudni, Raymond Cohen, Uri Bialer, Yaacov Bar Siman-Tov, Sasson Sofer, Arie Kacowicz, Michael Brecher, and Emanuel Adler. In addition to my faculty colleagues, a group of very able graduate students worked as my research assistants at different stages (some later became colleagues) and provided invaluable help with a lot of dedication and clever ideas. Among this wonderful group I would like to note the great help of Oded Lowenheim, Ram Erez, Boaz Atzili, Yoav Gercheck, Ohad Laslau, Shlomi Carmi, and particularly Korina Kagan, who was always extremely helpful in numerous areas of the research and the writing. Uri Reznick was a first-rate research assistant, and later collaborator, on a study of the nineteenth-century Balkans. Uri's great contribution is reflected in some of the key empirical portions of chapter 6.

During my stay as a visiting professor at Duke University, a number of colleagues posed tough challenges to my ideas and the direction my study was taking. I hope that, by forcing me to rethink some propositions and methods, they have helped me to improve the manuscript. I especially appreciate the regular meetings I held with Robert Keohane over lunch – always after he had read some portion of the study and was ready with written comments and suggestions. Extremely helpful and challenging were also Joe Grieco, Hein Goemans, Peter Feaver, Chris Gelpi, and Martin Seeleib-Kaiser. All read some important portions of the study and provided detailed and insightful comments. Other helpful and supportive colleagues at Duke included Don Horowitz, Bruce Jentleson, and Allan Kornberg. Also at Duke a group of graduate students was both demanding and helpful in its questioning and assistance. Among them were Jonathan Van Loo, Phil Demske, and the participants at a joint graduate seminar given by Hein Goemans and myself, who discussed the typescript at length.

My extended stay at Duke was also useful for delivering talks on the study in stimulating places such as Princeton University, the University of Chicago (PIPES), the University of Virginia, McGill University, Concordia University, James Madison College at Michigan State University, and of course a number of seminars at Duke. I thank the participants in these seminars, especially Aaron Friedberg, Richard Ullman, Charles Lipson, John Mearsheimer, Alex Downes, Charles Glaser, T. V. Paul, Dale Copeland, John Owen, Mohammed Ayoob, Norrin Ripsman, and Paul C. Noble.

The last stage of the long journey of writing and rewriting this manuscript took place when I came back to Israel, and colleagues and students at the University of Haifa and from other places gave much needed help for the final formulations of the study. Among them, Avi Kober, Jeremy Pressman, Zeev Maoz, and Ben D. Mor as well as Ranan D. Kuperman, Zach Levey, Sammy Smooha, Gabi Ben-Dor, Tal Dingott-Alkopher, Avi Ben-Zvi, and Uri Bar-Joseph were especially helpful. A number of graduate students provided a lot of badly needed help in many senses. Among them I would like to note Erez Shoshani, Moran Mandelbaum, and Zvika Kaplan, as well as Sharon Mankovitz in particular; above all Dov Levin was extremely helpful beyond the call of duty in numerous senses. Sharon was very instrumental in preparing the data-file on the post–1945 wars (see appendix B) while Dov refined and updated it as well as the comparative regional tables (see appendix A). I would also like to thank participants in seminars at the University of Haifa and the Hebrew University of Jerusalem as well as participants in the annual meetings and workshops of the Israeli Association for International Studies (IAIS) in Bar-Ilan, Haifa, Tel Aviv, and Jerusalem Universities. As the president of this association during 2003–7 I would like to thank my assistants there – Erez, Zvika, and Keren Raz-Netzer – and the members for their help and insightful comments.

Finally, many thanks to the very helpful team at Cambridge University Press – the editor, John Haslam, and his assistant Carrie Cheek. Both provided important assistance at various stages of the typescript preparation. Special thanks to the extremely helpful and cheerful copyeditor, Karen Anderson Howes, who has done a superb job in copyediting my typescript.

I am grateful for the generous financial assistance of the Israel Science Foundation (founded by the Israel Academy of Sciences and Humanities); the Tel Aviv University Institute for Diplomacy and Regional Cooperation; the Department of Political Science, Duke University; the National Security Studies Center at the University of Haifa; the Tami Steimnitz Center for Peace Research at Tel Aviv University; and the Jaffee Center for Strategic Studies at Tel Aviv University.

I have much revised earlier versions of some limited portions of this book which have been published before in "Between War and Peace: Systemic Effects on the Transition of the Middle East and the Balkans from the Cold War to the Post-Cold War Era," *Security Studies* 11, 2 (Winter 2001–2), 1–52; "Conflict in the Balkans, 1830–1913: Combining Levels of Analysis," *International Politics* 40, 3 (September 2003), 365–407, coauthored with Uri Reznick; "When and How Regions Become Peaceful: Potential Theoretical Pathways to Peace," *International Studies Review* 7 (2005), 229–267 © (2005) the International Studies Association; and "Balance of Power or the State-to-Nation Balance: Explaining Middle

East War-Propensity," *Security Studies*, 15, 4 (October–December 2006). I would like to thank these journals for permitting me to use material that first appeared in their pages.

Such a protracted and demanding process of writing a book is made easier by a supportive family. I would like to thank my wife, Liora, and my daughter Adi for their wonderful and warm love and support during the occasional crises related to writing the typescript. My daughter, in particular, inspires my curiosity at creating two-by-two tables to capture logically key arguments of the manuscript. My sister Eti and her lovely family were always a source of great encouragement. Any amount of words would not be able to capture the enormous support of my late parents, Zvi and Zunia Miller, and my late aunt and uncle, Tzipora and Yitzhak Sarfi. I dedicated my earlier book to my parents and to my wife and daughter. I would like to dedicate this book to my sister and my uncle and aunt for all their love and material and spiritual encouragement.

1 Why some regions are peaceful and others are not

This book offers a new theory of war and peace. I argue that if we approach the question of war and peace from the regional perspective, we may gain new insights which are otherwise obscured. The new theory developed here thus offers an explanation of the variations between war and peace within and among regions. It explains why some regions are particularly war-prone, while others are so peaceful that war among the regional states has become practically unthinkable. The theory also explains why regions become more or less war-prone over time.

The twentieth century was the stage on which two puzzling, not to say contradictory, phenomena were at play: some regions, such as the Middle East, were scenes of tense conflicts and numerous wars, while others, such as South America, suffered only a limited number of wars.[1] During the very same period, however, Europe profoundly transformed itself from an unstable, war-prone region into a peaceful, stable one. South America's move toward peace began at the end of the nineteenth century, but it has not yet attained the depth and institutional overlay that now characterize the European regional peace.

Thus, in the contemporary international system, some regions are peaceful (Europe, the Americas), while other regions either experience recurrent bloody conflicts, or are constantly on the verge of descending into war (East Asia, South Asia, the Middle East, and, at least until recently, the Balkans). These examples show that, over time, there is a

[1] See Geller and Singer 1998, ch. 5; Holsti 1996, Table 2.1, p. 22, Table 2.3, p. 24, and appendix pp. 210–224; and appendix B in this book. On territorial disputes, see Huth 1996, pp. 27–29, 195–251; 1999, pp. 48–50. For classifications of conflicts in different periods, see Luard 1986, pp. 421–447, esp. pp. 442–447; and Holsti 1991, especially pp. 140–142, 144–145, 214–216, 274–278, 280, 307, 308. On conflicts involving non-state rivals, see Gurr 1993.

marked variation in the level of violence among regions – and within regions.[2] In this book I explain this intriguing puzzle; a puzzle, moreover, that has not yet been systematically or satisfactorily examined in international relations scholarship.

I provide this explanation by proposing a theory of regional war and peace. This theory explains variations in war and peace among different regions – and also transitions from war to peace, and vice versa, within a region. In order to provide a more nuanced and powerful explanation, I further distinguish between "hot" and "cold" types of regional war and peace, depending on the intensity of the war or peace.

My explanation is based on three key concepts (I develop each concept in detail later): state, nation, and the international system. I argue that the specific balance between states and nations in a given region determines the more intense, or hot or warm, outcomes (that is, whether the region will experience hot wars or a warm peace). The international system – more specifically, the type of engagement in the region by the great powers – affects the cold outcomes, that is, whether the region will be the scene of a cold war or a cold peace.

What I call the "state-to-nation balance" is the key underlying cause that affects the disposition of a region toward war – in effect, determining the war proneness of the region. The state-to-nation balance refers to the degree of congruence between the division of the region into territorial states and the national aspirations and political identifications of the region's peoples. This balance also refers to the prevalence of strong versus weak states in the region. There is a state-to-nation imbalance when there is a lack of congruence between states and national identifications and at least some of the regional states are weak states.[3]

Some patterns of regional behavior and outcomes may appear to conform to more traditional realist expectations about the prevalence of

[2] See, for example, Zeev Maoz's 2005 Dyadic MID Dataset (version 2.0), psfaculty.ucdavis.edu/zmaoz/dyadmid.html. See also ch. 3 and appendix B in this book.

[3] For a more elaborate definition – and measurement – of the state-to-nation balance, see chs. 2 and 3. I draw here on Van Evera, who calls it "the state-to-nation ratio" (1994, 10–11). Van Evera's term is, however, too mechanical and relies too much on a numerical ratio between states and nations, whereas in my usage the number of states and nations in the region is not the only dimension. In contrast to Van Evera, who focuses on ethnic nationalism, I accept that nationalism can be either ethnic or civic (again see chs. 2 and 3). Moreover, given my conception of the state-to-nation balance, it is possible that in a region where the number of states is much smaller that the number of ethnic groups the state-to-nation imbalance may be low – for example, in North America. Conversely, a high state-to-nation imbalance may occur in a region where the number of ethnic groups does not vastly exceed the number of states – for example, the Balkans after 1991.

interstate conflict and the recurrence of war among the local states. The underlying explanation I offer for these phenomena, however, is not based on causal factors which realists usually highlight, such as the distribution of capabilities (Waltz 1979) or a quest for hegemony (Mearsheimer 2001), but rather on the state-to-nation balance within the region itself. Applying this logic to the dangerous conflict between China and Taiwan, for example, would lead us to expect that "the policy objective behind China's coercive diplomacy is national unification rather than regional hegemony" (Wang 2000, p. 61). Different approaches to addressing such a state-to-nation balance – crucially, whether such approaches or strategies derive from global factors or regional/domestic factors – would then produce different types and levels of regional peace.

In sum, the explanation I propose combines and integrates global factors and domestic/regional factors in a single theoretical construct. In other words, I argue that the old and apparently irreconcilable divide between systemic and regional/domestic explanations of state behavior may be bridged, and this book offers a theoretical synthesis that shows how a fruitful and compelling theoretical coexistence may be created within different schools of IR scholarship, and between IR scholarship and comparative politics.

Why there is a need for a new theory of regional war and peace: filling the gaps in the existing literature

Balancing the explanatory emphasis on great power rivalry with richer regional war and peace theories

Despite some recent notable developments, the international security field is still dominated by the traditional issues of great power rivalry and war. International relations theory has traditionally focused on the international system as a whole, emphasizing the role and influence of the great powers;[4] more recently, this emphasis has been augmented by appeals to international institutions and regimes as explanatory variables of state behavior.[5] The issue of regional war and peace is important

[4] See Miller 2002, in which I cite and discuss many of these works. See also Van Evera 1999, Copeland 2000, and Mearsheimer 2001.
[5] See Krasner 1983, Keohane 1984, Oye 1986, Grieco 1988, 1990, Mearsheimer 1995 and Keohane and Martin's response (1995), and Kagan 1997/8. For a more recent contribution, see Ikenberry 2001.

in general, especially in the post-Cold War period, but it has not enjoyed the kind of scholarly attention these other, more traditional, issues have. Conventional IR theories notwithstanding, most wars and war-related deaths are no longer attributable to great power conflicts, and can no longer be understood as the mere reflection or result of great power rivalry. This study, accordingly, develops a new theory of regional orders which is informed by the traditional literature on international conflict and international relations, but which takes advantage of the new literature on ethnic conflict, civil war, and small state behavior.

Lack of integration of regional and international factors

Neorealists emphasize the primacy of the international system in bringing about regional events and developments, while regional specialists argue that it is unique regional factors that are the most important in fostering the conditions that cause or drive regional events. Many analysts accept that both levels are important to one degree or another, but they do not offer modes for integrating the two levels which, at the same time, are theoretically rigorous and parsimonious. This study offers a novel way of doing this.

IR theory and regional conflicts: the conceptual limits of explanations

Realist and liberal approaches to war in general, and regional war in particular,[6] share a common problem: both are weakened by overlooking the political context of regional wars, most notably, the substantive issues over which wars are fought, especially issues related to nationalism, territory, and boundaries.[7] This weakness is the main reason why neither theory accounts very well for variations in the propensity toward war among regions and within regions. Both approaches treat the nation-state as an actor that either reacts to threats and opportunities in the international system (realism) or behaves in accordance with the nature of its regime and the effects of economic interdependence and international institutions (liberalism). For both theories, the nation-state is unified at least in the sense that states and nations are identical, and thus both theories use the terms "state" and "nation" interchangeably, as

[6] Realist and liberal approaches to war and peace are discussed below.
[7] This point is elaborated below. On the limitations in the treatment of nationalism by both realism and liberalism, see Hoffmann 1998.

the titles of major books in the field show.[8] There is an identity between states and nations in some regions (the Americas and Western Europe), but they are not the same in other regions (for example, the Balkans, Africa, the Middle East, and some parts of Asia).[9] This variation in the commensurability of state and nation among regions goes a long way toward explaining the war/peace variation among them. The imbalance between states and nations has crucial implications for international politics because of the centrality of the state as the key actor in the international system, and because of nations being the key political locus of identification at least since the late eighteenth century.[10] Moreover, national self-determination is a major norm legitimizing sovereignty in the international system, and a powerful motivation for people to fight for their independence.[11]

Neither realism nor liberalism can thus adequately explain the motivations of the regional actors to resort to violence, if such motivations are derived from problems of state-to-nation imbalance. It is the regional state-to-nation imbalance that provides a basic motivation for war, and therefore disposes certain regions to be more war-prone than others.

The state-to-nation balance – the underlying cause that determines regional war proneness – incorporates substantive issues of war (territory, boundaries, state creation, and state-making) and the motivations for war (hypernationalist, pan-national or secessionist revisionist ideologies). There are other influential ideologies and affiliations that play a role in shaping the war disposition of a region, but nationalism is an especially powerful ideology,[12] and the state-to-nation issue[13] bears

[8] For example, G. Snyder and Deising, *Conflict Among Nations* (1977); Grieco, *Cooperation Among Nations* (1990); Geller and Singer, *Nations at War* (1998); and Arthur Stein, *Why Nations Cooperate* (1991). These authors had in mind "states" but used "nations" interchangeably.

[9] For details, see chs. 4 and 6.

[10] Most modern scholarship dates nationalism, as a movement and ideology, as emerging with the Industrial Revolution and especially the French Revolution in the late eighteenth century. See, for example, Gellner 1983, B. Anderson 1991, Hobsbawm 1990, and Breuilly 1993. However, other leading researchers of nationalism argue that there has been a certain extent of continuity between traditional/old nations and modern nationalism. See H. Seton-Watson 1977 and A. Smith 1991, 1998, and 2000, pp. 25–51 (where he provides a comprehensive overview of the debate and references). See also Greenfeld 1992. On nationalism, see also chs. 2 and 3.

[11] On the connection between nationalism and popular sovereignty, and the implicit relations with international peace, see Mill 1861, cited also in Mayall 1990, pp. 27–29.

[12] Gellner 1983, A. Smith 2000.

[13] For ease of reading, I will generally use "state-to-nation" as a modifier instead of "state-to-nation balance": so "state-to-nation issue" rather than "state-to-nation balance issue."

directly on the key values of states – territorial integrity and, in some cases, state survival and independence.

Current treatments of territorial conflict: a useful framework but not a theoretical explanation

Since the early 1990s, more attention has been paid in the IR literature to territorial conflicts as a major source of war.[14] These discussions are useful, and they move us in the right direction for understanding war and peace, but they do not provide a theoretical explanation of *why* such wars occur so frequently, and under what conditions territorial conflicts are more likely to escalate to large-scale regional violence. Moreover, the argument in the literature on territorial issues that conflicts erupt over territory is correct, but it does not, by itself, offer an explanation as to whether the conflict owes to the territory's strategic location, its economic resources, or the state-to-nation issues involved with it.

From the dyadic level to regional outcomes

I argue that the state-to-nation imbalance is a major source of territorial conflicts, and especially of those regional conflicts that escalate to war and are hard to resolve peacefully. The literatures on territorial conflicts and enduring rivalries focus on the dyadic level (that is, the relationship between any two states in a region), but I suggest that the extent of the state-to-nation imbalance in a region affects the stability of the region as a whole because of the strategic interdependence among the constituent units. The primary security concerns of these units link them together "sufficiently closely that their national securities cannot realistically be considered apart from one another."[15]

Too high a divide between domestic and international conflict

The theoretical framework I offer overcomes the divide between domestic/civil and interstate conflict. Analysts have emphasized this divide especially since the end of the Cold War, arguing that civil wars were replacing international wars as the key conflicts in world politics. This study shows the common origins of numerous conflicts of both types. In many cases we have "mixed" internal and transborder

14 Holsti 1991, Vasquez 1993, 1995, Goertz and Diehl 1992b, Huth 1996, and Diehl 1999.
15 This is Buzan's (1991, ch. 5, p. 190) conception of a region, or what he calls a "security complex." This is further developed in Buzan and Waever 2003.

conflicts. Two examples are directly related to the post-2003 Iraqi crisis and its regional repercussions: the Kurdish problem involving Iraq, Turkey, Iran, and Syria; and the relations between Shiites and Sunnis in Iraq and their effects not only on Iraq's stability but also on many countries in the Middle East because of transborder ties among Shiites (in south Iraq, Iran, Lebanon, Saudi Arabia, Bahrain) and Sunnis (in numerous Arab countries).[16] Such conflicts – indeed, this type of conflict – are influenced by both systemic and regional/domestic factors. Thus, we need a theory that will integrate both types of factors in a rigorous and compelling way. This is what I do in this book: I offer a new, integrated theory of war and peace. I argue that a regional perspective is the most useful in explaining these *mixed* conflicts.

Explaining both war and peace

In the literature, the causes of war and sources of peace are usually treated separately, but it is not possible to understand transitions from war to peace without knowing the sources of regional wars and how different peace strategies address them. Different theories explain varying aspects of regional peace, but these theories are disconnected from each other, and as a result there is no single framework that integrates them into a coherent theoretical construct capable of accounting for differences among regions, or for differences within regions over time, that is, regional transitions from war to peace and vice versa.

9/11, the post-Cold War era, and regional conflicts

Following the end of the Cold War, many analysts expected that regional security would become separate from global security,[17] especially from the concerns of the great powers. This was because the great powers were no longer involved in an intense competition in all parts of the globe, as was the case during the Cold War. The events of 9/11 show, however, that there is a tight relationship between global security, US

[16] Other examples include the Balkans, both in the nineteenth century and in the post-Cold War era, and other post-Soviet crises; the Arab-Israeli-Palestinian conflict; Syria, Lebanon, the various ethnic communities there, the Palestinian refugees in Lebanon and Israel; India–Pakistan and Kashmir; Congo and the other states in the Great Lakes region in Africa; the Greek and Turkish communities in Cyprus, Greece, and Turkey; and North Vietnam, South Vietnam, and the Vietcong – a conflict that also spilled into Cambodia and Laos.

[17] See, for example, Lake and Morgan 1997.

national security, transnational terrorism, failed states, and issues of regional conflict (such as the relations among Afghanistan, its neighbors, and transborder ethnic groups; the Pakistan–India conflict over Kashmir; Iraq, Iran, and Gulf security; the Arab–Israeli conflict; and challenges to the stability of Arab regimes and other weak states). The US 9/11 Commission, set up by the US Congress to investigate the events leading up to the 9/11 terror attacks, agrees. Among its conclusions is this: "In the twentieth century, strategists focused on the world's great industrial heartlands. In the twenty-first, the focus is in the opposite direction, towards remote regions and failing states."[18] Thus, regional conflicts and their resolution should be addressed not only for their intrinsic importance, but also in order to advance the cause of international security and stability. The resolution of these regional conflicts, however, would be more likely were we to understand better the sources of such conflicts. The theory I offer makes a contribution toward such an understanding.

Indeed, one major reason why questions of regional war and peace have assumed added importance in the post-Cold War era is the growing salience of regional conflicts as a result of the end of the superpower rivalry, and the potential consequences of regional conflicts for international stability.[19] Militarily, the proliferation of weapons of mass destruction and their means of delivery to different regions may eventually pose a threat, if they do not already, not only to regional security, but to global security as well. Regional conflicts can place access to markets and resources at risk – Middle Eastern oil is a good example. As we have already witnessed in the Balkans, local conflicts may accelerate massive flows of refugees across state and regional boundaries, giving rise and added potency to xenophobic anti-foreigner extremism in Western societies.[20] These tendencies may, in turn, challenge the political stability in leading states such as Germany.

Regional developments may have gained importance in the post-Cold War era, but there is nothing new about the centrality of regional wars within the general phenomenon of international war.[21] Most of the interstate wars listed in the Correlates of War data, for example, were wars

[18] Quoted in *Financial Times*, July 23, 2004, 2. See 9/11 Commission 2004. See also the summary of the report's recommendations cited in *International Herald Tribune*, July 24–25, 2004, 1.

[19] Miller and Kagan 1997, p. 52.

[20] See, among others, Rudolph 2003.

[21] Vasquez 1993, 1995; Holsti 1991; and the literature review in Goertz and Diehl 1992b, pp. 1–31, citing especially the work of Starr, Most, and Siverson.

between neighbors, that is, regional wars.[22] More broadly, about two-thirds of the instances of threat to use force and of the actual use of force from 1816 to 1976 also took place between neighbors. As the level of threat increases, and that of violence escalates, so does the frequency of neighbors being drawn into the conflict.[23] Thus, with the exception of the great powers and their involvement in wars, war is largely a regional phenomenon – a neighborhood issue. Making peace among neighbors thus becomes even more important, because neighboring states are more likely than any other kind of states to get into a war with each other.

Some argue that the process of globalization has intensified with the end of the Cold War, and that this process leads to greater global uniformity which diminishes regional differences.[24] Others, however, point out that the end of the Cold War produced increasing regional variations, especially in the area of security.[25]

Indeed, the end of the Cold War has brought to the surface even greater variations among regions with respect to war and peace. In contrast to post-1945 international norms and practice (Zacher 2001), Iraq, a state with revisionist aspirations,[26] annexed a sovereign neighboring state, Kuwait, in summer 1990. The Iraqi action led to a major US intervention and to the First Gulf War in 1991. Following the 9/11 attacks, the United States came to see the Middle East, particularly Iraq, as a major source of terrorism and the proliferation of weapons of mass destruction. This brought about the Second Gulf War, in which the United States invaded and occupied Iraq in spring 2003. This time the United States had a wider agenda, one which called for bringing democracy to Iraq and, coupled with other US diplomatic initiatives, to the Middle East as a whole. Another example is the Balkans where, after forty-five years of relative calm, the collapse of the USSR led to an eruption of violence which eventually brought about US-led NATO interventions in Bosnia in 1995 and Kosovo in 1999. Violent eruptions also took place in other

[22] Cited in Vasquez 1993, pp. 134–135. See also the findings of Holsti 1991. The Correlates of War project is a major quantitative study of wars. It focuses on collecting data about the history of wars and conflict among states. The project has advanced the quantitative research into the causes of warfare. See, for example, Small and Singer 1982.

[23] Gochman 1990, cited in Vasquez 1993, pp. 135–136, Gochman et al. 1996/7, pp. 181–182.

[24] For an overview and citations, see Clark 1997, and Buzan and Waever 2003, pp. 7–10.

[25] See Friedberg 1993/4, p. 5. For a useful overview, see Hurrell 1995, and Katzenstein 1996a. See also Lake and Morgan 1997, pp. 6–7; Holm and Sorensen 1995, ch. 1; and Buzan and Waever 2003, pp. 10–13; in the rest of these three books the authors focus on different regions. From another perspective, see Huntington's critique of the globalization thesis and his notion of the "clash of civilizations" (1993, 1996).

[26] See ch. 4.

areas of the collapsing Soviet empire (for example, the war between Armenia and Azerbaijan), although they did not elicit Western military interventions.

At the same time other parts of the world had experienced more encouraging developments. The conflict-ridden Third World witnessed an encouraging process of conflict resolution in the late 1980s–early 1990s, as evident in the resolution of simmering conflicts in Southern Africa, the Horn of Africa, Southwest and Southeast Asia, and Central America. Moreover, for the first time in the long history of the Middle East conflict, most of the major parties, including Syria and the Palestinians – parties that had been reluctant to take part in the peace process with Israel – convened under US and Soviet auspices at the Madrid peace conference of October 1991. During the following five years, the adversaries met, now under the formal cosponsorship of the United States and Russia, for a series of bilateral and multilateral talks in Washington, Moscow, and other world capitals.[27] Since the Oslo accords of 1993, the peace process in the Middle East has led to a series of interim agreements between Israel and the Palestinians. These agreements facilitated the Jordanian–Israeli peace treaty of October 1994, and growing Israeli diplomatic and economic relations with Arab states from North Africa to the Persian Gulf. In the wake of the collapse of the summer 2000 Camp David summit between Israel and the Palestinians, however, violence between Palestinians and Israelis erupted again in fall 2000.

These diverging trends – toward peace in one region and war in another, and toward peace and then war within the same region – led analysts and practitioners to note two sets of differences: the difference between regions regarding the prospects of war and peace in the post-Cold War era, and the differences within the same region with regard to the propensity toward war between the Cold War and post-Cold War eras. Expressions such as "New Europe,"[28] "New East Asia,"[29] and, even more controversially, "New Middle East"[30] capture this new perspective. These variations in the tendency toward war among regions and

[27] Kaye 2001.

[28] See Mearsheimer 1990; Van Evera 1993; J. Snyder 1990; Hoffmann 1990/1; for an extended bibliography, see Lynn-Jones, and Miller 1993, pp. 396–397; Sheetz 1996.

[29] See R. Ross 1995 and M. Brown et al. 1996b.

[30] Former Israeli prime minister Shimon Peres (with Aori 1993) articulated a vision of a "New Middle East" in which Jews and Arabs live, cooperate, and grow rich together. Critics have argued that it is the same old Middle East in which the Arabs and their hostile intentions vis-à-vis Israel have not changed much.

within regions over time highlight the need for an innovative theoretical explanation.

A number of books have, indeed, addressed this issue, contributing to our understanding of the variety of regional orders which emerged in the wake of the Cold War.[31] These works are useful in offering an antidote to purely systemic/global approaches, especially now that these types of approaches seem to be bolstered by what is perceived as the hastening pace and scope of globalization. Even though these works show the importance of regional developments in understanding security trends in the post-Cold War era, and contribute to our understanding of such developments, they do not develop a coherent theory of regional orders, explaining variations in regional war and peace. Other helpful bodies of literature – on territorial conflicts,[32] enduring rivalries,[33] and civil and ethnic conflicts[34] – do a good job of focusing on the dyadic level, but typically do not address issues on the regional level.

Theory of regional war and peace: an overview

The purpose of this study is to address the missing aspect in the otherwise useful literature by offering a coherent theory of the causes of regional war and peace. A theory of regional war and peace should convincingly explain the different effects the end of the Cold War had on different regions. Such a theory, in other words, would explain the intriguing puzzles to which I pointed earlier: the *transition* from war to peace, or vice versa, in the same region in different periods, and the *variations* among regions with regard to their state of war or peace during the same period.

To develop such a theory it is necessary to answer two related questions: first, what are the substantive causes of regional war and peace? Second, are these causes located at the global/systemic level or at the regional/domestic level? In other words, is regional propensity toward war or peace influenced more by global developments in great power relations and the systemic distributions of power, or

[31] See, most notably, Buzan 1991, Job 1992, Wriggins 1992, Ayoob 1995, Holsti 1996, Maoz 1997, Lake and Morgan 1997, Solingen 1998, Kacowicz 1998, Barnett 1998, Adler and Barnett 1998, Lemke 2002, Diehl and Lepgold 2003, Buzan and Waever 2003, and Paul et al. 2004. For works sharing the regionalist theme but not dealing only with security, see Fawcett and Hurrell 1995 and Holm and Sorensen 1995. See also Katzenstein 1996b, 2005.

[32] See references in n. 14.

[33] Goertz and Diehl 1992a, Diehl and Goertz 2000, Huth 1999, and Maoz and Mor 2002.

[34] For recent works, see Walter 2002 and Toft 2002/3, 2003.

Table 1.1 *Types of regional outcome*

Dependent variables	Regional outcomes (according to the probability of the use of force)			
Type of outcome	Hot	Cold		Hot
Type of regional war or peace	Hot war	Cold war	Cold peace	Warm peace

by developments in the region and within the regional states? The theory I offer responds to these questions.

Hot vs. cold outcomes

The first step in presenting my theory is to define and develop the key distinction between "hot" and "cold" – that is, more or less intense – types of regional war and peace (see table 1.1). The more intense or "hot" outcomes include hot war and warm peace. In a hot war the two sides actually shoot at each other in order to resolve the conflict between them; in warm peace it is highly unlikely that the parties will use force regardless of the intensity of their differences. The "cold" – that is, less intense – outcomes refer to cold war and cold peace. In a cold war there is no ongoing violence between the two sides, but war may erupt at any moment. In cold peace the conflict is reduced but not resolved and, although the danger of war declines, its very possibility shapes the strategic landscape and the parties take the chance of war erupting into account in their behavior.

This study distinguishes between the effects of regional/domestic factors and global/systemic factors, and develops more refined and specified causal linkages between the two types of factors and different types of regional war and peace. The logic behind these linkages is that different types of causal factors (global or regional) account for different types of regional outcomes (hot war, warm peace, cold war, cold peace).

The state-to-nation balance in a region is the key underlying cause of regional war proneness. The extent of the state-to-nation imbalance determines under what conditions factors best explained by realist approaches, or factors best explained by liberal theories, would be more likely to obtain. In short, when the imbalance between states and nations in a region is high, factors highlighted in realist theory would play a greater role in shaping regional dynamics; when states and nations in a region are in balance, forces central to liberal theories become more influential.[35] There are different strategies – based on global or regional/domestic factors – to address the state-to-nation problem, and they produce different types and levels of regional peace.

In the remainder of this introduction, I outline the two core ideas of the theory of regional war and peace. The ideas provide answers to the two questions raised above: the relative influence of global/systemic vs. regional/domestic factors on regional outcomes, and the substantive causes of regional war and peace. These two questions are interrelated and, in chapter 2, I show how they are connected. For analytical clarity, however, in the following discussion I will address them separately.

Let me now introduce the two key ideas or propositions of this study. These propositions are further elaborated and examined in consecutive chapters.

Proposition 1: Regional/domestic factors are responsible for hot outcomes; global factors are responsible for cold outcomes

There is no doubt that the great powers' attitudes and policies contribute to regional war and peace, and that to understand the latter we have to study the former. The scope of great power influence, however, is limited to one-half of regional outcomes – cold war and cold peace. The other half – hot war and warm peace – is influenced more by regional parties and their domestic structures. To understand regional war and peace, then, we must integrate domestic/regional and global factors. This integrative approach thus shows that, with a few qualifications which I will note, cold phenomena are largely the result of systemic forces and

[35] A useful example is South Asia, a region which seems to conform to realist expectations, especially with regard to the India–Pakistan rivalry, and the resulting arms race and the recurring danger of war. But do realist factors, such as the distribution of capabilities in the region, constitute the underlying causes of the conflict? Moreover, do these factors explain the high war proneness of South Asia in comparison with other, more peaceful regions? My argument is that the underlying factors of the war proneness of South Asia are derived from the state-to-nation imbalance in the region, notably regarding the conflicting nationalist claims of India and Pakistan vis-à-vis Kashmir: "Kashmir is to Pakistan what Taiwan is to China: the missing piece whose absence calls into question the entire national project" (Beinart 2002). Under these conditions of imbalance, realist factors are more influential. Indeed, the three other most dangerous rivalries in contemporary world politics, which supposedly fit realist expectations regarding rivalry and the importance of the military balance of power, involve questions of state-to-nation imbalance: Korean unification, China–Taiwan, and the Middle East (on the latter, see ch. 4). The state-to-nation imbalance is also the underlying source of numerous conflicts in the Balkans (see ch. 6) and the former USSR. This was also the source of conflict, for example, in Vietnam until the 1970s.

that hot or warm phenomena are the result of regional/domestic forces. Moreover, a transition from a cold outcome to a warm one requires certain regional/domestic changes or developments to come to the fore.

The logic undergirding this argument is anchored by two related considerations: first, whether the regional outcomes depend on the capabilities or the motivations of the regional states; and, second, whether the balance of interests favors the great powers or the local states.

External powers may affect the capabilities of regional states (for example, through supplying or withholding arms and economic aid). In contrast, changing the basic motivations or objectives of the local states is beyond the power of states external to the region. Great power influence, therefore, is limited to those outcomes that may be affected or brought about without changing the basic motivations of the local actors.[36] The resort to arms in a hot war and the genuine and wholehearted termination of regional conflicts in a warm peace are extreme outcomes or options at the two ends of the war/peace continuum; these outcomes reflect the regional parties' own objectives and attributes. External powers cannot, by themselves, force regional states to adopt such extreme options. These end-of-the-spectrum options entail deep and costly commitments, the expenditure of resources, and the assumption of risks or the acceptance of drastic changes on the part of the local actors – and all these cannot be chosen without a very high motivation on the part of these actors. War is expensive in both human lives and material resources, and its outcome is not predictable. Warm peace entails a profound departure from traditional power-balancing, competition, and self-help behavior typifying state conduct under anarchy (Waltz 1979). Warm peace and the reconciliation on which it is based mean that states renounce the use of force even as a means of last resort to settle their disputes.[37] In warm peace there is always a risk that a state's neighbors might take advantage of its willingness to cooperate and exploit its lack of preparedness to meet potential military threats in the region. The great powers do not have the means, by themselves, to bring the level of motivation of regional states to a point so high that it would dispose them to go to hot wars or embark on warm peace. These drastic departures from the status quo are beyond the capabilities of external powers to affect, and depend on the goals and characteristics of the local

[36] For related points, see Ayoob 1995, pp. 58–59, and Rosecrance and Schott 1997.
[37] I refer here especially to the high-level subtype of warm peace; see ch. 2.

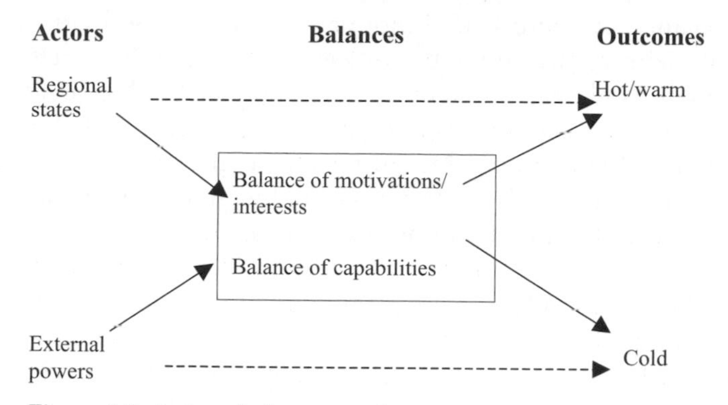

Figure 1.1 Actors, balances, and outcomes

parties themselves. The cold outcomes, on the other hand, are located more toward the center of the war/peace continuum, and selecting them does not entail a drastic modification in the basic motivations and perceptions of the regional parties.

The differential effects of the great powers and regional actors on regional outcomes also reflect different combinations of the balances of capabilities and interests between them at various stages of the war and peace continuum (see figure 1.1).[38] The great powers are superior to regional states in overall resources (qualified by limitations in power-projection capabilities). The local actors have, however, superior stakes in a conflict in which they are direct participants and in which their key interests, or even very survival, are at issue, while the great powers typically would have less than vital interests involved in remote regional conflicts. Even if the great powers have important stakes in a certain region (for example, because of geographical proximity to that region or the location of key resources or important allies there),[39] these stakes will still be lower than those of the local participants directly involved. Variations in these balances of capabilities and motivations with regard to the different regional war and peace outcomes determine the relative effects of the global and local actors on these outcomes.

[38] On the balance of interests or motivations, see George and Simons 1994, p. 15. Motivation "refers to each side's conception of what is at stake in the dispute, the importance each side attaches to the interests engaged by the crisis and what level of costs and risks each is willing to incur on behalf of those interests."
[39] On balances of great power interests and capabilities in different regions, see Miller and Kagan 1997 and Miller 1998.

The balance of interests and motivations favors the regional actors especially with regard to the hot outcomes, because these actors have much more at stake in a situation of a hot regional war,[40] or in the major transformation in relations resulting in warm peace, than do the distant great powers. At a certain point during a hot regional war, however, the balance of interests might shift in favor of the great powers because of rising threats to their own important interests in the region (for example, "losing" an important ally who is being defeated militarily), and the growing probability of being drawn into the regional hostilities on behalf of their allies, which might lead to a direct confrontation among the powers. Thus, the great powers' willingness to impose restraint on regional states in situations of war termination (which, in the absence of a peace process, brings about a state of cold war) is greater than at the initiation of hot regional wars. The balance of capabilities also changes in the great powers' favor toward the end of the local wars as the regional states become more dependent on the external powers, owing to the depletion of stocks and material during the war. The longer the war, the more vulnerable to great power pressure the regional combatants become. All this means that the great powers may affect the scope and duration of regional wars, but that they are not in a position to determine the outbreak of such wars.

Hot regional wars are caused by domestic and regional factors unrelated to the great powers. Thus, I refute the notion of "proxy wars," which is based on the assumption that the great powers have the ability to induce local states to fight for great power interests; in my view, the great powers do not have such an ability.[41] The great powers are also unable to impose warm peace if the regional parties are uninterested or are not ready for that high level of peace.

Without the willingness of regional states, the great powers are unable to produce hot regional outcomes. Are great powers necessary for cold regional outcomes? Could cold regional outcomes be achieved by the local parties alone, as a result of their own decisions and calculations, without external intervention? My answer is that the regional actors cannot bring about cold regional outcomes without great power involvement. Indeed, the great power's role in bringing about cold outcomes is crucial, for two reasons.

[40] A similar balance of motivation logic should lead us to expect that highly motivated regional actors, dissatisfied with the current state-to-nation balance, might initiate violence, even if they are inferior in the overall balance of capabilities.
[41] This point is discussed in ch. 3.

First, the great powers, because of their superior capabilities and the asymmetric relationship between them and the local actors, are well equipped to affect cold regional outcomes. The regional balance of power is directly related to cold outcomes, as it affects the cost–benefit calculations of local states and may motivate them to move from hot war to cold war, from cold war to cold peace, or back to hot war. Unless the great powers are not involved in the region, the regional balance of power is itself largely dependent on the great powers, especially in regions important to them.[42] Arms supply (or arms embargoes) by the great powers shape regional balances. The great powers may also use various economic measures to affect the regional balance, among them economic assistance, investment, and technology transfers or, conversely, economic sanctions, embargoes, and more. The great powers thus do not determine the propensity of a region toward hot wars, but they may sustain regional cold wars or foster the emergence of cold peace.

Second, great powers are especially important in encouraging a transition from cold war to cold peace. As I discuss in chapter 3, the security dilemma is exacerbated by proximity, and, as a result, regional (and, hence, proximate) states face great difficulties in arriving at regional peace on their own as long as the state-to-nation problems are not resolved. Indeed, the great powers are needed for helping the transition from cold war to cold peace only when the regional state-to-nation problems are unresolved; if these problems have been resolved, the regional states may even reach warm peace on their own. State-to-nation problems are not easy to resolve because, almost by definition, they involve proximate states with a history of bitter conflict. The difficulties regional states encounter in making the transition from cold war to cold peace offer the great powers an opportunity to use their superior military and economic capabilities to induce regional states to move toward cold peace. Cold peace does not involve a major transformation of attitudes and motivation – something which is not possible, in any event, until the state-to-nation problem has been completely resolved – and as such it is more susceptible to great power influence.

I said above that, if the regional state-to-nation problem is resolved, the states in the region may reach peace (even warm peace) on their own, without the help of the great powers. This does not mean that the great powers may not play a helpful role in promoting regional and

[42] For a related point, see Lake 1997, pp. 60–61.

domestic conditions that are conducive to the emergence of a warm peace. Later I discuss the regional/domestic factors contributing to the likelihood of warm peace, most notably, successful state-building and nation-building as well as the emergence of liberal democracy in the states of the region. These conditions, however, do not appear out of nowhere, and the transition from incoherent to coherent states, or from being a non-democratic regime to being a stable liberal democracy, is typically gradual and lengthy. The great powers may use their economic and political muscle to encourage regional and domestic developments more hospitable to liberal democracy, state-building, and nation-building, therefore helping to create the conditions necessary for the emergence of a warm peace. Yet the great powers cannot achieve this on their own without the minimal necessary regional/domestic conditions, especially a minimal level of a state-to-nation balance.[43] When these conditions fully take hold, the help of the great powers will no longer be necessary for regional warm peace to emerge.

Proposition 2: The state-to-nation imbalance is the underlying cause of regional war proneness

To go to war, regional states need both motivation and capabilities. The most compelling motivation regional states have to go to war is the state-to-nation balance in the region. The propensity of a region toward war depends on the degree of state-to-nation balance in the region. Following the definition above, a state-to-nation imbalance is present when at least some of the states in the region are weak and there is a lack of compatibility between the regional states (entities or institutions administering a certain territory) and the national sentiments of the peoples in the region (that is, their political aspirations of living as national communities in their own states).

[43] A current example refers to the Bush administration's "Greater (or Broader) Middle East" project which, together with the intervention in Iraq, aims at democratizing the Middle East. On this project, see the succinct summary in the *Economist* (June 12, 2004, 42). If this ambitious project had been successful, it might have been a good example of how external powers may try to create the strategic and political as well as the socioeconomic conditions that would allow regional states to reach warm peace. One of the key problems with this project is, however, the high extent of the state-to-nation imbalance in the Middle East, and specifically in Iraq (see ch. 4), which makes a transition to democracy an uphill battle. Such a regional/domestic transformation demands a lot of effort and costs from the great powers, and still success is far from being guaranteed in the absence of the appropriate conditions in the region. Notably, the higher the state-to-nation imbalance, the higher the difficulties and the costs.

The great powers are unable and, in many cases, unwilling to resolve regional state-to-nation balance problems on their own. A state-to-nation imbalance increases the power of revisionist/nationalist forces and the states which sponsor them, and lowers the level of state coherence in the region owing to the presence of powerful secessionist national groups within them.[44] The more powerful the nationalist/revisionist forces and the lower the level of state coherence, the higher the regional war proneness. Hypernationalist/revisionist states are dissatisfied with the existing regional order and, if they are powerful enough, they may use force in order to change it. State incoherence creates strong pressures by – and temptation for – dissatisfied groups, some of them minorities, for either irredentism or secession.[45] Irredentism threatens the territorial integrity of neighbors and thus intensifies the security dilemma in the region. Secessionism brings about domestic wars, producing opportunities for external intervention that may lead to regional wars. Insurgents in incoherent states may use the territory of neighboring states as a base from which to attack their government, thus involving the neighbors in the internal war. Leaders of incongruent states may also use diversionary wars to strengthen their hold on power – it has been argued, for example, that lack of domestic legitimacy affects war proneness by encouraging a regime to engage in scapegoating and initiate diversionary wars.[46] Weak and incoherent states – Afghanistan, Somalia, Pakistan, Yemen, Indonesia, the Philippines, and many African states come to mind – may become comfortable havens for guerrillas and terrorists, thus exporting instability across the region (and, indeed, violence throughout the world).[47]

Two of the major outputs of the state-to-nation imbalance – nationalist revisionism and incoherent states – reinforce each other's destabilizing effects on war proneness. When a revisionist state is guided by irredentist or pan-national ideologies, or is exploiting such ideologies to serve its interests, and it is neighbored by incoherent states, the latter would be further weakened by the former's appeal to dissatisfied domestic elements and recurrent transborder intervention in the weak states' territory.[48]

[44] For the specific relations between the imbalance and revisionism and state incoherence (or failure), see chs. 2 and 3.
[45] On the connections between the two phenomena, see Horowitz 1991.
[46] See Lebow 1981, J. Levy 1989b and 1989c, and J. Snyder 1991. For an overview of recent works on diversionary wars, see J. Levy 1998, 152–158.
[47] See 9/11 Commission 2004, pp. 361–383. See also Fukuyama 2004.
[48] For related points, see Walt 1996.

A state-to-nation imbalance is an *underlying* cause of regional wars, making some regions more prone to wars than other regions. Such an imbalance creates substantive issues pitting one state against another, and it exacerbates the security dilemma and power rivalries in the region. These power and security factors, which are at the center of the realist approach, are the *proximate* causes of specific regional wars.[49] The specific balance of power, offense/defense balance, and security anxieties determine when the underlying predisposition for war – or the region's basic war proneness – will be translated into actual wars.[50] Anxieties about security and power aspirations are less likely, in themselves, to plunge a region into a major war in the absence of the underlying state-to-nation imbalance. Addressing the state-to-nation issues may reduce the likelihood of hot wars in a region, and whether and how this is done will determine the other three regional outcomes defined in chapter 2 – cold war, cold peace, and warm peace.

The state-to-nation balance helps us differentiate among these three outcomes: in a situation of cold war, the regional imbalance remains unresolved, and as a result the likelihood of war is high; in cold peace, this imbalance is mitigated or reduced, but not fully resolved; in warm peace, the state-to-nation problem is resolved or transcended.

In sum, the regional state-to-nation balance, a relatively stable variable, can tell us *where* armed conflict is most likely, that is, which regions are most war-prone (regions with high state-to-nation imbalance) and which regions enjoy warm peace (regions with low state-to-nation imbalance). Yet, there are considerable variations in conflict outcomes over time even where the state-to-nation imbalance and the general high level of war proneness remain constant. It is the factor of great power involvement (including through its effects on the proximate cause of the regional balance of power) that interacts with the state-to-nation imbalance to produce the variations in conflict outcomes among hot war, cold war, and cold peace (and occasionally affecting the conditions for the transition to warm peace). That is, great power involvement can affect the *level* and *intensity* of the regional conflict. Thus, by integrating variables from different levels of analysis, this theory is able to provide a more detailed prediction of regional conflict outcomes.

[49] On the distinction between underlying and proximate causes of war, see Lebow 1981, Vasquez 1993, pp. 293–297, and Van Evera 1994.
[50] For further development of this argument and an application to the Middle East, see chs. 3 and 4.

My theoretical approach

The debates between the key schools in the IR field – realism, liberalism, and constructivism – have benefited the field. They have produced insightful and parsimonious explanations of many aspects of interstate behavior but, ultimately, have fallen short of offering compelling accounts of complex IR phenomena.[51] The neorealist variant of the realist school puts forth an elegant and parsimonious structural theory,[52] but two key groups of contemporary realists – defensive realists and neoclassical realists – acknowledge the need to enrich their analysis with nonstructural/realist variables.[53]

Theorists recognize, however, the need to avoid a "laundry list" of independent variables, which may provide a descriptive account of specific cases but not a useful theoretical explanation.[54] Even as we worry about an unwieldy list of variables, we should admit that there are excellent works that combine variables from different schools and levels of analysis,[55] although, predictably, these works are criticized as theoretically incoherent and inconsistent.[56] Critics charge that these works implicitly mix independent variables from different paradigms, and add variables to the explanation of specific cases in an ad hoc fashion, rather than stating in advance which variable best explains which phenomenon, based on an explicitly deductive logic.

My response to this quandary is to advance two strategies of synthesis which attempt to reconcile the tension between the "too few" and "too many" variables. These syntheses allow me to account for complex phenomena by appealing to multicausal explanations even as I keep the accounts tight and parsimonious. The two strategies, respectively, frame the two propositions advanced earlier.

[51] See, for example, Moravcsik 2003. This is one piece in a forum with a wide range of views on the feasibility and desirability of synthesis in IR. See Hellmann 2003. A special issue of *International Studies Review* (December 2003) also focuses on attempts at integration in IR.

[52] See Waltz 1979. For another major work in this direction, see Mearsheimer 2001.

[53] See Taliaferro 2000/1, at p. 135. On neoclassical realism, see Rose 1998. On defensive realism, see below.

[54] For such a recent critique, see Taliaferro 2004, p. 32, n. 20, who cites a number of recent works in IR, which use what he calls "a maximalist approach," namely, the usage of too many explanatory variables.

[55] This refers to some of the best, most innovative, and most influential works in contemporary IR theory: J. Snyder 1991, Van Evera 1999, Walt 1987, Schweller 1998, Zakaria 1998, Wohlforth 1993, and Glaser 1997.

[56] Legro and Moravcsik 1999.

The first strategy addresses the level-of-analysis problem by making a typology of the dependent variables, and then establishing causal linkages between different levels of analysis and different types of dependent variables.

The second strategy addresses the realist–liberal debate on the causes of war and peace by advancing an alternative explanation – the state-to-nation balance – that specifies the conditions under which realist factors (as causes of war) or liberal causes (as conditions for peace) are likely to exert more influence. When there is a state-to-nation imbalance, factors such as the balance of power and the security dilemma, which are central to realist approaches, are especially powerful. Under a state-to-nation balance, causes of peace, such as democracy and institutionalized conflict resolution, which are important in liberal theory, are more effective.

The question discussed in proposition 1 is a restatement of the levels-of-analysis problem with regard to regional war and peace. This problem refers to the question of the level on which the causal variables that best explain behavior and outcomes in international politics are located. Waltz's (1959) original formulation referred to three levels: the international system, the state, and the individual.[57] Following Waltz's later (1979) formulation, it is more common now to distinguish between two levels: system and unit. In this study I also distinguish between two levels: global and regional/domestic. This distinction is the most relevant to the issue of regional war and peace.

The question addressed in proposition 2 is related to the debates among competing perspectives in IR theory, which advance different approaches to the causes of war and peace in general, and to regional war and peace in particular.

The answer I give to these two questions is that neither a single theoretical perspective nor a single level of analysis can account for the variety of regional war and peace outcomes.[58] Rather, to explain regional transitions and variations in war and peace patterns, a number of major theoretical perspectives and both levels of analysis have to be integrated. Yet, the assertion that they all somehow "matter" in explaining regional outcomes is vague and underspecified. A coherent and compelling theory

[57] Other contributions to this debate include M. Kaplan 1957, Singer 1961, Jervis 1976, Larson 1985, Wendt 1987, Hollis and Smith 1991, and Buzan 1995. See also Miller 2002. For an overview of the systemic vs. domestic debate and related references, see Huth and Allee 2002, pp. 16–19.

[58] For a partly related argument, see Katzenstein and Okawara 2001/2.

of regional war and peace requires that the various perspectives and levels of analysis be integrated into a single framework in a specified and parsimonious manner.

To achieve this goal, I relate different approaches (realist, liberal) and levels of analysis (systemic, regional/domestic) to different types of regional war and peace outcomes (hot war, cold war, cold peace, warm peace). I specify what type of phenomenon is best explained by each causal factor. The proposed theory will first specify which type of regional security outcomes is best explained by global factors and which type is best accounted for by regional/domestic causes. Second, the theory will assess the combined effects of global and regional/domestic factors on regional orders.[59] If validated, both logically/deductively and empirically/historically, such a model should provide a powerful explanation of major regional patterns of war and peace; it will also offer the ability to predict the outline of possible future developments in different regions. This theory will also be helpful in highlighting the conditions under which each of the major IR schools offers more persuasive explanations, and in evaluating the likely effectiveness of global and regional mechanisms for managing regional security.

My theoretical approach bridges acrimonious and counterproductive divisions in the field of international relations. This approach synthesizes different levels of analysis, allowing me to integrate some of these competing perspectives. Phenomena that were previously explained by a host of distinctive and unconnected theories are now explained within a single coherent framework.

The key ideas and the existing literature

To show how my two core ideas – that global forces shape cold regional outcomes and regional/domestic forces shape hot regional outcomes, and that the state-to-nation balance determines regional war proneness – contribute to the current literature, it is first necessary to show why reliance on a single level of analysis or on a single theoretical perspective does not take us very far in accounting for transitions and variations in regional war and peace patterns. This section therefore offers a brief discussion of the existing literature and competing explanations.

[59] See Miller (2002) for the development of this method of distinguishing between the effects of different causal factors by specifying the type of phenomenon or outcome best explained by each.

The debate between outside-in vs. inside-out explanations of regional outcomes

Scholars of regional war and peace have tended to privilege either the global/systemic or regional/domestic level of analysis. These approaches are typically regarded as irreconcilable.

The systemic or "outside-in" logic[60] suggests that, to understand regional dynamics, we need to focus on the broader international context within which regional orders are embedded, taking into account the influence of external pressures and incentives on regional actors. It is also argued that, in the modern interconnected world, there can be no wholly self-contained regions, immune to outside influences.[61]

The systemic/global approach thus argues that the global environment shapes the behavior of the regional actors by offering inducements and punishments. The distribution of capabilities in the international system is unequal, so that the superior capabilities of the great powers and the dependence of small states on the great powers[62] force the small states to adapt to the international environment created by the great powers and to the dominant mode of interaction prevailing in it. Regional conflicts and wars are caused by frictions among the great powers; a variant of this approach is the argument that regional wars are only proxy wars – a reflection of the strategic and economic interests of major powers and their mutual competition (Vayrynen 1984, 351). Indeed, they may not be much more than an extension of great power competition. According to this logic, the bipolar Cold War brought about numerous regional conflicts from the late 1940s to the mid to late 1980s, whereas global developments such as US–Soviet cooperation under Gorbachev and later US hegemony have determined regional patterns since the late 1980s.

On the other hand, regional or "inside-out" approaches claim that regional states respond in the first place to local factors and developments because the region is the most important environment affecting their security interests. According to the regional approach, the immediate neighbors rather than remote global powers are the most critical actors on the security agenda of small states. The regional environment

[60] For a useful distinction between "outside-in" and "inside-out" approaches to regional orders, see Neumann 1994. See also Hurrell 1995, Hampson 1996, pp. 16–19, and Katzenstein 1996b.
[61] Hurrell 1995, pp. 339, 347–353.
[62] On the high economic and security dependence of Third World states on the great powers, see Ayoob 1995, p. 73.

creates the most direct external threats and opportunities for states (Wriggins 1992, p. 9). A group of neighboring states forms a "regional security system," which is characterized by high security interdependence and frequently by conflict (Buzan 1991, pp. 193–194; Wriggins 1992, pp. 3–13; Ayoob 1995, p. 57), especially among territorially contiguous states (Vasquez 1993).[63] The regional approach argues that there is a high degree of autonomy of regional dynamics from global developments (Doran 1992; Karsh 1997). To the extent that the global arena exercises influence, it is mediated by attributes of the region, such as the degree of intensity of the regional disputes and their characteristics (Buzan 1991, pp. 214–215; Ayoob 1995). Regional dynamics are shaped by patterns of relations among regional states (notably, those of amity and enmity),[64] by the nature of the regional conflicts (ideological, territorial, nationalist, hegemonic, security dilemma, etc.), and by the domestic attributes of the local states (democratic or authoritarian regimes, state–society relations, the demands of state-building and nation-building, regime stability, and elite security).[65] As a result, analysts of regional security must concentrate on regional conflict patterns and processes rather than assume that the causes of local conflicts can be attributed to the machinations of great powers or to the structure of the international system. Regional systems have their own structures and dynamics, and operate with their own sets of opportunities and constraints (Holsti 1992, pp. 44, 52).

Each of the two approaches provides plausible arguments for the importance of its preferred set of factors (global or regional). Indeed, the weakness of both approaches lies in their failure to accommodate the other set of factors. It is more reasonable to assume that both these types of factors (regional and global) affect regional conflicts (Vayrynen 1984; Wriggins 1992). Thus, the fact that dramatic changes have recently taken place in different regions more or less at the same time following a major international change – the end of the Cold War – shows the important effects of international factors on regional conflicts (Miller

[63] For a recent overview of conceptions of regional systems, see Lemke 2002, pp. 57–60. For his own conception, see ibid., pp. 61–66 and ch. 4.

[64] Buzan 1991, ch. 5. On the type of fundamental relations (amity and enmity) among regional actors, see especially ibid., pp. 189–190. The problem with his otherwise excellent analysis is that he does not provide a theoretical explanation of the emergence of these patterns of relations. More recently, Buzan and Waever (2003), however, have further developed their regionalist approach to security and applied it to a variety of regional systems.

[65] Migdal 1988, Ayoob 1995, Barnett 1992, Job 1992, S. David 1991a, 1991b.

and Kagan 1997; Miller 2002). At the same time, the different directions of these changes, and the great variations across regions in the post-Cold War era in terms of war and peace, notably between peaceful relations in Western Europe and armed conflicts in the Balkans and some parts of the Third World (Goldgeier and McFaul 1992), indicate the significance of regional factors in affecting regional war and peace.

Thus, it seems intuitive that both global and regional factors are influential in producing regional outcomes. The difficulty lies in building a coherent theoretical framework that integrates these global and regional factors in a single theory. This is one of the major objectives of this book.

The substantive debate on the causes of wars and conditions of peace

The second core idea of the theory of regional war and peace proposed in this study addresses the substantive causes of war and peace. My argument is that, rather than treating the causes of war and peace separately, as is often done in the literature, it is first necessary to inquire what makes certain regions war-prone, that is, why some regions are more prone to war than others. Indeed, without a coherent answer to this question, it is difficult to evaluate the utility of different conflict-management mechanisms and competing peace strategies. Without understanding the underlying causes of regional wars, it is difficult to know what are the most effective ways to manage regional conflicts and to reach regional peace. The way the underlying causes of regional war proneness are addressed, if at all, determines whether and what kind of regional peace will emerge, for example, whether it will be cold or warm peace.

In reviewing the approach of different perspectives in international relations theory to the causes of war and peace, we must note that two major competing perspectives – realism and liberalism – do not account adequately for the variations in the war proneness of different regions.[66]

Realists underline the impact of three factors on war proneness:[67] anarchy, which is a permissive factor for all types of war; the derived security dilemma and mutual fears, which produce unintended conflict

[66] For excellent overviews of realist and liberal approaches to war and peace, see J. Levy 1989a, 1996, 1998, and 2001.

[67] The two major modern works of the realist school are the classical realism of Morgenthau (1978) and the neorealism of Waltz (1979). For recent refinements, see M. Brown et al. 1995, Frankel 1996, Brooks 1997, and Rose 1998. For critiques of realism, see Keohane 1986 and Lebow and Risse-Kappen 1995.

spirals and inadvertent wars; and imbalances of power, which provide the opportunity for gains and thus cause wars of profit. While the focus on anarchy is shared by all realists, the latter two factors distinguish between two major strands within realist theory: "defensive realists" focus on the security dilemma and the effect on it of the offense–defense balance,[68] whereas "offensive realists" highlight the quest for power maximization under anarchy and power distributions which create incentives for wars of profit. Here the decisive elements are the opportunities related to power vacuums and changes in the balance of power that make war less costly and nonresort to force more costly.[69]

In contrast to the centralized authority within states, anarchy in international politics means the absence of global government or overall authority above the sovereign states in the international arena (Bull 1977, Waltz 1979, Buzan 1991). In the realist view, this situation explains why conflicts may lead to war: namely, because there is no supreme authority to stop the states from initiating wars, and no arbiter capable of enforcing a settlement (Waltz 1959).

Another effect of anarchy on the outbreak of wars is through the working of the security dilemma. In the absence of a reliable international law-enforcement agency, states have to take care of themselves and meet threats to their autonomy (Waltz 1979). The security dilemma refers to a vicious interaction whereby measures that a state adopts to increase its own security are seen as a threat by others who, as a result, take defensive steps of their own, which in turn reduce the sense of security of the first state.[70] In a self-help system, the quest to survive and the resultant security dilemma are sufficient to lead even status quo states to pursue arms races, construct opposing alliances, and occasionally even stumble into undesired and unintended wars.[71] The security dilemma is especially severe when offense has the advantage over defense, or when offense and defense are not distinguishable.[72]

[68] Defensive realists include Jervis 1978, Posen 1984, J. Snyder 1991, Glaser 1994/5, Van Evera 1998, 1999, and Taliaferro 2000/1. A related variant of defensive realism is balance-of-threat theory: see Walt 1987, 1996.

[69] On offensive realism, see Mearsheimer 1990, 1994/5, 2001; Gilpin 1981; Zakaria 1992, 190–196, 1998; Labs 1997; and Schweller 1998.

[70] On the security dilemma, see Herz 1950, Jervis 1978, Buzan 1991, p. 297, Miller 1994b, and Glaser 1997.

[71] Waltz 1959, p. 234; Jervis 1976, pp. 67, 94; 1978; 1979, 213, 217.

[72] For the initial formulation of this argument, see Jervis 1978; for an excellent review of the literature that has evolved on the security dilemma and the offense/defense balance, see Glaser 1997. See also Lynn-Jones 1995. For more contributions, see Van Evera 1998 and 1999, and Glaser and Kaufman 1998.

As a result of the lack of an effective overall authority, another factor that exercises crucial effects on the occurrence of wars is the balance of power or the distribution of capabilities among states. Yet, in contrast to the inadvertent nature of security dilemma wars, wars derived from imbalances of powers are usually intended.[73] Such wars are wars of profit or opportunity, and are made in accordance with cost–benefit calculations, namely, when the expected benefits of fighting outweigh the expected cost of fighting.[74]

In contrast to realists, liberals focus on the conditions for peace while neglecting to point out specific paths to war.[75] Still, through their focus on certain conditions of peace, one may deduce their conception of the causes of war proneness. Many liberals highlight domestic causes of war. A major liberal argument is that war among democracies is unlikely for two main reasons, one of which is normative and the other structural.[76] The normative explanation refers to the externalization of the domestic norm of peaceful resolution of conflicts within democracies to the relations among them (Russett 1993, pp. 30–38). As a result, a community of democratic states ensures peace. The structural explanation focuses on the more effective domestic constraints on the use of force in democracies in comparison with nondemocratic regimes. The liberal focus on the peace among democracies implies that the lack of liberal democracy increases the likelihood of wars either among authoritarian regimes or between them and democracies.

Liberals also point out that the presence of international institutions, a liberal economic order, and high economic interdependence reduce the tendency toward armed conflict. Institutions can help prevent conflict by stabilizing expectations; creating a feeling of continuity and an assurance that present collaboration will be reciprocated in the future; providing information on whether states are abiding by institutional norms; and creating mechanisms for resolving disputes.[77] A liberal economic order makes states more prosperous, and prosperous states have

[73] On intended and unintended wars, see Miller 1994b.
[74] On power maximization as a motivation for war, see Morgenthau 1978 and Mearsheimer 2001; on wars of profit, see Liberman 1993. For the formal logic of wars of profit, see Bueno de Mesquita 1981; for an informal version, see Waltz 1959, p. 60. Both are cited in Fearon 1995, 386.
[75] On liberalism in world politics, see Zacher and Matthew 1995, Russett 1993, Doyle 1997, Moravcsik 1997, and Russett and Oneal 2001.
[76] See Doyle 1986 and Russett 1993. For comprehensive discussions of this theory, see the collection edited by M. Brown et al. 1996a and Chan 1997. For a critique, see Gowa 1995.
[77] Nye 1996, 7. For an extended discussion of the effects of international institutions on cooperation, see Keohane 1984 and 1989.

fewer incentives to go to war and more to lose from the waste caused by war. A liberal economic order also fosters economic interdependence among states. When interdependence is high, each state is able to compel the others to cooperate. Furthermore, liberals assert that economic interdependence reduces the likelihood of war by raising the value of trading over the alternative of aggression: interdependent states would rather trade than invade.[78]

Both the realist and the liberal approaches to war proneness have major limitations. Both approaches are unable to account for variations either within a given region or among regions.

The realist focus on anarchy is unable to explain differences in war proneness among regions which are all under anarchy, such as the great variations between Western Europe and the Middle East, or South America and the Balkans. The key underlying factor that determines the extent of regional war proneness is not anarchy, because this factor is too general and underspecified.[79] It is a permissive factor allowing armed conflicts to occur, but it does not explain why these intense conflicts emerge in certain regions and not in others, and why peace endures in certain regions and not in others, despite the supposed absence of an overall authority in all of them.

In order to account for variations in war proneness among different regions, realism offers two additional factors: the distribution of power related to wars of opportunity, and the offense/defense balance which affects the security dilemma.[80] But these two factors are also problematic. There are two complications in using the distribution-of-power factor in accounting for regional variations. If we look at the global distribution of power, one difficulty is that there are great variations with regard to war proneness among different regions under the same international system, whether it is unipolar, bipolar, or multipolar (Miller and Kagan 1997). If we look at the regional distribution of power, another problem exists as to the extent that there are great variations among regions with the same power structure. Thus, the considerable differences in war proneness among regions that are all multipolar in their regional structure (East Asia, Western Europe, Balkans, the Middle East), and located under the same international structure, as in the Cold War era, pose a tough challenge to the distribution-of-power explanation.

[78] Copeland 1996, p. 5; for elaboration, see Rosecrance 1986. For an overview of the relations between interdependence and war, see McMillan 1997.
[79] See Wendt 1992, Milner 1993, and Schweller 1996.
[80] For an analysis of such variations drawing on Jervis, see Glaser 1997, 185–188.

Moreover, if the weaker parties initiate violence, this contradicts the logic of balance-of-power theory.

As for the security dilemma factors, even if there is a high correlation between the offense/defense balance and the tendency to war in a certain region, these factors are unable to account either for persistent differences in resort to force within the region (that is, in some parts rather than others), or for variations in war proneness among regions with a similar offense/defense balance. Thus, these factors are unable to explain both why the Middle East was more war-prone than other regions in the Cold War era, and why the Arab–Israeli conflict was more prone to escalating to war than other disputes in the Middle East.

Indeed, the explanatory power of the security dilemma is disputed by critics who argue that it is aggressive or greedy states rather than the offense/defense balance that produce the primary security problem for other states.[81] The offense/defense balance and the security dilemma provide the intervening variables and the proximate (rather than underlying) causes of regional wars or, in other words, the opportunity rather than the basic motivation for war.[82]

Liberalism, for its part, while being able to explain differences between democratic and nondemocratic regions, is unable to account for variations in war proneness among nondemocratic regions. Thus, it is unable to explain why the Middle East was more prone to interstate wars than other nondemocratic regions in the post-World War II era such as South America (Holsti 1996), West Africa (Kacowicz 1998), or post-1967 ASEAN (Association of South East Asian Nations: Khong 1997; Wriggins 1992). With regard to the liberal focus on the benign influence of international institutions and economic interdependence on state cooperation, realists have underlined the major influence of the balance of power (Mearsheimer 2001) and the quest for relative gains (Grieco 1988, 1990) on state inclination toward competitive behavior under anarchy. These factors minimize the independent effects of interdependence and institutions on regional outcomes.[83]

[81] See Schweller 1994, 1996. For a related critique of offense/defense theory, because it focuses on military capabilities while marginalizing the political context, see Butfoy 1997. Moreover, since almost all weapons can be used either for offensive or defensive purposes, it is extremely difficult to distinguish between offense and defense; thus it is impossible to establish the offense/defense balance in the first place (Mearsheimer 1994/5). In rebuttal, see the responses of Glaser 1997 and Glaser and Kaufmann 1998.
[82] This argument is further developed in ch. 3.
[83] See Ripsman and Blanchard 1996/7 and Kagan 1997/8.

The greatest problem of both realist and liberal approaches (and the main reason they cannot, on their own, account for regional variations in war proneness) is that both overlook the political context of regional wars, that is, the actors' motivations for going to war, the attributes that affect these motivations, and the substantive issues for which wars are fought,[84] most notably related to nationalism, territory, and boundaries.[85] Thus, neither approach can explain those motivations of the regional actors who resort to violence that are derived from problems of state creation, state-making and regime/elite survival,[86] state-breaking and failure,[87] ethnonational conflicts,[88] and revisionist ideologies (such as hypernationalism and fundamentalist religious movements).[89] Some of these factors, which are overlooked by both realism and liberalism, are related to a third major approach in international relations theory – the international society perspective, and especially its regional variant (I discuss this in the next chapter). It is this perspective that provides the best answer as to the basic underlying causes of the variations in regional war proneness.

On the face of it, realists, particularly some leading neorealists (Posen 1993a; Mearsheimer 2001, p. 365), recognize the powerful force of

[84] Luard 1986 argues that the issues and motives that dominate wars in each historical period vary fairly radically. For the frequency of different types of substantive issues in generating wars, see Holsti 1991, p. 308.

[85] For critiques of realism in this respect, see Goertz and Diehl 1992b, pp. 13–14, 23–25; Holsti 1991; Vasquez 1993; Donnelly 2000, pp. 64–65, 76. Reviewers criticized both variants of realism in this respect. For a critique of offensive realism, see Glenn Snyder's (2002, 157) critique of Mearsheimer 2001 for avoiding nonsecurity objectives which might be key causes of important wars. On defensive realism, see Betts's (1999) review of Van Evera's work. Holsti (1991, pp. 307–311) suggests that territory was the major cause of wars in the 1648–1815 period. As for the modern era, he argues that this issue has not lost its importance entirely, especially regarding strategic territory, but that its importance is in relative decline. At the same time, the issue of state-making has grown in importance, following the creation of numerous new states in the post-1945 era. However, Vasquez shows that even according to Holsti's findings, if one includes all the issues related to territoriality, then it is still the prevalent cause of wars in the modern period (1993, pp. 128–131). He (ibid., pp. 131–132) reaches a similar conclusion based on Luard's 1986 theoretical analysis.

[86] On these issues as major causes of war, especially in the post-1945 Third World, see Job 1992, Ayoob 1995, and Holsti 1991, 1992, and 1996.

[87] See Zartman 1995a. For an overview, see Ayoob 1996.

[88] See the articles in the volumes edited by M. Brown (1993, 1996). See also Horowitz 1985. Cagnon 1994/5 explicitly criticizes realism for its inability to explain ethnic conflict, particularly the war in Yugoslavia. But see Posen's realist explanation of the conflict in Yugoslavia (1993b). Steven David criticizes this line of analysis (1998, pp. 86–94), as does Stuart Kaufman (2001).

[89] On revisionism, see Wolfers 1962, Buzan 1991, and Schweller 1994, 1996, and 1998. On the effects of hypernationalism on war, see especially the work of Van Evera (1993, 1994).

nationalism and its relations with war. Yet, for realists, nationalism is an instrument used by the state to advance its interests in the competitive international system; for example, to motivate people to go to wars against the state's rivals (for defensive or offensive purposes). Under a state-to-nation imbalance, however, nationalism is a force that might be independent of the state and might even challenge it; it can take the form of secessionist and other ethnonational movements that do not identify with the state, or are oppressed by it on national grounds. Under a state-to-nation imbalance, moreover, nationalism may induce state leaders to endorse aggressive behavior, which could harm the state's power and its key security and economic interests. This may happen either when nationalism is used by the state leadership to further their own domestic standing even if it comes at the expense of key state interests, for example, the expansionist wars conducted by Saddam Hussein of Iraq (see chapter 4) and Slobodan Milošević of Serbia (see chapter 6). Or nationalism may constrain state leadership to endorse bellicose policies which might contradict the logic of *Realpolitik* and go against the logic of the balance of power, for example, the behavior of Israelis and Arabs in different phases of their conflict (see chapter 4).

"Post-neorealist" theories

In response to these limitations of the leading IR theories, at least three useful "post-neorealist" theories have emerged in recent years. These theories make an important contribution to IR theory by accounting for a substantial amount of the lacunae in the dominant approaches in IR, especially in realism: a territorial explanation, the revisionist state, and ethnic conflict.

The territorial thesis makes an important contribution by showing that territorial issues are the most important ones over which war is fought. Thus, variations among regions in war proneness could be explained by the extent of unresolved territorial disputes, because territorial disputes have more often ended in war than disagreements over other issues.[90] This thesis does not provide, however, a theoretical explanation of under what conditions such wars are likely to occur. Moreover, the territorial argument does not provide an explanation of the great variations among different regions in the intensity of territorial conflicts

[90] Vasquez 1993; 1995, 285; Holsti 1991; Goertz and Diehl 1992b; Huth 1996; Diehl 1999; and Hensel 2001.

and their escalation to violence. Thus, the territorial variable seems to be only an intervening variable. There seem to be some deeper causes – such as nationalism (White 2000) – that account for the great variations in the level of escalation to violence of territorial conflicts. Although quite useful, this thesis provides statistical correlations rather than a causal explanation.

By focusing on the greedy state, Schweller revived the classical realist idea about *the revisionist state* as being the key to explaining war. Schweller made a compelling argument that, in the absence of such a predatory state, it is hard to imagine how the supposedly destabilizing effects of the security dilemma are going to lead to war (Schweller 1996, 1998). This is a very innovative and important contribution. Yet he did not explain the emergence of revisionist states, especially on the regional level, and specifically under what conditions they are more likely to emerge and which factors cause the variations so that some states become revisionist while others follow status quo orientations.[91]

Ethnic conflict is a perspective that gained momentum after the end of the Cold War.[92] One theory that has been especially popular refers to "ancient hatreds" (R. Kaplan 1993), which supposedly lead ethnic groups to fight each other.[93] In the post-Cold War era, the number of conflicts that can be characterized in this way – for example, in the former Yugoslavia, the former USSR, and Africa – has increased, heightening the appeal of this thesis. Yet the focus on ethnic conflict as domestic/civil strife overlooks the phenomenon of the mixed conflict discussed above, namely, the transborder and international dimensions of the conflict.[94] Moreover, a major type of the state-to-nation imbalance, which leads to interstate conflicts, takes place precisely within the same ethnic group or Huntington's "civilization." This is the pan-national unification or "too-many-states" aspect of the state-to-nation imbalance. In this aspect some states challenge the independence of other states sharing the same ethnicity under the banner of national unification. Since states prefer

[91] See Donnelly 2000, pp. 64–65, 76.

[92] See M. Brown 1993, 1996; Lake and Rothchild 1998a. A useful review of different approaches to ethnic conflict is Kaufmann 2005.

[93] A partly related theory is Huntington's "clash of civilizations" (1996). For a recently sophisticated version of the "ancient-hatreds" explanation of ethnic violence, see Petersen 2002.

[94] Davis et al. 1997.

to maintain their sovereignty, such an imbalance leads to interstate conflicts.

In addition, many ethnic groups do not engage in violent conflicts and there are (generally) peaceful multiethnic societies such as the United States, Brazil, Switzerland, or Australia. "Ethnic group," based on common descent and a shared language and culture, is not identical with "nation," considered a politically conscious group, which claims the right of self-determination through statehood.[95] Only when ethnic *nationalism* – that is, the aspiration to establish states based on ethnic affiliations – becomes a major political force in the region, does the likelihood of violence rise to the extent that the division of the region into ethnonational groups does not coincide with the existing state boundaries in the region.[96]

Mainstream IR theory, including the more recent constructivist theory, however, overlooks the variations in the unitary nature of the key actor in the international system. The nation-state is in many regions not a unified actor.[97] Although IR theory uses the terms "state" and "nation" interchangeably, they are not identical. In practice, in some regions they are almost the same, but in other regions they are not, and there might even be big differences between them. This variation is a key factor in accounting for regional variations in war and peace.

Even though realism and liberalism are unable to account for the underlying problem – regional war proneness – they are very helpful with regard to the possibility of and the means for its solution. Indeed, I will show that all three perspectives suggest different ways of addressing the state-to-nation problem, and that their different strategies for peace determine what kind of regional peace (if any) will emerge.

To sum up, the second core idea of this study introduces the main underlying cause of regional war proneness, namely, the state-to-nation imbalance or asymmetry. Various types or levels of regional peace are the result of different ways of addressing this underlying cause. In other words, whether, how, and to what extent the question of the state-to-nation imbalance is resolved determines the type or level of regional peace. This is closely related to the first core idea with regard to levels

[95] See the more elaborate discussion in chs. 2 and 3. See also Gellner 1983, Jackman 1993, p. 102, Connor 1994, A. Smith 1999.
[96] The differences between ethnic and civic nationalism, and their sources and manifestations, are discussed in chs. 2 and 3.
[97] On some of the problems that the state-centric bias creates for major quantitative datasets in IR, see Lemke 2002, pp. 187–191.

of analysis, because the external great powers are able and willing at most to mitigate – rather than resolve – the state-to-nation problem, and thus they may only affect lower-level cold outcomes, which do not demand the resolution of the state-to-nation problem. In contrast, in the higher-level warm peace the state-to-nation problems are resolved (or transcended), and therefore such a peace has to be generated by the regional actors themselves. Thus, global elements can produce cold peace, but it will be of a different quality than a warm peace based on regional/domestic factors. The idea is that the higher the level of peace, the more demanding it is with regard to resolving the regional state-to-nation problems; in other words, in order to reach warm peace, the state-to-nation problems must be fully resolved or transcended. Hence, the requirement to move beyond global mechanisms and to rely on the appropriate regional/domestic factors.

Overview of the book

Chapters 2 and 3 focus on theoretical aspects, while chapters 4 to 8 consider empirical case studies. Chapters 5, 7, and 8, however, also contain conceptual introductions, which elaborate on their respective theoretical components.

Chapter 2 presents the theory of regional war and peace, that is, the independent and dependent variables and the causal linkages between them. I differentiate among five types of regional war and peace outcomes: hot war, cold war, cold peace, and two subtypes of warm peace (normal peace and high-level peace). The independent variables are divided into domestic/regional (the key variable is the state-to-nation balance; the secondary or intervening variable liberal compatibility among the regional states) and global (namely, the types of great power regional engagement: competition, disengagement, cooperation, and hegemony). Finally, I introduce the main propositions of the theory by linking the independent and dependent variables, that is, explaining the regional war and peace outcomes by the different causal factors. More specifically, the degree of the state-to-nation balance accounts for the extent of war proneness. In a situation of an imbalance, great power competition or disengagement from the region aggravate, or at least do not moderate, the level of the regional conflict, and produce a regional cold war punctuated by hot wars. Three strategies for addressing the regional state-to-nation imbalance account for the three types of peace: cold peace may be achieved by great power hegemony or cooperation in the region, which moderates (but does not resolve) the state-to-nation problem; normal peace is produced through directly resolving the state-to-nation issues, notably by a transition of the major regional states from revisionist ideologies to status quo orientations – the condition for this is the presence of coherent states and the related success of state-building and nation-building; and high-level warm peace is brought about by transcending (or resolving) the state-to-nation problem through achieving regional liberal compatibility. Yet a prerequisite for the success of such a process is a minimal degree of state-to-nation balance in the region. I formulate these propositions by combining the three substantive theoretical perspectives (realism, liberalism, and international society) and the two levels of analysis (global and regional/domestic). The following chapters further elaborate elements of this theory and examine them in empirical case studies.

Chapter 3 focuses on explaining hot regional wars. A high extent of the state-to-nation imbalance in a region is the underlying cause of regional war proneness. The state-to-nation balance has two dimensions: (1) the extent of congruence between geopolitical boundaries and national identities and (2) state strength in the region. The combined effect of these variables helps determine the war proneness of the regional states. Thus, a combination of incongruence and strong states leads to revisionist/expansionist orientation and the pursuit of wars of profit; the combined effect of incongruence and weak states leads to incoherent or "failed" states and the occurrence of civil wars and foreign intervention; congruence and weak states produce the "frontier state" and boundary wars; a combination of congruence and strong states leads to the emergence of status quo states, which are more likely to engage in peaceful conflict resolution. I offer brief illustrations of these patterns from a number of regions. At the same time, the major proximate (or intervening) causes of specific regional wars are mainly realist ones, notably related to the security dilemma and imbalances of power, which create motivations for wars of profit. Another proximate cause of regional wars is domestic/political, namely, domestic instability and elite insecurity, which produce the diversionary motivation for war. Chapter 3 also presents quantitative data from all regions in different periods, and I make some brief comparisons among them. These data show the correlation between the state-to-nation imbalance and war proneness. The causal relations between the independent variables and the outcomes are examined in the case studies.

Accordingly, the case studies are selected based on variations in the independent variables.[98] The outcomes are then expected to reflect the results according to the propositions advanced in the theoretical framework. For the cases in chapters 4, 7, and 8, the key variation is in the state-to-nation balance. Chapter 4 discusses a key region in which there is an imbalance (thus frequent hot wars are to be expected), while chapters 7 and 8 analyze regions with a state-to-nation balance (and thus I expect warm peace to take place). In chapter 5 the key variations are in the type of great power engagement, and as a result the study expects variations between cold war and cold peace. Chapter 6 examines the combined effects of variations in the state-to-nation imbalance and in the type of great power engagement. The expected outcomes should range between hot war, cold war, cold peace, and warm peace depending on whether there is a state-to-nation balance or imbalance and on the type of great power involvement.

The case studies in chapters 4, 5, and 6 are derived from two regions with high state-to-nation imbalances which lead to high war proneness: the Middle East during the post-1945 era, in which there have been frequent Arab–Israeli wars; the Balkans in the 1830–1913 period and again in the 1990s, notably the regional wars of 1885 and 1912–1913; and the wars of Yugoslav disintegration of 1991–1999. These regions present hard or even "crucial" cases[99] for my theory because they (especially the Middle East) are considered to be regions which "best fit the realist view of international politics."[100] IR analysts did not consider, however, that this so-called realist behavior might be derived from causes distinctive from realist factors such as state and nation issues.

Chapters 4 and 6 explain high regional war proneness by the high extent of the state-to-nation imbalance in the two regions. Such an imbalance, producing revisionist states and state incoherence, is the underlying cause of the frequent regional wars in both the Middle East and the Balkans. At the same time, the proximate causes of specific wars are the realist factors of mutual fears (due to the security dilemma) and power

[98] As King et al. remark (1994, p. 137): "selecting observations for inclusion in a study according to the categories of the key causal explanatory variable causes no inference problem. The reason is that our selection procedure does not predetermine the outcome of our study, since we have not restricted the degree of possible variation in the dependent variable."
[99] On the methodology of using hard cases for theory testing, see Eckstein 1975 and King et al. 1994, pp. 209–212. See also Van Evera 1997.
[100] On the Middle East, see Nye 1993, p. 147.

distributions providing incentives for territorial expansion or restoration (wars of profit), as well as diversionary motivations. In contrast to some popular perceptions, the regional wars were not caused by external great powers, but rather were initiated by local states, mostly against the great power wishes.

In order to increase the number of the examined observations, I use the theory not only to explain variations between regions but also to explain the following types of variations:

(a) Changes over time in war proneness in a region.[101]
(b) Variations among different locales inside a region, namely, spatial differences in war proneness.
(c) Variations among different states in the same region with regard to their resort to force and war involvement.

These variations are "observable implications" which I derive from my theory and test on new data.[102]

Chapters 5 and 6 examine the effects of variations in types of great power engagement on regional conflicts. Thus, I evaluate the effects of competition and disengagement on the persistence of regional cold wars. In a situation of a state-to-nation imbalance, the effects of great power competition are contradictory. On the one hand, competing great powers help prolong the regional conflict by aiding and supporting rival regional states. They are also unable to prevent the outbreak of regional hot wars. On the other hand, they are more able to effect the speedy termination of such wars. Thus, great power competition results in a pattern of cold war punctuated by short hot wars. Great power disengagement, on the other hand, leaves the states free to pursue their conflict in accordance with their interests and capabilities. In a situation of an acute state-to-nation imbalance, in the long run this will also result in a regional cold war pattern with occasional hot wars.

The major cases of great power competition prolonging regional conflicts are the Middle East during the US–Soviet rivalry in the Cold War, and the Balkans during Russian–Austro-Hungarian rivalry from 1880 until World War I. A major case of great power disengagement is the Yugoslav conflict from the early 1990s until late 1995. The Middle East and the Balkans are hard cases for examining the thesis about the key role of the regional, rather than the global, factors in the emergence of

[101] On the logic of within-case comparisons, see Van Evera 1997, pp. 58–63.
[102] On "observable implications," see King et al. 1994.

the hot outcomes, because they are usually considered areas where the great powers had decisive influence on outcomes. I demonstrate that, indeed, they had important effects, but mostly on the cold outcomes.

Chapters 5 and 6 also analyze the pacifying effects of great power hegemony or cooperation in regions suffering from basic state-to-nation problems, leading to regional cold peace. I address five cases of hegemony in the twentieth century (in addition to Austrian hegemony in part of the Balkans in the 1830–1913 era): two of them in the Middle East and three in Eastern Europe and the Balkans. The two Middle Eastern cases are the US hegemony vis-à-vis Egypt and Israel since the late 1970s, leading to the Camp David accords, and the US hegemony in relation to the Arab–Israeli arena as a whole in the post-Cold War era. The three cases of hegemony in the Balkans/Eastern Europe are Germany in the late 1930s–early 1940s, the USSR in the Cold War era, and the US assumption of the hegemonic role in Yugoslavia since 1995, leading to the Dayton peace agreements in that year and, in 1999, the pacifying intervention in Kosovo. The major case of great power cooperation is the post-Napoleonic Concert of Europe, culminating with regard to the Balkans during the 1878 Berlin Congress.

The transition from great power competition or disengagement to cooperation or hegemony changes the strategic environment for the regional actors through the influence of the great powers on their capabilities. This environment becomes more conducive to a peace process among the regional states under great power sponsorship and prodding. This process may lead to a significant reduction in the level of the regional conflict, but so long as the regional state-to-nation problems are not resolved, the peace will remain cold and will depend on the continuing engagement of the great powers.

Chapters 7 and 8 address the formation of a warm regional peace. Chapter 7 addresses the lower-level version of warm peace – normal peace, reached by a transition of the regional states to status quo orientations as a result of effective state-building and nation-building, leading to greater state coherence. A notable case in this respect is the transition of South America from a war zone in the nineteenth century to relative peace during the twentieth. Chapter 8 examines the higher level of warm peace achieved through regional integration, which is made possible, in turn, when the states are coherent (strong states and nationally congruent) and there is liberal compatibility. The leading case is Western Europe in the post-1945 era. The rapid and far-reaching transformation of Western Europe was heavily assisted in its formative stages by the benign US hegemony. Yet, following its consolidation, the high-level warm peace has proven able to stand on its own and to persist even while the United States partially disengages from Europe in the post-Cold War era.

The concluding chapter, in addition to summarizing the book's theory and findings, focuses on the feasibility and desirability of the competing roads to regional peace, in accordance with the integrative model developed in the book and examined in the empirical case studies. I explore the utility of various peace strategies with regard to the resolution of the state-to-nation imbalances and suggest some policy-relevant prescriptions in accordance with the components of the model presented here.

Appendix A defines the states included in each of the regions discussed in the book and compares the level of the state-to-nation imbalance among them. Appendix B lists all the wars in the post-1945 era and their causes. I draw on a number of sources and refine their findings in order to compare the explanatory power of the state-to-nation imbalance, as it is discussed in this book, with alternative causes of war.

2 A theory of regional war and peace

In this chapter I present in greater detail my theory of regional war and peace. I specify the dependent and independent variables and the causal relations between them. The various elements of the theory are developed further in subsequent chapters. Following the introduction of the phenomenon to be explained – typology of regional war and peace outcomes – I draw on the discussion in chapter 1 to introduce three major theoretical perspectives at two levels of analysis. The three theoretical perspectives are realism, liberalism, and international society, and the two levels of analysis are the global and regional/domestic levels. Although the three theoretical perspectives are useful for deriving the variables and propositions of my theory, none is able, by itself, to explain the key variations of the phenomenon. I thus introduce my synthesis as a single coherent explanation of regional war and peace. In subsequent sections I show under what conditions the expectations of each of the theoretical perspectives will be met.

The phenomena to be explained

Defining a region

The two key elements that transform a certain group of states into a region are (1) a certain degree of geographical proximity and (2) strategic interaction (Schelling 1966) or security interdependence (Morgan 1997, pp. 25–26).[1] Some geographical contiguity is a necessary element in defining a region. Still, it is the intense interactions and the extent of interdependence among a group of neighboring states, rather than mere

[1] Ayoob suggests that "geographic propinquity and intensity of interaction form the core variables that define a region" (1995, p. 56).

geographical considerations, that determine a region's boundaries.[2] These interrelationships are so consequential for the regional states that the behavior of any one of them "is a necessary element in the calculation of the others."[3] Buzan defines a region, or what he calls a "security complex," as "a group of states whose primary security concerns link together sufficiently closely that their national securities cannot realistically be considered apart from one another" (1991, p. 190).[4] Since proximate states are most likely to go to war with each other, and wars among neighbors have historically been the dominant type of interstate wars,[5] it is in regional settings that the danger of war and the necessity of peace primarily arise. Moreover, a number of studies have found that a war contagion/diffusion operates at the regional level. These studies explore the probabilities of both inter- and intraregional contagion and conclude that conflict spreads within but not across regions.[6] Other studies have found that border contact increases the probability of war contagion (reviewed in Geller and Singer 1998, pp. 106–107). The regional context is thus the most appropriate – and relevant – context for studying war and peace. Regional peace is a prerequisite for global peace.[7] Surprisingly, security studies have neglected the study of regional military conflict.[8]

A typology of regional war and peace

How can we explain the great variations in the state of war and peace between different regions, such as Western Europe, the Middle East, and South America, and how do we capture the historical and current changes in war and peace patterns in each of these regions? The use of the adjectives "hot" (or "warm") and "cold" in differentiating between situations of war and peace is a first step toward understanding these regional transitions and variations.

[2] For a partly related discussion, see Lake 1997, pp. 50–51. See also the excellent discussion in Wriggins 1992, pp. 3–13; and the discussion of the concept of PRIE (politically relevant international environment) by Maoz (1996, 2001).
[3] Bull 1977, p. 10.
[4] For an updated version, see Buzan and Waever 2003. See also Ayoob 1995, pp. 56–59. Thompson (1973) identifies four conditions for defining a regional subsystem, which are summarized in Lake 1997, p. 47. See also Russett 1967. On regional security complexes, see also Morgan 1997 and on regional systems see Lake 1997, pp. 46–48. See especially Lake's concept of externality (ibid., pp. 48–52) as defining a regional system. See also Solingen 1998 and Katzenstein 2005, pp. 6–13.
[5] See ch. 3 for the development of this argument.
[6] For a recent study, see K. Gleditsch 2002.
[7] Kupchan 1998, 45, citing also Nye 1971.
[8] See, for example, the discussion in M. Levy 1995, 58.

Actual use of force	War is possible in the short term	War is possible but not in the short run	War is unlikely (but not unimaginable)	War is unthinkable
1	2	3	4	5
Hot war(s)	**Cold war**	**Cold peace**	**Normal peace**	**High-level peace**
			Warm peace	

Figure 2.1 The dependent variables: a regional war–peace continuum
Note: The term "continuum" is used here to indicate the logical sequence of stages between maximum conflict (hot war) and maximum peace (warm peace). It is not intended to suggest a linear progression from war to peace. That is, a given region or group of states need not necessarily progress through all stages. Rather, stages may be skipped in accordance with the presence or absence of explanatory variables, and the process may be reversed (a regression from peace to war).

These terms have already been used in practice in different global and regional contexts. In the post-World War II era the term "cold war" became prominent in both academic and policy discourse. The idea was to contrast the type of relations that evolved between the superpowers after 1945 with the recurrent violent clashes among great powers before 1945. Even though US–Soviet interactions were highly conflictual, they never reached the stage of an armed conflict, in sharp contrast to the two world wars and numerous other "hot wars" among great powers in earlier eras.

On the regional level, the peaceful relations between Egypt and Israel since the Camp David accords of 1978, and the peace treaty of 1979, are commonly perceived to have remained at the stage of "cold peace," in contrast to the "warm peace" prevailing in Scandinavia, Benelux, or Western Europe as a whole. This cold peace, which in the aftermath of the Cold War and the 1991 Gulf War has begun to spread beyond Egyptian–Israeli relations to include additional Arab states and the Palestinians, also marks a significant departure from the previous state of regional relations, marked by occasional outbreaks of hot wars between Israelis and Arabs until the 1980s. The warm peace in Western Europe also emerged after 1945, following a long period of hot and cold wars among the European states.

Interestingly, international relations theory has not made theoretical use of the conceptual variation between hot and cold war or cold and warm peace. Most studies use a simple dichotomy between a state of war and a state of peace, but such a dichotomy is too broad and imprecise to describe the complex patterns of war and peace in regions such as the Middle East. Only a few studies have distinguished among types of peace,[9] but even they usually lack an intermediate degree between a state of nonwar (or negative peace) and full-blown peace (often called positive or stable peace).[10] The sheer distance between a state of war and full-fledged peace calls for recognizing distinct intermediate degrees, which would help us in comparing the proneness to war and peace in different regions. Such distinctions will also be useful in explaining historical transitions and predicting future trends about war and peace in the same region.

The advantage of the adjectives "hot" and "cold" is that they are simple and widely used terms. They make the analysis more differentiated, but they do not multiply by much the number of analytical categories. We thus gain additional richness and nuance without losing analytic power, a danger inherent in differentiations which are too rich. I argue that this differentiation captures significant phenomena that are lost if we look only at a dichotomous distinction between war and peace. Note that the category of warm peace is divided further into normal peace and high-level peace. The two main criteria for distinguishing among the five types of regional outcomes are the probability of the use of force, and the major foreign policy means employed by the actors. The combination of the two criteria yields the following five patterns.

1. *Hot war* is a situation of actual use of force aimed at destroying the military capabilities of adversaries.[11] This study focuses on interstate wars, but hot wars include domestic wars to the extent that other regional states get involved in one way or another in the hostilities.
2. *Cold war* is a situation of negative peace[12] – a mere absence of hot war in which hostilities may break out any time. It is characterized

[9] See Harkabi 1990, Rock 1989, and Holsti 1996, pp. 147–149.
[10] But see the works of Adler 1991, Boulding 1978, and Kacowicz et al. 2000.
[11] For the Correlates of War Project, see Small and Singer 1982, pp. 38, 54; see also Vasquez 1993, pp. 21–29, who suggests no fewer than 1,000 battle deaths from all sides as a part of the definition of war; see also Gochman and Maoz 1984 and Diehl and Goertz 2000. Although a strict adherence to such a precise figure is unnecessary in a qualitative study like most of the present one, it will be useful in chapter 6 where (with Uri Reznick) I conduct a semi-quantitative examination of the Balkans.
[12] On this concept, see Kacowicz 1995, 268.

by recurrent military crises and a considerable likelihood of escalation to war, either in a premeditated way or inadvertently.[13] The parties may succeed in managing the crises, avoiding escalation to wars while protecting their vital interests,[14] but they do not attempt seriously to resolve the fundamental issues in dispute between them. Such a conception of a cold war reflects Hobbes's idea of the nature of war as not necessarily consisting of "actual fighting but in the known disposition thereto during all the time there is no assurance to the contrary. All other time is peace" (cited in Rock 1989, p. 2). As to means employed by the parties, a cold war is characterized by the use of military forces for show-of-force purposes such as influencing the intentions of the regional rivals through deterrence and compellence.[15] Diplomacy plays an important role in the parties' relations, but it is largely a diplomacy of violence – the use of military means for diplomatic ends – for signaling and crisis management, and to clarify interests, commitments, and "red lines." An important component of cold war situations is the diplomacy of regional hot war termination, manifested in the establishment of ceasefires or armistices.[16] The presence of enduring rivalries in the region is a key indicator of a cold war there.[17]

3. *Cold peace* is a situation characterized by formal agreements among the parties and the maintenance of diplomatic relations among them. The underlying issues of the regional conflict are in the process of being moderated and reduced, but are still far from being resolved. The danger of the use of force is thus unlikely in the near future, but it still looms in the background, and is possible in the longer run if changes in the international or regional environment occur. In one or more of the regional states there are still significant groups hostile to the other states, and thus the possibility of belligerent opposition groups coming to power in these states may also lead to renewed hostilities or a return to cold war. The parties still feel threatened

[13] On inadvertent wars, see George 1991 and Miller 1994b.

[14] On crisis management, see George 1991, George and Simons 1994, and others cited in Miller 1995, 93, n. 34.

[15] On the distinctions between offense, defense, compellence, and deterrence, see Schelling 1960, 95 and L. Freedman 1998.

[16] A red line refers to the point beyond which the interests of the signaling state are greater than those of its adversary. Thus, the state attempts to deter its adversary by signaling that the crossing of these lines would lead to retaliation. On the termination of wars, see the useful articles in N. Oren 1982 and Goemens 2000.

[17] On enduring rivalries, see Goertz and Diehl 1992a and Diehl and Goertz 2000.

by increases in each other's power, and are concerned with relative gains.[18]

Military force is not used in the relations between the parties, not even for signaling and show-of-force purposes. Rather, the focus is on diplomatic means for the purposes of conflict reduction or mitigation,[19] and the parties seriously attempt to moderate the level of the conflict through negotiations and crisis-prevention regimes.[20] These efforts, however, stop short of a full-blown reconciliation among the parties. Foreign relations among the regional parties are conducted almost exclusively through intergovernmental diplomacy, and there are limitations on transnational activity involving nongovernmental players. The parties still develop contingency plans that take into account the possibility of war among them. Such plans include force structure, defense spending, training, type of weapons, fortifications, military doctrine, and war planning.

Warm peace refers to a low likelihood of war in the region and to much more cooperative relations among the regional states relative to cold peace. There are two types of warm peace – normal and high-level peace.

4. *Normal peace* is a situation in which the likelihood of war is considerably lower than in cold peace because most, if not all, of the substantive issues in the conflict between states in the region have been resolved. Regional states recognize each other's sovereignty and reach an agreement on issues such as boundaries, resource allocation, and refugee settlement. This peace is more resilient than cold peace. Still, war is not out of the question in the longer run, if the governing elite or the nature of domestic regime in one or more of the key regional states changes. Relations among the regional states begin to develop beyond the intergovernmental level, but the major channels of communication and diplomacy are still at the interstate level.
5. *High-level peace* reflects a still higher degree of stability of peace. It is a situation in which the parties share expectations that no resort to armed violence is possible in the foreseeable future under any circumstances, including government change in any of the states or a change in the international setting. There is no planning by the regional states

[18] On relative vs. absolute gains, see Grieco 1988 and 1990, Baldwin 1993, and Powell 1994. A concern over relative gains means, for example, that relative military power (and related economic resources) matters, and there is a fear of domination by a superior party.
[19] On conflict reduction, see J. Stein 1975, Zartman 1995b, and Ben-Dor 1982.
[20] On crisis prevention, see George et al. 1983 and George et al. 1988.

Table 2.1 *The three ideal types of regional peace*

	Cold peace	Normal peace	High-level peace
Main issues in conflict	Mitigated, but not fully resolved (conflict reduction)	Resolved (conflict resolution)	Resolved or transcended (conflict transformation)
Channels of communication	Only intergovernmental	Mostly intergovernmental; beginning of development of transnational ties	Intergovernmental and highly developed transnational ties
Contingency plans for war	Still present	Likely in the case of a rise to power of revisionist elites	Absent
Relative vs. absolute gains	Relative gains dominate the agenda	No clearcut domination of either absolute or relative gains	Absolute gains dominate
Return to cold or hot war	Possible in the longer run, unlikely in the short run	Unlikely (even in the longer run)	Unthinkable

for the use of force against each other, and no preparation for war fighting among them. There are institutionalized nonviolent procedures to resolve conflicts, and these procedures are widely accepted by the elites in government and outside it in all the regional states. None of the major political groups, either in government or in the opposition which may come to power in any of the regional parties, is likely to return the relations to cold peace, let alone cold war or hot war. The regional states thus no longer fear one another, are not concerned with relative gains, and can thus overcome the security dilemma among them. The regional states form a "pluralistic security community": "they have come to agreement on at least this one point: that common social problems must and can be resolved by processes of 'peaceful change,'" that is, "the resolution of social problems, normally by institutionalized procedures, without resort to large-scale physical force."[21]

[21] Deutsch et al. 1957, cited in Rock 1989, p. 3; Adler and Barnett 1998.

> The relations among the regional parties include extensive transnational transactions parallel to equally intensive intergovernmental and transgovernmental exchanges. The transnational relations take place in a multiplicity of areas and include open borders, a high degree of economic interdependence, a dense network of regional institutions, intense people-to-people interactions and tourism, and widespread cultural exchange.[22]

Table 2.1 distinguishes between cold, normal, and high-level peace.

Competing theoretical perspectives: system, society, and community at two levels of analysis

The theory of regional war and peace that I develop in this chapter is based on integrated insights from three major perspectives in international relations theory: realism, liberalism, and international society. These perspectives do not explicitly address the issue of transitions and variations in regional war and peace patterns, so insights into these issues must be deduced from these theories' underlying logic. For this purpose, I relate the three substantive perspectives to the question of level of analysis, by dividing each perspective into two variants – global and regional. The result is six distinctive images of regional war and peace. The global variants of all three perspectives stress the role of the great powers in influencing regional outcomes, and the regional variants highlight the effects of regional/domestic developments in affecting patterns of war and peace. Each perspective, however, differs with regard to the character of the great power involvement or the nature of the regional/domestic factors that are most relevant to war and peace. Indeed, the logic of the six images leads each to expect different regional war and peace patterns.

Realism: global system and regional system

The realist perspective sees the international system as characterized by rivalry and competition among states.[23] It focuses on states' quest for power and security in an anarchic international setting. Realism

[22] On intergovernmental, transgovernmental, and transnational relations, see Keohane and Nye 1972 and 1977.
[23] On the realist conception of system, see Waltz 1979, ch. 6 and Jervis 1979 and 1997.

contends that, in an anarchic self-help system, the most that is possible in cooperation among rival states are tacit rules which reflect balances of power and interest but do not have independent effects on state behavior and outcomes. As a result, state conduct is not determined by normative considerations.[24]

The global realist perspective focuses on the great powers because of the enormous capabilities at their disposal, which enable them to affect major international outcomes. Realism expects the great powers to compete rather than cooperate in important regions. This competition is manifested in efforts by one power to exclude rival powers from influence in the region, and in supporting regional parties who rival the other power's regional clients. Instead of peacemaking, which aims at resolving, or at least mitigating, the fundamental issues in a regional conflict, great power competition affords, at best, regional crisis management. "Crisis management" refers to efforts by the great powers to balance between protecting their vital interests in the region and avoiding an escalation to great power war, although without settling the underlying issues in the regional conflict.[25] The great powers avoid war among themselves by cooperating tacitly in trying to limit regional wars or end them early, and maintain the regional balance of power.[26] Realist logic also suggests that the great powers are likely to disengage from regions in which they do not have important interests.

The regional variant of the realist perspective focuses on the interaction and dynamics among the states that are part of the regional system, not on the involvement of external powers in the region.[27] This perspective emphasizes regional rivalry affected by the distribution of power, the balance of threats, and the security dilemma. Regional peace (or, more precisely, a situation of cold war) may emerge, but it is more a byproduct of a certain configuration of the offense–defense balance, the balance of power, or the balance of threat than a result of a purposeful policy and strategy of peacemaking.[28]

[24] For a realist discussion of norms and self-interests, see Gowa 1995, 514–516; see also Goertz and Diehl 1994, pp. 104–107. On tacit rules, see Miller 2002.
[25] The distinction between crisis management and conflict resolution is elaborated in Miller 2002, pp. 22–26.
[26] See Miller 2002, chs. 3 and 5. [27] See Wriggins 1992, ch. 1, and Evron 1994.
[28] On the balance of power vs. the balance of threat, see Walt 1987. For an excellent discussion of competing realist and nonrealist explanations for the emergence of peace, see Rock 1989.

The international society perspective: global and regional society of states

A second major theoretical perspective in IR theorizing is international society, also called the Grotian approach.[29] In recent times, the international society approach has been represented mainly by British scholars such as Herbert Butterfield and Martin Wight (1966) and Hedley Bull (1977).[30] The regime approach (Krasner 1983) is also related to the international society school as both highlight cooperation among states rather than focusing on conflict as in the realist perspective. Bull distinguishes between a system of states and a society of states. An international system exists when "two or more states . . . may be in contact with each other and interact in such a way as to be necessary factors in each other's calculations."[31] An international society goes further:[32] states' awareness of common interests or values gives rise to shared rules and institutions; these, in turn, enable states to cooperate in accomplishing common objectives. In contrast to realism, the international-society school regards states as informed by explicit international norms, specifying general "standards of behavior in terms of rights and obligations."[33] The major causal factor for the emergence of rules and institutions is cognitive-cultural.[34] Common ideas and values and a shared ethical code make possible the definition of international rules, the evolution of joint institutions, and the reinforcement of a sense of common interests. The international society perspective, too, is divided into two variants: global society of states and regional society of states.

The global society-of-states school emphasizes the unequal distribution of power between small states and great powers, and its major contribution to the international order. The global variant of this school focuses on the norms related to the primacy and leadership of the great powers (the "great responsibles") in the global society. The great powers enjoy a special status, having a voice in the settlement of regional disputes, but also responsibilities for promoting international order, peace, and stability.[35] The special great power status and role are recognized

[29] For a review of the Grotian tradition, see Cutler 1991 and Buzan 1993. A recent theoretical development partly related to the international society approach is the constructivist theory. See Wendt 1999.
[30] Thus, this approach is also called the English School. See Buzan 2004 and Devlen et al. 2005.
[31] Bull 1977, p. 14. [32] See ibid., pp. 5–18.
[33] Krasner 1983, p. 2; 1985, p. 4. A major work on norms is Katzenstein 1996a.
[34] For a qualification to this position, see Buzan 1993. [35] See Miller 2002, chs. 1 and 4.

by other states. Regional states accept the right of the major powers to have a voice in the settlement of local disputes if the external powers fulfill their responsibilities to the regional order and work to promote regional peacemaking. Great power responsibility and leadership thus have stabilizing worldwide effects. Concerted action by the great powers[36] or hegemonic leadership by one power[37] are the major means for regional peacemaking in the global society. Such mechanisms reduce the destabilizing effects of international anarchy and enhance the possibility for explicit cooperation of the great powers and the local states in promoting regional peace.

The regional variant of the international society perspective envisions a society of states on the regional level. This regional society is also norm-governed, but the substance of its norms is markedly different from that of global society. Thus, the norm of great power primacy, which the global society school advances, is in direct opposition to the norm of the sovereign equality of all regional states, irrespective of their size and capabilities, which the regional society-of-states perspective emphasizes.[38] In a regional society, ideologically diverse states coexist, interact, and cooperate by respecting the norms of mutual sovereignty, the territorial integrity of other states in the region, the sanctity of boundaries, and the principle of noninterference in their neighbors' domestic affairs.[39] Behavior in accordance with these norms ensures durable regional peace.

Transnational liberal community: global and regional

The regional society-of-states perspective focuses on interstate relations within a given region, but a competing liberal image of a regional community highlights the transnational social bonds which link the

[36] On great power concerts, see Kupchan and Kupchan 1991 and Richardson 1999. See also ch. 5 below. For a critique, see Kagan 1997/8.
[37] For overviews of hegemonic theories, see Nye 1990 and 2002, J. Levy 1991, DiCicco and Levy 2003, and ch. 5 below. Some hegemonic theories are also compatible with realist logic. For analytical clarity, in this study I classify them as part of the global society-of-states approach.
[38] On the contrast between the norms of great power primacy and sovereign equality of states, see Klein 1974.
[39] On these norms in the context of the post-1945 Third World, see Buchheit 1978, Jackson and Rosberg 1982, Jackson 1990, Ayoob 1995, ch. 4, and Zacher 2001. On a regional society of states, see also Buzan 1991, Job 1992, Wriggins 1992, Hurrell 1995, Holm and Sorensen 1995, Holsti 1996, and Lake and Morgan 1997. For a critique of the regional society thesis that focuses on the domestic politics of ethnic ties, see Saideman 1997 and 2001.

individual citizens of regional states.[40] In highlighting the possibility of a regional liberal community, this perspective emphasizes the domestic transformation of regional states, making them ideologically similar to each other, as well as the enhancement of transnational relations and communication in the economic, social, and cultural domains across borders. In a regional liberal community, interstate boundaries are not sacred, and intergovernmental relations are not the only relations that count. There is a high degree of interference or involvement in the domestic affairs of the other member-states in the community, accompanied by a process of creating powerful supranational institutions which challenge and diminish the sovereignty of states in the region.

A major difference between the regional perspectives of international society and liberal community is that a regional society may emerge regardless of the nature of domestic regimes and ideologies of the regional states. In a regional community, however, a common ideology is a necessary condition.[41] Mere ideological similarity, however, is insufficient for the creation of a meaningful regional community. Equally important is the content of the shared ideology, which should encourage a sense of affinity ("we-feeling") and mutual trust among the states of the region. Such trust is necessary for giving up some sovereignty by creating supranational institutions and encouraging transnational relations. Liberalism is the major ideology fostering such affinity and trust among the states which share it, and such an ideology is necessary for the emergence of a regional community.[42]

The global variant of the liberal approach is similar to the global society-of-states perspective in stressing the stabilizing role of the great powers (either a hegemonic leader or a concert) in shaping a global order. Unlike the global society approach, in which great powers may cooperate on the basis of shared norms despite differences in domestic regimes and ideologies, the global liberal perspective emphasizes the

[40] I partly rely here on Bull's (1977, pp. 25–27) so-called Kantian perspective, applied to the regional instead of the universal level.

[41] See the major work of Deutsch et al. (1957) on security communities. They argue that the compatibility of major values is essential for the emergence of such a community. On this point, see also Rock 1989, pp. 3–4. On security communities from a constructivist perspective, see the work of Adler and Barnett 1998.

[42] On the distinction between "unifying" and "divisive" ideologies, see Rock 1989, p. 16 (drawing on Walt 1987). Whereas unifying ideologies respect the autonomy, sovereign equality, and legitimacy of other like-minded states, divisive ideologies do not. Divisive ideologies include communism, fascism, hypernationalism, and fundamentalist religious movements. On hypernationalism, see Mearsheimer 1990, 21, and Van Evera 1994. Liberal democracy is the major example of a unifying ideology in the post-1945 era.

role of liberal democratic powers in promoting global liberal order.[43] The liberal powers may spread democracy, defend human rights and civil liberties, construct liberal international institutions, and promote a liberal economic order. Thus, liberal great powers may assist in the formation of regional liberal communities among new regional democracies, including through encouraging a process of domestic liberalization and democratization in key regional states, or even imposing such a process during military occupation (T. Smith 1994).

Each of these theories accounts for only a certain component of the phenomenon, leading me to present my integrative explanation as a general theory of regional war and peace.

Explaining regional war and peace

The independent variables: regional/domestic and global factors

The theory of regional war and peace has two sets of independent variables: regional/domestic and global. In this study I am interested in the combined effects of these variables on regional outcomes, rather than in the sources of the independent variables. The great powers may, under certain conditions, play a key role in affecting regional outcomes, but the focus here is not on explaining the great powers' regional policies as such, but on the consequences of these policies and types of involvement for regional events.[44]

Similarly, regional and domestic factors have important effects on regional war and peace, but my focus is not on explaining the origins of these factors, but on their implications for regional war and peace.

Regional/domestic causal factors: the state-to-nation balance and liberal compatibility

There are two regional/domestic characteristics that affect the patterns of war and peace in a region. The key independent variable is the *state-to-nation balance* in the region. An intervening variable is the extent of *liberal compatibility* among regional states.

[43] For a related discussion of a process by which smaller powers may experience a shift in value orientation through the influence and the example of the hegemon, see Ikenberry and Kupchan 1990, p. 55.

[44] In Miller 2002, I focused on explaining the sources of great power conflict and cooperation.

The regional state-to-nation balance There are two dimensions to the regional state-to-nation balance.[45] The first dimension refers to the prevalence of strong or weak states. This is the "hardware" of state-building. The second refers to the extent of congruence or compatibility between political boundaries and national identifications in a certain region. This is the "software" of nation-building.

I. The extent of state strength (or the success of state-building).[46] The strength of states is determined by the institutions and resources available to them for governing the polity.[47] Weak states lack effective institutions and resources to implement their policies and fulfill key state functions. Most notably, they lack effective control over the means of violence in their territory and an effective law-enforcement system. Weak states thus face difficulties maintaining law and order and providing security in their territory. This hobbles the economic activity in these states, making it difficult for them to raise sufficient revenues, to collect taxes, and to maintain an effective bureaucracy and provide vital, or even rudimentary, services to the population (mail delivery, regular water supply, road network, electricity, education, health care, etc.).

Strong states, on the other hand, control the means of violence in their sovereign territory[48] and possess an effective set of institutions. Tilly (1975b) focused on the ability of the state to coerce, control, and extract resources as the key to state-making. Thus state strength or capacity can be measured by the ability of the state to mobilize manpower for military service and to extract financial resources from their societies.[49] Another useful measure is the development of a communications and transportation infrastructure indicated, for example (especially in the nineteenth and early twentieth century), by total railroad mileage (Centeno 2002,

[45] Chapter 3 discusses at great length the details of the state-to-nation balance and its effects on state and regional war proneness.
[46] On state-building, see Migdal 1988, Ayoob 1995, and Holsti 1996.
[47] On institutionalization as a key to political development, see Huntington 1968. See also Nettl 1968, who developed the concept of "stateness," the institutional centrality of the state; for a more recent review of stateness, see Evans 1997. The relations between stateness and regional conflict are developed by Ben-Dor 1983. Mufti (1996, pp. 12–13) presents three characteristics of state strength: autonomy (from foreign pressures), efficacy (the elite's ability to use state power in seeking to manage and transform society), and legitimacy (general societal consent and support for the state). State-building as defined here comprises the second element, while nation-building includes the third.
[48] As Max Weber suggests: "the use of force is regarded as legitimate only so far as it is either permitted by the state or prescribed by it" (1978, p. 56).
[49] See Gause 1992, 457, and the references he cites.

p. 110) or railroad density per 1,000 km^2 (see ch. 7 on South America, especially table 7.3).[50]

II. The degree of congruence (or the extent of success of nation-building). The extent of congruence is determined by the ratio between the existing geopolitical boundaries in the region and the national aspirations and identities of the peoples in the region, that is, the extent to which the current division of a given region into territorial states reflects the national affiliations of the main groups in the region and their aspirations to establish states and/or to revise existing boundaries.[51] High congruence means that the regional states, as entities or sets of institutions administering certain territories, reflect the national self-determination sentiments of the peoples in the region, that is, their aspirations to live as national communities in their own states.[52] High congruence thus means that there is a strong identification of the peoples in the region with existing states, and that they accept these states' existing boundaries. Such an acceptance must not be based only on ethnic homogeneity

[50] While Tilly's indicators might broadly parallel Mann's "despotic power," the transportation measurement might roughly indicate Mann's "infrastructural power" 1993, pp. 58–61). Despotic power refers to the power of state authorities over civil society; infrastructural power is the institutional capacity of the state to penetrate the territory and carry out decisions effectively. See also the indicators in Rotberg 2003, esp. pp. 4–22, and Fearon and Laitin 2003, 80.

[51] This section draws especially on Van Evera 1994. See also Mayall 1990, Buzan 1991, M. Brown 1993 and 1996, Cederman 1997, Gottleib 1993, Holsti 1996, Kupchan 1995, Hoffmann 1998, and Gurr 2000.

[52] On the definition of state and nation, see Gellner 1983, pp. 3–7; Connor 1994, pp. 90–117; A. Smith 2000, p. 3; H. Seton-Watson 1977, pp. 1–5; Linz and Stepan 1996, pp. 22–24; and the very useful citations in Jackman 1993, pp. 99–107. See especially Barrington (1997), who emphasizes "the belief in the right to territorial self-determination for the group" as a central part of the definition of a "nation," distinguishing it from other collectivities. While many groups hold common myths, values, and symbols (including ethnic groups), nations are unified by a sense of purpose: controlling the territory that the members of the group believe to be theirs. Thus, nations need not even be based on a certain ethnic identity: cultural features link multiethnic civic nations. As Gellner suggests, "nationalism" is "a political principle, which holds that the political and the national unit should be congruent" (1983, p. 1). Thus, nationalism is the active pursuit of control by a national group over the territory which it defines as its homeland. As a result, every nationalist movement involves the setting of territorial boundaries (Barrington 1997, 714); and national conflicts must involve disputes over territory to be truly "national." Key works on nationalism include Gellner 1983, B. Anderson 1991, Connor 1994, A. Smith 1991 and 2000, and Hobsbawm 1990. See also Breuilly 1993. In Gellner's (1983) conception, nationalism is a construction of aspiring elites with instrumental goals who respond to the successful examples of national states in other places. Anthony D. Smith focuses more on persistent ethnic identities that create the basis for nationalist movements (1986a). My work is especially influenced by Smith, and at any rate I accept that even if national identities are "intellectually constructed," they are derived from preexisting group identities (Gurr 2000, p. 7). But see also Brubaker's (1996) constructivist conception of "nations" as socially constructed identities.

of the regional states, but can also be based on civic nationalism. Civic nations share cultural features but are generally multiethnic in their makeup, most notably in the immigrant societies of the New World (the Americas and Oceania), and also in many cases of the state-initiated nationalism of Western Europe.[53] In other "Old World" societies, however, nationalism and ethnicity are more closely related.

Avoiding tautology: measuring the state-to-nation incongruence as an independent variable There are two primary senses in which a region's geopolitical and national boundaries may be *incongruent* in relation to the ethnonational criterion of one state per one nation:

1. *Too few states*: A single geopolitical entity may contain numerous national groups. This is the internal dimension of incongruence.
2. *Too many states*: A single national group may reside in more than one geopolitical entity. This is the external dimension of incongruence.

Thus, one potential way of measuring the regional state-to-nation congruence is by combining the effects of the following two measures:

1. *Internal incongruence*: The proportion of states in the region which contain more than one national group.[54]
2. *External incongruence*: The proportion of states in the region in which the majority ethnic group lives in substantial numbers in neighboring and other regional states as well, either as a majority or a minority.

The higher the combined effect of the two measures, the higher the state-to-nation incongruence in the region.[55]

[53] In contrast to Van Evera (1994), who focuses on ethnic nationalism, I accept that nationalism can be either ethnic or civic. Civic nationalism focuses on citizen identification with the nation-state in its current territorial boundaries as opposed to a loyalty based on subnational or transborder ethnic ties which may challenge the existing boundaries. In ethnic nationalism, based on lineage and common ancestry, the nation precedes the state (the "German model"), whereas in the civic version the state precedes the nation (the "French model"). See Brubaker 1992. On the distinction between ethnic and civic nationalism, see Kohn 1967, A. Smith 1986a; 2000, pp. 15–20, and Greenfeld 1992. For a useful overview, see Kupchan 1995, ch. 1.

[54] Woodwell (2004, 206), who relies on various data-sets, uses the figure 3 percent of a population.

[55] For example, in region A there are ten states. Seven of them are multinational while in eight of them there is at least one ethnonational group which resides also in other regional states. In region B, there are also ten states, of which six are multinational while in only

A state-to-nation incongruence leads to nationalist dissatisfaction with the status quo and thus to the emergence of strong challenges to the existing regional state system either from within the states or from outside.[56] The lower the state-to-nation congruence in the region, the more powerful these challenges.[57] Challenges from within include sub-national ethnic groups aspiring for secession from the state and calling for the establishment of new states to reflect the right of national groups for self-determination. Challenges from outside include pan-national movements of unification or irredentist claims to territories held by other states.[58] These challenges are made on grounds of national affiliation of the population or national-historic rights on the territory. The secessionists claim that there are too few states in the region on national grounds, while the pan-nationalists argue that there are too many. The result is that the supply–demand ratio of states is unbalanced, with demand exceeding supply, leading to wars of secession, or supply exceeding demand, resulting in wars of national unification.

The leaders of such challenges might either believe in these nationalist causes or manipulate them for their own domestic political purposes because of the popular appeal of these ideas.[59] There are certain limits to the domestic political factor, however: political leaders will not be able to manipulate the nationalist causes unless such popular forces and movements exist in the region, and those who subscribe to these sentiments are committed to act to advance them. The greater the mismatch between state boundaries and the territorial extent of nations in the region imbued with ethnonational feelings, or with beliefs about national-historic rights to the territory, the stronger such nationalist forces will be.[60]

two of the regional states lives a national group which inhabits also other states in the region. The combined state-to-nation (s/n) measure for region A is $(7 + 8)/10 = 15/10$; the combined s/n for region B is $(6 + 2)/10 = 8/10$. Thus, the s/n incongruence is much higher in region A than in region B.

[56] According to Hugh Seton-Watson (1977, p. 3), nationalist movements usually have three main objectives: independence (the formation of a sovereign state in which the nation is dominant), unification (the incorporation within the boundaries of this state of all groups which are considered to belong to the nation), and what he calls "nation-building" (persuading the population as a whole that it constitutes a nation, a belief that was held before independence only by a minority).

[57] For specification of these causal relations and under what conditions incongruence results in revisionist challenges, see ch. 3.

[58] On revisionist territorial demands among states, see Goertz and Diehl 1992b, pp. 23–25.

[59] For a useful overview of ethnic politics, strategic politicians and foreign policy, see Saideman 2002, pp. 173–177.

[60] For the key components and indicators of the state-to-nation imbalance, see ch. 3.

Table 2.2 *Success and failure in state-building and nation-building: four types of states and their effects on the regional state-to-nation balance*

	State-to-nation congruence	
State strength	Congruent	Incongruent
Strong states	**Status quo states** Regional state-to-nation balance Europe Southern Cone in South America Oceania North America	**Revisionist states** Regional state-to-nation imbalance Asia/Middle East (China–Taiwan; North Korea–S. Korea; Pakistan–Kashmir; Syria; Iraq until 2003)
Weak states	**Frontier states** Regional state-to-nation imbalance (but a considerable likelihood of evolution of state-to-nation balance) Northern part of South America/Central America	**Incoherent or failed states** Regional state-to-nation imbalance Sub-Saharan Africa

The combined effect of state-building and nation-building leads to the emergence of the following four types of states. Table 2.2 shows these types and in which region in the current international system they are relatively most prevalent. The next chapter spells out the causal relations between these types of states and regional war proneness as well as the relevant examples.

Strong and congruent states tend to be status quo-oriented. The nation is satisfied by the territorial identity of the state and does not have any nationalist claims (based on ethnicity or history) on the territories of other states. There are also no national groups inside the state that prefer to secede from the state and, at any rate, the state is powerful enough to overcome such attempts and thus also to deter them. When a region is populated by this type of state, there is a high extent of state-to-nation balance in the region. In today's world, Europe, North America, Oceania (Australia and New Zealand), and the southern cone of South America (Argentina, Brazil, Chile) are good examples of this pattern.

In contrast, when any of the three other types of states are prevalent in a region, there is a state-to-nation imbalance. Strong and incongruent states tend to be irredentist states which have revisionist territorial claims vis-à-vis their neighbors. In Asia and the Middle East there are some important representatives of this pattern: China (regarding Taiwan); North Korea (South Korea); Pakistan (Kashmir); Syria; and Iraq (until 2003). Although they are able to prevent or even deter attempts at secession so long as they are strong, as soon as the central authority gets weaker, demands for secession are likely to emerge and generate clashes between different national groups and the state or among competing national groups with competing nationalist claims to the same territory.

Moreover, the combination of state weakness and national incongruence leads to incoherent or – in extreme cases – to "failed" states,[61] which invite intervention of neighbors out of fear (status quo states) or nationalist-territorial greed (revisionist states). In sub-Saharan Africa, there are quite a few such failed states, Somalia being a prime example.

The combination of state weakness and national congruence produces the "frontier state," which is not so fragmented on a national basis, but does not fully control its territory, while its boundaries are not clearly demarcated and agreed upon by the neighbors.[62] As we will discuss in chapter 7, nineteenth-century South America is a good example of this pattern. In more recent times, the northern part of South America (notably, Colombia and Venezuela) and Central America have hosted frontier states.[63] Although the prevalence of this type of state produces a state-to-nation imbalance in the region, this imbalance is more likely to change to a balance than when the other types of states are prevalent. This is because the major source of change that is necessary – strengthening of the existing states – is easier to create than the type of change necessary when the other two types are prevalent – namely, the task of nation-building – which is more demanding and problematic to manage.

Regional effects of the state-to-nation imbalance The two products of the state-to-nation imbalance – revisionism and state failure – are interrelated and mutually reinforcing. To the extent that a revisionist state calls for the subordination of the regional states to a larger

[61] On failed states, see Helman and Ratner 1992/3; Holsti 1996, pp. 119–122; *Foreign Policy* 2005; and the Failed States Index of the Fund for Peace, 2005.
[62] For a useful discussion of the concept of the "frontier," see Kimmerling 1982, p. 3.
[63] See, for example, Kurtenbach 2002, pp. 129–130, 137.

movement or authority, or advocates irredentist claims to the territories of neighboring states, it also undermines the internal coherence and the domestic legitimacy of the other regional states, especially if domestic groups within these states respond to the revisionist calls out of ideological/nationalist conviction or due to economic/political bribes and military assistance offered by the revisionist state.

Conversely, incoherent domestically unstable and illegitimate states invite aggression and intervention by strong revisionist neighbors, who are tempted to take advantage of the state's weakness, especially if there are transborder ethnonational ties between the intervening and the weak states. Weak and incongruent states also "export instabilities" to neighboring states.[64] Thus, domestic attempts at secession and border changes are likely to "spill over" and involve a number of regional states. Such spillovers may occur through a migration of refugees who seek shelter in neighboring states from the instability and turmoil within the incoherent state, or by the incoherent state hosting armed groups with secessionist or irredentist claims, which infiltrate into adjacent states. Terrorist groups may also take advantage of such states. Such hosting may be involuntary and result from the incoherence and weakness of the host state. Revisionist states, on the other hand, may host such groups by choice, in order to undermine their neighbors' domestic order.[65] Moreover, irredentist sentiments concerning one national group can be "contagious," diffusing to other groups and states in the region.[66]

To sum up, the state-to-nation balance in a region exercises important effects on the balance of power between the status quo states, on the one hand, and revisionist states and nonstate political movements (irredentist, pan-national, or secessionist), on the other. The greater the state-to-nation imbalance, the more powerful the nationalist-revisionist forces are in relation to the status quo forces in the region, and vice versa. A key point is that, if status quo states face one or more of the other three kinds of states in their regional system, they are also likely

[64] In Lake's (1997) terms, such effects constitute security externalities or transborder "spillovers."

[65] For a useful overview of both irredentism and the secession challenge, see Mayall 1990, pp. 57–63.

[66] With respect to war, a number of empirical studies have shown evidence of such "contagion" or "diffusion" at an intraregional, rather than interregional level; see the summary of findings in Marshall 1997, p. 91, as well as Geller and Singer 1998, pp. 106–108, for an overview. For a recent study of diffusion and escalation of ethnic conflict, see Lobell and Mauceri 2004.

to stumble into war even if they did not initially want the war to happen. This is because of the high strategic interdependence in a regional system irrespective of the desires of the regional states. In other words, they are mutually dependent in their security whether they want such interdependence or not.

The intervening variable: liberal compatibility Liberal compatibility refers to whether all the states in the region (or at least all the major states) are liberal. The term "liberal" refers both to the political and the economic domains,[67] but the most critical element is the political one, that is, whether the states in the region are liberal democracies. Liberal democracies are defined as states that not only hold free and fair elections but also respect human rights and maintain the rule of law, a separation of powers, and the protection of basic liberties of speech, assembly, religion, and property.[68] Economic liberalism, for its part, refers to free-market economies, free trade, and economic interdependence among liberal states.

Stable liberal democracies have a high degree of coherence and domestic legitimacy, and, since liberal democracy is a unifying ideology, a situation of liberal compatibility (a region composed of liberal democracies) will result in a status quo orientation of the regional states. The nature of the domestic regimes and the coherence of states are closely related because it is very difficult for incoherent states to become stable democracies (Ayoob 1995, pp. 194–196; Rothstein 1992). Yet coherent states may become status quo states even if they are not liberal democracies (for example, conservative monarchies). Thus, liberal compatibility is a sufficient, rather than necessary, condition for a status quo orientation.

The factor of liberal compatibility is an *intervening* variable between the state-to-nation balance and the level and type of peace. In other words, a certain degree of state-to-nation balance is a prerequisite for the liberal factor to exercise its effects. When at least a minimal extent of state strength and of national congruence are present, liberal compatibility will exercise important effects on the level of peace and also on the ways of addressing the remaining state-to-nation issues and their territorial manifestations.

[67] For references to liberalism in world politics, see ch. 1.

[68] See Zakaria 1997.

Global factors: types of great power regional involvement

This independent variable refers to the type of great power involvement in a region.[69] This global factor is the most important and is directly relevant for understanding transitions and variations in regional war and peace. The number of the great powers in the international system (polarity) is not an important factor in affecting the pattern of regional involvement by the great powers, because the polarity of the system does not determine the balance of great power interests vis-à-vis a certain region: different balances of interests might take place under the same international system, while a similar balance might hold even if the polarity of the system changes.[70] It is the balance of great power interests combined with their relative capabilities that determines the pattern of their regional involvement.[71]

More specifically, the distinction is between four major types of great power involvement: competition, cooperation, dominance, and disengagement.[72] In competition and cooperation several great powers are involved in the region. Dominance means that there is a single hegemon in the region, while in disengagement none of the great powers is involved in the region.

Great power *competition* with regard to a certain region means that the great powers focus on balancing each other in order to exclude one another from the region or at least prevent the emergence of the rival as a hegemon in a region in which they have important interests. Small regional allies are the key for achieving the great powers' regional goals, and therefore the critical "prize" in such a competition. Competing great powers thus bid for the support of the small states.

Cooperation means that, instead of competing, the great powers agree on common goals in the region and work together to promote them. The focus here is on "affirmative" cooperation, that is, active policy coordination and joint diplomatic, economic, and military action vis-à-vis the

[69] For an extended analysis of the sources and effects of different types of such involvement, see Miller 1995, 1997, and 1998, and Miller and Kagan 1997. See also ch. 5.
[70] Accordingly, there is a contradiction in Waltz's argument about great power interests in the Third World under bipolarity: see Miller and Kagan 1997, p. 62, n. 26.
[71] For elaboration of the sources and effects of such involvement, see Miller and Kagan 1997 and ch. 5 below.
[72] In reality there may, of course, be different combinations or "mixes" of different types of involvement. For a rather similar typology of patterns of great power regional involvement, see Spiegel 1972, pp. 145–165, although he deals more with great power involvement vis-à-vis a single small state, rather than a region.

region in question.[73] *Disengagement* means that the great powers are not involved diplomatically, and definitely not militarily in the regional conflict, apart from intervention on specific and limited grounds such as to rescue their citizens (Ullman 1990). At a minimum, the powers refrain from political-security commitments in the region in question, whereas economic interests there are perceived as not necessitating military-diplomatic intervention or at least not justifying the costs involved in such intervention.[74]

Hegemony (or dominance) means the dominant involvement of one great power in the region. Similarly to several cooperating powers, the dominant power can exercise a major influence on patterns and outcomes in the region in either a benign (Keohane 1984, p. 32) or a coercive manner (Gilpin 1981, p. 29).[75]

Theoretical linkages: the propositions

Chapter 1 presented the key ideas of the study. The first is that cold outcomes are determined by global factors while hot outcomes are affected by domestic/regional variables. The second key idea is that the state-to-nation balance in any region is a key factor determining the war proneness of that region. In this section I will relate each of the regional outcomes to the combination of independent variables affecting it. I start with a figure showing which type of outcomes are affected by which type of causal factors.

As figure 2.2 shows, the great powers can affect 2 and 5 (transitions from cold war to cold peace and vice versa), and also 1 (from hot war to cold war). However, the regional actors affect 3 (transition to warm peace), 4 (from warm peace to cold peace), and 6 (outbreak of hot war).

Table 2.3 and propositions elaborate the combined effects of the two types of factors (global and regional/domestic) on regional

[73] On "negative" versus "affirmative" cooperation, see A. Stein 1983, and Miller 1992a. Examples of great power affirmative cooperation include concerts, security regimes, and collective security mechanisms; see Kupchan and Kupchan 1991. On concerts, see ch. 5 below.

[74] For an advocacy of a strategy of disengagement for the United States in the post-Cold War era, see Nordlinger 1995.

[75] One variant of hegemonic theories underlines the benign or accommodative character of hegemonic leadership. This is hegemonic stability theory, which focuses on the international political economy, but the same logic may apply also to war and peace issues. See Keohane 1984 and Keohane and Nye 1977. Another variant, which has significant realist elements, advances a coercive type of hegemony. These are the hegemonic approaches to issues of war and peace. See Organski and Kugler 1980; see also Gilpin's (1981) theory of hegemonic war and change.

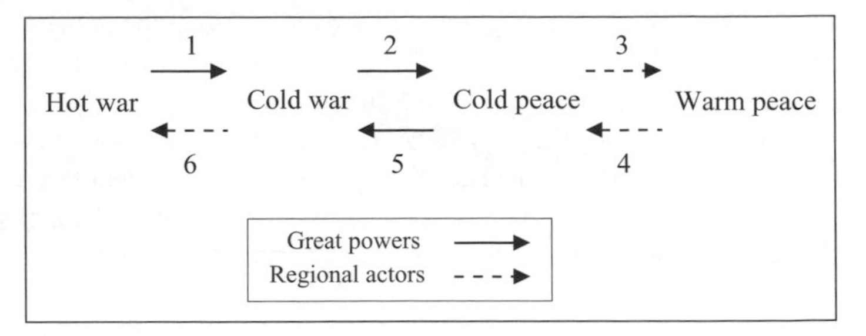

Figure 2.2 Who affects what and when: the type of outcome affected by the great powers and the regional states

outcomes. The empirical cases will be discussed in the following chapters.

In categories 1 and 2 the outcomes vary among hot wars, cold war, or cold peace but do not reach warm peace. The reason is that in both category 1 and category 2 there is a state-to-nation imbalance in the region manifested in some combination of powerful revisionist forces and state incoherence. In contrast, in both categories 3 and 4 the outcome is warm peace caused by a high state-to-nation balance, which reflects successful state-building and nation-building in the region. This regional balance leads to status quo orientations of the regional states and to state coherence, resulting in normal peace. When the regional state-to-nation balance is augmented by liberal compatibility, the regional outcome is high-level warm peace.

In general, a state-to-nation imbalance in the region is the major underlying cause of regional war proneness.[76] Great powers may mitigate or intensify it by their regional involvement, but – especially in the post-colonial age – they cannot change it. In other words, it is beyond their power to resolve the state-to-nation problem in the region. This may only be done by the regional states themselves. As a result, the type of great power involvement in the region makes a difference only so long as the state-to-nation problem in the region is still unresolved. Thus, the variation between great power cooperation or hegemony on the one hand and competition or disengagement on the other makes a difference with regard to the variation between categories 1 and 2 (in both of which there is a state-to-nation imbalance), but it does not affect the type of regional peace in categories 3 and 4, where the key state-to-nation issues are resolved or transcended by the regional actors. The main variation

[76] For data, see ch. 3 and appendixes.

Table 2.3 *Four categories of regional order: the combined effects of the type of great power involvement and the state-to-nation balance in the region*

Type of great power involvement	The state-to-nation balance in the region	
	Low	High
Hegemony/cooperation	Category 2 **Cold peace** – post-Camp David Israel–Egypt (hegemony) – post-1991 Middle East (hegemony) – the Balkans, 1815–1878 (cooperation) – the Balkans, 1939–1991 (hegemony) – post-1995 Dayton peace agreements (hegemony) – Asia/Africa following the end of the Cold War, (esp. during US–Soviet *cooperation* under Gorbachev, 1985–1991)	Category 3 **Warm peace** – Western Europe during the Cold War (**high-level peace** under US hegemony) – twentieth-century South America (**normal peace** under partial US hegemony)[a]
Competition/disengagement	Category 1 **Cold war punctuated by hot wars** – the Balkans, 1878–1939 (competition) – the Balkans, 1991–1995 (disengagement) – the Middle East in the Cold War era (competition) – East Asia/South Asia and Africa in the Cold War era (competition) – Africa in the post-Cold War era (disengagement)	Category 4 **Warm peace** – Western Europe during the post-Cold War era (**high-level peace** under partial US disengagement)[b]

Notes:
[a] On the limitations to US hegemony in South America, especially regarding the issues of regional war and peace, see ch. 7.
[b] See ch. 8.

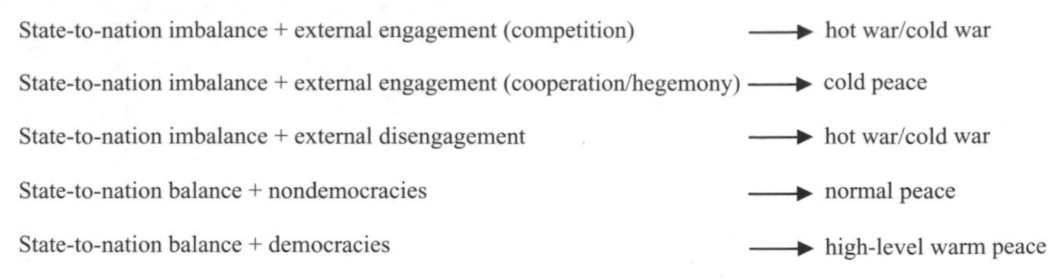

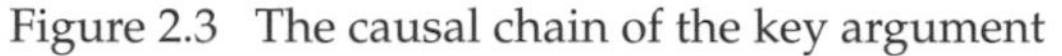

Figure 2.3 The causal chain of the key argument

within these two categories is the outcome of a regional/domestic factor rather than a global one: the extent of liberal compatibility in the region. A high extent of liberal compatibility produces a high-level warm peace, while a region with a state-to-nation balance but without liberal compatibility generates a normal peace. However, both these types of peace are warm in the sense of a low likelihood of war.

Figure 2.3 and the following propositions elaborate the combined effects of the two types of factors (global and regional/domestic) on regional war and peace outcomes.

Propositions

As for categories 1 and 2, the state-to-nation imbalance results in a high war proneness.

Category 1 *1. The combined effect of great power competition or disengagement under a state-to-nation imbalance leads to a regional cold war (punctuated by hot wars).*

Category 1 is a zone of cold war punctuated by hot wars. Great power disengagement from a regional conflict means the independence of the regional parties from the great powers. In a situation of a state-to-nation imbalance, the outcome will be an insulation of the regional conflict from great power influence, and its continuation without interference from the outside and in accordance with the resources and motivations of the regional states. As a result, regional wars may last for protracted periods without being interrupted and contained. They will end (and break out again) in accordance with the local balances of power and motivations of the rival states, and their cost–benefit calculations. The outcome will be a protracted cold war with occasional hot wars – a situation in which not only are the underlying state-to-nation problems not resolved, but they are not even moderated. As a result, war remains a likely option for addressing the conflicts among the regional states.

This outcome will be sustained in a situation of great power competition, in which the regional conflict will be aggravated and perpetuated by the great power involvement. Great power competition tends to sustain protracted regional conflicts through the support that the great powers provide to the local antagonists who are their clients (for elaboration, see chapter 5). The competition between the great powers for influence and allies in the region allows the local states to manipulate them by threatening to realign and thus extract more aid. It therefore helps the clients to sustain the costs of a protracted conflict. At the same time, worried about escalating regional wars into which they might be dragged by their clients, the competing great powers may cooperate tacitly in limiting the duration and scope of regional wars. As a result, the regional wars under great power competition will not change the regional status quo dramatically and will stop short of the emergence of regional hegemons. Yet, such limited great power cooperation in regional war termination will not go beyond crisis management, which sustains a regional cold war by making the local hot wars shorter. Since competing great powers tend to support rival regional parties and disagree on the terms of settling regional conflicts, their competitive involvement will tend to perpetuate cold war and prevent a transition to cold peace. The great powers will be unable (and probably also unwilling) to work together effectively to mitigate the regional dispute or even to prevent hot wars.

Category 2 *2. Great power hegemony or cooperation under a regional state-to-nation imbalance mitigates or reduces regional conflicts and thus brings about cold peace.*

In category 2 there is also a situation of regional state-to-nation imbalance, but the type of great power involvement changes from competitive to cooperative or hegemonic. As a result of this change, the region moves from a cold war to a cold peace under the stabilizing influence of a hegemon or cooperating great powers, which, unlike disengaging or competing powers, have both the capability and the interest to pacify the region. Once the great power competition ends, the ability of the regional actors to manipulate them declines dramatically. The great powers are then more able to move beyond regional war termination, which is possible even under great power competition, to the more ambitious task of war prevention and conflict reduction.

Indeed, a situation of hegemony means the ability and willingness of one great power to use its superior power to be the principal arbiter of regional conflicts. Such unilateral arbitration or brokerage corresponds to the notions of Pax Romana, Pax Britannica, or Pax Americana. Such a dominant power need not be a global hegemon. It might be one of several great powers in the international system which enjoys superior power resources and/or superior interests with regard to a certain region. In a situation of great power cooperation in a certain region, such brokerage will be undertaken by several powers acting in concert.

A concert of cooperating great powers or a stabilizing hegemon is unable to resolve the state-to-nation imbalance in the region that produces the basic motivations for war in the region. At best, they moderate the level of the regional conflict short of establishing state-to-nation balance. Still, they can deal effectively with the *capabilities* of the regional actors to go to war. As noted, the regional balance of power depends heavily on external support, notably arms supply by great powers. As a result, the great powers can constrain the regional ability to resort to force by imposing limitations on local military capabilities.

Beyond denying arms to the regional states, a hegemonic power or cooperating powers may undertake a variety of stabilizing measures that will advance cold peace in the region. They may help regional states to mitigate their dispute and moderate the level of regional state-to-nation incongruence by a combination of the following steps: diplomatic mediation, making it easier to reach at least a partial settlement of the substantive issues in conflict; financial assistance, providing incentives for the regional states to compromise with their local rivals, as well as economic sanctions against those who refuse to make concessions; security reassurance and guarantees, which reduce the regional security dilemma, while deterring, and occasionally coercing, aggressive revisionist powers; and the construction of regional arms control regimes. The absence of great power competition will reduce disagreements among the powers over these measures, and will also deny the regional states a realignment option and thus make them more amenable to moderating pressures from the great powers.

Great power hegemony or cooperation may take two forms, benign and coercive, depending on the means employed by the powers (Snidal 1985, Miller 1997).[77] The prerequisites for the success of this strategy

[77] These two forms are discussed in ch. 5.

for peace are the presence of a hegemonic power or a concert of cooperating great powers willing to stabilize the region in question (that is, seeing such a stabilization as being in their own interests) and able (having superior economic, military, and diplomatic resources vis-à-vis the region) to advance cold regional peace. Yet, the regional peace remains cold and the danger of war does not disappear because the regional states are still unable to overcome the major state-to-nation questions in the region. The major limitation of great power hegemony or cooperation is that, since the great powers are unable to affect the motivations of the regional states (stemming from the still unresolved state-to-nation problems), the regional outcome (cold peace) will depend on the continued presence and stabilizing role of the great powers. Without this, the situation is liable to revert to cold or even hot war.

To sum up, the two types of cold outcomes are related to two of the six competing images, global system and global society of states, both of which highlight the role of great powers in affecting regional outcomes. Great power competition, which sustains regional cold war, is in accord with the great power role in the realist image of the global system. Great power disengagement vis-à-vis unimportant regions is also consistent with realist logic. Great power hegemony or cooperation, both of which promote cold regional peace, is related to the global society perspective, with its benign image of the great powers as the "great responsibles" stabilizing regional conflicts. The regional variants of realism and the international society perspective, for their part, explain hot regional wars. The regional system is important for explaining the proximate causes of hot regional wars (as well as the conditions of cold war under great power disengagement), while the regional society of states explains the underlying causes of hot wars.

Categories 3 and 4 In contrast to great power involvement, the regional/domestic factors may address more effectively the *motivations* of the regional actors, and thus affect warm peace. This can be done either by changing those motivations directly related to the causes of regional wars, such as territorial disputes, or by transcending them through transforming the domestic attributes of the regional actors themselves, and as a result also radically changing their motivations regarding peace and war.

In both category 3 and category 4 there is a warm regional peace. The lower-level version of warm peace is normal peace, reached by effective state-building and nation-building, which produce greater state coherence, and as a result a transition of the regional states to status quo orientations. The notable case in this respect is twentieth-century South America and to some extent also post-1967 ASEAN.[78] The higher level of warm peace is achieved through regional liberal compatibility. The leading case is Western Europe in the post-1945 era. The rapid and far-reaching transformation of Western Europe was heavily assisted in its formative stages by benign US hegemony. Yet, following its consolidation, the high-level peace has been able to stand on its own and to persist even when the United States has partially disengaged from Europe in the post-Cold War era. That was made possible also by the relatively high degree of state strength and congruence in Western Europe (see chapter 8).

3. Successful state-building and nation-building in the region are conducive to the peaceful resolution of territorial conflicts and thus lead to normal regional peace. (This is the corollary to the proposition on the causal relations between the state-to-nation imbalance and a high propensity to regional wars.)

The growing coherence of local states directly addresses the underlying causes of regional wars by enhancing regional state-to-nation balance and thus leading to status quo orientations of regional states. Moreover, strong and congruent states are more likely to have a well-defined territorial identity and a greater capacity to control revisionist/nationalist forces. As a result, it is more likely to expect a peaceful resolution of territorial conflicts and other outstanding interstate questions and thus the emergence of a normal peace.

The growing state coherence in the region will take place as the result of the following three interrelated processes.

(1) *A decline of revisionism*, more specifically, a decline in the popular transborder appeal of revisionist/nationalist movements. This process may take place as a result of failed military or economic performance of the states representing these ideologies, leading to growing disenchantment with them. Such disenchantment is likely to bring to power more pragmatically oriented elites, supportive of the territorial status quo in the region, who focus on building their own states and on developing the national economies, rather

[78] On South America, see ch. 7.

than on spreading destabilizing pan-national/irredentist messages across interstate boundaries in the region.[79]

(2) *State-building (or state strengthening)*,[80] which comprises two processes.

(a) A decline in the power of subnational separatist/secessionist movements. This takes place as a result of a consolidation of state power over separatist groups, which may be achieved by monopolizing the instruments of violence in the state's hands (namely, power accumulation by the central government achieved by disarming the secessionist groups) and thus maintaining its territorial integrity against domestic challenges.[81] Yet, on those occasions in which the state is unable and/or unwilling to subordinate ethnonational secessionist movements for self-determination, a partition into two or more states may be necessary for the state to become more nationally coherent and thus to avoid protracted periods of ethnonational violence as was the case, for example, in Palestine and India–Pakistan in 1947–1948.[82]

(b) A growing ability of the regional states to extract resources from their societies, which are essential to support not only the war-making and policing activities of the state, but also to the growing effectiveness of state institutions/bureaucracy in providing material benefits for the citizens such as law and order, security, and socioeconomic prosperity and welfare (Ayoob 1995, pp. 22–23, 27; Ayoob 1996, pp. 38–39; Migdal 1988). Such material incentives are necessary for the development of citizen identification with, and loyalty to, the state.

(3) *Nation-building*, which refers to a growing loyalty of the citizens to the state due to nonmaterial symbolic functions provided by it. This is done through state-sponsored public education, the national media, and the propaganda of national myths (including the observance of national holidays, especially Independence Day,

[79] For a discussion of the extent of the focus of domestic coalitions on economic development as determining the likelihood of regional peace, see Solingen 1998.
[80] On historical dimensions of state-building, see A. Smith 1986b, Tilly 1975a and 1985, Cohen et al. 1981, and Jaggers 1992.
[81] See Cohen et al. 1981, 900; Ayoob 1995, pp. 182–184, and the sources he cites.
[82] See Kaufmann 1998. For a critique of partition, see Kumar 1997. For an overview of power-sharing arrangements among various ethnic groups as an avenue to avoid partition and to pursue peaceful integration, see Sisk 1996. For a powerful critique of such arrangements, see Downes 2001. This issue is discussed in ch. 9 of this book.

the designation of national heroes, and the commemoration of those who fell in the defense of the nation-state). In this process of nation-building there is a merging of the population into a more cohesive people with a common history, leading to the evolution of a national identity and the transformation of a centralized state into an integrated nation-state (Ayoob 1995, p. 30).[83]

Nation-building as defined in this study is a process that takes place within an existing territorial state and complements and reinforces state-building. Unlike state-building, which relies on material factors, nation-building refers to "soft" nonmaterial ones. This conception of nation-building is directly opposed to transborder pan-national movements that strive to unify in a single state entire ethnic nations located in a number of states by challenging existing territorial boundaries.[84] The process of nation-building may have destabilizing implications due to a potential need for external enemies to increase internal cohesion (Jackman 1993, p. 107), leading to a temptation to initiate scapegoat wars (J. Levy 1989b, 1998). Yet, the process will be much less destabilizing if it is confined to the existing territorial state, rather than aiming at transborder national unification. Most important, even if the process of nation-building itself has some destabilizing effects, once it is completed successfully and coherent states emerge, the motivation for both revisionist/nationalist wars and diversionary wars declines, and normal peace is more likely to be established.

As a result of the processes of state-building and nation-building, the population, irrespective of its ethnic origin, comes to accept the current territorial identity of the state and its boundaries, or at least is unwilling to resort to violence to change them either by seceding from the state or claiming the territories of neighboring states. Thus, the appeal of

[83] This notion of nation-building is consistent with Shils's conception of the state as not only able to impose exclusive sovereignty but also to articulate shared cultural values for its citizens, and claim their loyalty and obedience (Shils 1975, pp. 34–38). Nation-building can be closely related to civic nationalism to the extent that both focus on citizen identification with the nation-state in its current territorial boundaries.

[84] On the tensions between nation-building in the current boundaries vs. ethnically based transborder nationalism, and application to Central and Eastern Europe during the inter-war and the post-Cold War eras, see Brubaker 1996. On the tensions between nation-building and primordial ethnic loyalties especially in the Third World, see Jackman 1993, pp. 103–107. See Connor 1994 for a powerful critique of the literature on nation-building. Connor argues that modernization breeds ethnic awareness and conflict rather than national integration. Prescriptions for state-building and nation-building as avenues to regional peace are discussed in ch. 9.

separatist groups and revisionist ideologies declines, and the distinctive territorial identity of the state is respected both externally and internally. Under these conditions the peaceful resolution of territorial conflicts is more likely to succeed, leading to normal peace.[85]

The greater the state-to-nation balance, the more the supranational and subnational challenges to the regional states decline, which is the opposite of the process that takes place under a regional state-to-nation imbalance. In other words, the strengthening of the regional states and the decline of revisionist ideologies reinforce each other, thus reducing the power of the domestic and transnational factors conducive to war, and reinforcing those more favorable to the establishment of normal peace. The formation of coherent states makes it less possible for transnational movements to transmit revolutionary challenges across borders. Indeed, the decline of nationalist-revisionist ideologies is closely related to the process of successful state-building and nation-building in the region. The more effective the regional states and their institutions become (both in the coercive sense of suppressing domestic challenges and in the ability to provide socioeconomic services and symbolic functions to their populations), and the stronger the attachment of the citizens to them, the more limited will be the ability of transborder pan-nationalist ideologies to attract support and loyalty.

Coherent states will thus be both more stable internally and less vulnerable to domestic and transnational pressures to adopt hard-line positions which make a resort to force more likely and peaceful resolution of the regional conflicts less feasible. In other words, coherent states are more likely to endorse pragmatic international orientations and to behave cautiously according to cost–benefit calculations (both strategic and economic) rather than ideological or nationalist commitments and sentiments. Coherent states are also less hospitable to guerrilla / terrorist organizations which take advantage of weak states to conduct armed infiltrations from their territory into neighboring states. Because secessionist movements in coherent states are in decline, these states are also less likely to produce such guerrilla forces. Coherent states are also less likely to trigger destabilizing refugee movements across borders, or to invite armed intervention by neighbors bent on exploiting opportunities for expansion or worried about security threats from secessionist or

[85] Since state coherence is treated in this study as an independent variable leading to regional peace, I am interested in its effects rather than its causes. The factors affecting the success of state-making and nation-building fall beyond the research question posed here (the changes and variations in regional war and peace patterns).

irredentist elements present in unstable neighboring states. In this sense, the formation of coherent states decreases the security dilemma in the region. It also reduces the motivation of unstable elites for diversionary wars, as well as the motivation and opportunity for wars of territorial profit. All these processes reinforce the standing of status quo elites, who are more able and willing to reach normal peace based on mutual recognition of sovereignty and territorial integrity and noninterference in the domestic affairs of other states.[86]

4. Liberal compatibility is conducive to the resolution or transcendence of state-to-nation problems and thus is likely to produce a high-level peace.

The proposition that liberal compatibility brings about high-level peace is deduced from the democratic peace theory, which claims that democracies do not go to war against each other.[87] The democratic peace theory should be more appropriately called the liberal peace theory, because it is valid only among full-blown liberal democracies (Zakaria 1997; J. Owen 1997).

Because of the high degree of legitimacy of liberal democracies in the eyes of fellow liberal democracies, hostile mutual threat perceptions are much less likely to evolve or persist among them than among other kinds of regimes or between them and nondemocracies. In contrast to nondemocratic states with divisive ideologies, liberal democracies are also unlikely to go to war with each other over rivalries for regional leadership or hegemony. As opposed to divisive ideologies, liberal democracies preempt the question "who should rule other like-minded states?" with the answer that "no one should rule."[88] This reduces their fears of one another and the security dilemma, and thus makes a common and durable security cooperation among them more likely. Liberal democracies are also unlikely to harbor revisionist ambitions vis-à-vis other democracies, and especially to use force to achieve them. The high level of domestic legitimacy of liberal democratic regimes reduces the need for scapegoating, especially aimed at other liberal democracies. The evolution of nonethnic civic nationalism, which is much more likely in liberal democracies than in other types of regimes of nation-states,[89] is likely to reduce both revisionist/irredentist

[86] The state of normal peace is similar to what Buzan calls "a highly developed anarchy" (1984, 121).
[87] See references in ch. 1, n. 76.
[88] This is my refinement of Van Evera 1993, drawing on Walt 1987.
[89] See Kupchan 1995, and Hoffmann 1998.

territorial claims based on ethnic nationalism and the quest of ethnic minorities for self-determination. At any rate, even if ethnic groups claim this right and have other grievances, in a liberal democracy many avenues for nonviolent struggle to achieve their rights are available to them. This should minimize the likelihood of the eruption of ethnic violence, which may spread across borders, especially if all the regional states are liberal.

Consequently, territorial or other disputes among liberal democracies are transcended – that is, become less important and, at any rate, much less likely to be addressed by violence. Any remaining territorial problems are likely to be resolved by negotiations and peaceful means similar to the way domestic conflicts are resolved in these regimes (Russett 1993, pp. 30–38). Because of their high domestic legitimacy, liberal states can also tolerate intensive transnational relations much better than nonliberal states, which might see such transnational relations, and the associated spread of new ideas, as a potential threat to the legitimacy of their regimes and as an infringement on their sovereignty.

As a result of these factors, in a situation of liberal compatibility, in which all the key regional states are liberal democracies, high-level warm peace will emerge. Yet, this does not refer to the relations between liberal democracies and other states. Liberal democracies may not exhibit a similar benign attitude toward nondemocratic regimes that they fear or consider illegitimate. Thus, in the view of some liberals, there is a moral imperative to intervene in defense of human rights in illiberal states which infringe on the rights of their citizens (Doyle 1997, pp. 388, 396–402). Critics argue that such an interventionist tendency of liberal states may lead to an intensification of conflicts between them and nonliberal states. Another potentially destabilizing element in liberalism is that it regards the Wilsonian norm of national self-determination as superior, at least in principle, to the norm of maintaining the territorial integrity of existing states, especially if these states are not liberal democracies.[90]

High-level peace demands liberal compatibility in the political domain of liberal democratic regimes. Economic liberalism alone (in the sense of free-market economic systems and the potential for free trade and interdependence) cannot guarantee high-level peace, especially if some of the regional actors adhere to a divisive political ideology. Yet,

[90] For an extended discussion of the great variety of liberal views in favor of and against international intervention, see Doyle 1997, pp. 394–402. On self-determination in liberal thought, see Kegley 1995, p. 11, and Zacher and Matthew 1995, p. 115.

when coupled with political liberalism, economic compatibility among liberal market-capitalist states can be helpful in advancing and sustaining liberal regional peace. Liberal compatibility and its attendant mutual trust is also conducive to economic integration and the growth of supranational institutions.

While in both types of warm peace (normal and high-level) the likelihood of war is low, in some respects they are opposed to each other. This is especially clear with regard to the issue of boundaries. Normal peace entails the mutual recognition of boundaries. Indeed, major normative components of normal peace include a respect for the territorial integrity of other states and the sanctity of their boundaries.[91] In contrast, in a liberal regional community boundaries are rendered much less relevant by growing interdependence, intensive transnational relations, and supranational institutions, which entail some erosion of state sovereignty.

Also, normal peace derives from the conception of a heterogeneous regional society of states, all of which are mutually legitimate irrespective of domestic regimes and ideologies. Their legitimacy is reflected in the central norm of noninterference in the domestic affairs of states. In contrast, high-level peace stems from a homogeneous liberal community in the region, based on democratic institutions and mutual respect for human rights and civil liberties.

The prerequisites for the evolution of the two types of warm peace are also at odds with each other. This presents a dilemma for regional peacemaking, especially on the issue of democratization. Liberals wish to transcend the state-to-nation issues by a radical change in the domestic character of the actors and their objectives. As a result, liberals support a transformation of domestic regimes as the road to peace, and call for the democratization of all regional states, rather than the strengthening of authoritarian states and elites. In the liberal view, authoritarian states are a source of conflicts, and only democratic states can produce a lasting regional peace. But the proponents of the regional society approach argue that coherent authoritarian states with status quo ideologies are also able to achieve a durable peace. Moreover, critics of liberalism argue that, at least in the short run, rapid democratization in incoherent states may further weaken and destabilize them, bringing

[91] On these norms in the context of the post-1945 Third World, see Jackson 1990 and Ayoob 1995, ch. 4.

about a rise to power of radical/revisionist elites, a reinforcement of hypernationalism, and an acceleration of ethnic hatreds.[92] Thus, rather than achieving warm peace, democratization may create motivations for scapegoating and wars of profit, and intensify the security dilemma in the region, thus increasing the danger of regional wars. As a result, the logic of the regional society approach suggests that the road to regional peace lies through strengthening the existing states and their institutions irrespective of political regimes, in order to enhance state coherence and state-to-nation congruence.

A liberal reply to this argument, stemming from the global variant of liberalism, is that a liberal democratic hegemon or several liberal democratic powers acting in concert may help newly democratized regional states get through the initial difficulties and instabilities caused by the process of democratization, and achieve a smooth transition to high-level peace under the great power protective umbrella. Once the initial problems are overcome and the new democracies stabilize, high-level peace will endure without great power support, as demonstrated by the West European case.

However, liberal great powers are likely to play such an active role, and to make the necessary investment, only under certain circumstances, notably when they face a major common threat and when they fear instability spreading in a key region. Even then, if the regional states are incoherent, the great powers have to focus first on helping the new liberal states with the tasks of state-building and nation-building. These are not easy tasks; rather, they are quite costly for external powers, but they have to be carried out before the pacifying effects of the liberal compatibility are going to be noticeable.

The relationships between state coherence, democratization, and regional peace are discussed in chapters 7 and 8. I address this debate by suggesting that liberal compatibility is an intervening variable which

[92] Ayoob 1995, Holsti 1996, Zakaria 1997, 35–38, and Mansfield and Snyder 2005. For a useful overview, see Byman 2003, pp. 47–78. Another limitation of the liberal approach concerns the feasibility of democratization. The demanding prerequisites for successful democratization make it an inappropriate strategy for regional peacemaking for some regions, at least in the short run. For studies dealing with the prerequisites for democratization, see Lipset 1981, Dahl 1971, and Huntington 1991. For a review of research on the political and socioeconomic conditions for democracy and democratization, see Shin 1994. Key preconditions for democracy include high levels of literacy and economic development, and a relatively equal distribution of land, wealth, and income (Van Evera 1993, p. 212), namely the presence in society of a large middle class.

mediates between coherent states and the type of regional peace by raising the level of peace among them and by helping them to transcend remaining state-to-nation issues. At least a minimal degree of state strength and congruence is, however, necessary for these effects to take place. Full-blown liberal compatibility in a region leads to the highest degree of warm peace. Yet democratization in a region with a state-to-nation imbalance, populated by weak and incongruent states, can be destabilizing, at least in the short run. Moreover, deep ethnonational divisions, with a record of bitter conflicts, make both the initiation of democratization and the practice of democracy difficult.[93] The resolution of state-to-nation issues should precede democratization.[94] Democratization in a region with a high state-to-nation balance, however, can warm the regional peace considerably and result in a high-level peace.

Summary

This chapter has introduced the five types of regional war and peace outcomes to be explained in this study. I also presented the independent variables: the global ones – the types of great power engagement in a region; the key regional/domestic factor – the state-to-nation balance; and the intervening variable of liberal democracy. The propositions produce causal relations between the explanatory variables and the war and peace outcomes. The overall explanation draws on a rigorous integration of various elements derived from three key theoretical perspectives in IR. I also draw, however, on some key concepts usually associated with comparative politics, notably state and nation, thus allowing me to produce an integrative model of international, regional, and domestic factors. Chapter 3 will focus on the relations between the state-to-nation balance and war.

Tables 2.4 and 2.5 summarize the theory presented in this chapter, namely the causal linkages between the global and regional factors

[93] See Horowitz 1994, p. 37. Thus, most liberal democracies are either well-integrated societies (France, the United States) or divided societies in which several favorable structural conditions have moderated the effects of ethnic conflict (Switzerland, Canada, Belgium – see also ch. 8 below). Lepsius (1985, 49–50) analyzes the limitations imposed by ethnic nationalism on liberal democracy.

[94] See Linz and Stepan 1996, ch. 2, esp. pp. 26–27: "agreements about stateness are logically prior to the creation of democratic institutions . . . as Dahl argues, simple insistence on the majority formula per se will not do anything until the appropriateness of the unit is established."

Table 2.4 *Regional war and peace according to the six images*

Image	Causal factors	Effects on the state-to-nation imbalance	Regional outcome
1. Global system	GP competition or disengagement	Not addressed	Cold war
2. Regional system	Regional BOP/regional offense/defense balance	Not addressed	Hot wars/cold war
3. Global society of states	GP hegemony or cooperation (concert)	Moderated	Cold peace
4. Regional society of states	Coherent states: strong and congruent states	Resolved	Normal peace
5. Global community	Liberal democratic GPs (hegemon or concert)	Creating the prerequisites for transcendence	Emergence of high-level peace
6. Regional community	Liberal compatibility	Transcended or resolved	Endurance of high-level peace

Notes:
GP: Great power
BOP: Balance of power

derived from the logic of the competing approaches and the types of regional war and peace.

Let me now spell out the propositions derived from table 2.4.

1. The effects of the global system on regions with state-to-nation imbalance: under great power competition in the region or disengagement from it, state-to-nation issues are not addressed and the likely regional outcome is cold war. Great power competition aggravates the regional conflict but also limits the scope and duration of hot wars (discussed in chapter 5).
2. The effects of the regional system on regions with state-to-nation imbalance: the regional balance of power, the security dilemma, and the offense/defense balance do not address state-to-nation issues,

Table 2.5 *The type of regional outcome best explained by the different perspectives and levels of analysis*

The three schools/level of analysis	Realism (system)	International society	Liberalism (community)
Global	Cold war	Cold peace	Emergence of high-level peace
Regional	Proximate causes of hot wars/conditions for cold war (under great power disengagement)	Underlying causes of hot wars/ conditions for normal peace	Endurance of high-level peace

and the likely outcome is hot or cold war depending, among other things, on the success or failure of deterrence or compellence and the working of the security dilemma (see chapters 3 and 4).

3. Under a global society of states, great power hegemony or concert are likely to moderate the state-to-nation imbalance in the region and, as a result, cold peace is likely to emerge (see chapters 5 and 6).
4. If a regional society of states is composed of strong and congruent states, peaceful conflict resolution is likely to produce a normal inter-state peace by resolving state-to-nation issues (see chapter 7).
5. A liberal democratic hegemon or a concert of great powers in a global community provides the most effective mechanism for new liberal states to make the transition from war to warm peace (see chapter 8).
6. Regional liberal compatibility among coherent states in a regional community is likely to produce an enduring high-level warm peace by resolving or transcending remaining state-to-nation issues (see chapter 8).

Which type of regional war and peace outcome is best explained by the different schools of thought and levels of analysis? Table 2.5 addresses this question.

The global system – when the great powers compete in a region or disengage from it – best explains regional cold war. Global society – when the great powers cooperate or there is a stabilizing hegemon – accounts for cold peace. Global community led by liberal great powers encourages the transition to high-level peace of regions with emerging democracies.

The regional system explains the proximate causes of hot wars and provides the conditions for regional cold war when the great powers disengage. These causes and conditions are related to the regional balance of power, security dilemmas, and the offense/defense balance. The regional society, focusing on the state and nation factors, provides the underlying causes of hot wars. This approach also suggests the conditions for normal peace: strong states and state-to-nation congruence. A regional liberal community of coherent states is likely to produce an enduring high-level peace.

3 States, nations, and war

This chapter further develops the theoretical argument made in chapter 2 on the causal relations between the state-to-nation imbalance and regional war proneness. I argue that there is a need to distinguish between underlying and proximate causes of regional war. Regional factors, rather than global forces, account for regional war proneness; more specifically, the state-to-nation imbalance is the key underlying cause of regional war proneness. I then present the details of this balance: the various forces that reinforce the balance versus those that challenge it. Next, I introduce the combined effects of variations in the two main dimensions of the balance (state-to-nation congruence and state strength) on variations in state war proneness. This should produce "observable implications" of the theory (King et al. 1994). The chapter then presents the causal relations between the state-to-nation imbalance and regional war proneness and provides some empirical evidence to support these relations. I also elaborate on the effects of the two outputs of the state-to-nation imbalance – revisionism and failed states – and the linkages between them. Finally, I introduce the relations between the state-to-nation imbalance and the proximate causes of war, notably the security dilemma, profit, and scapegoating.

The argument

We have to distinguish between underlying and proximate causes of regional war. The key underlying factor that determines the extent of regional war proneness is the state-to-nation balance in a certain region. The greater the state-to-nation imbalance, the more powerful the revisionist nationalist forces in the region; as a result, there is a proportionally higher regional war proneness.

My alternative explanation has a greater explanatory power than either realism or liberalism. It predicts under what conditions a region will have a high war proneness: if it has a relatively low level of state-to-nation balance as compared to other regions and thus the revisionist/nationalist forces in the region are strong. While problems of state weakness are prevalent in large parts of the postcolonial Third World, a region will be especially war-prone if these problems are further aggravated by powerful revisionist/nationalist forces (see the causal chain in figure 3.1). This will be the case if there is not only internal incongruence in the region but also transborder external incongruence. Thus, the next chapter shows that such a combination of internal and transborder incongruence (as well as the presence of some weak states) has made the Middle East after World War II more prone to wars than most other regions.

Variations in the same causal factors that account for the differences between one region and others should also account for variations between different periods and various locales in the same region. Proximate reasons account for the timing of specific wars. The underlying causes are persistent over long periods; they cannot always account for the eruption of a specific war. Although the underlying causes are necessary for determining regional war proneness, they are insufficient to generate a war in the absence of the proximate causes. The war-causing effects of the proximate factors are, however, heavily affected by the extent of the regional state-to-nation balance.

Proximate causes of specific wars are mostly related to realist factors as they are advanced by the two main streams of realism – defensive realism and offensive realism (see the discussion in chapter 1). An additional proximate cause is domestic illegitimacy or vulnerability, producing incentives for diversionary wars. The sources of domestic illegitimacy are more directly related to the state-to-nation balance.

While these factors explain the eruption of particular wars, their relevance depends on the strength of the underlying factor – the extent of the state-to-nation balance in the region. If there is a high degree of imbalance, variations in the realist factors will affect the likelihood and timing of particular wars. If there is a high extent of balance, the realist factors will become much less relevant to the eruption of wars. Because regional wars are reflections of the problem of the state-to-nation imbalance in the region and not of global strategic interests, as chapter 5 argues, competing great powers affect the intensity, scope, and duration of regional

State-to-nation imbalance → revisionist nationalism and state incoherence → proximate causes of war → regional wars

Figure 3.1 The outbreak of hot regional wars: the causal chain

wars, but do not determine their outbreak.[1] The outbreak is determined by the balance of motivation, which favors the regional actors. Similarly, highly motivated regional actors might initiate violence if they are dissatisfied by the regional state-to-nation balance. In contrast to realist logic, such war initiation might take place even if these actors are inferior in the balance of capabilities. A more general point is that incoherent states (those that are weak and incongruent) are a much greater source of regional insecurity and instability than is expected by realism.

State-to-nation imbalance → hot wars

Hot wars are most likely in regions where there are severe problems of state-to-nation imbalance.

This section will focus on two related arguments highlighting the role of regional/domestic factors in bringing about hot wars:

(a) Most regional wars are initiated by the regional states, not by the great powers. Indeed, the causes of these wars are related to geographical proximity.
(b) The causes of these wars are conditioned by the extent of state-to-nation imbalance.

The regional sources of regional wars

Regional wars are undertaken by regional states against proximate (often contiguous) states, because geographical proximity is a key factor in determining the security agenda of states. A national security problem, which may require fighting a war, emerges once external threats to the state are present and the opponent is able to carry them out.[2] Both factors are heavily influenced by proximity. Since the ability to project power declines with distance, the capacity to wage wars is mainly local

[1] If there is a single hegemon vis-à-vis the region, however, it can promote a low level of regional peace and thus reduce the likelihood of regional wars. See ch. 5.
[2] On threats and vulnerabilities, see Buzan 1991, ch. 3.

or regional (except for great powers).[3] Thus, states that are proximate can pose a greater threat than those that are far away,[4] and threats are most strongly felt when they are at close range.[5]

One manifestation of a security complex or a regional system in the context of regional war is war diffusion: the war involvement of one state affects the likelihood that another state will become involved in war. Starr and Most found that a state with a warring neighbor was three to five times as likely to be at war as one that did not have a bordering state at war. A related finding is that the spread of war occurs primarily within regions, not across regions (Starr and his colleagues, cited in Goertz and Diehl 1992b, pp. 8–12). A second manifestation is that, in domestic conflicts in fragmented states, it is frequently the regional neighbors that intervene militarily.[6] This may then also lead to regional escalation; examples include the foreign interventions in Cambodia (Vietnam and China), Lebanon, Jordan, and Yemen.[7]

Proximity is also related to the security dilemma. The security dilemma is enhanced once offense has the advantage over defense or offense and defense are not distinguishable (Jervis 1978). These conditions are especially acute on the regional level because, even if regional powers have enough power-projection capability to be able to attack their neighbors, they are unlikely to have invulnerable retaliatory forces, territorial depth, and distance from sources of threat as is the case with more secure great powers. The resultant high vulnerability to surprise attacks and preemptive strikes enhances considerably the destabilizing effects of the security dilemma, as even supposedly defensive steps are viewed with alarm and thus trigger military reactions which may lead to an inadvertent escalation because of the mutual fear of being surprised or preempted while in an inferior position.

[3] For studies that show that most wars are fought between physically adjacent states, see the citations in Russett 1993, p. 26, n. 5. Empirical research has found that geographic contiguity makes war more likely. See Starr and Most 1976 and the studies they cite; Bremer 1992, 309, 338.

[4] Walt 1987, p. 23, citing Boulding 1962, pp. 229–230, 245–247, and others. Most relevant here is Boulding's idea of the "loss-of-strength gradient" (ibid.), that is, the degree to which a state's military (power-projection capability) and political power diminishes as the state tries to influence other states and events further away from its home base. On this point, see also Buzan 1991, pp. 190–195.

[5] Walt 1987; Buzan 1991, ch. 3; Goertz and Diehl 1992b, p. 17.

[6] Examples are provided in Levite et al. 1992; another example is Libya's attempts to take portions of northern Chad during that state's civil conflict, cited in Goertz and Diehl 1992b, p. 9.

[7] See the list of conflicts and interventions in Holsti 1996, pp. 210–224.

On the whole, it is less threatening for states to accept a power imbalance and even hegemony by a distant power than hegemony by a proximate power. Thus, local states especially fear domination by a regional power and, unless the regional power gap is completely unbridgeable (generating bandwagoning and a sphere of influence), they will try to oppose it by arming or establishing a countervailing coalition (Walt 1987). Such moves are likely to trigger the security dilemma and even lead to wars, especially if there is also a substantive conflict of interests among the regional states.

Indeed, most substantive sources of interstate conflicts are also related to proximity: they are conflicts over disputed boundaries, territories, resources, and populations, usually among contiguous states.[8] States are more willing to fight for a territory closer to home than they are for a distant territory even if they may want territorial control in many places.[9] As Kautilya observed long ago, proximity often generates friction.[10]

Proximity and territory are also closely related to ethnicity/nationalism[11] and state-making,[12] two major substantive causes of war. A contemporary analyst has observed that "the regional dimension of conflict is often determined by the process of state making undertaken concurrently by contiguous states in the Third World" (Ayoob 1995, p. 50).

A counterargument to my thesis is the notion of "proxy wars," which was popular during the Cold War.[13] According to this view, great power conflicts are exported to the Third World, whether as wars by proxy or as an exacerbation of indigenous Third World conflicts by the superpowers via political-military support, partially in order to moderate the core global conflict.

[8] On the strong linkages between territorial contiguity and war, see Vasquez 1993, ch. 4, pp. 134–135, and the many studies he cites. According to the Correlates of War data (Small and Singer 1982, pp. 82–95), there have been sixty-seven interstate wars from 1816 to 1980; all but eight were between neighbors or began that way. Twenty-four of the twenty-eight cases of enduring rivalries (states that have had at least five militarized disputes within a certain time frame) in the period 1816–1986 have been between neighbors (Vasquez 1993, pp. 134–135).

[9] Goertz and Diehl 1992b, p. 18.

[10] Cited in Wriggins 1992, p. 7, n. 10.

[11] M. Brown 1993, p. 4; 1996; Posen 1993b; Van Evera 1994.

[12] Ayoob 1995 and Holsti 1996.

[13] Gupta cited in Ayoob 1993, p. 37, n. 20; specific examples are cited in Holsti 1996, pp. 133–134.

Yet proxy wars, in the sense of wars caused by the great powers (as opposed to any war whose outcome has some implications for the global rivalry), are a relatively rare phenomenon because of two main reasons related to the balance of motivation and capabilities.

First, the asymmetry in the balance of capabilities in favor of the great powers is insufficient by itself to lead regional states to go to war unless it is seen to be in their own interest. External pressures and inducements are insufficient by themselves to induce a state to go to war if it has no reasons of its own. The stakes, commitments, costs, and risks involved in a decision to go to war are too high to make a proxy war a prevalent pattern.[14]

Second, under a balance-of-power system, the competing great powers have a strong interest in discouraging their allies from initiating hot wars because a regional war might spoil their relations with one another, might entrap them in the local conflict, and might even result in a great power confrontation under conditions neither planned nor favored and controlled by the great powers. However, as I discuss later, the great powers may fail in their attempts to prevent regional wars because the balance of motivation favors the regional players at the stage of war initiation and because their peacetime support of the regional states facilitates the resort to war by the small actors.

The combination of these two arguments leads to the conclusion that regional conflicts and wars are not fundamentally caused by external powers and their rivalries.[15] They are, rather, initiated by the regional actors in accordance with their characteristics, objectives, perceptions, and fears of the other regional actors. Thus, the conflict between India and Pakistan was not caused by the global US–Soviet rivalry, even though each of them was supported by a rival superpower during the Cold War. The independence of the regional conflict from the global competition can be seen most clearly when the regional conflict endures beyond the duration of the global rivalry, as is the case with India and Pakistan and in the post-Cold War Middle East, or when regional powers go to war in defiance of the wish of the great powers, as was the case several times in the post-1945 Middle East.

[14] For somewhat similar positions, see Ayoob 1995, pp. 58–59; 1993, p. 42; Vayrynen 1984, 346 ; Holsti 1996, pp. 128–236.
[15] For empirical support, see Vayrynen 1984; Kelly cited in Geller and Singer 1998, p. 102, n. 3.

The state-to-nation imbalance as the underlying cause of war proneness

The state-to-nation balance

The specific regional/domestic variable affecting hot wars is the degree of the state-to-nation imbalance rather than liberal compatibility. While liberal compatibility is a necessary condition for the emergence of high-level peace, and in a region composed of liberal democracies hot wars will not occur, it is a sufficient but not a necessary condition for the absence of hot wars.[16] In order to go to war, regional states need both the motivation and the capabilities to do so. The great powers affect the capabilities of the local states and thus affect the emergence and duration of regional cold war and cold peace. Yet, it is the state-to-nation imbalance, especially the level of national incongruence, that provides the basic motivation for war and therefore makes certain regions more war-prone than others.[17]

Forces affecting the state-to-nation balance

Table 3.1 presents the key forces that reinforce the state-to-nation balance and those that challenge it.

The forces in the left-hand column reinforce the regional state-to-nation balance by increasing the extent of congruence between states and nations and by strengthening the power of status quo states against revisionist nationalist forces. These status quo forces include ethnically congruent nation-states and civic nationalism. The latter is more likely to emerge under state-initiated nationalism or in immigrant societies in the New World. Finally, strong states reinforce the balance, even if they are not nationally congruent.

The forces on the right-hand side challenge the balance and increase the imbalance. They include two types of challenges: those from revisionists, who are more likely to emerge under external incongruence; and challenges of state incoherence which are more likely under internal incongruence and state weakness.

[16] For the development of this argument, see ch. 8.
[17] For related discussions, see Mayall 1990, Van Evera 1994, pp. 10–11, and Moravcsik 1997, 526. On changing international norms regarding the state and the nation, see Barkin and Cronin 1994. On the more specific effects of the two dimensions of the state-to-nation balance – state-to-nation congruence and state strength – on war and how to combine them, see below.

Table 3.1 *The forces affecting the state-to-nation balance*

Stabilizing forces that strengthen the state-to-nation balance	Destabilizing forces that weaken the state-to-nation balance	
Internal coherence: (internal congruence and state strength)	*Challenges of internal incoherence:* (internal incongruence and state weakness)	
1. Ethnically congruent nation-states	**1. Internally incongruent states**	a. Nations without states b. States without nations c. Stateless refugees
2. Strong states	**2. Weak states**	
Civic/territorial nationalism (national congruence):	*External incongruence-revisionist ethnic nationalist challenges:*	
1. State-initiated nationalism	**1. Majority–majority:** – Illegitimate states – Pan-national unifiers ("too many states")	
2. Immigrant societies (New World)	**2. Majority–minority:** – Irredentists – Settlers	

Forces that strengthen the state-to-nation balance

Ethnically congruent nation-states

Congruent nation-states are states in which there is a good match between the political boundaries of the state and the national loyalty of its population. The congruence and match can be derived from either ethnic or civic nationalism. Ethnic nationalism is based on blood ties, lineage, and common ancestry. Thus, in order to have a good match the state has to be both ethnically homogeneous and without either a transborder coethnic group in a neighboring state or nationalist-historical claims to neighbors' lands. Japan and Iceland are good examples but there are not too many others.[18] Even in a region in which there are states with few ethnic cleavages, others might face deep divisions. For example,

[18] Most states are multiethnic. Only some 10 percent of the world's states are nations by the criterion of 90 percent or more of their population speaking the same language (van den Berghe 1983, p. 221, cited in Jackman 1993, p. 107, n. 9); Connor (1972, p. 322) refers to 12 percent of states as ethnically homogeneous. See also Stepan 1998. For a useful classification, see Buzan 1991, ch. 2. Welsh suggests that of 180 states, fewer than 20 are

in post-Cold War Eastern Europe and the Balkans, Bulgaria, Slovakia, Romania, and especially the former Yugoslavia are more deeply divided than Poland, Hungary, and the Czech Republic (Horowitz 1994, p. 36). Regions with a high extent of state-to-nation balance are likely to be those dominated by civic rather than ethnic nationalism, most notably Western Europe, the Americas, and Oceania.

Strong states

Strong states possess a multiplicity of hardware resources, such as coercive and economic capabilities.[19] These states can weaken or suppress ethnic nationalism. However, to the extent that these states do not succeed in a genuine nation-building, they might lack the "software" of creating a common national identity. As a result, ethnic nationalism might reemerge once the capabilities of the central authorities get weaker. Examples include the post-Cold War USSR, Yugoslavia, and post-2003 Iraq (see ch. 4).

Civic/territorial nationalism

Civic nationalism refers to an inclusive membership in the nation according to territory or citizenship. Civic nationalism focuses on citizen identification with the nation-state in its current territorial boundaries as opposed to a loyalty based on subnational or transborder ethnic ties, which may challenge the existing boundaries. In ethnic nationalism, the nation precedes the state, whereas in the civic version the state usually precedes the nation. As a result, there is a greater likelihood of a better match between the state and the nation in those places where civic nationalism predominates.[20] Even though civic nationalism has created quite a few challenges to the interstate order (such as with Belgium, India, Nigeria, and Indonesia), ethnic nationalism has produced much more severe and enduring conflicts.[21] There are two types of nationalism conducive to civic nationalism.

– *State-initiated nationalism*: In Western Europe nationalism was initiated by the state (Cederman 1997, p. 142) and the concept of "nation" was

ethnically homogeneous, in the sense that ethnic minorities account for less than 5 percent of the population (1993, p. 45). I also use this percentage as a criterion in the comparative regional table in appendix A.

[19] For a conceptual and empirical analysis of state strength, see Jackman 1993. See also Organski and Kugler 1980, Buzan 1991, ch. 2, and Rotberg 2003.

[20] On the distinction between ethnic and civic nationalism, see references in ch. 2, n. 53.

[21] A. Smith 1993, p. 38.

framed directly within the existing territorial order that was accepted as a given (White 2000, p. 8; H. Seton-Watson 1977, pp. 8–9). Key Western European states (England, France, Sweden, Spain) have gone through the following gradual two-step evolution:

1 *State-building*, namely, the growth of monarchical power – of its military, fiscal, and bureaucratic controls – determined the boundaries within which the sense of community could develop.[22]
2 *Nation-building*, that is, a process of creation of a nation compatible with the state boundaries by reducing or eliminating cultural differences among the different parts of the population and creating a national consciousness through the education system, spreading a national language and awareness of shared history – including through mythmaking – and popular participation in the political process.[23]

In other words, in Western Europe the state usually preceded the nation, in contrast to many cases in the Old World outside Western Europe, where ethnic nations preceded the establishment of the new states in the late nineteenth century and during the twentieth century, notably in the cases of Germany, Eastern Europe, the Balkans, and the Middle East.[24] The preexistence of ethnic nations (sometimes called "tribes") also constrained state-building in many cases in Africa and various parts of Asia. Since in many of the new states boundaries did not coincide with the preexisting ethnic nations, a state-to-nation imbalance has emerged.

– *Immigrant societies in the New World*: One key distinction between different regions with regard to the state-to-nation congruence is between the Old World and the New.[25] For at least two reasons, the extent of congruence should be higher in the New World (with the notable exception of French Quebec in Canada) and the states in the New World should be powerful in relation to ethnic nationalist forces. The

[22] Tilly 1990; H. Seton-Watson 1977, p. 9.

[23] On state-building and nation-building, see Linz and Stepan 1996, pp. 20–24. On the importance of education in nation-building, see also B. Anderson 1991; on England, see Greenfeld 1992; on France, see E. Weber 1976.

[24] On the differences between the emergence of nationalism in Western and Central and Eastern Europe, see White 2000, pp. 8–9, A. Smith 2000, p. 72, and Gellner 1994, and many additional citations in J. Snyder 2000, pp. 186–188, nn. 151–160. Snyder himself partly challenges this dominant view. Particularly on the differences between the French and the German models of nationalism, see Brubaker 1992, esp. pp. 3–6. See also Schulze 1996, and an overview by Dawisha 2002b.

[25] See A. Smith 2000, pp. 71–72, who also cites additional useful references on nation-formation in the New World.

first reason is the national identity of immigrants (Walzer 1997, pp. 30–35). The second point refers to the balance of power between the European immigrants and the indigenous population. By immigrating, the settlers in the New World abandoned their ethnic-nationalist claims to a distinctive national territory in the Old World. Their new nationhood tended to form according to the existing boundaries of the new states in the Americas (or Oceania). Later waves of immigrants blended into the general population.

The second point, which enhances the congruence and strengthens the state in the New World, pertains to those elements within the population who could potentially have ethnic-nationalist attachment to certain territories, namely, the indigenous peoples. However, these peoples were technologically much weaker than the European immigrants. Thus, in many cases they were suppressed by the Western colonizers in the Americas and Australia.[26] As a result, state-to-nation conflicts were much less frequent in the New World as compared to Europe, the Balkans, the Middle East, Asia, and Africa, where many more of the rivals were comparatively equal in their capabilities, thus creating protracted conflicts of state-to-nation imbalance.

Destabilizing forces that weaken the state-to-nation balance

Chapter 2 presented the ethnic sources of the state-to-nation imbalance. There might be, however, variations in the translation of this imbalance to nationalist challenges to the regional status quo. Two key factors affect the likelihood that this incongruence will be translated to nationalist challenges to the existing state system. The first factor is demography or, more precisely, the geographical spread of the national groups in the region. The second factor is the history of the state and the nation in the region: which preceded which, and especially if some ethnonational groups lost the dominance they once had over the territories they have settled or in adjacent areas.

Demography: The first sense of incongruence – one state with a number of nations – is more likely to lead to secessionist challenges under the following two conditions:

[26] On the mass killings in the Americas, see Stannard 1992, J. Diamond 1999, ch. 3, and H. Seton-Watson 1977, pp. 378–379; but see also Lewy 2004.

I. The settlement patterns of ethnic groups in the region. Concentrated majorities of ethnic groups (i.e., the members of the group residing almost exclusively in a single region of the state) are more likely to risk violence to gain independence than other kinds of settlement patterns such as urbanites, dispersed minorities, and even concentrated minorities. Thus, the more concentrated ethnic majorities are in the region, the higher the number of attempts at secession.[27]
II. The state is more likely to oppose such endeavors violently if it is a multinational state that fears setting a precedent by the secession of one ethnic group, which would trigger secessionist attempts by other ethnonational groups in its territory.[28]

Thus, the combination of I and II – that is, the presence of multinational states with concentrated ethnonational majorities in a number of regions – is likely to lead to violence, as in Chechnya, whereas the binational nature of Czechoslovakia eliminated the fears that following the secession of Slovakia there would have been other such attempts.

The second sense of incongruence – of a single ethnic nation residing in a number of states – is magnified in proportion to the extent of the transborder spread of the national groups in the region: the greater the spread, the greater the imbalance. That is, the spread of a single ethnic nation into five neighboring states creates a greater imbalance in the whole region than the spread into two states which might create conflict only between these two states.

History, or more specifically, the history of state formation and of national independence:

If the state preceded the nation, it is more likely that there will be a state-to-nation congruence, and vice versa; if ethnic nationalism preceded the state, incongruence is more likely. More specifically, nationalist challenges are more likely to be mounted by national groups that have lost control they once held of territories in the region, especially if these territories are identified with a past "Golden Age" of national glory. These territories become major expressions of the nation's identity,

[27] On the effects of settlement patterns on the capacity and inclination of ethnic groups to secede as well as the legitimacy – in the eyes of the group's members – of their doing so, see Toft 2002/3. See also Gurr 2000, pp. 75–76.
[28] See Toft 2002/3, 95–96, on the importance of precedent-setting logic. See also Walter 2003.

both past and present. The Land of Israel for the Zionists and Kosovo for the Serbs are good examples.[29] The problem is that due to changing boundaries and ethnic demographics over the years, in many cases there are competing nationalist claims based on "history" vis-à-vis the same territory. Moreover, these claims might clash with present ethnic distributions. Thus, the Palestinians constitute a clear-cut majority in the West Bank, which is historically the most important part of the Land of Israel for the Jews, and Muslim Albanians are the majority in Kosovo, while the Serbs constitute the minority.

Finally, the translation of a state-to-nation incongruence into violence is influenced by the history of violence among the competing national groups. The less credible the connection between past nationalist violence and present threats, the lower the likelihood of the eruption of violence and vice versa. Such a variation might, for example, explain the more peaceful outcome in the case of the Hungarian minorities in Romania and Slovakia in contrast to the intense violence in the Yugoslav case in the 1990s.[30]

Political manifestations of nationalist dissatisfaction with the regional status quo

Key manifestations of the state-to-nation imbalance include the number and power of the following elements in the region.[31] Knowing the figures for each of these components in a certain region does not allow us to predict the precise likelihood of war. Yet, this knowledge enables us to compare the level of war proneness of different regions. In addition, changes in such figures in a certain region over time allow us to assess the rising or declining likelihood of armed conflict in the region. In general, the greater the presence of the following indicators in the region, the higher the imbalance.

More specifically, nationalist challenges can be divided into two types: domestic challenges from within states; and interstate challenges. Internal incongruence, based on demography and history, and reinforced by state weakness, produce the domestic challenges of incoherence, most notably the threat of *secession*. External incongruence, based on demography and history and reinforced by state strength, generate the

[29] For detailed case studies in Central and Eastern Europe, see White 2000.
[30] Brubaker 1998, pp. 282–283; and Csergo and Goldgeier 2004.
[31] For details on the strength of these elements in different regions, see appendix A.

revisionist challenges, most notably *pan-national unification* and *irredentism*.[32]

Internal incongruence and state weakness lead to challenges of incoherence

(1a) **Nations without states** ("illegitimate nations") or "too few states" in the region refers to substate ethnic groups aspiring for *secession* from the existing states. Too few states are said to be present when there are dissatisfied stateless national groups in the region, who claim their right of national self-determination, and especially demand to secede and establish their own states. The propensity for such claims will increase if the dominant national groups in the existing regional states are intolerant of the political, socioeconomic, and cultural rights of ethnic minorities. Examples of such dominant groups include the Sunnis in Iraq (until the US invasion of 2003), the Alawi in Syria (Hinnebusch 2003), the Sinhalese in Sri Lanka, the Thais in Thailand, and the Turks in Turkey (Ayoob 1995, p. 38).[33] Such intolerance and ethnicity-based discrimination tends to increase the desire of oppressed ethnic groups to have their own independent states.[34] This domestic challenge to the existing regional states undermines their coherence. Examples of quests for national self-determination include the Kurds in Iraq and Turkey; the Tamils in Sri Lanka; the Chechens in Russia; and Kashmiris in

[32] On secession and irredenta, see Weiner 1971; Horowitz 1985, ch. 6; 1991; Mayall 1990, pp. 57–63; Chazan 1991; Halperin and Scheffer et al. 1992; and Carment and James 1997.
[33] On the exclusionary policies of dominant ethnonational groups in the political, military, and economic domains, see Weiner 1987, pp. 35–36, 40–41.
[34] Buzan (1991, ch. 2) distinguishes between two types of multinational states: imperial and federal states. In the federal state no single nation dominates (such as Switzerland, Canada, and Belgium) whereas the imperial state uses coercion to impose the control of one nation over others (such as Austria-Hungary or the USSR). As multinational states, both types of states are potentially vulnerable to nationalist pressures to secede. In the case of the imperial state, its stability depends on the ability of the dominant nation to maintain its control as a strong state. The federal state constitutes, however, a middle category between deeply divided and well-integrated societies (Horowitz 1994, p. 37). Although ethnic groups have strongly held political aspirations and interact as groups, several favorable conditions have moderated the effects of ethnic conflict, among them the late emergence of ethnic issues in relation to other cleavages and to the development of parties, so that party politics is not a perfect reflection of ethnic conflict. Among these states are Switzerland, Canada, and Belgium – all, significantly, federations. These are also called consociational (Switzerland and Belgium) or semiconsociational (Canada) democracies – a power-sharing arrangement among ethnic groups (Lijphart 1977; Walzer 1997). In deeply divided societies, like Northern Ireland and Sri Lanka, the moderating conditions are absent. This issue is also discussed in chs. 8 and 9.

India (in addition to the irredentist claim of Pakistan on Muslim Kashmir); Nigeria and the attempt of Biafra to secede from it in 1967–1970; the Philippines and the Moros; Burma and the Karen; and at least until 2005 Indonesia and the Aceh province, among many other cases. Leading successful attempts of secession are Bangladesh from Pakistan (1971), Northern Cyprus from Cyprus (1974), Eritrea from Ethiopia (1993), and, more recently, East Timor from Indonesia (2002).[35]

(1b) **States without nations:** states that failed to build political communities which identify with their states as reflecting their political sentiments and aspirations and who accept their territorial identity. Many Third World countries mentioned in the previous category fit also here. Yet states which are relatively strong in their domestic coercive capabilities might also belong here, such as the USSR and Yugoslavia before their breakdown; it would potentially also include Indonesia and some Arab states, such as Iraq and Syria (discussed in chapter 4).

(1c) **Stateless refugees** who claim the right of return to their previous homes. They continue to see their previous place of residence as their national homeland from which they were unjustly evicted by force or had to leave under dire circumstances such as war. These refugees are not integrated with an alternative political community in the state in which they currently reside and continue to see their stay there as temporary. This applies, for example, to various victims of the ethnic cleansing in the recent wars in Yugoslavia during the 1990s such as Bosnians, Croats, Serbs, and the Kosovar Muslims in addition to the Palestinians discussed in chapter 4.

(2) **Weak or "failed" states:** states that lack a monopoly over the means of violence in their sovereign territory. An effective set of institutions is missing. These states are unable to extract sufficient military and economic resources from their societies to suppress ethnonationalist/separatist challenges. Numerous African states belong to this category along with Afghanistan, some post-Soviet and post-Yugoslav republics, and other poor and fragile Third World states from Central America, Asia, and the Middle East.[36]

[35] For a comprehensive list of secessionist attempts, see Gurr 2000. For a list of all secessionist and irredentist crises, 1945–1988, see Carment and James 1997, pp. 215–218.

[36] For a useful index of failed states and an updated and comprehensive ranking of sixty failed countries, see *Foreign Policy* 2005. See also the discussion and references in ch. 2, n. 61.

External incongruence and state strength lead to revisionist challenges When the second condition of external or transborder incongruence is present, one could expect challenges to the territorial integrity of other states, which include pan-national movements of unification or revisionist/irredentist claims to territories held by other states on the grounds of national affiliation of the population or national-historic rights on the territory.

More specifically, there are three patterns of transborder incongruence.[37]

1. *Majority–majority*: The presence of two or more states with a shared *ethnic majority* raises the likelihood of attempts at *national unification* led by revisionist states. A shared majority leads to conflicts derived from competing claims to leadership of the ethnic nation made by the elites of each state (Woodwell 2004, 200), and to attempts at national unification, including by coercion, based on the claim that there are "too many states" in relation to the number of nations. The nonrevisionist states are likely to resist the coercive unification by the revisionist state. Supra/pan-national forces (such as pan-Germanism, pan-Arabism, or pan-Slavism) challenge the legitimacy of existing states in the region and call for their unification because they all belong to the same ethnic nation. Such movements are especially dangerous to the existing regional order if they are championed by strong revisionist states.[38]

The presence of such revisionist forces generates the *illegitimate state* – a state whose right to exist is challenged by its revisionist neighbors, either because in their eyes the state's population does not constitute a distinctive nation which deserves a state of its own, or because its territory should belong to a neighboring nation on historical grounds. Examples include the illegitimacy of Taiwan in the eyes of China; South Vietnam in the eyes of North Vietnam; South Korea in the eyes of North Korea; Northern Ireland as part of the United Kingdom from the viewpoint of the Irish national movement; individual Italian and German states in the eyes of Italian and German nationalists in the nineteenth century; and individual Arab states in the eyes of Arab nationalists,

[37] See also Woodwell 2004.

[38] On revisionist vs. status quo states, see Wolfers 1962, pp. 18–19, 96–97, 125–126; and Schweller 1994, 1996 (which includes citations to other works that make similar distinctions on 98–99, n. 31), and 1998 (pp. 22–24, 84–89). See also Kupchan 1998 and Buzan 1991, ch. 8. On aspiring revisionist regional powers in the post-Cold War era, see Job 1997, p. 187.

specifically in different periods Kuwait (challenged by Iraq), Lebanon (challenged by Syria), Jordan, and Israel as discussed in chapter 4.

The likelihood of the emergence of pan-national forces and illegitimate states increases when the division of a single ethnic nation into a number of states was done forcibly via a military conquest by a rival regional state (supporting a competing national movement) or imposed by imperial powers.

2. *Majority–minority*: The presence of a state with an ethnic majority and neighbor(s) with the same ethnic minority increases the likelihood of attempts at *irredentism* by the former state vis-à-vis the territories populated by the minority.[39] The "revisionist/irredentist state" claims territories held by other states on the grounds of national affiliation of the population or national-historic rights to the territory.[40]

This type culminates in "the Greater state" ("Greater Germany," "Greater Syria," "Greater Israel," "Greater Serbia," etc.). The expansionist efforts of this type of state are likely to be opposed by the neighbors and thus lead to conflict. Because of the importance states attribute to their territorial integrity, such conflicts can escalate to violence. The likelihood of irredentism increases if political boundaries in the region cross ethnic nations so that a sizable portion of the ethnic nation is beyond the boundaries of the state which claims to represent this group or is dominated by it. Ethnic alliances – cases in which a majority group in one state is a minority group in a neighboring state – increase the likelihood of international conflict (Moore and Davis 1998) where the coethnics in one state (the majority group) are propelled by feelings of solidarity with their ethnic kin in a proximate state (the minority). As a result, the state hosting the transborder minority feels threatened by the majority state.[41] Likewise, this transborder minority, believing they have a greater chance of success due to this solidarity, is more likely to be emboldened and to attempt (or be persuaded to attempt) an armed rebellion. Such situations may lead to intended or unintended escalation.

[39] On other types of relations in this triangle, see Brubaker 1996.

[40] Irredentist conflicts include those between Iran and Iraq over the Shatt al-Arab; Afghanistan and Pakistan over Pakistan's North-West Frontier Province; Ethiopia and Somalia over the Ogaden; Pakistan and India over Kashmir; Serbia with Croatia and Bosnia in the 1990s; and the post-Soviet conflict between Armenia and Azerbaijan on Nagorno-Karabakh. For a list of all irredentist (and secessionist) crises, 1945–1988, see Carment and James 1997, pp. 215–218.

[41] For a recent empirical study that shows a significant increase in dyadic conflict when two states share an ethnic group and an ethnic majority exists in at least one of the states, see Woodwell 2004.

Similarly, irredentism is more likely to emerge if there are territories beyond the boundaries of the state to which there has been persistent and intense historical attachment as the homeland of the nation, where it was born and had glorified accomplishments.[42] What matters for this theory's purpose is not whether this nationalist account is based on historical facts or not–although it may well be, at least in part; what matters is that large groups of people believe in such a historical attachment and are ready to fight (and sometimes die) for it.

The international opposition to coercive changes of boundaries in the post-1945 era has, however, led to a growing support for secession of the ethnic kin as a partial substitute for irredentism.[43] Moreover, the trans-border minority itself might prefer secession to irredentism due either to the political interests of its leadership or to the unattractiveness of the putative irredentist state because of its authoritarian regime, economic backwardness, or low prestige (Horowitz 1991, pp. 16–18).

A subset of irredentists constitutes *settlers* – a nationalist group which resides beyond the state boundaries and advocates, with the support of irredentist groups back home, annexation to the homeland of the territories they settle. Illustrations include the Germans in Eastern Europe, the Protestants in Northern Ireland, and the French settlers in Algiers, in addition to the post-1967 Jewish settlers in the occupied territories discussed in chapter 4.

3. *Minority–minority*: a shared ethnic minority among contiguous states might result in a status quo orientation of these states. At any rate, this pattern makes it easier for states to act based on *Realpolitik* calculations because they are less constrained by domestic/nationalist considerations related to a certain ethnic majority. On the one hand, states might take advantage of a restive minority in a neighboring state and support the minority in order to weaken that state. For example, Iran supported the Kurdish insurgency against the Iraqi government in the early 1970s. On the other hand, the domestic/emotional commitment of a state to an ethnic minority is much weaker than to a group which is the majority in the state, and in this case an irredentist orientation is unlikely. Moreover, neighboring states might occasionally cooperate in suppressing common minorities which challenge their territorial integrity and

[42] For a variety of examples, see A. Smith 2000, pp. 67–68.

[43] See Chazan 1991; Saideman 2001; Woodwell 2004, p. 201. For examples of states that preferred to support a secession of their ethnic kin rather than irredentism because of *Realpolitik* considerations, see Horowitz 1991, p. 15. But at least some of these cases can be explained based on the minority–minority pattern discussed below.

Antecedent conditions	→	Independent variables	→	Manifestations	→	Outcomes
Demography and history	→	State-to-nation incongruence	→	Nationalist challenges	→	Hot war

Figure 3.2 The causal chain between incongruence and violence

pose a problem to regional stability. Thus, Iraq, Iran, and Turkey in some periods collaborated against the quest of the Kurdish minorities in their countries for self-determination, which threatened the territorial integrity of all three.

Figure 3.2 presents the causal relations between incongruence and violence. It especially underlines the role of demography and history as antecedent conditions which affect the influence that the independent variable is likely to have on producing nationalist challenges to the status quo and thus on the likelihood of violence.

Based on these manifestations we can distinguish between different regions, both whether they suffer from a state-to-nation imbalance in general and with regard to the two dimensions of the balance. South America and Western Europe currently have lower state-to-nation imbalances than most other regions. Thus, phenomena like "illegitimate states," strong pan-national movements, and the "Greater state" are almost nonexistent, although some weak states are present in South America and a few "illegitimate nations" exist in Western Europe.[44] Among the regions with a high state-to-nation imbalance, Africa is notable for a low state coherence due to the combination of internal incongruence and state weakness. The Middle East (see chapter 4) and Northeast Asia have, however, high extents of nationalist revisionism due to the combination of state strength and external incongruence.

Types of states and their war proneness

The state-to-nation imbalance affects both the motivation for resorting to violence and the opportunity to do so. The regional state-to-nation balance has two analytically distinctive dimensions (see chapter 2). The first is the extent of congruence between political boundaries and national identifications in a certain region. The second dimension is the prevalence in the region of strong or weak states.

[44] See appendix A.

Table 3.2 *State and regional war proneness: the effects of state-to-nation congruence and of state strength*

	Incongruence	Congruence
Strong states	1 **Revisionist states** (and pan-national movements) Wars of aggression or profit and diversionary wars: pre-1945 Germany (pan-Germanism) post-1949 China (Taiwan) Greater Serbia (pan-Slavism) North Korea (Korean unification) Pakistan (Kashmir) Iraq and Syria (pan-Arabism)	4 **Status quo states** Peaceful conflict resolution: post-1945 Western Europe twentieth-century South America post-1973 Egypt
Weak states	2 Civil war and intervention in **failed (or incoherent) states** Security dilemma post-Cold War former Soviet republics; Bosnia; Congo; Ivory Coast; Somalia; Liberia; Sierra Leone; Sudan; Afghanistan; Lebanon and Jordan; Yemen; Palestinian Authority	3 **Frontier states** Boundary/territorial wars Nineteenth-century South America

National incongruence motivates people to fight for issues that are affected by it, such as territory, boundaries, state creation, and state-making. External incongruence, in particular, affects motivations for interstate war related to nationalist revisionist ideologies, such as wars of national unification and irredentism. Thus, this aspect of the state-to-nation incongruence provides an explanation for many of the territorial conflicts among states. The extent of internal incongruence affects the motivation for domestic wars of secession.

The degree of state strength, for its part, exercises major effects on the capacity of states to wage international wars, on the opportunities to initiate civil wars, and on the possibility of external intervention in the territory of the state. Accordingly, we see the following four combinations of types of states and types of violent conflict in which they tend to be involved, if at all. Table 3.2 shows the combined effect of the two dimensions of the state-to-nation balance on state and regional war proneness.

In category 1 the combined effect of incongruence and strong states produces *revisionist* powers. Revisionist states are dissatisfied with the current regional order and are willing to use force to change the territorial status quo based on nationalist claims. Thus, state-to-nation imbalance leads to revisionism, which is a destabilizing force. The challenge to the regional order will be especially severe if there are powerful revisionist states in the region which experience state-to-nation incongruence and accordingly might face serious domestic challenges. These challenges can be directed against the legitimacy of the state and its boundaries from ethnic groups exerting pressure for secession or irredentism. Because of the external incongruence of these revisionist states, they may have irredentist claims toward their neighbors, which may lead to wars of expansion or profit. The internal incongruence produces domestic problems from which leaders may try to divert the public's attention with aggressive behavior and diversionary wars; they hope that these wars will result in domestic unity supporting their rule due to the production of the common external enemy – the scapegoat.[45] Revisionist states are also likely to aspire to regional primacy, generating countervailing coalitions of status quo states and struggles over regional hegemony. Even if these states do not always aim at domination, their challenge to the regional order markedly increases the intensity of the security dilemma in the region, thus raising the likelihood of inadvertent wars.

Examples of the emergence of revisionist states as a result of the combination of strong and incongruent states include both cases of unification and irredentism. A prominent historical case of unification is Prussia/Germany during the wars of national unification in 1863–1871.[46] Notable contemporary cases include China's unification claims on Taiwan and the cases of North Vietnam and North Korea toward South Vietnam and South Korea, respectively. Chapter 4 will discuss a notable attempt at national unification – pan-Arabism. In these cases relatively strong states pursue revisionist policies based on the "too many states" logic. There is a widespread national feeling, though it may be manipulated by leaders for their own political agenda, that the nation is

[45] See ch. 1 and below.
[46] For an overview, see Williams 2001, ch. 3. On German nationalism, see also ch. 8 in this book.

artificially and arbitrarily divided into a number of states. In this nationalist view, the nation should unify into one state, which would reflect the national aspirations and sentiments of the single unified nation. Such nationalists therefore tend to believe that, for this "noble" purpose of national unification, the strongest state of that nation should not hesitate to use force.

A related variant is the "Greater state," claiming territories beyond its boundaries based on national identity of the people or historical rights. A key example is Germany's interwar irredentist claims to the territories populated by Germans in Poland and Czechoslovakia. The irredentist policy is especially applicable with regard to the position of the German governments *before* Hitler in relation to the German areas of Poland.[47] A more recent case is Serbia's attempts in the 1990s to annex the Serbian-populated areas of Croatia and Bosnia and its ethnic cleansing in Kosovo and Bosnia.[48] Some cases of irredentism are particularly based on the historical national rights of neighboring states rather than the ethnic component (Ben-Israel 1991, pp. 24–25). For example, the nationalist claims in the cases of Italy (South Tyrol), Greece (Constantinople), and Israel (post-1967 Jerusalem and the West Bank) were based on supposed national heritage rather than on the ethnicity of the population in the claimed territories.

The examples discussed in chapter 4 are the revisionist policies pursued by Syria and Iraq, especially after these states became stronger in the 1970s.

In category 2, *incoherent or failed states* are the product of weak states in which the citizens also have a low level of identification with the state and with its territorial identity; they do not generally feel it reflects their national identity and aspirations. In other words, there are strong aspirations for either secession or irredentism. The weakness of incoherent states permits the violent actions of revisionist groups and encourages other groups trying to defend themselves. Such moves trigger a cycle of escalation which the weak state is unable to contain because it is unable to defeat or bribe the insurgents (Byman and Van Evera 1998, 37–39).

[47] Ben-Israel 1991. Although German revisionism vis-à-vis Eastern Europe under Hitler in the late 1930s seemed to be initially based also on state-to-nation imbalances, which were helpful in mobilizing domestic and international support for a policy of irredentism, Nazi policy went far beyond that, aspiring to world hegemony. For an extended discussion of the nationalist conflict over the Sudetenland and its international aspects, see Ben-Israel 1991, pp. 25–31. On German, Italian, and Greek irredentism in the interwar era, see Reichman and Golan 1991. On post-World War II German irredentism, see Stoess 1991.

[48] See Williams 2001, chs. 4, 5. On the Balkans, see also ch. 6 in this book.

The combined effect of weakness and incongruence may have unintended effects – making certain states arenas of armed conflict even if they have peaceful intentions. A good example might be multinational states, which prefer to maintain the status quo, but if they become weaker, various national groups try to take advantage and secede, including by violent means, thus also creating a situation which is conducive to external intervention. Illustrations include empires such as Austria-Hungary and the Ottoman Empire in the late nineteenth and early twentieth century.

Following the collapse of an imperial order, state creation will be conducive to hot wars when a number of national liberation movements compete for control of the same territory (Katz 1996, p. 29), which does not have legitimate agreed-upon boundaries (Van Evera 1993, p. 232).[49] The situation is especially explosive if each group is convinced of its own legitimacy based, for example, on historical or demographic rights, while delegitimizing the claims of the other movements. A victory of one of the movements will lead to revisionist claims by the defeated party, which will have destabilizing regional effects if they are supported by ethnic kin in other regional states. At the same time, the victorious movement may still be dissatisfied and exercise irredentist claims on the territories of neighboring states. The states created after imperial disintegration can also be incoherent or failed states to the extent that important groups inside the new state do not identify with it, delegitimize its boundaries, and seek to secede and establish an independent state or join a neighboring state. Comparative quantitative research has demonstrated that ethnolinguistic divisions, especially when reinforced by subjective feelings of political separatism, help to account for political violence and instability.[50]

The point is that incoherent or failed states may bring about challenges to the regional order precisely because they are militarily and domestically weak (vis-à-vis their own societies). In this case, one should expect the eruption of ethnic civil wars within these states, which also create temptations for their neighbors to intervene. Examples include incoherent/failed states in Asia (such as the recurrent interventions of Afghanistan's neighbors in its internal affairs in the past three decades)

[49] For overviews of imperial collapse, see Katz 1996; Van Evera 1993, p. 232; and Byman and Van Evera 1998. On state creation, see Ayoob 1996; Holsti 1996; and Goertz and Diehl 1992b, pp. 21–23 and ch. 3.

[50] References cited in Hudson 1977, p. 57. For a major quantitative study, see Huth 1996, 1999. See also Gurr 2000.

and Africa (such as the intervention of at least seven neighboring states in the Democratic Republic of Congo in recent years). Following the collapse of the USSR and Yugoslavia, new incoherent/failed states emerged in the Caucasus, in Central Asia, and in the Balkans (Bosnia and Macedonia). Indeed, these states were marked by a combination of civil wars and foreign intervention. Incoherent states in the Middle East – Lebanon, Jordan, and the post-Oslo Palestinian Authority – and their destabilizing effects are discussed below.

A related aspect is demographic revisionism – the demand that a country allows people of a nationality or ethnicity different than that of the group currently dominant in a state or colony to immigrate into it. These immigrants may alter the demographic nature of the entity in two main ways. First, the new settlers may significantly differ from the indigenous population and may therefore prefer alternative political arrangements. The second form demographic revisionism may take is as the fulfillment of the right of return of refugees to their country of origin as opposed to their resettlement in the new host countries. This right might be opposed by the country of origin due to fears that a massive return of refugees from another nation or ethnic group might challenge the existing national, ethnic, or cultural nature of the state as it emerged following a major relocation or displacement of people in the region.[51]

The more powerful the revisionist forces and the lower the level of state coherence in the region, the higher the regional war proneness. The issue is the outcome if the states are weak but nationally congruent: namely if the states are what I called in chapter 2 "frontier states." Such regions, populated by weak states and state-to-nation congruence, as in category 3, are still prone to regional wars, although they might have the potential for peaceful resolution at a later stage if state-building succeeds through the strengthening of the regional states. So long as the states are weak, there is a high likelihood of territorial and boundary wars because states' control over their territory is not complete and the boundaries are not fully fixed, unanimously agreed upon, or clearly drawn. As a result there are numerous boundary disputes and external interventions. A good example, as discussed in chapter 7, is nineteenth-century South America until the relative strengthening of South American states starting in the 1880s.

In contrast, the combined effect of congruence and strong states in category 4 results in a much lower likelihood of violence. As a result

[51] On migration, refugees, and security, see Weiner 1995.

of the state-to-nation congruence, states have less motivation to resort to violence and have fewer quarrels with their neighbors. They tend to be status quo states without ambitions of territorial expansionism. Thus, mutual fears and the security dilemma decline. As strong states, they are not only able to negotiate peaceful agreements with regional partners, but also to maintain their commitments and to guarantee stable peace. Thus, both wars of profit and security dilemma wars are less likely. Regimes in strong and congruent states, which tend to be more stable internally and are less likely to face threats of secession, also have less incentive to pursue diversionary wars and to maintain existing enduring rivalries than regimes in potentially unstable incongruent states. Since the nation is satisfied with its territorial identity, there are fewer opportunities or pretexts to initiate war than in incongruent states. Thus, politicians are less able and willing to manipulate nationalist issues in a way that might lead to resort to force. Chapter 7 examines whether such an analysis might provide a useful explanation of the regional peace which emerged in South America during the twentieth century.

Linkages between revisionism and failed states

Revisionism and state incoherence or failure are two major *outputs* of the state-to-nation imbalance. Although they are distinctive elements, there are also reinforcing linkages between them.

Revisionist ideologies and external interference in failed states

Supranational ideologies that challenge the legitimacy of the independence and sovereignty of existing states legitimize and encourage external intervention in domestic affairs of other states. This is especially the case if these ideologies subscribe to a pan-national divisive ideology that supports the subordination of the state to a larger entity. This will increase regional tensions and instability. The greater the appeal of this revisionist pan-national ideology, the weaker the regional states. The weakening and destabilizing effects are especially severe with regard to states which are incoherent due to their deep ethnic, religious, and/or ideological cleavages. Such states provide fertile ground for regional intervention in their domestic political systems by revisionist forces.

Irredentism and state incoherence

This is Weiner's "Macedonian syndrome" (1971),[52] in which irredentist states seek to revise international boundaries so as to incorporate an ethnic group which partly resides in a neighboring state along with the territory this group occupies. Revisionist/irredentist states desire to liberate what they view as oppressed minorities, to unite with their kinsmen in order to make whole a national people. A related and partly overlapping aspiration is to redeem "lost" territories of the historical homeland that are occupied by neighbors so as to make whole a national territory. As Weiner illustrates, many variants of this syndrome have been prevalent not only in the Balkans since the nineteenth century (1971, 669),[53] but also in postcolonial Asia and Africa (ibid., 670).

Such revisionist aspirations, demands, and interventions generate competitive pressures among regional states due to rivalries of power and ideology. Revisionism also generates security fears among neighbors of the target state and rivals of the intervening state. Moreover, external intervention by revisionist ideological forces may encourage revolutions in incoherent states. Revolutionary changes tend to have destabilizing regional effects (Walt 1996). Thus, the combination of revisionist pressures and incoherent states may bring about a growing likelihood of armed conflict among regional states.

Refugees, insurgents and regional wars

Refugees[54] who do not accept the legitimacy of the regional status quo and are willing to use force in order to revise it can be a major source of regional and domestic instability. This will be especially true if the refugees aspire to return to their homes in the country of origin and this country is a neighboring state. Refugees may use the host country as a base to launch attacks on the country of origin, triggering reprisals and

[52] See also Pillar 1983, pp. 24–26. See Brubaker 1996, esp. ch. 3, for a study that applies a similar type of relationship to interwar Eastern Europe and the post-Yugoslav and post-Soviet conflicts.

[53] For example, Albania demanded the Kosovo region of Yugoslavia, with its Muslim Albanian inhabitants; Hungary sought possession of the Vojvodina region of Yugoslavia and the Transylvania region of Romania, both with large Hungarian populations; Bulgaria claimed Macedonia consistently from the beginning of its national movement. The Balkans are discussed in ch. 6.

[54] For conceptual relations between refugees and security and for examples, see Weiner 1995. See also Posen 1996. On the example of the Internal Macedonian Revolutionary Organization in the Balkans in the 1920s and 1930s, see Weiner 1971, 678–679.

counteractions by that country on their host countries, thus producing regional violence which may escalate to full-blown wars. The situation may be especially conducive to wars if there is also a high degree of revisionism in the host countries. Thus, the host country may use the refugees for its own expansionist or hegemonic regional objectives.[55] Yet the host government may not support specific violent actions of the refugees. In this case, the latter may be able to drag the host countries to higher levels of violence than were their initial plans, at least regarding the timing and the scope of the wars. Transborder raids, for instance, can lead to a cycle of violence by triggering violent reactions of the country of origin and raising the security dilemma in the region (see chapter 4). The ability of refugees to drag local states into wars, or at least to make violence more likely and intense, will be especially marked if the host countries are incoherent. Moreover, massive flows of refugees may, by themselves, weaken the host countries, making them less coherent to the extent that the refugees are not well integrated (politically, economically, socially, and culturally) into the local societies and maintain their own distinctive identities and irredentist aspirations, especially if these countries arm them against their countries of origin. Guns can be pointed in both directions, and the host state takes the risk that refugees will affect the host state's policies toward their state of origin. For example, arming the Afghan refugees in Pakistan limited the options available to the government of Pakistan in its dealings with the governments of Afghanistan and the USSR during the Cold War. Arming refugees may also lead to internal violence and even to civil wars in weak states. Hence, Kurds, Sikhs, Armenians, Sri Lankan Tamils, and Palestinians, among others, are regarded by many intelligence and police authorities as threats to host countries.

The state-to-nation imbalance and regional war proneness

Regions populated by revisionist and incoherent states are more prone to wars than other regions for three reasons.[56] First, substantive issues of conflict may emerge on national grounds, most notably national

[55] Examples include the US armament of Cuban refugees and of the Contra exiles from Nicaragua; the Indian government arming the Tamil refugees from Sri Lanka and the Bengalis from Pakistan; and the Chinese support of the Khmer Rouge against the Vietnamese occupation of Cambodia.

[56] See also Lake and Rothchild 1998b, esp. pp. 30–32, and the references they cite.

independence, territories, and boundaries, or on demographic issues, such as refugees and settlers. As the territorial literature has shown, disputed territory is a major issue of international conflict. The question is, however, what does explain variations in the escalation of territorial conflicts to violence? I argue that, if the territorial issue involves state-to-nation imbalances, the likelihood of escalation is much greater than in other kinds of territorial disputes (such as economic and even strategic, which, in turn, might be aggravated by state-to-nation incongruence). This is because issues of nationalism and ethnicity tend to be less divisible than material issues. It is much harder to divide, in an acceptable way, the control of territories with symbolic and emotional importance among a number of contending parties than to divide the control of territories with material importance (containing minerals or oil, for example). It is also more difficult to find acceptable compensation for territory with emotional attachment to it than to land with mere material significance. Nations derive their identities to a large degree from particular places and territories, and the control of these is often essential to maintaining a healthy sense of national identity.[57] Thus, state-to-nation issues arouse strong emotions and passionate ideological commitments that make pragmatic compromise and bargaining more difficult.[58] As a result, domestic politics plays an especially powerful role in constraining the maneuvering room of political leaders on these issues. The strong commitment of domestic constituencies to ethnicity and nationalism generates pressures on and incentives for state leaders to maintain a hard line and even to go to war.[59]

Ethnic nationalism has more destabilizing regional effects than civic nationalism because the former is more likely to generate demands to annex neighbors' territories if these are populated by people of the same ethnic origin or if there are alleged historic ties between the nation and these territories. Such irredentism is the highest aspiration of nationalist groups; at the very least they will tend to support secession of their ethnic kin in the neighboring state (Chazan 1991; Saideman 2001). The fulfillment of such nationalist aspirations, however, threatens the territorial integrity of a neighboring state; and dismemberment is the

[57] White 2000, p. 10; Toft 2003.

[58] On the role of emotions in ethnic conflict, see Peterson 2002.

[59] For studies that show that ethnic/national claims are major sources of territorial conflicts, see Mandel 1980; Luard 1986, pp. 421–447, esp. pp. 442–447; Holsti 1991, esp. pp. 140–142, 144–145, 214–216, 274–278, 280, 308; Carment 1993; Carment and James 1997; Huth 1996, pp. 108–112; Huth 1999, pp. 53–57; White 2000; Woodwell 2004.

greatest nightmare of any state leader (Toft 2003; Woodwell 2004). Thus, crises born of transborder ethnic nationalism are more prone to violence than other types. In contrast, civic nationalism is less likely to produce territorial disputes even if there are transborder ethnic ties.[60]

Because of the strong passions and domestic incentives produced by a state-to-nation imbalance, it is likely to challenge the conventional realist logic of balance-of-power theory and deterrence. Highly motivated actors might initiate violence even if they are weaker in the overall balance of power. In other words, deterrence is less effective under a high state-to-nation imbalance because it produces highly dissatisfied state and nonstate players. It also produces leaders who have domestic incentives to resort to violence, even if their states are weaker. Such an imbalance also makes more likely asymmetric warfare, in which weaker states attack stronger ones[61] or nonstate organizations resort to guerrilla tactics and terrorism against stronger state opponents. A recent major example is the fight of the Chechen secessionists against Russia.

Second, a high state-to-nation imbalance provides fertile ground for the exacerbation of other causes of war such as the realist ones – the security dilemma and power rivalries as well as scapegoat/diversionary motives (i.e., externalization of domestic conflicts) in the region. I discuss below the effects of the state-to-nation imbalance on the rising likelihood of different types of wars.

Third, the presence of incoherent states produces regional insecurity through the effects of spreading transborder instability among a group of strategically interdependent state and nonstate actors. For example, failed or incoherent states produce regional instability because they provide targets for external intervention either from temptation for profit and expansion or due to insecurity and fear of instability spreading out of the incoherent states. In contrast, coherent states, in which the population identifies with the state and its territorial identity, are more likely to deter potential aggressors because the latter expect to meet stiff resistance. Such states are also likely to reduce the regional security dilemma because they enhance the sense that the current boundaries are permanent and irreversible and thus reassure regional actors about their territorial integrity.

[60] Lepsius 1985, 46.

[61] In a major book on wars initiated by the weaker state, most of T. V. Paul's cases (1994) involve state-to-nation conflicts: Korea, India–Pakistan, and the Arab–Israeli conflict.

Propositions derived from the state-to-nation imbalance as a key cause of regional war

Some of the key implications of the state-to-nation imbalance and its causal relations with regional war proneness are articulated in the following propositions.

Proposition 1: More wars are caused by state-to-nation issues than by other sorts (such as territorial, strategic, balance-of-power, ideological, and economic). State-to-nation issues are also more likely than other types to lead to regional cold wars, which are enduring rivalries made manifest.

Evidence: In light of all the major changes that the end of the Cold War has brought about, it is noteworthy that even this important watershed did not make any significant difference to the centrality of the state-to-nation issues as the leading causes of war. These issues, as defined in this book, constituted 62 percent of the causes of wars during the Cold War and 60 percent in the post-Cold War era, according to my coding. Thus, of 167 wars in the Cold War era, 103 were caused by state-to-nation factors.[62] Holsti found with regard to a similar conception of what are called here state-to-nation issues[63] that: "In terms of the relative frequency of issues it ranks highest by a considerable margin" (1991, p. 311).[64] According to Holsti,[65] state-to-nation issues accounted for about 40 percent of the issues that generated wars, while territory, including strategic territory and boundaries, constituted 18 percent of the issues, and ideological motives 14 percent. Other issues, such as commercial and national security (border threat), accounted for only a small percentage of the issues.[66]

[62] See appendix B in this book, which is based on Holsti 1996; Allcock et al. 1992; Holsti 1991; Huth 1996; SIPRI 2004; Eriksson and Wallensteen 2004; PRIO/Uppsala Armed Conflict Dataset (Version 2.1.); and Project Ploughshares 2004.

[63] Similarly to what is included in this cluster, Holsti refers to national liberation/state creation, national unification/consolidation, and secession. In appendix B I note the cases that I coded differently from Holsti as state-to-nation issues, based on the case studies of this research. For example, seemingly "territorial" conflicts, such as the Arab–Israeli conflict, might be better explained by state-to-nation issues. See ch. 4.

[64] For the 1945–1989 period, see table 11.1 in Holsti 1991, pp. 274–278 as well as table 11.2 (p. 280). See also the data in Holsti 1996 and Huth 1999.

[65] See table 11.2 in Holsti 1991, p. 280.

[66] Even during the interwar period, in which there was a relative decline in the proportion of state-to-nation issues, they still constituted up to 30 percent of all war-generating issues, while the next major issue – territory – accounted for 23 percent and empire creation and commerce/resources for 6 percent each (Holsti 1991, p. 218). Moreover, some of the empire creation was also related, at least initially, to state-to-nation imbalances, such as Germany's claims to the German-populated areas of Eastern Europe based on ethnic unification.

Similarly, in his comprehensive study of territorial disputes during 1950–1990, Paul Huth also provides strong evidence for the relations between state-to-nation imbalance and regional war proneness, focusing more specifically on enduring rivalries.[67] Huth found that those disputes "involving issues of ethnic irredentism or national unification were the most likely to develop into enduring rivalries" (1999, p. 53). These ethnonational issues are stronger predictors of a territorial dispute than the strategic location of the territory (ibid., p. 55).

In the post-Cold War era, thirty-eight of sixty-three wars were state-to-nation wars according to my coding.[68] Gurr and Harff (1994, p. xiii) found that ethnonational rivalries were a major cause of all but five of the twenty-two hot wars taking place around the world in 1993.[69]

The centrality of the state-to-nation issues is not, however, a new phenomenon. Similar trends were also prevalent in earlier eras. The findings of comprehensive research show that, apart from the 1914–1945 era, issues related to state-to-nation balance have been more often associated with war and armed intervention than any other issue since 1815.[70] Thus, in the period 1815–1914, following the rise of modern nationalism with the French Revolution and the Napoleonic wars, more than one-half of all the wars (55 percent) involved problems of state creation, according to Holsti's coding[71] (in my coding at least twenty of the thirty-one wars in his table 7.1 included state-to-nation issues).[72] From a related angle, state-to-nation issues constituted at least 37 percent of all issues that generated wars,[73] while other leading issues accounted for a much lower proportion; for example, contests over territory accounted for 14 percent of all issues, navigation/commerce for 4 percent, and dynastic/succession issues for only 3 percent.[74]

Proposition 2: Regions with higher levels of state-to-nation imbalance are more war-prone, producing both interstate wars (including external intervention) and domestic wars. Most of these wars are explained by state-to-nation issues. Thus, we should expect wars to be more frequent

[67] For a list of all enduring rivalries over disputed territories, see Huth 1999, pp. 48–50, Table 2.1. Table 2.3 (ibid., p. 54) presents the marginal impact of variables measuring the issue at stake on the probability of an enduring rivalry over disputed territory, 1950–1990.

[68] See appendix B. [69] Cited in Trumbore 2003, 183.

[70] Holsti 1991, p. 311. For summaries regarding the war-generating issues in the period 1648–1989, see the tables ibid., pp. 306–334.

[71] Ibid., p. 143. [72] This table is ibid., pp. 140–142.

[73] The percentage might increase to 46 percent if we include other subissues which are part of the state-to-nation agenda.

[74] For details regarding the issues that motivated all the wars in the 1815–1914 era, see Holsti 1991, pp. 140–145.

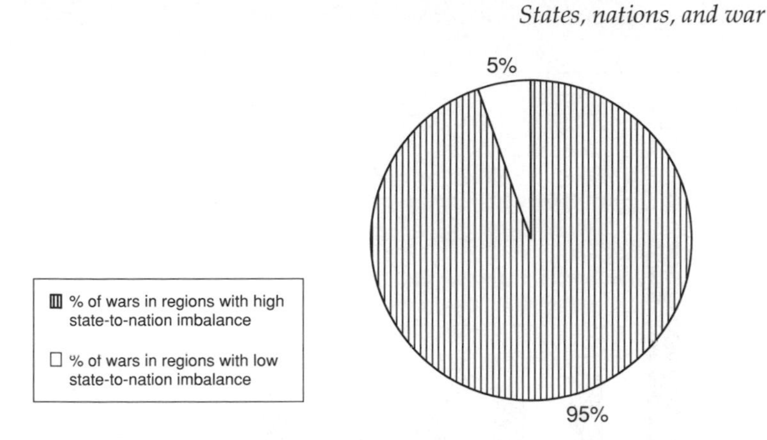

Figure 3.3 War frequency and state-to-nation imbalance, 1945–2004
Source: Appendix B.

in the post-1945 era in regions such as Africa, the Middle East, East Asia, and South Asia and less frequent in regions such as Western Europe and South America.

Evidence: Indeed, regions with high state-to-nation imbalances suffered many more wars than more balanced regions, and most of the wars in the former regions were caused by state-to-nation issues (see figures 3.3–3.5). Accordingly, in the period 1945–1991, of the forty-five armed conflicts in Africa, thirty-one were caused by state-to-nation issues;[75] and of the thirty-seven wars in the Middle East, twenty-eight were state-to-nation wars. In East Asia, including Southeast Asia, thirty-six wars broke out; twenty-four of these wars were state-to-nation wars; and of the twenty-two wars in South Asia, seventeen were state-to-nation conflicts.[76] Thus, the majority of conflicts in each region were state-to-nation.[77]

On the other hand, regions with a low state-to-nation imbalance, notably Western Europe and the Americas, experienced many fewer wars: three wars in Western Europe – all domestic; and nine in South America, eight of which were internal-ideological with only one interstate (and even this one with an extraregional force – the 1982 Falklands

[75] See appendix B. [76] See appendix B.
[77] This majority includes the relatively small number of anti-colonial conflicts because they are also a manifestation of state-to-nation issues; thus we should include these conflicts (eight in Africa, six in the Middle East, one in South Asia, and three in East and Southeast Asia) in the counting of the state-to-nation wars in the post-1945 era. At any rate, even if we exclude the anti-colonial conflicts, state-to-nation issues are still the leading cause of armed conflicts in the regions with state-to-nation imbalances.

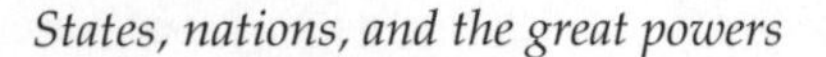

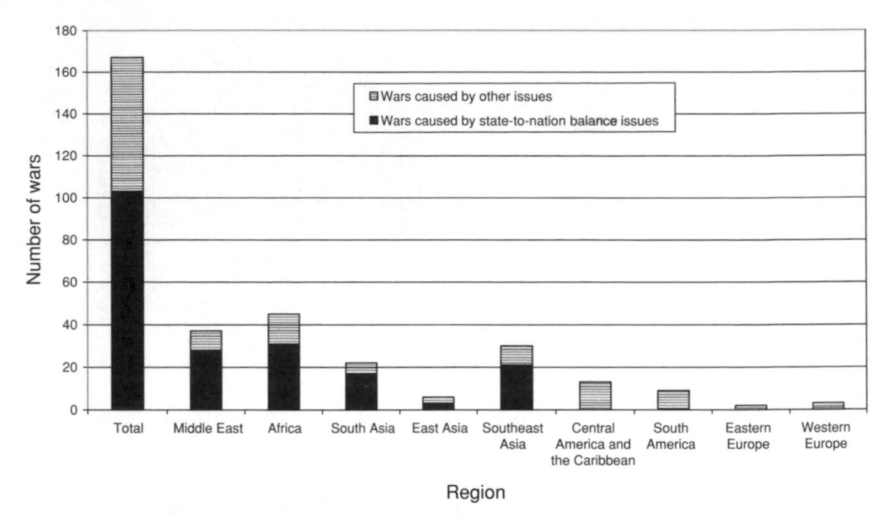

Figure 3.4 Wars caused by state-to-nation imbalance in the Cold War era (1945–1991)
Source: Appendix B.

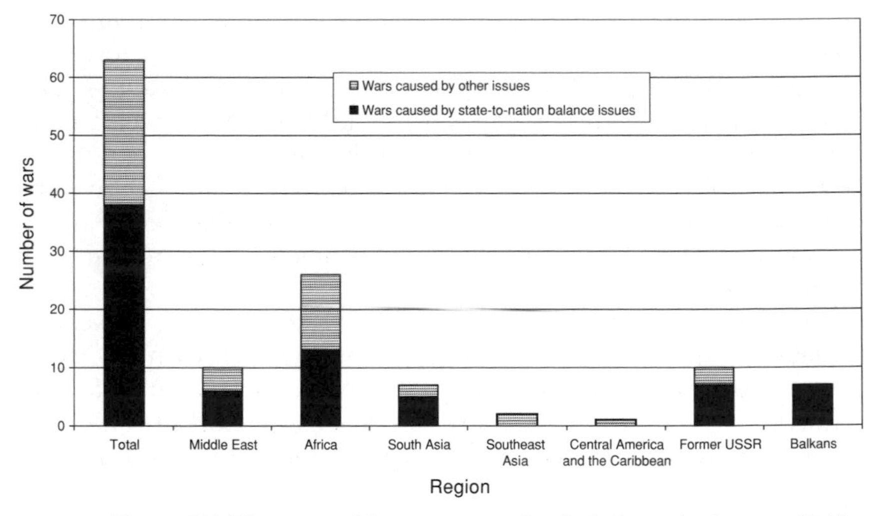

Figure 3.5 Wars caused by state-to-nation imbalance in the post-Cold War era (1991–2004)
Note: Numbers include only those conflicts beginning or recommencing since the start of the era.
Source: Appendix B.

Table 3.3 *The combined effect of external and internal incongruence on regional war proneness*

	External incongruence	
Internal incongruence	High	Low
High	1 **Interstate wars** **Civil wars & intervention** Post-1945 Middle East Post-Cold War Balkans	2 **Civil wars & intervention** Postcolonial Africa
Low	3 **Interstate wars** Europe in the 1930s East Asia in post-WWII era	4 **Interstate and civil wars are unlikely** South America Post-1945 Western Europe

War between Argentina and Britain). Liberal compatibility may have played an important role in preventing wars among West European democracies and especially in warming the peace there, but in South America most states were not liberal democracies, so this factor could not have played a key role in ensuring peace. This is especially true if we take into account the low number of wars in the region during the whole of the twentieth century despite the relatively weak presence there of liberal democracy during that period. The process of democratization that started in the last decades of the twentieth century cannot explain the regional peace, which has preceded the transition from authoritarian to liberal/democratic regimes. South America is further discussed in chapter 7.

Proposition 3: The distribution of interstate versus civil wars takes place in different regions according to the relative effects of the two aspects of state-to-nation congruence – external and internal. As noted, external incongruence may lead to destabilizing outcomes when in at least one of the states there is a clear-cut ethnic majority. When both dimensions of incongruence are high (see table 3.3), we should expect the occurrence of both civil and interstate wars. The Middle East and the Balkans represent this kind of region. In contrast, low levels of both dimensions of incongruence produce a low likelihood of either civil or international wars. South America during the twentieth century is an example of this pattern, especially with regard to the avoidance of interstate wars. The combination of a high level of external incongruence and a low level of internal incongruence generates domestic peace, but also proneness to interstate wars. Europe during the 1930s, under the assault of the revisionist powers, illustrates this tendency. When the combination is the opposite, that is, a relatively low degree of external incongruence and high domestic incongruence, we should expect high proneness to civil wars but low proneness to international wars. Countries in postcolonial Africa (where external incongruence is mostly of minorities and not majorities), some Asian states (Afghanistan, Sri Lanka, Burma, the Philippines, post-Suharto Indonesia), post-Soviet republics, and some other deeply divided Third World states represent this kind of pattern.

Table 3.3 focuses on the effects of the two aspects of the state-to-nation congruence (external and internal). In addition, I will refer here briefly to the effects of the second dimension of the state-to-nation balance – state strength – on this distribution of wars. Although these effects are not shown in table 3.3 in order to maintain the analytical clarity of the table, they are important when the regional states are weak: in category 1 the effects are varied – civil wars are more likely, but interstate wars less likely; in category 2 civil wars and external intervention will be more likely; international wars become less likely in category 3, while frontier/border wars are more probable in category 4. Thus, on the whole, state weakness makes civil wars and international intervention in these states more likely due to the fragility of the political center, which faces great difficulties in overcoming internal and external challenges, and is unable to deter them.[78] At the same time, such weak states are less capable of initiating external wars by themselves and of intervening in the domestic affairs of other states, although guerrillas and terrorist organizations might take advantage of weakness to launch attacks from their own soil on their neighbors and other targets.

Evidence: As was expected, regions populated by incoherent states (both incongruent and weak), most notably Africa, experience frequent wars, but most are civil wars (see figures 3.6 and 3.7). Although there are cases of external incongruence in Africa, the common combination of state weakness and internal incongruence tends to raise the proportion of civil wars in comparison to external wars in that region. Thus, of the forty-five armed conflicts during 1945–1991 in Africa, 70 percent were

[78] On the powerful linkages between weak states and civil wars, see Fearon and Laitin 2003.

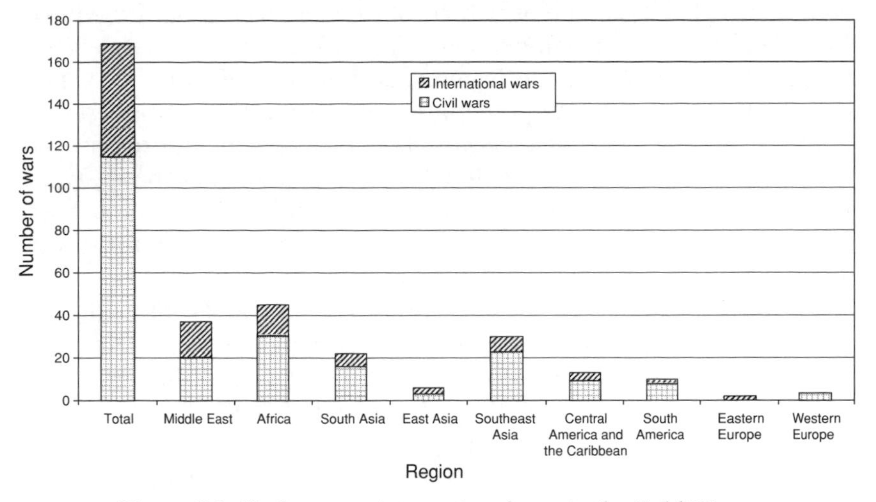

Figure 3.6 Civil war vs. international war in the Cold War era (1945–1991)
Source: Appendix B.

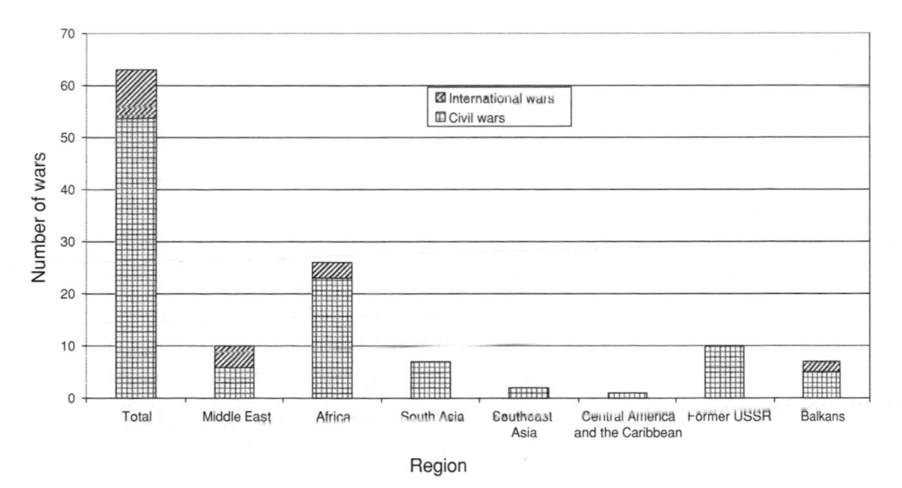

Figure 3.7 Civil war vs. international war in the post-Cold War era (1991–2004)
Note: Numbers include only those conflicts beginning or recommencing since the start of the era.
Source: Appendix B.

civil wars, while this type of war constituted 88.5 percent of the post-Cold War wars in that region (and one of the only three interstate wars in this era – the war in the Democratic Republic of Congo – was a combination of both). The potential for irredentism was fulfilled to a relatively limited extent also because in many cases the external incongruence is of minorities on both sides of the border, and none of the minorities regards either states as "theirs." The states, for their part, are also not committed to the cause of minorities, as was pointed out above.[79]

The Middle East, which suffers from both internal and external incongruence, though many of the states there are stronger than in Africa, also experiences numerous armed conflicts (thirty-seven in the 1945–1991 period and an additional ten through the end of 2004). These conflicts are both internal and external, but they are divided more evenly between civil and interstate wars (54 percent were civil wars to 1991 and 60 percent have been domestic conflicts since the end of the Cold War). The strength of external incongruence should also lead to a higher proportion of external interventions in civil wars, and indeed 50 percent of civil wars in the Middle East experienced external interventions, in comparison to 21 percent in Africa during the Cold War (in the post-Cold War era, however, there have been more external interventions in Africa – see figures 3.8 and 3.9).[80]

Regions with a state-to-nation balance tend to produce overall many fewer wars (three in Western Europe and nine in South America in the whole post-1945 period), almost all of them being domestic. These wars erupt in some cases because of the few instances in which there are nations without states, notably in Western Europe (the Basques in Spain and the Catholics in Northern Ireland), or due to internal wars which are unrelated to state-to-nation issues, but are instead associated with the nondemocratic nature of certain regimes and a few cases of state weakness in South America. For our purposes, it is noteworthy that these conflicts, in the absence of a regional state-to-nation imbalance, do not spread and do not lead to neighbors' intervention.

[79] See Neuberger 1991. On national boundaries in Africa, see the work of Herbst 1989.

[80] This change in the post-Cold War era might be at least partly related to the continuous state weakness in Africa. In the Middle East, however, there has been state strengthening in recent decades as well as a decline in pan-Arabism, and thus in external interventions, at least until the 2003 Iraq War, as discussed at the end of ch. 4.

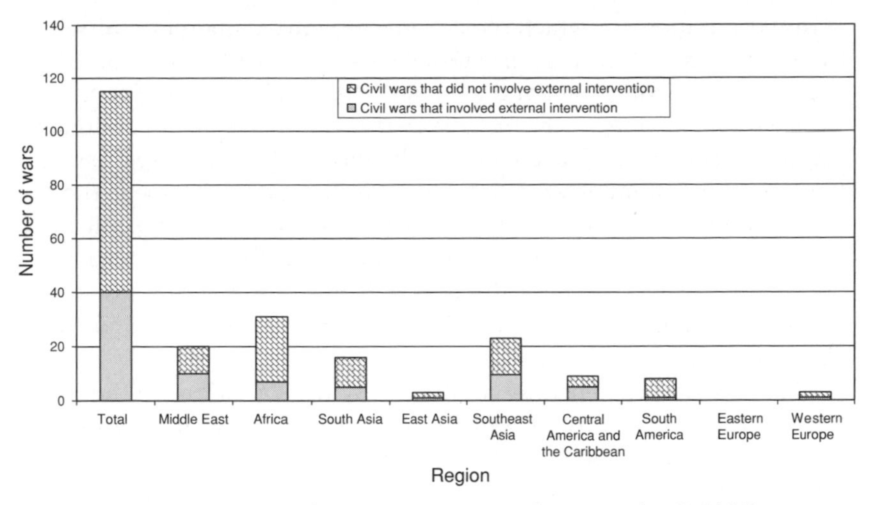

Figure 3.8 External interventions in civil wars in the Cold War era (1945–1991)
Source: Appendix B.

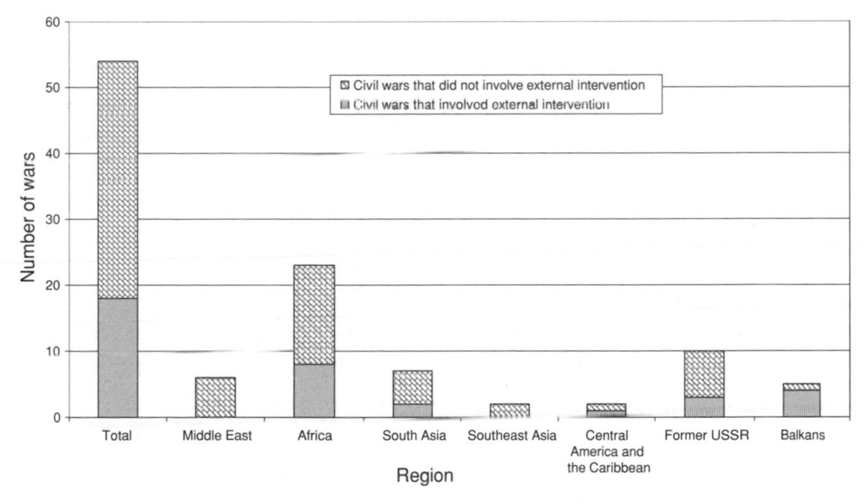

Figure 3.9 External interventions in civil wars in the post-Cold War era (1991–2004)
Note: Numbers include only those conflicts beginning or recommencing since the start of the era.
Source: Appendix B.

In those regions in which most states are fairly coherent, but where there are at least a few cases of external incongruence, based on an ethnic majority in a strong state and a shared ethnic majority or minority in the neighboring state(s), the theory predicts the emergence of nationalist revisionist powers with irredentist inclinations. Thus, these regions tend to produce major interstate wars. This was the case in Europe in the late 1930s with German expansionist policies based on national unification or irredentism. This logic also applies, at least partly, to East Asia in the post-World War II era with the national-unification policies of China toward Tibet and Taiwan, North Korea toward South Korea, and North Vietnam toward South Vietnam.

These results are generally reinforced by the variations in the intensity of cold wars in various regions, as measured by years of enduring rivalries between regional states during 1950–1990 (excluding rivalries with extraregional powers, which are mostly colonial disputes). Thus, the regions leading with the number of years of enduring rivalries are those with external incongruence and, as a result, the strongest nationalist revisionist forces: the Middle East (209 years altogether), East Asia (147 years), and South Asia (119 years).[81]

In contrast, Western Europe, as expected, has no years of enduring rivalries (apart from the dyad Greece–Turkey – fifty-two years of rivalry – but which might be seen as outside the region). The relatively low number of years of enduring rivalries in Africa (forty-three) can be accounted for by state weakness in the region while the problems of state incoherence lead especially to civil wars and external intervention. A somewhat anomalous finding is the not-so-low number of years of interstate rivalries in South America: eighty-five, but these are mainly accounted for by the enduring territorial rivalries between Argentina and Chile, and between Ecuador and Peru. Yet, apart from limited hostilities between the latter dyad in 1981 and 1995, no hot war has erupted in South America in the post-1945 period and there were only two wars during the whole twentieth century. Moreover, another study shows that South America is uniquely qualified among all the regions in the world to settle interstate disputes peacefully[82] – a phenomenon I explain in chapter 7 by the high state-to-nation balance in that region.

[81] Huth 1999, pp. 48–50.
[82] Simmons 1999, pp. 213–214.

The state-to-nation imbalance and the immediate causes of regional wars

Three major types of motivation for regional war may be distinguished: security dilemma, search for profit, and domestic vulnerability.[83] These are the immediate causes of specific regional wars. On the whole, the causal relations between state-to-nation imbalance and the immediate causes for the eruption of regional hot wars are the following:

- The state-to-nation imbalance intensifies the security dilemma.
- The state-to-nation imbalance produces substantive motives for wars of profit: boundaries and territory or hegemony and prevention.
- The state-to-nation imbalance produces diversionary wars to divert attention onto a scapegoat.

The following discussion will elaborate how the immediate causes of regional wars are conditioned or aggravated by the state-to-nation imbalance.[84]

Security dilemma wars (or "wars of strategic vulnerability"). It is true that anarchy brings about the security dilemma, but what accounts for the variations in the intensity of the security dilemma in different regions? Compare, for example, Western Europe and the Middle East; the relations between the United States and Canada vs. those between Greece and Turkey; or French–German interactions before World War II and after. The factor of anarchy by itself does not determine the basic level of the regional conflict and thus the underlying war proneness of the region. The state-to-nation imbalance is a key factor that accounts for regional variations in the intensity of the security dilemma.

The state-to-nation imbalance creates insecurity because the challenges to current boundaries and territories create a sense that the current regional order is temporary and each state has constantly to prepare to meet potential threats to it. This creates the conditions for the destabilizing effects of the security dilemma such as an arms race. Thus, the intensity of the regional security fears is affected more by the extent of the state-to-nation imbalance in the region than by the regional military balance. More precisely, because a high degree of state-to-nation imbalance produces competing territorial and demographic claims, it breeds insecurity, and thus leads to a regional arms race.

83 On these causes of war see Jervis 1978, Lebow 1981, Jervis et al. 1985, J. Levy 1989a and 1989c, George 1991, and Buzan 1991. In making this threefold distinction, I draw especially on J. Stein 1993.

84 See also Lake and Rothchild 1998b, esp. pp. 30–32 and the references they cite.

Therefore, the extent of the state-to-nation balance mediates between anarchy and the security dilemma. The extent of balance conditions the destabilizing effects of the security dilemma and the war proneness of different regions. In other words, when the extent of balance is high, the intensity of the security dilemma is lower, and it is less likely that mutual fears of being attacked and preempted will dominate the relations among the regional states and vice versa.[85] Thus, the security dilemma is less likely to lead to war among neighbors who enjoy a high level of state-to-nation balance. War is more likely among states that meet the criteria set by the independent variables, that is, high extent of state-to-nation incongruence and state weakness (see table 3.2).

These causes are antecedent to the technological and geographical factors that affect the strength of the offense/defense balance and thus supposedly the power of the security dilemma.[86] Thus, between the United States and Canada, between Australia and New Zealand, and in post-World War II Western Europe, the security dilemma is low irrespective of the objective military balance.[87]

In contrast, when there is a high degree of state-to-nation incongruence, it is more likely that the relations between offense and defense can exercise destabilizing effects. Thus, in the relations between Greece and Turkey, India and Pakistan, China and Taiwan, the two Koreas, Iraq and Iran, Israel and Syria, and the republics of former Yugoslavia, the balance of objective military capabilities is very important for determining the likelihood and timing of arms races, preemptive strikes, surprise attacks, or preventive wars. In the absence of challenges to the state-to-nation balance, the offense/defense balance is unlikely to lead people to fight hot wars even when an imperial order is replaced by anarchy. Thus, we should expect to see differences in war proneness among postimperial regions beyond the offense/defense balance and variations inside a certain region which cannot be accounted for by the offense/defense balance. Moreover, a state-to-nation imbalance, such as "too few states," might bring about the collapse of the imperial order in the first place due to nationalist aspirations for self-determination. At the same time, the offense/defense balance is likely to affect the timing and intensity of hot wars when a hegemonic order disintegrates, so long as the state-to-nation problems are powerful.

[85] For a partly related argument, see Schweller 1996.
[86] Jervis 1978. For an application of this argument to ethnic conflicts which emerge when a collapsed empire is replaced by anarchy and self-help, see Posen 1993b.
[87] See Butfoy 1997.

As evidence for the above claim that the two manifestations of the state-to-nation balance are mutually reinforcing, we may notice that not only revisionism but also state incoherence (weak and incongruent) have adverse effects on the security dilemma. This is because incoherence within a neighboring state produces instability and thus fears about potentially destabilizing changes in its regime, even if currently it is a status quo regime. Another concern is to preempt intervention of other neighbors because the instability creates temptations for making territorial or other profits at the expense of the incoherent neighbor(s). Such fears might lead to cycles of inadvertent escalation.

The presence of states that are considered illegitimate on nationalist grounds increases the security dilemma in a region because these states fear an attack and must prepare for it. But by so doing, for example, by arming themselves or making alliances, they make other regional states feel insecure. Examples in post-1945 East Asia include the tensions between China and Taiwan, and between North and South Korea.

Wars of power and profit (or "wars of opportunity") are attempts at maximizing power and profit by revisionist powers who challenge the legitimacy of the regional order on nationalist grounds and take advantage of opportunities to expand at the expense of weaker neighbors. Powerful regional states with external incongruence are especially prone to such wars. Leaders of these states can manipulate revisionist/nationalist ideologies in order to justify their expansionist aims abroad and to mobilize domestic support for these goals.

There are two types of motives for revisionist-offensive wars: the balance of power, traditionally emphasized by realism, and control over resources, most notably territories, underlined more recently by critics of realism (Holsti 1991; Goertz and Diehl 1992b, esp. pp. 12–14; Vasquez 1993) and related to the logic of the regional society approach, which was discussed in chapter 2. There are also two types of offensive actions in respect of the scope of the goals pursued by the military action: wide-ranging objectives of a major change in the (territorial or power-distribution) status quo, or limited aims of minor changes in the status quo or a return to a recent status quo ante (either territorially or the balance of power). The combination of the two variables (type of motive and the scope of the objectives) produces four types of revisionist-offensive wars (see table 3.4).

There are two types of wars with wide-ranging objectives: one type focuses on territorial ambitions; the other on the regional balance of power – in accordance with realist logic.

Table 3.4 *Types of revisionist-offensive-profit war*

	Motives for offensive action	
Scope of objectives	Control over resources (territory)	Power
Wide-ranging (major change in the status quo)	Expansion	Hegemony
Limited (return to a status quo ante)	Restoration	Prevention

Wars of expansion: The quest for profit is likely to be manifested in territorial ambitions vis-à-vis neighbors and in a desire to control resources that are located in the region. In this vein, the presence of weak and vulnerable powers in the region, which also lack a powerful and credible external protector, might serve as a temptation for strong and aggressive revisionist powers. Wars of territorial expansion are especially expected in regions with an *external* state-to-nation incongruence leading to strong irredentist aspirations as discussed earlier.

Hegemonic wars: While most regional states do not participate in global rivalries, powerful revisionist states may struggle for regional hegemony or dominance.[88] Both wars of conquest and hegemonic aspirations are more likely in a region where at least some states share the same ethnic majority. Shared ethnicity and culture make it easier for the revisionists to get support for their aggressive/hegemonic plans both among the population of the target states and in their own domestic base. Revisionists can present these plans as the fulfillment of long-held nationalist aspirations and as erasing artificial and imperially imposed boundaries rather than as naked aggression.

There are two types of limited offensive wars.

Wars of restoration: The objective of these wars is to return to the status quo ante, which is widely (internationally and regionally) seen as more legitimate than the new status quo based on state-to-nation criteria. Wars of restoration may be fought in order to reclaim territories seen as belonging to the nation which lost them in a war or under coercion. The war objective is to bring about not a dramatic change in the regional balance of power or distribution of territories, but only a relatively limited territorial change. Moreover, negotiated diplomatic alternatives to

[88] On aspirants for regional hegemony, see Ayoob 1995, ch. 3, esp. pp. 59–61; Wriggins 1992, pp. 9–13; Neumann 1992. On regional hegemons, see Myers 1991.

the use of force for returning to the status quo ante seem to be blocked by the intransigence of the current dominant power with a certain acquiescence of the external powers. Thus, the party that seeks to restore the previous boundaries feels that it has no choice but to resort to force if it wants the territories back.

Preventive wars: Such wars occur when a declining power attacks a rising power in the expectation that if it does not initiate war now, the balance of power will change in favor of its rising rival. Since the challenger is expected to attack the declining power in the future in a situation which will be much more favorable to the challenger, it makes sense to initiate the resort to force now – so long as the declining power has an advantage – because later the costs of resorting to force will rise dramatically.[89] This type of war is more likely under a state-to-nation imbalance because the parties believe that, due to the illegitimacy of the current regional order, war is expected in the future, so it is better to attack while the balance of power is still favorable.

In sum, national incongruence provides substantive issues for wars of profit, and revisionist (incongruent and strong) states take advantage of these issues and of incoherent (weak and incongruent) states in the region.

Diversionary wars (or "wars of domestic vulnerability") are also related to the extent of the state-to-nation incongruence in the region. The presence of incongruent states in the region provides not only many substantive issues for conflict (territory, boundaries), but also a potential motivation for aggressive policies, arising from domestic political weakness and elite insecurity.[90] It will be easier for an insecure elite in an unstable regime to initiate war in a region in which there is a state-to-nation incongruence than in a region which enjoys a high level of congruence. In this context, one has to bear in mind that even if the argument about the obsolescence of war (Mueller 1989) might be premature, nevertheless, especially in the post-1945 era, there is a strong need to legitimize going to war in all types of regimes. It is easier to mobilize domestic support for a diversionary war if the rival, or at least its boundaries, is widely seen, based on nationalist consideration, as illegitimate than it is against a legitimate opponent in a region where the boundaries are widely agreed upon.[91] Indeed, the state's external

[89] J. Levy 1987; Copeland 2000.
[90] For many examples, see J. Snyder 1991, 2000. For a useful detailed application of diversionary theory to the Yugoslav wars of the 1990s, see Cagnon 1994/5.
[91] Buzan 1983, p. 50.

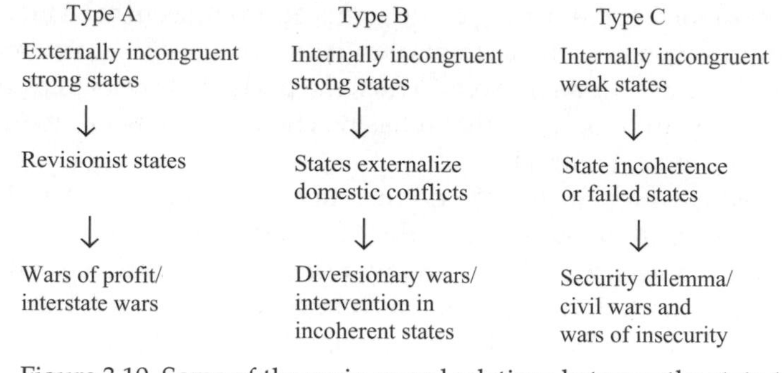

Figure 3.10 Some of the main causal relations between the state-to-nation imbalance and hot wars in regions in which there are both high incongruence and weak states

incongruence provides leaders with ready pretexts to divert the public attention from domestic problems to wars with foreign "enemies." They may also brand their domestic opponents as "traitors," who cooperate with this "state enemy," that denies the nation parts of its "fatherland." Such allegations may be helpful to them because the state's domestic incongruence provides a major incentive for its leaders to pursue a diversionary war, due to their expectation that a war with a foreign enemy will strengthen the state and especially help in the nation-building enterprise of an incongruent state,[92] although a certain minimal level of state strength is a prerequisite for the initiation of such wars.

Thus, the state-to-nation imbalance makes regions prone to all three types of hot regional wars: security dilemma, profit, and scapegoating. Figure 3.10 shows some of the main causal linkages. In Type A, strong states that are externally incongruent tend to be revisionist/irredentist; they initiate wars of profit to expand to territories which "should" belong to the nation on nationalist grounds. Some of the motivations for such an expansion might, however, be related to domestic politics, especially if the strong state is also internally incongruent, as in Type B, and its leaders believe that external conflicts (including intervention in the affairs of their neighbors, especially if these are incoherent ones) can divert attention from domestic conflicts. If the internally incongruent states are weak, as in Type C, these incoherent states produce security dilemmas inside the state that generate civil wars in the absence of

[92] This logic is related to Tilly's 1985 argument that war makes the state and the state makes war.

effective state institutions that can provide security to all ethnic groups (see Posen 1993b). Such incoherence may also increase the security dilemma in the region because status quo states worry that revisionist neighbors or guerrilla forces may take advantage of this weakness to harm their security and thus might preempt, leading to an inadvertent escalation.

The state-to-nation imbalance, democratization, and war

The state-to-nation incongruence is especially useful for authoritarian leaders to avoid democratization by providing emotionally laden issues, which can divert the attention of the public to wars against ethnonational enemies inside and outside the state. These leaders can also claim that democratization is not possible so long as the nation is threatened by the external and domestic enemies. Thus, the state-to-nation imbalance not only makes war more likely by providing seemingly credible pretexts for diversionary wars, but it also makes a key route to peace – democratization – less likely. Moreover, even if democratization takes place, politicians are able to manipulate nationalist conflicts to strengthen their popular appeal; thus, democratization will encourage more hard-line positions and may bring to power aggressive leaders.[93] Therefore, my expectation is that regions with high extent of state-to-nation imbalance will be less democratic than other regions, and democratizing states there will adopt war-prone policies. However, democratization does not have only destabilizing effects, as some critics charge;[94] if it takes place in regions with a considerable state-to-nation balance, it will warm the peace and produce a high-level peace (see chapters 7 and 8).

In sum, the state-to-nation imbalance makes regions more prone to all three types of hot regional wars: security dilemma, profit, and scapegoating.

Conclusions

This chapter has elaborated on the causal effects of the state-to-nation imbalance on regional wars. Regional wars are the result of regional forces. The most important of these regional forces is the state-to-nation imbalance. I present the various state and national forces that make the region more balanced between states and nations in contrast to those

[93] See Mansfield and Snyder 2005, J. Snyder 2000.
[94] See, for example, citations in Paris 2004, p. 180, n. 1.

forces that increase the regional imbalance. The combined effects of the two dimensions of the balance (state strength and state-to-nation congruence) explain variations in war proneness between different states and regions. The outputs of the state-to-nation imbalance – revisionism and state failure – are mutually linked and exercise important effects on the type of regional wars as civil or interstate wars. This should help to overcome the conceptual divide between civil and interstate conflicts by showing the common origins of many conflicts of both types, which result from variations in the extent of the state-to-nation balance in different regions (affecting the likelihood of hot wars but also of the evolution of peace, as discussed in chapter 7).

Lastly, the state-to-nation imbalance makes it much more likely that key causes of war – the security dilemma, the profit motive, and scapegoating – will produce regional armed conflicts. Thus, the state-to-nation balance in the region is the key for explaining variations in the level of regional violence. State weakness and state-to-nation incongruence in a region lead to insecurity, regional wars, and instability, whereas regions populated by coherent states (both strong and congruent) tend to be more stable and peaceful.

4 Explaining the war proneness of the Middle East

The collapse of the Arab–Israeli peace process and eruption of violence between Israelis and Palestinians in 2000–2004, and the recurrent Iraqi crises in the 1990s and the early 2000s, leading to the Iraq War in spring 2003, remind us that the Middle East has been one of the most war-prone regions in the post-World War II era in the sense of the intensity and recurrence of interstate warfare.[1] Some of the major hot wars of the post-1945 era took place in the Middle East:[2] six interstate Arab–Israeli wars in about fifty years, in addition to numerous other crossborder violent incidents between Arabs and Israelis; the eight-year Iran–Iraq war in the 1980s; the Iraqi invasion of Kuwait in 1990, which escalated to a major international crisis; and a number of supposedly civil wars internationalized by the involvement of regional states.[3] The war proneness of the

[1] In a comprehensive work on war proneness Geller and Singer cite a number of quantitative studies which underline the especially high war proneness of the Middle East as compared to other regions in the post-World War II era (1998, pp. 98–100). This high war proneness is also demonstrated in appendix B in the present work; see also Halliday 2005, p. 173; Sherman and Doron 1997, p. 72; and the sources cited in Maoz 1997, p. 35. In contrast to other regions, the risk of international war in the Middle East does not seem to have diminished. Three of the five international wars that took place from 1980 to 2000 were in the Middle East (Iran–Iraq, Lebanon, and the Gulf War), and a fourth (the Afghanistan war) was on the fringes of the region. The two post-9/11 US military interventions also took place in the Middle East (Iraq) or on its fringes (Afghanistan). The 1980s and 1990s also witnessed the spread of civil wars throughout the region; these have caused substantially more human suffering than the civil wars in other regions (Maoz 1997, p. 14). For the costs of Middle Eastern wars, see Ibrahim 1995, p. 46.

[2] For a recent discussion of definitions of the Middle Eastern regional system, see Gause 1999. A common definition would include the members of the Arab League and three non-Arab states: Israel, Iran, and Turkey. See Hinnebusch 2002b, p. 29. See also appendix A in the present book.

[3] Such as the Yemen war in the early 1960s, the 1970 Jordan civil war, the war in Lebanon between 1975 and the early 1990s, the recurring Kurdish insurgencies in Iraq and Turkey, the rebellion of the black south against the Arab north in Sudan, and the current conflict in the Darfur region of Sudan.

region influences states' conduct during peacetime as well. The danger of war looms large in the region almost constantly and the actors behave accordingly and prepare themselves for that possibility, mainly by arming themselves and building alliances. Thus, the Middle East surpasses other Third World regions in defense spending and in the deployment and import of various categories of weapons systems.[4] Indeed, the Middle East is the most highly militarized region of the globe.[5] The Middle East has also been notable for numerous competitive alliances among regional actors and between them and the superpowers (Walt 1987).

After I elaborate on the puzzle the Middle East poses to IR theory, the remainder of the chapter has four sections explaining different variations in war proneness through the main causal variable of the theory – the extent of the regional state-to-nation imbalance. These are the "observable implications" of my theory (King et al. 1994). The first section addresses the high war proneness of the Middle East as compared to other regions. In other words, why were there more wars, especially international ones, in the Middle East than in most other regions, including nondemocratic ones? The second section accounts for variations in war proneness among different Arab states. The third part addresses the spatial differences between different parts of the region, notably the high war proneness of the Arab–Israeli sector. The fourth part explains variations in regional war proneness over time. Another section addresses the mediating effects of the proximate causes – the realist factors of power and security (and also domestic vulnerability) – between the extent of the state-to-nation imbalance and the eruption of specific wars. The next chapter will address the effects the superpowers did – and did not – have on war and peace in the Middle East.

The Middle East puzzle

There is a widespread consensus among many analysts, both realists and nonrealists, that the modern Middle East is the region that more than any other manifests the predictions of realism in the international system, as evidenced by the dominance of conflict and the recurrence

[4] See Krause 1992, pp. 126, 132; Halliday 2005, pp. 153, 173. While in other regions there was a decline in arms purchases, in the Middle East they remained very high. Thus, defense spending for the region in 1998 was around $60 billion in comparison to $37 billion for Central and South America, $21 billion for Central and South Asia, and $9.7 billion for sub-Saharan Africa. At 7 percent of GDP, Middle Eastern defense spending was the highest for any region in the world. See Bronson 2005, 108.

[5] See Krause 1996, 330–331.

of rivalries, arms races, competing alliances, great power interventions, crises, and wars.[6]

At the same time, the recurrence of conflict and wars among illiberal regimes and especially between a democracy (Israel) and nondemocracies (the Arab states) could support the liberal approach in accounting for Middle East war proneness: liberalism expects that illiberal states will be aggressive and that relations between liberal and illiberal regimes will be particularly war-prone; additionally, it is expected that normally peaceful liberal states will be bellicose toward illiberal ones (Doyle 1986, 1997). The liberal explanation for the recurrence of war in the Middle East points out that most of the regimes in the region are nondemocratic.[7] In fact, almost all the states in the region, apart from Israel, have been something other than liberal democracies in most of the post-World War II era. Even following the wave of democratization in different parts of the globe in the post-Cold War era, the Middle East has remained the least democratic region in the international system (Rubin 2002). Liberals also point out that the absence of regional institutions (which would have also included the non-Arab states in contrast to the existing all-Arab organizations of the Arab League and the Gulf Cooperation Council) and low economic interdependence may increase the tendency toward regional armed conflict.[8]

As I argued in chapter 1, the two main families of IR theories – realism and liberalism – fail to provide an adequate answer to the variations in regional war proneness, and thus I try to provide an alternative explanation of these variations. Even though patterns of behavior and outcomes in the Middle East seem to conform to realist expectations about the dominance of international conflict, the key explanation is not based on realist factors such as the distribution of capabilities in the region. In terms of both realist and liberal explanatory factors, the Middle East is not so unique that the variations between it and other regions in war proneness could be accounted for by these differences. The Middle East has a multipolar structure,[9] but there are other similar regions, some of

[6] In addition to Nye 1993, p. 147, see citations in Kaye 2001, p. 238, n. 1. For an elaborate application of realism to the post-World War II Middle East, see Evron 1973, 1994; see also Mearsheimer 1983, ch. 6, and Telhami 1990. For a critique, see Barnett 1995, 1998.

[7] For an explanation of the frequency of Middle Eastern wars along these lines, see Sherman and Doron 1997. For a similar logic see also Garnham and Tessler 1995. For a critique, see Hudson 1995.

[8] This is the logic behind the former Israeli prime minister Peres's idea of a "New Middle East." See Peres 1993.

[9] The multipolar structure of the Middle East means that there are more than two regional powers: Egypt, Iran, Turkey, pre-2003 Iraq, Israel, post-1970 Syria, and Saudi Arabia.

them peaceful (notably, Western Europe and post-Cold War Europe as a whole). The Middle East is not democratic, but at least until recently such was the case with most other regions in the globe, and some of them were relatively peaceful (notably South America). What is special about the Middle East as compared to more peaceful regions (though shared to different degrees with other war-prone regions, notably South Asia, Northeast Asia, and the Balkans) is the great imbalance between states and nations in the region. Indeed, I argue in this chapter that the degree of imbalance is especially high in the Middle East compared to all other regions.

Although the multipolar structure of the Middle East had destabilizing effects on regional crisis management (see Miller 1994b), realism is unable to explain either why the Middle East was more war-prone than other regions or why the Arab–Israeli conflict was more prone to escalating to war than other disputes in the region. The Middle East has experienced a frequent recurrence of Arab–Israeli wars since the end of World War II in comparison to the lesser resort to force among other neighbors outside and inside the Middle East.[10] Although the Arabs have threatened the use of force against each other and have actually used it in limited military activities, a full-scale war was avoided until the 1990 invasion of Kuwait (Evron 1994, 124–125). Moreover, as we will see, both the limited uses of force and the Iraqi invasion are also closely related to the causal variables highlighted by my theoretical explanation.

Nor can realist factors account for the issues at stake in Middle East wars. These issues are determined by the two aspects of the state-to-nation imbalance, both of which are quite powerful in the Middle East: incongruence (both external and internal) and state weakness. External incongruence leads to nationalist revisionism, while internal incongruence, especially in weak states, produces the problems of state incoherence.[11] The powerful interrelationships between revisionism and incoherence in the Middle East have made the region especially war-prone. This explains why realist factors cannot account for the variations between the Middle East and those post-World War II regions where the same realist factors are presumably present. Despite this supposed "structural" similarity, in these other regions there have been fewer post-colonial interstate wars over state creation (as in the Middle East with

[10] Iraq and Iran, however, went to war for eight years (1980–1988).
[11] See the causal chain in ch. 3, fig. 3.1, and tabs. 3.2 and 3.3.

regard to Israel and a Palestinian state) and survival (especially the survival of Israel, as well as Lebanon, Jordan, and Kuwait). Realism also cannot account for the powerful appeal of transborder revisionist ideologies (pan-Arabism, Islamic fundamentalism, and Zionism) as motivating forces for war and for their attractiveness and usage in frequent interference in domestic affairs, including by military means (Gause 1992, 451–452). Realism also cannot account for the destabilizing effects of state incoherence and weakness; this is because realism underlines the destabilizing effects of imbalances of power among the strong states while underplaying the role of weak and incoherent states.[12]

The liberal factors of democracy, international institutions, and interdependence affect the quality and stability of peace, but are not causes of regional war. Domestic politics can provide a proximate cause of specific wars through the tendency toward scapegoating. Under a state-to-nation imbalance, the liberal factors are likely to be weaker, while illegitimate regimes are more widespread. Such regimes, in turn, tend to resort to scapegoating, especially if the states are relatively strong.

Application of the theory to the Middle East in the post-World War II era

Hot regional wars are initiated by the local states and not by the great powers, and are caused by the state-to-nation imbalance, rather than by systemic elements

The Middle East presents a hard or even a "crucial" case[13] for examining the thesis about the decisive role of regional, rather than global, factors with regard to war eruption, because this region has become "the most penetrated international relations subsystem in today's world."[14] This applies especially to the Arab–Israeli sector of the Middle East.

[12] In addition, in the Middle Eastern wars discussed here, there are no consistent relations between the distribution of capabilities and war outbreaks. Some of the wars were initiated by the stronger party (the 1982 Lebanon war, and the 1990 Iraqi invasion of Kuwait), but some were initiated by the weaker party (the 1969–1970 War of Attrition and the 1973 war). The latter outcome is inconsistent with both the balance of power and hegemonic versions of realism, and a nonrealist explanation is needed in order to account for it.

[13] On the methodology of using hard cases for theory testing, see references in ch. 1, n. 99.

[14] L. C. Brown 1984, pp. 3–5; see also Shlaim 1995, pp. 3–5; Gerges 1994, p. 1; Pervin 1997; Barnett 1995, 490, n. 39, and the citations he cites on the relative effects of the superpowers vs. inter-Arab dynamics on the regional order in the Middle East in the Cold War era.

There is a common perception of Arab–Israeli wars as wars by proxy closely related to and caused by the Cold War.[15] However, these wars were initiated by the local parties due to regional and domestic considerations rather than global strategic calculations.[16]

Despite the coincidence of the Cold War and the Arab–Israeli conflict and the tight connections between them, including superpower support of rival antagonists, the hot regional wars were not caused by external great powers but by the local parties' attributes, objectives, and mutual perceptions. Most importantly, these wars usually broke out against the wishes of the superpowers. The superpowers even made some unsuccessful attempts, in various degrees of intensity, to prevent them (see chapter 5). Not only did the superpowers fail to prevent wars at the height of the Cold War (for example, the 1956 war), but even greater superpower cooperation, as took place during the détente era in the 1970s, did not succeed in preventing regional wars such as the 1973 war. As a result, variations between global Cold War and détente did not affect the likelihood of regional wars.

The underlying cause of the recurrence of wars in the Middle East is the high level of state-to-nation imbalance in the region. The immediate or proximate causes of specific wars are likely to be the security dilemma and the search by regional states for power and profit (notably, control over territory). The state-to-nation incongruence, however, magnified the security and power problems and made it more likely for them not only to recur but to be addressed by the use of force. Domestic factors derived more directly from the problem of the state-to-nation incongruence also played a role in leading to an externalization of domestic conflicts and to diversionary wars. Moreover, the acute nature of the state-to-nation imbalance in the Middle East has motivated highly dissatisfied actors to initiate violence even when inferior in the balance of capabilities.

In the Third World in general there have been numerous challenges to the postcolonial order because of the absence of legitimate boundaries,[17] artificial division into states, and arbitrary allocation of peoples

[15] See Luttwak 1995, 109. For a more general argument about the primacy of global constraints in the case of the Arab countries, see Korany and Dessouki 1991b, pp. 20, 30–31, 37–44. For empirical support for the globalist argument, see Pervin 1998. For the regionalist view in the Middle Eastern context, see Gerges 1994 and Karsh 1997.
[16] See Bar Siman-Tov 1984, 266.
[17] Examples in Asia include Kashmir and the China–India border.

and territory to states, leading to irredentist interstate conflicts.[18] This process of artificial state-formation also took place in the Middle East in the post-World War I era.[19] Yet, most of the Third World accepted the colonial borders, despite their artificial nature, or at least rejected the use of force as a method for border change.[20] In contrast, the problem of the regional order's legitimacy was aggravated in the Middle East because of the strength of ideological revisionism based on external incongruence in the region, which challenged state sovereignty, in addition to the presence of incoherent states.[21] Thus, regional interstate wars also concentrated in the Arab–Israeli section of the Middle East because the challenges of powerful revisionism were especially prevalent there. The proximate causes of war can explain the timing and context of the eruption of specific wars. At the same time, changes in the underlying factors can account for the variations in war proneness between different periods in the same region. Thus, the strengthening of the states at the expense of nationalist revisionism should lead to a reduction in the frequency of wars. Indeed, this has happened in the Middle East after 1973. Yet the state-to-nation problems have remained powerful enough to prevent the emergence of normal, let alone high-level, warm peace. The best outcome that could be achieved is cold peace – and this only under US hegemony, and even then only haltingly.

Explaining the high war proneness of the Middle East: the combination of revisionist ideologies and state incoherence under a state-to-nation imbalance

The strength of the revisionist/nationalist ideologies and the presence of incoherent states pose tough challenges to the state system in the Middle East. Both are outputs of the high state-to-nation imbalance in the region. Two main revisionist ideologies are the two rivals – Zionism and Arab anti-Zionism. A third revisionist ideology is the broader framework to which the second is related: pan-Arabism. The fourth ideology – pan-Islamism – has been on the rise in the past two decades or so.

[18] Examples in Africa include conflicts between Ethiopia and Somalia, Libya and Chad, and over the Western Sahara (Ayoob 1995, p. 48). For a comprehensive list of territorial conflicts after 1945, see Huth 1996.

[19] On the artificial creation of states and borders in the Middle East by colonialist powers, see Fromkin 1989 and others cited in Ayoob 1995, p. 44, n. 35; Shlaim 1995; and Sela 1998.

[20] See Zacher 2001. See also Jackson 1990.

[21] See Gause 1992, 444. Graham Fuller (2000, 23) suggests that: "of all the peoples of the world today, it is Arabs – even at the popular level – who feel a longing for a greater sense of political or cultural union of some kind – while the rest of the Third World is thinking about how it can break apart into narrower ethnic units."

The state-to-nation balance in the Middle East is problematic in two major senses based on external and internal incongruences. From the point of view of external incongruence, specifically the wide spread of Arabs and Muslims beyond the boundaries of a single state, there are too many states in the region. The Arabs constitute a clear-cut majority in all the regional states apart from Turkey, Iran, and Israel, while there are also Arab minorities in Israel and Iran. Muslims are the overwhelming majority in all the states in the region except Israel. This spread has produced trans/pan-national revisionist ideologies, mainly pan-Arabism and pan-Islamism. "Too many states" refers to what they saw as the illegitimacy both of the artificial division of the Arab world into separate states and of the existence of Israel. In both cases, Arab nationalists claimed that Western colonialism was the perpetrator or guilty party. From the perspective of internal (and, not less important, transborder) incongruence, there were too few states for a number of dissatisfied national groups, which lacked states of their own. The key examples are the stateless Palestinians and the Kurds: both groups are spread throughout a great number of Middle Eastern countries. Thus, many states in the region have been incoherent due to a combination of supranational and subnational challenges, and ineffective domestic institutions and unstable regimes. There are strong interrelationships between revisionism and incoherent states. Pan-Arabism is a major source of revisionism; as a supranational ideology it has also weakened Arab states. On the other hand, the weakness and illegitimacy of Arab states have also increased the power and appeal of pan-Arabism (Mufti 1996). In another example, the stateless Palestinian refugees, a revisionist force, which is endorsed by pan-Arabists, also challenge the coherence of host Arab states. In an additional manifestation, the combination of incoherent Arab states and the illegitimacy of Israel in the eyes of Arab public opinion has produced incentives for and pressures on Arab regimes to resort to force against Israel, or at least to favor a hard-line approach toward it.

Table 4.1 applies the key sources of the state-to-nation imbalance to the Middle East. The application is elaborated in the next section.

The sources and manifestations of the state-to-nation imbalance in the Middle East

The illegitimacy of the state system in the Middle East

State incoherence is not unique to the Middle East, as numerous regimes and states in the Third World have faced domestic challenges to their

Table 4.1 *The sources of the state-to-nation imbalance in the Middle East*

Destabilizing forces: challenging nationalists	The Middle East
Dominance of ethnic nationalism	– Illegitimacy of state system – Even an immigrant society (Jewish-Israeli) is based on ethnic nationalism (Zionism) – Weakness of civic nationalism
Challenges of internal incoherence	
Nations without states	– Kurds; Palestinians
States without nations	– Lebanon; Iraq; some Gulf states
Stateless refugees	– Palestinian refugees and the "right of return"; post-2003 Iraqi refugees
Weak/failed states	– Lebanon, Jordan, Sudan, Yemen, Palestinian Authority, post-2003 Iraq
External incongruence: revisionist challenges	
Majority–majority	
Illegitimate states	– Kuwait, Lebanon, Jordan, Israel
Pan-national unifiers ("too many states")	– More than 20 Arab states – Muslims – majority in all states (except Israel)
Majority–minority	
Irredentists	– Greater Syria, Greater Iraq, Greater Israel, Greater Palestine
Settlers	– Jewish settlers in the occupied territories – Arab settlers in the Kurdish part of Iraq

legitimacy (Buzan 1991; S. David 1991b; Ayoob 1995; Holsti 1996). The European colonial powers exported the institutional structure of the territorial state and the idea of nationalism to the Third World, including the Middle East. Both the European state and nationalism were alien to these regions. In the Middle East these structures and ideas were especially alien, however, because people had for centuries been accustomed to a single unified political/religious entity – the Islamic universalism of the Ottoman Empire (Ben-Dor 1983, p. 231; Kedourie 1987, cited in Mufti 1996, p. 9, n. 16) and earlier Islamic empires (Hinnebusch 2003, p. 55). One of the key assumptions of the European state system is the modern belief in secular civil government. However, this belief is alien in a region where most people have subscribed for more than a thousand years to Islamic law as governing all of life, including political life (Fromkin

1989, p. 564). Thus, Islamic fundamentalists view the states as illegitimate imported solutions. Sunni Islamic fundamentalism is a response to the failure of the nation-state to take root in the Arab–Islamic region of the contemporary Middle East (Tibi 1998, pp. 7, 117).

What is unique about state legitimacy in the Middle East is the combined effect of the powerful pressures exerted on it both from below the state – by subnational, ethnic, and communal identities and related forces – and particularly from above – due to the special power of "pan" identities and related movements in the region – pan-Arabism and pan-Islamism.[22] As Hudson argues, "legitimate authority is hard to develop within state structures whose boundaries are inherently incompatible with those of the nation" (1977, p. 6). The challenge to the legitimacy of the regional order has been sharper in the Middle East than in other regions because it has come not only from the substate, subnational level, as is common in the Third World, notably Africa. In the Middle East, the challenge has also been on the supranational level, due to the strength of the transborder identities and the derived revisionist ideologies, pan-Islamism and pan-Arabism. These transborder identities are persistent and powerful, despite the emergence of new states in the post-World War I era, because they are founded on basic social elements. These include a shared language, facilitating communication among all Arabs, common history and memories of past Arab–Muslim glory, shared culture (similar food, music, art, family practices),[23] and a common religion (for the Muslims).

Even if the pan-Arabist challenge has become weaker today than it was before the 1970s, the pan-national challenge is still stronger than in other regions.[24] Forces of national unification have also been powerful in other locales: Korea, China–Taiwan, and Vietnam (until the 1970s). Indeed, they have made these areas very unstable and war-prone. Because of the regional spread of the pan-national identities (and the resultant movements) in the Middle East, however, this is the only whole region which is influenced by the destabilizing effects

[22] On the multiplicity of layers of identity in the Middle East, see Lewis 1998. See also Hinnebusch 2003, introduction and ch. 2; and Telhami and Barnett 2002b, esp. pp. 9–10, 13–14.

[23] Hinnebusch 2003, p. 58.

[24] Holsti (1996, p. 112) cites the results of a survey (Korany 1987, pp. 54–55) which shows that 80 percent of the respondents believed that there is a single Arab "nation" that is artificially divided and ought to be unified into a single state. See also the additional findings cited in Hinnebusch 2003, pp. 59–61.

of such forces. Moreover, these pan-national forces interacted with other elements of the state-to-nation imbalance to produce a war-prone region.

At the end of his book on the post-World War I creation of the modern state system in the Middle East by the European powers, David Fromkin argues that:

> in the Middle East there is no sense of *legitimacy* – no agreement on the rules of the game – and no belief, universally shared in the region, that within whatever boundaries, the entities that call themselves countries or the men who claim to be rulers are entitled to recognition as such. In that sense, successors to the Ottoman sultans have not yet been permanently installed, even though – between 1919 and 1922 – installing them was what the Allies believed themselves to be doing.
>
> (1989, p. 564; emphasis in original)

Two of the major challenges to the state system in the Middle East – pan-Arabism and pan-Islamism – saw this system as an artificial creation of Western imperialism. Pan-Arabists invoked past Muslim unity and glory as legitimizing the creation of a unified Arab state, while pan-Islamists saw it as justifying the political unification of all the Muslims (Karsh 2000, p. 20). Both movements rely on the prevalence in Arab culture and Islamic theology since the thirteenth century of a concept of leadership that acquires its legitimacy only through the quest for unity.[25]

"Illegitimate states" or "artificial nations which do not deserve a state"

Beyond the general challenges to the legitimacy of the regional state system, some states in particular are considered illegitimate by their neighbors, who raise irredentist/nationalist claims against them, arguing that these are artificial nations which do not deserve a state of their own, or that the land that these states occupy should belong to their neighbors on historical or demographic grounds or both.

The major cases, discussed in greater detail below, include the Arab claims on Israel, Iraqi claims on Kuwait, Syria's claims on Lebanon, and the claims at different times of Syria, Iraq, Israel, and the Palestinians on Jordan. Beyond these specific claims, however, such cases emerge in the Middle East (consistent with the argument made above), mostly due to the transborder spread of a single nation in the region and its

[25] Wurmser 2000.

long history in a unified entity there. The situation becomes especially explosive when demography and history interact with the settlement in the region of what the indigenous people see as an alien people. Indeed, the illegitimacy of Israel in the eyes of all its Arab neighbors (at least until the 1978 Camp David accords with Egypt or, more broadly, the 1991 Madrid Conference) has been an underlying source of the Arab–Israeli conflict which has brought about most of the hot wars in the region. The other key dimension is the Palestinian issue discussed below.

There are three key questions in this conflict:[26]

- Should Israel exist? A major component of pan-Arabism was the view of Israel as an illegitimate state in the midst of the Arab world.
- To the extent that the right of Israel to exist is accepted by the Arabs, then the major question is where its boundaries should be.
- Who will control the territories on the other side of the frontier with Israel: a Palestinian state, Jordan, or another Arab state like "Greater Syria" or Egypt (which until 1967 controlled the Gaza Strip)?

In the 1948–1973 era the Arab–Israeli conflict oscillated between hot and cold war. The source of the conflict was related to state-to-nation problems affecting regional legitimacy. On the one hand, these concerned the illegitimacy of Israel in the eyes of its Arab neighbors. The Arabs did not recognize the Zionist claim that the Jews should have the right to immigrate from all over the world and settle and establish a Jewish state in what the Arabs saw as Arab Palestine. The basic Arab concern since the early Zionist settlement in Palestine in the late nineteenth century has been that the Zionists are bent on continuous territorial expansion at the expense of the Arabs and on achieving dominance in the region. After 1967 the problem was magnified by the Israeli occupation of the West Bank and the Gaza Strip, thus supposedly confirming the Arab fears about Zionist expansion. The stateless status of the Palestinians compounded Israel's illegitimacy in the eyes of the Arabs.

On the other hand, the fundamental Israeli nightmare since its establishment in 1948 is that, due to the continuing illegitimacy of its existence in the Middle East, a grand coalition of Arab states might initiate a surprise two-front attack, utilizing its superior manpower resources. Such an attack would attempt to exploit the Israeli vulnerabilities of the lack of strategic depth and limited manpower (the military being composed largely of reservists). Such fears on both sides produce an intense security dilemma, which makes an inadvertent escalation in a crisis situation

[26] Lewis 1995, p. 368.

more likely than otherwise would have been the case. The most notable example of such dynamics is the 1967 crisis (see below). The mismanagement of this crisis had far-reaching implications which transformed the Middle East.

Nations without states: Palestinians and Kurds

The presence of two stateless nations, and their transborder spread in the region, has significant effects on the security situation in two major parts of the Middle East: the Palestinians in the Arab–Israeli sector, and the Kurds in the Iraq-Iran-Turkey triangle (and also Syria).

The Kurds are a non-Arab national people, mostly Sunni Muslims, who number about 20 million and live in Turkey, Iran, and Iraq, as well as Syria and the former USSR. Most Kurds are reluctant to be assimilated into dominant groups; instead they promote their own culture, preserve their own identity and language, and are determined to win regional autonomy, if not independence.

At different times the Kurds have conducted various levels of insurgency, particularly against Iraq and Turkey. This has had major implications for Iranian and Syrian security also. In southeastern Turkey, the Kurdish Workers' Party (known by its Turkish initials as PKK) has used guerrilla and terrorist tactics to pursue independence; over the past decade it has been the target of bombings and reprisals both in Turkey and in villages and camps in northern Iraq.

Due to the spread of the Palestinian refugees in many Arab states, especially those bordering Israel, and pan-Arab commitments to the Palestinian and the anti-Israeli cause, the Palestinian issue has had major implications for Arab–Israeli wars, and terrorist and guerrilla operations against Israel. In the aftermath of the establishment of Israel during the 1948 war, the Palestinians remained without a state and thus became a revisionist/irredentist force that did not have a stake in the stability of the regional order.

The 1967 war increased the number of Palestinian refugees and led to a growing Palestinian demand for an independent state in the occupied territories of the West Bank and the Gaza Strip. The Palestinians tried to achieve their objectives through the guerrilla and terrorist actions of the PLO and other Palestinian organizations, hoping also to involve the Arab states in fighting Israel. As these tactics failed to dislodge Israel from the West Bank and Gaza, the Palestinians in these territories revolted in the intifada of the late 1980s and early 1990s. Following Palestinian dissatisfaction with the Oslo peace process in the 1990s and

Israel's peace proposals, a second round of intifada erupted in September 2000 in the occupied territories.

At least until the Oslo Accords of 1993 there was an intensive debate in Israel over whether the Palestinians and their Arab supporters aimed only at the occupied territories or also at pre-1967 Israel proper. Even following Oslo, the right wing in Israel has continued to be skeptical about the Palestinians' ultimate intentions. This view was reinforced in the Israeli public by the recent second intifada (2000–2004), the failure of the Camp David negotiations in summer 2000, and the advocacy of the right of return of the Palestinian refugees to their former homes inside Israel proper (see below).

States without nations: incoherent states

National incongruence

While Israel and Iran, and to some extent Egypt, enjoy a historical sense of identity that facilitates civic loyalty to the state, none of the other Middle Eastern states can make that claim.[27] Most states in the region, especially in the Fertile Crescent, are superficial colonial constructs and many of their inhabitants have not identified with them and their colonially drawn artificial boundaries (Sela 1998, pp. 4, 11, 14; Hinnebusch 2002, p. 8).

The nation-building enterprise has not been successful in most Fertile Crescent states, such as Lebanon, Jordan, Iraq, and Syria, which are discussed in greater detail below. Most of the states in the Arab world are territorial states but still not nation-states (citations in Hinnebusch 2003, p. 55). This is partly due to ethnic fragmentation.[28] Moreover, the dominant ethnic groups in each state tend to exclude other groups and to discriminate against them while controlling the state resources and privileges. The pan-Arabist loyalties of large parts of the population also pose difficulties for constructing congruent nations in each state. In addition, the presence of a large population of stateless Palestinian refugees, especially in Jordan and Lebanon, has made nation-building

[27] Gause 1992, p. 461. Even these three states are, however, also problematic in their state-to-nation balance. Thus, the boundaries of Egypt – the strongest Arab state – were affected by the colonial powers. See Warburg cited in Ben-Dor 1983, p. 259, n. 16. Moreover, Egypt has a strong pan-Arab element – see Hinnebusch 2003, pp. 60–61. Israeli Arabs are about 20 percent of the population. In Iran only 51 percent of the population is Persian, while 24 percent is Azeri, 7 percent is Kurdish, and 3 percent is Arab. On the multiethnic character of Iran, see Hinnebusch 2003, p. 55. These three minorities have transborder ethnic ties.

[28] On the role of ethnicity in the failure of nation-building in most of the Arab world, see Ibrahim 1995, pp. 55–57.

a difficult task and has led to the eruption of civil wars in Jordan (1970) and Lebanon (1975–1991).

A key manifestation of the weakness of civic nationalism is the religious character of almost all the states in the region, apart from Turkey (Kumaraswamy 2006). Islam is the dominant identity of most Arab states (including nominally secular ones) and Iran, while Israel is a Jewish state. Such a religious identity excludes minority groups in many states, for example, the Copts in Egypt, the Christians and animists in South Sudan, the minority Shia in the orthodox Wahhabi-dominated Saudi Arabia, and Arabs in Israel. The narrow Shia–Islamic identity of Iran excludes Sunni (Kurds and Turkmen), non-Persians (Azeris) and non-Muslims (Armenians, Assyrians, and Bahais). Although not dominated by a single religion, Lebanon is highly fragmented by the sectarian tensions among its various denominations.

Almost all Arab regimes and states have faced the problem of low domestic legitimacy (Hudson 1977; Ayoob 1993, pp. 34–35; Shlaim 1995; Hinnebusch 2002, 2003). These legitimacy problems have often been translated into threats to the security of state structures and/or regimes, both from pan-Arab nationalist forces within and outside the boundaries of particular states and from local ethnic forces (such as the Kurds or the Shiites in Iraq) who have opposed the imposition of artificial political boundaries and, having in many cases a strong territorial basis, demanded secession.[29] Arab political culture is permeated with primordial sentiments and includes stigmatized groups – racial, tribal, religious, ethnolinguistic, and class-based. Minorities in the Arab world lack either the Arab or the Islamic character, or both, which define the majority community. At least half of the Arab states are heavily fragmented with conflict-ridden divisions: Iraq, Syria, Lebanon, Jordan, Yemen, Morocco, Oman, Bahrain, and Sudan. There are a number of examples of extremely violent conflicts between Arab-Sunni majorities and minority groups, which appear to be primordial in nature, even though political and economic interests are involved in the conflict. Examples include the civil war in Yemen during the mid-1960s (between the ruling Zaydi imamate and the orthodox Shafiis who supported the Republicans); the Lebanese civil war of 1975–1991 (between the ruling Christian Maronites and a coalition of mostly Muslim groups); the Kurdish struggle for self-determination in Sunni-dominated Iraq in the

[29] Salame 1990, p. 227, and Harik 1990, p. 21, cited in Holsti 1996, p. 112. On major ethnic divisions in the Arab world, see Ibrahim 1995, p. 47; Khoury and Kostiner 1990; Estman and Rabinovich 1988; and Bengio and Ben-Dor 1999.

1960s and 1970s, revived following the Gulf War of 1991 (joined at that time by a Shiite rebellion in the south); and in Sudan both a secessionist struggle in the south and ethnic cleansing in the Darfur region up to the present. Although they were supposedly internal conflicts, in all these cases there was an intense involvement by neighboring states: Saudi Arabia and Egypt in the Yemeni civil war, Syria and Israel in Lebanon, Israel and Iran in the Kurdish rebellion in Iraq (which, in turn, is also related to Turkey because of the Kurdish insurgency on its territory in which Syria, for its part, was involved), and Israel and neighboring African states in the Sudanese case (Hudson 1977, p. 11, ch. 3). Thus, these conflicts show the close relations between domestic illegitimacy and regional conflicts such that domestic weakness leads to external intervention[30] and as a result to confrontations between regional neighbors such as Syria and Israel in Lebanon.[31]

State weakness

While there is a dispute regarding the growing capacity of state institutions in many Arab states since the 1970s, reported by quite a number of analysts,[32] there is a consensus that the institutional effectiveness was very low in almost all Arab states until that time. As a result of the low levels of legitimacy and the weak and fractured national identities, a major mission of the armed forces in these countries has been defending the regime or a particular ruling elite against domestic threats to its control that emerge because of either its narrow base of support or a fragmented political system (Krause 1996, 333–334; Frisch 2002a). This distraction made the armed forces ineffective against external rivals such as Israel or the United States (in the 1991 and 2003 wars against Iraq).

The Palestinian Authority in the West Bank and the Gaza Strip is the most recent example of the ultimately weak (emerging) state, which lacks even a monopoly over the means of violence in its territory, let alone other effective institutions. Arafat's strategy of "state-building" has been quite unique – rather than monopolizing the means of violence in the territory under a single institutionalized authority, there is, even after Arafat's death in 2004, a multiplicity of competing armed militias. In other words, rather than building strong and effective state institutions, Arafat preferred to be the ultimate informal broker among competing factions, thus enhancing his personal power at the expense

30 Ibrahim 1995, p. 59. 31 Pressman and Kemp 1997, pp. 118–119.
32 See below on two key cases of weak states (Jordan and Lebanon); see also references in nn. 123–128.

of impersonal state institutions and bureaucracy. It is unclear whether Arafat's Authority has been able to control Palestinian violence against Israelis even if it wanted to. However, it is also uncertain whether Arafat was interested in stopping the violence or preferred to use it to get more concessions from Israel.[33]

In an acute state-to-nation imbalance, it is more difficult to maintain full control over the means of violence. A variety of groups has strong irredentist/nationalist aspirations, which enjoy some domestic support, although they go much beyond the policies of the state authorities. Thus, even though Israel is a much stronger state than the Palestinian Authority, the Israeli government also does not maintain full control over extremist groups of Jewish settlers in the occupied territories. These groups have an irredentist/nationalist/religious agenda of annexing Judea and Samaria (the West Bank) to Israel, based on the argument that these territories are the cradle of the Jewish nation and that God promised them to his chosen people. Those settlers who are highly committed to such an agenda might challenge the secular Israeli state.

"Too many states": the pan-Arabist revisionist challenge to the Arab state system and its interrelationships with weak states

There have been powerful interlinkages between pan-Arabism and state weakness in the Arab world. On the one hand, due to the spread of the Arabs as the majority group in most of the region, pan-Arabism has challenged the autonomy of the individual Arab states and undermined their legitimacy and the state-formation process. On the other hand, the weakness, permeability, and illegitimacy of the Arab states increased the appeal of pan-Arabism at the expense of territorial state identity and made it easier for a transnational ideology, and the powerful Arab states championing it, to penetrate the domestic systems of other Arab states. This appeal was both to elites, who were unable to consolidate their hold on power and who were pushed in a pan-Arab direction in search of legitimacy and support (Mufti 1996), and to minorities, who saw pan-Arabism as an instrument for their integration into the larger Arab nation and who hoped that their support of pan-Arabism would demonstrate their nationalist credentials and thus facilitate their social mobility.

[33] On Palestinian state-building, see Robinson 1997.

Pan-Arabism saw the Arab world as one nation sharing a common identity and a feeling of belonging, a single language and culture, and a shared glorious heritage, while the various sovereign Arab states and their boundaries were perceived as artificial colonialist constructs that only divided the culturally homogeneous Arabs (Korany and Dessouki 1991b, p. 33; Sela 1998, pp. 10–11). Accordingly, pan-Arabism, by underlining the unity of "one Arab nation," superseding the different Arab states, posed a tough challenge to the separate existence and legitimacy of individual Arab states.[34] Thus, the Arab agenda was full of calls for redrawing the regional political map, guided by the belief that there were too many colonially constructed states in the region. As a result, proposals for and attempts at unification of various Arab states,[35] along with the advocacy of the elimination of Israel, dominated regional politics.

The Hashemite family, who led the Arab revolt of 1916 and ruled Jordan and Iraq (until 1958), carried the banner of pan-Arabism from the 1920s to the 1940s and penetrated the domestic affairs of Syria, Palestine, and Saudi Arabia. Hashemite ideas of unity topped the Arab agenda in the 1940s. Since the 1950s, radical revolutionary movements have become the leading advocates of Israel's destruction and of Arab unity. The Baath party emerged as an important force in Syria, Iraq, and Jordan, all fragmented societies without a historical state identity, calling for a unified Arab state. In the heyday of pan-Arabism – led by Nasser in the 1950s and early 1960s – more than ever before, the Arab regional status quo, including the legitimacy of regimes, became politically threatened by militant pan-Arab alliances of transnational movements and official regimes. Nasser, for example, used the mass media, especially the "Voice of the Arabs" radio station, broadcasting from Cairo, in his campaign against the Baghdad Pact.[36] This propaganda, in cooperation with local groups, brought about mass opposition to governments in the Fertile Crescent and showed their states' weakness and permeable boundaries (Sela 1998, pp. 44–45).

A major manifestation of the pan-Arabist challenge was the "Arab Cold War" between the radical-progressive-military regimes (notably,

[34] See Sylvia 1976, pp. 147–153; Ben-Dor 1983, ch. 4; Gause 1992; Barnett 1995; Walt 1987; Sela 1998, pp. 6–7; Nafaa 1987, pp. 149–50; Mufti 1996, p. 3.
[35] Mufti 1996; Sela 1998; Ben-Dor 1983; Gause 1992; Porath 1986; Seale 1986.
[36] The Baghdad Pact is discussed in ch. 5. It was an anti-Soviet alliance, founded in 1955 that included Iraq, Iran, Pakistan, and Turkey. This alliance was a key component of the US/British strategy to contain the Soviet Union during the height of the Cold War.

Egypt, Syria, and Iraq) and the conservative monarchies (headed by Saudi Arabia and Jordan) in the 1950s and 1960s.[37] Even if specific cases of intervention by Arab states in other Arab states were motivated first of all by particularistic state interests rather than by a concern for the general Arab cause,[38] pan-Arabism has, in Arab opinion, provided a certain degree of legitimacy for interventions in the domestic affairs of other Arab states, such as the Egyptian intervention in the civil war in Yemen in the 1960s (Sela 1998, pp. 47–48; M. Oren 2002, p. 15); the Syrian intervention in Jordan in 1970 and in Lebanon in 1976; the Iraqi invasion of Kuwait in 1990; and many other cases of nonmilitary intervention in domestic affairs (Gause 1992, pp. 448–451; Sela 1998, pp. 44–47). Thus, pan-Arabism encouraged and made such interventions easier (Ayoob 1993, pp. 48–50, esp. p. 49). The radical-progressive camp was also divided, so that inter-Arab politics in the 1950s and 1960s was characterized by ideological rivalry, recurrence of *coups d'état* and numerous subversions of the domestic affairs of other states: "the sovereign norm of non-interference in the domestic affairs of other states was flouted with stunning and unapologetic regularity" (Gause 1992, p. 448).

On the whole, the effects of pan-Arabism were both an increase in the power of revisionism and a weakening of the Arab states, thus further reinforcing the state-to-nation imbalance in the region. More specifically, the main effects were the following interrelated processes (Ben-Dor 1983, pp. 197–198):

- destabilization of inter-Arab relations and aggravation of the struggle for Arab hegemony. This is because pan-Arabism has been a divisive ideology. Competing states, groups, and rulers have tried to dominate the Arab world by showing that they are more loyal to the nationalist cause than others and by intervening in the domestic affairs of other states in order to affect their policies and regimes.
- hindrance of the development of strong states in the region and increased domestic instability, both through interference in domestic affairs of other states and identification of large segments of the population with a supranational idea. Leading examples of transnational penetration and resultant destabilization were Jordan in the 1950s, Syria and its failed merger with Egypt between 1958 and 1961, and

[37] Kerr 1971; Seale 1986; Safran 1969, chs. 2 and 3; Ben-Dor 1983, p. 148; Sela 1998, p. 12.
[38] Sela 1998, pp. 19–20; Telhami 1990, pp. 92–93.

the radical nationalist revolution in Iraq and a Nasirit rebellion in Lebanon – both in 1958 (Sela 1998, pp. 44–46).

- placement of the Palestine conflict on center stage. From the late 1930s, the Palestine question had become a central component of the emerging doctrine of pan-Arab nationalism (Karsh 2000, p. 19). The issue was both unifying and divisive. On a fundamental level there was an all-out Arab consensus on the need to defeat Zionist objectives. On an operational level, Arab behavior was influenced by particularistic considerations of state power and interests (Sela 1998, pp. 37–38).
- the Palestinian problem as a leading pan-Arab issue becoming a major determinant of political legitimacy for Arab regimes and leaders (Korany and Dessouki 1991b, p. 34; Hudson 1977, p. 118; Sela 1998, pp. 27, 37). Incorporating Islamic, Arab nationalist, and anti-Western symbols, the Palestinian issue has become a major legitimizing mechanism for legitimacy-poor Arab regimes, both internally and regionally (Hudson 1977; Sela 1998, pp. 24, 27, 37). Notwithstanding the cynical abuse of the Palestinian cause by the Arabs on many occasions (Ben-Dor 1983, p. 211), a commitment to this cause became a major test of a pan-Arab loyalty, for not only is Palestine rich in national and religious symbolism for all Arabs, it is also a crucial geographical linkage between the eastern and western Arab world. Palestine being occupied by aliens was seen as a barrier to Arab integration. The occupation represented to all Arabs such a major national injustice that it had to be on top of the national agenda (Hudson 1977, p. 118). Indeed, the Arab failure to prevent the birth of Israel in 1948 brought about the violent removal of the rulers and regimes that were held responsible for the defeat and later for the continuing persistence and even prosperity of Israel (Lewis 1995, pp. 372–373).

Pan-Arabism has made the Palestinian issue both a constraint and an opportunity for Arab states, leading to hard-line policies. Pan-Arabism constrained the ability of Arab states to reach a comprehensive Arab–Israeli peace (Ben-Dor 1983, p. 212). At the same time, radical policies on the Palestine issue provided a shield against threats to the legitimacy of the regime. Thus, pan-Arabism exerted pressure on the individual Arab states to be loyal to the Palestine cause (Barnett 1995, 499), that is, to be hard-liners in the Arab–Israeli dispute and to adopt more intransigent positions than they would otherwise endorse (Safran 1969, p. 40), including a willingness to resort to military force, for example, regarding the Jordan River issue in the 1960s (Sela 1998, p. 59). This led to radicalizing Arab positions in the Arab–Israeli conflict, encouraging the resort to force against Israel and thus also increasing Israel's sense of insecurity and use of force.

Despite the decline of pan-Arabism as a force for Arab unification in recent decades and despite the expectation of rising state strength, the recent second intifada shows that the "Arab street's" support of the Palestinians constrains Arab leaders and moderate states from making peace with Israel, or from warming relations with it. Thus, even Jordan and Egypt, which signed peace treaties with Israel, had to return their ambassadors from Israel, and other states had to sever their relations with the Jewish state at least until a ceasefire was established in 2005. It is true that Arab states did not do much beyond that to help the Palestinian uprising economically or militarily.[39] Yet, Arab regimes constantly fear that a major escalation in the level of Israeli–Palestinian violence could fan sudden flames of militancy throughout the Arab world, leading to major disturbances which would pose a threat to Arab regimes and to regional stability.[40]

Such concerns are closely related to the recent emergence of the all-Arab satellite TV news network, Al Jazeera, and other similar networks, widely watched throughout the Arab world. The creation of such a transborder pan-Arab audience strengthens the Arab nation at the expense of the particular Arab state, which used to have a monopoly and full control over the sources of information.[41] This is especially the case since the eruption of the second intifada in September 2000. Al Jazeera broadcasts nightly images of Israeli soldiers seemingly gunning down Palestinian protestors.[42] Such messages reinforce pan-Arab solidarity with the Palestinians and a resentment at the lack of active support for them by Arab governments. The pan-Arab media have also inflamed Arab nationalist/anti-US messages in the aftermath of the US invasion of Iraq in 2003. These radicalization effects of the media contradict

[39] *Economist*, April 27, 2002, 44. On the poor record of Arab material support for the Palestinian struggle, see Rubin 2002, pp. 199–200.

[40] See the analysis of the veteran *Haaretz* Arab affairs commentator, Danny Rubinstein, who is cited on the *Haaretz* website (www. haaretzdaily.com/hasen/objects, Jan. 30, 2002).

[41] For related points and evidence about Arab solidarity with the Palestinians, and the strength of Arab nationalism across the Arab world, see Fuller 2000, 24, and Telhami 2002, esp. ch. 4.

[42] On the pan-Arabist orientation of Al Jazeera and its influence on the Arab street, see *New York Times*, Nov. 11, 2001, Week in Review, pp. 1, 3; El-Nawawy and Iskandar 2002.

liberal expectations that freer media, which transcend national boundaries, should have a moderating impact, facilitating the emergence of a more benign transnational community.

Some of the implications of this pan-Arab solidarity, despite the decline in the schemes for Arab unification, are the following:

(1) Israel must consider the possibility of an all-out war with the Arab world and to prepare for it by arming, training, and maintaining high readiness, etc. The Arabs see these steps as security threats and as a preparation for a potential attack, and thus have to respond by arming themselves and building alliances. Israel also feels it has to show resolve and to behave in a tough way to deter potential attack. This also creates fear and insecurity among the Arabs. The outcome is an intense security dilemma and a potential cycle of escalation (see below on the 1967 war).
(2) Arab regimes might be pushed to demonstrate support for the Palestinian cause due to domestic and transborder pressures even if they preferred not to.
(3) Pan-Arab solidarity has led Palestinians to expect support from the Arab world, even if it was not forthcoming in numerous cases. This encourages the Palestinians to resort to violence, expecting to draw the resources of the Arab world on their side and thus have much better chances of winning against Israel or at least to balance it.
(4) The support the masses give the Palestinians may tempt leaders who are in domestic trouble or who have leadership aspirations in the Arab world to initiate anti-Israeli moves in order to increase their popularity or to destabilize regimes of other Arab states.
(5) Authoritarian leaders may use a resort to anti-Israeli policies to avoid democratization. When democratization takes place, however, it might lead to more hard-line policies toward Israel rather than moderate ones.

Pan-Islamism: the Islamic "nation" is artificially divided into "too many secular states"

Until recently, radical Islam has been less active than pan-Arabism as a revisionist force with regard to the regional state system; it mostly acted to depose corrupt, secular regimes. Pan-Islamic forces, as manifested most recently by the rise of Al Qaeda and related Islamic fundamentalists, however, challenge the legitimacy of the division of the

Middle East into modern nation-states. In the view of these fundamentalists, the West imposed this division and an "Islamic system" in which God's rule, as manifested in His divine law, the *shari'a*, should replace it. They reject drawing boundaries among Muslims.[43] The Islamic "nation" or community of believers – the *umma* – should be unified under the rule of God in a new caliphate. In an Islamic world order the current state system would be transcended by the territorial broader entity of the *umma*.[44] This would be the first stage of an Islamicized humanity under the banner of Islam.[45]

Before Al Qaeda, Islamic fundamentalist movements opposed secular Arab regimes, notably Egypt, Algeria, and Jordan. These movements were inspired and supported by the Islamic republic of Iran after the 1979 revolution (and later also by the Islamic regime in Sudan). Iran has challenged the legitimacy of the regimes in Saudi Arabia, Bahrain, Kuwait, Egypt, Iraq, and Jordan. Its questioning of the sovereignty of these states aimed not so much at redrawing state boundaries in the region, as was Nasser's quest; rather, it wanted to change the character and sources of legitimacy in existing states.[46]

The Iranian-led Islamic revolution, and Islamic movements throughout the Arab world, also challenge the legitimacy of Israel, support violence against it, and oppose the peace process with it. The most active in the resort to violence of these movements are under the weak Palestinian Authority in the occupied territories – Hamas, which in early 2006 won the elections to the Palestinian Parliament, and the much smaller and more militant Islamic Jihad. Militant Islamic movements are also active in weak states neighboring Israel: Jordan and especially the Iranian-supported Shiite organization, Hezbollah, in Lebanon. The 2003 US invasion and the resultant weakening of the Iraqi state have provided a great opportunity for jihadists from all over the Arab world to join the anti-US fight in Iraq.

[43] The aspiration of Islamic fundamentalism is pan-Islamic: "All fundamentalist groups have one goal: setting up an Islamic state with no borders," said Muhammad Salah, a journalist who writes about Islamic movements in Egypt. Hassan al-Banna, who founded the Muslim Brothers in 1928, set a very ambitious goal for Islamic groups: "it is the nature of Islam to dominate, not to be dominated, to impose its law on all nations and to extend its power to the entire planet." See *New York Times*, Jan. 20, 2002, p. 3.

[44] Karsh 2000, 21; Kumaraswamy 2006.

[45] Tibi 1998, pp. 119–120, chs. 7, 8.

[46] On the Islamic challenge to Arab states, see references cited in Gause 1992, pp. 446, 449–451; Barnett 1995, p. 509, n. 108; Lewis 1995, pp. 376–387; Tibi 1998, p. 117; Karsh 2000, pp. 20–22. For a recent useful analysis, see Sivan 2005.

Ethnic fragmentation and the endorsement of radical pan-Arab positions

When in power, members of ethnic minority groups have sought to demonstrate their nationalist credentials by endorsing militant pan-Arab stances on Arab unity and the Palestinian question. One example is leading members of the Syrian Baath party from the minority Alawi sect, who pursued a militant policy against pro-Western Arab states and especially against Israel. In the case of Iraq, the leadership also pursued an aggressive foreign policy, its quest for hegemony serving as a means of diverting the public's attention from domestic conflict. The prospect of Arab leadership was expected to induce the Shiite majority to support the Sunni Arab rulers and thus lead to a radical Iraqi foreign policy (both the Syrian and Iraqi cases are discussed below).

The Palestinian refugees: the "right of return" of stateless refugees

The stateless Palestinian refugees raised the level of both revisionism and incoherence, especially among Israel's Arab neighbors.[47] By proclaiming their right to return to their homes in what they define as occupied Palestine, the refugees are a revisionist/irredentist force that undermines the legitimacy of the regional order and of post-1949 boundaries. Because these refugees maintain their separate Palestinian identity and are not allowed to integrate into the local societies in the Arab states where they reside,[48] the refugees also jeopardize these states' coherence. Moreover, as the Palestinians organized to fight Israel, they also presented a challenge to the sovereignty of the host Arab states.[49] These states tried to control the Palestinians, but they were constrained in their ability to do so because too tight a control would contradict the pan-Arab commitment to the Palestinians to regain their occupied homeland.

Thus, the refugees constrain state- and nation-building in these states, most notably in the most incoherent and weakest of Israel's neighbors – Jordan and Lebanon[50] – where they constitute a large portion of the population. They were also a revisionist/irredentist force in Syria and Egypt (especially before the 1967 war when Egypt still controlled the

[47] On the Palestinian refugee problem, see Alpher and Shikaki et al. 1999.
[48] The most receptive state is Jordan, but the Palestinians have faced major problems of integration even there (Benny Morris 1996, p. 20).
[49] Hudson 1977, pp. 295–296; Benny Morris 2001, p. 260.
[50] On the Palestinians in Lebanon, see Harff 1993, pp. 236–238.

Gaza Strip, which was densely populated by refugees); in a different way, they were also a restive element in the Israeli-occupied territories after the 1967 war. The Palestinian paramilitary/insurgent challenge to state authorities led to a civil war in Jordan (Black September in 1970) and contributed to the eruption and longevity of the protracted civil war in Lebanon (1975–1991). These civil wars, in turn, led to regional escalation, with Israel and Syria intervening. The stateless Palestinians also revolted in the first intifada against the Israeli occupation between 1987 and the early 1990s. Palestinian revisionism contributed to the eruption of wars between Israel and Egypt (1956) and Syria and Egypt (1967), and to the Israeli invasion of Lebanon (1982). The escalatory dynamics involved crossborder infiltrations and raids by Palestinian guerrillas against settlements inside Israel, and Israeli retaliatory actions against targets in the Arab host countries. Such action–reaction dynamics aggravated the security dilemma between Israel and its neighbors which, in turn, contributed to large-scale violence in 1956, 1967, and 1982.[51]

During the Oslo process, Israelis expected that a final settlement would include the resettlement of refugees outside Israel. Yet, during the Camp David negotiations of summer 2000, and mostly at other talks around that time, the traditional Palestinian demand for the right of return to Israel resurfaced. Since Israel rejects this demand, which could threaten its ethnonational Jewish character, it helped stalemate the negotiations, which, in turn, led to the eruption of the second intifada in September 2000.[52]

Explaining variations among different states in the same region with regard to resort to force and war involvement

The argument in this section is that the theory presented here will account not only for the differences between the Middle East and other regions regarding war proneness, but also for variations inside the

[51] For a detailed study of this pattern before the 1956 war, see Benny Morris 1996, and before the 1967 war, see M. Oren 2002. See also Safran 1969, p. 48.
[52] For a recent analysis, by a key American participant, of what happened in the 2000 Camp David summit, see D. Ross 2004, pp. 650–758. For a critique of this analysis, see Malley 2004.

region, notably, among the states' inclination to resort to force based on their level of national congruence and state strength (see figure 3.2).[53]

The combination of state strength and national incongruence leads to revisionism: Syria and Iraq in the Middle East

Syria and Iraq, both key actors in regional insecurity in the Middle East, have pursued revisionist foreign policies.[54] These policies can best be accounted for by a combination of relative state strength and national incongruence.[55] Measured by state ability to coerce, control, and extract resources from society, both the Syrian and the Iraqi states have become much stronger during the post-World War II period, especially since the 1970s.[56] They mobilized big militaries, and especially built effective security services which made it possible to maintain the state against external and internal threats; the top priority has been to keep the regimes in power and to exercise increasing control over society.[57] The extraction of resources also made it possible for the state to bribe and maintain the loyalty of key elites supporting the regime, such as the Baath party, the army, and the security services. However, they were much less successful in the software of nation-building and creating a common national identity of the peoples in their states.

Lacking domestic legitimacy, many Third World regimes are repressive and rely on kinship ties. The pre-2003 Iraqi and the Syrian regimes are prime examples of this phenomenon in the Middle East. The dominant groups in Syria and pre-2003 Iraq – the Alawi and the Sunni Muslims – constitute only 13 percent and 22 percent of their respective

[53] The "Greater Israel" case is discussed on pp. 176–177. For additional cases of the "Greater state" in the region, see Halliday 2005, pp. 207–209.

[54] I refer to Iraq before its occupation by the United States in March 2003; since then it has not been a fully independent country.

[55] On this combination in Iraq, see Baram and Rubin 1993a. See also Tripp 2000. On Syria, see Rabinovich 1998 and Maoz 1996. On both, see Mufti 1996. On their foreign policies, see the chapters on Iraq and Syria in Korany and Dessouki 1991a and in Hinnebusch and Ehteshami 2002. On identity and Iraqi and Syrian foreign policies, see the respective chapters in Telhami and Barnett 2002a.

[56] For example, in 1955 there were 6.4 and 6.7 members of the regular armed forces per 1,000 of total population in Syria and Iraq, respectively. By 1977, there were 29.4 and 15.9, and in 1987 36.2 and 62.9 for the two countries. In 1957 government expenditures were 12.6 percent and 30.3 percent of GDP in Syria and Iraq, respectively; by 1978 the expenditures were 41.2 percent and 66.4 percent. The figures in 1957 in Syria refer to the expenditures as a percentage of GNP, not GDP. For data, analysis, and references, see Gause 1992, pp. 456–462. See also Mufti 1996.

[57] On the linkages between domestic politics, systemic factors, and Third World security structures, see Frisch 2002a.

populations.[58] Such regimes trigger violent opposition because they do not allow legitimate opposition activity. This leads to a vicious cycle of violence and counterviolence that aggravates the already high levels of internal insecurity. Such domestic instability is conducive to diversionary wars. Nationalist causes have provided multiple targets for such wars. Thus, members of minority groups, when in power, have sought to demonstrate their nationalist credentials by endorsing militant pan-Arab stances regarding Arab unity and the Palestinian question.

Iraq and Syria have alternated between entertaining strong pan-Arabist inclinations and hegemonic aspirations in their subregion: "Greater Syria," or an Arab union of the Fertile Crescent under Iraqi domination. Both were heavily involved in regional wars and initiated some of them. Syria was involved in the Arab–Israeli wars of 1948, 1973, and 1982, and most notably contributed to the escalation of the 1967 war. Syria also engaged in armed interventions in Jordan (1970) and Lebanon (from 1976 to 2005). Iraq has also been at war with Israel (1948, 1973), but has especially initiated wars in the Gulf against Iran (1980–1988) and Kuwait (1990–1991). The latter war escalated to a major international crisis which also included Iraqi Scud missile attacks on Israel.

Syria's incongruence and revisionism

Since the aftermath of World War I and Syria's independence, Syrian nationalists have been frustrated that historic Syria was dismembered into four mini-states (Syria, Jordan, Lebanon, and Palestine) and that the state of Israel was established in Palestine. "The resulting powerful brew of anti-imperialist, anti-Zionist, pan-Arab, and pan-Syrian sentiment has imparted an enduring revisionist and irredentist thrust to Syrian foreign policy."[59] This revisionism peaked in the attempt of the radical faction of the Baath party (1966–1970) to make Syria the bastion of a pan-Arab revolution and a war of liberation in Palestine. The result was the 1967 war (as well as the armed intervention in the Jordanian civil war of September 1970).

Indeed, Syria was the key state in the escalation to the 1967 war. Following its 1961 secession from the union with Egypt, Damascus had a hard time defending the legitimacy of its separate existence in the face

[58] See the chapters on Iraq and Syria in Bengio and Ben-Dor 1999; Ibrahim 1995, p. 57; Ayoob and the references he cites, 1995, p. 41, n. 54; Hudson 1977; and Ben-Dor 1983, pp. 164–173. For the argument that the state has been strengthening in recent decades in Syria and Iraq, see Mufti 1996.
[59] Hinnebusch 1991, p. 374.

of Nasser's pan-Arabist challenge. Even if the first attempt to realize the idea of Arab unity failed, the idea was so powerful that Syria had to defend its independence. The tactic used by the Syrians was the pursuit of a hard-line policy on Israel, which would expose Nasser as a soft-liner on Palestine, particularly regarding the water issue (Rabinovich 1998).

This hard-line policy can be explained by national incongruence leading to scapegoating. Leading members of the ruling Syrian Baath party, who belonged to the minority Alawi sect, were opposed by the majority Sunni public.[60] Especially unpopular was the radical faction of the Baath party, which took power in February 1966. In addition to its ethnic composition, there were also socioeconomic sources of tension between this secular, socialist group and large segments of the more conservative public. The ruling group itself was intensely factionalized. To strengthen domestic control, these tensions were externalized in a militant policy against the pro-Western Jordan and Saudi Arabia. The main target, both rhetorically and militarily, however, was Israel,[61] leading to the escalation which culminated in the Six-Day War. Indeed, adopting pan-Arabist ideology and a militant policy against Israel seemed an effective means for a minority like the Alawi to increase their legitimacy among regional and domestic audiences while not opening the political system to real democracy.

The next Syrian ruler, Hafiz al-Asad, who ruled from 1970 until 2000, even if more pragmatic in his behavior,[62] persisted vigorously with the idea of "Greater Syria."[63] He saw Lebanon, Jordan, and Palestine as integral parts of Syria, all of them undeserving the right of self-determination (Karsh 2000, p. 15). This accounts for Asad's denial of Israel's legitimacy and his relentless efforts to dominate the Palestinian national movement;[64] it also provides the background for Syria's expansionist policy vis-à-vis Lebanon. Moreover, the pan-Arabist/nationalist leanings in Syria go much beyond the personal preferences of one leader. As Bassam Tibi argues, the "national ideology of Arabism serves as a

[60] The sectarian distribution in Syria is as follows: 60 percent Sunni; 13 percent Alawi; 10 percent Christians; 10 percent Kurds; and about 5 percent Druze.

[61] Kimche and Bavly 1968, pp. 63, 72; J. Stein 1993, pp. 62–63; Rabinovich 1998; Bar Siman-Tov 1983.

[62] On the *Realpolitik* character of Asad's behavior in foreign policy, see Sadowski 2002, p. 151.

[63] Pipes 1990.

[64] On the domestic constraints – arising from membership in the Alawi minority – on Asad's ability to make peace with Israel, see Pipes 1996, cited in Rabinovich 1998, p. 240. More generally, on Asad and his policies, see Seale 1988 and Maoz 1996.

legitimizing formula in the tribal set-up in Syria."[65] The opposition to Israel and to its policies has been the key component of Arabism since the establishment of Israel. As a result, Syria was involved in four Arab–Israeli wars: 1948, 1967, 1973, and the 1982 war in Lebanon in addition to numerous low-intensity exchanges and the sponsorship of terrorism and guerrilla warfare against Israel.

Syria's hegemonic aspirations in Lebanon

In the eyes of successive Syrian rulers, the Muslim-inhabited territories annexed to Lebanon by the French were an integral part of Syria. It was also difficult for Syria to accept the Christian Maronites' pro-Western political-cultural orientation and economic independence. Therefore, Syria maintained patronage over Lebanon, manifested by coercive interference in Lebanon's domestic and foreign affairs and by close ties with Lebanese opposition groups (Sela 1998, p. 35). Even though Lebanon was recognized officially in the 1944 Alexandria Protocol by all Arab states including Syria, the Syrians refused to establish diplomatic ties with Lebanon to avoid recognizing it as a separate entity. Since the rise to power of the Baath party in 1963, the Syrians emphasized their special relations with Lebanon and wanted to establish their tutelage over it.[66] The stabilization and strengthening of Syria under Asad since 1970 reinforced its hegemonic aspirations toward its weaker neighbors: Jordan, the Palestinians, and Lebanon. The eruption of the civil war in Lebanon in 1975–1976 was seen by Syria as both a threat (a premature confrontation with Israel that had its own interests in Lebanon) and an opportunity for consolidating its hegemony over the PLO and Lebanon. After a long hesitation, Asad decided in March 1976 to use military force in the Lebanese civil war in support of the Christian forces and against the Lebanese left and the PLO. Through its considerable military deployment in Lebanon, Syria became the de facto referee of Lebanese affairs. This led to a clash between the Syrians and the Maronites, who wanted to secede and establish their own state (Ajami 1978/9, 362). The growing Syrian involvement also intensified the rivalry with Israel, which allied with the Maronites, over dominance in the Levant. At the same time, the "red-line" agreement, based on a tacit understanding with Israel of the balance of power and deterrence, limited Syrian entry to the south

[65] Cited in Zisser 1999, p. 143, n. 14. For an account that stresses the emergence of Syrian identity in place of subnational and pan-national loyalties (although the elite is still committed to pan-Arab ideology), see Sadowski 2002.
[66] Avi-Ran 1986, pp. 11–21.

of Lebanon and thus helped to contain the conflict with Israel even if it did not prevent the military clash initiated by Israel during the 1982 invasion of Lebanon.[67]

The de facto Syrian control of Lebanon ended the civil war in the beginning of the 1990s, pacified the country, and made possible some economic revival after the upheaval of the fifteen-year civil war. Yet the iron-fist policies of the Syrians have generated resentment, which peaked following the assassination in February 2005 of the former Lebanese prime minister, Rafik Hariri, by suspected Syrian agents. The combined effect of the massive anti-Syrian demonstrations following Hariri's murder, and international pressures led by the United States and France, brought about the withdrawal of the Syrian army from Lebanon in spring 2005. Still, many analysts suspect that, through its remaining intelligence agents and various pro-Syrian groups, Damascus might continue to meddle in Lebanese politics despite the rising power of the anti-Syrian forces in Lebanon.

Iraq as an incongruent and revisionist state

Iraq, created by Britain after World War I, suffered from a combination of domestic and foreign impediments, making it an unstable society while giving it a perennial urge to change the regional status quo.[68] The crucial point is Iraq's internal instability – due largely to divisions in a population composed of around 55 percent Shia Arabs, 20 percent Sunni Arabs, and 18 percent to 20 percent Kurds:

> the state of Iraq was established in the teeth of social rejection. For their own imperial and strategic reasons, the British marked out the boundaries of a collectivity which had never existed before and which lacked the minimal sense of social cohesion thought to be a necessary attribute of statehood . . . The Kurdish nation, the world of Shi'i Islam, and the domain of the Sunni Arabs represented three civilizations which were contiguous on the terrain of modern Iraq.
>
> (Chubin and Tripp 1988, pp. 14–15)

Due to this artificial joining of these three ethno-national-religious groups by British imperialism,[69] Robert Kaplan calls Iraq a "Frankenstein's monster of a country."[70]

By the late 1990s, Iraqi nationalism was still in its infancy (Bengio 1999). Most Kurds preferred to secede, and to most of the Shiites the

[67] Seale 1988; Rabinovich 1985; 1998, pp. 48–49; Evron 1987.
[68] Baram and Rubin 1993a; Mufti 1996; Hinnebusch 2003, pp. 206–210.
[69] Dawisha 2002a, p. 119. [70] R. Kaplan 1998.

Iraqi nation-state was acceptable only on the condition that they be given equal opportunities in the political and socioeconomic spheres. The Sunni ruling elite distrusted both the Kurds, whom they suspected of wanting to secede, and the Shiites, because they might support neighboring Shia Iran, in order either to undermine or to take over the Sunni-controlled state.[71] Because of the Sunni–Shia cleavage, religion has not served to promote common identity in Iraq; quite the reverse. The Kurds differ from the Iraqi Arabs regarding some of the key components of nationhood: language, race, common history, and a territorial framework (Bengio 1999, p. 150). Externalization of domestic conflict played a key role in the Iraqi hegemonic quest. The prospect of Arab leadership was expected to induce the Shiite majority to support the Sunni Arab rulers.[72] Although Iraq had no common border with Palestine before 1948 and with Israel after that, it has been consistently engaged in the Arab–Israeli dispute. This can also be explained by the relationships between national incongruence and revisionist and hegemonic aspirations, related to pan-Arabism. The Sunni elite tried to legitimize their dominant position by highlighting the Arab identity of Iraqis (rather than sectarian or religious identity) as the basis for nationhood. Thus, every pan-Arab issue, including notably the Palestine question, has become a major domestic issue for Iraq. The first mass anti-Zionist demonstration in the Arab world took place in the Iraqi capital in 1928. Since the 1930s, Iraqi elites have seen the Palestinian issue both as an important element in the vision of an Iraqi-led Fertile Crescent and as an ideological common denominator for the Sunnis and Shiites inside Iraq. Thus, Iraqi regional behavior has been closely intertwined with the building of an Iraqi nation-state and the persistent domination of the Sunni Arab elite.

Apart from this domestic challenge, Iraq had long, partly disputed borders with two far more powerful non-Arab nations: Turkey and Iran. To achieve a strategic balance with these two powerful neighbors and to dilute the Shiite/Kurdish majority in a Sunni Arab ocean, Iraqi leaders aspired to create an Arab union of the Fertile Crescent – including Palestine, Jordan, Lebanon, and Syria – that would guarantee its regional dominance. Another consideration for this aspiration was the need for

[71] An even more fundamental problem for nation-building than the sectarian rivalry is the strong loyalty to the clan or the tribe, which supersedes allegiance to the state or to civic commitment. One manifestation of this allegiance to the clan is the popularity of cousin marriages in Iraq. See *International Herald Tribune*, Sep. 29, 2003, 7.
[72] Baram and Rubin 1993a.

access to the sea, of which Iraq had little. In this context, Iraq sought to annex Kuwait, which Baghdad saw as part of its territory taken away by British imperialism. This has been a persistent Iraqi demand which emerged a long time before the 1990 invasion.

An additional Iraqi concern relates to a boundary suffering from persistent legitimacy problems. This refers to the struggle to control the Shatt al-Arab waterway. This territorial conflict has both dimensions of a nationalist conflict: competing historical claims and ethnic incongruence. The struggle between Sunni Iraq and Shia Iran on this strategic waterway is an ancient quarrel, which preceded the regimes in Iran and Iraq in 1980. It dates back to the struggle between the Ottoman and Safavid dynasties as early as the sixteenth century (Ghareeb 1990, pp. 24–25).

One key element in the Iran–Iraq escalation was that both intervened in the domestic affairs of the other by backing ethnic minorities, taking advantage of their neighbor's incongruence and of some transborder ethnic kinship: Iran supported the Kurds in northern Iraq; Iraq backed the Arabs in the southwestern Iranian province of Khuzestan. In this sense the Iraqi invasion of Iran in 1980 manifests how transborder *external incongruence* encourages a revisionist/irredentist policy: the presence of a significant Arab minority facilitated Iraqi claims to the territory surrounding the Shatt al-Arab waterway. Moreover, Iraq expected that the local Arab minority would support its takeover of the region.[73]

Particularly destabilizing was the post-1979 Iranian belief that they could spread their revolution to Iraq with the help of their Shiite brothers as well as the Kurds, who jointly constituted a clear-cut majority of the Iraqi population. This Iranian threat was an important motivation for Saddam's decision to attack Iran in September 1980 (Halliday 2005, pp. 179–180).

External incongruence has also played an important role in irredentism in the Kuwait crisis. Thus, it is not surprising that the major case of inter-Arab war (rather than just intervention in civil wars as in Yemen, Jordan, and Lebanon), which violates the Arab League principle of not settling inter-Arab disputes by the use of force (Lewis 1995, pp. 360–361), is the Iraqi invasion of Kuwait in 1990. Iraq has not recognized the legitimacy of the Kuwaiti state and has seen it as a province of Iraq. The Iraqi historical claim is that Kuwait had been an administrative subdistrict of the Iraqi province of Basra in Ottoman times and was

[73] Cordesman and Wagner 1990, pp. 36–38.

therefore an integral part of modern Iraq. In 1921, the British founded the Iraqi state which included Kuwait. In the following year, they separated Kuwait from Iraq, although it remained under their protectorate. The Iraqi historical claim has been fairly consistent on the part of very different Iraqi regimes and ideological orientations.[74] It was first expressed under the Iraqi monarchy in the late 1930s (before Kuwait became oil-rich or independent) by the nationalist King Ghazi (1935–1939). The claim was renewed by the revolutionary Iraqi president Qassim (1958–1963) when Kuwait became independent in 1961. Only a deployment of British troops (and, to a lesser extent, Arab League opposition) deterred him from invading Kuwait at the time. When the Baath party came to power in 1963, Iraq recognized Kuwait's independence, but it continued to challenge the country's legitimacy and its boundaries until the invasion of 1990.[75] In 1973, a contingent of Iraqi troops crossed the frontier and occupied a Kuwaiti military post. They subsequently disengaged, but the event indicated the continuity of the subject of frontier delineation. Similarly, as early as 1973, the Baathist regime in Iraq had pressed Kuwait to lease to it the uninhabited islands of Warba and Bubiyan which are important for facilitating Iraq's access to the Gulf. In light of the durability of the Iraqi claim to Kuwait, when Saddam voiced it again in 1990, it had a certain resonance among the Iraqis in general and especially among those military and governmental elites who were expected to implement it (Tripp 2002, pp. 180–181).

It is noteworthy that Iraq became more aggressive in carrying out its revisionist aspirations (Iran in 1980; Kuwait in 1990) following the strengthening of the state in the 1970s. This strengthening was reflected in the massive growth of the army and the rising governmental share of the GNP due to the oil boom. Such strengthening was not accompanied by a comparably successful nation-building. Thus, once the state was consolidated, its leaders could try to fulfill their dream of being the Prussia of the Arab world (Hinnebusch 2003, pp. 207–209; Mufti 1996). Revisionist behavior of a strong and incongruent state fits the expectations of the model presented in chapter 3.

Saddam used the Israeli card to enhance his appeal in the Arab world, drawing on Israeli illegitimacy among the Arabs. The culmination of this came during the Gulf War when Iraq shot about forty Scud missiles at Israeli cities. This use of force against Israel gained Saddam considerable

[74] G. Joffe 1997, pp. 69–70; Baram and Rubin 1993a; Schofield 1991; Tripp, 2002, pp. 180–181.
[75] Bahbah 1991, pp. 50–51; Evron 1994, 132.

support among the Arab masses, especially the Palestinians. Saddam's ability to mobilize such support indicates the persistent appeal of pan-Arabism at the popular level.

Like Nasser before him, Saddam raised the Arab banner against the legacy of European imperialism and what pan-Arabists saw as the goals of Western neocolonialism, that is, an Arab nation "divided in order to be mutilated, fragmented and weakened."[76] In contrast to most Arab governments, popular opinion was inspired by his move and his message.

The case of Egypt: from revisionism to status quo?

In the 1950s and 1960s, Egypt under Nasser, as the strongest Arab state, led the revisionist pan-Arab movement, which advocated the unification of all Arabs in a single state, and called for the elimination of Israel as an illegitimate state that had been established on Arab lands and had displaced the Palestinian Arabs.

As a result, Egypt was intensely engaged in Arab–Israeli wars in 1948, 1956, 1967, 1969–1970, and 1973, in addition to its intervention in the Yemen civil war in the 1960s. Cairo was also engaged in transborder revolutionary messages to the populations of the other Arab states, notably in the conservative monarchies of Saudi Arabia and Jordan (the so-called Arab Cold War).[77]

While being incongruent as part of the Arab (and Islamic) nation,[78] however, in contrast to Syria and Iraq, Egypt is a relatively coherent state with its own distinct identity: "Of all the Arab states, Egypt is the largest, the most politically stable, the most legitimate within her boundaries."[79] Egypt is historically the most centralized and developed state in the Arab world and has a stronger national identity than other Arab states (Ben-Dor 1983, pp. 237–239; Lewis 1995, p. 372). Thus, it was easier for Egypt – being relatively less vulnerable – to move away from the path of war

[76] Cited in Lustick 1997, 672, n. 68. See also Kuttab 1990 for a view of the invasion as a liberation from the imposed fragmentation of colonial borders.
[77] Kerr 1971.
[78] The only significant minority are the Coptic Christians – about 6 percent of the population.
[79] Ajami 1978/9, 358. Ben-Dor (cited in Mufti 1996, p. 10, n. 18) suggests that Egypt is a relatively coherent state because of its geographical isolation, social homogeneity, and longer history of functioning bureaucratic institutions. On Egypt as a relatively coherent state, see also Ben-Dor 1983, Telhami 1990, p. 94, and Gause 1992. On its foreign policy, see the chapters on Egypt in Korany and Dessouki 1991a and in Hinnebusch 2002c. On its identity and foreign policy, see the chapter on Egypt in Barnett and Telhami 2002.

on its own than for the other Arab states, which are domestically much weaker and are less congruent. Following the disastrous defeat of the expansionist, pan-Arab aspirations in the 1967 war and the partial success of its limited restoration goals in the 1973 war, a status quo elite came to power in Cairo in the 1970s; they were mostly interested in addressing the country's huge economic problems through closer links with the West, and thus were inclined to make peace with Israel. Still, there were remaining problems of state-to-nation balance between Israel and Egypt (regarding the resolution of the Palestinian problem and a full-blown acceptance of Israel in the Middle East), which Egypt could ignore only at the expense of its traditional aspirations for Arab leadership. Even if they are less constraining than in other Arab states, Egypt also has domestic vulnerabilities (including a militant Islamic opposition and lingering pan-Arab constituencies such as among the intellectuals and professionals). As a result, the peace between Israel and Egypt has remained a cold one and has required intensive and persistent US engagement in order to reach and to maintain even this level (see chapter 5).

Weakness and incongruence lead to incoherence and civil wars and external intervention: the cases of Lebanon and Jordan

I focus here on two main cases from the Middle East because of their relevance to the war proneness of this vital region. There are, however, numerous other cases of the destabilizing effects of state weakness and incoherence such as in the Balkans in the nineteenth century and in the post-Cold War era (see chapter 6), in postcolonial Africa, and in the post-Cold War Soviet republics. Afghanistan in the past three decades is an additional example of the dynamics analyzed in this section.

Two incoherent Arab states – Lebanon and Jordan – have provided a "sanctuary" or a launching ground for guerrilla activities, notably for Palestinian refugees demanding their right to self-determination, as well as a battleground for armed interventions by expansionist or insecure neighbors. In these weakest and most incoherent states, the Palestinian refugees aggravated the levels of both domestic and regional violence.

The incoherence of the Lebanese state

Despite the overall process of state-building in the Arab world in the 1970s and 1980s, which somewhat reduced the threat of Arab–Israeli wars, Lebanon is a leading exception which has been prominent well into the 1990s. In contrast to other Arab states, where states exercised a growing control over their societies, in Lebanon the state remained very weak in relation to society. The society remained open to penetration by outside powers whose support was sought by local groups (Gause 1992, p. 461, citing Hudson 1968). Indeed, Lebanon's severe incoherence generated a high degree of regional instability, culminating in the Syrian and Israeli invasions.

Lebanon is deeply fragmented between the Maronites (15 percent), other Christians (10 percent), Muslims (divided between Sunnis, 25 percent, and the underprivileged Shiites, 45 percent), and Druzes (5 percent).[80] The political-social-economic fragmentation of Lebanon produced the Lebanese civil war between 1976 and the early 1990s and invited outside intervention. Every Arab regime, especially Syria, as well as Israel, has been involved to some degree in the domestic affairs of Lebanon, while the Palestinian presence has exacerbated the domestic turmoil. The PLO move to Lebanon after its defeat in the 1970 civil war in Jordan was a major factor contributing to the country's slide into civil war in 1975. The PLO set up a virtual state-within-a-state (Lewis 1995, pp. 365–366), which Israel aimed to destroy in its 1982 invasion of Lebanon. This invasion brought about a clash with the Syrian army stationed in Lebanon. The invasion also reinforced the emergence of militant Shiite organizations, notably Hezbollah, which were inspired by the 1979 Islamic revolution in Iran. Hezbollah fought against the military presence of Israel in south Lebanon until the unilateral withdrawal of the Israeli army in May 2000. Even after the withdrawal, however, Lebanon has continued to be a weak state; this is demonstrated by the lack of control of the Lebanese army over the southern section of the state adjacent to the border with Israel. Thus, this area persists in being a tinderbox which might explode at any time. Indeed, following a Hezbollah crossborder attack in July 2006, the conflict between Hezbollah and Israel escalated to a major clash which included thirty-three days of massive Israeli attacks on Hezbollah targets in Lebanon as well as Hezbollah firing thousands of missiles into northern Israel. Although the ceasefire is still holding at the time of this writing, there is a potential for future escalation which might include in some scenarios the supporters of Hezbollah – Syria and potentially even Iran. The Palestinians interpreted the 2000 Israeli withdrawal as a military defeat of Israel, and some argue that it encouraged the eruption of the second intifada against Israel a few months later, in September 2000.

[80] Zamir 1999; Rubin 2006.

Irredentist refugees and incoherent states – the example of Jordan

The transformation of Transjordan into Jordan[81] with the annexation of the West Bank, following the 1948 war, illustrates the difference between state power in the sense of capabilities and state coherence in the sense of national congruence and identity. The addition of the West Bank and of hundreds of thousands of educated Palestinians potentially increased the power and importance of Jordan, but also made it a less congruent and coherent state. Moreover, at least until 1970 Jordan was also a weak state in the basic sense of a lack of control over the means of violence in its territory. Instead of having simply a loyal and coherent population of traditionally oriented Bedouins, the society became much more diversified and much less identified with the state. The majority (70 percent) became Palestinian, half being dissatisfied and dispossessed refugees. For decades the crux of the Jordanian–Palestinian divide was rooted in the divergent interests and policies of the Jordanian state and the Palestinian national movement in the Arab–Israeli conflict.[82] The Palestinization of the kingdom made it much more vulnerable to interference by hostile elements such as radical Palestinians, Nasserites, and pan-Arabists (Benny Morris 1996, p. 21; Sela 1998, pp. 44–45), culminating in the Syrian military intervention in the civil war between the Palestinian guerrilla organizations and the Jordanian army in September 1970.

Before he disarmed the Palestinian guerrilla organizations in the civil war, and especially before Israel took over the West Bank in 1967 with its large Palestinian population, King Hussein had a difficult time controlling his long and highly penetrated border with Israel. Actions by Fatah – the Palestinian guerrilla organization – encouraged by a radical Syria (Gerges 1994, p. 210), brought about Israeli retaliation on November 13, 1966, in the West Bank village of Samu. Palestinians in Jordan rioted against Hussein. Jordan, in turn, accused Nasser of not acting as a good pan-Arabist: Egypt did not come to its aid and hid behind the "skirts" of the UN Emergency Force (UNEF), set up following the 1956 war as a buffer between Egypt and Israel (J. Stein 1993, p. 63; Ovendale 1992, pp. 193–194; Gerges 1994, p. 211; M. Oren 2002, pp. 33–37). Allegations of this kind exerted pan-Arab pressures on Nasser to escalate his

[81] On Jordan's domestic environment and foreign policy, see the chapter on Jordan in Korany and Dessouki 1991a.
[82] Susser 1999.

behavior against Israel in order to maintain his Arab leadership claims, generating the 1967 crisis.

Jordan joined the radical Arabs in the anti-Israeli coalition of that crisis – despite an expected military defeat – because of fears of a civil war that would have threatened the Hashemite monarchy if it had remained on the sidelines rather than joined the war: "political legitimacy superseded any strategic considerations" (Gerges 1994, p. 216).[83] The important point is, however, that the survival of the vulnerable Jordanian regime was closely related to its standing in the Arab–Israeli conflict: the conflict with Israel was a crucial subject of inter-Arab and domestic legitimacy in the Arab world, especially in an incoherent state such as pre-1967 Jordan.

Following the 1967 Israeli occupation of the West Bank, the Palestinian guerrillas deployed their forces in Jordan, creating a "state within a state." Jordanian sovereignty was steadily eroded until the armed confrontation between the PLO and the Jordanian army in September 1970 in which the Palestinian challenge was defeated. The presence of the Palestinian guerrillas created fear among Jordanians that the Palestinians had a hidden agenda to take over Jordan and transform it into their "alternative homeland" (Susser 1999, p. 97). By defeating this challenge on the battleground, the Jordanian state was strengthened considerably. However, on the national congruence level, there are still major challenges to the Jordanian state identity: the majority of the population is of Palestinian origin, with strong loyalty to the Palestinian national cause, while important segments of the society are Arab nationalists and Islamists.[84] Thus, even if the state is stronger today than it was in the 1950s and 1960s, it is still vulnerable to national unrest in the case of major upheavals in the Israeli–Palestinian conflict or other parts of the Arab world as was the case in the 1991 Gulf crisis. As a result of this vulnerability, King Hussein bandwagoned out of fear with Saddam Hussein in that crisis despite his pro-Western leanings and dependence on the West and the oil-rich Gulf states.

There are currently major concerns about the potential implications for the stability of Jordan of the post-2003 Iraq crisis and the US occupation, as well as of the Israeli–Palestinian confrontation. This is due

[83] See citations of King Hussein and other important Jordanians in Gerges 1994, pp. 215–216; see also J. Stein 1993, pp. 64–66.
[84] On the challenges of forging a national identity in Jordan since its creation by the British, see Massad 2001.

to the transborder ties so typical of the Middle East: the Sunni majority in Jordan has embattled brethren who are a minority in Iraq; they both fear the rising Shiite power and presumed alliance of the Shiites in Iran, Iraq, and Lebanon. Further, the Islamists in Jordan support the anti-US insurgency in neighboring Iraq; and the Palestinian majority in Jordan supports the Palestinian struggle against the Israeli occupation across the Jordan River.

Explaining spatial differences: the high war proneness of the Arab–Israeli arena

This section explains the especially high war proneness of the Arab–Israeli arena, as compared to the other parts of the region, by the especially high state-to-nation imbalance in this area, manifested by mutual illegitimacy on nationalist grounds.

Manifestations (indicators) of mutual Arab–Israeli illegitimacy

Both the Arabs/Palestinians and Jews/Israelis have expressed in words and deeds a high degree of mutual illegitimacy in terms of state and nation over the decades of conflict among them. The Arabs had denied the legitimacy of the Jews' right to establish a state in Palestine and to immigrate and settle there. Later, once the Jewish state was established, the Arabs rejected its legitimacy and were unwilling to accept any partition plan. The Zionists, for their part, claimed to have historical national rights on territories inhabited by Arabs, and Israel denied that the Palestinians were a nation.[85] Having evicted some of the 1948 Palestinian refugees, Israel did not allow any of them back. The Arabs supported the right of return of the refugees and discouraged them from settling in their new Arab countries. Arab states sponsored terrorist actions and infiltrations into Israel, which, in turn, generated Israeli reprisals, sometimes disproportionately. Israel also confiscated land, on ethnonationalist grounds, from Palestinian Arabs in Israel and the occupied territories, and settled Jews on these lands. The Arabs manifested

[85] Thus, the former Israeli premier, Golda Meir, stated in 1969: "It was not as though there was a Palestinian people and in Palestine considering itself as a Palestinian people and we came and threw them out and took their country away from them. They did not exist" (Hirst 1984, p. 264).

their view of Israel's illegitimacy by forming anti-Israeli Arab coalitions with sharp anti-Israeli rhetoric, by closing the Straits of Tiran and the Suez Canal to Israeli navigation and Arab airspace to Israeli air traffic, and by boycotting Israel in economic, cultural, professional, tourist, and sport exchange domains, thus producing a besieged Israeli mentality (Sela 1998, p. 52).

The temporal evolution of rival revisionism in the Middle East: Zionism and Arab anti-Zionism

Zionism and anti-Zionist Arab nationalism have pursued conflicting revisionist agendas since the start of the Zionist emigration to Palestine in the late nineteenth century. Having achieved the Jewish right to self-determination in 1948–1949, however, Zionism became mostly status quo oriented, especially in the period between the war of Israel's independence and the Six-Day War. In the aftermath of that war, aspirations for expansion into the occupied territories emerged among some significant elements of Israeli society.

The evolution of Zionist positions and those of their Arab opponents may be subdivided into three periods. However, in all of them, the nationalist elements of territory (in the sense of competing claims for the control of territory) and people (namely, their right to migrate, settle new lands, or return to old ones) have played the central role (see table 4.2).

The three main stages in the national/ideological struggle are the following:

(a) Before 1948 and the establishment of the State of Israel, the Zionists, though their settlements in pre-1948 Palestine still did not constitute a state, were the revisionist force, while the Arabs aimed to forestall their immigration to Palestine and their further settlement there.
(b) Between 1948 and 1967, the Arabs were the revisionists, while Israel was mainly the status quo party, although it did reveal some aspirations for revisionism in 1949–1956.
(c) In the post-1967 era, both parties are qualified revisionists due to the addition of the problem of the territories occupied by Israel in the 1967 war. Israeli revisionism is manifested in the settlements beyond the 1967 boundaries and limited annexations of occupied territories (notably East Jerusalem). Yet, Israel has also shown a willingness to make concessions and to withdraw from most of the territories in exchange for peace settlements with the Arabs, even if the extent of

Table 4.2 *The evolution of Zionist/Israeli and Arab/Palestinian positions: control over territories and settlement of people*

	Territories		People	
	Zionists/Israel	Arabs/Palestinians	Zionists/Israel	Arabs/Palestinians
Pre-1948	Acquisition	Deny acquisition by Zionists	Jewish immigration	Refusal of immigration
1949–67	Mostly status quo (though some revisionism in 1949–56)	Revisionism to pre-1948 abolition of Israel	Refusal of right of return of Palestinian refugees	Right of return of refugees
Post-1967	Settlements and partial withdrawals from occupied territories	Minimalists: restoration to pre-1967; maximalists: restoration to pre-1948	Limited transfer of population to occupied territories	Right of return to territories; in principle also to pre-1948; opposition to Jewish settlements in occupied territories

the pullout is highly disputed inside Israel. The Arabs have become divided between those who only want to restore the pre-1967 situation, that is, to get back all the occupied territories while being ready to accept Israel in the pre-1967 boundaries, versus those who still entertain full-blown revisionism, that is, Israel's annihilation. Also, the demand for the establishment of a Palestinian state has grown: parallel to the general debate among the Arabs, they have been divided between those who advocate a Palestinian state alongside Israel and those who prefer to establish such a state instead of Israel.

The state-to-nation issues and revisionism with regard to the regional territorial order have played a critical role in making the Middle East more prone to hot wars than other regions in the post-World War II era. What is exceptional about the Middle East is the strength of the competing claims for legitimacy by two national movements which seek an exclusive control of the same piece of postcolonial land in order to establish their own national state in that territory.[86] Each side's claims are based on a belief in the legitimacy of its own aspirations and a lack

[86] On some of the characteristics of the Arab–Israeli conflict, see Ben-Dor 1982. For recent major revisionist histories of the conflict, see Benny Morris 2001, Shlaim 2000, and Pappe 2004.

of legitimacy for those of the other side, and thus any victory by one side leads to powerful revisionist demands by its neighbors.

Before the establishment of the State of Israel, the Zionists, especially since the first World Zionist Congress in 1897, claimed that Jews should have the right to immigrate from all over the world and settle and establish a Jewish state in the area Arabs saw as Arab Palestine but that Jews saw as their historical homeland. Moreover, the Jewish claim for legitimacy also relied on Jewish persecution through the ages in exile, culminating in the Holocaust. The Arabs countered, however, that the Palestinians should not bear the responsibility and pay the price of Jewish suffering and rejection in Europe.

While the claim for a state by a national group during the post-1945 decolonization was a common phenomenon, the intense opposition to it by a majority of the local population and by all neighboring states was quite unique[87] because Zionist immigration peaked when colonization by immigrant settlers of European origin was already in decline (Kimmerling 1982, pp. 9–13).

Arab anti-Zionist revisionism

Arab anti-Zionist revisionism came in three main stages with the following changing nationalist objectives:

Before 1948 The Arabs rejected the legitimacy of the Zionist objective to settle in Palestine and aimed to forestall the establishment of a Jewish state in what they saw as Arab Palestine. The Arabs rejected the Zionist claim that the Jews were a nation deserving the right to self-determination in general and in Palestine in particular, due to an alleged historical-national connection.[88] Thus, the Arab efforts before 1948 were mainly preventive in nature – denial of the realization of the alien Zionism and its major manifestations through immigration and settlement, which in Arab eyes posed a threat to the Arab character of Palestine (Harkabi 1977, p. 5; Kimmerling 1982; Nevo 1979; Ovendale 1992, pp. 11–12; Sela 1998, p. 36).

The Arabs were alienated by Zionism's (and later Israel's) Western character, an image reinforced by the fact that Jewish immigration

[87] Other major examples are the white minority governments in South Africa and Rhodesia. But even in these cases, the delegitimization was only of the white minority control of the government, not of the state itself and its territorial identity. Indeed, these states and their boundaries stayed in place following the removal of the white governments from power.
[88] On Muslim attitudes to the Jews before Zionism, see Benny Morris 2001, pp. 8–13.

and settlement were accelerated under British colonialism (Ayoob 1993, p. 51; Shlaim 1995; Butenschon 1992; Safran 1969, p. 21) following the 1917 Balfour Declaration, which stated that Britain viewed "with favor the establishment in Palestine of a national home for the Jewish people" (cited in Safran 1969, p. 24; Hudson 1977, p. 116; and Ovendale 1992, p. 37). The Arabs regarded the declaration as a violation of the pledges made to the leaders of the incipient Arab nationalist movement by Britain through its high commissioner in Egypt, Sir Henry McMahon, that it would support Arab independence in most of the Arab-inhabited territories of the Ottoman Empire in exchange for their launching a revolt against the Ottoman authorities (Safran 1969, p. 24; Hudson 1977, pp. 116–117; Ovendale 1992, pp. 23–25). The Arabs opposed the establishment of a Jewish national home under the British mandate and saw it as an illegitimate colonial enterprise that infringed on the Wilsonian right to self-determination of the indigenous population (Ovendale 1992, p. 46). Zionism was seen as an extension of the colonial world (Sela 1998, p. 32) which invaded the "non-white" parts of the globe in order to exploit them. The Zionists focused on the causes of Jewish immigration (which they claimed were different from other colonial movements, due to the ancient and continuous attachment of the Jews to the Land of Israel), while the Arabs highlighted its effects – dispossession and uprooting of the indigenous population of Palestine (Nevo 1979, pp. 163–164; Kimmerling 1982, pp. 28–29).

The Arab opposition was expressed in violent resistance in 1920, 1921, and 1929, and especially in the Arab revolt against British authority in 1936–1939. The Arabs also opposed the British (1937) and UN (1947) plans for partition of Palestine into Arab and Jewish states, consistently insisting on absolute Arab sovereignty over Palestine (Ben-Dor 1983, pp. 196–197). The Arabs refused even to negotiate with the Jewish community because they feared that such talks could be interpreted as recognition of the national/political rights of the Zionists, which they vehemently opposed (Nevo 1979, p. 171). Even if this intransigence reflected political ineptness, it also reflected the Arab belief in the absolute justice of their cause and the total illegitimacy of the Zionist one.

Apart from their focus on preventing Jewish settlement and the creation of a Zionist political entity in Palestine, there was also a more purely revisionist element in the Arab position even before the Jews achieved sovereignty. In the aftermath of World War II, Arab leaders demanded that citizenship rights (but not national/political rights) be granted only to those Jews who arrived in Palestine through 1919; Jews who arrived after that date would be denied equal rights and might even have to be deported. This demand was later inserted into the Palestinian National Charter of 1964 and 1968 (Nevo 1979, p. 171).

1948–1967 The objective in this period was to reverse the consequences of the 1947–1949 war as manifested in the formation of Israel and its boundaries and the birth of the Palestinian refugee problem (this stage will also be discussed below in the context of the 1956 and 1967 wars).[89] Following the creation of Israel, the Arab position in the 1950s was a continuation of its pre-1948 stance (Harkabi 1977, pp. 3–8), although it now became a revisionist claim. This revisionism referred in the first place to the illegitimacy of Israel's existence, and more pragmatically (though still on state-to-nation grounds) to the questions of boundaries (namely, that Israel had to make considerable territorial concessions to neighboring Arab states) and people, that is, the Palestinian refugees and their "right of return" to Palestine (Benny Morris 1996, pp. 29–37).

Israel's neighbors did not recognize its legitimacy as a state and as the political homeland of the Jewish people. As a result of the colonial legacy, they regarded Israel as a "cancer in the body of the Arab nation"[90] and as a Western imperialist outpost and bridgehead in the Middle East (Lewis 1995, p. 373); that is, Israel was seen as "in but not of the region" (cited in Sela 1998, p. 15). The Arabs believed that Israel was doomed to share the fate of the Crusaders in the Medieval Ages – to suffer a defeat, to disintegrate, and to disappear (Benny Morris 1996, p. 437). In the 1950s, the Arab purpose was described as the liquidation of Israel as a polity, i.e., "politicide" – the destruction of a state because, on the one hand, it would right a wrong done to the Arabs (since the country might be restored to its Palestinian owners and become Arab), and, on the other, it would remove an alien element disrupting the homogeneity of the area and threatening further incursion and expansion (Harkabi 1977, pp. 3–4; Sela 1998, pp. 50–51).

This is partly because, in the eyes of the Arabs, Israel is an extraterritorial actor, which maintains intense and crucial institutionalized links with diaspora Jews (Korany and Dessouki 1991b, pp. 41–42), rather than with its Arab neighbors. For the Arabs, Israel failed to convince its neighbors of its legitimacy and to persuade the Palestinians to abandon their cause and accept the Zionist state.[91]

[89] On the birth of the Palestinian refugee problem, see Benny Morris 1988.
[90] Eytan 1958, pp. 87–88. [91] Hudson 1977, pp. 303–304.

At the same time, in the aftermath of the establishment of Israel in the 1948–1949 war, the Palestinians remained without a state and thus did not have a stake in the stability of the regional order (Ayoob 1993, p. 42). This is especially true for the Palestinian refugees who fled or were deported from their homes in what became Israel.[92] The refugees numbered between 600,000 and 760,000. Most of them wanted to go back to their homes. Half of the refugees settled in Jordan, most of them in the West Bank. The other half were spread between the Gaza Strip (200,000), Lebanon (100,000), and Syria (60,000).[93]

The Palestinian refugees shared the fate of millions of other refugees in Eastern Europe, India, and other places who fled their homes or were deported during the post-World War II and postcolonial turmoil. Yet, the position of the Palestinian refugees was unique in that, unlike the others, they were neither repatriated nor resettled but were left or kept in camps as stateless refugees. Although Arab states viewed the dispersion of the Palestinians as a blatant case of injustice against all Arabs, their responses to the problem varied considerably.[94] Egypt and Jordan, which occupied the West Bank and the Gaza Strip from 1948 to 1967, did not allow the creation of a Palestinian state in these territories. Only Jordan formally annexed the Jordanian-held territories on the West Bank and later offered citizenship to all Arab Palestinians.

Post-1967 The goal has been to reverse the consequences of the 1967 war, which is to say, to restore Arab sovereignty to the territories occupied by Israel in that war, if not to undo the outcome of the 1947–1949 war (I will return to this point at the end of the chapter). After 1967, the problem was seemingly compounded by the Israeli occupation of the West Bank and the Gaza Strip. This occupation added a new dimension to the dispute through the active involvement of a Palestinian leadership. The total defeat of the Arab states in 1967 increased the importance of the PLO, established three years earlier and serving until then as an instrument in inter-Arab politics (Lewis 1995, p. 365). There has been a growing Palestinian demand for a Palestinian state, expressed in the 1970s mainly in guerrilla and terrorist attacks against Israel and its citizens, alongside worldwide diplomatic activity for international support of the Palestinian cause. Palestinian nationalism culminated in the intifada in the occupied territories from 1987 to 1993 (Schiff and Yaari

[92] Hudson 1977, pp. 297–298. [93] See Benny Morris 1996, pp. 19–20; 2001, p. 260.
[94] See Hudson 1977, pp. 298–299; Korany and Dessouki 1991b, p. 34.

1990; Lewis 1995, p. 366), and more violently in the second intifada of 2000–2004.

However, besides these aggravating developments, the outcome of the 1967 war, and even more so that of the 1973 war, moderated some elements of Arab revisionism, while creating a division between moderates who were willing to accept Israel in the pre-1967 boundaries and radicals who continued to oppose Israel's right to exist. The occupation of the territories produced the possibility of a compromise based on the formula of "land for peace." Yet, thus far, even the moderate elements have been unable to reach a comprehensive resolution of the conflict with Israel that would directly address the underlying legitimacy sources of the dispute, partly also due to Israeli revisionism (for recent developments see the end of the chapter).

Zionist/Israeli revisionism

Zionist/Israeli revisionism also came in three main stages according to a similar division of time spans.

Pre-sovereignty (pre-1948) Zionism The objective of Zionism was to resolve the "Jewish question," namely, to find a solution to the problems resulting from the presence of an ethnic-religious minority which had been scattered over the globe for almost two thousand years and which could not be assimilated as a group within the "host" societies. The Zionist solution was to construct a Jewish society or a state in their ancient land – Zion or Eretz Israel – by encouraging as many Jews as possible to immigrate, acquire territory, and settle there (Benny Morris 2001, pp. 14–26). Although the Jews continued to be attached to Zion over the many years of their exile, its boundaries were unclear and undefined, except for its center, Jerusalem (Kimmerling 1982, pp. 8–9, 16–17). When the Jewish settlement began, the Zionists incorrectly estimated that the country was almost uninhabited. In fact, there was very little free land available in Palestine (Benny Morris 2001, pp. 42–45). As a consequence of this land scarcity, the acuteness of the conflict was intensified. Since the Jewish immigration coincided with the first signs of political awakening among the local population (Porath 1974, 1977), and since the Zionist settlement contributed to triggering the awakening,[95] the Zionists faced an intense conflict with the Arabs. Although the

[95] Lewis 1998b.

conflict was aggravated by major cultural and economic differences, it was essentially a conflict of competing nationalist objectives.[96]

Territory has been central in the dispute. From the beginning to the present, Zionist settlement has involved a Jewish–Arab dispute over land because of the desire of both parties for exclusive political control of the land. The most intense element in the interaction between the two parties has been the struggle for land ownership.[97] The acquisition of land, a foremost objective for the Zionists, required the transfer of land from one national ownership to another, dispossessing some of the Arabs living there. This provoked national resistance of the Arabs to Jewish land acquisition in Palestine (Porath 1974, pp. 7, 18; Benny Morris 2001, p. 37), although until the establishment of the State of Israel Jews had acquired only around 10 percent of the total land area of Palestine. More important, the acquisition was attained only through purchase rather than the use of force (Kimmerling 1982, pp. 15–19), and at least some of the acquired areas were uninhabited (Benny Morris 2001, p. 38). Finally, despite the Zionist aspiration to accumulate as much land as possible in Palestine, the majority of the Jewish community was willing to accept partition plans both in 1937 and 1947. In other words, the Zionists were ready for significant territorial compromises in order to gain sovereignty even if only in part of the promised land (Kimmerling 1982, pp. 58–65).

Following statehood – 1949–1967: Israel in the aftermath of its War of Independence The Israeli policy was to reach peace with the Arab states based on the territorial and demographic status quo, that is, without territorial concessions to the Arabs or the return of any significant number of Palestinian refugees to their previous homes in Israeli territory (alongside encouragement of massive Jewish immigration to Israel). At the same time, there was a certain degree of dissatisfaction of some leaders and groups, notably in the military, with the 1949 borders of the newborn state and aspirations for territorial revisions (Benny Morris 1996, pp. 26–28, and 2001, p. 261; Miller 1981, pp. 27–28). This dissatisfaction lasted until the 1956 Sinai campaign, in which Israel occupied the Sinai, only to return it, after a

[96] For an overview of the emergence of the conflict between the settlers and the indigenous Arabs as a nationalist conflict due to the "objective historical conditions and the conflicting interests and goals of the two populations," see Benny Morris 2001, pp. 42–66.

[97] Kimmerling 1982; Nevo 1979. See also the revisionist histories of Shlaim 2000 and Benny Morris 2001.

short while, to Egypt under US pressures and reassurances. Until the 1967 war Israel accepted the territorial status quo.

Post-1967 – Did state strength and national incongruence produce a "Greater Israel"? In accordance with the model presented in chapter 3 (see table 3.2), one should expect Israel to have revisionist/irredentist tendencies. Israel is a strong state, notably in its capacity to mobilize armed forces.[98] It is internally incongruent – 20 percent of the population are Arabs, who are torn between their loyalty to the state as good citizens and their ethnonational identity as part of the transborder Arab/Palestinian nation which is in intense national conflict with their state. In addition, the Jewish population itself is very heterogeneous – coming from numerous diasporas. Indeed, the focus of Zionist Israel was on building a nation of the Jews themselves with a strong transborder ethnonational connection to the world Jewish diaspora. This nation-building was based on ethnic nationalism rather than an inclusive civic one – it excluded the Arab minority who, for its part, had great difficulty identifying with the Jewish character of the state and its Jewish national symbols. While Israel's democracy has facilitated political integration of the Arab citizens, they suffer from some discrimination in a Jewish state that has been somewhat suspicious of their loyalty to a state which is in a war with their ethnic nation.[99]

Most important, Israel is externally incongruent due to the mismatch between sovereign Israel (in its 1949 boundaries) and the historic homeland of the Jewish people, which largely coincides with the territories occupied in 1967, notably East Jerusalem and the West Bank. This incongruence is based on the historical component of ethnic nationalism, which is an important legitimacy provider in the Israeli/Zionist case.

The uniqueness of the Israeli case is that, although it is an immigrant society, its legitimacy is derived from ethnic nationalism. This contrasts with other immigrant societies such as those in the New World, where the immigrants endorse civic nationalism in accordance with the territorial identity of their new homeland. Although the Zionists had a realist objective – securing a sanctuary for the persecuted Jewish

[98] Thus, Israeli forces that can be mobilized within seventy-two hours included 145 per 1,000 of total population in 1987; in Egypt the figure for regular forces was 8.6, and in Iraq it was 62.9. See Gause 1992, p. 458.

[99] For a comprehensive discussion of nationalism and democracy in Israel, see Yacobson and Rubinstein 2003 and the numerous references they provide of the competing views on this issue.

people – the rationale for the chosen territory was nationalist rather than realist. In other words, Palestine was not necessarily the safest place for Jewish settlement, but the Zionists had emotional ties to it as their ancient homeland. These emotional ties limit territorial flexibility, as compared to other immigrant societies, but they did not prevent territorial compromise: most Zionists accepted the 1947 UN Partition Resolution. The nationalist-historical commitment makes it more difficult to compromise on Jerusalem and the West Bank, especially after Israel became stronger and occupied these territories in the 1967 war. Although realist considerations of security played a role, the ideological attachment to these places reinforced the settlers' moral appeal and their domestic political power in collaboration with right-wing irredentist allies even if left-leaning parties opposed settlements in the midst of Arab population centers.[100]

Until the unilateral disengagement from the Gaza Strip in summer 2005, Israel had seemed unwilling or unable to make concessions regarding Jewish settlers and their nationalist right to settle the occupied territories of the West Bank and the Gaza Strip. This aggravated the conflict between Israel and the Palestinians because it challenged the latter's aspiration for their own state. The settlements signaled Israeli nationalist irredentism at the expense of the Palestinian right to national self-determination.

The effects of the state-to-nation imbalance on regional war proneness: power and security as the proximate causes of specific Middle East wars

The state-to-nation imbalance, by generating revisionism and incoherent states, accounts for the high war proneness of the Middle East as compared to most other regions in the post-World War II era. Such an imbalance does not explain, however, the timing and circumstances leading to specific wars. In other words, the state-to-nation imbalance is a necessary condition, but it is insufficient to bring about a resort to force without the presence of additional factors, which are mostly realist, having to do with power and security considerations. If the state-to-nation imbalance led directly to wars, then we should expect that there would have been continuous hot wars in the region because there

[100] For a comprehensive – and critical – study of the Jewish settlements in the occupied territories, see Zertal and Eldar 2004.

was little variation in this factor, especially until the 1970s. For most of the period between 1948 and the 1970s, there were cold wars, not hot ones. The timing and specific context of particular wars are explained by the proximate causes: first, the security dilemma and, second, power or profit. A third proximate cause is diversionary/scapegoating. The state-to-nation imbalance in the Middle East increased the likelihood of these three kinds of wars.

The Arab resort to violence has been either in order to expand at Israel's expense (1948) or to restore lost territories (1969–1970, 1973). The combined effect of domestic vulnerability of Arab states and regional illegitimacy of the "Zionist entity" prolonged a state of war which increased Israeli security concerns and thus the level of the security dilemma in the region. This brought about a security dilemma war (1967) and led to a preventive war initiated by Israel (1956), which was also partly induced by Israeli revisionism and its quest for territorial profit. Israeli revisionism resulted, in addition, in the 1982 invasion of Lebanon.

Arab–Israeli wars: situational vs. state-to-nation

Under the conditions of a state-to-nation imbalance, the security dilemma in the Middle East was exacerbated by the geographical and technological attributes of the region which favored taking the offensive (J. Stein 1993, pp. 58–62). Without a high degree of state-to-nation imbalance, however, these conditions by themselves would not have led to recurring wars. Thus, in other regions such conditions by themselves do not lead to wars. The geographical and technological factors exacerbating the security dilemma in the region are:

- Many borders are not separated by natural obstacles and thus are easy to cross. Notable in this sense are all of Israel's pre-1967 borders.
- Israel's lack of strategic depth makes it more costly to absorb a first strike by the enemy and thus favors a preemptive strategy. Such a strategy emphasizes offensive capabilities and thus increases the security dilemma (Jervis 1978, Van Evera 1999).
- Weapons systems in the region, which are mostly land-based and are deployed a relatively short distance from enemy territory, have been highly vulnerable to a first strike. A major example is the high vulnerability of the Arab air forces to the Israeli preemptive strike in the early hours of the Six-Day War.
- The systemic difficulty of distinguishing between offensive and defensive weapons and military postures (Jervis 1978) is especially notable

in the Middle East because of the large-scale mobilization of standing forces in the region. In addition, the widespread deployment of sophisticated weapons systems can be used for either defensive or offensive purposes. For example, supposedly defensive anti-aircraft missiles were crucial for the Egyptian offensive in 1973.

The Israeli security dilemma was also sharpened by several structural or situational factors.[101] The quantitative disadvantages in military spending and manpower reserves constrained its ability to wage a protracted war as compared to its rivals (J. Stein 1993, p. 58). Notable features of Israel's strategic situation include a high degree of vulnerability due to the small size of the country, the fact that its frontiers have few obstacles, and the proximity of major population centers to the borders. Israel's territory is also not conducive to guerrilla resistance.[102] These factors dictate an offensive strategy designed to preempt and defeat rivals before they move into Israeli territory. Such a strategy encourages mobile forces, like airplanes and tanks, able to move quickly and capture the enemy's territory. By posing a high threat to the other side's capabilities (Walt 1987), they enhance the security dilemma.

The situational attributes of the Middle East, however, did not bring about recurring inter-Arab wars. There is, no doubt, an unusual recurrence of use of force between Israel and the Arabs. Yet, war has occurred also when the situational factors were not conducive to war. Thus, Israel was attacked by the Arabs even when its strategic depth had increased drastically and its vulnerability had declined. Such attacks took place in the 1969–1970 War of Attrition and especially in the 1973 war, that is, following the victory in 1967 and the occupation of the Suez Canal, the Golan Heights, and the Jordan River. In other words, the Arabs resorted to force even though control over these territories increased the distance between Israel's major population centers and the borders, and the borders also had more formidable natural obstacles. Similarly, the Palestinians fought against Israel, notably in the two intifadas, even when they were much inferior in the conventional balance of capabilities.[103] At the same time, the peace with Egypt (which reflected a reduction in the legitimacy problems) persisted even after Israel evacuated its strategic assets in the Sinai in 1982 (by returning the Sinai to Egypt as part of the 1979 peace treaty, Israel evacuated strategic assets such as

[101] On the Israeli security dilemma, see Mandelbaum 1988, ch. 5.
[102] Van Evera 1998, 19.
[103] On the Palestinian struggle against Israel, see Sayigh 1997.

airfields, oil fields, and especially the natural obstacles of the Suez Canal and the large, sparsely populated Sinai desert, which provided strategic depth and lowered Israel's vulnerability). Accordingly, the pattern of recurrent Arab–Israeli wars has to do more with the state-to-nation issues, such as the persistent legitimacy problem of Israel in the Middle East, Arab and Israeli revisionism, and the absence of agreement on boundaries and on state-creation for the Palestinians.

Thus, because of the regional hostility toward Israel and the lack of regional legitimacy accorded its existence, or at least its boundaries, Israeli security fears have been very strong. Such fears led it to assume uncompromising positions in the Arab–Israeli conflict (most notably in the pre-1973 period), regarding both questions of territory and the right of return. In addition, they have led Israel to resort frequently to retaliation and also prevention (notably the 1956 war).

The 1967 war: a security dilemma war?

The state-to-nation imbalance exacerbated the security dilemma and thus led to an inadvertent resort to force. The 1967 war is the foremost example of an inadvertent "security dilemma" war in the Middle East.[104] The 1967 war, in which four regional states – Israel, Egypt, Jordan, and Syria – took part directly and a few others – Lebanon, Iraq, Saudi Arabia, and a non-state actor, the Palestinians – were involved indirectly, transformed the region as a whole and has had far-reaching repercussions for it, and beyond, to the present (M. Oren 2002). A brief account of the crisis which led to the war follows.

Israel's persistent insecurity was exacerbated when a radical Baath regime came to power in Syria in February 1966 and started agitating for a war to liberate Palestine. Israel's insecurity increased with the signing, with strong Soviet prompting, of the defense pact between Egypt and Syria on November 4, 1966 (Ovendale 1992, p. 193; Gerges 1994, p. 211). Moreover, Syria was sponsoring raids on Israeli territory (M. Oren 2002, pp. 42–46). The beginning of 1967 saw an increase in the intensity of the actions of Fatah (the Palestinian guerrilla movement) against Israel. This contributed to an escalation of hostilities along the Israeli–Syrian border and to Arab fear (agitated by the Soviets) of an imminent Israeli attack

[104] On the June war as an inadvertent war, see J. Stein 1991a and Miller 1994b. The most updated and comprehensive is M. Oren 2002. In his book (1969, p. 49), King Hussein of Jordan reiterated the belief that Nasser did not want a war. On Syria's unwillingness to go to war despite its bellicose behavior, see Rabinovich 1998, pp. 37–38.

on Syria. In order to deter such an attack, on May 14 Egyptian troops entered the Sinai, and in reaction Israel started to call up its reserves. The Israeli security dilemma increased dramatically as the country became besieged by concentrations of troops along its borders, especially those with Egypt, while UN troops, which had been serving as a separating force between the two armies, were removed.

The Israeli feeling of encirclement was intensified by the closure of the Tiran Straits on May 23 and the establishment of a hostile pan-Arab alliance, including Jordan, along most of Israel's borders at the end of the month.[105] Jordan, for its part, joined the alliance because of the state weakness and domestic political vulnerability of the regime; thus, it was bandwagoning out of fear.[106] Israel's sense of insecurity was heightened by extreme anti-Israeli statements by Arab leaders, most notably Nasser, calling, during the crisis, for the destruction of Israel.[107] Coming on top of hostile strategic actions at a time of crisis and especially following a long record of anti-Zionist revisionism, such rhetoric was very threatening for Israel and created a sense of imminent danger to its very existence. This sense of clear and present danger provided Israel with the political incentive to strike first, out of fear that if it did not, the other side might have done so.[108] Furthermore, there was a widespread feeling in Israel that, even if Nasser did not initiate an attack, the price of a continuing siege by the large Arab coalition surrounding the country would be unbearable to a small state with limited manpower that would have to maintain a very large force mobilized for an indefinite period. There was a consensus in Israel that Nasser, assisted by the armies of other Arab states, which were providing military reinforcements, was planning to exert pressure on a besieged Israel and to impose on it, at a minimum, a pullback to the 1947 partition boundaries as a stage toward destroying it completely.[109]

Thus, it seems that what led to the June war was essentially a process of action and reaction that led to escalation and eventual hostilities. Although Nasser probably miscalculated in believing that his moves

[105] On Israel's alarm that this alliance raises the danger of an Arab attack, see Bar Siman-Tov 1987, p. 121.
[106] J. Stein 1993, p. 66. On alternative sources of alliances, see Walt 1987, S. David 1991a and 1991b, and Schweller 1994.
[107] Citations in Gerges 1994, p. 214; J. Stein 1991a, p. 215; Ovendale 1992, p. 202; Yariv 1985, pp. 19–20.
[108] On the preemptive character of the Israeli strike in 1967, see Walzer 1977, pp. 80–84.
[109] Yariv 1985, pp. 20–21.

would not lead to an Israeli attack, the establishment of the pan-Arab pact boosted his confidence and encouraged him to escalate his threats against Israel. The initiation of war by Israel was a case of preemption, based on an overestimation of the probability of Egyptian attack (J. Stein 1991a, pp. 141–142). Indeed, when Nasser barred Israeli shipping from using the Tiran Straits, Israel became convinced that war was inevitable. Thus, after the failure of international diplomacy to open the straits, it felt compelled to resort to military means. At the same time, the emergence of the pan-Arab alliance sharpened Israel's security dilemma; it felt encircled and thus obliged (by June 5) to attack preemptively, before it was too late and the costs of war had become intolerable.

Thus, seemingly, the June war was a security dilemma war caused by Israel and Egypt reacting to each other's defensive moves. The combination of military moves by Egypt and other neighbors and statements calling for Israel's destruction created an intense insecurity, which compelled Israel to preempt. Especially important for such a defensive realist analysis is that Israel's insecurity was exacerbated by its situational vulnerability, thus pressuring Israel to move combat operations to the soil of the enemy as soon as hostilities started.

In the absence of a sharp state-to-nation imbalance, the kinds of crisis and escalation that took place in 1967, however, were unlikely to occur despite the conducive structural-situational elements. So how did the nationalist manifestations of this imbalance lead to the outbreak of the war? My answer is that it was through the interacting effects of the following five manifestations of the state-to-nation imbalance discussed above.

Illegitimate states: The surrounding Arab world's rejection of Israel's right to exist as the national homeland of the Jewish people was the key to the emergence of an intense Israeli insecurity. This illegitimacy was signaled not only by statements calling for the destruction of Israel, but also by a total Arab boycott and by sponsorship of Palestinian guerrilla operations. This created mutual expectations of an imminent and decisive "second round" of fighting to come after each war had ended (M. Oren 2002, pp. 8, 13; Benny Morris 2001, p. 261). Facing such a situation compelled Israel to adopt an offensive strategy of muscular retaliation, prevention (as was exercised in 1956 and again in the 1981 destruction of the Iraqi Osirak nuclear reactor), or preemption, aiming to attack first in times of crisis. These are all destabilizing strategies that increase the regional security dilemma. Still, the key source of Israel's security fears was derived from the awareness that its neighbors rejected its right to exist and would attack in order to destroy it whenever they got the opportunity. Such existential fears are not typical in the post-1945 international system and, at any rate, are a very extreme case of fear based on the fact that all the neighbors viewed Israel as illegitimate.[110] The anarchy of the international system and even the vulnerable geopolitical conditions are far from sufficient to explain the origins of Israel's security dilemma and its offensive behavior without taking into account its illegitimacy.

Pan-Arabism, which advocated both Arab unity and a fight against Israel and for Palestinian national rights, compelled Nasser, as an aspirant to Arab leadership, to show his commitment to the pan-Arab cause. Thus, he deployed his army in the Sinai in order to deter what appeared to the Arabs (at least partly under the influence of Soviet disinformation) as an imminent Israeli attack on Syria, which was sponsoring Palestinian attacks on the common enemy, Israel (M. Oren 2002, p. 45). Under pressures from other Arab states, notably Syria and Jordan, Nasser followed a much more militant policy against Israel in the May–June crisis than he initially wished, in order to demonstrate his commitment to the pan-Arab cause (Ayoob 1993, p. 49), notably, by expelling the UN force from the Sinai and by closing the Tiran Straits. Nasser's loss of control over aroused Arab public opinion both in Egypt and in the Arab world in general was a major factor influencing his escalatory policy (J. Stein 1991a; M. Oren 2002, p. 65). Nasser was severely constrained in his later moves by his concern that steps toward deescalation would lead to an allegation in the Arab world that he had deserted Syria and the Arab cause and yielded to Israeli pressure.[111] Thus, in some sense he lost control over the situation and continued the escalatory moves, culminating in the signing of a pact with Jordan on May 30, which was expanded to include Iraq in early June. Nasser became, to some extent, the victim of the pan-Arabism he had previously used for his own purposes. In this critical crisis, pan-Arabism constrained his freedom of maneuver and pushed him toward actions which led to war, against his intentions. As the leader of the Egyptian state, Nasser felt that, based on cost–benefit calculations, Egypt was not ready for war. He eventually had to

[110] Thus, weak African states, for example, persist due to external recognition of their "juridical statehood" and despite their empirical failure. See Jackson and Rosberg 1982.
[111] On earlier Jordanian and Saudi allegations about the pan-Arab credentials of Nasser which touched his "rawest nerves," see M. Oren 2002, pp. 36, 82–83.

pursue aggressive moves, however, due to pan-national incentives and pressures, and the related domestic implications, which generated an unintended escalation.

Nations without states: The irredentist Palestinian guerrillas, especially Fatah, conducted anti-Israeli sabotage operations in the mid-1960s in order to provoke an Israeli retaliation which would ignite an all-Arab offensive to destroy the Zionist entity. They succeeded in bringing about such a war in 1967,[112] although the outcome was completely different from their expectations.

Weak states hosted Palestinian guerrillas involuntarily. Lebanon and Jordan provided bases for Palestinians because of their state weakness and despite their unwillingness to get entangled in a war with Israel. This contributed to the escalation in the security situation.

Incongruence and irredentism: Syria's incongruence and revisionism played a crucial role in the escalation. Syria was a revisionist state, entertaining irredentist/historical "Greater Syria" claims vis-à-vis its neighbors – Lebanon, Jordan, and Israel. As noted, members of the minority Alawi sect, who dominated the governing Baath party, were resented by the majority Sunni public. The radical faction, which had attained power in February 1966, was particularly resented. To strengthen its hold on power, the internal quarrels were externalized in a militant policy against Israel, leading to the escalation which culminated in the 1967 war.

In sum, defensive realist factors, notably the security dilemma, offense/defense balance, and the related logic of inadvertent escalation (and also the multipolar structure of the Middle East) can account for the dynamics of the 1967 crisis. Such factors can also account for the dynamics of other crises in the region. Yet, these factors on their own can not explain the fundamental origins of this and other crises, the basic propensity toward war and crisis in the post-1945 Middle East, and why this problem has been especially severe in this region as compared to most other regions. It is the high extent of the state-to-nation imbalance in the region, especially the high external incongruence, that created the basic predisposition toward escalation to regional war; indeed, high extents of such external incongruence have created the conditions for war in the other major hot spots in the post-war international system (Taiwan, Korea, Vietnam, Kashmir, and other conflicts).

[112] M. Oren 2002, p. 1.

Offensive wars of power and profit

The two major motives for offensive/aggressive wars – territorial expansion and a quest for hegemony – have been salient in the Middle East. But only under the condition of such a high level of state-to-nation imbalance could they so frequently have resulted in hot wars.

Territorial profits: The regional illegitimacy of Israel and its boundaries produced a substantive territorial issue for the Arab–Israeli conflict, generating a desire for territorial expansion and profit expressed in the pan-Arab attack on Israel as soon as it was established in 1948 in what was, in the eyes of the Arabs, an illegitimate way. Illegitimacy of boundaries has also led to the more limited goal of the restoration of control over previously held territories (the 1969–1970 War of Attrition and the October 1973 war). Egypt (in 1969 and 1973) and Syria (in 1973) attacked Israel on these two occasions despite Israel's overall military superiority. What motivated the attacks was the Arabs' intense dissatisfaction with the territorial status quo following the occupation of their territories by Israel in 1967 and the lack of diplomatic progress to regain control over them. Thus, Israel's deterrence failed despite its military advantages, although the timing and the scope of the Arab offensives were influenced by balance-of-power considerations related to arms supply from the USSR and military strategies designed by the Arabs to bypass Israel's overall superiority (J. Stein 1985; Paul 1994).

Israeli dissatisfaction with the outcome of the 1948–1949 war and its boundaries contributed to the 1956 war, while Israeli unwillingness to make territorial concessions in the post-1967 era made the 1973 war more likely.

Separate from the Arab–Israeli disputes, the illegitimacy of Kuwait's independence in the eyes of successive Iraqi governments has been the underlying cause behind Iraq's threat of force against it in 1961 and of its occupation in 1990. It is quite safe to assume that Iraqi leaders might have been motivated first of all by profit considerations related to the quest to control the oil-rich territory of Kuwait which was too weak to deter Iraqi superior power. Yet, the historically grounded and ethnically based nationalist claims to Kuwait, and the latter's artificial creation by Western imperialism, provided Iraqi governments with domestic and regional legitimacy (on the mass rather than the elite level) to the resort to force.[113] Thus, Iraqi leaders could see such a move as an effective

[113] See Halliday 1991a, pp. 395–398, cited in Hinnebusch 2003, pp. 211–212.

means both to mobilize support for themselves at home and to achieve Iraqi leadership in the Arab world. In the absence of such legitimacy, it is much less likely that Iraq would have resorted to the use of force in an international system which sanctifies international boundaries and opposes territorial conquests.

Regional hegemony and balance of power: The other major proximate cause is related to the balance of power either in the purely offensive sense of aspirations for hegemony or more qualified offensive concerns for preventing deterioration in the balance of power.

In the Middle East, there is an intense mismatch between overall regional (especially military) capabilities, and status and legitimacy: Israel, as the superior military and the most economically advanced power, should supposedly be the regional leader, but in the eyes of its neighbors, because of its national identity, it lacks the legitimacy necessary to be an equal partner, let alone the regional leader (Ayoob 1995; Ben-Dor 1983, pp. 208–209).

The hegemonic battle in the region focused on a keen struggle for hegemony in the Arab world, intensified by the divisive/revisionist ideology of pan-Arabism. Even if pan-Arab ideology was not the major factor which motivated Egypt's Nasser and other aspirants for hegemony, and power considerations did play a much more significant role, pan-Arabism could serve as a useful legitimizing force for these aspirants and help them gain support in inter-Arab politics and in the public opinion of other Arab states in the struggle for Arab hegemony (Sela 1998). Indeed, "the dominant feature in the modern history of inter-Arab relations is the struggle for leadership in the name of Arab unity" (Vatikiotis 1976, cited in Ben-Dor 1983, p. 141).

The traditional protagonists in the struggle for Arab leadership and hegemony were Egypt, Saudi Arabia, and the Hashemites in Iraq and Jordan. One serious rivalry was between Egypt and Iraq (Sela 1998, p. 15), for example, regarding the establishment of the Baghdad Pact in the mid-1950s (Podeh 1995). Later, the post-Hashemite regime in Iraq continued to play a significant role, while Jordan's importance has declined and Syria's has increased (Ben-Dor 1983, p. 144). Thus, the issue of regional leadership has been a contested one, and no contender has achieved widespread regional acceptance for an extended time period, let alone full-blown hegemony (Podeh 1995, ch. 1). This is true even of Egypt's Nasser, who came the closest to achieving the status of hegemon (Sela 1998, pp. 17–19).

The recurrent pattern of regional competition for hegemony was between revisionist and status quo powers (Sela 1998, pp. 34, 49). From the 1920s to the 1940s the struggle was between the revisionist Hashemite rulers of Iraq and Transjordan and a status quo coalition of the Saudis and the nationalist movements in Syria, Lebanon, and Palestine, led since the mid-1940s by Egypt (Sela 1998, p. 39). In the 1950s and 1960s, the main battle took place between the revisionist/revolutionary camp led by Egypt's Nasser (including Syria and post-1958 Iraq) and the status quo conservative regimes (Saudi Arabia, Jordan, and Morocco), notably regarding the Yemen war. Yet, as can be expected among regimes sharing a divisive ideology such as pan-Arabism, there was also an intense rivalry among the radical states themselves while Syria, and especially Iraq, were resisting Nasser's attempt to claim hegemony (Sela 1998, pp. 48–49; Hinnebusch 2003, pp. 159–163).

The fight against Israel did not moderate this leadership struggle. The anti-Israeli front was far from being a unifying force in the Arab world but, rather, was divisive, creating controversies and disputes (Ben-Dor 1983, p. 145; Sela 1998, pp. 37–41). At the same time, inter-Arab rivalries over power and hegemony (strengthened by pan-Arabism) aggravated and reinforced the Arab inclination to use force against Israel. Any fight with Israel was used by Arab states to buttress the position of their state in the Arab world (Sela 1998, pp. 37–40). Examples include the 1948 invasion of Palestine, the 1967 crisis, the October 1973 war, and the 1991 Gulf War. Another example is the armed infiltrations into Israel from Egypt, Syria, and Jordan preceding the 1956 and 1967 wars. Indeed, this was part of the sponsorship of Palestinian groups by many Arab regimes to further their particularistic interests among the divided Palestinians (Gause 1992, p. 449) and thus also in the Arab world at large, by showing their pan-Arab credentials. Similar widespread intervention by numerous Arab states (and Israel and Iran) in an incoherent society took place in Lebanon, exacerbating the domestic conflict there as well as the clash with Israel, resulting in the 1982 war.

At the same time, Israeli power considerations, either in a preventive fashion or in a hegemonic manner, led to the 1956 and 1982 wars respectively. The objective of the 1956 Sinai war was to prevent deterioration in the balance of power against Israel under the expectation that a "second round" of an Arab–Israeli war was inevitable so long as Israel suffered from illegitimacy in the region on nationalist grounds. Thus, Israel preferred to attack in fall 1956 before Cairo became stronger by

Table 4.3 *Revisionist-offensive-profit wars in the Middle East*

	Objectives of offensive action	
	Control over resources (territory)	Power
Wide-ranging (major change in status quo)	**Expansion** 1948 by the Arabs; Iraq invasion of Iran 1980 and of Kuwait 1990	**Hegemony** Israel's 1982 Lebanon war
↑ **Scope of Objectives** ↓		
Limited (preservation of or return to status quo ante)	**Restoration** Egypt 1969–70 and 1973; Syria 1973	**Prevention** Israel's 1956 Sinai war

absorbing the arms acquired from the Soviet bloc a year earlier.[114] The incentive for the timing of the attack increased because Israel had a unique opportunity at that time for an alliance with two Western powers (France and Britain) against Egypt.

The Israeli "grand design" for the 1982 invasion of Lebanon was to address some of the key state-to-nation problems in the region by imposing the Israeli nationalist agenda and thus to create a new regional order under Israeli military hegemony. The key components of such a new order were supposed to include the control over the West Bank by a "Greater Israel"; a Palestinian state on the East Bank instead of the nationally "artificial" Hashemite Kingdom of Jordan; and a pro-Israeli Maronite-led state in a Lebanon free of the Syrian presence.[115]

Table 4.3 illustrates the main types of wars of profit with Middle Eastern examples.

Illegitimacy, domestic vulnerability of regimes, and diversionary wars

The state-to-nation imbalance produces legitimacy deficits and challenges for stability of states and regimes. Under such conditions, rulers

[114] On the 1956 war as a preventive war, see J. Levy and Gochal 2001.
[115] Schiff and Yaari 1984, pp. 42–44; see also Yaniv 1987.

of stronger states have incentives to resort to diversionary wars. The weaker states tend to become arenas of civil wars and targets of intervention by their neighbors. A number of studies have found strong linkages between domestic instability and the initiation of regional wars in the Middle East. Because of the combination of the low legitimacy of Arab regimes and states and the illegitimacy of Israel in the eyes of Arab masses and their support of the Palestinian cause as the leading Pan-Arab issue, fighting against Israel could be used by Arab rulers to buttress the position of their regimes internally. Maoz (1995, p. 176) highlights the strong linkage between domestic and international instability in the Middle East. He found that, in the case of Egypt and Syria, the intensity of conflict initiated toward Israel seems to be affected by the level of violence within their own societies. At the same time, the greater the domestic stability in Egypt (under a liberalizing regime) or Syria (under an authoritarian rule), the lower the level of Arab–Israeli conflict in the late 1970s and 1980s (ibid., pp. 187–189). Bar Siman-Tov (1983, p. 171) similarly found that, in the 1960s, Syrian ruling elites used the Syrian–Israeli and Arab–Israeli conflicts to divert attention away from the highly unstable internal situation and domestic conflicts. Lawson (1996) also argues that the diversionary theory, extended by political-economic motives, best explains Syria's participation in wars. Janice Stein (1993, pp. 62–66) highlights the crucial impact of domestic political vulnerability on decisions to resort to force in the Middle East in the post-World War II era. Tessler and Grobschmidt (1995, pp. 144–145) point out that Arab leaders have sometimes deliberately involved themselves in regional conflicts, notably the Arab–Israeli dispute, in an attempt to enhance their legitimacy and deflect attention away from domestic grievances (see also Shlaim 1995).

In weak states, regimes are very much constrained from endorsing dramatic initiatives and changes by the extent to which powerful groups in the society oppose such moves. In the case of making peace with Israel, Arab regimes faced great domestic difficulties because of opposition from the military (Krause 1996, 344), from many intellectuals and professional groups, and from large segments of public opinion (Hudson 1977, 1995). Such intransigence made it, in turn, more difficult for Israel to make concessions.

At the same time, authoritarian Arab elites could manipulate pan-Arab ideology and the struggle against Israel (and the West) to justify their opposition to the opening of their political systems by diverting the attention of the public to these ideological and nationalist battles rather than addressing domestic problems. They could also argue that their states could not afford democracy so long as the nationalist enemies were at the gate threatening their most cherished national values, and thus that they must focus first on the nationalist struggle. As a result, the Middle East is not only more war-prone than most other regions, but it is home to many fewer democracies, and it is lagging behind, even while other regions made progress in all indicators of freedom, especially in the post-Cold War era.[116]

Nation-building by Israel, as noted, attempted to create a cohesive Israeli/Jewish nation out of the diverse immigrant Jewish groups. This nation-building, especially in the 1950s, produced some hard-line positions in Israel's security policy, notably manifested in the military actions of the early 1950s against neighboring Arab states, culminating in the 1956 Sinai campaign. Although these actions were in retaliation for transborder terrorist/guerrilla infiltrations by Arab/Palestinian *fedayeen*, partly supported by the Arab states, they were occasionally overreactions influenced also by domestic politics – solidifying support for the ruling party – and ideological considerations related to nation-building in Israel.[117]

Explaining change over time: The decline in war frequency in the post-1973 era due to the growing state coherence/strength at the expense of pan-Arabism

Since 1973, there has been only a single interstate Arab–Israeli war: the Lebanon war of 1982, although Iraqi Scud missiles were fired at Israel during the 1991 Gulf War. Most of the violence shifted from high-intensity to low-intensity conflict: the two intifadas, numerous terrorist actions inside Israel including suicide bombers, and guerrilla-type skirmishes in southern Lebanon, the West Bank, and the Gaza Strip, and

[116] For an extended discussion, see Rubin 2002. The references to the much more limited democratization in the Middle East as compared to other regions are on p. 23. On the failure of liberalization – both political and economic – to take hold and overcome underlying conflicts and to produce peace in the Middle East since the 1990s, see Hinnebusch 2003, pp. 229–231.

[117] See Benny Morris 1996. See also Miller 1981 which is based, among other sources, on the diaries of Moshe Sharett (1978) – the Israeli foreign minister, and briefly also prime minister, in the early 1950s.

Israeli attempts to suppress them. Thus, it seems that since 1973 the Arab–Israeli conflict was transformed from an interstate conflict to a Palestinian–Israeli ethnic conflict.[118]

Are the causal factors of my theoretical framework able to account for the decline in the frequency of hot wars in the Arab–Israeli conflict in the post-1973 period? Indeed, there has been a decline in some of the sources of the state-to-nation imbalance in the region: pan-Arabism has become weaker, while individual Arab states have become stronger and to some extent more coherent; thus, Arab revisionism has declined. At the same time, some other sources of the state-to-nation imbalance are still quite powerful, and the danger of hot war has therefore not disappeared from the region. Indeed, as noted, a major armed clash erupted in summer 2006 between Israel and Hezbollah. This asymmetric clash between a state and a guerrilla/terror organization caused hundreds of military and civilian casualties and very heavy material damage in both Lebanon and Israel. Still, it did not escalate to a full-blown interstate war between Israel and Lebanon or any other Arab/Muslim state, even though Syria and Iran support Hezbollah politically, financially, and militarily.

I first address the decline in the major nationalist manifestation of revisionism in the region and then address a key cause – the strengthening of the individual Arab state at the expense of pan-Arabism, although there are limitations to these changes.

Revisionism

As noted, some important elements of Arab revisionism shifted from a demand for the elimination of Israel to a restoration of Arab control over the occupied territories, that is, a shift from the issue of Israel's legitimacy to the question of boundaries (Sela 1998, pp. 27–28). Yet, there are still very powerful forces in the Arab world and among the Palestinians that delegitimize Israeli existence.

In the aftermath of the 1967 defeat, there has been a growing split in the Arab world (and among the Palestinians) between the moderate camp, focused on restoring the occupied territories, and the rejectionist front, which challenged Israel's right to exist as a Jewish state

[118] For documentation and analysis of this argument, see Ben-Yehuda and Sandler 2002. I argue that the Arab–Israeli conflict has been since its outset an ethnonational/state-to-nation conflict, including both interstate (at least since the 1930s) and communal dimensions (since the late nineteenth century; see Benny Morris 2001).

(Ben-Dor 1983, p. 199; Harkabi 1977; Ajami cited in Ben-Dor 1983, p. 190, n. 15). The former included both Egypt and Jordan, which accepted Security Council Resolution 242 in 1967, implicitly recognizing Israel's right to exist. Syria joined them by accepting Resolution 338 following the Yom Kippur War in 1974. The peace process made progress in the aftermath of the 1973 war, culminating in the 1978 Camp David accords and the 1979 Egyptian–Israeli peace treaty. Yet without resolution of the Palestinian demand for self-determination and the right of return of refugees, and with Israel's permanent borders still undecided, the remaining legitimacy issues – even with the moderates – still require external involvement and mediation, which can at best have reached only cold peace. This is to say, such mediation could have striven only for conflict reduction rather than for conflict resolution.

The questionable/ambiguous nature of the moderation in the revisionist goals of the Arabs was manifested in the June 1974 Cairo "ten-point program" of the National Council of the PLO to establish a "Palestinian Authority" on territories to be evacuated by Israel. On one hand, it represented a major reduction in the revisionist objectives – from an unconditional demand for Arab control over all of Israel's territory to a claim for Palestinian control only over the territories occupied in 1967. In this sense, it was part of the more general reduction in revisionism in the Arab world through a transition from revisionist/radical pan-Arabism to a more pragmatic/moderate state nationalism (Ben-Dor 1983, pp. 198–203). This was a necessary condition for a transition from a "paradigmatic" to a "normal" conflict (Sela 1998, pp. 27–30), in which individual Arab states after 1967 focused on gaining back their occupied territories from Israel rather than on a pan-Arab struggle on behalf of the Palestinian cause. This shift culminated in the peace process between Egypt and Israel in the late 1970s. In the 1980s, the focus seemed to shift to the Iran–Iraq war and the resultant splits in the Arab world, such as Syria's alliance with Iran versus the support for Iraq of most Arab states.

This reduction in revisionism had moderating effects on the Arab–Israeli conflict. The Arab defeat in 1967 contributed significantly to the weakening of pan-Arabism because this revisionist ideology was at least partly responsible for the Arabs' resort to the belligerent behavior that led to the war. The outcome of the war was viewed, thus, as a defeat of pan-Arabism (Ajami 1981). More specifically, the policy of the Egyptian government to weaken the ties of its citizens to pan-Arabism led to "an increasing passiveness toward" Arab causes in general and toward the

Palestinian cause in particular.[119] The Palestinians themselves, led by the PLO, moved in the aftermath of the 1982 Lebanon war toward a diplomatic avenue, culminating in the 1988 decision to accept the two-state solution of a Palestinian state in the West Bank and the Gaza Strip alongside Israel (Karsh 1997, 287; Sela 1998).

On the other hand, at least until the 1993–1995 Oslo Accords, it was not completely clear to the Israelis that the Palestinians, even with the 1974 plan, had deserted the objective of destroying Israel. Thus, the term "Palestinian Authority" was apparently chosen in 1974 by the PLO in order to evade calling it a state, which might have signified a more final arrangement (Harkabi 1977, pp. 37–39). There were various statements indicating that the Palestinians still aimed to annihilate the Zionist presence in Palestine (Ben-Dor 1983, p. 204). Indeed, the Palestinian National Charter still called for Israel's elimination, and it was debatable whether this had been fully abandoned even following the Oslo Accords. A major outstanding issue – in addition to the still intense disputes over territories, final boundaries, settlements, the scope of the sovereignty and authorities, and the size of the future Palestinian state – is the right of return of the 1948 Palestinian refugees. In the domain of symbols, sentiments, and attitudes, the Palestinians see and mark Israel's Independence Day – the most important national holiday for Israel – as Al Nakbeh or the Disaster, the defeat and dispossession of the Palestinian Arabs in 1948. Commemorations are held by Palestinians both in the occupied territories and inside Israel. While the declaration of independence is celebrated in Israel, for the Palestinians, especially those who became refugees, it is a traumatic and catastrophic event.

On the whole, revisionist forces are still powerful in the Middle East. Important manifestations have occurred in the Gulf with the two Gulf wars in the 1980s and early 1990s. Some researchers claim that pan-Arabism is still powerful in the Arab world at large.[120] The main recent manifestations of revisionism include the following elements:

a. Before the US occupation of Iraq in April 2003, Saddam Hussein's expansionist aspiration for hegemony and irredentism was expressed by his offensive against Iran and his occupation of Kuwait. He is also presumed to have attempted to accumulate nonconventional weapons of mass destruction, at least until the 1991 Gulf War.

[119] See Brynen 1991, 613.
[120] See, for example, Nafaa 1987. For more evidence, see Telhami 2002.

b. The Iranian Revolution and the threat it, as a divisive ideology, poses to many regimes in the Arab world and Turkey (Gause 1992). It opposes the Israeli–Palestinian peace process and supports guerrilla and terrorist attacks against Israel, especially from Lebanon. Iran strongly opposes US hegemony in the region; it is trying to become a regional superpower, seeking to fill the void left by the collapse of Arab nationalism and by the absence of any one dominant state.[121] For that purpose, Iran uses harsh anti-Israeli rhetoric, including denial of the Holocaust and calling for Israel to be wiped off the map, presumably to mobilize transborder pan-Islamic support in the region, somewhat similar to what Arab nationalists such as Nasser and Saddam Hussein have done in the heyday of pan-Arabism. Hegemonic aspirations, as well as security fears in an unstable region, might explain Iran's alleged efforts to develop nuclear capability.
c. The radicalization of pan-Islamic forces: the emergence of non-state radical Islamic forces that challenge pro-Western regimes in the Middle East and the US hegemony that protects them. Some of these organizations resort to asymmetric warfare, most notably the anti-American Al Qaeda transborder network, which committed the 9/11 attacks on New York and the Pentagon. Al Qaeda challenges the legitimacy of the post-World War I division of the Arab-Islamic world into states which was sponsored by the infidel – the Western imperial powers. Alleging that the division of the Muslims among these states is artificial, the ultimate objective is to unify the *umma* (the whole community of the Muslim faithful) into a single political entity, a resurrection of the medieval Islamic caliphate. In other words, they see a state-to-nation imbalance in the region based on the external incongruence of all the states due to their Islamic majorities; the one state that does not enjoy a Muslim majority – Israel – belonged to the Muslims for over a thousand years, and then was taken over by force by the infidel – the Jews and their Christian "crusader" sponsors. Bin Laden and his cohorts also challenge the legitimacy of numerous oppressive regimes in the Islamic world, especially the pro-American ones such as Saudi Arabia, Egypt, and Pakistan. Thus Al Qaeda can mobilize support in these states based not only on their affiliation with the United States but also on their denial of political freedom and economic opportunities to their people.

[121] *New York Times*, Feb. 5, 2006.

The Islamic militants believe that, if they succeed in bringing about US disengagement from the Middle East, these regimes will collapse because they do not enjoy real popular support, but rely mainly on US assistance. Therefore, the Islamists desire to cause as many American casualties as possible, which will be associated with US policies and involvement in the Middle East and will thus bring about domestic pressures in the United States for a departure from the region. Although the hard core of these militants is only a small minority in the Islamic world, they are a highly committed group which can take advantage of modern technology and communications in order to commit their terrorist actions and to cause havoc. Since they are willing to commit suicide, they are nondeterrable. Moreover, because of the illegitimacy of some pro-Western regimes and the broad-based resentment of US policies in the region (such as US support for these regimes and for Israel), the radicals enjoy a level of public support for some of their anti-Western goals, even if not in their means of mass destruction.

d. Israeli revisionism (in relation to the internationally sanctioned 1949 boundaries), marked since 1967, especially during the 1980s, by expansionist Israeli policy in the occupied territories, notably by building settlements. This revisionism causes especially acute problems for compromise between Israel and its neighbors, because it is based not only on pragmatic security considerations, but also on the much more indivisible historical and ethnic elements of the state-to-nation imbalance. Israeli expansionism was also expressed in the 1982 war. The Arab resentment of what they see as the Israeli occupation of Arab national territories could, in turn, stimulate a hot war as it did in the 1969–1970 War of Attrition, the 1973 war, and the low-intensity conflict of the Palestinian intifadas of the past two decades.

Such expansionist policies have been supported by a powerful right-wing coalition of nationalists and religious groups. At the same time, the left-of-center sectors of Israeli society have moderated their position toward the Arab–Israeli conflict due to the lessons of the limits to Israeli military power arising from the 1982 Lebanon war and the guerrilla war in its aftermath, the intifada, and the perceived indications of moderation in the PLO. Still, until the early 1990s, there was almost a consensus among the major parties against the establishment of a Palestinian state, against negotiations with the PLO, and against a withdrawal to pre-1967 borders. This consensus was broken by the Oslo Accords and replaced by a de facto acceptance of the emergence of an independent Palestinian entity in the West Bank and Gaza, even though its future authorities, its final boundaries, and the status of the Jewish settlements are still disputed between Israel and the Palestinian Authority and among Israelis. Following the eruption of the second intifada in fall 2000, large segments of the Israeli public are willing to entertain further concessions in the framework of a final-status peace agreement with the Palestinians or as a unilateral disengagement from the territories like the 2005 withdrawal from Gaza. The unilateral approach – comprising disengagements and the construction of a separation fence between the West Bank and Israel – has become especially popular recently in Israel. This is because of two developments. On the one hand, there is a widespread feeling that there is no credible partner on the other side who is willing and able to make peace. This feeling has been reinforced by the victory of Hamas in the January 2006 Palestinian elections. On the other hand, the rising costs of the occupation due to the Palestinian resistance discredits the settlers and their supporters. This is reinforced by the demographic fear that the Jews will lose their ethnodemographic majority if Israel continues to control the occupied territories with their overwhelming Palestinian majority. The combined effect of these developments leads me to expect conflict management rather than resolution, a long interim agreement rather than a peace accord, and a cold peace, if not a frozen one, rather than warm peace.

e. A persistent absence of full legitimacy of Israel as an equal member in the Middle East. There is still a considerable extent of rejection of Israel's legitimacy partly because of pan-Arab solidarity with the Palestinians so long as their right to self-determination is denied,[122] partly in response to Israel's intransigence and territorial aspirations, and partly due to a persistence in some quarters of the Arab world in the rejection of the moral right of a Jewish state to exist in the midst of the Arab world, even if there is an acceptance of the fact of its existence. This is one of the elements of the cold peace in the Middle East, especially in Egypt–Israel relations.

All these elements make international engagement, notably US leadership of the Arab–Israeli peace process and the containment of the radical/revisionist elements in Iraq and Iran, still crucial for the

[122] For evidence, see Telhami 2002.

achievement of peace and for war prevention despite the overall decline of revisionism.

Growing state-to-nation balance: rising state strength and decline in pan-Arabism since the 1970s

A key cause of the relative decline in revisionism is arguably the growing strength of individual Arab states, partly at the expense of loyalty to the Arab nation in recent decades. This leads to a greater state-to-nation balance in the region. Some observers argue that there has been a process of gradually growing legitimacy and strengthening of Arab states and rulers since the 1970s (see Ben-Dor 1983, pp. 150–176; Sela 1998, pp. 12–13), parallel to the decline in pan-Arabism.[123] Schemes for Arab unity were replaced by inter-Arab cooperation on a state-to-state basis. The strengthening was in an external sense – growing noninterference in domestic affairs[124] and respect for sovereignty and boundaries by the other Arab states – as well as in an internal sense – growing identification of populations with their state and its boundaries. Indeed, the greater degree to which Middle Eastern states can control their societies (measured by the ability to extract and control social resources – manpower and money), due to oil revenues and the growth of bureaucratic structures, increases state capacity to resist military intervention and domestic subversion from the outside (Gause 1992, pp. 457–459).

State-building has been achieved through material incentives, external threats, and a manipulation of a variety of symbols to create state-national identity (Barnett 1995, 497–498).[125] The outcome is that populations have greater loyalty to the state, citizens increasingly have a state-based identity, and Arab leaders have fewer incentives to appeal to pan-Arabism to enhance their legitimacy (ibid., 499).[126] Increased state capacity since the 1970s oil boom has helped stabilize regimes in the Arab world, making them less susceptible to pressures based on

[123] See Ajami 1978/9; 1981; 1982; Ben-Dor 1983, ch. 4; Salame 1988; Luciani 1990; Noble 1991, p. 51; R. Owen 1992; Gause 1992, pp. 453–454, 456–462; Barnett 1995; 1998; Sela 1998. See the brief summary and many citations in Pervin 1997, pp. 278–279.

[124] Noble 1991 and Dessouki 1991.

[125] See also Mufti 1996. Analyzing state consolidation in Iraq and Syria since 1970, Mufti traces the expansion of state institutional and mobilizational capacity, the growth in fiscal stability, and the successful repression of political opposition in both Syria and Iraq. Growing state strength brought about a decline in pan-Arabism, manifested in a reduction in attempts at Arab unity. Mufti cites also other studies on p. 10, n. 20.

[126] Sadowski (2002) argues that there is not only successful state-building but also growing state-to-nation congruence in Syria, based on the schools, courts, and universal military conscription.

transnational ideological challenges originating from external sources (Gause 1992, p. 461; Hinnebusch 2003, p. 67). State authority and symbols of power have been internalized through widespread coercion and socialization (Sela 1998, p. 13). Although radical Islam has been on the rise, it does not have a common supranational institutional or spiritual authority.[127]

Some limitations to the growing state-to-nation balance

There has not necessarily been, however, growing legitimacy of specific regimes, and there are still many subnational problems in Syria, Iraq, Jordan, and Lebanon resulting from the high internal incongruence in these states. The Islamic external incongruence in the region generates Islamic revolutionary challenges in Saudi Arabia, Egypt, Jordan, and other Islamic states. Especially in Syria and Iraq (notably under Saddam Hussein), the element of coercion in bringing about civic loyalty to the state is still crucial, and this indicates the limits to the supposed emergence of a state-to-nation balance based on territorial/civic nationalism. On a comparative scale, many of the Arab states, with the notable exception of Egypt, might still be relatively weak or incoherent even if they have been considerably strengthened in the past decades.[128]

The Kuwait crisis raised again on the Arab agenda the issue of the permeability of the Arab state. Saddam Hussein enjoyed considerable success in his attempt at transnational political mobilization, although there were important limits to such mobilization, which was on a smaller scale than during Nasser's era. Hence the evidence with regard to permeability is mixed. Although in the past decades the Arab state has become stronger, it is too early to suggest that there has been an end to permeability and a resultant consolidation of the Arab state system along the lines of the post-Westphalia European system (Hinnebusch 2003, p. 72). There are still agenda-shaping common, transnational (or more precisely, transborder or trans-state) issues in the Arab world, most notably the Palestinian issue.[129] This is reinforced by the new free

[127] Sela 1998, p. 13, and the sources he cites.

[128] See Hinnebusch's comprehensive and updated survey on the limitations to state- and nation-building in various Arab states (2003). See also Kedourie (1987) who claims that the Arab state is still weak; Migdal (1988) argues that Egypt and Syria were weak by the late 1980s; for a similar view, see Ayoob 1995.

[129] See, for instance, the findings of a study commissioned by Shibley Telhami in five Arab states. In each country, about 60 percent of the public reported that the Palestinian issue "is the single most important issue" to them personally; about 85 percent of people in the five states ranked the Palestinian issue among the top three issues. See Telhami 2001.

transborder media, such as Al Jazeera, which have been highlighting the Palestinian issue especially during the recent intifada. Islam also has a strong appeal and Islamic regimes could rise to power. Indeed, Islamic parties have done very well in recent elections in Iraq, Palestine, Iran, Egypt, and Lebanon (Hezbollah). "Any of these factors could lead to a new round of transnational political warfare and renewed state permeability in the Arab system" (Noble 1991, pp. 91–92). Moreover, there are still major problems of national (external and internal) incongruence in quite a number of Middle Eastern states. These states include Lebanon, Syria, Jordan, and Iraq – especially in the post-Saddam era. They all face the destabilizing effects of transborder ties (Shiites in Iraq, Lebanon, and Iran; Palestinians in Jordan, Lebanon, the West Bank, and the Gaza Strip; Kurds in Iraq, Syria, Iran, and Turkey; Islamists in all countries) and the potentially destabilizing effects of democratization under these state-to-nation imbalances.

Conclusions

The high extent of the state-to-nation imbalance in the Middle East causes the high war proneness of the region. The Middle East shares with other Third World regions state weakness and strong subnational forces, or what I call internal incongruence. The uniqueness of the region is, however, the extent of external incongruence, which strengthens the power of the pan-national and transborder forces and revisionist states and movements. Power and security considerations affect the timing and context of the occurrence of specific wars and their conduct, but do not explain the basic tendency of the region to go to war. Moreover, regional wars erupted against the conventional logic of the regional balance of power: Israeli military advantage (superb conventional capability and nuclear deterrence) deterred Arab revisionist plans, although by itself Israel's military power could not deter the Arab resort to force if there was sufficient motivation such as in the 1969–1970 War of Attrition, the 1973 war, and the two intifadas. Wars also erupted against the will of the global powers (see chapter 5). Notably, in 1956 and 1967, as well as in 1973, Egypt made crucial decisions without bothering first to inform its patron, the USSR.

The high level of the state-to-nation imbalance in the Arab–Israeli sector accounts for the strength of revisionist Zionism and of anti-Zionist revisionism in the Arab world and as a result also for the concentration of wars in this sector. In the past two decades, the focus of the revisionist forces partly moved from the Arab–Israeli core of the Middle East to the Gulf. Indeed, interstate Arab–Israeli wars became less frequent while wars erupted in the Gulf. A major cause for the decline in Arab–Israeli wars is related to the decay of pan-Arabism and the related growing strength of the particular Arab state, which is much more able to resist radical revisionist and domestic pressures to go to war against Israel. Exemplifying this, the Arab members of the anti-Iraqi coalition did not defect when Saddam fired missiles at Israel. Arab states also did not join the Palestinians in their struggles against Israel in Lebanon in 1982 and in the two intifadas in the late 1980s and in 2000–2004.

However, despite the decline in Arab revisionism and the growing state strength, which were helpful in bringing about a decline in hot wars, there is still a high degree of state-to-nation imbalance, not only regarding boundaries, but also in relation to the questions of the establishment of a Palestinian state and the legitimacy of Israel as a Jewish state in the region. Due to the transborder ethnic affinity between the Palestinians and the Arab world, violence can potentially spread beyond borders. It can especially involve the country with the highest extent of transborder incongruence with the territories: Jordan, with its large Palestinian community.[130]

It was mainly the emergence of US hegemony in the post-Cold War and post-Gulf War era, discussed in the next chapter, that made possible a move beyond merely war avoidance to an active regional peace process. This process has been, however, only a cold one, precisely due to the remaining unresolved state-to-nation questions. The lack of resolution of these issues, moreover, delayed the emergence of democracy in the region. Authoritarian elites found a seeming substitute for democracy as a legitimacy-enhancing mechanism. They could enhance their domestic and regional legitimacy by appealing to nationalism and ethnicity instead of opening their political system to allow the representation of competing views and interests.

Post-2003 Iraq and its effects

What are going to be the effects of the US occupation of Iraq in 2003 on Middle East stability? The jury is still out in light of the ongoing struggle to stabilize Iraq. The two types of challenges to the status quo addressed here – nationalist revisionism and state incoherence – might, however, provide a useful guide. Pan-Arabist revisionism suffered a major blow

[130] On the challenges facing nation-building in Jordan, see Frisch 2002b.

with the fall of one of the leading advocates of an aggressive Arab and Greater Iraq nationalism. The devastating defeat of Iraq's army showed the great weakness of such a revisionist state as well as the lack of broad-based public support for this oppressive nationalist regime. The overall effect might be to discredit radical Arab nationalism, and thus to enhance Middle East stability, at least in the short run. Yet, the fundamental problems of Iraq's external incongruence with all its neighbors remain in place, and thus the potential for instability and irredentist conflict is considerable. Under the regional state-to-nation imbalance in the Middle East, each of the key communal groups has transborder ties which might be destabilizing and pose a threat to the other groups and to the region. For example, a potential Shiite Islamic alliance among Iranians, Iraqis, and Lebanese (Hezbollah) might frighten the Sunnis in Iraq and the neighboring Arab states with a Sunni majority such as Jordan and Saudi Arabia. Thus, Jordan's King Abdullah said that he was worried by the prospect of Iraq's Shiite-led government allying with Iran, Syria, and Hezbollah to form a Shiite crescent threatening regional stability. The king's statement generated an outraged Shiite response in Iraq (Rubin 2006). In early April 2006, President Mubarak of Egypt raised doubts regarding the Shiites' loyalty to their respective Arab states because of their alleged greater allegiance to Iran.[131] Saudi Arabia might be especially concerned because its Shiite minority, which although small (about 10 percent of the population) is both underprivileged and located in a vital oil-rich area of the kingdom. At the same time, the Iraqi Shiites are aware that the Sunni violent campaign against them is supported by Syria and Saudi Arabia (Rubin 2006).

The persistent problem of Iraq's internal incongruence, for its part, poses challenges to its territorial integrity, with potential implications for regional stability. The internal incongruence and the lack of a coherent Iraqi nation produce divisions among the Shiites, the Sunnis, and the Kurds about the governance of Iraq. These challenges are further aggravated by the weakening of state strength following the US invasion and the collapse of Saddam Hussein's regime, which held the country together with an iron fist. Law and order are challenged by the ongoing insurgency against the United States and its Iraqi allies. The lawlessness has negative implications for the revival of economic activity and the functioning of the infrastructure (electricity, water, etc.). Although the United States and its allies are trying to establish order, they face some

[131] Interview on Al-Arabiya satellite television, April 8, 2006.

major problems. There is a nationalist and Islamist resistance supported by militants from other Arab states. The struggle against the United States and its allies provides a magnet for jihadists from across the region, who at a later stage may destabilize their own countries, as did the "Afghan Arabs," the veterans of the war against the Soviets in Afghanistan in the 1980s.

The "shadow of the future" (Oye 1986) for the United States as a security provider is limited, due to the widespread expectation that it will eventually withdraw from Iraq. Thus, under a weak state, the security dilemma among groups is high, which encourages the resort to violence.

While democratization, encouraged by the United States in the post-9/11 Middle East (see chapter 5), provides mechanisms for conflict regulation among competing interests, it may aggravate conflicts under a state-to-nation imbalance (see also chapters 8 and 9). Minority groups fear dominance by the majority group. This is especially severe in Iraq because the minority Sunnis, who had been Iraq's rulers since its independence, fear being dominated by the majority group, the Shiites, who were the underprivileged until 2003. Under a state-to-nation imbalance, the mechanism of federalism might also be problematic. The Sunni region is the poorest in oil; thus the Sunnis would be the losers in a federalist arrangement, and would become a dissatisfied revisionist force. Federalism under these conditions also poses the problem of secession. This especially applies to the long-time aspiration of the Kurds for self-rule, which is opposed by other groups in Iraq as well as by those neighbors with large Kurdish communities, notably Turkey, Iran, and Syria. There is also a fear that the Shiites, with the oil resources in their southern region, might have their own semi-independent entity with close relations with Shia Iran and potentially destabilizing implications for neighboring states.

Yet, if the democratization succeeds, potentially through federalism and autonomy for each group, and a government that is more representative and tolerant than that of Saddam Hussein emerges in Iraq, it might produce a more coherent state, even if a federal one, and it might serve as a positive model of democratization for the other Arab states. Indeed, there were most recently some positive developments toward democratization in a number of Arab states.[132] Yet, under a regional

[132] See *Economist*, March 5–11, 2005, pp. 24–26. For an analysis, see Bronson 2005, 107–111. But for the recent slowdown in the drive for democracy in the Arab world, see *New York Times*, April 10, 2006, 1.

Table 4.4 *The Middle East: the effects of the state-to-nation imbalance on regional security problems*

Dimensions of s/n imbalance	Security problems
Weakness of civic nationalism	Ethnic fragmentation leads to ethnic conflict and extremism; incoherent states
Transborder intervention in domestic affairs	Egypt in Yemen in the 1960s; Islamic Iran and its Shiite allies in Iraq and Lebanon
Even an immigrant society is based on ethnic nationalism	Protracted conflict between Zionist revisionism and Arab/Palestinian nationalism
Challenges of internal incoherence	
Nations without states	– The Kurds (insurgencies against Iraq, Turkey, Iran) – The Palestinians (guerrillas, terrorism)
States without nations	– Lebanon (protracted civil war); Iraq; Some of the Gulf states (unrest in Oman, sectarian tensions in Bahrain)[1]
Stateless refugees	– The Palestinian refugees (destabilizing Lebanon, Jordan, and the occupied territories)
Weak/failed states	– Lebanon, Jordan, Sudan, Yemen, post-2003 Iraq (civil wars, insurgencies); Palestinian Authority
External incongruence: revisionist challenges	
Majority–majority	
Illegitimate states	Security challenges to Kuwait, Lebanon, Jordan, Israel
Pan-national unifiers ("too many states")	Radicalizing effects of pan-Arabism: Nasser, Saddam; pan-Islamists like Al Qaeda
Majority–minority	
Irredentists	– Revisionism of Greater Syria, Greater Iraq, Greater Israel, Greater Palestine (PLO and Hamas charters)
Settlers	– Jewish settlers (conflict with Palestinians and Arab nationalism) – Iraqi Arab settlers in Kurdistan (conflict with Kurdish nationalism)

[1] On the Sunni–Shiite tensions in Bahrain, see Rabi and Kostiner 1999 and *New York Times*, April 16, 2006.

state-to-nation imbalance like the one that exists in the Middle East, democratization, at least in its first stage, might bring to power militant forces. Although it is too early to judge the lasting impact of recent elections, religious parties have done very well. This does not bode well for regional stability, since most of these parties are anti-Western/Israel (the Muslim Brotherhood in Egypt, among others) and nationalist-religious (Iran, and Palestine – Hamas), or ethnic-religious (Shiites in Iraq and Lebanon). Specifically in Iraq, under the shadow of the external and internal state-to-nation incongruences, it will be quite difficult to reach a stable democracy: it will demand a persistent long-term investment of a lot of resources by the United States as well as considerable international support. Indeed, I turn in the next chapter to an analysis of international involvement in the region.

Table 4.4 summarizes the main effects of the state-to-nation imbalance in the Middle East on regional security problems.

5 The great powers and war and peace in the Middle East

The end of the Cold War affected various regional conflicts differently. Some dormant conflicts erupted violently, while others, violent during the Cold War, moved toward peaceful resolution. The contrast between the Middle East peace process and the eruption of war in the Balkans in the 1990s illustrates these trends. During the Cold War, the Middle East was one of the more volatile war zones in the world. In contrast, during the same period the Balkans, a region famed for its instability before the two world wars, was relatively stable and peaceful. In the 1990s, the character of both regions changed: an Arab–Israeli peace process was under way, even if haltingly, while conflict and war returned to the Balkans (see chapter 6).

Why? How does a zone of war become more peaceful while a zone of peace becomes volatile and combustible in such a short time? Does this variation testify to the limitations of the global system's influence on regional developments? If a global change such as the end of the Cold War leads to more violence in some regions and to less violence in others, is this evidence that indigenous regional/domestic factors, rather than systemic ones, determine regional events? Here, then, is the puzzle: Regional variations under post-Cold War unipolarity may suggest that the structure of the international system is indeterminate with regard to regional outcomes, which are influenced more by nonsystemic characteristics. Indeed, following the end of the Cold War, the regionalist literature has burgeoned owing to the expectation that the decline in systemic constraints will lead to greater regional autonomy and differentiation. At the same time, however, the significant changes taking place in different regions after the end of the Cold War may evince the influence of systemic changes on regional war and peace.

The end of the Cold War and the end of bipolarity – a major systemic transformation and consequent regional changes – afford us an opportunity to specify the effects of the global system on regional war and peace. This chapter develops further the argument made in chapter 2. The main thesis is that systemic factors, chiefly the type of great power involvement in a region, affect what I term "cold" regional outcomes (cold war and cold peace), while regional and domestic forces determine "hot" or "warm" regional outcomes – hot war and warm peace. This is the result of the differential effects of two different sets of balances (balance of motivations/interest and balance of capabilities) of two different sets of actors (regional states and external powers) on two different types of outcomes (hot and cold). The more intense or hot the outcome (that is, hot war or warm peace), the larger the influence regional states will have exerted owing to their greater motivation. In contrast, the great powers' superior capabilities are reflected in their influence on the less intense outcomes – cold war and cold peace. The specific influence of the great powers on cold regional outcomes is conditioned by the type of great power involvement in regional affairs. I distinguish among four ideal types of great power regional involvement: hegemony, cooperation, competition, and disengagement. Competition and disengagement are likely, in different ways, to bring about regional cold war. More specifically, great power competition or disengagement may prolong and aggravate a state of regional cold war, making it more susceptible to punctuation by regionally inspired hot wars. Hegemony and cooperation, on the other hand, are likely to lead to regional cold peace, diminishing the prospects for hot war.

Great power effects are prominent in conflict-prone regions with high war proneness, either in aggravating the level of conflict – which is the case when the great powers compete with each other in the region – or in reducing the intensity of the conflict – which happens under conditions of great power cooperation or hegemony. Thus, the shift of the Middle East from being a tense war zone to one of emerging cold peace was the result of the systemic change vis-à-vis the region: from US–Soviet competition during the Cold War to US hegemony in the post-Cold War period (see table 5.1). The superpower rivalry, which had exacerbated the Arab–Israeli conflict during the Cold War, ended, in the process reducing the level of the regional conflict. The second factor was the rise of US hegemony, which has further facilitated a transition to cold peace. Conversely, the change from peace to war in the Balkans was made possible by the decline of Soviet/communist hegemony and the

Table 5.1 *The effects of the type of great power involvement on regional war and peace in war-prone regions*

	Type of great power involvement	
	Competition/disengagement	Hegemony/cooperation
Regional outcomes	Cold wars (punctuated by hot wars)	Cold peace
Empirical cases	The Middle East during the Cold War Post-Cold War Balkans	Post-Cold War Middle East The Balkans during the Cold War

transition to great power disengagement from the region in the 1990s (see chapter 6).

The chapter is organized as follows. After showing that a focus on the four types of great power regional involvement is able to resolve debates in the literature on great power–small power relations, I discuss the sources of these types of engagement. The chapter then analyzes the effects of unipolarity on regional systems. The next section links great power competition and disengagement with cold regional war, and great power cooperation and hegemony with cold regional peace. The empirical section applies these links between types of great power involvement and regional outcomes to the Middle East in the Cold War and the post-Cold War eras and also in the current post-9/11 and post-2003 Iraq War period.

Global factors: types of great power regional involvement

This chapter investigates the effects of the following four major patterns of great power regional involvement on regional war and peace: competition, disengagement, cooperation, and hegemony. These patterns were introduced in chapter 2. Analyzing state behavior and its outcomes in terms of alternative ideal type patterns is not a novel theoretical approach.[1] Such an approach constitutes an antidote to systemic analysis, with its assumption of uniformity of behavior induced

[1] For example, Walt (1987) discusses two basic types of responses to security threats: balancing and bandwagoning; Schroeder (1994) elaborates these responses into four types: balancing, bandwagoning, hiding, and transcending.

by the international structure. The present study adopts this approach for studying great power regional involvement and its outcomes. By distinguishing among different types of great power regional involvement, the present model will be able to resolve some disagreements in the realist literature. For example, there is a disagreement among realist scholars as to the degree of the expected autonomy of small states in their relations with great powers (for elaboration, see Kagan 2000). Classical realists have argued that great powers tend to dominate the behavior of small powers and that they often abuse their superior power at the expense of the weak states (Thucydides 1950; Vital 1971; Pearson et al. 1994, p. 207). In contrast, some newer versions of realism highlight the ability of small powers not only to maintain a high degree of autonomy but also to manipulate the great powers through the "power of the weak," or the "tyranny of the weak" (citations in Handel 1981).[2] These disagreements were, in turn, derived from treating great power–small power relations as a single unified phenomenon rather than distinguishing among different types and patterns of relations. The present model will help to suggest some of the conditions under which each of these alternative patterns is more likely. The key is the type of great power involvement in a region. Let us now turn to the sources of these types of involvement.

The sources of great power involvement in regional conflicts: the balances of interests and capabilities

The four types of great power regional involvement are determined by the nature and balance of great power capabilities and of their interests in regional conflicts.

Capabilities refers both to overall capabilities in all key issue areas (military, economic, sociopolitical cohesiveness, etc.) and to power-projection capabilities with regard to specific regions, influenced by the factor of geographical proximity. Great power capabilities may be (roughly) equal or unequal (superior/weaker powers). Whereas some patterns of great power regional involvement (competition and cooperation) tend to take place under a more or less equal distribution of capabilities, other patterns (dominance and disengagement) tend to reflect power asymmetry.

[2] On the contradiction in Waltz's position on this issue, see 1979, pp. 184, 194–195, cited in Kagan 2000.

The level of great power *interests* at stake in a given region (high/low) is affected by two factors: material interests in the region and geographical proximity to the region. Whether the interests in question are converging or conflicting is also affected by two factors: the general status quo or revisionist orientation of the great powers, and the degree of ideological similarity and polarization among them. Together, these four factors affect the balance of great power interests with regard to regional conflicts.[3]

The following discussion will analyze the four patterns of great power regional involvement in terms of balances of capabilities and interests.

(1) *Competition*: equal capabilities, conflicting (symmetrical high) interests.

(2) *Cooperation*: equal capabilities, converging (symmetrical high) interests.

Significant cooperation in regional conflict reduction is likely to take place among ideologically similar, status quo powers, whereas ideological polarization and the division of great powers into status quo and revisionist will result in intense competition in regions where all the powers have symmetrical high interests. Status quo powers are likely to be interested in stabilizing turbulent regions and at least containing regional conflicts, which may escalate and undermine the stability of the international order. In contrast, revisionist powers may not necessarily be interested in stabilization, and may even exacerbate regional conflicts precisely in order to exploit them and to upset the existing order. Moreover, even if they are interested in containing or reducing the regional conflict, the global rivalry is likely to limit the possibilities for enduring cooperation and joint efforts at conflict reduction with status quo powers. Both cooperation and competition are likely to take place under a rough

[3] For analytical clarity, the level of great power stakes in a given region is assumed here to be intrinsic in the sense of being independent of the general state of great power relations. In practice, global great power competition, especially if it is ideological, may result in inflated importance accorded to certain regions because the rival is or may become involved there. As a result, the great power will also become involved in the region to contain and balance the rival and to maintain its prestige and credibility in the eyes of its allies (a reputational interest). According to neorealists, this was the case with US interests in the Third World during the Cold War (see Van Evera 1990; Walt 1989; Desch 1993). With the end of great power competition, those regions that lack intrinsic interests will tend to lose their inflated importance. As will be discussed in ch. 6, this has been the case with US interests in the Balkans in the post-Cold War era.

equality of capabilities and a symmetry of interests of several great powers, since a marked imbalance in favor of one power is likely to lead to its dominance in the region.

(3) *Dominance* may result from the superior capabilities and/or superior interests of one power. Thus, it is most likely to take place in regions where a single power has clear-cut advantages in both the balance of capabilities and the balance of interests relative to the other great powers. These regions are usually proximate to one of the great powers (and distant from the others) and fall within its exclusive sphere of influence.[4] But dominance can also take place in more remote regions when there is a single power that has both superior overall capabilities relative to the other powers (including the most effective power-projection capability in the global arena) and high interests in these regions. For example, these might be the sources of US dominance in the post-Cold War Middle East.

(4) In contrast to dominance, *disengagement* by a single great power from a regional conflict may take place as a result of either low interest and/or low capabilities (relative to the other great powers). Accordingly, all or some of the great powers may fail to become involved in a regional conflict because of one of two principal situations:
   (a) *Equal capabilities, low interests*: this situation is relevant to remote regions unimportant to any of the great powers.
   (b) *High capabilities, low interests vs. low capabilities, high interests*: the superior great power has low intrinsic interests in the region, while the relatively weaker powers might have the interest to intervene in the regional conflict but lack the capabilities for effective involvement in the region without the leadership of the stronger power. This may result in a situation whereby those who are able to stabilize the region are unwilling to do so, while those who are willing are unable.

The effects of unipolarity

A unipolar world, like the post-Cold War era, should not necessarily lead to hegemony of the sole pole in every region. The main point is that in a unipolar or a semi-unipolar system for the hegemon there are both declining constraints on intervention and declining incentives to intervene in regional crises.

[4] On great powers' spheres of influence, see Keal 1983, p. 15, and Kagan 2000.

Systems theory expects declining constraints for the hegemon in a unipolar system because of the disappearance of the major limitation on its freedom of international action under bipolarity – the other pole. This disappearance means that there is no countervailing force whose possible military responses to its own actions the hegemon has to anticipate. This should make intervention by the hegemon far more likely than in a bipolar or even a multipolar world, where the presence of other great power(s) constrains the maneuvering freedom of all the great powers of the day.

However, structural theory also leads us to expect declining *incentives* for international engagement by the hegemon under unipolarity. According to this theory, a major motivation for international engagement by the great powers is derived from their balancing of the other great powers in order to maintain their security and autonomy and to avoid being put in an inferior position in an anarchic world. The disappearance of the other pole means that there is no more need for intense competition and costly balancing in different parts of the world. As a result, we may derive the expectation of *less* intervention by the hegemon across the globe.[5]

Thus, a unipolar model, while helpful in suggesting important differences from a bipolar world, is indeterminate in its expectations with regard to the likelihood and scope of the hegemon's regional engagement.[6] Such indeterminacy should lead us to recognize the influence of regionally derived incentives based on the hegemon's interests in different regions. A critical distinction in this context is between intrinsic, extrinsic, and low interests.[7] Intrinsic interests refer to the geostrategic importance of the region, the economic resources located there, and the importance of the region for trade, investments, and financial links with the hegemon.[8] In other words, control of such regions directly affects the world balance of power. Intrinsic interests notably include security threats posed by actors in a certain region to the great power. In a unipolar system, in which there is no great power, let alone regional power, that can pose a direct security threat to the superior hegemon,

[5] On the effects of 9/11 on changing incentives with regard to interventions, see below.
[6] For balanced assessments of the indeterminacy of structural analysis for explaining certain outcomes, see J. Snyder 1991, Van Evera 1993, and Buzan 1991, ch. 4. See also Miller 2002, ch. 4.
[7] In making this distinction I partly draw on Desch 1993, esp. p. 10.
[8] See Papayoanou 1997, who especially emphasizes the importance of great power economic interests (trade and financial links) in a region.

these threats might be related to asymmetric warfare such as terrorism or weapons of mass destruction. Extrinsic interests refer to the geographical proximity of the region in question to the hegemon or to its most important allies. Extrinsic interests are important but less vital than intrinsic interests because they do not directly affect the global balance of power. Low-interest regions contain neither intrinsic nor extrinsic interests. Such regions lack key geostrategic or economic importance and are also distant from the hegemon or its major allies.

The hegemon's involvement will vary between high-level engagement in regions with intrinsic interests and disengagement from low-interest regions. The level of engagement in regions with extrinsic interests will be influenced by the expected costs of military intervention there. The more costly such intervention is estimated to be, due to the power of expected resistance and its ability to inflict heavy casualties, the greater will be the hegemon's inclination toward partial or even complete disengagement. The less the expected costs, the greater the hegemon's inclination to intervene. Yet, under unipolarity, the high freedom of action allows the hegemon to work actively to reduce the expected costs of its intervention by conducting intensive air raids on the local adversary or by supplying arms to the latter's local rivals or both. Such pressures can induce the challenger to accept diplomatic proposals which will transform the hegemon's ground deployment from a coercive "peace enforcement" to a more benign "peacekeeping" – which is acceptable to the local parties; this will reduce the expected costs considerably and make possible such a deployment.

The effects of types of great power involvement on regional war and peace

Great power competition or disengagement in highly conflictual (war-prone) regions leads to cold war (punctuated by hot wars)

When the great powers *disengage* from a regional conflict, the conflict will continue in accordance with the resources and motivations of the regional states. As a result, regional wars may last for protracted periods without being interrupted and contained (see the discussion in chapter 2).

A *competitive* great power involvement in regional conflicts leads to the persistence of protracted regional cold wars, because of the combination of the following three elements:

(a) Great power competition prolongs local conflicts and thus blocks the transition to cold peace and beyond.
(b) Competitive great power involvement produces incentives for the great powers to discourage regional hot wars. They are unlikely, however, to succeed because the balance of interests at the initiation of regional wars favors the local powers, and also because the great power competition produces disincentives for them to engage in regional conflict reduction, or at least tends to weaken great power attempts at regional war prevention in peacetime.
(c) In contrast, the balance of motivation shifts in favor of the great powers at the stage of war termination; thus, regional war termination occurs relatively early as a result of great power intervention, which, in turn, leads to a new round of cold war.

Thus, under competitive great power involvement the outcome would be long periods of regional cold war punctuated by short regional hot wars, which the great powers are unable to prevent (and are, at most, able to terminate early).

I will now elaborate on the logic of these propositions.

a. Competitive great power involvement in a region can intensify and prolong local cold wars even if the great power competition did not bring about the regional conflict in the first place The more intense the competition among the great powers in the region, the greater the autonomy of the small states and their ability to manipulate the powers and extract military and economic aid.[9] Because of the keen superpower rivalry during the Cold War, the ability of regional actors to manipulate the great powers was especially strong in the post-1945 era.[10] The intense global competition during the Cold War hindered the mitigation of local conflicts and reduced the likelihood of stable settlements. The diplomatic support, financial aid, and massive arms supplies provided by the superpower patrons to their respective Cold War clients produced disincentives for the regional parties to show the flexibility and moderation needed to resolve disputes. Rather, such generous aid made it easier for the local actors to persist in their quarrels.[11] The assistance granted

[9] I draw here on Miller and Kagan 1997. [10] For examples and citations, see ibid.
[11] See, e.g., the cases in MacFarlane (1992, p. 225) with regard to the effects of Soviet assistance to Somalia (1969–1977) and later to Ethiopia on the choice of military options by these regimes.

by the patrons to their regional clients shields these clients from the costs of the regional rivalry and thus reduces their incentives to make the concessions necessary for a diplomatic compromise. In other words, great power aid enables small states to persist in regional conflict and even intensify it.[12] Thus, to some extent, regional conflicts during the Cold War were fueled by the global contest (Wriggins 1992, pp. 293–294), even if in most cases the origins of these conflicts were indigenous and unrelated to the East–West rivalry (Kanet and Kolodziej 1991, p. 24).

We should thus expect that a termination of great power rivalry in a region, most notably through a transition from competitive balance of power to hegemony, will lead to a reduction in local conflict and bring about a process of cold peace.

b. The great powers may try to prevent regional wars, but under a competitive involvement they will be unable to accomplish war prevention The great powers are frequently interested in preventing local wars (Zartman 1995b, p. 14), especially those involving their allies, because of the fear that these wars will spread, eventually entangling the great powers themselves in situations not under their own control, and thus escalating to an inadvertent great power clash.

In general, great powers cannot resolve the problems of the legitimacy of the regional order (notably those derived from the state-to-nation imbalance), which are too complex and fundamental to be addressed by foreign powers. There is a considerable asymmetry of motivation on these issues in favor of the local actors, and it is also difficult for an external power in the postcolonial age to control and determine basic internal developments in another state. The major exception to this generalization in the postcolonial era is the rare phenomenon of an extended occupation by a great power after a major war. During the occupation the great power may transplant a new political system into the occupied country, although this transplantation can reasonably succeed only to the extent that the state-to-nation (and also socioeconomic) prerequisites had been present in the occupied land (see chapter 8). Apart from this demanding and exceptional option, so long as the local powers themselves do not address the regional state-to-nation questions, the region will remain war-prone (although, as discussed below, a hegemon or a

[12] See also Buzan 1991, p. 222.

concert can facilitate the establishment of intergovernmental diplomacy that mitigates the underlying sources of the conflict, and thus indirectly address the state-to-nation problems).

Thus, a balance-of-power system is unable by itself to prevent the eruption of local wars. The competition between the great powers reduces their effectiveness in thwarting a regional eruption of violence and providing an alternative mechanism to the use of force for resolving regional conflicts. Because the great powers balance, check, block, and neutralize each other, they are less effective in preventing the resort to violence, leaving room for determined local actors to address their conflicts by a resort to force. In effect, competitive great power involvement in regional conflicts is a permissive condition for the occurrence of hot regional wars.

c. Relatively early termination of regional wars Even if the great powers prefer to prevent local violence, the balance of motivation works in favor of the regional actors with regard to issues that are much more directly related to their interests than to the interests of the great powers. Thus, the causes of local wars will have a more concrete and immediate relation to the concerns of the regional actors than those of outside powers. The balance of motivation starts to change only when there is a growing probability of escalation of the local conflict to the international level because the local protagonists are about to cross certain red lines which may lead to a great power confrontation. This change usually takes place only after the regional war has already started and may help bring about its termination earlier than would otherwise have been the case.

In other words, at the stage of war termination, the balance of motivation shifts in favor of the great powers. The reason is the growing great power fear of entanglement and direct confrontation toward the end of regional wars among their allies.

Thus, in times of regional war between the allies of competing great powers, whenever there is a serious danger to the survival of the regime of a major ally because it faces a strategic defeat, the great power patron of the defeated ally may threaten to intervene on its behalf. Because such intervention can lead to a counter intervention by the other power on behalf of its ally, and consequently to an escalation of the local conflict to the global level, the great powers have an incentive to cooperate, at least tacitly, in terminating the regional war before any local party is decisively defeated.[13] The dependence of the local allies on their great power patrons also rises at the stage of war termination because of their depleted weapons stocks; therefore the local allies are unlikely to defy great power wishes at this stage.

As a result of this de facto cooperation in regional war termination, the superpowers during the Cold War period helped to preserve the basic postcolonial status quo in Third World areas and the territorial integrity of Third World states.[14] Moreover, because of superpower support of their respective allies, the United States and the USSR helped to maintain the regional balance of power in many Third World regions (Rosecrance 1991, 373–374), and to constrain the emergence of regional hegemons (MacFarlane 1992, p. 226).[15]

The result of the combined effect of these three aspects of competitive great power involvement in regional conflicts (prolonging local conflicts; inability to prevent the outbreak of local hot wars and inability or unwillingness to engage in peacemaking; and relatively early war termination) is a regional cold war in regions where there are severe conflicts due to problems of state-to-nation imbalance.

Two regions in such a situation are the Middle East during the post-1945 era, in which there were frequent Arab–Israeli wars, and the Balkans from 1880 to 1914, and again in the early 1990s, periods in which notable regional wars took place (such as the wars of 1885 and 1912–1913, and the 1991–1999 wars of Yugoslavia's disintegration).[16] The regional wars in both regions were not caused by external great powers, but rather were initiated by the local states, mostly against great power wishes.

Both regions also illustrate the effects of great power competition on prolonging regional cold wars. In the Middle East, it was the US–Soviet rivalry during the Cold War, and in the Balkans it was the Russian–Austro-Hungarian rivalry from 1880 to World War I. At the same time, the superpowers played an important role in terminating Arab–Israeli wars during the Cold War. A major case of the effects of great power disengagement on regional conflicts in a region with severe state-to-nation problems is provided by the Yugoslav conflict from the early 1990s to late 1995.

[13] On the nature and content of the tacit rules underlying this cooperation between the superpowers in the Cold War era, see George et al. 1988 and Miller 2002, ch. 5.
[14] See Ayoob 1995, p. 82, n. 28. [15] See also Kanet and Kolodziej 1991.
[16] The Balkan cases are discussed in ch. 6.

A concert or hegemony in regions with high war proneness leads to cold regional peace

There are two variants or modes of great power regional involvement that are conducive to the advancement of cold regional peace: a great power concert and hegemony of one power. While there are important differences between the two modes, they are broadly similar in terms of their effects on regional peace, and therefore for the purposes of this study may be regarded as two variants of a single type of engagement.

A concert refers to cooperation among a group of more or less equal great powers in resolving international conflicts, both among themselves and among third parties, thereby making peaceful change possible.[17] The emphasis in a concert is on *collective* consultation, decisionmaking, and action with respect to the diplomatic agenda.[18]

In principle, a concert should include all the great powers of the day. In contrast to this approach, which emphasizes cooperation among several powers, the logic of the hegemony proposition draws on the hegemonic-stability perspective.[19] This perspective, drawing on collective goods theory, suggests that the production of "common goods" such as peace and stability requires the presence of a single hegemon that is both able (has dominant capabilities in important issue areas) and willing to lead (is ready to offer "side payments" to get other states to join it). The leader sees itself as a major long-term beneficiary of regional peace, and is also able to shape and dominate the regional environment. For this purpose, the hegemon provides a flow of services and benefits to the small states that include diplomatic "good offices," "honest brokerage," or mediation, as well as security guarantees, construction of arms control and crisis-prevention regimes, and deterrence and compellence of military aggressors. Leadership and mediation by a single broker should, according to this perspective, be more efficacious than that by several great powers, even if they concert their actions, because transaction and information costs are lower.[20] All in all, a single dominant country will be better able and more willing to provide these "goods" than a number

[17] Clark 1989, pp. 121, 126–127. On great power concerts, see Jervis 1986, Kupchan and Kupchan 1991, and Miller 1994a; 2002, ch. 4.
[18] On the high frequency of joint consultation and collective decisionmaking in the post-Napoleonic Concert of Europe, see Elrod 1976, 162–163, and Lauren 1983, pp. 35–36.
[19] For overviews of this perspective and references to key works, see citations in ch. 2, n. 75. See also Miller 1992b, 1996. For a security version, see Webb and Krasner 1989. For applications to regional orders, see Zartman 1995b, Papayoanou 1997, and Buzan and Waever 2003.
[20] On these types of costs, see Keohane 1984 and Oye 1986.

of comparatively equal powers, who are more likely to compete among themselves for regional influence than cooperate to ameliorate regional disputes.

Benign vs. coercive hegemony and concert Each of the two variants of international engagement – great power hegemony and concert – may take two forms, benign and coercive, depending on the means employed by the great powers.[21] A benign or accommodative strategy emphasizes negotiated diplomacy for promoting regional peacemaking; the local actors actively participate in the negotiating process and can voice their concerns and bargain among themselves and with the great power(s). The talks between the power(s) and the small actors tend to be of a persuasive nature, characterized by compromise and give-and-take rather than sheer *diktat* by the dominant power(s) to the smaller states. Indeed, accommodative diplomacy by the great power(s) attempts to advance peace and stability in the region, while minimizing the encroachment on the local states' sovereignty and autonomy. In contrast, in the coercive[22] approach, the great power(s) impose a regional order on the small states regardless of their wishes.[23] A threat of intervention by the regional "policeman" may deter the local disputants from resorting to force against each other. It may also unify them against the common external threat[24] or at least mitigate the disputes among them. In any case, as long as the threat of hegemonic intervention is credible, it tends to reduce the violent manifestations of the local conflict because the protagonists avoid providing pretexts for external intervention such as having a bloody quarrel among themselves.

The form of concert or hegemony will depend on the nature of the domestic regimes of the powers and on their proximity to the region. Democratic and distant great powers will tend to be less abusive and more benign than authoritarian and proximate powers.[25] With regard to

[21] See Snidal 1985; Miller 2002, ch. 4. On the benign or accommodative variant of hegemonic theories versus a unilateralist-coercive conception of hegemony, see Miller 1997.
[22] On coercive diplomacy, see Lauren 1994 and Craig and George 1995, pp. 196–213. This concept corresponds to Schelling's "compellence." See Schelling 1966, pp. 70–71.
[23] On imposed orders, see Young 1983, pp. 100–101, and 1986, 110.
[24] This argument is based on the in-group/out-group proposition, which suggests that conflict with an out-group reinforces the cohesion of an in-group (J. Levy 1998, 152).
[25] For some of the differences in regional peacemaking between a democratic and a non-democratic great power, see Miller 1997. Proximate powers tend to be coercive because they have greater stakes in their immediate environment than in faraway places. Even more important, their ability to coerce is greater because of the adverse effects of distance on power-projection (see Walt 1987 and Buzan 1991).

democratic powers, they will be most accommodative when the regional states are also democratic (or undergoing a transition to democracy), thus sharing a common ideology. A shared ideology between the great powers and the regional states is not a necessary condition for the emergence of hegemony or concert. Nevertheless, the endurance of these patterns of engagement legitimizes the ideologies associated with the powers and delegitimizes rival ideologies, and vice versa: the decline of hegemony or concert discredits the ideologies the great powers advance.[26]

In either of the two situations (concert or hegemony), the great power(s) are likely to be *willing* to invest in regional conflict reduction and to effect a transition from a state of hot or cold war to cold peace for two major reasons: the intrinsic importance of a region, and a shared threat. A distinction has to be made between different regions according to their standing in the great powers' balance of interests. Intrinsically important regions, whose value for the great powers stems from major material resources and also from geographic proximity to the powers, will draw great power involvement and attempts at stabilization.[27]

A major factor that enhances the willingness of the great power(s) to engage in promoting conflict reduction is the presence of a shared threat both to the great power(s) and to the status quo regional states on the part of an aggressive revisionist power, or weaker regional states with divisive ideologies.[28] The presence of such a shared threat will motivate the power(s) to invest considerable resources in forming and leading a countervailing coalition, in deterrence and compellence of the aggressor, and also in a more general brokerage of disputes among the regional states.

Great power strategies to advance regional cold peace

As for the great power *ability* to stabilize the region, a hegemon or a great power concert is able to prevent local wars and to advance regional peace, albeit a cold one, in regions vital to the great power interests. This is because both situations reduce the maneuvering room of the small states and enable the great powers to exert coordinated moderating pressures (diplomatic, economic, and military) on their regional allies, as well as to broker settlements and mediate between the local parties.

[26] For a related point, see Ikenberry and Kupchan 1990, p. 55.

[27] For the debate on the importance of various regions to the United States, see Van Evera 1990, S. David 1992/3, Desch 1993, Posen and Ross 1996/7, and Gholz et al. 1997. For the importance of different regions to the great powers, see Miller and Kagan 1997 and Miller 1998.

[28] On unifying and divisive ideologies, see ch. 2.

As a result, peacemaking efforts by the great powers will be much more effective than in a competitive type of involvement.

Moreover, a concert and hegemony produce a strategic-economic environment which makes it highly profitable, for both security and economic reasons, to join the regional peace process and raises the costs for those who oppose the regional peace. Thus, a regional peace process under the great powers includes a "bandwagoning" dynamics which attracts local states that are interested in reinforcing their security and economy. The latter are status quo players, while revisionists reject the regional peace unless they are subdued by the great powers. Thus, in contrast to the claims of both current variants of realism: the defensive (in the form of Walt's balance-of-threat theory) and offensive (as expressed by Schweller's neoclassical realism), such bandwagoning under a benign hegemony/concert is a stabilizing process.[29] At any rate, under hegemony those who oppose the peace are likely to pay a heavy price both economically and in their strategic situation so long as they reject the process. Thus, many players are expected to become more supportive of the regional peace because of the combined offer by the hegemon of rewards or positive sanctions for those who support the peace and punishment or negative sanctions to those who oppose it.

More specifically, a hegemon or a concert can advance cold peace through the following four interrelated mechanisms.[30]

Restraint: of aggressive local clients intent on wars of expansion, through imposition of diplomatic, economic, and, if necessary, military sanctions. Unlike a situation of several great powers competing for regional influence, in a concert or hegemonic involvement, the small states do not have a realignment option.[31] As a result, the great power(s) need not worry about losing their clients. The client states, for their part, have less maneuvering room and are unable to escape the great powers' restraining pressure.

Reassurance: of local states and reduction of their security dilemmas by the extension of security guarantees, preferably manifested in a regional

[29] For a review of neoclassical realism, including Schweller's work, see Rose 1998. Walt (1987) suggests that bandwagoning dynamics are destabilizing, and Schweller (1994) argues that revisionists "bandwagon for profit."
[30] On the potential role of a hegemon in reducing regional conflicts, see Zartman 1995b, pp. 4–8, and Papayoanou 1997. The ultimate expression of regional hegemonic order is what Buzan (1991, p. 198) calls "overlay." See also Buzan and Waever 2003. On the European Concert's pacific amelioration of conflicts, see Lauren 1983, pp. 40–42, 48–50; Craig and George 1995, pp. 25–31; and Clark 1989, p. 121. Schroeder (1986, 3) lists the Concert's diplomatic accomplishments in ameliorating disputes.
[31] See Miller and Kagan 1997.

deployment of troops.[32] Peacekeeping forces of the great powers can separate the regional parties, minimize the prospects of clashes, and deter any offensive inclinations on their part. In the absence of trust among regional actors, the military presence of external power(s) is conducive to overcoming the security dilemma and mutual fears. Such a presence reassures the regional parties that the great power(s) will minimize the chances for blackmail, surprise attacks and preemptive strikes, hostile alliances, and arms races among the local parties by penalizing the violators of agreements and settlements.[33] Another strategy that the power(s) may employ to reassure the local states concerns leading the efforts to construct regional security and crisis prevention regimes and confidence-building measures, thus minimizing the likelihood of inadvertent wars.[34]

The deployment of advanced reconnaissance technology by the great power(s) can help in building regional security regimes. The powers have the best technical means and the greatest political leverage to monitor the military actions of the regional parties and their adherence to agreements. Thus, the powers can reduce the incentives of the local parties to cheat on agreements to the extent that they are able and willing to penalize the violators. Such monitoring can also reduce the chances of misunderstanding and miscommunication among the regional parties, which may lead to inadvertent wars.

Thus, regional stability is increased by the reduction in the fears of being attacked, and the increase in the costs that an aggressor is likely to pay by having to face great power sanctions. The regional troop deployment necessary for effective reassurance is possible under a concert or a hegemony because the powers in either of these situations face no constraints from rival great powers and need not fear escalation.

Deterrence and containment of potential aggressors: under a concert or hegemony, potential regional aggressors do not enjoy the strategic backing of a rival great power that could neutralize and deter other great powers from intervening. The credibility of the great power commitment to ensure stability in the region is high because of the large degree of maneuverability in the absence of countervailing great powers. Thus, the great powers should be able to deter potential regional

[32] On the concept of reassurance, see J. Stein 1991b. On reassurance provided by the United States through the forward deployment of its forces in Europe and East Asia, see Art 1992, pp. 96–98.
[33] See Waltz 1979, pp. 70–71, and Mearsheimer 1990.
[34] On inadvertent or unintended/undesired wars, see Miller 2002, pp. 27–31. On regional security regimes, see Inbar 1995.

aggressors and revisionist powers intent on wars of profit. Moreover, in case of deterrence failure, the lack of rival great power constraints on their ability to act militarily should enable the powers to demonstrate their resolve and compel the aggressor to desist through threats of force and military deployments. If short-of-war coercive diplomacy also fails, the great powers' freedom of action allows them to use force to maintain the regional order and roll back aggression.

Conflict reduction: the external power(s) may also engage in conflict reduction and war prevention in the following ways.

(a) *Mediation and reduction* of the level of the basic regional conflict and thus encouragement or imposition of a cold peace. A hegemon or a concert can help the local states overcome the collective goods problem by being able and willing to pay disproportionate costs for achieving regional peace through the provision of valuable services as an "honest broker": the great power(s) can serve as mediator(s) able to employ powerful pressures and incentives which no other potential mediator can offer.[35] The powers can provide compensation for the painful concessions that the parties must make in the conflict-reduction process. This may include diplomatic recognition, membership in international organizations, technology transfers, financial aid, trade benefits, credit, arms supply, security guarantees, and the presence of their troops as peacekeepers. At the same time, the powers can impose sanctions on intransigent parties who delay progress in the regional peace process. Indeed, the role of the powers is especially vital when the parties (or some of them) are intransigent. Against extremely intransigent actors, they may have to resort to heavy diplomatic and economic pressures and even use military force.

(b) *Guaranteeing* of regional arrangements. The powers can guarantee a regional settlement and serve as final arbiters in case of disagreements among the parties about its interpretation. Concerns about the potential reactions of the powers would motivate regional parties to adhere to the agreement and to follow its rules and procedures. Thus, the enforcement of cold peace is more reliable under a concert or a hegemony.

[35] On third-party mediation, especially by great powers, see Touval 1992; on third-party conflict management, see Dixon 1996.

Although every concert or hegemon may promote cold regional peace by employing these basic strategies, benign and coercive concerts or hegemons are likely to stress different strategies and use a different "mix" of foreign policy means. A benign concert or hegemon will serve as a mediator who takes into account the wishes of the local parties, and will focus on reassurance and positive sanctions. A coercive concert or hegemon, in contrast, will emphasize deterrence and negative sanctions, and is likely to abuse its power and impose a solution of the regional conflict on the parties regardless of their wishes. While a benign concert or hegemony leads to a negotiated, accommodative regional peace (albeit cold), a coercive concert or hegemony leads to an imposed cold peace. For the effectiveness of an accommodative order, its acceptability by the regional states is crucial, while an imposed order depends more on the durability of the coercive power of the concert or the hegemon.

The main problem with the international mechanism for regional peace is that by itself it is unable to proceed beyond cold peace. It is beyond the capabilities of external powers to resolve state-to-nation problems or to induce domestic liberalization, unless the regional states themselves are willing to undertake these tasks. Thus, neither concert nor hegemony – whether benign or coercive – is able, by itself, to resolve the underlying issues in conflict and to bring about warm peace in the region.

Cold peace is not expected to survive changes in great power regional involvement. Thus, potential problems with the international mechanism include the difficulty the powers have in sustaining domestic support for a long-term and costly regional engagement because of public demands to focus on internal affairs. Another danger is the collapse of the concert or the hegemony due to international rather than domestic factors. Changes in the global balance of power, due to a weakening of the hegemon's power or a rise in its competitors' capabilities, may lead to the loss of the hegemon's capacity to stabilize the region, because revisionist local states will be able to receive support from the hegemon's international competitors. The expectation of realist balance-of-power theory is indeed that any hegemony will be at best temporary because new great powers will rise or a counterhegemonic coalition will be formed. According to this theory, long-term hegemony is not feasible because of the effective functioning of the equilibrium mechanism which results in the recurrent formation of balances of power.[36]

[36] See Wight 1973, p. 100; Rosecrance 1986, pp. 56–58; Layne 1993; Waltz 1979, ch. 6.

Balance-of-power theory also expects great powers to compete for influence in different regions rather than cooperate in joint peacemaking efforts.[37] As a result, a concert is also regarded by this theory as, at best, a short-term phenomenon that is likely to disintegrate into great power rivalry.[38] Another possibility is that in the absence of a hegemonic leadership, the great powers may act as "free riders," that is, each of them expects the other powers to pay the price for providing the collective good of regional peace, while it disengages and thus avoids paying the price, although benefiting from the collective good. Yet, if each of the powers expects the others to do the hard work while it disengages, the end result will be great power disengagement from the region. As a result of any one of these developments – collapse of hegemony, disintegration of a concert, or great power disengagement – the cold regional peace is likely to collapse and the region revert back to war.

To sum up, while the great powers can be helpful in promoting regional conflict reduction, as long as they, rather than the local parties, play the critical role in the peacemaking process, this process will amount to no more than a mitigation or moderation of the dispute, namely, a cold peace: it will fall short of full-blown indigenous reconciliation among the local parties. Moreover, the durability of the cold peace depends on the strength and continued presence of the powers in the region. A collapse of the concert or a decline of the hegemon or disengagement of either from the region may bring about a decline of the cold peace and a return to either cold or hot war.

The Middle East during the Cold War period

The Middle East during the Cold War saw competitive great power involvement which sustained a regional cold war, but did not cause regional hot wars.

The superpowers did not cause the hot wars in the Middle East. These wars were caused by state-to-nation issues as discussed in the previous chapter. In almost all cases, the superpowers wanted to prevent the hot wars. Yet, competitive great power involvement in regional conflicts results in the persistence of protracted regional cold wars because of the combination of the following three elements. Competitive great power

[37] On the differences between the balance-of-power, the concert, and the hegemonic perspectives, see Miller 1992b, 1996.
[38] See Mearsheimer 1994/5 and Kagan 1997/8.

involvement produces incentives for the great powers to discourage regional hot wars. They are unlikely, however, to succeed in at least some cases because the balance of interests at the initiation of regional wars favors the local powers. In addition, great power competition produces disincentives for the great powers to engage in regional conflict reduction or at least tends to weaken great power attempts at regional war prevention in peacetime.

In contrast, the balance of motivation shifts in favor of the great powers at the stage of war termination; thus, regional war termination occurs relatively early as a result of great power intervention, which, in turn, leads to a new round of cold war. Deliberately or not, great power intervention also tends to maintain the territorial status quo and the regional balance of power. Yet great power competition results in the prolonging of local conflicts and thus blocks the transition to cold peace and beyond.

Thus, under competitive great power involvement, the outcome is expected to be long periods of regional cold war punctuated by short regional hot wars that the great powers are unable to prevent, but are, at most, able to terminate. These three types of regional effects of great power competition leading to a regional cold war can resolve the debate between the two perspectives on the effects of the global Cold War on regional conflicts: the "conflict suppression" and the "conflict exacerbation."[39]

Competitive balance of power prolongs regional conflicts

The global Cold War and the competitive superpower balance of power in the Middle East since the mid-1950s and until the Soviet collapse prolonged the Arab–Israeli conflict and made it difficult to move beyond a regional cold war to cold peace, that is, to reduce the level of the regional conflict. Thus, the superpowers had major effects on the persistence and longevity of the Arab–Israeli conflict (Krasner 1997, p. 202); they helped to sustain it by supplying arms,[40] along with diplomatic and economic support of their respective clients.

[39] See A. Stein and Lobell 1997.

[40] For figures on the much higher proportion of superpower arms deliveries to the Middle East as compared to other regions, see A. Stein and Lobell 1997, p. 115, nn. 30, 31. US arms deliveries to the Middle East in the years 1964–1991 were nine times greater than to Latin America and fifteen times greater than to Africa. During the same era, Soviet military deliveries to the Middle East were four times greater than to Latin America and two times greater than to Africa. There were only negligible deliveries to Oceania. See Neuman 1986, cited in A. Stein and Lobell 1997 who provide quantities of arms delivered to the different regions on p. 116, n. 31.

Some regional effects of the superpower competition

(1) Superpower competition increased the autonomy of the local states and raised their ability to manipulate their patrons.

The superpower regional competition increased the maneuvering freedom of the regional actors and facilitated the manipulation of the superpowers by key local states.

An example of the ability of local states to play off and manipulate the great powers in a competitive international system, and thus to continue and intensify the regional conflict, is Egypt's turn to the Soviets in 1955. US officials were involved at that time in attempts to resolve the Arab–Israeli conflict. The United States conditioned its military assistance on Egypt's readiness to make concessions in the peace settlement with Israel (and also on Egypt's joining the pro-Western regional defense system – the Baghdad Pact, discussed below). Nasser believed that these demands would undermine his regional standing. In a competitive international system, Egypt could avoid making the concessions without having to pay a price – by turning to the USSR, which was willing and able to supply major arms to its new ally. This resulted in the $250 million Czech arms deal of September 1955 (Gerges 1994, pp. 31–32; Golan 1990, p. 45). This advanced weaponry enabled Egypt to embark on military adventures that the USSR considered undesirable, even dragging the superpower itself into wars it did not want. This was the case with Soviet arms delivery before the 1956, 1967, and 1973 wars, with the accompanying danger of the Soviets being dragged into them.[41]

Another major example of manipulation of a superpower by its client was the pressure exerted by Nasser on Moscow to intervene in the 1969–1970 War of Attrition following the deep penetration bombing by Israel: "When president Gamal Abdel-Nasser confronted Soviet leaders with the choice of either accepting the political and military risks of direct military intervention in the War of Attrition or losing Egypt as a client, the Soviets agreed to intervene militarily" (Bar Siman-Tov 1987, p. 9). The USSR subsequently decided to assume responsibility for Egypt's air defense. To carry this out, they were to deploy about 15,000–20,000 military advisers, including personnel to handle a SAM-3 air defense

[41] R. Freedman 1991, p. 17. On the manipulation of the United States by the Shah of Iran through his use of the threat of defection to the Soviets during the 1970s, see Karsh 1997, 277–279.

system and Soviet pilots who would actually fly Soviet aircraft in the Egyptian air force (Golan 1990, p. 73).

(2) Competition between the superpowers reduced their capacity to exert pressures on the local states to moderate their diplomatic positions even though the superpowers preferred this moderation.

The fear of "losing" their client to the other superpower reduced the superpower's capacity to moderate the stance of their small allies. Thus, despite the joint sponsorship by the superpowers of UN Security Council Resolution 242, which laid the foundations for a comprehensive resolution of the Arab–Israeli conflict, the superpowers were unable to exert effective moderating pressures on their clients to carry out this resolution. This was clearly the case in Soviet relations with Egypt and Syria regarding their positions on the Arab–Israeli conflict.[42] The Soviets sought a political settlement, but they also intended to remain a superpower and therefore did not want just any settlement, but only one that would recognize, preserve, and legitimize their ongoing presence and role in the Middle East. For this purpose, the Soviets needed to maintain close relations with their regional allies. As none of the superpowers was ready to make its economic and military aid to its clients dependent on their concessions in the peace process, the peace effort collapsed (Slater 1990/1, 567–569).

On the US side, Henry Kissinger,[43] for example, was in favor of ensuring Israel's military superiority, so that the Arabs would realize that Soviet arms could not bring about the recovery of the occupied territories. Thus, Kissinger strongly opposed what he saw as a "premature" US responsiveness to Arab demands, by exerting moderating pressure on Israel through various diplomatic initiatives – unilateral US proposals or in cooperation with the Soviets.[44] Only when the Arab position became more flexible could the American ally, Israel, be expected to reciprocate. Most importantly, the United States would be willing to pressure Israel only when the credit for this newly won flexibility was given to

[42] On the USSR and the settlement of the Arab–Israeli conflict, see Golan 1990, ch. 7. On the USSR and Syria, see ibid., p. 144.
[43] See the Middle East chapters in his memoirs (1979, 1982).
[44] This was Kissinger's perception of the two-power talks and even of the State Department (led by Secretary of State William Rogers and his assistant, Sisco) attempts to accomplish partial agreements between the regional parties under unilateral US leadership (1970–1971).

Israel's patron; the United States would thus emerge as the regional peacemaker.

(3) Patron–client relations increased the risk-taking propensity of the local states.

The superpowers established intense patron–client relations with key Middle East states. The United States and the USSR wanted their clients to win or at least avoid a total or major defeat. For this purpose, the superpowers backed their protégés militarily (by supplying arms, providing military advisers, or operating sophisticated weapons), economically (by stepping up economic aid), and diplomatically (Bar Siman-Tov, 1987, p. 18).

Such a pattern and the commitment it entailed increased the self-confidence and risk-taking propensity of the recipients. The commitment, especially the arms supply, also raised the fears of its regional adversaries. Since the transfers tended to be of offensive weapons, they reinforced the security dilemma of the local protagonists, thus generating a regional arms race (Wriggins 1992, p. 294) and encouraging balancing moves and preventive wars such as Israel's collusion with the British and French in 1956 (Kinsella 1994, 572).

Indeed, every major regional cycle of violence was preceded by the receipt of major military supplies by the superpowers. The Czech arms deal between the USSR and Egypt emboldened the latter and frightened Israel, leading to the 1956 war. By the late 1950s, the Soviets were providing large amounts of arms to the key radical states: Egypt, Iraq, and Syria. The Kennedy administration tried to respond to the developing alliance between the Soviets and Arab radicals by appeasing Nasser, but this strategy failed because of Egypt's intervention in the Yemen war, which brought the potential for Soviet influence to the borders of oil-rich Saudi Arabia. The Johnson administration thus responded to the threat of Soviet encroachments by increasing arms supply to Israel and a number of conservative Arab states (Spiegel 1988, pp. 200–201). The Soviets, for their part, became highly involved with the radical new regime in Syria and attempted to use Egypt's deterrence to defend Syria against growing Israeli assertiveness. The background was thereby set for the action–reaction cycle between Egypt and Israel, which led to the 1967 war. In 1973, Soviet weapons transfers enabled the Egyptian–Syrian offensive on October 6. The US airlift made it easier for Israel to counterattack later in the war.

Moreover, the superpowers' strategic backing of their clients – namely, the commitment to come to their aid in times of crisis, through arms resupply and issuing threats of intervention when the clients were attacked and the survival of their regimes was threatened – reduced the costs and risks of continuing the conflict for the client states, including by resort to force. As a result, even when the superpowers did not actively encourage regional wars, their guarantees encouraged clients to initiate adventurous behavior (Rubin 1988).

In both 1956 and 1967, Nasser gambled on Soviet support to escape entanglement and defeat. In 1967, Nasser even believed that the Soviets were ready to fight on Egypt's behalf if necessary (Gerges 1994, pp. 217–218; Karsh and Karsh 1996, 385). This expectation made it easier for him to take serious risks by deciding on escalatory moves – even without consulting Moscow in advance (M. Oren 2002, pp. 116–119). Indeed, because the Soviets were especially worried about alienating their clients, the Arabs became quite confident that the Soviets would thwart their complete defeat by Israel. Such confidence made it easier for them to decide to go to war and reinforced the Arab diplomatic and military position (Spiegel 1992, pp. 160–161).

During the 1967 crisis, Israel was confident that the United States would countervail any Soviet steps to intervene in the event of hostilities and that it would support Israel in the UN (Gerges 1994, p. 221, citing then Israeli defense minister Dayan and then Israeli foreign minister Eban). Israel thus believed it was less risky to go to war, although it still might have followed this course if Washington had opposed it.

(4) Superpower support provided disincentives for the kind of diplomatic compromises that would have made possible a transition from a cold war to a cold peace.

Superpower patronage permitted Middle Eastern regimes to avoid compromises with local rivals since the option was always present that a patron would fund or support attempts to reach regional hegemony or finance losses from such a bid by supplying more weapons (Krause 1996, 344).[45] For example, the Soviet replacement of Egypt's and Syria's arms losses following their defeats in 1956, 1967, 1973, and 1982 helped the Arabs to avoid peace talks with Israel.[46]

[45] For a general conclusion along these lines based on a study of four regions during the Cold War, see Wriggins 1992, p. 294.
[46] See Slater 1990/1, 565; Rodman 1994, p. 484.

Thus, following the devastating defeat of the Arabs in the 1967 war, the Soviets embarked upon a massive resupply of arms to the Arabs.[47] This delivery not only exerted pressure on the United States to transfer arms to Israel to preserve the regional balance, but also made it easier for Nasser to initiate the War of Attrition along the Suez Canal in 1969. In the aftermath of the 1967 war, the Soviets were also intensely involved in training and support of the PLO, which accelerated its violent activities against Israel (Spiegel 1988, p. 201) and led to Israeli retaliations. In the aftermath of the Israeli invasion of Lebanon, the blows it inflicted on the PLO and the Syrians, and the US proposal to intervene as part of a multilateral force in July 1982, the Soviets initiated a major resupply of arms to Syria (D. Ross 1990; Golan 1990, p. 137; Spiegel 1992, p. 158).

On the other hand, US supplies to Israel, which were intended to counterbalance Soviet supplies to the Arabs, and thus to maintain its qualitative military edge over them, reduced Israel's incentives to make the necessary concessions for diplomatic progress (Slater 1990/1, 572). Paradoxically, superpower support reduced the incentives for the local parties to reach a diplomatic solution along the lines of UN Security Council Resolution 242, which was based on a land-for-peace formula, although such a solution was supported by both Moscow and Washington.

(5) Both superpowers obstructed diplomatic initiatives and attempts at moderating the level of the conflict.

Due to competitive pressures, rather than cooperating in resolving the Arab–Israeli conflict, the superpowers tried to weaken each other's position in the region and thus obstructed attempts at reaching a settlement. The first example is from the early 1950s. Following the 1948–1949 Israeli War of Independence, the Western powers sought to limit the level of the regional conflict by the 1950 Tripartite Declaration, which limited arms deliveries to regional states. However, the declaration excluded the USSR from the region by leaving it out of the agreement. The Western strategy of containment also attempted to establish an anti-Soviet multilateral alliance: the Baghdad Pact, established in 1955 and comprising Iraq, Iran, Pakistan, and Turkey. These "northern-tier" states, all proximate to the USSR, were intended to serve as a geographic barrier to prevent Soviet penetration into the Middle East. The Soviet response

[47] See Golan 1990, p. 69. On the details of Soviet resupply of Syria after the 1973 war, see ibid., p.148.

to these attempts of exclusion was a countervailing strategy of establishing close ties with radical Arab regimes in Egypt and Syria, which regarded local rivals supported by the "imperialist" West as their major threats. The USSR's diplomatic "leapfrog" over the northern tier and its penetration into Arab lands, beginning with the 1955 Czech arms deal, increased the freedom of action of Arab states; as a result, Egypt could rebuff Western pressures to join the Baghdad Pact as well as the Western desire to contain the conflict with Israel (Golan 1990, p. 45; Gerges 1994, pp. 24–40). Thus, Moscow's massive aid to the radical states, designed to balance Western attempts to reach hegemony in the region, accelerated a polarization of the region from the mid-1950s until the outbreak of the 1973 Arab–Israeli war.

In another example, in spite of serious Soviet plans and suggestions for a diplomatic settlement during 1968, Kissinger exerted his influence on Nixon not to accept them. In Kissinger's view, the Soviets were seizing upon the Arab–Israeli conflict to advance their geopolitical global goals and to drive the West from the Middle East. Therefore, the United States had to exclude the Soviets from Middle Eastern diplomacy, and avoid cooperation with them, especially since the successful completion of a comprehensive Arab–Israeli settlement would legitimize and institutionalize the Soviet presence in the region. There was no gain for the United States, Kissinger believed, in collaborating with the Soviets in reaching a settlement until a stalemate demonstrated that the Soviets were unable to generate progress. Such a stalemate would lead the Arabs to turn to the United States to bring about an Israeli withdrawal under what would amount to a unilateral-exclusive Pax Americana (Kissinger 1979, pp. 351, 379, 559).

The Soviets, for their part, worked hard to obstruct US-led peace initiatives, especially if they were excluded. Notably, they helped to construct an anti-Camp David coalition by increasing their support of Syria – a pivotal actor, whose support is essential for achieving a comprehensive Arab–Israeli peace. Syria's absence from the US-led peace process considerably weakened the possibility of establishing Pax Americana until the end of the Cold War. Thus, while arms imports to Syria, mainly from the USSR, are estimated to have averaged some $570 million per year between 1970 and 1978, they increased sharply from $900 million in 1978 to $2 billion in 1979, the year of the Egyptian–Israeli peace treaty. In the first half of the 1980s, arms imports remained extremely high, averaging more than $2.8 billion annually. Only after Gorbachev came to power and changed Soviet policy – in the second half of the decade –

did they decrease, averaging only half of that amount (Perthes 1995, p. 32).

Superpower attempts at war prevention: some fateful failures punctuate the regional cold war with hot wars

The superpowers have generally opposed the resort to force by their clients. They tried to avert most of the Arab–Israeli wars but they were unsuccessful in at least some fateful cases.[48] The two major reasons for these failures are: the balance of interests/motivation and the competitive international environment. At the stage of local war initiation, the balance of motivation favored the local actors. The motivations of the local powers were unrelated to the global cold war. They were related, rather, to their own security and power considerations, domestic politics, and the substantive state-to-nation issues of competing nationalisms, boundaries, and territories. The fear of losing its clients to the rival superpower limited the patron's ability to restrain its clients (this applies especially to Soviet relations with Egypt and, to a lesser extent, with Syria). Even if the superpowers occasionally succeeded in preventing wars, since their competition exacerbated the conflict, war remained an imminent option which they could not always control in light of the asymmetry in the balance of motivation. The main successes of the superpowers were in delaying their clients' resort to violence, because the clients tended to avoid alienating their superpower patrons so long as doing so did not come at the expense of what they saw as their key interests. In almost all cases, however, regional wars did erupt within a relatively short time, because the basic parameters of the regional conflict, intensified by superpower competition, did not change.[49]

Thus, for instance, the expectations of the first Israeli prime minister, David Ben-Gurion, of a US response delayed the Israeli military plans for a preventive war against Egypt.[50] These plans were reinforced after the Czech arms deal of 1955. Although Ben-Gurion initially rejected pressures from Moshe Dayan, then chief of staff, for a preventive war, Israel attacked Egypt in late October 1956 despite superpower opposition, because it perceived that a key security interest was at stake. Israel felt that it needed to prevent deterioration in the balance of forces with a revisionist neighbor, which at that time challenged its legitimacy as an independent state, and thus was seen as likely to use, in the near

[48] See J. Stein 1988 and Karsh 1997. [49] See Pervin 1998.
[50] Bar Siman-Tov 1987, p. 28; citations in Pervin 1998, p. 5.

future, its newly acquired arms against Israel. In Israeli eyes the United States did not provide an effective response to its security problems; thus, it could not comply with US requests to avoid attacking Egypt (Bar Siman-Tov 1987, p. 48), especially when the alliance with France and Britain seemed to provide a great opportunity to carry out a preventive war against Egypt (ibid., pp. 27, 48; Bar-On 1992, p. 293).

Even if the superpowers were successful in defusing the 1960 Egyptian–Israeli crisis (Pervin 1998, pp. 7–8), they were unable to prevent the 1967 war (Johnson 1971, p. 291; Whetten 1981, p. 49). The United States especially tried to restrain Israel (Spiegel 1985, pp. 137–141; Rusk cited in Gerges 1994, p. 221; J. Stein 1988, pp. 178–183), but failed to give Israel the one thing that might have kept it from acting on its own – a firm guarantee to use force, if necessary, to reopen the Tiran Straits. The failure of the attempts to open the straits and the emergence of a pan-Arab coalition exerted heavy pressure on Israel to resort to preemption, out of fear that, otherwise, war would be too costly for its society (Walzer 1977, pp. 80–84). While the United States was willing to agree to almost any diplomatic compromise to defuse the crisis, Israel felt that its vital security interests were at stake (breaking the blockade, restoring the credibility of its deterrence, and reinforcing its defensive power), and the major way to advance them was by resorting to force (J. Stein 1988, pp. 182–183).

The Soviets, for their part, pressed Nasser both to avoid initiating the War of Attrition in 1969 (Bar Siman-Tov 1980, pp. 46–47) and, once the war began, to stop shooting. Not only did they not succeed,[51] but the Egyptians actually dragged them into assisting by sending air defense systems.[52] During the peak years of détente in the early 1970s the superpowers sought to prevent Arab–Israeli wars. This preference was expressed in the decisions of the summits of May 1972 and June 1973 to cooperate in crisis prevention, to avoid unilateral advantages and to prevent nuclear war (George et al. 1983; George et al. 1988). The Soviets also imposed limitations on the supply of offensive arms to the Arabs (Golan 1990; Breslauer 1983, 1990; Miller 2002, pp. 147, 193–194). Although the USSR succeeded in compelling Egypt to avert its planned attack on Israel in May 1973 (Ben-Porat 1985; J. Stein 1988),[53] in

[51] Sadat 1977, p. 196; Riad 1981, p. 102; Heikal 1978, ch. 11.
[52] Heikal 1975, pp. 79–83; Golan 1990, p. 73.
[53] Even this presumed case of superpower success in hot war prevention is disputed by Bar-Joseph (2001, pp. 148–149), who claims that it was the lack of Syrian preparedness that prevented war in May 1973 and not Soviet pressures.

October 1973, despite superpower opposition to war, Egypt and Syria jointly attacked Israel.[54] This is because they were highly motivated to gain back the territories Israel occupied in 1967. In Arab eyes, Israel held intransigent views, and the superpowers, constrained by détente, were unwilling to apply effective pressure on it. The Arabs calculated that, even if they failed to regain the territories by resorting to force, the fighting and the attendant risk of a superpower crisis would compel the superpowers to advance Middle Eastern peace and thus to exercise pressure on Israel to make territorial concessions (J. Stein 1985; 1988, pp. 176–178; Sadat 1977, p. 238; Paul 1994, pp. 130–131; Shlaim 1995, p. 230).

The superpowers had to walk a tightrope between supporting their allies, notably by arms supply, and restraining them from resorting to force, in order to avoid a superpower clash. While the former enhanced the clients' capability to go to war, the latter alienated the clients and harmed the superpowers' reputation as credible protectors, potentially bringing about their client's – and perhaps others' – defection. This tension limited the capacity of the great power patron to restrain its clients from going to war and even forced the patron sometimes to approve or at least not to oppose the resort to force by the client when it had important interests/motivations at stake. This was the case with the United States and Israel in 1967 after the US failure to open the Tiran Straits; it thus had to give a circumscribed permission to Israel, which felt highly threatened, to resort to force in order to do the job by itself (Quandt 1993, p. 42; Ovendale 1992, p. 203). Similarly, the Soviets could not vehemently oppose the Egyptian resort to force in 1969 and 1973 because they were highly motivated to get their territories back and the Soviets could not accomplish this goal by other means. Nasser even succeeded in bringing about Soviet involvement in the War of Attrition after he issued a threat to resign in favor of a pro-Western leader unless Moscow deployed air defense units in Egypt to contain Israel's air superiority (Heikal 1975, pp. 79–83).

Similarly, the expulsion of the Soviet advisers from Egypt in July 1972, in reaction to the Soviet arms restraints, clarified to the USSR the high price it was paying for its restraint and the fact that it was going to lose a major ally if it continued to be so cautious. Thus, the Soviets had to resume arms deliveries to Egypt (Shamir 1980, p. 282; George et al. 1983, p. 145). Although the Soviets still tried to prevent a war (Golan 1977,

[54] On Soviet opposition to Arab war plans in 1973, see Israelyan 1995, pp. 2–11.

pp. 39–42; Porter 1984, pp. 116–125), the Arab attack on Israel in October 1973 was facilitated by Soviet arms.

Effective regional war termination by the superpowers

Despite the superpowers' lack of success in preventing wars, they were more successful in war termination. The relatively early termination of most Arab–Israeli wars was effected by superpower intervention, which prevented major changes in the prewar status quo (Miller 2002, ch. 5). These interventions took place when the balance of motivation shifted in favor of the superpowers because of the growing danger of the local war's escalation to a direct superpower confrontation, due to the risk of the Arab states' strategic defeat at the hands of Israel. Since such an outcome was bound to result in Soviet intervention against Israel to save its Arab clients and in an American counterintervention in support of Israel, both superpowers intervened to end the war and prevent a decisive Arab defeat. This pattern was manifested most clearly in the wars of 1956 and 1967, the 1969–1970 War of Attrition, the 1973 war, and the 1982 Lebanon war.[55] The shifting balance of motivation made it easier for the superpowers to control their regional allies at the end (rather than at the beginning) of the local wars.

Thus, the United States was much more successful in influencing the termination of war in 1956 than in its attempts to prevent the war erupting (Atherton 1994, p. 240; Spiegel 1992, p. 152). The United States exerted effective pressure on Britain and France during the war and even used the Soviet threats of intervention at the end of the war as a subtle form of further pressure on its two West European allies and on Israel (Spiegel 1985, pp. 66–82). The US clarification that it would not prevent Soviet intervention had a decisive influence on the Israeli responsiveness to the great power pressures to stop the fighting and eventually to withdraw from the Sinai (Bar Siman-Tov 1987, pp. 58, 64).

This pattern was also clearly manifested in subsequent Arab–Israeli wars. On the last day of the 1967 war, when Israel's intentions toward Syria were unclear, the Soviets threatened to "intervene militarily" if Israel did not stop advancing immediately. Again, the United States used the Soviet threat to pressure Israel to accept a ceasefire.[56]

[55] On the tacit rules of US–Soviet intervention in these and other Arab–Israeli crises, see Miller 2002, ch. 5. For a related argument, see A. Stein and Lobell 1997, pp. 104–105.
[56] On the joint termination of the 1967 war, see Whetten 1981, p. 54, Bar Siman-Tov 1987, pp. 85–145, and Gerges 1994, p. 225, and citations.

Following the escalation of the War of Attrition in early 1970, culminating in the Soviet intervention with their own air defense crews, the United States embarked on the Second Rogers Plan designed to bring about a ceasefire on the Suez Canal. The Soviets helped to secure Egyptian acquiescence by exerting pressure and denying them enhanced military aid (Whetten 1981, p. 61; Sadat 1977, p. 128; Heikal 1978, p. 199). Through a combination of incentives and pressures, the United States brought about Israel's agreement to the plan (Spiegel 1992, p. 154).

In contrast to their lack of success in preventing the 1973 war, the superpowers were more successful in its termination. After the tide of battle turned in Israel's favor, Premier Kosygin of the USSR came to Cairo to show Sadat satellite photographs demonstrating that the Egyptian army was being defeated.[57] The Soviets also exerted restraining pressures on the Syrians to agree to a ceasefire and, most important, cooperated with the United States in setting it up. When the Israelis seemed to violate the ceasefire, the Soviets threatened intervention. Although the United States deterred such intervention, it also took advantage again of the Soviet threat in order to put heavy pressure on Israel to comply.[58]

Thus, Israel could never win any conflict outright. At the same time, the Arab states knew that if they posed a threat to destroy Israel the United States might intervene or take dramatic measures. No war could end definitively because the superpowers would not allow complete surrender (Spiegel 1997, p. 303; Lewis 1995, p. 368; Krasner 1997).

As a result of these combined effects of competitive great power involvement on the perpetuation of the regional conflict – the enabling of local wars coupled with effective war termination – the pattern of Arab–Israeli relations in the 1955–1991 period was one of a protracted cold war punctuated by short, hot wars, determined by regional and domestic factors.

US hegemony in the Middle East results in a transition to Arab–Israeli cold peace

In the post-1973 period, the United States gradually managed to exclude the USSR from involvement in the Arab–Israeli conflict and to establish partial hegemony over the region, becoming the common great

[57] Heikal 1975, p. 237; Sadat 1977, pp. 252–254.
[58] Kissinger 1982, pp. 576, 602–605; Dayan 1977, pp. 551–552; Eban 1977, p. 537.

power patron of Israel, Egypt, Jordan, and the Gulf states. US hegemony became much more complete with the end of the Cold War and Soviet disintegration:[59] other Arab parties to the conflict, notably the Palestinians and Syria, had lost the possibility of recourse to a rival superpower patron who could shield them from the adverse effects and costs of opposition to US-led peacemaking efforts.

Since the 1973 war, US leadership has helped to moderate the Arab–Israeli conflict and to initiate an Arab–Israeli peace process, thus "cooling" the regional conflict. It specifically made a major contribution to the establishment of a cold peace between Israel and Egypt in 1978–1979 which coincided with a growing dependency of both Egypt and Israel on the United States (since the 1973 war) in the diplomatic, economic, and military domains.[60] On the diplomatic front, the United States was the only actor able to broker the crucial disengagement (January 1974) and interim (September 1975) accords between the two ex-combatants following the inconclusive outcome of the 1973 war.[61] The disenchantment in Egypt with the state socialist road of development and the transition under Sadat to a more open capitalist economy induced a realignment of Egypt from the USSR to the United States, which had much more to offer Egypt, economically, than the Soviets. The dire economic conditions of Egypt in the 1970s produced a dependence on stable and predictable US aid.[62] The food riots in Egypt in early 1977 showed Sadat the urgency of economic reforms in Egypt and the need for external assistance. He viewed the United States as the key to both issues.

The necessity to save scarce resources for Egypt's increasing development needs encouraged a shift to diplomatic means of recovering the Sinai, instead of expensive military spending. The United States was viewed by Sadat as the only actor who could potentially influence Israel to give up the Sinai (Dessouki 1991, p. 167). A major Egyptian objective in the 1973 war was to engage the superpowers in a diplomatic process which would restore the Sinai to Egypt (Sadat 1977; Telhami 1990, p. 68). Following the outcome of the 1973 war, it became clear that force alone would be insufficient to regain the Sinai, especially so long as Israel received US support. This US support, however, also provided Washington with powerful leverage over Israel. Thus, Sadat became convinced

[59] See Miller 1997; Hudson 1996. On US global hegemony in the post-Cold War and its limitations, see Krasner 1997, pp. 203–204; Wohlforth 1999; Huntington 1999; Nye 2002; Ikenberry 2002; and Paul et al. 2004.

[60] See Ajami 1982, 23–25; Dessouki 1991, pp. 166–168, 175–179; Shamir 1980; Touval 1982, chs. 9, 10; Telhami 1990, esp. pp. 105–106; Ben-Zvi 1993; Quandt 1993.

[61] See J. Stein 1987, pp. 70–71.

[62] See Telhami 1990, chs. 3 and 4, and Sela 1998, p. 212.

of the necessity of a rapprochement with the United States, which held "the key to peace" in the area and "99 percent of the cards of the game," in order to make it a full partner in the peace process (Dessouki 1991, p. 167; Telhami 1990). Sadat also realized that the way to Washington passed through Jerusalem. Thus, "one is tempted to argue that the target of his visit to Jerusalem was not only the Israelis but equally the American people" (Dessouki 1991, p. 176).

For Israel's part, its rising defense burden following the 1973 war increased its dependence on the growing American economic and military aid. The US airlift during the war demonstrated the great Israeli security dependence on the United States. The growing dependence of both sides on the US patron, and particularly their competition to be the major US regional ally,[63] made it easier for Washington to broker the Camp David accords (1978) and the Egyptian–Israeli peace treaty (1979).[64] Although Egypt and Israel started their peace contacts in the summer of 1977 without US involvement, by the end of the year it became clear that active US engagement was essential (Sela 1998, p. 198). Indeed, President Carter of the United States played a key mediating role during the Camp David conference and the peace treaty negotiations in its aftermath; without his involvement the parties might not have reached peace agreements (Quandt 1986).

Following the Gulf War, a more comprehensive cold peace was established, manifested in the Madrid process involving Israel, the Palestinians, Jordan, and most Arab states.[65] It is extremely hard to imagine the progress in the Arab–Israeli peace process since 1973 without the active mediation and the financial assistance of the United States both to Israel and to the two parties which signed peace treaties with it, Egypt and Jordan. The end of the Cold War, the collapse of Soviet power, and the blow inflicted by the United States on Iraqi military power – and thus on Arab radicalism – in the Gulf War are essential for understanding the accomplishments in Arab–Israeli diplomacy in the 1990s.

The transformation from a competitive to a hegemonic international system has limited the maneuvering room of the Middle Eastern actors, especially the Arab radicals. During the Cold War Arab radicals could turn to the USSR for diplomatic assistance as well as arms supply and resupply during crises, especially when the tide in regional wars turned

[63] This point is highlighted by Telhami 1990, pp. 70, 105–106.
[64] Telhami 1990; Quandt 1986 and 1993, chs. 10–12.
[65] See Indyk 1992; Quandt 1993, chs. 15, 16; Lieber 1995.

against them. This made it possible for the radicals to persist in the conflict against Israel and to intimidate those who wanted to make peace with it. Soviet disintegration terminated this support and thus weakened the ability of the radicals to continue the conflict and to prevent progress in peacemaking under US sponsorship.[66]

The US victory in the 1991 Gulf War further neutralized the ability of the radicals, led by Iraq, to sabotage the peace process. Jordan and the PLO, which bandwagoned with Iraq during the crisis, changed their orientation following its defeat and were ready to join the US-led peace process.[67] The Gulf War dramatically demonstrated the security dependence of Israelis and most Arab states on US military power. The inability of the Arab states to defend Kuwait showed the high dependence of many states in the region, especially the oil-rich Gulf states, on the United States for their security. The Gulf War also showed the limitations that the United States can impose, under crisis conditions, on Israel's freedom of military action, such as in the deployment of US Patriot missile batteries in Israel (in addition to US air raids on the Iraqi army) as a substitute for an Israeli military response to the Iraqi Scud missile attacks.

The massive US intervention both by airpower and on the ground, including a willingness to absorb considerable casualties, showed a very powerful American commitment to supporting Middle East stability and to fighting revisionist forces. US economic power has also provided it with important leverage, both through direct financial assistance to key regional players and through the provision of credit and technology transfers. Thus, US hegemony has created a powerful *Realpolitik* logic in favor of peace, even if only a cold one: those who join the peace camp benefit in the security, economic, and diplomatic fields, while those who oppose the peace pay a heavy price in these domains without being compensated by a countervailing force. This explains why not necessarily idealist but rather pragmatic leaders joined the Pax Americana in the 1990s,[68] while ideologues in both sides (Arab radicals and Islamic

[66] On the effect of the Soviet collapse and the Gulf War on Syrian international reorientation, see Rabinovich 1998, pp. 36–43. On the key role of the United States in the regional peace process following the Gulf War, see Faour 1993 . On the key US role in convening the 1991 Madrid Conference, see Baker and DeFrank 1995 and Sela 1998, p. 333.

[67] Faour 1993, p. 111. On the enormous economic and political difficulties of the PLO following the collapse of the USSR and the end of the Gulf War, and before the Oslo process brought it back to relevance, see Robinson 1997, pp. 175–177.

[68] For example, the global changes led Israeli premier Rabin to change his long-held positions against negotiating with the PLO and to accept the Oslo process of peace negotiations with it (Makovsky 1996, p. 112; Inbar 1999).

elements and right-wing nationalists in Israel) rejected the peace process and therefore faced heavy diplomatic, economic, and military sanctions imposed by the hegemon.

The central role of US hegemony in bringing about a transition to cold peace is especially significant if we take into account the limitations of the expected stabilizing effects of regional and domestic changes such as the decline of pan-Arab ideology and the strengthening of the sovereignty norm in the Arab world.[69] First, these are long-term and gradual changes which are unable to account for major changes over short periods of time, as is the case with the transition to an active Arab–Israeli peace process in the post-1991 period. The Middle Eastern leaders and regimes involved in the Madrid process following the Gulf War were the same ones who, only a short time before, spearheaded hardline policies in the Arab–Israeli conflict. Second, the regional/domestic changes have had very limited effects in bringing about regional stability and domestic order in the Arab world (Barnett 1996/7, 606–618; Faour 1993; J. Stein 1993; Inbar 1995). There are many unresolved border disputes in the Arab world (G. Joffe 1997) and difficult state-to-nation issues (see chapter 4). Many Arab states suffer from problems of severe domestic instability, which exercise negative effects on the regional order (Ayoob 1993, 1995; Maoz 1995; J. Stein 1993). Third, in the post-Gulf War era there has still been strong rejection among the Arabs of the acceptance of Israel as an equal and normal member in a "New Middle East" (Barnett 1996/7, 604–606; Sela 1998, ch. 16; Korany 1997). This rejection, in addition to intransigence on the part of some Israeli governments, made it impossible for the parties to advance in the peace process without third-party intervention. Fourth, had the Iraqi occupation of Kuwait not been reversed, the fate of the sovereignty norm and the fortunes of pan-Arabism could have been completely different; thus, the purported stabilizing effects of the regional changes would not have occurred. Moreover, Iraq was evicted mostly by US power, while the Arabs provided only minor assistance to the military campaign. The Arabs were unable by themselves to liberate Kuwait and to contain the expansionist drive of Saddam Hussein (Sela 1998, p. 326), which could have severely destabilized the Middle East in the absence of US intervention.

[69] See the discussion in ch. 4. See also Ben-Dor 1983; Ajami 1978/9; 1981; Pervin 1997; Sela 1998; Barnett 1998.

The United States has employed the various strategies available to a hegemonic power for promoting a transition from a regional cold war to cold peace:

- restraining its client Israel (notably in times of local wars, when it posed a threat to Arab capitals, such as at the end of the 1967 and 1973 wars, or when its use of force could potentially have caused an escalation of the conflict, such as during the 1956 war and the Gulf War) and applying diplomatic and economic pressure to induce its moderation in the regional peace process, for example, during the reassessment crisis of spring 1975.[70] The Ford administration decided to reassess its policy toward Israel following Secretary Kissinger's abortive effort of March 1975 to mediate an interim agreement between Israel and Egypt. The new policy included several punitive measures in the form of implicit threats as well as limited sanctions.[71] The George Bush Sr. administration also exerted heavy pressure on the right-wing Shamir government to take part in the 1991 Madrid peace conference (Ben-Zvi 1993; Arens 1995, pp. 242–243; Baker and DeFrank 1995).
- reassuring its allies through arms supply and security cooperation and assistance (to Israel, Jordan, the Gulf states, and post-Camp David Egypt), crucial financial assistance (to Israel, Egypt, and Jordan), and security guarantees (to the Gulf states). Indeed, following the insecurity in the Gulf, generated by the Iraqi invasion of Kuwait and the resurgence of other regional rivalries, the Gulf states have preferred to rely more on US security assistance than on their fellow Arabs.[72] In the post-Gulf War era, and even before the 2003 occupation of Iraq, American military forces and equipment were stationed in six Middle Eastern states, including the most populous (Egypt) and the richest (Saudi Arabia). Until the 2003 Iraq War about 20,000 US troops were deployed in the Gulf region as a whole. The United States is also the patron of the most militarily powerful state in the region (Israel). This security assistance creates dependence of the armed forces of the recipient states on the United States and, especially in the absence of a credible alternative, minimizes the likelihood of a defection from the US-led coalition. The persistent US security commitment to Israel played a crucial role in convincing initially Egypt and later other

[70] See Spiegel 1985, pp. 291–305; Ben-Zvi 1993, ch. 4.
[71] For details, see Ben-Zvi 1993, pp. 97–98.
[72] Barnett 1996/7, 608 and the references he cites; Buzan and Waever 2003.

Arab states that they would not be able to overcome Israel militarily. This commitment thus encouraged the turn to peace by the Arabs.[73]

- coercion of revisionist regional powers by sanctions and use of force. In contrast to its attitude toward its friends in the region, the United States has imposed economic sanctions and arms embargoes on states perceived to be hostile toward it, its regional interests, and the advancement of the peace process; these states, specifically, are Iraq, Libya, Iran, and Sudan.[74] A notable example of a containment strategy toward revisionist powers by the imposition of diplomatic and economic sanctions and an arms embargo is the Clinton administration's dual containment of both Iran and Iraq.[75] When diplomatic and economic means seemed to be insufficient for defending its key interests, the United States was willing to resort to military means to maintain the regional order. Washington exercised deterrence[76] and later compellence; when both of these strategies failed to prevent aggression, ultimately it was willing to fight and defeat a regional aggressor (Iraq in the 1991 Gulf War and in spring 2003).[77]
- playing a crucial mediating role in moderating the level of the Arab–Israeli conflict. Since 1967, successive US administrations have undertaken a long series of unilateral diplomatic efforts intended to promote the reduction of this conflict under exclusive US auspices.[78] The

[73] See Faour 1993, p. 15. [74] Feldman 1996, p. 35. [75] Hudson 1996, p. 340.

[76] On US deterrence policy in the Middle East, see Craig and George 1995, pp. 186–188.

[77] For an analysis of US coercive diplomacy in the First Gulf War, see Herrmann 1994 and Miller 1998.

[78] Eisenberg and Caplan note that "almost every major peace initiative since Camp David can be linked with an American president or secretary of state, and in those cases where actual US mediation was minimal . . . the parties still found it necessary to sign their agreements in the presence of the American president and with his full and public support" (1998, p. 135). For a short survey, see Miller 1997, 116–120. Examples include the diplomatic initiatives made in 1970–1971 by the State Department in the first Nixon administration, dubbed Rogers I, II, III, and IV; Kissinger's unilateral, step-by-step "shuttle diplomacy" which produced the disengagement accords of 1974 between Israel and Egypt (Sinai I, January 1974), between Israel and Syria (May 1974), and the Sinai II interim accord between Israel and Egypt (September 1975); Carter's mediation of the Camp David accords (September 1978) and the Egyptian–Israeli peace treaty (March 1979); Reagan's "fresh start" initiative of September 1, 1982; the diplomatic efforts made by the George Bush Sr. administration in the wake of the Gulf War, manifested by Secretary of State Baker's eight trips to the region following the Gulf War (Baker and DeFrank 1995), leading to the convening of the Madrid peace conference in October 1991; and the Clinton administration's active brokerage of the agreements between the Palestinian Authority and the Netanyahu government, the Hebron Agreement (January 1997) and the Wye accord (October 1998) and later, during the Barak government, the Sharm-El-Sheikh accord (September 1999). Although the Clinton administration did not initiate the Israeli–Jordanian peace treaty (1994) and the Oslo process (1993–1996), its support of these agreements was very

United States made it easier for the regional parties to make painful concessions in the peace process by "bribing" them through the provision of major financial aid. Israel especially was compensated for its major territorial concessions by generous financial and security assistance. Thus, the United States assisted Israel to build new airfields in the Negev as a replacement for its airfields which had to be abandoned because the Sinai was returned to Egypt (Quandt 1986). Accordingly, following the "step-by-step" agreements, and later the Camp David accords between Egypt and Israel, these two states top, by far, the list of recipients of US foreign assistance.[79] Jordan and the Palestinian National Authority have also received substantial amounts of assistance following their signing of peace agreements with Israel (the Palestinians in 1993, followed by Jordan in 1994).[80] Forty percent of all US foreign aid goes to the region. No other state comes close to these levels of regional involvement.

- playing the roles of a guarantor and a referee: the United States serves as the guarantor of the accords reached between Israelis and Arabs since 1973 and as a final arbiter/referee in case of disagreements among the parties about the interpretation of a settlement. For example, an important component of the Israeli–Egyptian disengagement agreements in the Sinai in the aftermath of the Yom Kippur War has been the US role in monitoring and verifying the implementation of the agreements, including an American commitment to administer early-warning stations at the buffer zone and to conduct regular

important for their sustainability and implementation. The Clinton administration was also intensely involved in the failed Camp David negotiations of summer 2000 and the follow-up attempts to reach an Israeli–Palestinian accord in the last few months of the administration.

[79] For example, in 1988 the figures in millions of dollars were 1,800 and 1,301.5 in military aid to Israel and Egypt respectively and 1,200 and 873.4 in economic aid to the two countries. For a comparison, a large recipient of US aid such as Turkey received in that year $493.5 million in military aid and $32.4 million in economic aid (Agency for International Development, cited in Congressional Quarterly 1991, p. 77).

[80] The secretary of state at that time notes that the United States led the international economic support provided for the implementation of the Israeli–Palestinian accords. See Christopher 1998, p. 196. In the aftermath of the Gulf War, both the Palestinians and the Jordanians were in dire economic need. See Sela 1998, pp. 328, 334. This increased their dependence on the United States, especially because the Arab oil-rich countries suspended their aid in anger at the support that the PLO and King Hussein gave to Saddam Hussein during the crisis. This dependence increased their desire to join the peace process in the expectation of getting US assistance, that is, based on the logic of "bandwagoning for profit" (Schweller 1994), though in this case the bandwagoning with the hegemon was stabilizing, as expected by hegemonic stability theory and in contrast to Schweller's offensive realist theory.

reconnaissance flights over the demilitarized area established by the accord.[81] In the Camp David accords, the United States was active in establishing and manning the international force that was deployed in the Sinai.[82] Such a situation moderates the destabilizing effects of a lack of supreme authority under anarchy and the associated fears of defection (Jervis 1978; Waltz 1979). The United States could be a credible referee especially in this case because of the high dependence of both parties on continued US assistance in key security, diplomatic, and economic domains.

As for the US willingness to play the role of the hegemon in the Middle East, it stems from the intrinsic importance of the region to US interests due to the location of vast oil resources there. This produces an American interest in stabilizing the region and thus containing radical anti-American forces, promoting regional security arrangements and peace processes. More specifically, the presence of oil in the Arab world generates an interest in maintaining good relations with the Arab states. Such an interest conflicts with American political/ideological/moral commitment to Israel's security. The United States tries to reconcile this conflict of interest by advancing the Arab–Israeli peace process. US attempts during the Cold War to construct an Arab–Israeli grand alliance against the supposedly shared Soviet threat failed because local parties tend to focus on regional threats rather than on global ones. In contrast to the highly dubious and disputed Soviet threat to the regional states, following Iraq's 1990 invasion of Kuwait, Iraqi revisionism posed a true shared threat to the United States (because of the threat to the regional oil resources), Israel, and status quo Arab states. Thus, the United States was able to lead a multinational coalition, which included most Arab states, and in the aftermath of its 1991 victory over Iraq, to promote the Arab–Israeli peace process. The dual threats of Iraqi radicalism and the Islamic revolution (inspired by Iran but having multiple local manifestations in Arab states, and in the occupied territories) led to a convergence of threats for the United States, Israel, and the status quo Arab states; this facilitated the regional peace process led by the United States.[83]

As the United States is both democratic and distant from the region, the form of its hegemony has been relatively benign, with an emphasis

[81] See J. Stein 1987, pp. 71–73.

[82] See Mandell 1990, Mandell and Tomlin 1991, and Quandt 1993.

[83] On the importance of the Islamic threat in the territories (Hamas) for Rabin's decision to go to the Oslo process with Hamas's rival, the PLO, see Makovsky 1996, p. 112.

on encouraging (rather than imposing) a regional order and peace. However, this interest became much more concrete following the 1973 war when the Arab oil embargo disrupted the world economy. This can account for the much more aggressive US promotion of the peace process following that war. That war also generated a dangerous US–Soviet crisis, and thus demonstrated that lack of progress in the peace process is dangerous both for world peace and the world economy.

While US involvement has been conducive to the establishment of cold peace in some parts of the Middle East, peacemaking has not progressed much beyond this level. Thus, the threat of war has not disappeared completely from Egyptian–Israeli relations (despite their having been at peace since 1979), let alone from the Syrian–Israeli arena, where the US-sponsored peace talks collapsed in 2000 because of the unresolved substantive issues related to the recognition of Israel, normalization of Israeli–Syrian relations, security arrangements, water issues, and the legitimacy of boundaries.[84] Even in the two Arab states that have signed peace agreements with Israel (Egypt and Jordan), there are still significant elites that continue to regard Israel as illegitimate and oppose the development of normal relations with it, at least partly because of the lack, thus far, of a permanent settlement of the Palestinian problem. There are also limitations on transnational activity in areas such as trade, investment, and culture.[85] Moreover, the progress made in the Middle Eastern peace process is still reversible, as was demonstrated by the general deterioration of Arab–Israeli relations after the right-wing nationalist Netanyahu government came to power in Israel in mid-1996.

This reversibility was most dramatically demonstrated by the eruption of violence between Israel and the Palestinians in fall 2000 (the El Aqsa Intifada) following the collapse of the Camp David negotiations. This violence testifies to the severity of the still unresolved state-to-nation problems in the Israeli–Palestinian arena, which forms the core of the Arab–Israeli conflict (these issues are discussed in chapter 4). US hegemony on its own was unable to produce a change in the basic nationalist (and related religious) motivations of the parties, and was therefore unable to prevent the recent outbreak of violence between them.

At the same time, the United States was extremely helpful in preventing a regional escalation of the violence despite powerful domestic

[84] See Faour 1993, pp. 116–118.
[85] On the cold Israeli–Egyptian peace, see Yaari 1987, Dowek 1998, and Gerges 1995.

pressures on Arab states to join the struggle against Israel and actively to support the Palestinian struggle. US allies in the region, notably Egypt and Jordan, who are heavily dependent on US aid, were strongly encouraged by the United States to oppose the escalation of the violence beyond the Israeli–Palestinian confrontation. Thus, neither the Arab League nor the Islamic Conference, their anti-Israeli rhetoric notwithstanding, has adopted the extreme resolutions introduced by the anti-US forces in the region. Moreover, despite strong domestic pressures against the continuation of peace with Israel, Jordan and Egypt persist in the US-supported cold peace with their Jewish neighbor.

In a unipolar world, with no countervailing force to US hegemony, it is much more difficult to bring about regional escalation, in contrast to a situation in which other great powers are competing with the United States for dominance in the Middle East. Thus, the absence of serious international challengers to the United States helped to prevent the spread of violence to a regional war. A major case is the Syrian–Lebanese frontier on the northern border of Israel. Attacks by the Lebanese group Hezbollah on Israel could easily have escalated into a regional war because of the Israeli reactions by sending fighter jets firing missiles into Syrian-controlled Lebanon. US pressures on Syria to moderate the attacks from Lebanon on Israel were very important in preventing escalation. This was especially important during Secretary of State Colin Powell's visit to the area in April 2002. Although Powell failed to reach a ceasefire on the Israeli–Palestinian front, he was more successful defusing the attacks on Israel over the Lebanese border, which were supported by Syria. Before Powell visited Damascus, Vice President Cheney called Syria's president, Bashar Asad, and President Bush wrote him a "strong letter" urging him to stay out of the conflict.[86]

US restraining power was also important in the case of Iraq. Before the outbreak of the second intifada in fall 2000, Saddam Hussein had already made a series of startlingly belligerent speeches, as he did before the invasion of Kuwait in 1990. Iraq also mobilized several divisions on its western border, offering to step in if Syria needed military help. Yet, the United States, aided by a number of Arab states, including Syria,

[86] *New York Times*, April 19, 2002, A1, A8. A day earlier the *New York Times* cited Israeli sources who indicated that, while the eighteen-month-old conflict with the Palestinians did not menace the region, Powell managed a much more dangerous issue – the northern border – "the real tinderbox that could potentially lead to regional escalation" (Dore Gold, an adviser to Sharon, cited in *New York Times*, April 18, 2002, A1, A10).

ordered him to pull back, which he did.[87] More indirectly, the US-led international environment has also helped to moderate Iran's behavior when the intifada erupted. While issuing extreme anti-Israeli statements and encouraging calls by volunteers to go and fight the Zionists, Iran's desires to improve its relations with the West and to join the global economy contained the level of Iranian support of the Palestinians and limited it to the provision of arms and money to extreme Islamic organizations, preventing the escalation of its involvement beyond that level.

This combination of low-intensity conflict such as the second intifada and the nonescalation to the regional level shows both the limitations and the opportunities of the hegemon with regard to the scope of its influence on regional war and peace. While a hegemon has proved unable to prevent the eruption of communal violence between national groups competing for control of the same territory and its nationalist-religious symbols, it is much more capable of exercising moderating pressures for the prevention of the spread of this violence to the interstate regional level, where *Realpolitik* logic is more inclined toward moderation under hegemony. Moreover, the United States has succeeded in inducing the parties to resume peace negotiations relatively quickly, even before the cessation of violence, although the talks were not fruitful. President Clinton's active role in these negotiations testifies that the United States remains the only reliable broker for peacemaking between Israel and the Palestinians. Thus, we should expect that the United States would play a leading role in brokering any future peace agreements between the two parties. The US hegemony continues to provide strong incentives to the parties to pursue peace, even if a very cold and unstable one. Given the US special leverage on Israel, which holds the territorial cards, the Palestinians realize (similarly to Sadat and Jordan's King Hussein in the past, and potentially Syria's Asad in the future) that, once they are ready to make peace with Israel, the United States provides the most effective avenue for the pursuit of a land-for-peace formula.

Progress in the crucial Israeli–Palestinian track will go a long way toward resolving a key state-to-nation issue in the region. Together with the formation of legitimate boundaries between Israel and Syria, the resolution of these national/territorial problems will allow the establishment of a comprehensive peace in the Middle East. Even under optimistic scenarios, however, intensive diplomatic-security-economic

[87] *New York Times*, November 5, 2000.

engagement of the United States will be crucial for creating an environment conducive to any progress, at least in the initially critical stages.

The effects of 9/11 and the war in Iraq

Although a unipolar world emerged following the collapse of the USSR, the materialization of US hegemony was only partial until 9/11. While the disintegration of the USSR has weakened the constraints on US dominance and thus allowed greater freedom of military action, the disappearance of the Soviet threat has also reduced the US motive for an intensive worldwide US military engagement.[88] A major manifestation of the partiality of US hegemony in the Middle East was the continued challenge posed by a defiant Saddam Hussein who survived in power in direct contrast to US preferences. Such a signal of the lack of resolve of US hegemony has supposedly undermined its ability to promote American objectives in the region, notably advancing Arab–Israeli peace.

The 9/11 attacks have changed this situation by increasing the US motivation for a resolute international engagement, a motivation which was missing after the end of the Cold War. US hegemony changed its character to a more unilateralist orientation, ready to ignore the UN, the Europeans, the Russians, and the Chinese whenever its perceived key security interests were at stake. The US also changed its security doctrine, endorsing a strategy of preemption or even preventive war against rogue states that sponsor terrorism, or develop weapons of mass destruction, or both. Moreover, the United States adopted the idea of regime change by force in order to democratize this kind of state. While some neoconservative thinkers in the United States advanced similar ideas well before 9/11, the political support these ideas could garner became much stronger after that attack. This new and far-reaching revisionist grand strategy could not find considerable domestic support before such a traumatic experience for American society.[89]

These changes are especially relevant to the Middle East because of the heavy presence there of the new security threats: rogue states which supposedly sponsor terrorism and develop weapons of mass destruction. Following 9/11 it seemed that the core interests of US national security, notably homeland defense, are tightly related to issues such as: the stability of the Middle East; the type of nonconventional arsenal

[88] Miller 1998. See also the discussion on US intervention in the Balkans in ch. 6.
[89] See Miller 2004 and the references cited there.

that certain rogue regimes in the region developed, and these regimes' relations with terrorist organizations. In the aftermath of 9/11, it even seemed to some key players in the George W. Bush administration that key US security interests were affected by the nature of the regimes in the region, specifically, whether they were democratic or not. These perceived interests led to a major military intervention in Iraq in spring 2003, with the goals of preventing its supposed attempts to acquire weapons of mass destruction (WMD) and, even more fundamentally, replacing Saddam Hussein's regime with a democracy. The objective of this post-9/11 strategy is not only to change the capabilities of rogue regimes, namely to destroy their WMD, but also to change their intentions by transforming the nature of the political system. The idea is that the regime change in Iraq would have bandwagoning effects on the other states in the region. Namely, to the extent that a democratic regime emerges in a prosperous and stable oil-rich Iraq, such a change would have the "power of example" and serve as a model for other Arab states.

This liberalization of Arab-Muslim regimes would not only reduce their incentives to acquire WMD, but would supposedly also drain the swamp in which terrorists like Al Qaeda thrive. In the view of key officials of the George W. Bush administration, Al Qaeda emerged in the Arab-Islamic world because of the authoritarian nature of the regimes, which silenced dissent effectively. This lack of political space pushed radicals to use violent means, while the regimes followed a scapegoat strategy, even if indirectly (through the education system, the media, and the religious establishment). This strategy focused on diverting the people's attention away from the local oppressors toward the allegedly external enemies of Arabism and Islam: the "Great Satan" – the United States – and the little one – Israel. The Bush administration expected that the liberalization of the Arab regimes would end this diversionary strategy and thus remove the type of security threat to the United States manifested on 9/11. In addition, it was hoped that liberalization would reduce the danger that these regimes would acquire WMD and then provide them to terrorist organizations which might use them against the United States. Democratization of Arab regimes would also arguably increase the prospects of peace with Israel based on the logic of the democratic peace theory.[90] This would remove a threat to US national security, because the Palestinian issue supposedly produces resentment

[90] On the democratic peace theory, see chs. 1 and 2. In contrast to this theory, in the view of the new US doctrine, democracy becomes not only a sufficient condition for peace, as is expected by the theory, but a necessary condition for regional peace.

against the United States due to its support for Israel. Thus the Bush administration hoped that the regime change in Iraq (and Afghanistan) would weaken the appeal of radical terrorist organizations and make it much harder for them to act in the Middle East and to recruit volunteers and raise funds.

Indeed, at first glance it seemed that the removal of Saddam weakened the radical forces in the region and increased the likelihood of progress in the peace process. The Bush administration seemed more determined to promote the process and, following the military victory, had more leverage to pressure the parties to make concessions. Thus, following US pressures, both the Palestinians and Israelis endorsed the US-sponsored "road map" to peace which focuses on resolution of the state-to-nation issues, security arrangements, and political reforms in the Palestinian Authority. Israel is more reassured because the removal of Saddam undermined the so-called Eastern Front, which could have potentially posed a major security threat by combining the forces of Syria and Iraq. Because of this reassurance, as well as to avert expected US and international pressures, Israel now seems more willing to make some territorial concessions. Although these concessions have been confined until now to the unilateral disengagement from the Gaza Strip (and an evacuation of a few Jewish settlements from the northern West Bank), the March 2006 Israeli elections signaled a willingness to implement considerable withdrawals also in the West Bank.[91]

The pro-US Arab moderates, Egypt, Jordan, Saudi Arabia, the Gulf states, and Morocco, are more willing to join again the US-led peace coalition. Saudi Arabia in particular put on the regional agenda a relatively moderate peace plan in March 2002, at least partly in order to maintain good relations with the United States following the worsening of their ties in the aftermath of the participation of fifteen Saudi nationals in the 9/11 attacks.[92] The United States also made some limited gains even with some of the radicals, although Syria and Iran continue to be hostile to the US war in Iraq and to the continued occupation of that country. The United States together with France and a Lebanese coalition succeeded in bringing about a Syrian withdrawal from Lebanon,

[91] Yet, following the Israel–Hezbollah war in summer 2006, there are growing domestic constraints on future Israeli withdrawals, particularly unilateral ones, due to the disappointment in the Israeli public arising from the unilateral withdrawal from southern Lebanon in May 2000, which failed to produce peace and security along the Israeli–Lebanese border; moreover, the unilateral disengagement from Gaza also failed to result in greater stability along its border with Israel.
[92] See Podeh 2003.

even if Syria continues to meddle there (see chapter 4). Libya recently made an especially drastic change in its policy by giving up its programs for development of weapons of mass destruction and its ties with terrorism. Moreover, as noted in chapter 4, at least partly as a result of US attempts to bring democracy to this region, which had fewer democracies than other regions, relatively free elections were held not only in Iraq, but also in a host of other states and in the Palestinian territories, even if there have been quite a few setbacks.

The rising challenges to US hegemonic management

Yet, the challenges to US hegemony in the Middle East persist, and are even reinforced, in the aftermath of the 2003 Iraq War.

First, it is inherently difficult for an external power to pacify communal violence derived from an intense state-to-nation imbalance such as the Israeli–Palestinian clashes or to stabilize, let alone democratize, an occupied country like Iraq with an ethnically divided society that had been held together for decades by an iron fist. Indeed, despite US efforts, the low-intensity violence in both Palestine–Israel and in Iraq continues. If Iraq continues to be unstable and US forces are bogged down there or alternatively if the US disengages from Iraq without stabilizing it and Iraq remains a failed state, all such scenarios will pose a major problem for US standing not only in Iraq but also in the region as a whole. The difficulties in stabilizing Iraq have already seemed to divert US attention away from promoting the Arab–Israeli peace process.

Second, there are some countervailing forces that, even though they are still weak militarily, oppose US hegemony; thus, they engage in asymmetric balancing through terrorism and the acquisition of WMD:[93] Iran, Islamist forces, other radical movements including some inside Iraq and Palestine, terrorist organizations such as Al Qaeda, and Syria. An especially difficult challenge is the attempt by oil-rich Iran to acquire nuclear weapons, which might lead to a destabilizing nuclear arms race in the region. A nuclear Iran could also more effectively resist US coercion and limit the US freedom of action in the Gulf. Thus far, it seems that Iran is the state which has benefited most from the war in Iraq. On the interstate level, due to the weakening of Iraq – its traditional regional counterbalancer – Iran emerges as the potential hegemon in the Gulf, especially when US forces disengage from Iraq. Iran also has a rising leverage vis-à-vis the United States because of its transborder ties with

[93] On asymmetric conflict, see Arreguin-Toft 2005.

the Shiites in Iraq; thus, Iran's cooperation is needed to stabilize Iraq. At the same time, Iran has recently accelerated its anti-Israeli rhetoric, while continuing to support radical Islamic groups in Lebanon and Palestine.

Third, some of the great powers with traditional and present interests in the region also oppose US hegemony even if they engage in much "softer balancing" than the radical Muslims.[94] This includes the Russians and the Europeans, notably the French, who seek a greater role for themselves in Middle East diplomacy as equal participants. At any rate, there is an increasing economic and diplomatic engagement of the European Union in the Middle East; the Russians are also involved in the Iranian nuclear issue and recently with Hamas following its victory in the Palestinian elections.

Fourth, there is a rising popular resentment, on nationalist grounds, across the Arab world and the region against the United States and its heavy military presence in the Middle East. This resentment is intensified by what is seen in the Arab world as an unjustified invasion of Iraq and the continuing occupation of the country.[95] There is a widespread feeling in the Arab world of a "double standard" in the American attitude toward the Arabs in comparison to Israel, especially following the eruption of the second intifada, because of the supposedly pro-Israeli bias of the United States under the influence of its domestic politics. In addition, the United States is seen as supportive of repressive pro-US regimes, notably Egypt and Saudi Arabia. Moreover, the US objectives of "regime change" and "democratization" in Iraq (and in Palestine) not only pose a potential threat to many nondemocratic Arab regimes, but also are perceived as manifestations of US imperialism. On the other hand, if democratization takes place in Iraq and other Arab states, societies with state-to-nation imbalances might bring to power radical forces such as anti-US Islamist parties at least initially. Indeed, this has happened in a number of recent elections, as reported in chapter 4. This poses tough dilemmas for the United States, which has encouraged the elections and then has had problems dealing with some of the winners, notably, in the case of Hamas. It is designated as a terror organization and does not recognize Israel's right to exist, but it won the elections in a major case of state-to-nation imbalance – Palestine (see chapter 4). The United States must decide (1) what to do about economic assistance to

[94] On "soft balancing" against US hegemony, see Paul et al. 2004, and the debate in the Summer 2005 issue of *International Security*.

[95] For a critique of the post-9/11 US policy in the Middle East as neocolonialism, see Khalidi 2004.

a Palestinian Authority that is controlled by such a militant movement, but that desperately needs external support in order not to completely collapse and create instability; and (2) how to promote the hoped-for Israeli–Palestinian peace process under such dire conditions. Indeed, the United States is still the key player for promoting regional peace.

Conclusions: systemic effects – possibilities and limitations

This chapter shows how the global balance of power influences regional balance in the Middle East. It also shows the dramatic transformation of the regional balance at the end of the Cold War. During the bipolar US–Soviet standoff, the superpowers balanced each other and supported their regional clients, making it possible for them in turn to balance the clients of the rival superpower. Indeed, attempts at forming hegemony, either through pro-Western alliances or through US exclusionary peacemaking, failed. At the same time, the United States achieved a significant goal when Egypt made its move from the Soviet sphere to the US orbit, culminating in the US-sponsored Camp David accords in the late 1970s. US efforts to extend American influence in the Middle East failed, however, while the USSR remained a superpower.

Following the Soviet collapse and the Gulf War, most of the states in the region bandwagoned with the United States because of the prospects of financial and territorial gain and the chance to come under the American security umbrella. This bandwagoning helped the Arab–Israeli peace process make some important gains. Once under the US security umbrella, status quo states were willing to help contain their revisionist neighbors, Iraq and Iran.

To maintain its influence in the Middle East, the United States uses the traditional tools of military alliances and arms sales, but significantly also makes extensive use of less threatening, more positive inducements such as economic incentives, diplomatic mediation, and regional security regimes to bolster its influence and to advance its interests in the region. American officials also wield great influence as arbiters and guarantors of agreements among regional actors.

The military victory in the Iraq War bolstered US hegemony in the region by removing from power a key anti-US leader and by showing US commitment and capability to advance its interests even against strong international and regional opposition. This seemed to create a new window of opportunity to advance the American-inspired order in the region by making progress in resolving the Israeli–Palestinian conflict and by stabilizing a more moderate pro-US regime in Iraq.

In terms of the model presented here, however, the United States overplayed its hegemonic hand when it went beyond the domain of capabilities and regional stabilization associated with the "cold" outcomes affected by great powers. With the attempt to democratize Iraq, the United States tried to affect the "hot/warm outcomes" by changing intentions and domestic regimes and embarking upon nation-building, which were supposed eventually to lead to warm peace in a democratic Middle East. These are very tough challenges even for a powerful hegemon, especially in light of the resentment against the United States in the Arab world. There is a great complexity of the forces as well as the state-to-nation imbalances to deal with. These include the tension and suspicion among the Kurds, Shiites, and Sunnis in Iraq as well as the intervention – through Iraq's porous boundaries and transborder ties – of neighboring states such as Turkey, Syria, Iran, Jordan, and Saudi Arabia, and of terrorists from across the Arab world.

Lack of progress in resolving these problems, especially if the violence persists, may jeopardize US standing in the region and may even make it easier for radical and terrorist organizations to recruit more people and resources against US interests in the region and beyond. Yet, despite the opposition to US policies in the region, it is only Washington that can play the decisive role in shaping the regional agenda. Thus far, in the absence of an external balancer, no countervailing coalition has been able to form against US hegemony. The Europeans, the Russians, and the UN, as they should, play important roles in regional diplomacy alongside the United States, as members of the Quartet, which tries to advance the Israeli–Palestinian peace process; the European Union especially also plays a key role in economic development.

Yet, these actors, with all their importance, do not have the military, economic, and diplomatic resources required to balance US hegemony in the region (the EU is an economic superpower but not a strategic one, especially as long as it does not become a unified actor in the security field). Thus, most Arab states might appear willing to go on bandwagoning with the United States because of their high dependence on American military protection and economic assistance and because of its key role in brokering the Palestine issue. However, Arab governments will try to hedge their bets and will at most be very cautious in this bandwagoning because of the anti-US nationalist sensibilities of their publics and because at this stage it is still unclear whether the US will be able successfully to resolve the Iraqi and Palestinian issues.

This chapter has specified the type of regional outcomes best explained by systemic factors and also identified those regional outcomes that are not determined by systemic causes. "Hot" outcomes, such as hot war and warm peace, are not determined by international elements but rather reflect regional and domestic causes, because in these domains the balance of motivation favors the local parties. Thus, the hot wars in the Middle East (chapter 4) and in the Balkans (chapter 6) are the result of the multiplicity of state-to-nation problems in these regions. While peace may be achieved in these regions based on the help of the great powers, the state-to-nation problems make it difficult to move beyond the level of cold peace.

The great powers affect the "cold" outcomes of cold war and peace in accordance with the type of their regional involvement. While hegemony is conducive to cold peace, great power competition helps to sustain a cold war situation in regions with state-to-nation problems, although the decision to embark on a hot war will be up to the regional actors. Great power competition intensifies regional conflict but also contains the duration and scope of regional wars. This was the case in the Middle East in the Cold War era. While the great powers were unable to prevent wars due to advantages of the local powers in the balance of interests during war initiation, the superpowers were able to bring about early war termination because of their superior capabilities and the shifting balance of motivation in their favor at the end of the regional wars. With the decline of the Cold War and the emergence of US hegemony, especially after the 1991 Gulf War, the situation in the Middle East became conducive to the emergence of a cold peace, even if a reversible one, as the recent outbreak of violence – both Israeli–Palestinian (2000–2006) and Israeli–Hezbollah (summer 2006) – demonstrates.[96]

To sum up, the analysis in this chapter shows the strength of systemic factors in accounting for the transition of the Middle East from a war zone in the Cold War era to a zone of (partial and tenuous) peace since the 1990s. The next chapter will discuss the simultaneous reverse transition of the Balkans from a zone of imposed peace in the Cold War era to a war zone in the early 1990s (and back to a zone of still tenuous peace since the US-led interventions in 1995 and 1999).

[96] Although the second intifada is considered, as noted, to have lasted between 2000 and 2004, intermittent violence between Israel and the Palestinians has continued until the end of 2006.

6 War and peace in the Balkans: states, nations, and great powers

The gradual disintegration of the vast multinational empires that controlled the Balkans – the Ottoman and Habsburg Empires – since the beginning of the nineteenth century has produced a multiplicity of nationalist rivalries in the region. Competing national groups have sought to fulfill their right to self-determination and to establish their own national states. The Balkan ethnonational groups have striven for their states to include both as many of their ethnic brethren as possible and lands to which they have had historical claims. Due to the high extent of intermingling of populations of different ethnic origins, as well as to a mismatch between historical "rights" and demographic realities, the nationalist aspirations of different groups have frequently clashed. These conflicts have made the Balkans an extremely war-prone region.

A major factor that reduced the frequency of hot regional wars, even if it did not resolve the fundamental state-to-nation problems, was great power intervention. The latter came either in the form of great power cooperation during the nineteenth-century Concert of Europe, or in the form of hegemony of Germany and later the USSR. Conversely, in other periods, great power competition and great power disengagement exacerbated the regional conflicts and exposed the region to the eruption of hot regional wars.

In the first part of the chapter, which focuses on the 1830–1913 period, there will be an investigation of the effects on regional violence of the different types of great power involvement in combination with those of the extent of the state-to-nation imbalance.[1] The second part of the chapter focuses on the effects of variations in great power engagement on the level of regional conflict from the end of World War I to the post-Cold War era.

[1] This part of the chapter was written jointly with Uri Reznick.

To assess how well this theory performs in the Balkans between 1830 and 1913, we divide the peninsula into seven areas: the Aegean, the Epiro-Albanian Coast, the Lower Danube, the Vardar and Drin Valleys (Macedonia), the Central Continental Core, Bosnia-Herzegovina, and Croatia-Slavonia, Dalmatia, and Carniola (or the north west).[2] For each of these regions, we trace the pattern of state-to-nation incongruence over time. We then divide the period under study into five subperiods – 1830–1856, 1856–1870, 1870–March 1878, March 1878–July 1878, July 1878–1913 – reflecting the variance in great power involvement concerning the different regions. Superimposing this pattern of great power involvement on the spatial delineation of incongruence, we derive a prediction as to the expected pattern of conflict, which we then compare with what happened historically. This prediction consists of three basic empirical expectations: (1) any large-scale violence ("hot" war) ought to have erupted in regions characterized by state-to-nation incongruence; (2) hot war ought to have occurred in such regions either when the great powers were competing over, or were disengaged from, them; (3) cooperation between the great powers, or hegemony of a single great power, is expected to have mitigated the severity of conflict, shifting it from cold war to cold peace,[3] and even creating conditions conducive to the establishment of high-level warm peace (see chapter 8).

Our findings are essentially consistent with these expectations. That is, the state-to-nation balance and great power involvement together offer an explanation of conflict patterns that fares rather well in this region.

[2] We have chosen the period 1830–1913 for reasons of scale. Substantial geopolitical changes occurred in 1830 and in 1913, such that extending this research beyond these dates would require a significantly longer study.

[3] For the purpose of the "semi-quantitative" examination in this chapter, we adopt the following operational definitions. *Hot war* – the Correlates of War definition of at least 1,000 battle-related deaths, to ensure a reasonable scale in the events we designate as wars. *Cold war* – if the average number of annual militarized incidents is at least 0.2, corresponding to two such incidents per decade. We adopt this "annual average" measure since we have divided our study into uneven intervals, reflecting the pattern of changing great power involvement. This definition affords some measure of "density" to the militarization of the area and is reminiscent of accepted definitions of "enduring rivalry." See, for example, Geller and Singer 1998, pp. 150–152. A quantitative study of broader scope can help to refine this measure. *Cold peace* – if two conditions are met: (1) militarized incidents are too infrequent to count as cold war; (2) there are parties in the region that possess – or are constructing – military forces that they might conceivably use in the future against other regional parties. Operationally, a given region and year is considered to be in *warm peace* if there have been no militarized incidents in the region in the ten years preceding the year in question. The resort to military force is highly unlikely and thus there is no planning by the regional states for the use of force against each other, and no preparation of appropriate capabilities for war fighting among them.

Although high degrees of state-to-nation imbalance have persistently characterized the Balkans, there have been major variations in the type of great power involvement in the region. This enables us to assess the distinctive effects of great power engagement on regional outcomes beyond the 1830–1913 period. A key challenge is to explore whether these systemic variations are able to explain the variance in regional war and peace outcomes, which is not addressed by the state-to-nation imbalance, notably when there is a high extent of continuity of this variable. Indeed, the history of the Balkans provides us with additional variations in great power engagement over time: competition (France–Italy in the 1920s and early 1930s); disengagement (the status quo powers vis-à-vis Eastern Europe in the late 1930s and in the early post-Cold War era); and hegemony (Germany in the late 1930s–early 1940s; the USSR in the Cold War era; and the United States in the late 1990s). Indeed, we can observe the distinctive effects of these variations in engagement on the conflict outcomes in the Balkans.

Assessing the theory in the Balkans (1830–1913)

Our first task is to describe the distribution of state-to-nation incongruence throughout the Balkans during the period under study. We can think of this task in terms of the region's geographical layout, its ethnonational makeup, and its geopolitical boundaries.

Geography of the Balkan peninsula

Excluding Romania, the Balkan peninsula is bounded in the north by the Danube River and its tributary, the Drava. It is surrounded by the Adriatic and Ionian Seas on the west, and by the Aegean Sea on the east. Within these boundaries, six basic regions can be distinguished: the Aegean, including its numerous islands; the Epiro-Albanian Coast, including the Pindus mountain range and its littoral; the Lower Danube plateau and the Maritsa Basin in the east; the Continental Core; the Vardar Valley in the south; the Dinaric Alps, Vardas and Drina Rivers and Adriatic coast in the central-western region; and Carniola in the northwest, extending roughly from Trieste to the Drave River.[4]

[4] This description is based on Jovan Cvijić's authoritative works on the subject. See Cvijić 1918a; 1918b. For a recent discussion of what is included in the Balkans, see Glenny 1999, pp. xxi–xxvi.

Ethnonational makeup of the Balkans

Seven ethnonational groups of substantial numbers may be distinguished as having resided in the Balkan peninsula during the period in consideration: Greeks, Albanians, Turks, and four strands of Yugo (South)-Slavs, Serbs, Croats, and Slovenes in the west (areas that are later to be constituent parts of Yugoslavia) and Bulgars in the east (Cvijić 1918a, 345). Each of these groups was mostly concentrated in a well-defined geographical region, though substantial areas of intermingling existed as well.

Greeks

Despite the diverse ethnic groups from which modern Greeks were comprised, Hellenic culture had long been rather uniformly imprinted upon them. In fact, they constituted a distinct, collectively self-aware group long before their political emancipation in the nineteenth century (Cvijić 1918a, 345–346).

The geographic dispersion of the Greeks encompassed the Aegean region, including the Cyclades and Dodecanese archipelagoes. In the north, the Greeks were bounded by the Slavs, with varying degrees of definition between the peoples, depending on the specific region. In the eastern areas (the Maritsa Valley and the Rhodope Mountains) that became independent Bulgaria in 1878, Greeks fled or were expelled southward, effectively emptying these regions of Greek inhabitants. This process occurred over the course of the several decades studied here, and resulted in a better-defined border between the Greek and Slavic populations of this region.

Along the Thraco-Macedonian coast, the Greek population was intermingled with communities of Turks, Bulgarians, and Serbs. Areas in Macedonia contained the most poorly defined ethnic boundaries, with Greek, Slav, Turkish, and Albanian villages interspersed in close proximity to one another (Cvijić 1918a, 348).

Albanians

The area populated by the bulk of the Albanians – 28,749 km^2 or roughly 6 percent of the total area of the peninsula – was relatively homogeneous ethnographically. In 1920, the population was 82.4 percent Albanian, 6 percent Serb, 5.7 percent Romanian, and 5.7 percent Turk (Singer 1997).

The Albanians – descended from the different Illyrian tribes of antiquity – have resided in the vicinity of the Epiro-Albanian Coast and the Pindus Mountains since before the Yugoslav invasion. In terms of lifestyle, they traditionally have been more similar to the Slavs of the interior and northern parts of the Balkan peninsula than to the Greeks in the Aegean region.

The main Albanian pockets outside this rather well-defined region lay to the east, in Kosovo and Metohiya, reaching as far east as the Morava River, in the town of Leskovats and its environs. The Albanians of Kosovo have resided there to the present day, and were intermingled then, as now, with the region's Slavic population.

The inhabitants of Albania had a long tradition of conflict with the Ottoman authorities, dating back to rebellions of Albanian feudal lords prior to and during the 1423 invasion of Sultan Murad II (Skendi 1967, p. 3). Yet, despite periodic rebellions throughout the centuries of Ottoman rule, which were mostly sporadic, localized occurrences, for the most part the Albanians formed an integral and basically loyal part of the Ottoman Empire. This remained true until the upsurge in Albanian national feeling and organization in the 1870s (ibid., p. 21).

Turks

For centuries, the Turks, through their administrative and military presence, constituted the majority of the urban population in much of the Balkans. In addition to Turkish immigrants, some of the local inhabitants became "Muslimized." Muslimized Serbs, concentrated mostly in the regions of Bosnia and Herzegovina, and Muslimized Bulgarians or Pomaks of the Rhodope Mountains, had adopted Turko-Oriental customs and beliefs. By the nineteenth century, these people had become instrumental in spreading the influence of these cultural attributes alongside the other influences competing for attention in the region (Cvijić 1918b, 476).

Since the early stages of the Ottoman Empire's decline in the late 1600s, however, the Turkish population of the Balkan peninsula decreased substantially. By the late nineteenth century, the rural Turks lived in "pockets" mostly in the Thraco-Macedonian and Pontic regions. The four main Turkish pockets were in eastern Bulgaria, Thrace, the Vardar Valley, and the two towns of Kailar and Djuma and adjacent villages (Cvijić 1918a, 349). In addition, some 4,500 Greek Orthodox Turks lived in eastern Macedonia.

Western Yugoslavs: Serbs, Croats, and Slovenes

The distinctions between the constituent peoples of twentieth-century Yugoslavia are only partly rooted in past centuries. These distinctions have been heavily influenced by geopolitical developments, from the Congress of Berlin in 1878 through to the establishment of the Socialist Federal Republic of Yugoslavia (SFRY) and its ultimate dissolution in the 1990s. In the nineteenth century, meaningful distinctions could be drawn between the Serbs/Montenegrins, Croats, and Slovenes.

Serbs In 1911, there were 2,900,000 Serbs in Serbia and Montenegro, 850,000 in Bosnia-Herzegovina, and 750,000 in Croatia-Slavonia and Dalmatia (R. Seton-Watson 1969, p. 1). The Serbian state was itself quite homogeneous ethnically. By the end of the nineteenth century, Serbia, spanning roughly 48,620 km^2 (roughly 10 percent of the total area of the peninsula), was over 90 percent Serb, after Turks, Albanians, and Bosnian Muslims had departed, as well as a sizable number of Greek traders (Lampe 1996, p. 47).

The Serbs were (and are) concentrated in the central regions of the Continental Core. These areas included Montenegro, and the large area roughly bounded by the Drin River in the west, the Danube in the north, and the Southern Marava Basin in the east. A large concentration of Serbs also resided in a pocket within Bosnia, alongside Croats and Muslimized Slavs, and Serbs were interspersed with large concentrations of Albanians in Kosovo and Macedonia.[5]

Modern Serbian nationalism first broke out into open rebellion in 1804 under Karageorge Petrovic, but was a direct continuation of a national Serbian identity which dated back to the medieval state last ruled by Stephen Dusan (Auty 1965, pp. 26–27). Though the Serbian national movement was by no means monolithic in outlook, it was nevertheless dominated by a vision of South Slavic political unity within a singularly Serbian framework. That is, the Serbs were basically striving to establish a "Greater Serbia" that would extend Serbian identity and geopolitical control over the other Slavic peoples in the Balkans (Lampe 1996, p. 52). Also, of the western Yugoslavs, only the Serbs belonged to the Eastern Orthodox faith. Some scholars have attributed the exclusivist nature of Serbian nationalism to this ecclesiastic inclination.[6]

[5] See the ethnographic map in Cvijić 1918a.
[6] See, for example, Banac 1984, pp. 66–67, 107 (citing Ivo Pilar).

Croats Croatia-Slavonia and Dalmatia span roughly 42,436 km^2 (approximately 9 percent of the total area of the peninsula). In 1911, there were 2,450,000 Croats in Croatia-Slavonia and Dalmatia, and 400,000 in Bosnia-Herzegovina (R. Seton-Watson 1969, p. 1).

Like the Serbs, the Croats had established an independent political entity in the Middle Ages. Yet, modern Croatian nationalism developed differently from its Serbian counterpart, no doubt due in part to the geographic proximity of Croatia to West European – essentially Habsburg – influence (Auty 1965, p. 38).

The Croats were predominantly Roman Catholic, an attribute which dated to the schism between the Roman and Byzantine Empires (R. Seton-Watson 1969, pp. 15–16). Croatian nationalism reflected this "cosmopolitan" western bent, in the emphasis placed on inclusionary "Illyrianism," which drew primarily on similarity of speech as the basis for a broadly defined South Slavic community (Pavlowitch 1971, p. 41). In contrast with the Serbian nationalist outlook, Croatian Illyrianist nationalism envisioned some manner of Yugoslav confederation that would respect the unique characteristics of the different Slavic groups, as expressed in their distinct vernacular or national appellation (Banac 1984, pp. 78, 106).

Slovenes The Slovenes populate a fairly small section of the northwestern corner of the Balkan peninsula, formerly known as the Habsburg Duchies of Carniola, Styria, and Carinthia (Rogel 1977, p. 3). In 1910, there were 500,000 Slovenes in Carniola (93 percent of the population), 1,200,000 in Austria, and 67,000 in Hungary (Pavlowitch 1971, p. 46 [citing the 1910 Austro-Hungarian census]).

By virtue of their proximity to Austria, Slovenes were always susceptible to a strong German influence, and like the Croats they were predominately Roman Catholic. Historically, the ethnographic dispersion of the Slovenes extended considerably further north – reaching Salzburg and Lungau – but these Slovenes became Germanized over the centuries.

Though Slovenes sometimes attribute an early national awakening to the religious works of Primoz Trubar in the sixteenth century, it was not until after the French Revolution that "the idea of 'nationhood' [came to be identified with] the idea of 'homeland'" (Rogel 1977, p. 7). With Napoleon's annexation of Carniola in 1809, the idea of a separate Slovenian political unit was strengthened and, in the wake of French administration, which ceased in 1813, Slovene intellectuals became engaged in linguistic rejuvenation and nationalist discourse.

Bulgarians

In 1911, there were 3,501,000 Bulgarians in Bulgaria (81.2 percent of the total population) and 501,000 Turks (11.6 percent) (Singer 1997). Bulgarians lived in the eastern reaches of the peninsula, rather homogeneously inhabiting the Lower Danube Basin.

The Bulgarians, like the Serbs, had established a state in the Middle Ages which was later crushed by the Turkish invasion (Lang 1976). The idea of attaining Bulgarian political independence through force of arms was gaining adherents as early as the 1850s, but drew on latent feelings of nationalism from previous decades (Macdermott 1962, p. 188). The first significant, practical steps toward bringing the Bulgarian revolutionary movement to fruition were undertaken in the 1870s by Vasil Levski, who began to construct an extensive conspiratorial organization (Kosev 1976, pp. 54, 55). With the establishment of the independent Bulgarian exarchate in 1870 and increased revolutionary activity in its wake, Bulgarian nationalism matured into a collective focus of identity, fusing ecclesiastical, linguistic, and cultural characteristics into a politically mobilized whole (Pundeff 1969, p. 115).

Geopolitical boundaries and the distribution of state-to-nation incongruence

Geopolitical boundaries were significantly altered only once during this period, through the dictate of the great powers at the Congress of Berlin (1878). Thus, it is convenient to describe the 1830–1878 and 1878–1913 periods separately.

1830–1878

Three geopolitical entities controlled areas in the Balkan peninsula between 1830 and 1878: the Ottoman Empire, the Austro-Hungarian Empire, and Greece, which had attained its independence in 1830. The Ottoman Empire still controlled much of the region, though Wallachia and Serbia achieved some measure of autonomy in 1829 through the Treaty of Adrianople (Thomson 1990, pp. 86–87). In the Aegean region, the Peloponnesus, Attica, and part of the Morea were controlled by Greece, while Macedonia and Thrace were still under Turkish rule. Crete, Rhodes, and Cyprus also were still governed by the Ottomans. The provinces of Rumelia, which later became Bulgaria, were still under the Ottomans, as were Bosnia and Herzegovina. The Albanian coast too was controlled by Turkey. Croatia, Slavonia, and the Dalmatian coast, which together formed a crescent-shaped area framing the peninsula from the northwest, had been under Habsburg rule since 1815, following a brief occupation by the Napoleonic empire.

In this period, the areas with the most acute incongruence were those that were inhabited by groups that were possessed of political ambitions: the Serbs and Montenegrins in the central regions of the Continental Core, the Bulgarians in the eastern environs of the Lower Danube, and the Croats and Slovenes of Croatia-Slavonia and Dalmatia.

The primary focus of these groups was on freeing the central hubs of their societies from imperial control, Ottoman or Habsburg. Consequently, these national movements were initially less concerned with relatively peripheral regions such as Macedonia. To a great extent, this prevented the latter from becoming embroiled in issues of territorial revisionism during this period.

Macedonia itself contained an ethnically mixed, but mostly politically unaware population. During the 1870s, the inhabitants of Macedonia began to undergo a far-reaching change in their outlook, affected by the beginnings of competition between Bulgaria, Serbia, and Greece for influence over the area.

The Greeks had attained independence in 1830 over the Peloponnesus, Attica, and much of the Morea, and constituted an ethnically homogeneous community, thus freeing these regions of revisionism and intercommunal instability. Nevertheless, the Greeks still entertained ambitions concerning regions occupied by the Turks, in Macedonia, Thrace, and the Aegean islands; a large number of ethnic Greeks still resided outside the boundaries of the Greek state, contributing to the basic incongruence between their ethnic dispersion and political borders (Clogg 1979, p. 70).[7]

The crescent-shaped northwestern region of the peninsula, inhabited by the Croats and Slovenes, marked the boundary between the Ottoman and Habsburg Empires. Early manifestations of Croat nationalism in these areas erupted in 1849, with the brief achievement of Hungarian independence under Kossuth in that year (Thomson 1990, pp. 217–219). Serb visions of a "Greater Serbia," which was to include

[7] While the population of the Greek kingdom was roughly 800,000, 2.5 million ethnic Greeks still inhabited Macedonia, Constantinople, Asia Minor, Crete, and the Ionian islands (M. Anderson 1966, p. 76).

Croatia-Slavonia and the Dalmatian coast, contributed to the incongruence characterizing the region.

As noted above, the Albanian residents of the Epiro-Albanian Coast had traditionally been loyal Ottoman subjects, despite frequent rebellions on socioeconomic grounds. The 1870s witnessed a notable upsurge in Albanian nationalism, culminating toward the end of the decade in organized reflections of collective mobilization. This change was signified, for example, by the establishment of the "Albanian League" at Prizren on June 10, 1878 (Skendi 1967, p. 368; Logoreci 1977, p. 40), and the issuing of the Shkodër memorandum to Lord Beaconsfield on June 18, 1878, affirming that the Albanians were intent to "oppose with all our might anyone who would like to make us Slavs, or Austrians, or Greeks" (Skendi 1967, p. 45; see also Pollo and Puto 1981, pp. 114–121; Jelavich 1983, pp. 361–366; Wolff 1956, pp. 91–92). Thus, this region became incongruent during the 1870s.

1878–1913

At the Congress of Berlin in 1878, the great powers of Europe redrew the geopolitical map of the Balkans. Bulgaria, Serbia, and Montenegro were founded as independent entities, free of Ottoman suzerainty. In the wake of the Treaty of Berlin, the Austro-Hungarian Empire occupied the provinces of Bosnia and Herzegovina, establishing effective control over them. Greece also gained some lands at the expense of dwindling Ottoman territorial possessions in the region.

The issues underpinning state-to-nation incongruence underwent considerable change as a result of the Treaty of Berlin. The major issue concerning the Serbs and Bulgarians – independence – had been largely resolved. The bulk of those people identifying themselves as Serbs or Bulgarians had achieved a realignment of the political borders, which now matched their ethnonational dispersion. A relatively small region along the Serbo-Bulgarian frontier was still in dispute. Notably, the inhabitants of this region were substantially more ambiguous about their national affiliation than their western and eastern counterparts.[8]

Areas still held by the Ottomans – primarily in Macedonia – came to the fore as the subject of conflicting ambitions of the Greeks, Serbs, and Bulgarians (Wolff 1956, p. 87). The reasons for this development were manifold but can be summarized briefly as follows. For the Serbs, apart from their historical claim to these southern areas, Macedonia

[8] See the detailed ethnographic map in Cvijić 1918a.

represented a vital outlet to the sea, which, denied them in the Adriatic, they now sought in the northern Aegean (Pavlowitch 1971, p. 47; Banac 1984, pp. 92–93; M. Anderson 1966, p. 212). This development was consolidated in 1881 with a secret convention between Serbia and Austria-Hungary (Banac 1984, p. 93; M. Anderson 1966, p. 231).

The Bulgarians had been actively trying to foster national awareness among the residents of Macedonia by trying to expand the ecclesiastic influence of the newly founded autocephalous Bulgarian exarchate (1870), and by founding schools geared to entrenching the Bulgarian language and Bulgarian national ideology among the local population. These efforts were met with Russian encouragement and approval (Petrowich 1956, pp. 198–240; see also Mackenzie 1967, pp. 17–18).

Bulgarian ambitions regarding Macedonia were magnified by the reversal of the terms of the 1878 Treaty of San Stefano, which would have created a much larger "Greater Bulgaria," including much of Macedonia and Thrace. This treaty was forced upon Turkey by Russia in the final days of the Russo-Turkish War (1877–1878), and was replaced by the Treaty of Berlin, at the behest of the great powers (Jelavich 1973, pp. 111–113; M. Anderson 1966, pp. 203–205; Marriott 1917, pp. 335–341). Under the Treaty of Berlin, a much smaller Bulgaria was created, leaving most of the coveted regions – under the name of Eastern Rumelia – in the hands of the Sublime Porte.[9]

Greece, too, had long entertained ambitions with respect to Macedonia and Thrace, but these ambitions became aggravated by the outcome of the Congress of Berlin. Greece felt excluded from the "spoils" granted to the Balkan peoples by the great powers, and renewed the fervor of its outstanding claims in the aftermath of the international convention.[10] Thus, the revisionist ideologies in the centers of Balkan nationalism ultimately spread out to Macedonia, which previously had been relatively benign.[11]

The other area still a subject of territorial ambitions was Bosnia-Herzegovina, which lay at the core of the Serb-populated regions. Serbian ambitions regarding this region were even more deeply held than those concerning Macedonia (Jelavich 1983, p. 350). Habsburg control

[9] Bulgaria as defined by the Treaty of Berlin was roughly one-third the size of Bulgaria as stipulated by the Treaty of San Stefano (Marriott 1917, p. 342).

[10] These claims mainly concerned Thessaly and Epirus to the north, and the island of Crete (Thomson 1990, p. 470).

[11] See Banac 1984, p. 313, and Clogg 1979, p. 95, on the transformation undergone by Macedonia.

of the province did not eliminate these ambitions, which continued to be salient throughout the period under study and which, by virtue of the relative size and proximity of the province to the existing Serbian polity, constituted a major source of state-to-nation incongruence (Auty 1965, pp. 35–36; Singleton 1985, p. 104).

As we have seen, the Epiro-Albanian Coast became infused with strident nationalism during the 1870s, a development that culminated in the formation of the Albanian League at Prizren in 1878. The Austro-Hungarian occupation of Albanian-inhabited regions in the north, and provisions for Greek annexation of the Salamyrias–Kalamas Rivers in the south served to augment this development (Skendi 1967, p. 52). Similarly, Croat and Slovene dissatisfaction with their position within the Habsburg Empire continued to grow in the decades following the Berlin Congress (Rogel 1977).

In summary, one may say that state-to-nation incongruence was not eliminated by the Congress of Berlin in any of those areas which were marred by it prior to 1878. Moreover, those two areas which still had been basically free of incongruence in the first period – the Epiro-Albanian Coast and Macedonia – rapidly became embroiled in the virulent revisionist nationalism long characterizing adjacent regions. This development was felt both in terms of the local inhabitants' ambitions and in terms of neighboring states' expansionist goals.

Great power involvement

Relations between the great European powers during the nineteenth century, sometimes referred to as the Concert of Europe, are generally regarded as having being cooperative (Miller and Kagan 1997, pp. 66–69; Hinsley 1963; Elrod 1976; Lauren 1983; Craig and George 1995; Schroeder 1986; Clark 1989). This cooperation is usually considered to have consisted of joint international congresses and treaties, and joint military operations.

Yet, looked at more closely, this period is better described as one of protracted and often acute competition between the powers, broken by several notable instances of cooperative diplomacy, such as in the much celebrated great power conferences which resulted in regional treaties. In the Balkans specifically, conflicting great power interests date back to well before the nineteenth century.

The primary great power rivalry in the region was between Russia and Austria. However, Russia and Turkey were also significant adversaries: Russia's contest with Turkey in general, and over its Balkan possessions in particular, dates back to Ivan the Terrible's rule in the sixteenth century (Marriott 1917, p. 131). With strengthening Russian power in the seventeenth and eighteenth centuries, the conflict between Russia and Turkey grew progressively more acute. This conflict was a reflection both of Russia's ethnic and religious ambitions in seeing itself as the protector of the Slav race and custodian of the Byzantine heritage in Constantinople, and of the country's strategic requirement of controlling the Bosporus and the Dardanelles (Marriott 1917, p. 130). The Habsburg Empire, which had previously been Turkey's main antagonist, became Russia's primary competitor for influence in the Balkan peninsula. During the nineteenth century, Austria vacillated between exploiting Turkey and supporting it as a buffer against Russian incursion.

With the emergence of Russian "pan-Slavism," first in the late 1820s, and then with renewed fervor under Tsar Alexander II during the Crimean War (1854–1856) (Petrowich 1956, p. 3), the conflict between Russia and Austria attained new heights, Russia using the Balkan Slavs to gain a foothold in the region and Austria trying to maintain the cohesion of its multiethnic imperial holdings.

Britain and France added an additional layer of complexity to the basic Austro-Russian rivalry. In the eighteenth century, extensive commercial interests in Russia guided Britain's foreign policy toward supporting that country. As these interests declined in importance in the early nineteenth century, Britain shifted support to Turkey, wary of Russian encroachment upon its vital interests in the Levant, the Mediterranean, and India.[12]

France, after a long history of influence in Constantinople, found itself realigning to some extent against Turkey.[13] Nevertheless, for much of the nineteenth century, France remained aligned with Britain and Turkey, sharing their fears of an expansionist Russia.

The Crimean War – in which Britain, France, and Turkey fought against Russia – was one of the more visible reflections of these great power alignments.[14] The Treaty of Paris, concluded at a peace conference held between February and March 1856, was made possible by a broad coalition of European powers: Britain, France, Turkey, Sardinia, and Sweden, as well as Prussia, which convinced the Russian tsar to

[12] See Stavrianos (1958, p. 227) on changing British interests in the nineteenth century, especially the enactment of the Corn Law in 1815, which curtailed Russian imports.

[13] France's traditional policy had been to support Turkey in order to weaken one of its main rivals – Austria – from the rear (Stavrianos 1958, p. 228).

[14] On the Crimean War, see Bartlett 1996, pp. 55–68, and M. Anderson 1966, pp. 132–135.

attend (Stavrianos 1958, p. 336). The provisions of the treaty settled some of the territorial issues underlying the Crimean War and reinforced the European concert's ambitions of fostering peace in Europe. Of most significance were the provisions of the treaty to "respect and guarantee the [Ottoman] empire's independence and territorial integrity" by virtue of having recognized the reform edict promulgated by the sultan in February 1856 – the Hatt-i Humayun (ibid.).

The commitment of the powers to preserve the territorial integrity of the Ottoman Empire was doubtless not lost on the regional players within the Balkans, as elsewhere. This spirit of great power unity lingered for some time, but once again became undermined toward the late 1860s, primarily due to the rise of Prussian power and the ultimate achievement of German unity in 1871, a harbinger of the increasingly polarized international environment that lay in store in subsequent decades.[15] The rise of the new German and Italian states is often identified as the beginning of a more competitive international atmosphere, with the major powers coalescing into opposing blocks, ultimately to mature into the Triple Alliance between Austria-Hungary, Germany, and Italy, and the Triple Entente between Britain, France, and Russia (Seaman 1963, pp. 130–156; Bartlett 1996, pp. 93–99).

With several exceptions – most notable of which was the Congress of Berlin – the period between the 1870s and the outbreak of World War I was characterized by virulent and acrimonious competition between rival great powers. No small amount of this tension revolved around events in the Balkans, driven primarily by Austro-Hungarian and Russian competition.

Russia was eager to capitalize on Prussia's defeat of France in the 1870 Franco-Prussian War, in light of Russia's "benevolent neutrality" toward Prussia at the time. This development was seen as an opportunity to reverse the "humiliating" terms of the Treaty of Paris and to reopen the path toward Russian encroachment upon the Balkans (Jelavich 1983, p. 352).

In July 1875, an uprising broke out against Turkish authorities in the Herzegovinian village of Gabela; it quickly spread across Herzegovina and Bosnia (Mackenzie 1967, p. 30). In the following months, Serbia and Montenegro joined the fray, with Russia as the sole great power backing the rebels. Britain, fearing Russian encroachment upon its vital interests

[15] On the collapse of the concert, see Thomson 1990, p. 311, and Bridge and Bullen 1980, pp. 81–111.

in the Turkish Straits, and Austria, fearing the disruption of its empire's cohesion, initially backed Turkey (M. Anderson 1966, p. 180; Clayton 1971, p. 132). As of autumn 1875, the powers were unable to calm the situation, while in Russia there was significant popular support for the rebels. The great powers tried several times to mitigate the Balkan strife, but these attempts were invariably met with "defections," most notably by Britain (Seaman 1963, p. 131).

The Andrassy Note, jointly prepared by Germany, Russia, and Austria in Budapest on December 30, 1875, represented the great powers' first significant failure in trying to induce quiet in the region (Marriott 1917, p. 324). This was followed several months later by the Berlin Memorandum, again issued jointly by the Austrian, Russian, and German chancellors on May 11, 1876, in Berlin. The memorandum gave the Turks an ultimatum, demanding reforms that had been promised by the sultan the previous fall. Britain subsequently refused to endorse the note, leading Marriott to conclude that: "There can be no question that the European Concert, whatever it was worth, was broken by the action of Great Britain" (ibid, p. 325).

Alongside and perhaps in light of the fecklessness of the great powers, Russia was directly involved in regional hostilities, entering into open war with Turkey in 1877. Yet, the competing great powers were unable to prevent the ongoing strife in the region, even when war between Russia and Turkey appeared imminent (ibid., pp. 332–334).

By March 1878, Russia had forced Turkey to sign the Treaty of San Stefano, in an attempt to establish a large and loyal Bulgarian state which would be instrumental in furthering Russia's commercial and strategic interests in the Balkans, as well as being confluent with the pan-Slavic ideology then fashionable in Russia (Stojanović 1939, p. 233; Skendi 1967, p. 33). This, naturally, was viewed as a threat to the interests of the other powers (Clayton 1971, pp. 148–159; M. Anderson 1966, pp. 202–203; Seaman 1963, pp. 122–123).

Germany, an important source of the European concert's diminishment, was instrumental in achieving cooperation at this critical juncture. It was the combination of Bismarck's decision to side with Austria against Russia, and Disraeli's positioning of 7,000 Indian troops in Malta, that brought Russia to agree to a congress in Berlin, subjecting the terms of the Treaty of San Stefano to the scrutiny of the powers (Marriott 1917, p. 340).

The Congress of Berlin itself was an exemplary instance of effective great power cooperation. Between the first calls for a European congress in March and the signing of the Treaty of Berlin on July 13, 1878, the great powers of Europe cooperated in altering the terms of the Treaty of San Stefano, to the detriment of the new Bulgarian state and its patron, Russia (Heppell and Singleton 1961, p. 127; Auty 1965, p. 36). The settlement effectively put an end to open hostilities in the region – in the short term. Under the terms of the Treaty of Berlin, Serbia, Romania, and Montenegro were granted independence (M. Anderson 1966, p. 217). Nonetheless, it was not long before rivalries between the great powers resurfaced and overshadowed the brief cooperative interlude at Berlin.

Russia's designs for the Greater Bulgarian vassal state envisaged by the Treaty of San Stefano did not cease with the signing of the Treaty of Berlin in July 1878 (Marriott 1917, p. 352; see also Jelavich 1983, p. 370). Britain, wary of increased Russian influence in the region, also began to involve itself in regional affairs. One of the more visible signs of Britain's involvement in the region was the marriage of Queen Victoria's daughter, Princess Beatrice, to the brother of the Bulgarian Prince Henry of Battenberg, on July 23, 1885 (Marriott 1917, p. 358), adding a dynastic aspect to Britain's regional interests. The election of Gladstone, with his anti-Turkish outlook, as prime minister of Britain in 1880 led to a deterioration in Britain's relations with Turkey, which had flourished under Disraeli's tenure (Birch 1966, pp. 13–17). This development, in turn, eased Germany's "infiltration" into Turkish affairs, reflected, for example, by its training of the Turkish army.

Another important development was the change in the cooperative relations between Germany, Austria, and Russia, manifested since 1872 in the Dreikaiserbund (namely, the League of the Three Emperors of these countries). The first indication of this change was Bismarck's preference of Austria over Russia, which had opened the path to the Berlin Congress (Marriott 1917, p. 341). The formation of the Triple Alliance between Germany, Austria-Hungary, and Italy in 1882 contributed an additional dimension of competition to the relations between the major European powers (Thomson 1990, pp. 524–528).

These great power rivalries concerned those regions in the Balkan peninsula which were controlled by Turkey, the "sick man of Europe." Unlike the regions in its vicinity, the northwestern region of the peninsula was considered by the great powers of Europe to be an integral part of the Habsburg Empire. Whereas the Ottoman Empire was on the verge of collapse, propped up almost entirely by Britain, the Austro-Hungarian regime still had effective control over its territory, having withstood the wave of unrest in 1848.[16] As such, there were no substantial questions of competing interests in this region. With Austria-Hungary's occupation of Bosnia-Herzegovina in the wake of the Congress of Berlin, its hegemony was extended over this area as well.

Thus, broadly stated, great power involvement in the region was essentially competitive throughout this period, with two distinct periods of significant cooperation. The first began with the 1856 Treaty of Paris, which signaled the great powers' commitment to the territorial inviolability of the Ottoman Empire, including the Balkan peninsula. Despite several altercations, this great power commitment remained essentially intact until the upsurge in Prussian, and then German, power during the 1860s. By 1870, Germany was united, Austrian ambitions in the Balkans had been amplified, Russia's pre-Crimean War territorial aims were renewed, and French and British anxiety over German power and Russian expansionism was growing.

Competition between the European powers, soon to be evinced in rigid, countervailing blocs, eventually culminated in World War I. The only significant, albeit relatively brief, exception to this post-1870 competitive trajectory occurred at the Congress of Berlin in the spring of 1878. The effects of the cooperation achieved at Berlin were relatively brief, however, in comparison with those achieved at Paris twenty-two years earlier. Immediately at the end of the international conference, Russia resumed its pan-Slavist attempts to infiltrate the Balkans.

At no time were the great powers truly "disengaged" from any of the areas of the peninsula, which was the core of the much celebrated Eastern Question. The only areas in the peninsula that were exempted from the changing relations between the great European powers were Croatia-Slavonia and Dalmatia during the entire 1830–1913 period and Bosnia-Herzegovina after 1878. Both of these regions were under the effective, hegemonic control of the Habsburg Empire until its dissolution in the aftermath of World War I.

Conflict outcomes

Conflict varied greatly from area to area in the peninsula, in terms of both intensity and timing, such that all four of the conflict outcomes forecast by the theory were in evidence. Only some of the areas witnessed hot war

[16] Part of the Habsburg Empire's ability to remain intact was no doubt due to its flexibility, evidenced by such measures as the creation of the Dual Monarchy.

at some point during the period under study. Some areas maintained the same conditions throughout, while others witnessed fluctuation in the level of conflict. The conflict outcomes in each of the seven geographic zones making up the peninsula are described below, with an assessment of how well the exhibited pattern fits with the expectations generated by the theory.

The Aegean

Between 1830 and 1897, the Aegean was essentially free of violent conflict, with newly independent Greece focusing primarily on building its national institutions. Outstanding territorial claims – which came to be known collectively as the Megali or Great Idea (see Clogg 1979, p. 76) – gave rise to periodic diplomatic tensions, but these were not translated into action.

Nevertheless, Greek territorial claims were not forgotten, and the prospect of an ultimate resort to armed force for addressing these claims was well within the limits of conceivable policy options.[17] Notably, Greece was not involved in the violence of the Great Eastern Crisis in the 1870s, aside from some minor border incursions toward the end of the Russo-Turkish War of 1877 (Clogg 1979, pp. 88–89). After 1878, tensions rose over Greek territorial claims in Macedonia, Thessaly, and Crete (Singleton 1985, p. 99; M. Anderson 1966, p. 270).[18] Incidents involving implicit and explicit threats and shows of military force became more frequent (Clogg 1979, p. 95).[19]

In 1897, war broke out between Turkish and Greek forces over Crete, followed by a thirty-day war in Thessaly (Marriott 1917, p. 381). After these crises, tensions in the Aegean once again returned to a state of precarious cold war, which lasted until the fall of 1912, with the assault of the Balkan League – comprising Greece, Serbia, Bulgaria, and Montenegro – on Turkey. The hostilities of the first Balkan war continued intermittently and melded into those of the second Balkan war, which ended in the Treaty of Bucharest in July 1913. Greek casualties in the first Balkan war have been estimated at 5,000 dead, with an estimate of 2,500 dead in the second (Small and Singer 1982, p. 88).

[17] For example, on Greece's alliance with Serbia, which was directed at Turkey, see Clogg 1979, p. 87.

[18] Limited and localized uprisings had already occurred in Crete in 1858 and between 1866 and 1869 (Clogg 1979, p. 87).

[19] Tensions with Serbia and Bulgaria had already been on the rise over Macedonia subsequent to the establishment of the autocephalous Bulgarian church in 1870 (Clogg 1979, p. 87).

Thus, the Aegean progressed from a state of cold peace before the 1870s to a state of cold war punctuated by hot war in the subsequent period. This pattern reflects to some extent the theory's expectations, though there is some measure of discrepancy. Prior to the perceived injustice of the Berlin Congress, the territorial issues facing Greece did not inspire much in the way of active policy, even though there was still a large population of ethnic Greeks outside the boundaries of the Greek state, constituting a significant source of state-to-nation incongruence. On the basis of the theory, we might have expected competitive relations between the great powers before the 1856 Treaty of Paris to have opened the path to substantial Greek violence, but this did not occur. Nevertheless, with increasingly competitive great power relations after 1878, the Aegean did witness a degenerating situation of cold war with actual eruption into hot war in 1897 and 1912, as expected.

The Epiro-Albanian Coast

Signs of burgeoning Albanian rebellion were already evident in the context of the Greek war of independence in the 1820s, with the *agas* and *beys* of southern Albania abandoning the battlefield because they had not been paid by the Ottoman government. After the revolution, the Turkish commander in the region – Mehmed-Reshid Pasha – tricked the Albanian leaders into coming to Monastir, where 500 were murdered on August 26, 1830 (Skendi 1967, p. 23).

Successive uprisings occurred in 1835 in Shkodër, in 1844 in Skopje, Tetovë, and Priština, in 1845 in Gjakovë, and in 1847 in Laberia; each focused on dissatisfaction with Ottoman policies on taxation, conscription, and centralization in general, but were not nationalistic or separatist in outlook (Pollo and Puto 1981, p. 109). With the enactment of the reforms promulgated by the Hatt-i Humayun of 1856, tensions appeared to be reduced for a time (Skendi 1967, p. 25).

Despite sporadic revolts against the Turks during the Great Eastern Crisis, overall Albania did *not* participate in the hostilities, its contribution being felt mostly in the refusal of many Albanians to join the Turkish war effort (Pollo and Puto 1981, pp. 116–117). In the subsequent months, there were numerous diplomatic initiatives geared to achieving Albanian autonomy, which culminated in the Assembly of Gjirokastra in July 1880, where the claim for an independent Albanian state became explicit (ibid., p. 126).

A military clash between the Albanian and Turkish armies in 1881 resulted in a resounding Albanian defeat. The Turkish victory did not, however, succeed in ending the sporadic Albanian attacks carried out during the following decades, particularly in the late 1890s, in tandem with the rising tide of unrest in neighboring Macedonia (Pollo and Puto 1981, p. 136). These attacks and countervailing military actions taken by the Turks continued after the Young Turks deposed the sultan in 1909; they culminated in a series of rebellions, beginning in March 1910 in Priština and ending on the eve of the first Balkan war in August 1912.

This pattern only partly corresponds with the theory's expectations. Though there was no eruption of hot war between 1830 and 1878, coinciding with the region's basic congruence in this period, there were repeated militarized incidents before 1856, giving rise to an extended period of cold war. This discrepancy could be reconciled by broadening the definition of incongruence to include dissatisfaction with existing economic policies, but to do so is in some sense to empty the concept of its primary meaning: nationalist dissatisfaction with prevailing geopolitical boundaries. It is probably better to view this case as illustrative of the theory's limitations, in the sense that violence sometimes does occur without direct relation to state-to-nation incongruence.

Nevertheless, as expected, the cooperation achieved through the Treaty of Paris – and accompanying endorsement by the great powers of the Hatt-i Humayun – did coincide with a remarkable cessation of the numerous Albanian rebellions that had erupted in the previous decades. This is consistent with the theory that suggests that the great powers' influence on regional conflict patterns should not hinge crucially on the *motivations* underlying the conflict, acting as it does on the regional parties' *capabilities*.

With increasing competition between the powers after 1870, combined with a growing sense of separatist nationalism, we should not be surprised that minor violent episodes occurred in the region in the context of the Great Eastern Crisis. The as yet nascent state of the Albanian nationalist movement – which began to flourish only with the 1878 formation of the League of Prizren – explains the minor involvement of Albania at that time. After 1878, the return to cold war and eventual eruption of violence in the region coincide with the upsurge in nationalism and highly competitive great power relations.

The Lower Danube (Bulgaria)

The Lower Danube and Maritsa Basin were the scene of frequent militarized incidents from early in the nineteenth century. A series of rebellions and peasant risings began in 1835 in western Bulgaria, in 1841 in Niš, in 1842 and 1843 in Braila, and in 1850 in Vidin (Macdermott 1962, pp. 169–178; Pinson 1975; Jelavich 1983, p. 341). These uprisings were socioeconomic rather than political in nature, focusing primarily on land ownership, intolerable taxation, and misdeeds of the local Turks. Nevertheless, some of the battles or massacres that occurred in this context involved thousands of casualties, and were fought between semi-organized rebel army bands, and Turkish irregular *bashibazouks*. During the 1850s and 1860s, the region entered a period of relative calm in which no notable militarized incidents were reported.

In April 1876, Bulgaria joined the regional turbulence in what has become known as the April Uprising. The Bulgarian rebellion was swiftly defeated by the Turks and was followed by the infamous "Bulgarian atrocities" in which thousands of Bulgarians lost their lives (Macdermott 1962, p. 276; Jelavich 1983, p. 348).

On November 13, 1885, a full-scale war between Serbia and Bulgaria ended in a decisive Bulgarian victory (Jelavich and Jelavich 1965, p. 57). Military preparations geared for the pursuit of outstanding territorial claims subsequently continued (Stavrianos 1958, pp. 440–441). Bulgaria was particularly active in Macedonia, fostering paramilitary activity from within Bulgarian territory and in Macedonia itself. Low-level military incidents continued over the Macedonian issue throughout the 1890s and increased in frequency and severity with the turn of the century.

Outright war broke out in 1912 within the context of the Balkan League's attack on Turkey, where Bulgaria, Greece, Serbia, and Montenegro gained territory at Turkey's expense. Dissatisfied with the results of the first Balkan war, Bulgaria attacked Serbia and Greece in June 1913, beginning the second Balkan war. This second war ended in July 1913 with the signing of the Treaty of Bucharest, confirming the territorial losses sustained by Bulgaria. Bulgarian fatalities in the first Balkan war are estimated at 32,000 with an estimated 18,000 dead in the second (Small and Singer 1982, p. 88).

Thus, the Lower Danube area never proceeded beyond cold peace throughout the period in question and witnessed hot war on four separate occasions: 1850, 1876, 1885, and 1912–1913, in addition to numerous lower-level rebellions and militarized incidents. This pattern fits well with the theory's expectations. The region was characterized by state-to-nation incongruence throughout the entire period, so that we might expect a protracted period of cold war, punctuated by hot wars.

Moreover, the outbreak of hot war coincided with competitive relations between the great powers.

Competitive relations between the powers prior to the 1856 Treaty of Paris were accompanied by an incessant chain of violent uprisings. Great power commitment to Ottoman territorial integrity – as affirmed by the Treaty of Paris – lasted for a number of years and coincided with relative calm in the region. By contrast, resurgent competition between the great powers in the 1870s enabled Bulgaria to become embroiled in the Great Eastern Crisis, where pan-Slavist Russian agitation actually played a major role in instigating Bulgarian involvement. When the powers did finally succeed in coordinating on a joint regional strategy in March 1878, war in the region ceased, though its underlying instability remained. Unchecked by renewed competition between the great powers in the following decades, this instability erupted into hot war twice more.

The Vardar and Drin Valleys (Macedonia)

The Vardar and Drin Valleys remained largely outside the Great Eastern Crisis. Aside from several minor insurrections in the late 1870s, in which few casualties were sustained, Macedonia was relatively tranquil prior to the 1880s (see also Poulton 1995, pp. 48–49). Before the 1870s, there are few traces of militarized incidents occurring in Macedonia and the very idea of resorting to violence to further some political goal was virtually unheard of among the politically unaware populace.

In fact, there was only one uprising in Macedonia prior to the Berlin Congress. This peasant revolt, which occurred in Razlog in 1876, was triggered by a similar uprising in Bulgaria in the same year (Djordjevic and Galati 1981, p. 163). Three more uprisings occurred in this period in Macedonia (Poulton 1995, pp. 49–50).

After the Berlin Congress, the increasing involvement of Bulgaria, Serbia, and Greece in Macedonia elevated the political self-consciousness of the different components of Macedonian society (Poulton 1995, pp. 50–64). In tandem with these developments, a steadily escalating intercommunal conflict was unfolding, which grew into a semi-organized, paramilitary guerrilla war (M. Anderson 1966, p. 269; Wolff 1956, pp. 87–88).

Violent insurrections against Ottoman rule became more and more frequent by the 1890s (Stavrianos 1958, pp. 522–523). By 1904, the English Blue Book reported the average number of monthly political assassinations in Macedonia as 100 (Report of the International Commission 1914, p. 32). Following a series of bombings in Salonika in 1903, there was an

IMRO revolt which was suppressed by the Turks.[20] This situation of protracted cold/hot war finally erupted into full-fledged hot war in 1912 with thousands of casualties sustained by all the belligerents, many of whom were Macedonian inhabitants (ibid.).

On the whole, the pattern of conflict in Macedonia conforms with the theory's expectations. When the region's inhabitants were still largely politically unmobilized, prior to the 1880s, there was little violent conflict, and few militarized incidents of any kind, despite increasingly competitive great power relations before 1856 and from 1870 on. Notably, Macedonia was basically left outside the Great Eastern Crisis, which engulfed most of the surrounding areas. With the rise of intercommunal political awareness, mostly instigated by the surrounding states, Macedonia quickly became embroiled in severe cold war which eventually erupted into hot war. The pattern of conflict changed with changes in state-to-nation incongruence, despite competitive systemic influences during most of the period under consideration.

The Central Continental Core

The central regions of the peninsula witnessed hot war on three occasions: during the Great Eastern Crisis (1875–1878), during the brief Serbo-Bulgarian War of 1885, and during the two Balkan wars lasting intermittently from October 1912 to July 1913.[21]

The main geopolitical unit in the region – Serbia – did not proceed beyond an uneasy cold peace with adjacent areas. The possibility of military action, both as a conceivable policy option and in terms of actual preparedness, was never removed from the contemporary agenda.[22]

After achieving some limited measure of autonomy in 1829, Serbia was left with the open question of Bosnia-Herzegovina, the Sanjak of Novi-Bazar, and "Old Serbia" (northern Macedonia), over which it still had territorial ambitions (Marriott 1917, p. 314). Though relative quiet followed in the wake of the Treaty of Paris in 1856, Serbia became embroiled in the Great Eastern Crisis in the 1870s. Serbia entered the

[20] The Internal Macedonian Revolutionary Organization (IMRO), founded in 1893 in Salonika, represented the nascent "Macedonian" self-consciousness.

[21] The region also suffered from internal instability, such as in the 1883 Timok rebellion, in which peasants rose up against the increasingly centralized government (Lampe 1996, p. 54).

[22] On Montenegro's involvement in militarized incidents such as the brief "war" that the Turkish governor of Bosnia – Omer Pasha – declared on it in 1852, see M. Anderson 1966, pp. 119–120.

hostilities in June 1876, after the infamous Bulgarian massacre at the hands of the Turks (ibid., p. 330).[23]

Russia's entry into the fray in 1877 played a significant role in influencing Serbia's behavior during the crisis. By October 1877, Serbia had joined Russia's war effort which had, by then, taken on larger proportions. Montenegro, too, soon found itself the object of a massive Turkish attack, which it managed to repel by June 28, 1877 (Mackenzie 1967, p. 212).

After attainment of Serbian independence at the Berlin Congress, tensions between Serbia and its neighbors came to revolve around relatively marginal issues, concerning Serbian expansion into territories still coveted by other entities, such as Austria-Hungary, Bulgaria, and Turkey. These territorial ambitions flared up into hot war on two occasions, the Serbo-Bulgarian War of 1885 and the two Balkan wars of 1912–1913, even though the great powers themselves were interested in preventing these wars. Serbian losses in the first Balkan war have been estimated at 18,500 dead with an estimated 2,000 dead in the second (Small and Singer 1982, p. 88).[24]

This pattern is essentially consistent with the theory. Given some form of state-to-nation incongruence in Serbia throughout the period, we would not expect to see its conflict patterns proceed beyond cold peace. Moreover, escalation of the latent tension in the region to cold and hot wars tended to occur in tandem with periods of heightened competition between the great powers.

Bosnia-Herzegovina

Bosnia and Herzegovina, like the Central Continental Core, had long been simmering with political tension. Much of the immediate disaffection was rooted in socioeconomic issues, primarily the overbearing mismanagement of the Muslim rulers over the Christian peasantry. Local rebellions of the Christian peasants against the Muslim governors broke out in 1861 (M. Anderson 1966, p. 178; Heppell and Singleton 1961, p. 121). In addition, the local Muslim administration repeatedly rose up against the central Ottoman government, rebelling in 1831 and again in 1847–1850, resulting in roughly 6,000 dead (Jelavich 1983, p. 349). Aside from the 1861 rebellions, violent turbulence in the region was subdued

[23] One estimate of Serbian casualties during the Great Eastern Crisis is of 150,000 dead or dislocated people (Lampe 1996, p. 65).

[24] Lampe, however, lists a total of 61,000 Serbian casualties in these wars (1996, p. 94).

in the 1850s and 1860s, much as was the case in neighboring areas of the peninsula.

As noted above, the Great Eastern Crisis originated in Herzegovina. In the wake of the Treaty of Berlin, with Austria-Hungary's occupation of the provinces, three months of sustained fighting between Habsburg and Bosnian Muslim forces ensued (Lampe 1996, p. 65).

Austro-Hungarian domination of Bosnia-Herzegovina after 1878 coincided with an absence of organized eruptions of violence, despite a progressively more nationalistic domestic atmosphere. Until the first decade of the twentieth century, this nationalistic activity was primarily nonviolent in character. After 1910, Sarajevo was witness to burgeoning terrorist activity (Lampe 1996, p. 88). The Serbo-Croat Progressive Organization, founded in 1911, was eventually to become renowned for the assassination of the Habsburg heir Franz Ferdinand, by its infamous member, Gavrilo Princip (ibid., p. 89).

Bosnia-Herzegovina illustrates the forecasted pattern rather well. The area's consistently acute state-to-nation incongruence is expected to have precluded a progression beyond cold peace. Moreover, the timing of violent conflict closely reflected changes in great power regional involvement.

Prior to 1856, under great power competition, the area witnessed repeated armed confrontations, some of which reached the level of hot war. Great power cooperation in the wake of the Treaty of Paris did not coincide with a disappearance of instability, as evidenced by the 1861 rebellions, but was definitely accompanied by a substantial lowering of tension. Renewed competition between the powers in the 1870s coincided with the eruption of the Great Eastern Crisis, which then ceased through great power cooperation at Berlin in 1878. Notably, during the period of Austro-Hungarian hegemony subsequent to 1878, there was virtually no violence, despite the domestic surge in fervent nationalism and growing irredentism of neighboring Serbia.

Croatia-Slavonia, Dalmatia, and Carniola

Apart from siding with Austria against the bid for Hungarian independence in 1849, Croatia-Slavonia and Dalmatia did not witness notable militarized incidents during the period under study. There was no large-scale violence (hot war) in the area at all, unlike the surrounding areas. Notably, the Great Eastern Crisis did not sweep the area into the strife that had erupted in neighboring Bosnia, Herzegovina, Serbia, Montenegro, and Bulgaria. Nor was the area involved in the Balkan wars of 1912 and 1913. Aside from several incidents, such as the 1883 peasant revolt (Lampe 1996, p. 62), nationalist tension did not result in militarized outcomes. Nevertheless, there can be no question of the acute salience of the nationalist issue, as evidenced by countless demonstrations and political maneuverings revolving around the question of independence. Toward the end of the period, the tense atmosphere attained violent expression. Organizations such as the Croato-Serbian Radical Progressive Youth Movement, which after 1910 began a campaign of terrorist attacks against Habsburg targets in Zagreb, were indicative of this new development (ibid., p. 88).

During the Balkan wars of 1912 and 1913, some Croats entertained the possibility of enlisting in the Serbian army and certain Croatian leaders called for a "second round" to liberate the region from Austro-Hungarian rule (Lampe 1996, p. 92). Yet the reticence of Croatian leaders such as Nikola Pašić to confront the Habsburg authorities with separatist demands, despite broad domestic support for the nationalist cause, attests to the restraining influences of effective hegemony, even in the face of acute incongruence (ibid., p. 93).

As in the case of Bosnia-Herzegovina, Croatia-Slavonia and Dalmatia fit well with the basic forecast drawn from the theory. The area, consistently subject to the hegemonic control of the Habsburg Empire, did not witness conflict on a scale comparable to those areas in its vicinity under the nominal suzerainty of the Turks. This variation cannot be attributed to a variation in the acuity of state-to-nation incongruence between the areas. Unlike the inhabitants of Macedonia and the Epiro-Albanian Coast, separatist nationalism had long been fermenting among the Croats. The Slovenes, though somewhat later in developing their nationalist "awakening," also reached a point in which separatist territorial ambitions existed, but had to be suppressed in the face of Austro-Hungarian dominance. Only on the eve of the Balkan wars did the prolonged state of cold peace in the region give way to low-level militarized incidents and cold war.

Summary of the theory's success

Table 6.1 summarizes the values of the independent variables alongside the predicted and actual conflict outcomes. If we compare the revealed pattern with the pattern forecasted by the theory, the theory appears to perform well overall. Of thirty-five predictions, thirty-one outcomes (88.6 percent) fit the expected pattern. The theory fails to predict the outcome in the Aegean (1830–1856), in the Epiro-Albanian Coast

Table 6.1 *Evaluating the theory: pre-World War I Balkans*

Period	Region	S/N[a]	GP[b]	PRED[c]	CON[d]	Fit
1830–1856	Aegean	Incong[e].	Comp.[f]	Cold war/hot war	Cold peace	×
	Epiro-Alb. Coast	Cong.[g]	Comp.	Warm peace	Cold war	×
	Lower Danube	Incong.	Comp.	Cold war/hot war	Cold war/hot war	✔
	Vardar Valley	Cong.	Comp.	Warm peace	Warm peace	✔
	Cen. Cont. Core	Incong.	Comp.	Cold war/hot war	Cold war	✔
	Bosnia-Herz.	Incong.	Comp.	Cold war/hot war	Cold war/hot war	✔
	Northwest	Incong.	Heg.[h]	Cold peace	Cold peace	✔
1856–1870	Aegean	Incong.	Coop.[i]	Cold peace	Cold peace	✔
	Epiro-Alb. Coast	Cong.	Coop.	Warm peace	Cold peace	×
	Lower Danube	Incong.	Coop.	Cold peace	Cold peace	✔
	Vardar Valley	Cong.	Coop.	Warm peace	Warm peace	✔
	Cen. Cont. Core	Incong.	Coop.	Cold peace	Cold peace	✔
	Bosnia-Herz.	Incong.	Coop.	Cold peace	Cold peace	✔
	Northwest	Incong.	Heg.	Cold peace	Cold peace	✔
1870–1878 (Mar.)	Aegean	Incong.	Comp.	Cold war/hot war	Cold war	✔
	Epiro-Alb. Coast	Incong.	Comp.	Cold war/hot war	Cold war	✔
	Lower Danube	Incong.	Comp.	Cold war/hot war	Cold war/hot war	✔
	Vardar Valley	Incong.	Comp.	Cold war/hot war	Cold war	✔
	Cen. Cont. Core	Incong.	Comp.	Cold war/hot war	Cold war/hot war	✔
	Bosnia-Herz.	Incong.	Comp.	Cold war/hot war	Cold war/hot war	✔
	Northwest	Incong.	Heg.	Cold peace	Cold peace	✔

	Aegean	Incong.	Coop.	Cold peace	Cold peace	✔
	Epiro-Alb. Coast	Incong.	Coop.	Cold peace	Cold peace	✔
1878 (Mar.)–1878 (Jul.)	Lower Danube	Incong.	Coop.	Cold peace	Cold peace	✔
	Vardar Valley	Incong.	Coop.	Cold peace	Cold peace	✔
	Cen. Cont. Core	Incong.	Coop.	Cold peace	Cold peace	✔
	Bosnia-Herz.	Incong.	Coop.	Cold peace	Cold peace	✔
	Northwest	Incong.	Heg.	Cold peace	Cold peace	✔
	Aegean	Incong.	Comp.	Cold war/hot war	Cold war/hot war	✔
	Epiro-Alb. Coast	Incong.	Comp.	Cold war/hot war	Cold war/hot war	✔
1878 (Jul.)–1913	Lower Danube	Incong.	Comp.	Cold war/hot war	Cold war/hot war	✔
	Vardar Valley	Incong.	Comp.	Cold war/hot war	Cold war/hot war	✔
	Cen. Cont. Core	Incong.	Comp.	Cold war/hot war	Cold war/hot war	✔
	Bosnia-Herz.	Incong.	Heg.	Cold peace	Cold peace	✔
	Northwest	Incong.	Heg.	Cold peace	Cold war	×

Notes:
[a] S/N – State-to-nation balance; [b] GP – Great power involvement; [c] PRED – Predicted conflict outcome; [d] CON – Actual conflict outcome; [e] Incong. – Incongruent; [f] Comp. – Competition; [g] Cong. – Congruent; [h] Heg. – Hegemony; [i] Coop. – Cooperation

(1830–1870), and in the northwest (Croatia-Slavonia and Dalmatia) (1878–1913). In the first case, the area was more peaceful than expected. In the latter two instances, the areas experienced more conflict than expected.[25]

Of course, these "predictions" do not constitute independent observations and are too few in number to draw substantive statistical conclusions.[26] Moreover, to keep the size of this comparative case study feasible, we have adopted somewhat arbitrary time intervals for the variables, choosing them in terms of the variance in one of the variables – great power involvement.[27] It may be worthwhile to conduct a thorough, quantitative replication of these findings, using annually measured variables. Yet these results are suggestive of the basically sound empirical framework provided by the theory. On the whole, it succeeds in encapsulating much of the variance in conflict witnessed in the region, and is able to do so within the confines of a rather parsimonious theoretical framework.

The effects of the type of great power engagement on regional outcomes in the post-World War I era

This section further investigates the effects of changes in great power involvement on variations in conflict outcomes in the Balkans and Eastern Europe from the end of World War I to the post-Cold War era.[28]

[25] Another point worth mentioning is the relative volatility of the independent variables. An underlying premise of the theory is that the state-to-nation balance is fairly constant, whereas great power involvement fluctuates more. The findings support this idea: the average number of changes in the state-to-nation balance experienced by a region is 0.29, with five of seven areas remaining unchanged throughout the entire period. By contrast, the average number of changes in great power involvement concerning an area is 3.42, with only one of seven regions experiencing a constant form of great power involvement. Though we are unable to assess whether these differences are statistically significant, they are nonetheless suggestive of the basically sound premises of the model.

[26] The thirty-five observations produced by the combination of the different areas and periods are no doubt correlated both spatially and temporally, leaving us with at most seven observations, and perhaps even fewer.

[27] This is particularly noticeable for the relatively brief March 1878–July 1878 period. Since this period is shorter than a single year, the conflict variable – coded on the basis of the average number of annual militarized incidents – could produce a misleading result. As it happens, however, there were no MIDs (militarized interstate disputes) in the period in any of the regions, so this methodological problem has no practical consequences in the current study.

[28] Although the northern part of Eastern Europe (Poland, Czech Republic, Slovakia, Hungary) is distinctive in many senses from the Balkans or Southeastern Europe, for analytical purposes this section refers to both regions as Eastern Europe/Balkans because the main

Competition: France–Italy in the 1920s and early 1930s

Beyond the Austro-Russian competition, a second example of great power competition is the Franco-Italian rivalry in Eastern Europe and the Balkans in the 1920s and early 1930s. Eastern Europe and the Balkans in the interwar period were characterized by a sharp division between status quo and revisionist small states. While the former fought on the victors' side in World War I and consequently were the beneficiaries of the Versailles territorial settlement in Eastern Europe, the latter (namely, Austria, Hungary, and Bulgaria) were on the losing side, and therefore the Versailles settlement was concluded largely at their expense. This division paralleled the division of the great powers into status quo and revisionist, according to their attitude to the post-World War I international order. Thus, the interwar period in Eastern Europe and the Balkans was characterized by persistent territorial claims by the revisionist states against the status quo states, compounded by territorial claims of status quo states on one another (such as the Polish–Czechoslovak conflict over Cieszyn/Český Těšin), and the dissatisfaction of ethnic minorities within existing states.

As for the great powers, two powers proximate to the region (Germany and the USSR) were in eclipse in this period, due to Germany's defeat in World War I and the USSR's preoccupation with domestic affairs following the 1917 revolution. Their temporary weakness allowed France and Italy to play the leading role in the region. (The attitude of Britain and the United States to the region will be discussed below, in the illustration of great power disengagement.)

France, as the major continental status quo power, had a high interest in the region. It regarded the small states of the area as a potential bulwark against both potential German expansion eastward and Soviet expansion westward (Mandelbaum 1988, ch. 2). Therefore, in the 1920s and early 1930s it sought to erect a "cordon sanitaire" of small status quo states by concluding a series of agreements with Poland and the states of the Little Entente (Czechoslovakia, Romania, and Yugoslavia) and the Balkan Entente (Romania, Yugoslavia, Greece, and Turkey). France's alignment with these states made it the major guarantor and protector of the Versailles order in Eastern Europe and the Balkans in this period.

type of great power engagement in the period from the 1920s until the end of the Cold War was the same and applied equally to both areas, thus increasing the potential number of observations regarding the effects of the great powers on regional conflicts (also enabling us to include Romania, which is excluded from the above definition of the Balkans).

While French interests made it uphold the territorial status quo in the region, Mussolini's revisionist self-aggrandizing ambitions in the Balkans (a region proximate to Italy) dictated the opposite policy of disrupting the existing order in the area and attempting to undermine the French system of alliances. The means employed by Italy for this purpose were championing the revisionist small states (the 1934 Rome protocols with Austria and Hungary), attempting (without success) to woo the status quo small states away from France, and encouraging separatist terrorist groups in existing status quo states in order to disrupt them from within (notably, the Croatian Ustaše and the Macedonian IMRO within Yugoslavia). In 1934 terrorists funded by Italy assassinated the status quo-oriented king of Yugoslavia. The Italian policy contributed to the perpetuation of territorial conflicts in the area by encouraging the revisionist small states and dissatisfied separatist groups within states to persist in their claims, thus undermining attempts at regional reconciliation (Stavrianos 1958, pp. 734–736). Unlike the earlier period of Austro-Russian competition, however, the Franco-Italian rivalry did not bring about the escalation of the regional conflicts to local wars or great power crises. One reason was that the permanent identification of the small states with either the status quo or the revisionist camp precluded realignment, and thus gave them less room to maneuver between the great powers than in the earlier period. A second reason was the relative weakness of Italy vis-à-vis France, which made Italy no more than a major irritant to the French diplomacy and system of alliances in the region. Thus, this illustration diverges from the ideal type in that there was an imbalance in the competitors' capabilities. However, this imbalance was not so marked as to result in French hegemony in the region. Despite its relative weakness, Italy "succeeded in keeping alive and even intensifying existing hatreds between Eastern European states, and maintained all Eastern Europe in a condition of unrest and tension . . . The importance of Mussolini's Eastern European policy from 1922 to 1936 cannot therefore be overestimated . . . Italy had done a good job by keeping the wounds open for sixteen years and by turning the knife from time to time" (H. Seton-Watson 1962, pp. 368, 378).

Disengagement: the status quo powers vis-à-vis Eastern Europe and the Balkans in the late 1930s

The historical example of great power disengagement is Eastern Europe in the late 1930s in the face of the resurgence of German power. The conflicts among the regional states from the 1920s and early 1930s continued unabated in this period. Indeed, the small states were unable to overcome their rivalries and to maintain a united front even when facing the threat of a German encroachment. However, it was not the small states but the major status quo powers which were capable of resisting German expansion in the region. Therefore, this illustration is useful for demonstrating the effects of great power disengagement, as the noninvolvement of the Western powers allowed Germany to prevail and establish its hegemony over the region.

Indeed, the theoretical conditions stated above as conducive to disengagement seem to have existed in the interwar era. Although I lump all the status quo powers together as disengaging, there was a significant difference between the interests and capabilities of the French and those of the British and the United States in Eastern Europe. Thus, the United States and Britain might have possessed the capabilities necessary for containing German expansion and maintaining stability in Eastern Europe but, being remote from the region, they, especially the United States, lacked the interest to do so. At the same time, France as the most proximate Western power had the interest but lacked the capability to deter German aggressiveness toward the small East European states. This mismatch between the balances of capabilities and interests with regard to Eastern Europe led to Western disengagement from the region in the late 1930s, even if reluctantly on the part of the French. This disengagement, in turn, contributed to German ascendancy in the region and the collapse of the collective security system and the post-World War I international order.

The Senate rejection of US membership in the League of Nations was obviously a major blow to President Wilson's plans for a new world order. As E. H. Carr comments: "in 1918, world leadership was offered, by almost universal consent, to the United States . . . (and was declined)" (1946, p. 234). In addition to American isolationism from conflict management in the Old World, Britain during most of the 1920s and 1930s was also unwilling to commit itself to the defense of Eastern Europe – the most problematic region of the interwar order (see Craig and George 1995, pp. 55–57). Politicians and domestic opinion in the United States and Britain supported disengagement policies because of short-run benefits associated with saving defense expenditures, avoiding seemingly undesirable alignments (such as with the USSR), and shunning what appeared to be unnecessarily dangerous entanglements in faraway places and expensive commitments (against the fascist powers).

Britain's relatively low interest in Eastern Europe was given a blunt expression by Prime Minister Chamberlain, who referred to the Sudetenland crisis as "a quarrel in a far away country between people of whom we know nothing" (Palmer 1970, p. 237).

This left France as the only major status quo power with sufficiently high interest to make a credible commitment to the East European states. Yet French resources, which were significantly weaker than Nazi Germany's, were insufficient for sustaining such a commitment and for deterring German aggression in Eastern Europe in the face of the growing might of the revisionist powers, especially given the ideological-domestic constraints on cooperation between the Western powers and the USSR. Therefore, in the late 1930s France was unwilling to act on its own; it tended to follow Britain's lead, lest Britain abandon it (Mandelbaum 1988, ch. 2).

The direct result of the Western disengagement from Eastern Europe and the Balkans in the late 1930s in the face of rising German power was the breakdown of the French alliance system and the defection of the regional small states to the German camp. Germany remained virtually unopposed in the region, and by 1939 had established its hegemony over the entire area. In its ascendancy, Germany deliberately exploited the territorial disputes in the region and skillfully played off the rival states against each other by posing alternately as the champion of revisionist small states and dissatisfied separatist minorities within existing states (notably the Slovaks in Czechoslovakia and the Croats in Yugoslavia) and as the only power capable of controlling and restraining revisionism, and thus as the only protector of status quo states such as Romania and Yugoslavia (Hitchens 1983, pp. 13–15). Thus, Hitler achieved the enthusiastic cooperation of Poland, Hungary, and the Slovaks in the dismemberment of Czechoslovakia in 1938–1939 by encouraging them to take a share of the spoils. In a similar manner, Hungary, Bulgaria, and the Croats actively participated in the destruction of Yugoslavia in 1941.

Yet, the most important cause of the realignment of the regional status quo states with Germany was Western disengagement, which overshadowed the skillful German tactics of exploiting the regional conflicts in Eastern Europe (H. Seton-Watson 1962, pp. 368, 412). As France and Britain repeatedly failed to counter the moves of the revisionist powers in Eastern Europe and elsewhere and, moreover, engaged in an active appeasement of Germany, the small status quo states in the region came to regard the alignment with France as an ineffectual guarantee of their security against the potential German threat. The decisive event in this respect was Western acquiescence in the German reoccupation and remilitarization of the Rhineland, which effectively prevented France from giving prompt military aid to its East European allies if they were attacked by Germany; it thus rendered France's guarantee to their security practically useless (Mandelbaum 1988, pp. 103, 109; Hitchens 1983, pp. 11, 17). The prestige of the Western powers and of the collective security system they presided over was further undermined by Italy's occupation of Ethiopia, and in Eastern Europe itself by the Anschluss, the Sudetenland–Munich crisis, and the dismemberment of Czechoslovakia. As a result, the regional small states behaved in accordance with alliance theory: they showed the tendency of small states to bandwagon with a proximate threatening great power, especially when such a threat is compounded by the unavailability of great power allies (Walt 1987, p. 30). The small states defected one by one from the French alliance system, and moved into the German political orbit (except for Czechoslovakia, which was destroyed). "Greater German primacy was thus already established in the Danube Basin and the Balkans before the first Panzer divisions moved against Poland in September 1939" (Palmer 1970, p. 228).

The disengagement of the Western powers thus provided the opportunity for the gradual establishment of German hegemony over Eastern Europe, which finally made Britain and France reverse their policy and oppose further German expansion against Poland. Thus, such disengagement at best only delayed the war and may have considerably aggravated its eventual scope or even contributed to its outbreak (Taylor 1961).

Dominance: Germany in the late 1930s–early 1940s and the USSR in the Cold War era

The first example of dominance in the post-World War I era is the German hegemony in Eastern Europe and the Balkans in the late 1930s–early 1940s. Germany's dominance in the region arose because it was the only power that possessed both sufficient interests and sufficient capabilities for effective intervention there, as a result of the proximity of the region to its borders. Chamberlain admitted that, "geographically, Germany must occupy a dominating position in central and southeastern Europe" (Hitchens 1983, p. 34).[29] It regarded the establishment of

[29] The only other great power that was equally proximate to the region and possessed both high interests and high capabilities for intervention there was the USSR, potentially

political, economic, and military control over the region as a necessary step toward the attainment of longer-range goals, whether vis-à-vis the USSR or the West (ibid., p. 260). By the beginning of Operation Barbarossa (the invasion of the USSR), Germany successfully imposed its "new order" on the entire region. The "new order" included a sweeping redrawing of the territorial map of the region, whereby five states (Austria, Czechoslovakia, Poland, Yugoslavia, and Greece) were occupied and/or dismembered, two new states (Croatia and Slovakia) were created, and these two together with the remaining states (Romania, Hungary, and Bulgaria) formally acceded to the Tripartite Pact. Romania and Hungary also took part in Hitler's war against the USSR. In addition, territorial changes were effected between the existing states in a coercive manner, which reflected the totalitarian German regime. For example, in 1938, following the Munich agreement, Hitler settled the boundary conflict between autonomous Slovakia and Hungary by arbitrarily dictating the "First Vienna Award." Similarly, in 1940, after Hungary, Romania, and Bulgaria failed to settle their territorial disputes on their own, Hitler imposed the "Second Vienna Award," which made Romania cede part of Transylvania to Hungary and southern Dobruja to Bulgaria (H. Seton-Watson 1962, p. 401). Thus, German hegemony resulted in the containment, although not the resolution, of regional conflicts. While German power was in place, it was inconceivable for the small states to attempt to change unilaterally the new territorial order imposed by Germany. This order, which lasted until 1944, was achieved at the price of reducing the small regional states to satellite status with very limited autonomy. German hegemony was, of course, not accepted by the West, and was eliminated with Germany's defeat in World War II.

With the end of World War II, the region passed from German to Soviet hegemony, because in the new bipolar international system the USSR's interests and interventionary capabilities in this region – due to its proximity – were superior to those of the United States. Soviet hegemony in Eastern Europe and in most of the Balkans in the Cold War era (Pax Sovietica) shows the proposed effects of coercive great power dominance: very limited autonomy for the lesser actors, and the

Germany's main rival in the region. Yet, in the late 1930s it was still preoccupied with domestic affairs and concentrated on building its internal power base. Therefore, it was content for the time being to leave most of the area under German hegemony, except for its immediate periphery (Finland, the Baltic states, eastern Poland, and Bessarabia), assigned to it in the Molotov–Ribbentrop pact of 1939.

creation of a highly effective imposed cold peace (in the sense of freezing the status quo and keeping a lid on the region).

Indeed, Eastern Europe and the Balkans, having become part of the Soviet sphere of influence, ceased to be a powder-keg of Europe in the Cold War era, as Soviet power created an imposed zone of cold peace in the area. Under Pax Sovietica, no full-blown ethnic war was allowed to break out in that part of the world, which for centuries had been a crucible of clashing nationalisms (Avineri 1994, p. 31).

Moreover, unlike the earlier German hegemony, the fact (although not the moral right) of Soviet predominance in the region was tacitly recognized by the United States. This tacit recognition was expressed by its not intervening militarily in regional or domestic conflicts in Eastern Europe (parallel to the Soviet respect of this tacit rule regarding US predominance in Central America).[30]

Thus, the Soviet sphere of influence in Eastern Europe was an important element of the international order in the postwar era. As in the earlier German case, however, this effective conflict management by the Soviet hegemon[31] was achieved at the expense of the freedom of the East European nations. Moreover, the USSR did not promote the resolution of the many territorial conflicts in its sphere of influence, but rather suppressed them and kept the situation "frozen": [32]

> None of the prewar Balkan disputes can be said to have been resolved by the agreement of the contesting parties. If the Balkans have ceased to be the tinderbox of Europe, it is not because the Hungarians no longer desire Transylvania from Rumania, or because Bulgaria is content to see Macedonia remain a part of Yugoslavia, or because Albania and Greece are satisfied with their existing boundaries . . . Rather, it was only in the postwar era, when the Soviet Union emerged as the dominant power in the Balkans, willing to intervene to prevent one or another Balkan state from using force to assert its border claims – and militarily capable of such intervention – that peace was established in the region.[33]

Moving beyond imposed cold peace was well beyond the power of the hegemon, and remained contingent upon the internal attributes of the regional states. This question could not be examined as long as the coercive Soviet dominance over the region endured and limited the

[30] See Bull 1977, pp. 223–225; George et al. 1983, pp. 384–385; and Keal 1983, p. 115.
[31] See J. Joffe 1992, 46; Larrabee 1992, 31–32.
[32] Lundestad 1992, p. 198; Tomaszewski 1993.
[33] Weiner 1971, 682; see also Bull 1977, pp. 218–219. On the management of the Transylvanian Question, see Hupchick 1995, pp. 91–95.

autonomy of the regional actors, either in terms of engagement in hot war or in terms of movement to a warm peace. The collapse of Soviet hegemony and the communist order produced a great variation in the region. In those parts of Eastern Europe in which democratization and liberalization have taken root and state-to-nation problems have been resolved – thus marginalizing aggressive nationalism – we should not expect the reappearance of hot or cold ethnic-nationalist wars, and this indeed seems to be the case in Poland, Hungary, and the Czech Republic.[34] As these states evolve into stable democracies, the emergence of high-level warm peace among them is likely.

In contrast, as predicted by some observers,[35] with the disintegration of Soviet power, violent conflicts have broken out again in other places in the former Soviet sphere. These are locales in which state-to-nation problems have been especially severe, such as in the Balkans, as well as areas in the periphery of the former USSR itself (primarily the Caucasus). The disintegration of Pax Sovietica and of communist regimes throughout Eastern Europe has resulted in the reemergence of regional conflicts in these places in the 1990s, most notably the wars in the former Yugoslavia.

The decline of Soviet hegemony and the emergence of a war zone in the Balkans

Yugoslavia was not a part of the Soviet sphere of influence in the Cold War era as were the members of the Warsaw Pact, and it maintained a much higher degree of autonomy from the USSR than other East European states. However, its fate was very closely linked to developments in the Soviet sphere. Thus, there are strong links between the collapse of the USSR and the eruption of war in the Balkans. It is no coincidence that the two happened more or less simultaneously; Soviet decay made the breakout of large-scale violence in Yugoslavia more likely, for two major reasons.

The external Soviet threat had led to greater internal cohesion. The USSR had played the role of the regional "policeman" or bully in the Cold War era, and the threat of Soviet intervention deterred regional states and ethnonational groups in Eastern Europe and the Balkans from fighting each other and from trying to revise the regional territorial order. More

[34] On these factors as leading to peaceful transformations in Central and Eastern Europe, see Vachudova 1996.
[35] Licklider 1976/7.

specifically with regard to Yugoslavia, it also deterred domestic ethnonational leaders and groups from attempts at secession because such attempts could have provided an opportunity for Soviet intervention. The fear of Soviet meddling in Yugoslavia helped to unite the southern Slavs behind Tito and minimized the likelihood of internal fighting to avoid providing an excuse for Soviet intervention.[36]

Thus, a bid for independence by Slovenia or Croatia (and also by the Muslim leadership of Bosnia) was much less likely during the Soviet era because such a bid might have brought about Soviet intervention. Tito legitimized his harsh suppression of nationalist demands by citing fear of Soviet involvement. Confronted with Croatian nationalist demands in 1971, Tito said: "Others are watching. Are you aware that others would immediately be present if there would be disorders? But I'll sooner restore order with our army than allow others to do it."[37] As Gow notes, "Whereas during the Cold War, the threat of Soviet annexation might always discipline fractious republican leaders, with the fall of the Berlin Wall that shadow no longer loomed."[38]

Moreover, in the Cold War era secession could also have triggered a superpower war because unrest in the Balkans leading to Soviet intervention might have brought about a counterintervention by NATO to contain Soviet expansion. Thus, there was a shared interest of the superpowers during the Cold War in preventing a breakdown of Yugoslavia and in ensuring that violence did not erupt there.[39] With the weakening of the USSR, Western states became much more willing to recognize the independence of Slovenia and Croatia.[40]

The sources of legitimacy were changing. Soviet regional domination in the Cold War era legitimized the rule of communist parties and delegitimized hypernationalism in Eastern Europe and the Balkans. Tito was always a loyal communist, and Yugoslavia maintained close economic links with the Comecon members. By the same token, the collapse of the USSR and the anti-communist revolutions in Eastern Europe in 1989 discredited communist rule[41] and legitimized the militant aspirations of

[36] For example, on the effect of the Soviet intervention in Czechoslovakia in 1968 on the consolidation of national Yugoslav feeling, see Wilson 1979, p. 186.
[37] Jelavich 1983, p. 397.
[38] Gow 1997, p. 20; see also pp. 12, 21. See also Banac 1992, 141; Ullman 1996a, pp. 13, 27; Dragnich 1954, p. 302; Lampe 1996, p. 294; Pavlowitch 1971, pp. 343–344.
[39] Dragnich 1954, p. 202; Ullman 1996a, p. 12; Mandelbaum 1996, pp. 36–39; Krasner 1997, p. 201.
[40] Woodward 1995, p. 178; Gompert 1996, p. 125.
[41] Di Palma 1991, 49; Bernard Morris 1994; Caratan 1995; Ullman 1996a, p. 13; A. Stein and Lobell 1997.

nationalist leaders and movements. Nationalist ideology filled the ideological vacuum created by the decline of communism. These nationalist aspirations clashed in the former Yugoslavia because different ethnonational groups sought to control the same pieces of territory, which were populated by intermingled ethnonational groups that, moreover, had a recent history of extreme nationalist violence during World War II. In addition, former communist leaders such as Serbia's Milošević or Croatia's Tudjman remained without a legitimizing ideology. Thus, in order to mobilize support for the continuation of their rule, they turned to militant nationalism, which also served to divert attention from socioeconomic problems.[42] This led to aggressive behavior toward other nationalities and brought about the eruption of violence between these groups.

Disengagement: the great powers and the former Yugoslavia in the post-Cold War era

Many analysts expected the decline of Soviet hegemony in Eastern Europe and the end of the Cold War to bring about great power cooperation as the dominant strategy in local conflicts such as those in the Balkans. Such cooperation could take place in the form of either a revitalized great power concert or of pan-European collective security institutions such as the Organization for Security and Cooperation in Europe (OSCE), or some combination of the two.[43]

Although there have been some elements of concerted great power diplomacy in the conflict in the former Yugoslavia,[44] the dominant strategy of the great powers, until summer 1995, was disengagement (or at most a relatively low level of involvement, which included sending some limited peacekeeping forces, especially from Europe, imposing UN economic sanctions on Serbia, and enforcing the UN-declared no-fly zone over Bosnia and an arms embargo on former Yugoslavia). As a

[42] Gagnon 1994/5; Djilas 1995.
[43] See Kupchan and Kupchan 1991, esp. 115, n. 2. See also Zelikow 1992. For a critical analysis of the OSCE (in its former incarnation, the CSCE, the Conference for Security and Cooperation in Europe) as well as other regional organizations, including the European Community, in the area of regional security, see MacFarlane and Weiss 1992. To continue the discussion from ch. 5, the great powers in the post-Cold War era are of two classes: the hegemon or the sole global superpower, the United States (see Wohlforth 1999); and the next tier, all of which are inferior to the United States in overall capabilities, though they are roughly equal among themselves, China, the EU, and Russia (and in the foreseeable future potentially also India). The limits on a fully common foreign and security policy of the EU that still exist, however, somewhat weaken Europe's standing on the great power stage. At the same time, China is the key rising power for the foreseeable future.
[44] See Ullman 1996a; Gow 1997; Jakobsen 1997.

result, international institutions, whether European (such as the OSCE and the European Union) or global (the UN), failed in their attempts to resolve or at least contain the conflict. Consequently, the conflict continued uninterrupted, causing many casualties, a massive flow of refugees, and continuous fears of escalation and spreading instability. Many analysts argue that "more decisive and intrusive action by the West, including the use of military force, would have stopped, if not prevented, this most recent round of conflict in the Balkans."[45]

There are three factors that encourage great power disengagement from the conflicts in the Balkans: the mismatch between the hegemon's balance of capabilities and interests in the region; the mismatch between the balance of capabilities and interests of the United States and the Europeans in the Balkans; and the high expected costs of ground intervention in the Balkans. At the same time, two elements encourage partial engagement: the extrinsic interests of the United States in the region; and the ability of the hegemon to reduce the expected costs of intervention due to its high maneuvering room under unipolarity. Thus, despite strong reservations against intervention, especially on the ground, these two factors allowed for limited US deployments in later stages of the crises in Bosnia and in Kosovo.

Mismatch between the hegemon's capabilities and interests. The Balkans are a good example of a region where the United States can act much more freely in the post-Soviet era than during the Cold War, but, with the disappearance of the main threat to its security, it has much less interest in doing so. Although the disappearance of the USSR has made US military intervention in the Balkans much more feasible and much less costly than during the Cold War, the decline of the rivalry with the Soviets has also weakened the interest of the United States in that part of the world. Both the Bush Sr. and the Clinton administrations have shared the view concerning the low intrinsic US interests in the former Yugoslavia.[46] The absence of intrinsic geopolitical or economic US interests in the Balkans did not provide incentives powerful enough for

[45] Djilas 1995, p. 86.

[46] See Doder 1993, 4; Mandelbaum 1996; Ullman 1996a. The statement "we don't have a dog in this fight" is attributed to Bush Sr.'s secretary of state James Baker. See, for example, *International Herald Tribune*, June 18, 1999, 8. A senior official in the first Bush administration suggested that the "American strategic interest in the integrity of Yugoslavia, per se, ended with the collapse of the Soviet threat to Europe." See Gompert 1994, 33. In a memo to US ambassadors on March 7, 1993, Secretary of State Christopher suggested that Bosnia was of no vital interest to the United States: *New York Times*, June 16, 1993, A13, cited in C.-P. David 1994, p. 8, n. 27.

implementing a costly military intervention in the local conflict there, in contrast to its interests in Central America due to its proximity to the United States or in the oil-rich Middle East–Gulf region. Accordingly, there have been two considerable US interventions in Central America in the lead-up to and aftermath of the collapse of the USSR, in Panama (1989) and in Haiti (1994), along with two major US interventions in the Gulf region: the 1990–1991 Gulf War, and the 2003 invasion of Iraq (and the subsequent presence there). The two interventions in the Gulf included a major deployment of ground forces.[47] In contrast to the widespread perception that a lack of military response to the Iraqi invasion of Kuwait in 1990 would have threatened the flow of a key resource – oil – and destabilized the whole Middle East region, in the early stages of the Yugoslav crisis Washington did not view even a violent disintegration of Yugoslavia as likely to engulf Europe and destabilize Eastern Europe. Thus, neither preemptive military action nor a major economic aid program to help the Yugoslav federal government was seriously considered.[48]

Mismatch between the United States and the Europeans regarding their capabilities and interests in the Balkans. In the post-Cold War era, the powers that want to intervene in the Balkans because they have high interests at stake there (that is, the West Europeans) are unable to do so, while the power that is able to do so (that is, the United States) is less interested. In the 1990s the European powers seem to have had a higher interest than the United States in ending the war in Bosnia, at the very least because of their proximity to the conflict and the fear of spreading instability and chaos, the emergence of a major refugee problem, or the establishment of an Islamic state in the middle of Europe.[49] The Europeans, however, still need US leadership for carrying out a major military or diplomatic engagement. A major weakness of the Europeans compared to the United States is that they are unable to formulate a single coherent foreign policy because of conflicting interests among the members of the European Union, which were clearly demonstrated in the Yugoslav crisis.[50] As a result, "not only have the Europeans been unable to stop a civil war on their doorstep, but some of their contradictory responses have aggravated it."[51] On the military side, as the 1999 Kosovo crisis shows, Europe is still almost totally reliant on the United

[47] See Miller 1998, and 2004. [48] Gompert 1996, p. 124.
[49] See *New York Times*, March 13, 1994 (Weekly Review), 2; and Ullman 1996a, esp. 16–20.
[50] See *Economist*, Feb. 26, 1994, 21–24; see also MacFarlane and Weiss 1992.
[51] Doder 1993, 4.

States in several key fields, including electronic intelligence gathering, the ability to airlift large quantities of troops and equipment, and command and control capabilities.[52] Over four-fifths of the air strikes in Kosovo were carried out by the United States.[53]

US extrinsic interests in the Balkans. Although moral and humanitarian considerations have played an important role in the Western policy toward the Balkans in the 1990s, they are insufficient to explain why there was an intensive debate in the United States on intervention in the Balkans almost from the outset of the crisis there, while such a debate was absent in the cases of other humanitarian disasters, for example, in local conflicts in Africa or in post-Soviet republics. Such a difference between Bosnia and these other crises indicates that it would be wrong to portray US material/strategic interests in Bosnia as completely absent. Rather, the tangible US interests in Bosnia should be conceived of as "extrinsic" or secondary and based on Bosnia's proximity to the most crucial allies of the United States – the West Europeans.[54] This proximity led to a growing fear in the United States that the spread of instability in the Balkans would indeed adversely affect European stability,[55] for example, that massive flows of refugees would reinforce the power of various xenophobic and extremist movements in Western Europe and thus have negative effects on European integration. In addition, the involvement of the West Europeans in Bosnia entangled the crisis with the future of the main US alliance, NATO, and with the security commitment of the United States to the key region of Western Europe.[56]

Yet, these extrinsic interests were insufficient to generate a US military intervention alongside its allies until fall 1995.[57] Even after Serb forces began to overrun some of the UN-protected "safe areas" in July 1995, thereby posing a severe challenge to the credibility of the UN mission in Bosnia, the Clinton administration continued to resist US combat intervention beyond air strikes. Accordingly, the United States objected to the French plan to mount an aggressive defense of the besieged enclaves in Bosnia, at least partly because it could have led to a deeper US military involvement.

52 See *International Herald Tribune*, June 4, 1999, 1; and L. Freedman 1999.
53 *Economist*, July 17, 1999, 12.
54 On extrinsic interests, see Desch 1993.
55 See Gati 1992, 76; Larrabee 1992, 45–46; and C.-P. David 1994, p. 12.
56 On this point, see President Clinton's address cited in *International Herald Tribune*, Nov. 29, 1995, 6. See also Ullman 1996a, pp. 31–34; and the citation of Assistant Secretary of State Holbrooke in Mastanduno 1997, 69, n. 66.
57 For elaboration of this point, see Miller and Kagan 1997.

The high expected costs of intervention. The reason for this consistent refusal to engage militarily on the ground was the high expected costs, due to severe regional constraints, of intervention in terms of casualties. Such high costs acted as a deterrent against intervention in a place where the United States has only extrinsic, rather than intrinsic, interests. The mountainous terrain made a possible intervention in former Yugoslavia a much more difficult and expensive proposition than the Gulf War. The harsh geography acts to neutralize the effectiveness of air power, thus forcing the need for higher levels of ground forces.[58] The Yugoslav army was considered to be a modern European army that had been trained to fight the Soviet Army. It was expected that an American interventionary force would have to face a Serb force at least 90,000 strong, probably assisted by the Serbian air force.[59] Moreover, the Serbs proved themselves to be courageous guerrilla fighters in World War II against Nazi forces and succeeded in tying down forty-four German divisions.[60] The civil–ethnic nature of the Yugoslav conflict produced an additional constraint on intervention by making the attainment of US objectives much more complicated than in the case of the purely interstate Iraqi aggression against Kuwait. All these constraints combined led to an estimated need for a force of 200,000 to 500,000 in order to quell the situation in Bosnia[61] and to the expectation of very high casualties in case of such intervention.

In addition to the military constraints, there were also diplomatic constraints on military intervention. These were primarily the expected adverse effects on relations with Russia.[62] Whereas in Central America and in the post-Cold War Middle East the United States did not have to take into account a possible hostile reaction by a major power, this was not the case in the Balkans even in the post-Cold War era[63] because of the proximity of Russia and its historical ties there, especially with the Serbs.[64]

The outcome of the major power disengagement from the Balkans until 1995 was the inability to contain or ameliorate the violent local conflict, which continued uninterrupted.[65] The United States did not even respond to alarming developments such as, for example, the Serbian

[58] C.-P. David 1994, pp. 10–11. [59] Mearsheimer and Pape 1993, 22.
[60] On the limitations of this analogy, see L. Freedman 1994/5.
[61] Mearsheimer and Pape 1993, 23; Dewar 1993, 33.
[62] L. Freedman 1994/5, 54. [63] Maynes 1995.
[64] On the complexities of these ties in the past and at present, see Globe 1996.
[65] See J. Joffe 1992, pp. 36–50; L. Freedman 1994/5; Ullman 1996b.

offensive against the UN-designated "safe area" of Goražde in spring 1994, and especially the taking of UN peacekeepers hostage in May 1995 and the occupation of the "safe areas" of Srebrenica and Žepa in July 1995 by the Bosnian Serbs. This lack of response indicated the powerful limits to the US commitment to Bosnia, thus making possible unrestrained aggression by the local parties, especially the most powerful ones – the Serbs.

A decline in the expected costs and limited US involvement. In regions where major powers have only extrinsic interests, the likelihood of ground intervention depends on the expected costs. The above calculation of high expected costs of intervention was derived from the conception that a military intervention in Bosnia would be an aggressive peace enforcement or robust peace maintenance, that is, enforcing peace on reluctant local parties.[66] The nature of a proposed US military intervention in Bosnia, however, changed drastically in August–November 1995 because of three developments that transformed the objective of the intervention from peace enforcement to the much less costly one of peacekeeping. These developments were:

- A changing local balance of forces, namely, the growing military power of the Bosnian Muslims and especially the Croats vis-à-vis the Bosnian Serbs. The main manifestation of the new balance was the Croatian army's reoccupation of the Krajina from the Serbs in August 1995. In addition, a joint Muslim–Croat offensive took much of northwest Bosnia in September.
- These local changes were assisted by a US-led NATO air bombardment against the Bosnian Serbs in late August–September 1995 that was much more effective than previous air raids.
- The previous two developments increased the effectiveness of a vigorous US-led diplomatic mediation conducted by Richard Holbrooke. This resulted in a ceasefire on October 12 and a peace agreement initialed in November 21 in Dayton, Ohio, and signed in Paris on December 14 by the leaders of Serbia, Croatia, and Bosnia.

Following these events, President Clinton decided to fulfill his pledge to help keep the peace after a cessation of hostilities and after a peace agreement between the local protagonists had already been reached. Thus, the United States has deployed 20,000 troops within a 60,000-strong NATO force, with an initial commitment to stay in Bosnia for

[66] Ullman 1996a, p. 19.

one year; this has been continuously extended since then. In light of the changes in Bosnia, the mission of the force has become one of keeping the peace rather than of enforcing it, and accordingly, the expected costs have become much lower, bringing about a much higher US willingness to sustain its involvement. The limited US involvement has helped establish the conditions for the emergence of a cold regional peace, which would still depend on a continued major power military presence, at least in the short term.

The Kosovo crisis erupted in March 1999 after Serbia rejected the US–NATO peace proposals in Rambouillet. As in Bosnia, the absence of a credible threat of ground intervention and the US insistence on a casualty-free air operation initially undermined NATO ability to compel Serbia.[67] Yet, the combination of US extrinsic interests in the Balkans[68] and the great freedom of US military action under unipolarity given the absence of a powerful countervailing coalition allowed NATO to bomb Serbia massively for almost eighty days; it eventually compelled Serbia to accept somewhat similar conditions to those it rejected before the air campaign, including a deployment of a NATO force in the newly formed permissive environment in Kosovo.[69] To the extent that such a deployment is sustained and accompanied by a massive effort at economic reconstruction and intensive diplomatic efforts to ameliorate state-to-nation problems in the region, this may signal a strong commitment on the part of the United States and the Europeans to the Balkans; as a result a cold regional peace may emerge under US–NATO hegemony. Indeed, some argue that the US-led bombing helped in the removal of Milošević from power in fall 2000, thus ending the era of an aggressive leader who contributed quite considerably to the instability in the Balkans in the 1990s.[70]

The change from Western disengagement to NATO military interventions in Bosnia and Kosovo under US hegemony created the conditions for transition from war to peace in the Balkans. Since these interventions, power has been vested in the hands of international forces – NATO, the EU, and the UN. Those forces were charged with enforcing reforms and upholding the peace. As expected by the theory presented here,

[67] See, for example, *International Herald Tribune*, June 7, 1999, 9; J. Joffe 1999.

[68] On such interests motivating the US intervention in Kosovo, see *International Herald Tribune*, June 11, 1999, 1.

[69] On the causes for the apparent submission of Serbia, see, for example, *International Herald Tribune*, June 5–6, 1999, 4; *Newsweek*, July 26, 1999, 47–49.

[70] *New York Times*, Dec. 25, 2000, A6.

this internationally supported peace has remained cold while state-to-nation problems are still unresolved. Thus, there is a risk of renewed violence, especially if power is transferred back to local authorities without resolving the outstanding state-to-nation issues. In Bosnia, despite efforts by international officials to forge a more unified state and a coherent nation, the country's Serb, Muslim, and Croat populations remain deeply divided. The powers of the federal parliament and prime minister are weak in relation to the ethnic groups, each of which has its own president. Leaders of Bosnia's Republika Srpska (Serb Republic) have persistently opposed efforts to create a more centralized state at the expense of their own "entity," as it is known. Particularly controversial is the future sovereignty of Kosovo – whether it will become an independent state, as the Albanian majority hopes, or continue to be part of sovereign Serbia, as most of Kosovo's Serb minority prefers and in which it is supported by Serbia.[71]

In other parts of Eastern Europe, nationalist conflicts derived from state-to-nation imbalances were moderated by the stabilizing role of Western cooperative engagement. Thus, the enticing prospect of membership in NATO and the EU led to bandwagoning of East European states with the West. Under the Western economic and security umbrella, these states had strong incentives to resolve their outstanding nationalist conflicts – such as that between Hungary and its neighbors, Romania and Slovakia, over the status of the Hungarian minorities in these countries. In the Caucasus, Armenia and Azerbaijan, which, in contrast, lacked such systemic incentives, went to an irredentist war.[72]

The need for an "integrated" explanation

The importance of understanding conflict patterns in terms of both of the proposed independent variables is evident in this case study. The Great Eastern Crisis began as an insurrection against Ottoman rule, occurring in a region where national awareness and basic feelings of injustice had existed for many decades. Before a united great power front came to guarantee Turkish territorial inviolability in 1856, there had been numerous violent rebellions in the region. With the signing of the Treaty of Paris, this region entered a peaceful phase, largely at the behest of the European powers. The 1870s witnessed a tangibly altered arena of great power relations, with an emergent Germany drastically changing the

[71] *International Herald Tribune*, Oct. 15–16, 2005, 2.
[72] Linden 2000; Mychajlyszyn and Ripsman 2001.

European balance of power. This development, coupled with Russian efforts to stir pan-Slavist sympathies, emerged into a striking example of state-to-nation incongruence matched by competitive great power interference (Marriott 1917, pp. 320, 322).

Nevertheless, basically absent from the violent conflict were Macedonia and the regions of Croatia-Slavonia and Dalmatia. The former had not yet advanced internally to a condition in which political ambitions were articulated, and had not yet evolved into the focus of heated competition between Serbia, Bulgaria, and Greece it was destined to become. The people of Croatia-Slavonia and Dalmatia, though no less nationalistic than their Bosnian or Serbian counterparts, were left outside the violence since they were still subject to the effective hegemony of the Habsburgs, which precluded independence.

Only when state-to-nation incongruence became coupled with great power competition did the conditions for escalation to cold and hot war materialize. Thus, neither variable is sufficient on its own to explain the pattern of conflict, whereas together they appear to offer a reasonable account. State-to-nation incongruence tells us which regions are inherently war-prone; great power involvement tells us when this inherent war proneness is likely to erupt into war.

Conclusions

This chapter shows the usefulness of combining levels of analysis into a coherent explanation of regional conflict patterns. Neither unit-level nor system-level variables on their own provide a satisfactory framework for understanding the different dimensions of the phenomenon.

The Balkan peninsula between 1830 and 1913 provides a good illustration of the patterns expected by the present theory. Looked at through the prism of the proposed theory, the Balkan case reveals a measure of regularity and order which transcends the insights provided by the many excellent historical works on the region. Above and beyond the conventional wisdoms, which regard the Balkans as a perpetual cauldron of simmering hatred and unrest, the theory offers us insights as to where, when, and in what manner conflict can have been expected.

Those areas of the peninsula that were essentially congruent at certain periods of time – due to an absence of organized political mobilization among their inhabitants – witnessed considerably less conflict than adjacent areas. Thus, neither the Epiro-Albanian Coast nor the Vardar and Drin Valleys witnessed hot war prior to the development of acute state-to-nation incongruence in the post-1878 period. Notably, prior to the late 1870s, state-to-nation congruence in Macedonia resulted in warm peace, irrespective of the changing pattern of great power involvement. In the Albanian-inhabited lands, where limited conflict had erupted during the first half of the nineteenth century, great power cooperation evinced by the Treaty of Paris resulted in relative calm.

Those areas which were incongruent throughout the entire period – the Lower Danube and Maritsa Basin, and the central-western part of the Continental Core, plus the provinces of Bosnia and Herzegovina and the Adriatic coast – never proceeded beyond cold peace, and all experienced hot war at some point. Moreover, hot war erupted only in these areas when the great powers were competing fiercely. Cooperation between the great powers, in the context of the Treaty of Paris in 1856, prevented the outbreak of hot war, despite the severe incongruence in these areas which had previously resulted in violence. In the context of the Congress of Berlin, such cooperation put an end to the hot war witnessed during the Great Eastern Crisis.

Most notable among these examples, in terms of illustrating the interplay between the two independent variables, are the cases of Macedonia and Bosnia-Herzegovina. The great powers were pursuing conflicting interests in Macedonia both in the 1870s and in the 1900s. At the same time, Macedonia was being transformed in the course of several decades from a relatively benign province to a cauldron of intercommunal hatred. The frequency and extent of militarized violence in the province escalated in tandem with the latter development, despite the essentially constant array of external influences. In contrast, Bosnia-Herzegovina had been fiercely and consistently incongruent since the early nineteenth century. When the great powers cooperated in containing local tensions – between 1856 and 1870 and during the spring of 1878 – militarized incidents, indeed war, abated. When the great powers clashed over competing interests – such as before 1856 and during the 1870s – violent rebellions erupted. Once it was under Austro-Hungarian hegemony, subsequent to July 1878, the area once again was left out of the circle of militarized incidents and war, despite the fact that incongruence, if anything, had grown more severe with the presence of an independent Serbia pursuing irredentist claims.

Following the analysis in chapters 4 and 5, this chapter has also showed the type of regional outcomes best explained by systemic factors and also identified those regional outcomes that are not determined by systemic causes. "Hot" outcomes, such as hot war and warm peace, are not determined by international elements but rather reflect regional and domestic causes, because in these domains the balance of motivation favors the local parties. Thus, the hot wars in the Middle East and in the Balkans are the result of the multiplicity of state-to-nation problems in these regions. While peace may be achieved in these regions based on the help of the great powers, the state-to-nation problems make it difficult to move beyond the level of cold peace.

The great powers affect the "cold" outcomes of cold war and peace in accordance with the type of their regional involvement. While hegemony and cooperation are conducive to cold peace, great power competition and disengagement help sustain a cold war situation in regions with state-to-nation problems, although the decision to embark on a hot war will be up to the regional actors. Thus, the Austro-Russian and the Franco-Italian competitions intensified regional conflicts; great power disengagement in the 1930s and early 1990s made the region prone to violent conflicts.

The collapse of the Soviet/communist order in the Balkans with its imposed cold peace was conducive to the outbreak of aggressive nationalism in the Balkans. The great power disengagement from the Balkan wars in the early 1990s made it possible for Yugoslavia to become a major and protracted battlefield of the post-Cold War era. Limited US intervention in Bosnia in 1995 and in Kosovo in 1999 helped to bring about a tense peace there. US interests in the Balkans, however, are limited as is its willingness to play the role of a full-blown hegemon, including a willingness to commit ground troops and to tolerate casualties. This unwillingness to commit troops in the absence of a "permissive environment" (that is, only for peacekeeping purposes rather than for war-fighting/peace enforcement) stands in contrast to the massive US intervention on the ground in the Gulf crisis – an intervention that was crucial for the initiation and progress in the Arab–Israeli peace process during the 1990s. Thus the global US hegemony may be insufficient to produce a cold peace in a certain region in the absence of a commitment to intervene on the ground in that region.

Since US interests in the Balkans are lower than those of the Europeans and the latter are also interested in the integration of their foreign and security policy, it made sense that a semi-division of labor has emerged in recent years. The United States assisted the Europeans in gradually taking responsibility for the stabilization of the Balkans, notably deploying European Union troops as peacekeepers in the region (Macedonia, Bosnia). At the same time, the United States continues to fulfill its security obligations in the Middle East–Gulf region and in East Asia (although the Europeans have also taken part in the international security force in Afghanistan in recent years, while some states opposed US intervention in Iraq). To the extent that Europe integrates its security and foreign policy and develops military capabilities independent of those of the United States, in addition to its enormous economic assets, then it could become the key security provider in the Balkans. Fulfilling these conditions, however, will not be an easy task given the experience of European integration in the strategic field thus far.

While the state-to-nation imbalance in the Balkans is the underlying cause of the war proneness in the region, the analysis in this chapter also shows the strength of systemic factors in accounting for the transition of the Balkans from a zone of imposed peace in the Cold War era to a war zone in the early 1990s and back to a zone of still tenuous peace since the US-led interventions in 1995 and 1999.

Thus, this case study appears to provide substantial support for the proposed theory. State-to-nation incongruence and great power involvement together offer predictions as to where, when, and in what manner militarized conflict can have been expected. These predictions fit the revealed historical patterns in the Balkans in the past two centuries rather well.

7 The state-to-nation balance and the emergence of peace in South America during the twentieth century

Potential pathways to regional peace

Chapters 7 and 8 focus on the *effects* of two major mechanisms for regional peace – conflict resolution and integration – and on the domestic *conditions* for their success. I use the regional cases of South America (in this chapter) and Western Europe (in chapter 8) to illustrate these potential theoretical pathways to peace.

The degree of state-to-nation balance conditions the effectiveness of different peacemaking strategies. When there is a high state-to-nation imbalance in a region, strategies that focus on changing the capabilities of the local antagonists tend to be the most effective. In a regional context, those strategies are related to the type of involvement of the great powers in the region, especially hegemony or cooperation, which are discussed in chapters 5 and 6. However, when there is a relatively high extent of state-to-nation balance, peacemaking strategies that focus on changing the intentions of the regional parties can be effective. There are two major types of such regional strategies: conflict resolution and integration.

I make a distinction between the *effects* of approaches to peacemaking and the *conditions* for their success. Different peacemaking strategies may bring about a transition from war to peace, but each strategy will be successful only if certain distinctive conditions exist in the region. The conditions for the effectiveness of the different strategies vary considerably and stem from three levels of analysis. Chapters 5 and 6 analyzed the global level – the presence of a great power hegemon or concert in the region in question (for the strategy of great power engagement). Chapters 7 and 8 analyze the regional/domestic level – the presence of coherent, namely, strong and congruent states (for the strategy of conflict resolution); and the (purely) domestic level – the presence of liberal

Table 7.1 *The theoretical framework of peacemaking strategies*

The theoretical approach	The derived strategy	The strategy's effects – the level of peace	The conditions for the strategy's effectiveness
Global society	Great power regional engagement	Cold peace	A great power hegemon or concert
Regional society	Regional conflict resolution	Warm peace – normal	Coherent (strong and congruent) states
Regional community	Regional integration	Warm peace – high-level	Liberal democracies

democracies (for the integration option). Chapter 7 shows that the presence of coherent states in twentieth-century South America reduced the likelihood of hot wars and facilitated conflict resolution. Chapter 8 argues that when the coherent states are also liberal, the strategy of integration is likely to succeed and high-level peace will emerge.

The strategies are derived from the discussion in chapter 2 of major approaches to international relations: one is globalist and two are regionalist. The two regional-level approaches are regional society and regional community. The peacemaking strategy derived from the regional society approach is conflict resolution, while the strategy of integration is derived from the regional community approach (see table 7.1). The third strategy of great power engagement stems from the global society approach.[1] Moreover, different peacemaking strategies bring about different levels of peace. Thus, even if different strategies may be successful, there will still be dramatic differences in the level of regional peace they will produce and, thus, in the likelihood of returning to a state of war; these distinctions arise because of their varying treatments of the regional manifestations of the state-to-nation problem, notably, territorial and boundary questions (on types of peace, see chapter 2).

Whereas the global-level strategy can bring about only cold peace, the regional strategies may result in warmer peace. More specifically,

[1] As indicated in ch. 2, some components of this approach are closely related to the realist international system approach, especially regarding the role of a coercive hegemon. Thus, it can be seen simply as the "globalist" approach; for analytical clarity, however, I classified it in ch. 2 as a global society in order to differentiate it from the competition – or disengagement – associated with the realist international system.

conflict resolution tends to result in normal peace, and integration in high-level peace. The reason that the global strategy can bring about only cold peace is related to the way it addresses the situation of state-to-nation imbalance. Since the global strategy only moderates the manifestations of this imbalance in the region, being unable to resolve it fully, the resulting peace is only a cold one. Strategies that focus on changing the intentions of the actors can bring about higher or "warmer" levels of peace, although only under certain conditions. Where such conditions pertain, these strategies can either directly resolve the outstanding issues in conflict (the regional conflict resolution strategy) or transcend them (the integration strategy).

In the main, chapters 7 and 8 investigate the pacifying value as well as the disadvantages of the two mechanisms, through comparative illustrations from two regions, each exemplifying a specific strategy leading to a transition to or from a certain level of peace based on the presence of certain conditions: South America during the twentieth century (normal peace evolved following the strengthening of the regional states); and post-1945 Western Europe (high-level peace evolved as a result of successful regional liberalization promoted by US hegemony).

There is a trade-off between the regional and the global strategies for advancing regional peace. While the regional/domestic strategies are more desirable than the global one in that they are conducive to higher levels of regional peace, they are less feasible, since state-to-nation problems are hard to resolve and liberalization depends on prerequisites that are demanding to establish. In contrast, the global strategy is more feasible (to the extent that the necessary global conditions are present), but is unable to take regions beyond cold peace to higher levels. Yet, while the global strategy can bring about only a relatively low level of peace (cold peace), such a cold peace can be conducive to enhancing the efficacy of the regional/domestic-level strategies of peacemaking, starting from the regional conflict resolution strategy that results in normal peace. Normal peace, in turn, is conducive to domestic liberalization and as a result to the emergence of the high-level warm peace. Thus, the proposed framework suggests an integrated-gradual approach to regional peacemaking. The framework provides an analytical tool for evaluating the current and future (short-term and long-term) progress in the Middle East peace process and in peacemaking in the Balkans in comparison with successful past peace processes in other regions, most notably, Western Europe and South America.

Table 7.2 *Strategies for regional peacemaking*

Strategy for regional peace	Changing intentions or capabilities of regional states	Way of addressing state-to-nation imbalance	Level of regional peace
Great power concert or hegemony	Capabilities	Imbalance moderated	Cold peace
Regional conflict resolution	Intentions	Imbalance resolved	Warm peace – normal
Regional integration	Intentions	Imbalance transcended	Warm peace – high-level

There are two basic interrelated differences among the three mechanisms for regional peacemaking: whether they focus on regional states' capabilities or motivations for war, and how each addresses the state-to-nation problem (see table 7.2). The global strategy does not resolve the state-to-nation balance problem; at best, it moderates the level of conflict. One advantage of the global mechanism is that it can deal effectively with the *capabilities* of the regional actors to go to war. The regional balance of power depends heavily on external support, and notably on arms supply by great powers. As a result, the great powers can constrain regional actors' ability to resort to force by imposing limitations on local military capabilities and by constructing an effective arms control regime. But this can be successful only if a concert of cooperating powers or a stabilizing hegemon is present. If, on the contrary, the great powers are competitively engaged in the region, the state-to-nation problem will not only not be moderated, but will be aggravated, encouraging a situation of regional hot or cold war.

The regional/domestic approaches may address more effectively the *motivations* of the actors, either by changing those motivations directly related to the causes of regional wars such as territorial conflicts (through the strategy of regional conflict resolution) or by transcending the causes of such wars through transforming the general motivations and capacities of the regional actors regarding peace and war (the strategy of integration).

The regional conflict strategy confronts the state-to-nation question directly and puts it center stage by addressing and aiming to resolve the outstanding territorial and boundaries issues in the region. Agreement is achieved among the parties on nonintervention in the domestic affairs of the other states, on respect for their sovereignty and territorial integrity, and on peaceful resolution of conflicts. However, the lasting success of the conflict resolution process and the maintenance of a stable normal peace depends on the presence of strong and congruent states in the region, namely, on the success of state-building and eventually nation-building processes. Under these conditions the incentives to go to war will be much lower, and the type of involvement of the great powers will be much less crucial. The higher the level of state-to-nation balance and the more conflicts are resolved peacefully by coherent regional states, the less likely it is that great power competition will spill over into the region and that it will have a major impact on regional outcomes. Because they are unable to achieve strategic gains in the region by meddling in its conflicts, the competing great powers are likely to disengage from strategic intervention there under the conditions of regional conflict resolution and the presence of coherent states.

The regional integration path transcends the state-to-nation problem by aiming at a radical change in the ability and motivation of states to act unilaterally, especially constraining their resort to force (see chapter 8). In this strategy the high level of warm peace is reached by successful regional integration, in which there is a voluntary transfer of certain authorities from the regional states to supranational institutions as well as pooling of sovereignty. Necessary conditions for this particularly high level of peace are successful democratization and liberalization; that is, all the key regional states have to be liberal democracies. For the initial stages of such liberalization, the presence of a great power hegemon or concert might be necessary as well, because democratization may lead, at least in the short run, to greater instability and conflict (Mansfield and Snyder 2005), especially in regions where there is a high extent of state-to-nation imbalance. However, following the completion of the liberalization process, the leadership of the great powers will be much less needed, if at all, for maintaining the high-level peace. After this level of peace is stabilized, ethnic conflicts are less likely to lead to internal armed disputes, and are sure not to spread regional instability across borders.

As a result, the big advantage of the regional/domestic approaches is that they can establish warm peace (normal or high-level), whereas the global strategy can at best bring about cold peace. Regional strategies are also less dependent on the continuing engagement of external powers in the region. Yet, the prerequisites for the success of the regional/domestic strategies (the presence of strong and congruent states or liberal democracies) are very demanding to establish and sometimes extremely hard to achieve. If these conditions are unattainable while the conducive global conditions exist, the global strategy can be helpful in advancing peaceful regional settlements under state-to-nation imbalance, even if only cold ones. These cold regional settlements may, in turn, prove conducive to the later success of the regional/domestic strategies for promoting higher levels of regional peace.

The strategy of regional conflict resolution

The resolution of regional state-to-nation problems, and their territorial manifestations, reduces the likelihood of wars in a region quite considerably. But as long as there are incoherent states in the region, successful conflict resolution is less likely. Moreover, the presence of coherent states in the region is necessary for the stability of the peace accords, for their implementation, and for reaching the level of regional normal peace for an extended period.

The strategy of conflict resolution leads to normal peace

This strategy suggests that, rather than relying on external powers, the regional parties should focus on directly addressing the state-to-nation issues in dispute among them through negotiation and conflict resolution.[2] More specifically, the parties should settle the substantive manifestations of the state-to-nation issues in dispute; such moves might include recognizing all the other states in the region, agreeing on acceptable boundaries, resolving territorial conflicts and problems of refugees, and negotiating a fair division of scarce resources (such as water).

Resolution of these problems will lessen the motivation of the regional states to go to war, and thus will markedly reduce the likelihood of the outbreak of wars in the region.[3] More specifically, conflict resolution will make less likely the occurrence of the three major types of regional wars:

[2] On negotiations and conflict resolution, see, for example, C. Mitchell 1981, pp. 275–277, Patchen 1988, Kriesberg 1992, Hopmann 1994, Zartman 1995b, and Zartman and Rasmussen 1997. For an overview and references, see Craig and George 1995, pp. 163–179.

[3] For empirical findings about the connection between resolved territorial disputes and declining likelihood of war in comparison with unresolved territorial conflicts, which are an extremely potent predictor of interstate war, see Kocs 1995. Although these findings

security dilemma wars, profit wars, and diversionary wars (see chapter 3). With regard to security dilemma (or inadvertent) wars, in accordance with the logic of the conflict resolution strategy, it is the extent and severity of unresolved issues that account for regional variations in the intensity of the security dilemma. The extent of unresolved problems conditions the security dilemma and the war proneness of different regions. In other words, when there is a high state-to-nation balance, and thus the territorial division among the states is widely accepted, the intensity of the security dilemma is lower, and it is less likely that mutual fears of being attacked and preempted will dominate the relations among the regional states.[4] The security dilemma on its own is unlikely to lead to war among neighbors; a high level of state-to-nation imbalance, which results in sharp territorial disagreement, is also required.

Nationalist irredentism provides substantive issues for wars of profit or expansion, namely, for boundaries, for territory, or in a struggle for hegemony. The resolution of these disputes will directly reduce the likelihood of wars of profit. Diversionary wars, on the other hand, are produced by problems of domestic illegitimacy, related in many cases to state-to-nation problems. The resolution of state-to-nation problems decreases secessionist demands, which may have previously posed a major challenge to ruling elites, increasing their insecurity; this therefore strengthens local states and increases their domestic stability. Thus, mutual recognition and the acceptance of boundaries strengthen the regional states not only externally but also internally, and increase the stability of their political regimes. As a result, the likelihood of scapegoat wars will also be lower if the territorial manifestations of the state-to-nation imbalance are resolved.

The conditions for the effectiveness of the conflict-resolution strategy: the presence of coherent states in the region

The relationship between stable and strong states and regional conflict resolution is a complex one. While regional conflict resolution

make a lot of sense, the question is whether there are causal relations or only correlations. In other words, what explains the variations between resolved and unresolved conflicts? Moreover, while Kocs focuses on interstate dyads, I deal with regional war and peace, which is affected also by civil/ethnic conflicts, since these may have transborder regional security effects. In this context, the state-to-nation balance plays a key role.

[4] For a partly related argument, see Wendt 1992 and Schweller 1996.

strengthens local states because of the acceptance of their sovereignty and boundaries by their neighbors, the other side of the coin is that the effectiveness and durability of conflict resolution are heavily dependent on the prior presence in the region of strong and congruent states.[5] Strong states have effective institutions; in congruent states there is a high level of identification of the citizens with the state; and key domestic groups accept the territorial identity of the state, namely, the permanence of its boundaries.[6] In contrast, a low level of citizen identification and a lack of firm territorial identity may result in attempts at secession and border changes which may spill over and involve a number of regional states. In other words, the weaker the regional states on these two dimensions, the greater the state-to-nation problems, the less the regional and domestic stability, and the greater the obstacles to effective conflict resolution; conversely, the stronger the states on these two dimensions, the greater the likelihood of successful conflict resolution and thus for normal peace.[7]

Weak states are a source of regional instability because of the low credibility of their commitments to implementing peace accords. They are unreliable partners, and neighbors cannot trust that they are able to carry out their commitments.[8] Alternatively, the regime might change and because of the lack of institutional continuity, the new regime may not feel obliged to honor previous agreements; thus, negotiated accords are less likely to take place or to endure even if they do take place.

There is a difference, however, depending on whether the weak states are congruent or incongruent. If they are weak and congruent ("frontier" states), then they are unable to control their sovereign territories. This lack of control leads to border wars and external intervention, but there is no powerful nationalist opposition to conflict resolution. Thus, the strengthening of the state is sufficient to encourage moderation and successful peacemaking.

Under state-to-nation incongruence, however, the same logic that provides incentives to go to war (see chapter 3) also produces domestic and transborder constraints on the ability of elites to make peace even if they believe that it is in their state's best security and economic interests to

[5] On the possible values of the two dimensions of the state-to-nation balance (state strength and state-to-nation congruence), see chs. 2 and 3. Coherent states are both institutionally strong and nationally congruent.

[6] See Buzan 1991, ch. 2, Ayoob 1995, and Holsti 1996.

[7] See Ayoob 1995, pp. 194–196.

[8] Similarly, in the absence of third-party guarantees, the lack of credibility of commitments will have negative effects on the implementation of peace agreements in civil wars. See Walter 2002.

do so. Nationalist/ethnic forces oppose making territorial concessions either on demographic grounds (the territories are populated by ethnic kin) or due to national-historical-religious attachments to these territories. Nationalists manipulate such causes against moderate elites, who have limited room to maneuver in incongruent states. Weak states are also vulnerable to pressures from other states, which are able to intervene in their domestic affairs and can make it difficult to pursue moderate policies. Under the pressure of secessionist movements, it is difficult to reach stable peace agreements with neighbors who may also face nationalist and ethnic pressures. Irredentist forces, for their part, fight against concessions. Ambitious politicians use the nationalist/ethnic card to promote themselves and thus to make it difficult to pursue moderate policies. Mobilization against external national/ethnic enemies is a major diversionary tactic used by political leaders to mobilize mass support in incoherent states. This is especially the case in regions populated by states that are considered illegitimate by some of their neighbors or by peoples who are not seen as qualified to have their own states (for examples, see chapters 3, 4, and 6). State-to-nation imbalance produces conflict-prone regions with deep-seated animosity among neighbors. Such neighbors with a long history of rivalry have a hard time overcoming a legacy of mutual fears and suspicion by themselves, and it will be difficult for them to resolve conflicts without external support, mediation, and assurances and to agree on issues like boundaries, on which they have incompatible positions.

To overcome these obstacles to regional conflict resolution, state-building is necessary. Thus, the strategy of conflict resolution may also be called the "statist" strategy, because it gives priority to strengthening the state and consolidating its power over separatist groups. This is done by monopolizing the instruments of violence in the state's hands (namely, disarming the secessionist groups) and maintaining its territorial integrity.[9] At a minimum, for attempts at conflict resolution to be effective, the regional states should be in the process of strengthening their institutional base. Major areas of institutional state-building include law and order (in particular, professional police and an independent judiciary); an effective bureaucracy and a professional military force; tax collection; constitutional arrangements; and the provision of

[9] See Ayoob 1995, pp. 182–184, and the sources he cites.

socioeconomic services.[10] In order for conflict resolution to bring about stable peace, state-building should be followed by a nation-building process, which, if successful, will lead to identification of the major groups within the state with its existing territorial identity at the expense of revisionist/nationalist and ethnic/secessionist forces. Nation-building includes the provision of nonmaterial symbolic functions to the population through a national educational system, the media, and myth-making. It may also include the promotion of a national language and the manipulation of identities so as to form a more cohesive nation. Although many cases of nation-building in the Third World have failed (Connor 1994; L. Diamond and Plattner 1994, p. xvi), a recently successful example in the Middle East is the growing national identity in Morocco between 1956 and 1999 (Byman 2002, pp. 100–124).

In regions populated by institutionally strong and nationally congruent states, regional conflicts are more likely to be resolved and wars are more likely to be prevented. The combination of national congruence and institutional strength, which leads to coherent states, enjoys domestic legitimacy and citizen support for the territorial integrity of the state. Thus, these states are not a temptation for conquest and can deter attacks more effectively because nationalism can mobilize popular resistance to conquest.[11] The greater state congruence also makes it more difficult for transborder forces to penetrate the state and to challenge pragmatic policies. Coherent states will thus be both more stable domestically and more able to resist domestic and transnational pressures to endorse hard-line policies. As a result, coherent states are more likely to endorse pragmatic international orientations and to behave cautiously according to *Realpolitik* considerations rather than emotional nationalist commitments.[12] Such commitments and symbols make it more difficult to bargain and to reach compromises and accommodation, in comparison to materialist/rationalist considerations, according to which it is more profitable to negotiate peaceful arrangements rather than go to a costly war (Fearon 1995).

The problem is that state-building and nation-building are difficult to accomplish in regions with a state-to-nation imbalance where many states are weak and lack firm territorial identity. At the same time, the possibilities for state-building by internal or external coercion as well

[10] Weiner 1987, p. 59. For an extended discussion, see Rotberg 2003, Paris 2004, and Fukuyama 2004.
[11] Van Evera 1994. [12] This is the idea of "stateness" according to Ben-Dor (1983).

as by economic bribes are constrained by the economic and military weakness of the central authorities in many states. This weakness also produces economic and security dependence on the Western powers, which, in turn, exerts pressure against violent policies and massive violations of human rights, thus making it even more difficult to build states through coercion.[13]

The difficulty in state-building poses severe problems for the conflict resolution strategy: as noted, this strategy depends on strong states, but under a state-to-nation imbalance, state-building is difficult. In other words, state-building is least feasible where it is most needed.

A possible solution involves democratization: a democratic regime can strengthen national congruence in the long term by increasing the population's identification with a state that gives them political rights; the regime can also reduce ethnic-based discrimination. Yet, in the short term, democratization in weak states may further weaken the state and bring about its disintegration. For this reason, the conflict resolution/state-building strategy gives priority to consolidating state power over domestic groups at the expense of, and as a prior prerequisite for, democratization. Thus, regional integration/liberalization and regional conflict resolution/state-building constitute distinct and competing approaches to regional peacemaking. One possible way to make them complementary is in the framework of an integrated-gradual approach (discussed in chapter 9).

The following case study shows how relatively successful state-building can lead to an effective regional conflict resolution – even in the absence of democracy – when there is a predisposition for national congruence in the region. The major change that pacified South America in the transition from the nineteenth century to the twentieth was not the rise of democracy, but state consolidation or strengthening, which came on top of national congruence. Democracy (or the lack thereof) and national congruence remained relatively constant from the nineteenth century to the twentieth. Thus, I can isolate the effects of the variable of state strength and show that, while state weakness brings about wars among "frontier" states, state-building can generate status quo orientations and thus lead to normal peace when it is combined with the low national incongruence of immigrant societies. In other words, the formation of a regional state-to-nation balance leads to the emergence of a regional peace.

[13] Ayoob 1995.

Explaining the emergence of peace in South America

The frontier state: state weakness in nineteenth-century South America leads to a war zone

Nineteenth-century South America was an area of chronic war and armed intervention: the war of Argentina, Brazil, and Uruguay against Paraguay in 1865–1870 (Lynch 1993, pp. 40–46); the Pacific war among Chile, Bolivia, and Peru (1879–1883); and armed conflicts over boundaries between Brazil and its southern neighbors, Argentina, Uruguay, and Paraguay.

More precisely, six postcolonial wars took place between 1825 and 1883, in addition to some undeclared confrontations:

1. The First Argentine–Brazilian War (Cisplatine War) of 1825–1828;
2. The Peru–Grand Colombia War of 1828–1829;
3. The War of the Peruvian–Bolivian Confederation (1836–1839), engaging Chile and Argentina against Peru and Bolivia;
4. The "Great War" (1836–1852), involving different factions of Argentina and Uruguay, Brazil, and short interventions by Britain and France;
5. The War of the Triple Alliance (1865–1870): Argentina, Brazil, and Uruguay against Paraguay;
6. The War of the Pacific (1879–1883), pitting Chile against Peru and Bolivia.

Other hostilities took place between Peru and Bolivia (1841); Peru and Ecuador (1859); and Ecuador and Colombia (1862).[14]

The underlying cause of the wars in the nineteenth century was state weakness in the region. Nineteenth-century South American states were inherently weak, including the ambiguity of their boundaries, which were neither marked clearly nor agreed upon with their neighbors (Holsti 1996, p. 153). While pan- and subnationalism and their destabilizing effects were much weaker than in Europe, still the nineteenth-century South American states were very weak and not consolidated; thus, most boundaries were not clearly defined and some states seized territories belonging to their neighbors. Power was mostly in the hands of local landowners or warlords. Weak central states and powerful centrifugal

[14] See Burr 1965, pp. 1–2; H. Seton-Watson 1977, p. 220; Seckinger 1984; Kacowicz 1998, p. 71; 1996, p. 19; D'Agostino 1997, p. 52; Fraser 1997, p. 158; Centeno 2002, pp. 37, 44; Dominguez et al. 2003, pp. 21–22.

propensities led to the emergence of local rule systems, contrary to the states' laws and constitutions (Wiarda and Kline 1979, pp. 61, 67). The regional wars were closely related to the domestic political instability, civil wars, and external intervention that characterized the states in the region (Kacowicz 1998, pp. 71–72, and the references he cites).

Argentina, for example, was highly fragmented during most of the nineteenth century.[15] There was no effective central government whose authority was accepted by all. Monopoly over the use of force was lacking: every city and province had its own militia, and different warlords (*caudillos*) had their private militias. The provinces not only had standing armies and warred against each other, they sometimes even signed treaties with neighboring states.[16] Also absent were a central constitution and a common judiciary, and there was no central education system apart from that of the church. The period was characterized by a continuous struggle between the hegemonic attempts of Buenos Aires and the aspirations of the provinces for autonomy and independence from the center. During the 1870s, there was intensive fighting between the white settlers and the Indians in the frontier, as well as armed conflicts between the different regions and *caudillos*. Indeed, the fragility of the Argentinean state, together with the weakness of the neighboring states at that time, made the region conducive to wars. Thus, the weakness of Argentina brought about the intervention of its neighbors in its territory, Brazil as well as forces from Uruguay and Paraguay (Shumway 1991, pp. 169–170). Moreover, state weakness generated diversionary wars, such as Argentina's participation in the war against Paraguay (ibid., pp. 237–240).

Although the other key state in South America, Brazil, was already stronger than Argentina in the nineteenth century, it was not a strong state at that time. There were many rebellions against the central government, especially in the 1830s and 1840s. These rebellions were derived in part from social motives – against the suppression and exploitation of the lower classes and the slaves. Another part was separatist-oriented. In the southern province of Rio Grande do Sul, cattle owners and *gauchos* fought against the central authorities, demanding the independence of their province. With the support of most of the large landowners in the region and occupying territory that was geographically defensible, the Farrapos rebellion took ten years for the Brazilian central government to defeat. Caxias, the son of General Lima e Silva, the leading military

[15] See Merquior 1987; Lynch 1993. [16] Escude 1988, esp. 143.

commander under Pedro I, Emperor of Brazil and King of Portugal, during Brazil's battles for independence in 1822–1823, rose to military prominence in Brazil during this period after successfully suppressing several rebellions, including Maranhão in September 1831 and São Paulo in 1842. Caxias was called in to put down the Rio Grande do Sul rebellion, but was able to accomplish the task only over the course of two to three years, during which time the Brazilian army reached a peak size of 23,000 in 1845 (Schneider 1991, pp. 49–50).

In 1837–1838 army officers, merchants, and professionals rebelled in the city of Rasifa (located in the province Bahaia), demanding independence from the center in Rio de Janeiro. This demand was later modified to a call for autonomy within the state (Barman 1988, pp. 170–195). Similar rebellions were common during the nineteenth century.

The center's monopoly on the means of violence was far from complete in Brazil, although it was more effective than in Argentina. Control was especially incomplete in the first decades of Brazil's independence, when every province's president had a military force under his command. This situation led to problems such as Brazilian interference in the Bolivian district of Chiquitos; this arose from an independent 1825 initiative of the Mato Grosso province in Brazil, and was not endorsed by the Brazilian crown (Seckinger 1984, pp. 73–79; see also below on this crisis).

Brazil's boundaries were also not fixed and clear-cut; it had boundary disputes with Venezuela, Colombia, Ecuador, Bolivia, Peru, Paraguay, Uruguay, and Argentina (see map in Burr 1965, p. 1). Brazil's imperial and hegemonic aspirations as well as its ideological conflicts with its republican neighbors further reinforced these disputes. Boundary disputes occasionally escalated to wars, especially along Brazil's southern frontier with Argentina, Paraguay, and Uruguay (Seckinger 1984, pp. 20–28, 55–98).

The outcome of state weakness was that every state constantly faced the danger of intervention, territorial conquest, and attack by its neighbors. More specifically, state weakness brought about an intense security dilemma, wars of profit, and diversionary wars.

Security dilemma wars

This situation created an intense security dilemma: defensive capabilities were perceived by others as a threat to their own territorial integrity. The results were arms races, regional balancing, and war (Holsti 1996, p. 172).

The Paraguay War, in which Brazil, Argentina, and Uruguay fought against Paraguay between 1865 and 1870, illustrates these dynamics. The war resulted from a gradual escalation of conflicting interests, which got confused due to a range of mistaken, but understandable, perceptions of the parties (Graham 1989, p. 152). The war started when Brazil and Argentina intervened militarily in the domestic politics of Uruguay (a common practice in that era), creating a grave perception of threat in Paraguay: Cardinal Lopez of Paraguay feared that Brazil would take over Uruguay and deprive Paraguay of its sole access to the sea (Shumway 1991, pp. 231–232). Furthermore, in the Treaty of Montevideo, signed between Brazil and Argentina in 1864 and dealing with domestic order in Uruguay, there was also a clause about a common action against Paraguay if it intervened in favor of the Blancos, the Uruguayan party opposed by Brazil and Argentina. Lopez saw it as a vindication of his worries about Brazilian–Argentinean plans to divide Paraguay between themselves.

Lopez, therefore, stated his support for the Blancos and declared a war on Brazil. In order to fight Brazil, Lopez's army had to go through Argentinean territories, which he did in spite of the refusal of President Mitre of Argentina. The outcome was Argentina's declaration of war against Paraguay. Argentina and Brazil signed an alliance against Paraguay which included the client government they established in Uruguay. In this way started the bloodiest war since the liberation of South America from colonial rule. Less than half of Paraguay's population – and only a small portion of the men – remained alive at the end of the war (Shumway 1991, pp. 231–232).

Wars of profit (wars of opportunity)

A weak state is, naturally, a convenient arena for external intervention especially when not only a certain regime but the state itself does not enjoy the legitimacy of its citizens (or at least important population groups, which might identify with neighboring states). This creates a temptation to expand on the part of neighboring states (especially if their military power is greater). The lack of clarity and the legal ambiguity of boundaries facilitated the eruption of violence. An example is the First Brazilian–Argentinean War of 1825–1828.

War broke out between Argentina and Brazil over the upper portion of the Rio de la Plata estuary, also referred to as the Eastern Bank or Banda Oriental, modern-day Uruguay. Prior to the independence of Argentina and Brazil, this territory was the subject of disputes between the colonial powers of Portugal and Spain, because, as Thomas Millington has described, the territory "lay astride the Plata river system, which drained large portions of the Brazilian interior" (1996, p. 8). The territory is also located immediately across an estuary from Buenos Aires, making it strategically important for both countries. During the first decade of the 1800s, a local leader, José Artigas, organized an insurgency in the Eastern Bank against both Spain and Portugal. Like João VI, Prince Regent of Brazil and King of Portugal, Buenos Aires was opposed to Artigas because he threatened Argentinean plans to create a united state from the Plata viceroyalty, ruled by Spain: João invaded the Eastern Bank in 1811 to remove Artigas from power, but soon agreed to withdraw his troops in response to British objections. However, Brazilian troops invaded the territory once again in 1817, taking advantage of the weakness of military forces in Buenos Aires and growing local opposition to Artigas. The Brazilian army was able to consolidate control over the region and formally annexed the territory in 1821 (Millington 1996).

In 1825, a group commanded by a local military leader invaded the Eastern Bank and forced the Brazilian army to evacuate the countryside. Leaders in Buenos Aires saw an opportunity to regain the territory that they believed was rightfully theirs, and therefore declared it Argentinean. Brazil and Argentina fought to a standoff, and, submitting to British mediation, they agreed to create the buffer state of Uruguay in 1828 (Schneider 1991). The war with Argentina demonstrated the weakness of both states. The naval forces of both opponents, for example, were commanded by British citizens, and most of the sailors were also British (Bethell and Carvalho 1989, p. 54). The war had caused a great economic strain and embarrassed the Brazilian government, especially after a mutiny by Irish and German mercenaries briefly took over the capital of Rio de Janeiro in June 1828 (Bethell and Carvalho 1989).

The attempted coup during the Cisplatine War indicated the weakness of Brazil's monarchy, and local landowners and political leaders were growing increasingly dissatisfied with Pedro's autocratic and centralized control. Dom Pedro was forced to abdicate in 1831, and the country was ruled by a line of regents before Pedro II assumed the crown in 1840 at the age of fourteen.

The Paraguay War (1864–1870) is also an excellent example. The alliance treaty among Brazil, Argentina, and Uruguay in 1865 stipulated that after the victory in the war the parties would redraw the boundaries of Paraguay and would force it to open the Paraguay River to free navigation and international trade. This clause and its implementation made the Paraguay War a classical example of a war of opportunity (Shumway 1991, p. 237; Graham 1989, p. 152). The other side, for its part, also tried to use state weakness and fragmentation to its advantage at the expense of its rivals: Lopez, for example, thought that he would get support for his war against Buenos Aires from the *caudillos* who governed the Argentinean province of Entre Rios.

There are other examples of weak states in nineteenth-century South America that attracted the intervention of their neighbors, such as Ecuador. Following its secession from Colombia, it was in an eternal state of coups d'état and civil wars. This weakness encouraged frequent intervention of Peru and recurrent attempts on its part to annex territories from Ecuador. Nineteenth-century Bolivia is another illustration of a weak state. It included geographically distinct and diverse regions (whose population identified more with neighboring states), it had significant separatist movements (in Tarija and Santa Cruz), and the central government was weak and ineffective. The outcome was constant intervention by its neighbors (Peru, Chile, Argentina, and especially Brazil), who all swallowed some Bolivian territories at one time or another in the nineteenth century (Holsti 1996, p. 152). Bolivia's weakness and incoherence made it possible for Chile, in the Pacific War (1879–1883), to annex the desert zone of Atacama, a zone with a mostly Chilean population and whose natural resources, especially fertilizers, were controlled by Chilean entrepreneurs (Collier 1993, pp. 28–31).

The weakness of Uruguay since its founding in 1828, its political cleavages, and the presence of many Brazilians (who owned about a third of the land) created a convenient background for endless Brazilian intervention in its internal affairs. A similar situation existed in the area of Uruguay bordering Argentina. These were some of the main reasons for the outbreak of the Paraguay War in 1864 (Graham 1989, pp. 150–151). Brazil, in general, took advantage of the weakness of its Hispanic neighbors: during the nineteenth century (at least until the last quarter), all of Brazil's boundaries were contested (see map in Burr 1965, p. 1). Brazil took advantage of its demographic and territorial superiority and eventually reached agreements in its favor (Seckinger 1984, pp. 55–98).

An example of the effects of incoherence on an international confrontation (though it did not reach a full-blown war in this case) was Brazil's attempt to annex the Chiquitos province from Bolivia in 1825. The royalist governor of the district, who fought against a republican Bolivian general, proposed the annexation to the governor of the Brazilian province Mato Grosso in order to prevent a republican takeover of his district. The governor of Mato Grosso sent military forces to the Bolivian district on his own initiative without authorization of the central government in Rio de Janeiro. This move created an international crisis, which was solved only after many months by the withdrawal of the Brazilian forces (Seckinger 1984, pp. 73–79). This crisis (like many others in nineteenth-century South America) shows, on the one hand, the influence of the lack of legitimacy of the state (Bolivia) and, on the other hand, the lack of control of the center on distant provinces and the absence of a monopoly on the use of force (Brazil).

There were similar cases in other places in nineteenth-century South America. In different provinces of New Granada (today's Colombia) the local leaders entertained the idea of seceding from the state in the first years of its establishment and of joining Ecuador (in the south) or Venezuela (in the north), states which themselves had seceded not long ago from "Grand Colombia." To the extent that the regimes in Ecuador or Venezuela would have been tempted by these transborder proposals, an international war was quite likely (Bushnell and Macaulay 1994, p. 90).

Nineteenth-century Argentina was also split into separate provinces, which were only loosely tied to each other and which were governed by different *caudillos*. This situation invited an intervention by its big neighbor, Brazil, as well as of some elements in Uruguay and Paraguay. At various times the leaders of the different provinces made alliances with Brazil and Uruguay against other *caudillos* or against the center in Buenos Aires. A salient example was the removal of Rusas by an alliance between Urquiza, the *caudillo* of the province Entre Rios, and Brazil (Shumway 1991, pp. 169–170; Graham 1989, pp. 150–151).

Diversionary wars

As Holsti suggests: "some of Brazil's conflicts with its southern neighbors derived more from internal considerations, needs, and threats, than from external security problems" (1996, p. 152). Some researchers attribute the initiation of the War of the Pacific by Chile against Peru and Bolivia in 1879 to domestic political reasons, although the war was fought ostensibly over nitrate deposits. Chile at that time was a weakly institutionalized state undergoing an incomplete democratic transition.[17] Sater (1986, pp. 15–16) writes that the Chilean president was pushed to war by the opposition which condemned his "appeasement" of Argentina (in the 1878 Fierro–Sarretea treaty) and

[17] Mansfield and Snyder 2002, pp. 308–309.

urged him to avoid a similar mistake in relation to Bolivia. The approaching elections in Chile increased domestic pressures and made a compromise with Bolivia impossible, although the president wanted to avoid war with Bolivia and its ally, Peru, just as he had with Argentina. The frustration arising from the economic crisis, which Chile faced at this time, was one of the main reasons for the popular support for the war (Collier 1993, pp. 29–30). Thus, the Chilean president was pushed to declare war reluctantly by an inflamed public (Sater 1986, pp. 9, 16).

Shumway argues that since Paraguay was not a real threat to Buenos Aires, Argentina's war against it (together with Brazil and Uruguay, 1865–1870) can best be explained by domestic factors. He cites Alberdi, one of the key opponents to President Mitre's regime, who contended that the problem of the interior provinces was the main cause of the Paraguay War. Paraguay was seen in the context of the challenge posed by the periphery to the central authorities in Argentina (Shumway 1991, pp. 237–240).

State consolidation enables conflict resolution: from war to normal peace

Since 1903 there have been, however, only two interstate wars: the Chaco War between Bolivia and Paraguay in 1932–1935 and the war between Peru and Ecuador in 1941. Since 1941 there has been no interstate war in the region, although military clashes between Peru and Ecuador took place in 1981 and 1995.[18] Moreover, as Holsti (1996, ch. 8) suggests, in the twentieth century, this region has become a no-war zone where mutually peaceful relations and nonviolent modes of conflict resolution are the norm.[19] Thus, a recent major study concludes that "no matter how

[18] The 1982 Falklands War is not counted here because it engaged Argentina with an external power – Britain – and without the involvement of other regional states. The two regional wars involved weak states and the three states with state-to-nation imbalances reflected by nonintegrated indigenous populations: Peru, Ecuador, and Bolivia. Bolivia, the initiator of the Chaco War, suffered problems both of domestic legitimacy and of disputed boundaries. In the Peru–Ecuador War both sides suffered disputed boundaries, and Peru was a weak state in respect of its domestic legitimacy and ethnic conflict as well.

[19] Kacowicz (1998) calls it a zone of "negative peace." Mares (1997) disputes the characterization of South America as a peace zone. But in the introductory comparative chapter of the volume containing Mares's chapter, Morgan suggests that even if war is sometimes contemplated among Latin American states today, this contemplation is limited. In terms of the amount of military spending and the number of real wars and casualties since 1945, Latin America is much more peaceful than most other regions and may be seen as a pluralistic security community (Morgan 1997, pp. 36–37, n. 8). See also Hurrell 1998.

measured, Latin America appears remarkably peaceful . . . Latin American states have only rarely fought one another."[20] Indeed, there was a major decline in the number of territorial conflicts from the nineteenth century to the twentieth.[21] Except for North America, South America has been the most peaceful region in the world in the twentieth century.[22] Especially noteworthy for this study is that, even though civil wars were much more common than interstate wars in the last century, "in a notable exception from the European pattern, we see little evidence of internal struggles enveloping neighbors. Violence rarely crossed borders" (Centeno 2002, p. 47).

The region has shown a marked inclination toward conflict settlement as compared to other regions, for example, by frequently using arbitrage procedures[23] and subscribing to many multilateral treaties.[24] No regional state has disappeared or has been born as a result of violence in the twentieth century, and there have been only few minor territorial changes in the region. Thus, South America as a region has moved during the twentieth century toward normal peace, even if an incomplete one, as some pairs of states did not maintain normal peace during some periods (Holsti 1996, pp. 158–161). But on a comparative regional basis, the number of territorial conflicts that were resolved peacefully

[20] Centeno (2002, pp. 35–37) bases his conclusion on the quantitative data of comparative regional warfare in the last two centuries in Small and Singer 1982.

[21] See Hensel 2001, esp. p. 93. Thus, in the last two decades of the nineteenth century and the first two decades of the twentieth, twelve territorial conflicts among South American states (excluding conflicts with colonial European powers) ended while only five conflicts continued well into the twentieth century.

[22] Based on the quantitative data, Centeno reports that "Latin America appears to become more peaceful over time – the twentieth century has episodes of warfare, but it is generally nonviolent" (2002, p. 37).

[23] Since the 1820s and until 1970, Argentina, Bolivia, Brazil, Colombia, Chile, Ecuador, Peru, and Venezuela used arbitration procedures 151 times (Holsti 1996, p. 156). Beth Simmons reports (1999, pp. 213–214) that "one of the most interesting aspects of territorial-dispute resolution in this region is the unusual propensity of independent countries to submit to authoritative third-party legal rulings. With one small exception, there has never been a legally constituted third-party ruling on a land border in continental Europe, there have been two between independent countries in Africa, two in the Middle East, three in Asia, the Far East and the Pacific, and twenty in Latin America."

[24] Among the most prominent are the Treaty on the Maintenance of Peace (Lima 1865), the General Treaty of Arbitration between Argentina and Chile (Pacto do Mayo) of 1902, the Bogota Pact of 1948, the 1948 Charter of the Organization of American States (Puig 1983, pp. 11–13), and the 1967 Treaty of Tlatelolco, ratified in the 1990s by Chile, Argentina, and Brazil, making the entire Latin American region a zone free of nuclear weapons (Kacowicz 1996).

in South America remains unique (Kacowicz 1994, pp. 265–294; 1998; Holsti 1996, p. 156; Centeno 2002, p. 37).[25]

Thus, in contrast to the continuous domestic instability in most countries of the region,[26] *regional* stability in South America has been strengthened since the end of the nineteenth century due to a process of conflict resolution. The normative basis for the peaceful settlement of the vast majority of border disputes in the region was established through the common recognition of the principle of *uti possidetis*, according to which the South American states accepted the colonial boundaries as their postindependence international frontiers.[27] The regional states also accepted the norms of the sovereign equality of states and of nonintervention in the domestic affairs of sovereign states. The Estrada Doctrine (1930) held that, if a particular government controlled population and territory, it deserved to be accorded diplomatic recognition and no normative evaluation or criterion should be applied (Fraser 1997, p. 160).

An especially important factor in the evolution of normal peace is that the most powerful state in the region, Brazil, has been a status quo state and has not entertained expansionist aspirations (Calvert 1969, pp. 39–40).

Alternative explanations for the emergence of regional peace

Alternative explanations for the peacefulness of South America in the twentieth century are undermined because the causal factors that supposedly produced peace according to these explanations were also present in the nineteenth century; yet these factors did not succeed in preventing the frequent wars in that period and in producing peace. Such factors include the tough terrain in the region as a major obstacle to going to war (McIntyre 1993, cited in Kacowicz 1998, pp. 96–98),[28] the supposed peacefulness of authoritarian/military regimes (Andreski 1992, cited in Kacowicz 1998, pp. 97–98), or a shared Spanish culture

[25] Dominguez et al. (2003, pp. 22–23) provide a brief overview of the early evolution of mediation in Latin America during the twentieth century. Even when other regional organizations began to be active in mediation after World War II, the Organization of American States "was more effective than the Organization of African Unity, the Arab League, and the United Nations in addressing the outbreak of wars and other international crises in their respective domains."

[26] Yet, "even when one looks at civil conflicts . . . Latin America appears benignly peaceful" (Centeno 2002, p. 37).

[27] See Child 1985; Ireland 1938; Kacowicz 1998.

[28] For a useful critique of the physical-constraints explanation, see Centeno 2002, pp. 75–76.

and normative consensus (Kacowicz 1998, pp. 102–105; Hurrell 1998; Dominguez et al. 2003, p. 22).[29] The continuous civil wars in the region also debunk the validity of the idea that these factors prevent war.[30] The democratic peace theory cannot provide a satisfactory explanation, because most of South America was not a democratic zone during most of the twentieth century. Moreover, researchers found that most of the time the existence of democracy was unrelated to the evolution of territorial disputes.[31]

An alternative explanation which has a certain utility in explaining the emergence of peace in South America is the formation of a balance of power in the region in the period 1883–1919 (Dominguez et al. 2003, p. 20; Kacowicz 1998, pp. 91–94). Although quite useful, this explanation has powerful limitations. First, it cannot account for the peace in other periods in the twentieth century, apart perhaps from the 1970s. Second, this explanation contradicts the argument about Brazilian superiority in the region. And, third, an especially important point for the thesis advanced in this book is that the balance-of-power explanation does not directly address the sources of those wars in the nineteenth century related to state weakness. Moreover, it seems that a certain degree of change in the variable highlighted here – state strength – was necessary for the effective functioning of the balance of power. Finally, the balance-of-power system in the region was quite complex and convoluted (see the figure in Kacowicz 1998, p. 93). Thus, it is difficult to imagine that it could guarantee the peace on its own without the explanation offered here.[32]

Instead, we need to focus on a causal factor which has undergone a major transformation from the nineteenth century to the twentieth: state-building and consolidation.

The necessary conditions: consolidation of nationally congruent states

A major explanation for the emergence of normal peace in South America is growing state strength and coherence during the twentieth century

[29] Centeno criticizes the shared cultural account in 2003, p. 74.
[30] For the long list of major civil wars in Latin America, see Centeno 2002, pp. 44–45.
[31] Dominguez et al. 2003, pp. 16, 31, and the sources they cite. See also Centeno 2002, p. 74.
[32] This point draws on the argument made by Waltz (1979) and Mearsheimer (2001) that complex unequal multipolar systems are the least stable.

in the region. This is especially true with regard to the territorial identity of the states in South America. This evolution stands in contrast to both the state weakness in the region during the nineteenth century and the domestic illegitimacy of many political regimes, which lasted at least until the recent wave of democratization in the 1980s.

South America was better disposed than Europe to enjoy peace relatively early because it entered the twentieth century with a higher level of state-to-nation balance than Europe did. This balance reflects the emergence of territorially based, nonethnic (or civic) nationalism and the relative weakness of both ethnic/subnational secessionist forces and pan-national revisionism. Benedict Anderson writes about the emergence of national identities ("nation-ness") in South America, well before most of Europe, which were compatible with the territorial boundaries of the colonial administrative units that became independent states. He argues that "the original shaping of the American administrative units was to some extent arbitrary and fortuitous, marking the spatial limits of particular military conquests. But, over time, they developed a firmer reality under the influence of geographic, political and economic factors" (1991, p. 52). Thus, the European settlers (the Creoles) consciously redefined the nonwhite populations in their territorial states as "fellow-nationals" (ibid., p. 50).[33] At the same time, "the 'failure' of the Spanish-American experience to generate a permanent Spanish-American-wide nationalism reflects both the general level of development of capitalism and technology in late eighteenth century and the 'local' backwardness of Spanish capitalism and technology in relation to the administrative stretch of the empire" (ibid., p. 63).

In South America, state formation (based on the territorial identity of the former colonial units) nearly always preceded the formation of the nation.[34] With a few exceptions of nonintegrated indigenous populations in Peru, Bolivia, and Ecuador,[35] there were no ethnic conflicts.[36] The

[33] For a comparative discussion and qualifications, see Connor 1994, esp. p. 79.

[34] See Centeno 2002, p. 24, although he also shows some of the limitations to the state-to-nation balance in the region.

[35] On the high proportion of Indians in these three states, see H. Seton-Watson 1977, pp. 222, 380–381. In the 1970s, there were 6 million Quechua Indians in these three states, but there was (and still is) no indication of the formation of a Quechua national consciousness transcending state frontiers. The case of the new indigenous/Indian president of Bolivia – Evo Morales, elected in 2005 – shows the tendency of underprivileged Indians, once more empowered, to try to address their grievances by making the state more representative and attentive to their needs rather than by seceding from it.

[36] As Gurr (1993) shows, the proportion of ethnic, irredentist, separatist, and transnational grievances is the lowest in South America as compared to all other regions in the globe.

emergence of a relatively high extent of state-to-nation congruence can be explained by the combination of immigrant societies who abandoned their territorial-national-historical roots in the Old World of Europe with the suppression of those elements of the society who could have certain territorial attachments – the indigenous population in the New World of the Americas.[37] Thus, indigenous people were destroyed in Argentina and to a lesser degree in Brazil and Chile, or were politically marginalized in their societies (Holsti 1996, p. 154; Centeno 2002, pp. 64–65). In addition, the emerging nations could be congruent with the colonial boundaries because the identification of the new nations with the pre-Columbian states and cultures was minimal at best (Barman 1988, p. 4); as a result there were no grounds for revisionist/irredentist claims based on historical/nationalist arguments.

Thus, with the consolidation of the states in South America in the late nineteenth century, the region could move from being a war zone to enjoying regional peace. Indeed, toward the end of the nineteenth century (1870s–1880s) and the beginning of the twentieth, the South American states became relatively stronger and more consolidated. As Calvert suggests: "In 1900 the great countries of Latin America seemed to have attained an almost unprecedented degree of stability" (1969, p. 32). State-building or consolidation in Latin America included three major components:

(1) pacification: establishing a state monopoly over the means of violence (Centeno 2002, pp. 108–110);
(2) "civilizing" the vast isolated interior (by populating it);
(3) extending the central government's authority over the entire national territory.

This process of strengthening was achieved through national police agencies, which enforced the state's authority at the local level; roads and communications grids (see Centeno 2002, p. 110 and table 7.3 in the current book); and centralized economies. Moreover, powerful bureaucracies were created, and national armies replaced the local ones (under the control of the *caudillos*). The army functioned as an integral part

See also Mares 2001, p. 31: indigenous people, as well as descendants of Africans brought to the Atlantic coast in Central America, have demanded their rights as citizens and, in cases where communities are split physically by national boundaries, dual citizenship. Not even the recent political movements for varying degree of autonomy by some of these communities call for full independence. The exceptions are ethnic cleavages within Guyana and Suriname (Kacowicz 1998, p. 106).

[37] On this combination as contributing to state-to-nation balance, see ch. 3.

Table 7.3 *State strengthening indicators: South American railroad density (track in use per 1,000 km^2; select years)*

Year	Argentina	Brazil	Chile
1854[a]	–	0.001	–
1870	0.3	0.09	1.43
1885[b]	1.71	0.82	2.94
1900	6.13	1.81	5.81
1914	11.4	3.08	10.9
1929	13.7	3.8	11.72

Notes:
[a] The first year in which railroads were in use in any of the three countries.
[b] Between 1870 and 1885 all three countries grew significantly in size (and from this year onward railroad density is calculated accordingly): Argentina by about 84,000 km^2, Brazil by about 56,000 km^2 (both of them due to the results of the War of the Triple Alliance), and Chile by about 240,000 km^2 (due to the results of the War of the Pacific).
Sources: CIA World Factbook; B. Mitchell 1999.

of the state apparatus, and had the power to defend national integrity and preserve order. Armies and bureaucracies were the main tools in that historical process of centralization and expansion of the center's authority and influence (Wiarda and Kline 1979, pp. 67–68, 70–71).

Another major instrument in the struggle to concentrate authority in the hands of the central government was the government corporations or the autonomous agencies. Some agencies had been set up in order to stimulate economic growth and development, and to increase state efficiency and, hence, its legitimacy. Many were regulatory agencies, others administered vast government corporations (such as steel, electricity, coffee, tobacco), and still others were involved in social programs (such as education and social security) or in the administration of new state services (such as water supplies, agrarian reforms, and family planning). These official agencies tended to serve as agents of centralization in the sense of "civilizing" and bringing order to the interior. The growth of these centralized state agencies and corporations led to a significant increase of state control and even ownership of the means of production (Wiarda and Kline 1979, pp. 68–69).

Since the 1880s, political stability began to prevail in Argentina through the dominance achieved by the center over the provinces.[38]

[38] Gallo 1993; Kacowicz 1996, p. 19; Escude 1988, p. 115.

This superiority was based first of all on a monopoly on the use of force reached by the national army which disarmed the militias (Centeno 2002, p. 109). State coherence was augmented by an expansion of the central administrative-judicial control into the provinces supported by an impressive economic growth in the late nineteenth and early twentieth centuries. Moreover, the elites succeeded in helping to construct a common Argentinean identity and unifying national myths. Even though there were conflicts between liberal and nationalist variants and sharp ideological disagreements about political and socioeconomic affairs, all shared a collective Argentinean identity, including support for a common territorial identity for the nation-state (Shumway 1991). This is also essentially true for Chile and Uruguay: "for all the internal weaknesses and contradictory forces pulling society apart, three nations had arisen, and national consciousness extended downwards to the great majority of the population" (H. Seton-Watson 1977, p. 222).

Although nineteenth-century Brazil was more stable than most of its neighbors, it still was not a strong state. It had a despotic power – the power to impose the center's decisions – but only a limited capacity to penetrate society and to implement political decisions in practice (Merquior 1987, p. 277). In the first decades of the nineteenth century, there was not yet a Brazilian nation. Yet, by the middle of the century, a nation had been forged and Brazil was consolidated as a nation-state (Barman 1988, p. 217). The suppression of the Farroupilha revolt in 1845 ended the threat of separatism in the far south, with Rio Grande do Sul being reintegrated into the nation. The cycle of local revolts against domination of the central government, which had started with the 1817 insurgency in the northeast, was eradicated in 1849. After a generation of turmoil, by the 1850s the nation was consolidated and its institutions were functioning; henceforth, power would be concentrated in the national capital (Barman, p. 218; Centeno 2002, p. 109). Despite the persistence of social injustice, there was little doubt of the formation of a Brazilian nation: "immigrants had been absorbed into a national culture based on the Portuguese language and thus easily distinguishable from that of Spanish or English-speaking neighbors" (H. Seton-Watson 1977, p. 226).

The growth of Brazil's legal, extractive, and coercive state administration can be traced to the 1830s. Public expenditures for the Justice Ministry consistently outstripped growth in that for the Interior, War, and Economy Ministries during the 1830s and 1840s (Uricoechea 1980, pp. 45–47). "Obviously, this dramatic increase reflects the attempt to create an adequate institutional apparatus for the operation and organization of the new legal order" (ibid., p. 47). During the second half of the nineteenth century, the provincial areas experienced a dramatic growth in the bureaucracy. Ministries and provinces grew at approximately the same rate during the period 1850–1888 (ibid., 48).

In the last decades of the nineteenth century and in the early part of the twentieth, the Brazilian state became stronger due to the expansion of elementary education (Viotti da Costa 1989, pp. 166, 183), the gradual development of the economy and the transportation and communication infrastructure (Dean 1989, pp. 217–251; Viotti da Costa 1989, pp. 164–167), and the stabilization of Brazil's international boundaries, especially the problematic southern border, following the Paraguay War and the settlements with Argentina in its aftermath. Even if Paraguay remained dissatisfied, it was too weak to revise the boundaries. In the early twentieth century, Brazil reached agreements on its boundaries with Uruguay, Bolivia, Peru, Colombia, and the Guyanas. As a result, only a few contested boundaries remained in peripheral districts, and Brazil gained considerable territory, which made it a status quo power during the twentieth century (Calvert 1969, pp. 39–40; Rachum 1990, p. 84).

Another example of the process of state strengthening is provided by Chile during the 1880s. Domingo Santa Maria was Chile's president from 1881 to 1886. He took some very drastic measures in religious affairs, namely, a direct confrontation with the church, which resulted in the expansion of the state's jurisdiction to three critical realms – birth, marriage, and death – through legislation. The Chilean government had to face the still formidable power of the church, which opposed those measures, but despite fierce opposition the liberal laws were increasingly applied. This legislation marked a decisive decline in the power and influence of the church and a parallel increase in that of the state. The Radicals and the National party supported the president's anti-clerical policies in Congress, since they shared his strong conviction that the power of the church should be reduced; their support contributed considerably to this process (Blakemore 1993, pp. 36–38).

Moreover, both Domingo Santa Maria and José Manuel Balmaceda (minister of the interior and president from 1886 to 1891) were particularly strong men (especially in comparison with Anibal Pinto, whom Santa Maria had succeeded). They were determined to maintain presidential prerogatives according to the written constitution, and "saw the presidency as the dynamic motor of the whole machine" (Blakemore 1993, p. 39).

Most other states in the region saw their domestic consolidation develop in a similar way; the exceptions are Colombia and Bolivia.[39] Thus, in the twentieth century, the territorial identity of the states in South America became more firmly established and there was growing state strength and coherence in the region. Citizens may have been alienated from particular governments, as many were before the democratization of the 1980s, but they generally accepted and defended the overall identity of their states, including their territorial integrity and dimensions. Despite a great variety of powerful domestic grievances, and in contrast to other Third World and Balkan states, disaffected domestic groups in South American states have not sought secession as a solution to their problems. Rather, levels of citizen identification with their states have been progressively strengthening (Holsti 1996, pp. 173–75). Thus, "even if the self-satisfied claim of Brazilians to have 'solved' racial problems was premature, there seemed little doubt that both blacks and whites felt themselves to belong to one Brazilian nation" (H. Seton-Watson 1977, p. 369).

While state incoherence in South America is lower than in other Third World regions, state-making has been less successful than in Europe (despite what several elites and militaries would have liked, Chile most obviously).[40] This medium level of success in state-building might have been a cause of peace:[41] on the one hand, twentieth-century South America could avoid the regional instability generated by weak states in the Third World, while refraining from the excessive resort to force by the strong European states, whose surplus of resources might have led to the eruption of World War I.[42] Another major difference, however, is

[39] See Kacowicz 1998, p. 106, and the citations he cites on p. 217, n. 28, on the definition and the role of the state in South America in general.
[40] For the considerable limitations on state capacity in Latin America, see Centeno 2002. On the other hand, Centeno cites a number of researchers who might hold critical views of the Latin American state, but in fact view it as so strong that they interpret it as "overpowering, centralizing, and coercive" (ibid., p. 12, n. 33).
[41] See also Kacowicz 1998, pp. 106–107.
[42] This is a key argument of Centeno (2002), who focuses on comparing the Latin American state to the much stronger West European states. While being able to provide an explanation of the lower level of warfare in Latin America in comparison to Western Europe, the limited state capacity highlighted by Centeno is unable to account for the two puzzles addressed here by the state-to-nation variable: the decline in warfare from the nineteenth to the twentieth century in South America and the tendency to resolve conflicts peacefully.

nation-building. The imbalance between state and nation was much greater in Europe than in South America, particularly because of the German question at the heart of Europe. This imbalance contributed to excessive nationalism and major wars in the Old World, including the Wars of German Unification in the nineteenth century and World War II. The lower extent of the state-to-nation imbalance in South America can explain why domestic struggles enveloped neighbors less in South America than in other regions. This is further evidence for the theory in this book that when nations extend across state borders the likelihood that internal violence will cross these borders increases; conversely, high state-to-nation congruence decreases the chances of the spread of such violence.

Neither the change from the war-prone nineteenth-century South America to a much more peaceful region in the twentieth century, nor the comparative differences between South America and other regions, can be explained by the international factor of US hegemony (Mares 2001, ch. 3; Centeno 2002; Dominguez et al. 2003, pp. 24–25). First of all, South America has been a secondary arena for all the great powers[43] in comparison with Asia, the Middle East, and Europe. Even US engagement in the region, especially in the strategic domain, was much more limited than in the US sphere of influence in Central America and the Caribbean. In contrast to the numerous military interventions in the latter region, the United States did not intervene militarily in South America and even clandestine interferences (like in Chile in the early 1970s) were rare.[44] In the absence of a credible and persistent threat of intervention, it is difficult to see the United States as a hegemon in South America (in contrast to Central America and the Caribbean). Had the US hegemony been the major cause of regional peace, recent international changes should have had destabilizing effects on the region, because US influence in South America has been steadily declining over the previous thirty years, with the rise of regional powers such as Brazil, Argentina, and Venezuela, and with the consolidation of international links between South American states and Europe, Japan, the former USSR,[45] and most recently with growing economic ties with China.[46] And, yet, not only has peace in

[43] Fraser 1997, pp. 160–161; Kacowicz 1996, p. 20; Mares 2001; Dominguez et al. 2003, pp. 20–21.
[44] Thus, President Theodore Roosevelt confined his amendment to the Monroe Doctrine to the Caribbean Basin alone. See Schoultz 1998, pp. 192–197, 203–204, cited in Kagan 2000, ch. 5, p. 8.
[45] See Pastor 1992; Kacowicz 1996, pp. 19–20; 1998, p. 67.
[46] See *Economist*, Jan. 1, 2005, 42–43; *International Herald Tribune*, Jan. 17, 2005, 1–2 at 2.

South America persisted: it has been upgraded in recent years despite these international changes. Indeed, the character of the regional peace goes beyond internationally produced cold peace in that most substantive issues in conflict among the regional states have been resolved rather than merely mitigated or reduced. As noted, the achievement of such a level of peace is beyond the capabilities of external powers.

While a normal peace has evolved in South America during this century, until recently it did not go much beyond an interstate peaceful resolution of territorial disputes. However, in the past few years a process of upgrading the normal peace and the evolution of warm regional peace has begun in the southern cone of South America. This warming of the regional peace follows the recent wave of democratization and liberalization there. The major manifestations of this process are increased economic interdependence and the enhancement of economic and political integration, notably, the emergence of a common market, Mercosur, which includes Brazil, Argentina, Uruguay, and Paraguay.[47] There is also growing cooperation on common transborder problems such as the environment and drug trafficking. Rising regional cooperation and integration stand in complete contrast to the failure of previous attempts at economic cooperation and integration, which collapsed when the domestic regimes in South America were authoritarian (Schmitter 1991, pp. 115–116).

The regional integration seems to have been enhanced most recently with the gathering of leaders of eight South American states in São Paulo to declare the founding of a "South American Community of Nations," which is to include all twelve of the continent's countries, encompassing 360 million people and a GDP of $1 trillion. The summit continues a series that started in the beginning of the 2000s to draw up plans for building bridges, roads, and energy connections among South American countries. The community's second leg is a series of free-trade agreements connecting Mercosur to the five Andean states. The focus of the summit was to integrate all of these pieces into a political framework, along with commitments to cooperate on security, poverty, and the like. Despite some serious disagreements among the South American leaders, one useful outcome of the summit is talks between the leaders of Chile and Bolivia, two states which have been quarreling since Bolivia lost its coastline in the 1879–1883 war with Chile.[48]

[47] See Schmitter 1991, pp. 108–121; Holsti 1996, pp. 175–180; Kacowicz 1998; Solingen 1998.
[48] See *Economist*, Dec. 11, 2004, 47.

Conclusions

Nineteenth-century South America shows that state weakness leads to regional instability, and to wars and armed interventions in neighboring states even if there is relative national congruence in the regional states. The presence of weak states produces security dilemma wars, wars of profit, and diversionary wars. The combination of immigrant societies and the suppression of the indigenous peoples is, however, conducive to the emergence of at least relative national congruence. Due to the legitimacy that it conveys to the territorial identity of the state, though not necessarily to a specific political regime, such congruence may facilitate the strengthening or consolidation of the regional states, even if congruence cannot guarantee state strength in all cases. Indeed, since the late nineteenth century, key South American states have been strengthening to various degrees. The combined effect of national congruence and state consolidation makes it easier for states to resolve territorial and other conflicts peacefully. The record of South America is impressive in this respect, and the outcome has been normal regional peace during most of the twentieth century. Democratization under such conditions can produce more effective regional integration than among authoritarian states. Thus, following the recent wave of democratization in the region, South American states have embarked on integrative regional frameworks which made considerable progress, even if many problems must still be addressed. This shows that democratization in a region with congruent and consolidated states can warm the regional peace and bring about a higher level of regional cooperation.

8 The emergence of high-level peace in post-1945 Western Europe: nationalism, democracy, hegemony, and regional integration

This chapter presents a third strategy of regional peacemaking – regional integration – and its application to Western Europe in the era following World War II. This strategy has produced high-level warm peace in the region. The conditions for its success are, however, quite demanding to establish and include both domestic factors – at least a minimal extent of state-to-nation balance and liberalization – and external ones – in particular, a benign great power environment. The external conditions are especially crucial in the early stages of the regional integration when the internal conditions are still evolving. As these conditions (liberalization and state-to-nation balance) reach a high level, however, the role of the external factors becomes less crucial for maintaining the integration and high-level warm peace. Thus, US hegemony, motivated by the Soviet threat common to both the United States and Europe, was a key to the emergence of a cold European peace in its early stages when state-to-nation problems were addressed and democracy was emerging, especially in Germany. Following the resolution of the state-to-nation issues and the consolidation of democracy, regional integration developed and US hegemony became less necessary to maintain the high-level warm West European peace.[1]

[1] For a recent explanation of the West European peace, see Ripsman 2005, which also provides a review of key theories of peace. Although Ripsman draws on some of the themes of this chapter (which he saw, as my colleague, in earlier draft versions), the "conventional approaches to regional pacification," reviewed comprehensively in his study, do not address the issues of nationalism and stateness, considered by this book to be crucial to the questions of regional war and peace.

Rising interdependence > Low-politics institutions > Spillover to high politics > Shifting loyalties from the states to regional institutions

Figure 8.1 The process of regional integration

The effects of regional integration

Partly in response to the difficulties of the conflict-resolution approach in regions with a state-to-nation imbalance, this third approach prescribes that the best strategy to achieve regional peace is not to focus on the substantive state-to-nation and related territorial issues that are in conflict between the parties but to *transcend* them by regional integration. In other words, the best way to reach peace is by establishing effective regional institutions for collective security and arms control, regional economic integration, and cooperation in other issues of common concern such as the environment. More specifically, the leading theory of integration, neofunctionalism, suggests that growing interdependence would lead to the establishment of supranational institutions. These institutions, led by technical elites and international bureaucrats, would initially deal with the management of technical "low-politics" type of problems (see figure 8.1). But the rising complexity of interdependence and the self-sustaining process of institution-building would eventually lead to the "spillover" of the regional integration to the domain of "high politics." Thus, regional institutions would have increasing jurisdiction over the preexisting national states. This would result in a transfer of loyalties from the nation-state and the redefinition of collective identities toward a regional identity.[2]

Another method for strengthening peace according to the integrative approach is by creating a regional community through advancing transnational contacts among the regional societies and nongovernmental groups, and encouraging people-to-people ties through social communications, tourism, and cultural exchange.[3] Thus, this approach differs markedly from, and goes much beyond the governmental, state-to-state character of the regional conflict-resolution strategy. Indeed, regional integration and transnational contacts might be seen by non-liberal, nationalist elites as posing a threat to the independence and

[2] See Haas 1958, 1964; Lindberg 1963; Lindberg and Scheingold 1971. For a useful overview, see Hurrell 1995, pp. 59–61.

[3] See Deutsch et al. 1957. For a recent development and revision of Deutsch's approach to community-building along constructivist lines, see Adler and Barnett 1998.

autonomy of their states, which are a mainstay of regional peace according to the conflict-resolution/state-building approach. In contrast to the focus of the conflict-resolution/statist approach on the strict preservation of state sovereignty and on noninterference in the domestic affairs of other states as a prerequisite for peace, the integration strategy is based on significant compromises to state sovereignty and on the transfer of authority from the states to supranational institutions, leading to joint decisionmaking and the pooling of sovereignty.[4]

Some of the predicted effects of regional integration on the emergence of high-level warm peace are:

(1) *Political*: joint decisionmaking and pooling of sovereignty would diminish the capacity of national governments to act unilaterally, including in the area of war and peace, especially in regard to the other members. At the same time, a certain degree of freedom of action may remain vis-à-vis third parties.
(2) *Economic*: interdependence would make it very difficult to act alone and would limit the independent war-making ability of the individual states. Interdependence would increase mutual prosperity and thus raise the stakes of many key groups and the public at large in the continuation and intensification of the economic relations; it would incline such groups away from war, which would disrupt such relations. Thus, on a cost–benefit calculation, territorial gains would not be worth the loss incurred by the disruption of the economic interdependence (in addition to the costs of the war itself). Even if the integration starts in "low politics" (economics, environment), over time there will be a spillover to "high politics" (security and foreign policy).[5]
(3) *Sense of community*: common supranational institutions, strong economic ties, and intensive transnational interactions in the areas of culture, tourism, and commerce lead to the construction of a sense of community and shared identity and mutual identification at the expense of exclusionary and aggressive nationalism. Thus, it becomes unimaginable that the members of the community will fight each other along national lines.

[4] Keohane and Hoffmann 1990, p. 276. See also Kupchan 1998.
[5] Haas 1958, 1964, summarized by Schmitter 1969, cited in Russett and Starr 1992, p. 384.

The conditions for the effectiveness of the integration strategy: the prevalence of liberal compatibility

Although rarely explored explicitly, liberal democracy is a necessary, even if not always sufficient, condition for successful integration.[6] Thus, the neofunctionalist approach to regional integration presumed – without stating it explicitly – that the states undergoing integration would be pluralist democracies. This is because the core integrating mechanism of the neofunctional approach – the autonomous action of specialized interest groups pressing for further integration in order to capture greater economic benefits – can operate only in a liberal democracy.[7] Moreover, liberal democracy can mitigate the aggressive and destabilizing aspects of nationalism. Where democratic norms are closely related to national self-images, nationalism may support peaceful democracy by advancing identifications with civic institutions.[8] Such identification will, in turn, inhibit the appearance of virulent forms of ethnic nationalism; thus, democracy and moderate civic nationalism are mutually reinforcing.

There is a qualitative difference between democracies and authoritarian regimes with respect to integration, because the latter type of regime is in itself a major obstacle to integration. They tend to suppress or distort negotiations among transnational interest groups and to assert their passionate defense of national sovereignty as the major source of domestic legitimacy (Schmitter 1991, p. 115). A major reason for the necessary connection between democracy and regional integration may be deduced from the democratic peace theory: only among liberal democracies is the security dilemma sufficiently reduced to allow the states to surrender part of their sovereignty without the fear that today's partner may become tomorrow's enemy. As a result, democracies are relatively more willing to concede some sovereignty to a supranational authority voluntarily – on the condition that all the states involved in the integration are democracies. Even then, the concession of sovereignty will initially be quite limited, the process of integration is likely to be very lengthy and painstaking, and reversals are quite possible. Thus, despite numerous obstacles, regional integration is successful in liberal democratic

[6] Schmitter 1991, p. 114; Hurrell 1995, pp. 68–69.
[7] See Schmitter 1991, p. 114; Hurrell 1995, p. 59.
[8] J. Snyder and Ballentine 1996, p. 11, and the sources they cite in n. 21; Brubaker 1992, chs. 2, 5.

Europe, and it is clearly more effective than in regions populated, at least partly, by authoritarian regimes such as the Middle East, Africa, and Asia. A similar logic can explain, as noted in chapter 7, why after the democratization wave in the 1980s regional integration became more effective in South America than in earlier periods, in which most of the regional states were not liberal democracies.

The cornerstone of the liberal approach is democratization, and all the other elements (economic interdependence, regional institutions and integration, and transnational ties) ensure high-level warm peace only when the regional states are liberal democracies.[9] The great advantage of the liberal strategy is manifested in the empirical record of liberal democratic states not fighting each other,[10] while high economic interdependence, for example, did not prevent the great powers from going to war with each other in 1914, and nondemocracies do not go very far in building effective regional institutions (as noted in chapter 7). Even if some substantive issues remain unresolved among liberal democracies, they do not resort to force in order to resolve them but use peaceful means only; as a result, the security dilemma among them declines drastically. Consequently, high-level warm peace will only be established in regions populated by liberal democracies. Indeed, a liberal democratic Western Europe has succeeded in establishing a high-level warm peace among its regional states in the post-World War II era.

The interrelationships between liberalism and nationalism

The shortcoming of the liberalization approach is that the political and socioeconomic prerequisites for successful democratization are quite demanding to establish[11] while, for this strategy to work, all the major regional states have to become stable liberal democracies. Major preconditions for a stable democracy are the existence of both a strong state and a high state-to-nation congruence, namely, a state which has been through successful state- and nation-building.[12]

[9] For references on the liberal school, see ch. 1, nn. 75–78.
[10] See references in ch. 1, n. 76.
[11] See the references cited in Byman 2003, 48, n. 9. See also Huntington 1991. For a review of the research on the political and socioeconomic conditions for democracy and on how states become democracies, see Shin 1994. But see also L. Diamond 2005, pp. 314–336.
[12] Rustow 1970; Rothstein 1992; Ayoob 1995, p. 195. See also Linz and Stepan 1996, pp. 16–37, esp. p. 25: "these conditions are met only if there is no significant irredenta outside the

There is a major difference in this respect between democracies and nondemocracies.[13] In nondemocracies there is no need for a prior agreement on the territorial identity of the state because separatist or irredentist aspirations can be suppressed by force. In contrast, if a significant group in a democracy does not accept the legitimacy of the state and its territorial integrity, this poses a severe challenge to democratization and especially to democratic consolidation.[14] Similarly, the lack of a clear definition of the people and the citizens in a democracy makes democratization more difficult than in a state in which there is congruence with the nation. In order for a democratic state with majority voting to function well, a powerful sense of national identity that is congruent with the state is required. As Cooper suggests, "democracy entails the definition of a political community. In many cases, this is provided by the idea of the nation."[15] When such an idea is missing, democratization might lead to the breakup of a state, as happened in the former USSR and Yugoslavia.

Thus, one of the obstacles to successful democratization and the emergence of a stable democracy is the presence of severe ethnonational cleavages,[16] especially in weak states, which lack strong political institutions (J. Snyder 2000). A key norm of a democracy is the peaceful transfer of power from one party to another according to election outcomes. Yet, in such divided societies there might be reluctance to transfer power or even to share it out of fear that the other groups will abuse their power to harm their ethnic rivals or to secede from the state. This creates a lack of trust and a sense of insecurity which may result in violence. Examples from the past fifteen years include Armenia, Burundi, Congo, Ethiopia, Indonesia, Nigeria, Rwanda, Russia, Sri Lanka, the former Yugoslavia (Mansfield and Snyder 1996, 2002, 2005; J. Snyder 2000), and currently Iraq. Yet such divided societies are precisely the places where the supposedly pacifying effects of democratization are most needed, not only

state's boundaries, if there is only one nation existing (or awakened) in the state, and if there is low cultural diversity within the state."

[13] Linz and Stepan 1996, p. 27.

[14] See also Rustow 1970, p. 351: "In order that rulers and policies may freely change, the boundaries must endure, the composition of the citizenry be continuous." For a discussion of this issue and references to leading scholars who make a similar argument about the difficulty of democratizing under what I call here a state-to-nation imbalance, see Stepan 1998, pp. 220–222. Stepan cites Gellner 1983, Mill 1861, and Dahl 1989, p. 207.

[15] Cooper 2003, p. 14.

[16] For an overview, see L. Diamond and Plattner 1994, p. xiv; Horowitz 1994; Linz and Stepan 1996, ch. 2.

because of the domestic ethnic conflicts, but also because of the close relations between these conflicts and regional ones, due to the spread of ethnic groups across existing borders in many regions, especially in the Third World and the Balkans.[17]

Another major problem with the liberalization strategy is that, as noted, in the short term democratization may increase domestic instability and provide insecure elites with incentives to pursue the scapegoat strategy by initiating diversionary wars against their neighbors. Indeed, Mansfield and Snyder (2005) show that at least until all the regional states become full-blown liberal democracies, the process of democratization itself may encourage the use of force and thus aggravate regional conflicts. Elites left over from the old regime compete for political power among themselves and with new democratic elites. One of the major strategies available to all these elites for gaining mass support is appealing to nationalist feelings. Once mass support for this strategy is mobilized, leaders have a hard time controlling it in democratizing states, which tend to lack effective institutions. A nationalist public and belligerent pressure groups may push for a militant policy and constrain the freedom of maneuver of foreign policy elites.[18] Especially bellicose are interest groups from the old regime that benefit from imperialism, military expansion, and war (Mansfield and Snyder 1996, pp. 303, 315–331). The model presented here specifies under what conditions this thesis is particularly applicable, namely, under a state-to-nation imbalance (see chapter 3). On the other hand, democratization under a high state-to-nation balance can warm the peace, by facilitating a higher degree of integration, as in South America since the 1980s (see chapter 7).

Democratization can also increase the citizens' identification with their state; it thus strengthens regional states and makes them more coherent in the long term.[19] However, a related negative effect of democratization in the short term is that in fragmented societies, notably in Africa and some other parts of the Third World and the Balkans, it may not solve social cleavages but may rather exacerbate existing ethnic

[17] See L. Diamond and Plattner 1994, p. xxviii; and Ayoob 1995.

[18] For the argument that nationalism is both necessary for democracy and can also push democracies toward belligerent behavior, see Kupchan 2002, pp. 112–118. But I argue that the first part is applicable mainly under a state-to-nation balance, while the second is valid especially under a state-to-nation imbalance.

[19] For various ways and mechanisms for achieving this, see Linz and Stepan 1996, pp. 33–34; Stepan 1998; and Byman 2003, 50–52.

problems,[20] and even embolden ethnic minorities openly to oppose their state boundaries and seek self-determination and secession.[21] One major route to democratization is federalism – decentralization of political power along territorial lines. In weak states, a loose federal system may reinforce separatist forces by guaranteeing them assets they can employ for the secessionist cause, such as local police forces and government revenues.[22]

Under a state-to-nation imbalance, democratization may weaken moderate/status quo regimes and elites, which are the key to regional peace processes, and make it more difficult for them to make concessions to long-time adversaries. Through an appeal to nationalist and religious emotions, a domestic opposition may use these concessions against the moderate elites and undermine their political base of support. Democratization may also bring to power radical forces that oppose regional reconciliation, for example, fundamentalist Islamic forces in the Middle East (see chapter 4).

Thus, democratization may bring about the disintegration of the regional states, especially weak ones, or the intensification of ethnic and regional conflicts, or both. If there is a stark choice between maintaining the territorial integrity of the state and democratization, state elites are bound to prefer the former.[23]

In the absence of a minimum extent of a state-to-nation balance and of strong and coherent states, democratization is unlikely to enhance peace and may even destabilize the region, at least in the short term. A minimal extent of successful state- and nation-building, which increase the state-to-nation balance, is required for the consolidation of democracy and thus to ensure the pacifying effects of integration based on the compatibility of liberal states. Thus, democracy has made the greatest advances in those East European states that face the fewest severe ethnic cleavages (Poland, Hungary, and the Czech Republic) and progressed more slowly or not at all in those that are deeply divided (most notably

[20] For a specification of the conditions under which this may happen, see De Nevers 1993. For a study that shows the destabilizing effects of political and economic liberalization in war-shattered states, see Paris 1997, 2004. See also Byman 2003, pp. 52–54, 58–61.

[21] Ayoob 1995, p. 182; Chipman 1993; Holsti 1996; and R. Kaplan 2000.

[22] Holsti 1996, pp. 184–185, who cites the examples of Congo, Chad, and Sudan; Downes 2001; Byman 2003, pp. 54–58. For more on the various solutions to the state-to-nation problem and their various drawbacks, see ch. 9.

[23] Ayoob 1995, pp. 182–184, who cites the example of democratic India and its record in Punjab and Kashmir.

former Yugoslavia, Romania, Bulgaria, and Slovakia).[24] Closely related is the observation that an agreement about the borders of a state is critical to democratic consolidation. For example, in postcommunist states, countries with well-defined borders, such as Poland, Hungary, and even Mongolia, have made the transition to democracy much quicker than places where borders are contested, for example, Armenia, Georgia, and most of the states that emerged from Yugoslavia.[25] Similarly, territorial disputes derived from state-to-nation imbalances in Kashmir, Palestine, Chechnya, and Iraq continue to block democratic consolidation in all of these regions.

State- and nation-building must include a decline in revisionist nationalism, leading to a greater acceptance of the territorial status quo. A major source for this decline is a military defeat and economic collapse of the revisionist ideology, producing disenchantment in its supporters. The large-scale wave of refugees, which results from these calamities, must be well integrated socially and economically into the new postwar national societies in order to reduce the appeal of irredentist forces. This integration must also include settlers who have to vacate their homes beyond the frontier as part of the postwar settlement.

The criteria for the definition of the nation suggest political consequences for the determination of its external boundaries. Thus, a conflict between nations over boundaries is more likely if the definition of nationhood, as in ethnic nationalism, includes people who live outside the state boundaries based on ethnic or cultural criteria (Lepsius 1985, 46), namely, cases of external incongruence (see chapter 3). The criteria for the definition of the nation also have implications for the type of domestic order – whether it is democratic or not; and especially whether it is a liberal democracy with full-blown civil rights, or an "illiberal democracy" which maintains free elections, but is not constrained by the rule of law and the separation of powers, and does not respect individual rights and liberties.[26] Lepsius (1985) claims that there are three conceptions of nationalism, each based on a different element and each having implications both for the domestic order and for war and peace with the neighbors.[27] While the first kind challenges the state-to-nation

[24] Horowitz 1994, p. 36. [25] McFaul 2002. See also Brubaker 1996, esp. ch. 3.
[26] On illiberal democracy, see Zakaria 1997, 2002.
[27] This is a refinement of the key distinction introduced in ch. 3 between ethnic and civic nationalism. This refinement is especially useful for the key German case discussed later in this chapter.

balance, and thus makes peace less likely, the third reduces the state-to-nation imbalance. The third conception, most closely related to liberalism, also makes regional integration of liberal democracies more likely and hence increases the prospects for high-level warm peace.
The three kinds of nationalism are:

- Folk nation or ethnic nationalism: The folk nation is based on the ethnic descent of a collectivity of human beings (Lepsius, 1985, 47). The elements on which the folk nation is based are also common language, religion, culture, historical fate, etc.[28] The properties through which a people becomes a nation concern a collectivity; civil rights are not considered a leading principle. Moreover, the fundamental higher status of the folk in relation to the individual can even serve to justify the limitation of individual civil rights in the name of the realization of the interests of the folk. This can legitimize authoritarian regimes so long as it is accepted that they serve the interests of the collectivity of the folk while the opposition can be delegitimized as lacking national loyalty (ibid., 50–51).

  A major problem with this kind of nationalism is that it usually produces situations of a state-to-nation imbalance in which populations within the state boundaries are regarded as outsiders, while other populations located outside the state boundaries are regarded as a part of the nation. The first type of situation leads to discrimination against minorities and, if the state weakens, to ethnic conflicts, which might spread across boundaries; the second is likely to lead to territorial conflicts.
- Cultural nation: The cultural nation is based on the principle of the cultural unity of a group of human beings, without requiring concurrent political/territorial unity in a single state. This apolitical (or more precisely, aterritorial) conception of a nation highlights the strong cultural connection among people with a shared language and culture even if they live in different communities, politically independent of each other (Lepsius, 1985, 53).
- The nation of citizens or civic nationalism: The nation of citizens is constituted on the basis of equality of civil rights and the democratic legitimization of rule by the citizens (Lepsius, 1985, 58). The boundaries of this kind of a nation are determined by the geographic domain of the state. Factors such as ethnicity, history, or culture do not produce

[28] Other studies define folk nation as a mixture of nation, race, and people (Mosse 1964).

political demands for changes in the current boundaries of the state. Civil rights are based on the constitution, and the main principle is the equality of individuals irrespective of their ethnicity. Immigrant societies such as the United States tend to follow this path rather than that of ethnic nationalism (ibid., 49).

New liberal states under benign hegemony/concert

The major challenge presented by the liberalization strategy is how to dampen the negative effects that the democratization process creates in the short term, before states can become stable liberal democracies and arrive at high-level warm peace in the longer term. In addition to the prerequisite of a certain degree of successful state- and nation-building, one possibility for solving this dilemma involves combining the liberalization strategy with the international strategy of great power involvement, if the great powers are liberal. The great power hegemon or a concert of powers may then prevent regional wars and maintain cold peace, thus allowing the liberalization process to develop and ripen into high-level warm peace.

Although an enduring high-level peace depends on regional/domestic factors, under some conditions international factors may be helpful in its initial emergence. More specifically, a benign liberal hegemony (or concert) may be useful for facilitating the transition to high-level warm peace of new liberal states which are emerging from a long history of bitter enmity. The role of the hegemon/concert is especially important when some of the regional states are still in the process of completing the transition from an authoritarian regime to a young democracy, and the durability of their democratic identity is still uncertain in the eyes of their neighbors.[29]

In the absence of a benign hegemony/concert, new liberal democracies that were formerly bitter opponents (in a situation where some of them were nondemocratic just a short time before and democracy has not been fully consolidated) may face difficulties in moving beyond cold peace. Although, in accordance with the democratic peace theory, they will not go to war with each other, mutual suspicions and distrust as a result of their history of conflict may be strong enough to derail the emergence of high-level warm peace among them. Concerns about

[29] On young democracies, see Russett 1993, p. 34.

relative gains may be powerful enough to constrain regional cooperation. Young democracies emerging out of former authoritarian or totalitarian regimes might be suspected by their neighbors because of the fear that the new democratic regimes will not hold; thus, the security dilemma between them may still be in effect, especially if there are still lingering state-to-nation disputes.

A benign hegemon/concert can facilitate the transition of newly liberal states from intense conflict to high-level warm peace by reassuring them and reducing their mutual fears and the security dilemma, thus reducing the costs of reciprocal concessions and taking risks for peace. As noted, under hegemony or concert, fears of being cheated and the problem of relative gains will be less consequential than under a competitive balance of power because the security of all the regional partners is guaranteed by the hegemon/concert, and thus the need for self-help is reduced. As a result, the "shadow of the future" (Axelrod 1984; Oye 1986) is getting longer. Thus, it will be much safer and easier for liberal states to pursue full-blown reconciliation.

A hegemon/concert can facilitate the following regional developments, which provide a solid basis for high-level warm peace:

(a) Encourage democratization in regional states, or even impose it in the special circumstances of occupation of some of the regional states by the hegemon's forces after a major war.
(b) Promote economic development and integration by providing financial assistance and free trade in order to bolster the local economies and as a result also increase domestic and regional stability. The hegemon or concert may encourage and pressure local states to move toward economic integration by using its economic leverage.
(c) Provide a security umbrella that will moderate the security dilemma and mutual suspicions by deploying military forces of the hegemon/concert in the region, thus weakening the need of regional states for independent military forces. The hegemon or concert may also encourage the establishment of multilateral security organizations that include the former regional opponents in the same framework under the great power leadership.

Thus, in an initial period of transition to democracy and reconciliation among states that have just emerged from a long period of hostility, the presence of a benign hegemon or concert will be useful for reassurance. Such a presence provides the regional states with a window of opportunity to make progress in the domestic liberalization and regional reconciliation process, and helps in constructing effective regional institutions which also enhance their economic interdependence, further reinforcing regional peace. In the absence of hegemony or concert, the reconciliation process might be bumpier, take longer, and face severe problems and obstacles. However, only when the appropriate domestic prerequisites exist in the regional states will the high-level warm peace endure. If these prerequisites are lacking, any efforts on the concert's or hegemon's part to establish such high-level regional peace will fail. Thus, democratization will take root if certain domestic prerequisites mentioned above are present, such as high levels of literacy and industrial development, and a relatively equal distribution of land, wealth, and income (citations in Van Evera 1993, p. 212, n. 48; Byman 2003, 48, n. 9), in addition to at least a minimal extent of state-to-nation balance. Economic measures to promote regional integration will not succeed without a prior high level of development and economic compatibility among the regional states. Even if the hegemon or concert helps to establish regional security organizations, the democratic character of the participants is essential for durable security cooperation.

When the regional/domestic prerequisites exist, following the establishment of high-level warm peace with the help of the hegemon or concert, a community of liberal states can sustain it through their own efforts. Therefore, when a high-level peace is well established, the decline of the concert or hegemony should not undermine this peace, even if it had been beneficial for its initial emergence. The indigenous reconciliation among the liberal democracies in the region will endure even "after hegemony" (Keohane 1984).

The road to peace in post-1945 Western Europe is the most relevant case through which to examine the effects on the emergence of high-level peace of these systemic and domestic factors, which help states transcend nationalism and embark on regional integration.

Post-1945 Western Europe: transition from war to high-level warm peace

The state-to-nation problem in Europe and its transcendence after World War II

In comparison with South America before World War II, Europe was both much more of a war zone and had suffered from many more state-to-nation problems. Europe was the major war zone in the international system until 1945.[30] Most great powers were European and competed among themselves for power, hegemony, security, and influence on the continent and in overseas colonies. The state-to-nation imbalance affected many of the key rivalries and armed conflicts on the continent during the nineteenth and twentieth centuries: the two world wars, the wars for German and Italian unification, the competing irredentist/nationalist claims of Germany and France on Alsace-Lorraine,[31] pan-Slavic aspirations and struggles for self-determination in Eastern Europe and the Balkans leading to World War I, nationalist conflicts in Eastern Europe after World War I, and German demands for irredentist/nationalist unification in Central and Eastern Europe producing tense crises before World War II.

The deportation of millions of Germans from Eastern Europe, the imposed division of Germany, and Soviet control over Eastern Europe following World War II helped to reduce or at least to manage the national, especially the German, problem on the continent.[32] Over time, the German deportees were integrated into West German society, in stark contrast to the lack of integration of the Palestinian refugees into Arab societies (see chapter 4). This is one of the reasons that, although they were deported at a similar time period, "the right of return" continued to be much higher on the agenda of the Palestinian refugees than on the agenda of the Germans expelled from Eastern Europe.

A key explanation for this difference is that the pan-Arabist support in the Palestinian cause gave the Palestinian refugees some hope that achieving the "right of return" was not unthinkable. In contrast, the imminent Soviet threat and the division of Europe between the superpowers made German revisionism an impractical option and removed it from the political agenda (Stoess 1991). Although the continuous division of Germany meant that the "German problem" was not resolved

[30] For example, twenty-five of seventy-five interstate wars that occurred during 1815–1993 took place at least partly in Europe. In thirty-one wars, one or more European states participated on both sides. These wars accounted for 25 million dead or 80 percent of the battle casualties in all interstate wars since 1815. In forty-six wars, at least one European state participated (N. P. Gleditsch 1995, 539–540).

[31] On this nationalist rivalry, see Gutmann 1991.

[32] On the deportation of 12–14 million Germans from Eastern Europe between 1944 to 1947, see Naimark 2002, esp. pp. 108–138; Ther and Siljak 2001; and Rieber 2000. On the unmixing of nations in Eastern Europe and the Balkans in the twentieth century as a result of World Wars I and II, and thus the emergence of ethnically more homogeneous states, see Brubaker 1996, ch. 6. On the pacifying effects of Soviet control of Eastern Europe and the Balkans, see ch. 6 in this book.

until 1990, the control of Germany by the superpowers made it clear that German unification and "the right of return" of German refugees were not feasible so long as the bipolar order and the Cold War persisted.

Western Europe did not, however, focus only on direct conflict resolution of state-to-nation problems, even if some of these issues were addressed successfully. Western Europe transcended the state-to-nation issues through regional integration, which generated high-level warm peace. What made this possible was the combination of the related phenomena of liberalism and postnationalism, especially in the state which historically provided the key state-to-nation problem on the continent – Germany. Some state-to-nation issues in Western Europe persisted (see appendix B) – Northern Ireland; the Basques in Spain; Spain's irredentism vis-à-vis Gibraltar – but they were relatively marginal issues and were mostly transcended by European integration, which made interstate wars between Ireland and Britain, or Spain and Britain, unthinkable, although the low-intensity struggles of the Catholics in Northern Ireland or the Basques in Spain continued for an extended period.

Thus, post-World War II Western Europe is an example of a region dominated by states with a status quo orientation even though some of them are ethnically incongruent (United Kingdom, Belgium, Switzerland, and Spain).[33] Some of the reasons for the status quo tendency are derived directly from factors that reduce the state-to-nation imbalance (as discussed in chapter 3): the strength of civic nationalism, the early

[33] The cases of Belgium and Switzerland in particular might support the argument that power-sharing can function well in states with ethnic cleavages if they are democracies; this would potentially challenge the argument about the destabilizing influence of the state-to-nation imbalance. However, these countries (as well as Canada) are federations based on the congruence of the autonomous regions with the key ethnic groups (O'Leary 2003, pp. 63–64). Moreover, power-sharing was not originally developed to address ethnonational conflicts; where it was applied successfully, it was to cases of other cultural-ideological-religious cleavages (McGarry 2005). This neglect of ethnonationalism is related to the origin of Lijphart's (1977) model of power-sharing or consociationalism in small West European democracies (Switzerland, the Netherlands, Austria, Belgium) that were divided culturally, socioeconomically, and religiously, but not nationally. Moreover, they were not divided deeply or violently. Ethnonational groups, in contrast to the kind of groups addressed by Lijphart and his associates, prefer territorial autonomy or independence to power-sharing. Additionally, they have powerful emotional/ideological connections to a certain territory – their "homeland," which they want to control; power-sharing would not satisfy that desire for national territorial self-determination. Thus, there have been serious problems in recent years with the implementation of power-sharing in the ethnonational conflict of Northern Ireland. As I argue in this book, ethnonational conflicts are especially severe and are more likely than other types of conflict to bring about large-scale violence. Critiques of power-sharing are also discussed in ch. 9.

emergence of state-initiated nationalism, and the presence of strong states. Another factor is related to liberal compatibility in the region, which was completed in the 1970s when Spain, Portugal, and Greece went through a successful transition to democracy (Linz and Stepan 1996). Based on the democratic peace theory, well-established liberal democracy may help to overcome the problems associated with state-to-nation imbalance and may lead even incongruent states to pursue a status quo orientation versus their liberal neighbors and to resolve conflicts peacefully. Liberal compatibility, moreover, provides to democratic states the option of pursuing the strategy of regional integration, which helps to transcend remaining state-to-nation disputes and to bring about high-level warm peace. The liberal European states could accomplish this because of the conducive international security environment under the benign US hegemony during the Cold War. Also helpful was the reduction in state-to-nation problems in the aftermath of World War II: the outcome of the war both discredited revisionist nationalism and helped the unmixing of ethnic nations.

The integration strategy's effects: the postnational state and high-level warm peace

The first major West European supranational institution was the European Coal and Steel Community, established in 1951 by the initiative of the French foreign minister, Robert Schuman, with the explicit goal of limiting the independent war-making ability of the West European states, most notably the former archenemies France and Germany; enhancing economic welfare was only a secondary goal.[34] Thus, he stated that "the French Government proposes to put the whole of the Franco-German coal and steel production under a joint High Authority, in an organization which is open for the other European countries to enter . . . The solidarity between the two countries established by joint production will show that a war between France and Germany becomes not only unthinkable but materially impossible" (cited in Russett and Starr 1992, p. 379). One of the major motivations for Schuman's initiative was the worsening Franco-German relations at the time, mainly due to the dispute over the Saar region (see below). The French were particularly anxious about the progress of German economic and political revival and the calls for German rearmament. Schuman's idea

[34] Wyatt-Walter 1997, p. 19.

was not so much to focus directly on addressing the bilateral issues in conflict between France and Germany, but rather to transcend them by a reconciliation of Germany within a transformed European framework. Indeed, the integration of coal and steel made possible new relations between France and Germany and gave France the leading role in building a European Community, the driving force of which would be Franco-German. More specifically, in the context of integration, it is easier for democracies to transcend territorial issues. Thus, France returned the Saar region to Germany following the outcome of a referendum in which most of the region's population expressed its will to return to Germany.

The next major step of West European integration was the establishment of the Common Market or the European Economic Community (EEC) in 1957, later transformed into the European Community (EC). This institution had broad supranational authority, notably to eliminate barriers to trade within the Community and to make possible free movement of capital and people among the member states, thus fulfilling Jean Monnet's vision of binding the economies and eventually the people of Western Europe inextricably by economic union, making war unthinkable (Russett and Starr 1992, p. 379).[35] After a slowdown between 1967 and 1985, the integration process regained powerful momentum with the successful negotiation and ratification of the Single European Act in the mid-1980s.[36]

Beyond a certain point of stabilization, high-level warm peace among liberal democracies should stand on its own. Thus, even though the US presence is still very important for the security of the West European states (Art 1996), the present study (as opposed to realist predictions)[37] does not expect that the potential US military disengagement from Europe, or at least the reduction in its presence, following the disappearance of the Soviet threat will dramatically affect the high-level warm peace in the region (see also Ripsman 2005, 686). On the contrary, the tendency in recent years, in the aftermath of the Cold War, has been the reinforcement of the West European high-level warm peace

[35] For a succinct analysis of the West European integration within a broader European and international context, see Wallace 1995. Jean Monnet, a French official, was a leading advocate and founding father of the joint West European institutions in the early 1950s.

[36] For an extended analysis of the recent stages of the evolution of European integration, including the act and its effects, see Keohane and Hoffmann 1991 and Wallace 1995. For a leading explanation of European integration, see Moravcsik 1998.

[37] See Mearsheimer 1990, 2001; Sheetz 1996.

and the deepening of regional integration (though the focus was also on enlargement, to include East European states in 2004).

The tendency toward deepening is manifested in the 1992 Maastricht Treaty; the creation of a single currency – the euro – in 1999 and its introduction in 2002; the agreement to enlarge the Western European Union (WEU), the military arm of the EU; the Schengen Group of eight (originally five) countries attempting to move more rapidly toward common policies on policing and border controls; and the Franco-German "Eurocorps" with its stated aspiration to create the nucleus for a future European army.

Following NATO air war over Kosovo, the European Union decided in late 1999 to construct its own European security force of 60,000 troops.[38] Thus, the Kosovo conflict demonstrated the dual face of European security in the post-Cold War period. On the one hand, it showed Europe's military inferiority in relation to the United States and the great military dependence of the Europeans on the United States for coping with external threats of spreading instability related to ethnic conflicts such as those in the Balkans. At the same time, the Kosovo crisis exerted pressure on the Europeans further to upgrade their security cooperation, even if it is still questionable how fast and how effectively they will implement their new commitment toward increased integration in the security field.[39]

The conditions for the strategy's effectiveness: liberalization under US hegemony

The effectiveness of the integration strategy has been due to the liberalization process in all the key states of Western Europe as well as to US hegemony, which was crucial especially in the early stages of the transition from war to high-level warm peace.

The main historical example of the influence of liberal democracy on the success of regional integration and the emergence of high-level

[38] *International Herald Tribune*, Dec. 10, 1999, 4; and Dec. 13, 1999, 5.

[39] The Iraq crisis of 2003, with the cleavages between the supporters of the US war in Iraq (the UK, Italy, and the East Europeans) and its opponents (notably France and Germany), demonstrated some of the limitations to the EU objective of pursuing a common foreign and security policy. For a skeptical analysis of the foreign and defense policy aspects of the EU's recent draft constitution, see *International Herald Tribune*, July 18, 2003, 8. Moreover, the rejection of the EU constitution by the French and Dutch referendums in May 2005 indicates that European integration still faces major challenges despite its remarkable accomplishments.

warm peace among liberal states is the West European peace established in the aftermath of World War II. Such a warm peace could not have been established without the major West European states being liberal democracies, with West Germany undergoing a forced democratization during the Allied occupation. Indeed, the level of supranational integration has remained limited in all nondemocratic regions outside the liberal democratic Western Europe. Although US hegemony over the region was crucial for the initial establishment of peace in Western Europe in the late 1940s and early 1950s, it was unable by itself to produce a normal, let alone a high-level, warm peace.[40] Without the conducive international factor of US leadership, peace among the West European states might not have developed, as French–German relations in the late 1940s–early 1950s might suggest.

From hot war to cold war: the aftermath of World War II, 1946–1950

In the late 1940s these relations were close to a cold war. Immediately following the war, France's greatest fear was that a resurgent Germany would once again challenge the legitimacy of the political and territorial order in Europe. Such a danger was to be prevented by the dismemberment of Germany, its demilitarization, and French control over the Rhine. Moreover, the French demanded control over German resources, especially its production of coal and steel, in order to repair their own economy and to prevent Germany from gaining ascendance once again.[41] This explicit demand was bound to cause serious conflict between France and Germany if implemented, because it involved not only the Saar region, but also the Rhineland and the Ruhr. These are all regions that were important in economic and cultural terms to Germany.

However, the dynamics of the Cold War and its own weakness forced France to change direction in terms of its "German" policy. This did not mean, however, that the French attitude toward Germany changed abruptly. When it became clear that France could no longer afford attempts to balance, or contain, Germany, other options were developed.

[40] For an alternative explanation of West European integration, see Kupchan 1998.
[41] See Geraud 1947, 33. On de Gaulle's demands regarding the Rhine as the French border, see Freymond 1960, p. 6.

From cold war to cold peace: global factors, 1950–1954

Global factors produced a transition in the early 1950s from cold war to cold peace.[42] This cold peace was created by the US pacifying role as a benign hegemon,[43] which was in turn made possible by the common Soviet threat to the United States and to Western Europe.[44] This threat motivated a bipartisan consensus in the US administration and Congress to support a security commitment to the defense of Western Europe (manifested by NATO) and to pay the heavy costs necessary for the initial stages of the economic reconstruction of Europe (reflected in the Marshall Plan and in the opening of the American market to European goods).

During the Franco-German "cold war," France tried to dismember Germany, to keep it weak and powerless. With the emergence of "cold peace" between them, the two states accepted each other's existence and reached formal agreements and maintained diplomatic relations, despite the presence of unresolved, substantive conflicts and a high extent of mutual insecurity. France chose the option of attempting to control Germany by drawing it into an alliance rather than leaving it outside. Necessity, created by the global rivalry between the United States and the USSR, dictated the change in French policy. At the same time, the US involvement had a mitigating influence on the French–German relationship, although it did not solve the underlying sources of conflict between the two states.

Thus, in the early 1950s, French military planning continued to treat Germany as a potential enemy. The French president and the public both continued to be very suspicious of Germany.[45] As a result, in 1954 France did not join the European Defense Community (EDC), which excluded the United States and Britain, because in that framework France would have been left essentially alone with its former archenemy.[46] In contrast, American and British membership of NATO provided guarantees against potential German aggression. Thus, only four months after

[42] Ripsman shows convincingly that the causes of peace, according to the liberal school (the democratic peace, economic interdependence, and liberal institutionalism), did not bring about the transition to what I call here "cold peace" in the early 1950s. See Ripsman 2005, 675–679.

[43] See Hurrell 1995, p. 48; and J. Joffe (1984), who also cites Nerlich 1979, 88.

[44] See Lundestad 1990, p. 57; Gaddis 1992, pp. 26–27; Buzan 1991, pp. 220–221; Wallace 1995. On the common Soviet threat as a unifying factor for West Germany and its European neighbors, see Gerbet 1996, p. 58.

[45] Citations in Ripsman 2005, 676–679.

[46] See J. Joffe 1984, pp. 69–73, and 1987, ch. 5. See also Gerbet 1996, pp. 72–75, and Gillingham 1991, p. 250.

rejecting German participation in Western defense by defeating the EDC, the French National Assembly approved German rearmament within NATO after the United States and Britain extended guarantees that they would not withdraw their troops unilaterally from Europe.[47]

On the whole, the United States has played a crucial role in regional conflict reduction in Western Europe by helping to reassure West Germany and its neighbors of each other's peaceful intentions, thus reducing the security dilemma in a once volatile region. Since the United States took upon its shoulders the role of security provider to the Europeans, they did not have to ensure their own security; this fact dramatically weakened the security dilemma among them and made possible a separation between high and low politics. The Europeans could focus on the economic dimension, more precisely on mutual or absolute gains in this domain, while the US security umbrella weakened the concern about relative gains among them.[48]

Moreover, the United States also spurred European integration by direct encouragement and pressure (Beloff 1963, p. 28; Treverton 1992, ch. 4; Hurrell 1995, p. 48; Ikenberry 1989, 388–389; Gerbet 1996, p. 60). Thus, the American Marshall Plan for the recovery of Europe after World War II provided the basis for the cooperation between the former enemies. US policy initiated the regional integration by insisting that aid funds had to be distributed among the European actors by themselves. Thus, it provided the first step toward economic and political cooperation and integration. According to Kunz, the American administration saw the reconstruction of Germany in a framework of European integration as a means of "assuaging French fears of the resurgence of German expansionism. Moreover, integration, first economic and then political, could cut the costs of Europe's recovery to the United States while creating ties among belligerent leaders that they would later find difficult to sever" (1997, 165).

Most important, the United States induced the democratization and social reform process in West Germany in the immediate aftermath of World War II,[49] and thus made possible the benign effects of liberal compatibility on the emergence of high-level warm peace. As noted, the state-to-nation problem of the ethnic German expellees from the East could be potentially destabilizing to the new West German democracy. Indeed, West Germany recognized the post-1945 Oder–Neisse line de

[47] Ripsman 2005, 682; Trachtenberg 1999, pp. 117–118.
[48] On relative vs. absolute gains, see ch. 2 in this book.
[49] See T. Smith 1994.

facto only in 1970; even then there was high-level opposition to the move, which nearly caused the government to fall. The United States was, however, helpful in mitigating this key problem of the refugees: it extended relatively generous aid to the German expellees after the war, thus helping their successful integration into the emerging German democracy (Rynhold 2005, pp. 7–8).

From cold peace to normal peace: conflict resolution by coherent states, 1954–1957

The American hegemony cannot explain the transition from cold peace to normal peace between France and Germany in the middle of the 1950s. The United States did not force or pressure France to warm its relations with Germany. In order to achieve warm peace between the two states, an acceptable agreement regarding their territorial disputes was needed. The end of the dispute over the Saar region completed the process that created a balance between the German nation and the political boundaries of the two German states, thus creating a greater state-to-nation balance in Europe. In the east, the Soviets expelled Germans from lands east of the Oder–Neisse line to East Germany. This movement of population made states such as Poland, Czechoslovakia, and East Germany more coherent in their state-to-nation balance.[50] In the west, an understanding was achieved between France and Germany to annex to France the regions of Alsace-Lorraine (a region that was regarded by its inhabitants as French) but not the Ruhr or the Saar. This understanding helped to reduce the tension and to strengthen the state-to-nation balance in both of these strong and highly developed states. Only after reducing the state-to-nation imbalance could the two states reach high-level warm peace, starting from the late 1950s.

The Saar problem

The Saar province, a coal-rich German province, was annexed by France at the end of the war, as a part of de Gaulle's plan to protect France's security.[51] The USA and Britain agreed that France would have economic control of the Saar, until a peace treaty with Germany was signed. After the end of the war, France tried to bind the province to it by creating a customs union and signing long-term leases on the province's coal mines

[50] Lepsius 1985, p. 48.
[51] For an overview of the Saar conflict, see Stoess 1991, pp. 71–73. See also the discussion in Gerbet 1996, esp. pp. 66–70; Freymond 1960; Friend 1991; Hannum 1990, pp. 394–400; and Ripsman 2002.

and railroads. On July 18, 1946, France declared that the Saar boundaries of 1935 were not satisfactory, and increased them by 48 percent, at the expense of the adjacent Rhineland. Only after the United States and Britain declared their objections did France withdraw its forces; it still enlarged the Saar territory by 33 percent (Freymond 1960, pp. 16, 32; Willis 1968, pp. 71–72). Germany condemned the French policy and opposed the existing status of the Saar. The first time Germany raised the Saar problem was in January 1950, during a visit by Robert Schuman to Bonn. The next day Chancellor Adenauer of Germany declared that if France would not show more flexibility regarding the Saar, Germany would strongly protest the unilateral fixing of Germany's eastern frontier by the USSR. The French became concerned about reawakening German nationalism; the Germans referred to the hypocritical French, willing to accept the Germans into the Council of Europe but still intent on controlling the Saar (Friend 1991, p. 16). By 1952, the residents of the Saar felt that they were being exploited by France. This opinion was expressed by the creation of the political party Demokratische Partei des Saarlandes (DPS), which demanded an end to the French exploitation. The French response to these demands was the dissolution of the DPS (Willis 1968, pp. 75–76, 197–198). During 1952, Germany and France conducted negotiations over the future of the Saar. A 1954 proposal urged Europeanization of the Saar: the Saar would become a European Territory when the European Political Community came into existence, subject to the terms of the peace treaty or settlement in lieu thereof. In the interim period, the interest of the Saar in external and defense questions would be entrusted to a European Commission (ibid., p. 202).

This proposal was an example of the change in the French policy toward Germany. In contrast to the previous policy, France did not insist on controlling the Saar, but was content with Europeanization of the region. France conducted a referendum in the Saar in October 1955, in order to ratify the proposal. Although both Germany and France believed the proposal would be ratified, 67.72 per cent of the Saar electorate voted against the Europeanization process (Willis 1968, pp. 204–207; Wiskemann 1956, 287–288). Two days after the referendum, France and Germany began negotiations on the compensation Germany would give France for the Saar. In January 1956, the negotiations were accelerated after a European-minded government was established in France, under the leadership of Guy Mollet. By June 1956 an accord on the Saar was achieved; at the beginning of 1957, the Saar officially became a German territory (Gerbet 1996, p. 71).

Germany: from revisionist ethnic nationalism to postnationalism?

The post-1945 democratization in West Germany could lead to the emergence of high-level warm peace in Western Europe because it took place concurrently with the growing state-to-nation balance due to the demographic changes in the East, conflict resolution in the West, and the transformation in the nature of German nationalism following the decisive military and moral defeat in World War II. This rising congruence came on top of other prerequisites for stabilizing democratization: Germany was a developed and strong state with a tradition of effective institutions and a good socioeconomic infrastructure. Yet these latter factors by themselves, without changes in German nationalism, did not guarantee the success of peaceful democratization before World War II; the Weimar Republic of the interwar era thus collapsed.

Lepsius (1985) claims that the history of Germany can be seen as a process, in which Germany shifted the character of its nation. Van Evera argues that there is a close connection between certain kinds of nationalism and war; thus, the kind of hegemonistic nationalism that existed in Germany until 1945 increased the war proneness of Europe (1994, 13).[52] One major source of such an aggressive attitude might have been related to the state-to-nation imbalance caused by the presence of numerous ethnonational Germans beyond the boundaries of the German state. On the other hand, the post-1945 changing character of German nationalism made possible the acceptance of the territorial losses of World War II. This changed character was partly derived from demographic changes (discussed above) that reduced the state-to-nation imbalance, although it was also influenced by the superpower control, domestic liberalization, and Germany's decisive defeat in World War II.

In contrast to the "French model" of state-initiated nationalism, conceived in relation to the institutional and territorial frame of the state, the "German model" of nationalism stressed the particularistic characteristics of an ethnic community of common origin and descent which revealed itself in the national spirit and its language, culture, or even landscape.[53] In France, a bureaucratic monarchy engendered a political and territorial conception of nationhood; in Germany, the disparity in scale between supranational empire and the subnational proliferation of

[52] Van Evera (1993) claims that the attitude of German nationalists toward other groups as inferior was the main cause of the aggressive German foreign policy until 1945.
[53] Brubaker 1992, pp. 1–6; Knischewski 1996, p. 126. For a useful overview, see Dawisha 2002b.

sovereign and semi-sovereign political units fostered the development of an ethnocultural conception of nationalism that preceded the state. Nationhood and statehood in Germany were sharply distinct; in France they were fused.

Until the late nineteenth century Germany was divided into numerous territorial states, which included mainly German-speaking populations. Because of major political obstacles, uniting all of these states was impossible. As a result, the idea of a German *cultural nation* emerged which underlined the cultural *apolitical* connection among German-speaking populations in the various German states. The conception of a cultural nation combined the cultural unity among the Germans with the political independence of the German-speaking states, based on the dynastic legitimacy of political rule.

With the demise of dynastic legitimacy, notably following the French Revolution, the cultural nation acquired political content through the movement for German national unity in the nineteenth century.[54] This movement proclaimed the idea of the *folk nation* as a community, with homogeneous ethnic and cultural roots and a common language, which should realize its popular sovereignty by unifying in a single national state (though parts of the movement still combined its demand for unity with that for an elected government and a democratic constitution). This was the ideological background for German unification in the late nineteenth century, although it was the Prussian "Realpolitiker" Bismarck who, based on balance-of-power calculations, unified Germany following three successful wars against Denmark, Austria, and France between the years 1862 and 1871 (Knischewski 1996, p. 127). Political boundaries and the borders of German settlement, however, were not identical even in this supposedly unified German state.

The ethnocultural distinction between Germans and Slavs throughout the zone of mixed settlements in Central and Eastern Europe has been basic to the self-conception of German nationalism. This frontier has no parallel in the French case. Massive migration of Germans in the High Middle Ages and in the early modern period had created numerous pockets of German settlement in Slavic lands which, to a considerable extent, did not assimilate with the Slavic population (Brubaker 1992, pp. 5–6).

[54] This is related to the point made in ch. 1 that most modern scholarship dates nationalism as a movement and an ideology from the time of the French Revolution.

The continuous mismatch between state and nation made German nationalism revisionist – aspiring to align German boundaries with the German nation based on ethnic criteria (Lepsius 1985, p. 48). The state-to-nation imbalance was further magnified after German unification in 1870 by the annexation of Alsace-Lorraine in that same year and the intolerance toward national minorities, such as the Poles in Prussia. German nationalism claimed national (or racial) superiority of the German people, which also led to imperialism.

After Germany was united during the nineteenth century, the national state transformed into a folk nation, and not a citizen nation.[55] Under the leadership of the kaiser, the national idea was seized by the ruling elites for the justification of conservative interests opposed to those furthering democracy. Even during the Weimar Republic, the elements of civil rights were not considered the foundations of the state (Lepsius 1985, p. 60). The Nazi regime strengthened the elements of the folk nation and ethnic nationalism, a policy that led to World War II.

Nazism carried revisionist nationalism to its most extreme form by going beyond the initial demands to revise the state-to-nation imbalances of the Versailles Treaty, to expansionist imperialism and a quest for hegemony. The Nazi conception of nation was exclusively ethnic/racial – based on blood and lineage. The unconditional military and moral defeat of the Nazi regime brought about a major decline of revisionist nationalism. The horrible results of World War II and the Nazi regime caused the German people to reexamine their nationalism. As a result of the war, nationalism was equated with National Socialism, which had awful associations and was widely discredited. Nationalism was considered a negative value opposed to highly positive values such as democracy, human rights, etc. (Alter 1992, p. 156).[56]

The feeling that the German people needed to replace nationalist values with democratic ones encompassed not only intellectuals, but also leading politicians.[57] The first chancellor of West Germany, Konrad Adenauer, was often troubled by the problem of nationalism. When a group in Germany resisted the Schuman plan, Adenauer explained it as

[55] See Lepsius 1985, p. 60. Verheyen (1991, p. 17) claims that the reason German nationalism evolved on the basis of folk and not liberal ideas, as in France or Britain, is that the dominant philosophy in Germany was Romanticism, not the ideas of the Enlightenment. According to Romanticism, nationalism is based on culture and not on the state.

[56] A good example of the negative attitude toward national symbols is the debate over the anthem of the German Federation; see Alter 1992, pp. 173–175.

[57] See, for example, the powerful statement in 1946 in favor of democracy by Theodor Heuss, who became the president of West Germany in 1949, cited in Alter 1992, p. 159.

an example of the difficulty "of liberating this section of the Germans from the nationalistic thinking they have so far been pursuing" (Adenauer 1965, cited in Alter 1992, pp. 163–164). In 1951, Adenauer claimed that "the overwhelming majority of the German people have outgrown nationalism" (ibid., p. 164). In his memoirs he labeled nationalism the "cancerous sore of Europe" (ibid., p. 164).

According to Alter (1992), the plan to eliminate the aggressive nationalism of the Germans succeeded, and a postnational identity emerged. Contradicting the opinion that nationalism ceased to exist in the German identity, some scholars assert that nationalism changed only its character. Verheyen claims that "This does not mean, of course, that nationalism completely disappeared from German political life" (1991, p. 65).

A major transformation took place, however, in the character of German national identity. The major manifestations of this changing postnational/civic identity are the following (Knischewski 1996, p. 131):

- The relatively low national pride of the Germans, in comparison to other European nations, particularly among the younger generations (Schulze 1996, p. 316).
- Strong emphasis on *economic* prosperity, trade, and social welfare as core elements of national pride.
- Growing acceptance of *democratic* norms and institutions. The establishment of the German Federal Republic transformed Germany into a *civic nation* – a nation of its citizens. Elements such as democracy, free self-determination, civil rights, and a liberal economy became the main sources legitimizing the new state, while the ideas of folk and cultural nation are supplementary and politically subordinate (Lepsius 1985, pp. 60–61). Thus, according to Lepsius, even if there were no realistic alternatives, the German acceptance of its territorial losses after World War II, in contrast to previous historical periods, was made much easier by the changing national basis from a folk nation to a nation of its citizens.[58]
- *The rule of law* and civil rights. Simultaneously with the change in/decline of German nationalism, a new political ideology was developing in the German state. Its basis was the supremacy of the law, which would protect citizens from all abuses of power. The law was rewritten so that it would secure all the citizens' rights. The new German Basic

[58] See Knischewski (1996, pp. 134–136) on the rise of substitutes for nationalism and the resulting acceptance of postwar boundaries in the 1970s.

Law emphasized the fundamental superiority of the individual civil rights over the state.[59] A new institution, the Federal Constitutional Court (Bundesverfassungsgericht), was established to ensure that the state would not abuse the Basic Law.
- Especially for the ideological *Left*, which achieved cultural dominance in parts of the media and education system for a considerable period, anti-fascism replaced German unity as the overriding ideology, and the official demand for reunification was regarded as a revisionist, conservative objective (Knischewski 1996, pp. 137, 138). Indeed, when the Left came to power in the late 1960s–early 1970s, West Germany recognized the postwar boundaries, and reunification was practically removed from the agenda.
- *European integration*: nowhere else was the European idea greeted as enthusiastically as in West Germany. On an institutional level, European integration introduced itself as a substitute for national identity (Knischewski 1996, p. 134).

From normal peace to high-level warm peace: European integration by democracies, 1958–2005

The international factor of US hegemony was insufficient by itself to produce the high-level peace that has gradually emerged in Western Europe since the late 1950s. The liberal democratic nature of the West European states was necessary to upgrade the cold peace (and later normal peace) and turn it into the high-level warm peace of the European Community and the European Union through the strategy of regional integration, starting from the Schuman plan and the European Coal and Steel Community, which helped to transform Franco-German relations.

Accordingly, domestic liberalization in formerly authoritarian West European states, especially in West Germany, in the post-World War II era was critical for the evolution of the high-level warm peace because it permanently removed the traditional causes of war on the continent,[60] notably state-to-nation issues. The American security umbrella facilitated this evolution and allowed it to take place. Yet, even if the United States had imposed democratization, the socioeconomic prerequisites for democracy had to be present in West Germany (and in Italy) for

[59] Article 1 says: "The following basic rights shall be binding as directly valid law on legislation, administration and judiciary." For more on citizens' rights in the German Basic Law, see Grosser 1971, pp. 83–84.
[60] See Van Evera 1993, esp. pp. 206–211; Buzan et al. 1990, pp. 107–115.

democratization to succeed. Most important in this respect, the nationally homogeneous nature of German society made it easier for democratization to take root, in contrast to deeply divided societies where democratization faces an uphill battle, such as today's Iraq. While the United States induced European integration, for high-level integration to be successful, economic *and* political compatibility were necessary. Indeed, a key prerequisite for joining the EU is for a country to be a functioning democracy.[61]

General de Gaulle and Prime Minister Thatcher have shown that there can be powerful opposition to integration even among democracies. Yet, it is difficult to imagine the regional integration in Western Europe without the factor of liberal democracy, which reduced mutual fears to the point of making the regional states willing to give up a part of their sovereignty and set up supranational institutions. These, in turn, have helped to build institutionalized procedures for peaceful conflict resolution. Such developments have conspired to make a return to violent conflict in Western Europe unthinkable.

The moderating influence of liberal democracy on mutual fears can be seen in the changing mutual perceptions between the two previously archenemies, France and Germany, especially the rising positive perception of the Germans by the French following the consolidation of liberal democracy in Germany. At the end of World War II, the French regarded the Germans with distrust. In 1956 the French public still exhibited little confidence in West Germany as an ally. The French also held a negative opinion of West Germany by a ratio of almost three to one.[62]

However, two decades after France's liberation the responses to the question "What is your opinion of West Germany?" were completely different: "good," 52 percent; "neither good nor bad," 29 percent; "bad," 9 percent; no response, 9 percent. These findings put Germany ahead of all other countries in French sympathies. In addition, some fairly remarkable increases in "net trust" occurred within both national populations between the mid-1950s and the early 1960s. The French public confidence in Germans as allies expanded by a factor of seven and German confidence in the French increased more than ten times.[63] A series of public opinion polls taken from December 1968 to January 1971 persistently showed that, apart from Belgium, the French public regarded West Germany as France's best ally in Europe. In March 1972, 86 percent

[61] See Cronin 2002, 143–144.
[62] See the citations in Ripsman 2005, pp. 685–686. [63] Puchala 1970, 188.

of the French believed that Germany no longer constituted a threat to France.[64] The most common explanations of this reduced fear cited by the French public were related to liberal factors: Germany's membership in the EU (35 percent) and its democratization (23 percent).[65]

The emergence of a stable liberal democracy in West Germany seems to be intrinsically bound to this change of heart on both sides of the border. The emergence of liberal democratic structures has enabled transnational interactions between French and German individuals regardless of the content of the interactions of the governments of these countries at any single time. A prime example of this is the fact that levels of mutual trade and confidence did not decrease during the early 1960s when conflicts between the French and German governments were on the rise.[66] Moreover, the emergence of such liberal democratic structures seems to have increased the confidence of German and French policymakers in their mutual reliability.[67] Both countries developed a clear-cut preference for alliances with democracies and an opposition to alliances with nondemocracies.[68]

The key test case of German–French reconciliation took place in the context of German reunification at the end of the Cold War in 1989–1990.[69] With the disappearance of the shared Soviet threat, French decisionmakers worried about the reunification of Germany. They made an effort to delay it with Soviet help. However, they expressed a willingness to accept the reunification if Germany continued to be democratic and integrated into liberal Western institutions. Moreover, public opinion polls found that 80 percent of the French accepted German reunification.[70]

Conclusions

The relations between nationalism and democracy are critical for issues of war and peace, although the interaction between the two factors is complex. On the one hand, a minimal extent of state strength and

[64] See the citations in Ripsman 2005, p. 686.
[65] Only 38 percent suggested realist factors such as the common threat shared by France and Germany (30 percent) and the division and occupation of Germany (8 percent) (cited in Ripsman 2005, p. 686, n. 31).
[66] Some very interesting data are provided in Puchala 1970.
[67] For an overview of the evolution of the French–German alliance, see Ripsman 2005, 683–687.
[68] Grosser 1963, 570; Fritsch-Bournazel 1989, p. 66.
[69] Ripsman 2005, 685. [70] Cited in Ripsman 2005, p. 686.

national congruence is necessary for the pacifying effects of democratization to be effective. On the other hand, successful democratization can transcend remaining state-to-nation issues and generate high-level peace. What can be critical in complex situations is the international security environment, at least for the initial emergence of cold peace.

In the case of post-World War II Europe, there were several state-to-nation factors that were conducive to the success of democratization in Germany, the key state for European security. These factors include: the basic strength of the German state, as well as of the other West European states; the homogeneous character of German society (high internal congruence); the reduction of external incongruence in Eastern Europe with the expulsion of the Germans; and the decline of revisionist ethnic nationalism. This last resulted from the decisive defeat of Germany in World War II, which clarified the costs of such nationalism; civic nationalism conversely became even stronger than before the war in the other West European states, which had created the "state-initiated nationalism" in the first place.[71]

At the same time, the remaining major state-to-nation imbalances – the division of Germany and the "right of return" of German refugees – could not spoil the emergence of peace because of the conducive international security environment: a benign and helpful hegemon, the common Soviet threat, and the imposed division of Europe, which made the reunification of Germany and the "right of return" completely impractical. The combination of all these factors enabled the pacifying effects of democratization by transcending the remaining territorial and state-to-nation issues in the context of successful regional integration and thus producing high-level peace.

Even though some distrust remained among the foreign policy elites, as was expressed by French anxieties regarding German reunification, liberal mechanisms, notably democracy and integration, have been instrumental in entrenching the peace and stability that were initially generated by the systemic/realist factors (US hegemony and the shared Soviet threat) and consolidated by the decline in revisionist nationalism, especially in Germany. Confidence in the greater explanatory power of the liberal factors with regard to the high-level warm peace is enhanced due to the inverse relationship between the power of the realist factors and the warming of the regional peace. Although the peace-inducing realist factors have become weaker (with the decline in the Soviet threat

[71] On variations in national identity in contemporary Europe, see Jenkins and Sofos 1996.

and in US hegemonic engagement in Europe, especially since the end of the Cold War),[72] not only has the high-level warm peace persisted, but the peace in Western Europe has become even warmer, most notably following the end of the Cold War, with the further deepening of regional integration, such as with the creation of the common currency.

The high-level warm peace itself contains some elements which go far beyond a realist peace and have a much better fit with liberal expectations about interstate relations, especially among democracies:

- the scope of the cooperative relations goes much beyond a military alliance against a common enemy and includes high-level economic, legal, cultural, and other dimensions of cooperation;
- integration is deepening and certain elements of national sovereignty are being transferred to a supranational authority, culminating in the European monetary union;
- relations have a strong transnational component, including people-to-people exchange, mass tourism and cooperation among interest groups and NGOs, and free transborder flow of people, jobs, ideas, goods, and services;
- in the military field, joint German–French units have been established;
- changes in relative capabilities do not lead to a security dilemma, irrespective of the offense/defense balance, notably the acquisition by France of its independent nuclear force in the 1960s and German reunification in 1990.
- a Common Defense and Foreign Policy of the European Union has been established, though there are still important foreign policy differences among the member states, as the Iraq crisis of 2003 has clearly shown, and the formation of joint military forces is quite slow.

[72] On the decline in US hegemonic commitment to Europe already during the latter stages of the Cold War, see the data cited in Ripsman 2005, 682–683.

9 Conclusions

This concluding chapter has two main parts. The first part summarizes the main theoretical argument and some of the key findings. The second part examines the utility of competing peace strategies with regard to the resolution of the state-to-nation imbalance and suggests some policy-relevant recommendations. I explore the strategies, which are related to the logic of key IR theories, in accordance with the integrative model presented in the book.

Summary of the theory and findings

This book addresses two main puzzles on the regional level: (1) What best accounts for the transition from war to peace and vice versa in different regions at different times? (2) What is the best explanation for variations in the level of regional peace that exists in different regions in a particular time period? Consider, for example, the differences that exist today in the Middle East, South America, sub-Saharan Africa, East Asia, and Europe.

The book's response is that regional conflict outcomes are determined by two main factors: (1) the state-to-nation balance, the degree to which ethnic/national and political boundaries in a region are congruent as well as the extent of state strength, and (2) the form of great power involvement in the region. On the first variable, regions may be either balanced or imbalanced;[1] on the second, I distinguish among four types of great power involvement: competition, cooperation, disengagement,

[1] However, the independence of the two components of the state-to-nation balance – state strength and national congruence – allows also a more refined differentiation, as discussed in ch. 3 and below.

and hegemony. In various combinations, these factors produce outcomes that include hot war, cold war, cold peace, normal peace, and high-level warm peace. Among the principal hypotheses offered by the study are the following: (1) the state-to-nation balance determines the basic war proneness of a region; regions characterized by congruence of national and political boundaries and the presence of strong states will be in a condition of normal or high-level warm peace regardless of the form of great power involvement; and (2) when national and political boundaries are not congruent, then the form of great power involvement determines the outcome. Specifically, great power hegemony or cooperation produces cold peace, while competition or disengagement results in hot or cold war. Especially when state-to-nation imbalance becomes coupled with great power competition (and occasionally disengagement), the conditions for escalation to cold and hot war materialize. Thus, neither variable is sufficient on its own to explain the pattern of conflict, whereas together they appear to offer a reasonable account. State-to-nation imbalance tells us *which* regions are inherently war-prone; great power involvement tells us *when* this inherent war proneness is likely to erupt into war.

This book illustrates the usefulness of integrating levels of analysis into a coherent explanation of regional conflict patterns. Neither unit-level nor system-level variables on their own provide a satisfactory framework for understanding the different dimensions of the phenomenon.

Regional attributes, such as the type of political regime in the region, its ethnonational makeup, and its geographical and natural resource-related features, all tend to be relatively constant characteristics; change is possible but slow (such as changes in state- and nation-building over time). Such variables are often quite successful in identifying which regions are more or less "war-prone." Yet, conflict outcomes vary considerably over time, even where such unit-level features and the overall level of war proneness remain constant. Influences external to a region – systemic variables – are a possible avenue through which such variance can be explained.

Systemic characteristics are essentially determined by the capabilities, interests, and behavior of the great powers. The great powers' engagement in regional conflicts, due to their overwhelming advantage in terms of power resources, often plays a vital role in how regional events develop. Yet, different regions respond to the same systemic influences in different ways. Attributes unique to each region can suggest reasons for why this is so.

Thus, unit- and system-level variables complement one another and together can provide a suitable framework for understanding regional conflict. This book has proposed two such causal factors – the state-to-nation balance and great power involvement – that capture the essence of the phenomenon.

Systemic factors

Through cooperation, great powers can force regional powers to desist from open conflict, in much the same way as a regional hegemon can. Competing great powers, by contrast, can be manipulated by regional powers for the furtherance of their own interests. Through arms provision, diplomatic support, and new regional alignments, such manipulation can lead to more severe conflict. Moreover, patterns of conflict in regions neglected by "disengaged" great powers are likely to reflect regional conditions.

Neither international anarchy by itself nor system polarity determines the type of strategy pursued by the great powers with regard to regional conflicts. Different patterns of great power behavior are possible in different regions under anarchy, even under the same international structure. Thus, we have seen four distinct patterns of great power involvement in Eastern Europe and the Balkans under a multipolar structure (in the period 1815–1945 – see chapter 6). Although only one pattern was analyzed under bipolarity with regard to Eastern Europe/Balkans (hegemony in chapter 6), there was a high regional variance also during the bipolar era: competition in the Middle East (see chapter 5), hegemony in Western Europe (chapter 8), and cooperation between the superpowers in some parts of the Third World toward the end of bipolarity (see below).

This argument is, on the whole, in accordance with the work of Schroeder (1994). Indeed, the four patterns of great power regional involvement identified in this study are somewhat compatible in their logic with Schroeder's four strategies of responding to security threats. More specifically, cooperation has certain logical similarities with Schroeder's "transcending"; disengagement with "hiding"; hegemony with "bandwagoning"; and competition with "balancing."

The best explanation of the variations among these patterns is, however, based on the logic of what might be called "integrated realism":

the integration of the two main factors highlighted by the two streams of realism (see chapter 5), interests (classical realism) and distribution of capabilities (neorealism). Although the balance of great power interests is of critical importance, we cannot overlook the impact of the balance of capabilities for explaining variations in great power regional involvement and their regional and international effects.

This study has shown the critical importance of knowing the type of great power involvement in various regions in explaining the considerable variations in the intensity of regional conflicts, even if the sources of these conflicts and their full-blown reconciliation are accounted for by local elements, most notably, the state-to-nation imbalance.

The state-to-nation balance

Military conflict and militarized incidents in general are considerably more likely in those regions where the political borders and national dispersion are incongruent than where they are congruent. Some of the key causal mechanisms are related to the effects of the state-to-nation imbalance on key causes of war. Such an imbalance increases the security dilemma in the region, and raises the incentives for scapegoating and for wars of profit (see chapter 3).

If we also take into account the effects of the second component of the state-to-nation balance (the extent of state strength) and introduce the distinction between strong and weak states, the following patterns emerge:

(1) Strong states that are nationally congruent tend to be status quo states. Regions populated by this kind of state are conducive to peaceful conflict resolution. A key example is twentieth-century South America following the state consolidation at the end of the previous century (chapter 7). Western Europe also fits this pattern, although here US hegemony (especially in the initial stages) and later democracy played an important role (chapter 8).
(2) Weak states that are nationally congruent tend to be frontier states. Regions populated by these states are engaged in boundary and territorial wars. The Americas of the nineteenth century, including South America, are a good case of this pattern (chapter 7).
(3) Regions are unstable if at least some of the states in the region tend to be weak and incongruent. Such failed states are engaged in civil wars and encourage crossborder intervention by neighboring states. Africa is a major example. Chapter 4 discussed the applicability

of this pattern to the Middle East (such as the examples of Jordan and Lebanon, the Palestinian Authority, post-2003 Iraq, and their regional repercussions). Chapter 6 applied it to the Balkans in the nineteenth century and in the post-Cold War era.

(4) Strong states that are nationally incongruent tend to be revisionist and initiate armed conflicts on nationalist grounds, notably under one of these conditions of external incongruence:
   (a) The revisionist state may pursue political unification when one or more of its neighbors shares the same ethnic majority. If the neighbors resist, the revisionist state may resort to violence legitimized on nationalist grounds: neighbors are seen as illegitimate states that do not have the right of self-determination (North Korea and South Korea; North Vietnam and South Vietnam; China and Taiwan; Prussia and other German states; Egypt under Nasser, Iraq under Saddam Hussein, and other Arab states as discussed in chapter 4).
   (b) Revisionist states may pursue irredentism vis-à-vis their neighbors' territories populated by minorities from the same ethnicity of the majority of the revisionist state. "Greater Iraq," "Greater Syria," "Greater Israel," "Greater Serbia," and "Greater Germany" were discussed along these lines in chapters 4, 6, and 8. Settlers may encourage such policies, presenting themselves as pioneers on behalf of the national cause, occupying territory that should be annexed to the homeland.
   (c) A shared ethnic minority among contiguous states might result, however, in a status quo orientation of these states and makes it easier for states to avoid nationalist revisionism. Together with state weakness, this explains the relative infrequency of irredentism in Africa despite the high extent of incongruence in this continent. The combination of state weakness and internal incongruence, in turn, leads to numerous civil wars and trans-border interventions.

Democracy

When there is a fairly high degree of state-to-nation balance in the region, a third factor – democracy – can warm the regional peace through the mechanisms of democratic peace and by making possible regional integration. The integration, in turn, further marginalizes the questions of nationalism and related territorial conflicts or at least makes the use of force to resolve them highly unlikely. Western Europe is the best example of these dynamics, as discussed in chapter 8. South America since the 1980s also shows the warming effects of joint democracy, and Central and Eastern Europe shows it since the 1990s.

However, under state-to-nation imbalance in those regions where ethnic nationalism is strong, partly because it preceded the state, and state institutions are weak or get weaker, premature democratization might lead to state collapse and civil wars (in African, post-Soviet, and post-Yugoslavian states in the 1990s) and to ethnonationalist wars of irredentism (Serbia, Pakistan, and Armenia in the 1990s) or secession (post-Soviet Chechnya, and post-Yugoslavia Croatia, Bosnia, and Kosovo).

Some of the findings with regard to the six propositions listed at the end of chapter 2

Proposition 1: The effects of the global system on regions with state-to-nation imbalance: under great power competition in the region or disengagement from it, state-to-nation issues are not addressed and the likely regional outcome is cold war. Great power competition aggravates the regional conflict but also limits the scope and duration of hot wars (discussed in chapter 5).

Findings: The regions with the highest state-to-nation imbalances, especially those with external incongruence, are the most war-prone regions in the international system. These include especially the Middle East, East Asia, and South Asia. These regions experienced superpower competition during the global US–Soviet Cold War at least until the mid-1980s. Global competition aggravated the regional conflicts; the outcome was protracted cold war, manifested by high duration of enduring rivalries, and interrupted by relatively frequent hot wars.

Indeed, these three regions lead with the number of years of enduring rivalries: the Middle East with 209 years altogether, East Asia 147 years, and South Asia 119 years.[2] The global Cold War had prolonging effects on disputes such as Korea, Vietnam, China–Taiwan, India–Pakistan, and the Arab–Israeli conflicts, even though the superpowers tried to prevent or at least to contain the use of large-scale violence in hot wars. The outcome has been mostly extended regional cold wars.

[2] Huth 1999, pp. 48–50.

The Middle East illustrates the effects of great power competition on prolonging regional cold wars. The global Cold War and competitive superpower involvement in the Middle East from the mid-1950s to the Soviet collapse prolonged the Arab–Israeli cold war and made it difficult to move beyond it to cold peace, that is, to reduce the level of the regional conflict. Thus, the superpowers helped to sustain the Arab–Israeli conflict by arms supply, along with diplomatic and economic support of their respective clients. Superpower support increased the risk-taking propensity of the local states. The superpowers established close patron–client relations with key Middle East states that included a commitment to help them win or at least avoid a major or total defeat in regional wars. For this purpose, the superpowers backed their protégés militarily (by supplying arms, providing military advisers, or operating sophisticated weapons), economically (by stepping up economic aid), and diplomatically.

Despite the superpowers' lack of success in preventing regional wars, they were more successful in war termination due to the balance of motivation shifting more in their favor in these latter situations. When there was a risk, for example, of Arab–Israeli wars ending in defeat of the Arab state(s) by Israel, the superpowers were more motivated to intervene at this stage to prevent major changes in the prewar status quo. That was so because such changes in the regional balance of power would be bound to result in a Soviet intervention against Israel to save its Arab clients and in an American counterintervention in support of Israel, escalating to a direct superpower confrontation. To avoid such an escalation, the superpowers intervened to end the regional war and prevent a decisive Arab defeat; the result was the relatively early termination of most Arab–Israeli wars. This pattern was manifested most clearly in the wars of 1956 and 1967, the 1969–1970 War of Attrition, the 1973 war, and the 1982 Lebanon war. In addition to the shifting balance of motivations, a change in the balance of capabilities in their favor also made it easier for the superpowers to control their regional allies at the end (rather than at the beginning) of the local wars due to the growing dependence of the clients on superpower arms resupply.

A major case of the effects of great power disengagement on making possible protracted regional wars under a state-to-nation imbalance is provided by the Yugoslav conflict from the early 1990s until the US-led intervention in Bosnia in late 1995 (see chapter 6).

Proposition 2: The effects of the regional system on regions with a state-to-nation imbalance: the regional balance of power and the offense/defense balance do not address state-to-nation issues, and the likely outcome is hot or cold war depending, among other things, on the success or failure of deterrence or compellence and the working of the security dilemma (see chapters 3 and 4).

Findings: Realist factors such as the regional balance of power and the offense/defense balance affect the dynamics and the management of the conflict even if they do not cause it or bring about its resolution.

The high state-to-nation imbalance in a region such as the Middle East made it conducive to either offensive wars of expansion (1948), preventive wars (1956), or defensive/security dilemma wars (1967). A major factor which helped to translate this proneness to specific wars was the high vulnerability of pre-1967 Israel which increased the likelihood of aggression by the Arabs (1948), of preventive wars by Israel (1956), or of inadvertent escalation as in 1967.

The decreasing vulnerability of post-1967 Israel and its growing deterrent capability should presumably have reduced the level of violence, but the continuing state-to-nation imbalance has led to additional wars, due to high motivation of Arab states to recapture their occupied land (1969–1970, 1973) or Israeli ambitions to resolve the conflict by its superior arms (1982). But gradually since then large-scale wars have become less likely due to the working of the regional balance of power. The Arabs were dissuaded from attacking Israel because of its military superiority, its widely perceived nuclear option, and its informal alliance with the United States. The Israelis have also seen the limitations to their ability to translate military force to political objectives. However, the continuing state-to-nation imbalance brought about lower-level violence between Israelis and Palestinians in the late 1980s and especially in the early 2000s, despite the huge military gap between them.

Similarly, the regional balance of power and deterrence play a role in reducing the prospects of large-scale violence in other key rivalries of state-to-nation imbalances, such as China–Taiwan, India–Pakistan, and the Koreas, though in the Taiwanese and Korean cases the US security umbrella also plays a role in deterring the use of force even if not in resolving the underlying problems.

Proposition 3: Under a global society of states, great power hegemony or concert are likely to moderate the state-to-nation imbalance in the region and, as a result, cold peace is likely to emerge (see chapters 5 and 6).

Findings: In the late 1980s, after Gorbachev came to power and US–Soviet relations improved, a change occurred in the type of great power engagement in some of the most war-prone places – from competition to some degree of cooperation. This change resulted in a reduction, though not a comprehensive resolution, of conflicts in a number of trouble spots in the Third World: Angola, Mozambique, Cambodia, Afghanistan, and Iran–Iraq. Yet, following the disintegration of the USSR in 1991, it disengaged from regional conflicts all over the globe, while the United States disengaged more selectively, especially from Africa. Thus the pattern expected by proposition 1 (cold war interrupted by relatively frequent hot wars) dominated Africa in the 1990s and the first few years of the twenty-first century, with numerous civil and transborder wars in the Great Lakes region, between Ethiopia and Eritrea, and in West Africa.

The Middle East and the Balkans provide major cases of the pacifying effects of great power hegemony or cooperation in regions that suffer from a severe state-to-nation imbalance, thus leading to regional cold peace. There are five cases of hegemony in these two regions in the twentieth century, two in the Middle East and three in Eastern Europe and the Balkans. The two Middle Eastern cases are the US hegemony vis-à-vis Egypt and Israel since the late 1970s, leading to the Camp David accords, and the US hegemony in relation to the Arab–Israeli arena as a whole in the post-Cold War era, leading to a vigorous, even if problematic, peace process.[3] The three cases of hegemony in the Balkans and Eastern Europe are Germany in the late 1930s–early 1940s, the USSR in the Cold War era, and the US assumption of the hegemonic role in Yugoslavia since 1995 (leading to the Dayton peace agreements in that year and to the pacification of the region more recently). The pacifying effects of Soviet hegemony in the post-1945 era were manifested in a major reduction in the number of conflicts in this conflict-prone region. Only when Soviet hegemony disappeared in the early 1990s did major armed conflicts erupt in the Balkans. All of these were state-to-nation conflicts. While not fully resolved, their violent manifestations ended when the United States assumed leadership in the late 1990s. The major case of the stabilizing effects of great power cooperation is the

[3] See chapter 5, Quandt 2001, and Hudson 1996.

post-Napoleonic Concert of Europe, culminating with regard to the Balkans during the 1878 Berlin Congress.

A recent case of the pacifying effects of a semi-concert is demonstrated by the moderating effects exercised on nationalist conflicts in Eastern Europe by the lure of joining the EU and NATO. A good example is the conflicts between Hungary and its neighbors – Slovakia and Romania – which host large Hungarian minorities. The United States might be seen as the hegemon in this environment because of its leadership of the key security institution – NATO – and its role as a security provider, mitigating the destabilizing effects of anarchy. Yet the key role played by the EU and its economic incentives changed the situation in post-Cold War Europe at least partly to a US–EU concert. At any rate, the effects of the international system here were very benign and reduced the level of nationalist conflicts.[4] In these cases concert and hegemony produce a strategic-economic environment which makes it highly profitable, for both security and economic reasons, to join the regional peace process (see chapter 5 on the greatly enhanced US aid to Israel following the peace agreements with Egypt in the 1970s, the large annual US assistance to Egypt since the Camp David accords, and the US assistance to Jordan following the peace treaty with Israel; see also chapter 8 for the Marshall Plan to Western Europe as a major incentive for integration and reconciliations). At the same time, such an environment raises the costs for those who oppose the regional peace, such as Iraq under Saddam or Serbia under Miloševič; both men were deposed directly or indirectly by the use of US military power following years of economic sanctions.

Proposition 4: If a regional society of states is composed of strong and congruent states, peaceful conflict resolution is likely to produce a normal interstate peace by resolving territorial disputes (see chapter 7).

Findings: The evolution of peace in South America during the twentieth century is an example of these dynamics, even if not perfectly so. The relative consolidation of South American states, especially in the southern cone, led to a major decline in the frequency of interstate wars since the end of the nineteenth century. Not only were there relatively very few wars in the region during the twentieth century, while Europe had two

[4] Csergo and Goldgeier 2004.

world wars (in addition to more limited wars), but South America has also shown remarkable ability to resolve territorial conflicts peacefully.

Proposition 5: A liberal democratic hegemon or a concert of great powers provides the most effective mechanism for new minimally congruent liberal states to make the transition from hot war to high-level warm peace (see chapter 8).

Findings: If the hegemon or the concert is composed of liberal states, the effect might be not only pacification of the regional conflict, but also support in the consolidation of the new liberal regimes, thus making it possible for them to reach high-level warm peace later on. Such liberal regimes become more attractive to the local population because of the expected security umbrella provided by the liberal great powers against regional opponents. The liberal powers can also reinforce the appeal of the local liberal regimes by offering economic benefits and free trade agreements.

Such a process took place at the end of World War II in Western Europe with the hegemonic role of the United States, and in Eastern Europe in the post-Cold War era with the joint role of the United States as the security provider against a potential Russian threat in the future and the EU as the economic provider offering the possibility of joining the economic club of affluent states. Such joint Western provision helped both to smooth the transition to democracy and to reduce tensions in state-to-nation conflicts, thus preparing the ground for the emergence of high-level warm peace in the region when all states join the EU and NATO.

Proposition 6: Regional liberal compatibility among coherent states is likely to produce an enduring high-level warm peace by resolving or transcending remaining state-to-nation issues (see chapter 8).

Findings: Post-World War II Western Europe is the most successful example of these dynamics. The recent integrative acts in South America in the aftermath of the wave of democratization there in the 1980s might also follow this path (see chapter 7). The relatively high state-to-nation balance there facilitates this process. These dynamics could also apply to post-Cold War Central Europe and to growing parts of Eastern Europe. In this case, the expectation of joining the security umbrella of NATO and the economic benefits associated with joining the EU helped to consolidate democracy and to dampen regional conflicts. It is instructive that democratization and liberalization have been most successful in the most coherent states in Eastern Europe: Poland, the Czech Republic (following its peaceful separation from Slovakia), and Hungary (although it faces the problem of Hungarian minorities across the border with Romania, Slovakia, and Serbia). The expectations of joining NATO and the EU were crucial here in damping these potential conflicts.

Table 9.1 summarizes the six propositions and their application to the cases. Table 9.2 summarizes some of the main findings of the study with regard to the Middle East, the Balkans, South America, and Western Europe; it presents the combined effects of the three key factors (the state-to-nation balance, great power engagement, and democracy) on variations in regional war and peace and the major pathway to peace in the respective regions.

In the Middle East and the Balkans the high state-to-nation imbalance created a considerable space for the influence of the great powers. Under these conditions, the type of involvement of the great powers became a crucial factor. When the engagement was competitive as well as under disengagement, the regional outcome was hot or cold war. Under hegemony or cooperation, in contrast, the outcome shifted to cold peace. So long as the state-to-nation imbalance remained high, there were no prospects for warm peace.

The case of South America shows that the presence of relatively coherent states and a relatively high degree of regional state-to-nation balance enables a successful process of conflict resolution to generate a normal peace, even if not a perfect one. Under these conditions, the role of the great powers is not as critical as under the conditions that prevailed in the Middle East and the Balkans. Democratization under these conditions brings about a more successful regional integration than among authoritarian states and, as a consequence, a gradual emergence of a high-level warm peace. Western Europe demonstrates that democracy is indeed the key for effective integration and the emergence of such warm peace. But it also shows that a benign hegemon may be needed in the early stages to play a crucial role in the evolution of this warm peace: it will facilitate the transition of former archenemies like France and Germany to peaceful and cooperative partners. Intensive engagement by a hegemon in Europe in the post-World War II period was more critical than in twentieth-century South America; it made possible the dramatic transition from a long history of hot and cold wars to a high-level warm peace, with only relatively brief intermediate stages of cold

Table 9.1 *Regional war and peace according to the six images*

Image	Causal factors	Effects on state-to-nation imbalance	Regional outcome	Empirical cases
1. Global system	GP competition or disengagement	Not addressed	Cold war	Middle East 1948–74/91; Balkans post-1878
2. Regional system	Regional BOP/regional offense/defense balance	Not addressed	Hot wars/cold war	Middle East 1948–91; Balkans 1991–95
3. Global society of states	GP hegemony or cooperation (concert)	Moderated	Cold peace	Camp David; 1878 Berlin Congress
4. Regional society of states	Coherent (strong and congruent) states	Resolved	Normal warm peace	South America in the twentieth century
5. Global community	Liberal democratic GPs (hegemon or concert)	Creating prerequisites for transcendence	Emergence of high-level peace	United States, Western Europe 1946–58
6. Regional community	Liberal compatibility	Transcended or resolved	Endurance of high-level peace	Western Europe 1958–2005

Notes: GP: great power; BOP: balance of power.

Table 9.2 *Summary of the findings on the causes of war and peace in the four regions*

Region	State-to-nation balance	Great power engagement	Are all the key states liberal democracies?	State of regional war/peace	Pathway to peace
Middle East					
1945–90	Imbalance	Competition	No	Hot/cold war	None
1991–2005	Imbalance	Hegemony	No	Cold peace	US hegemony
The Balkans					
1945–90	Imbalance	Hegemony	No	Cold peace	Soviet hegemony plus control by Tito in Yugoslavia
1991–94	Imbalance	Disengagement	Democratizing	Hot/cold war	None
1995–2005	Imbalance (though some unmixing)	Hegemony/concert	Democratizing	Cold peace	Great power intervention[a]
Western Europe					
Pre-1945	Imbalance	Competition	No (Germany)	Hot/cold war	None
Post-1945	More balanced (decline of German revisionist nationalism; expulsion of Germans from Eastern Europe, though Germany still divided until 1990)	Hegemony	Yes	From cold peace to high-level warm peace	From US hegemony to integration by democracies
South America					
Nineteenth century	Nationally congruent but weak states	Competition	No	Hot/cold war	None
Twentieth century	Nationally congruent and consolidated states	Partial US hegemony	No (though democratization since 1980s)	Normal peace	Conflict resolution by consolidated/congruent states

Note: [a] On the effects of the great variations in great power involvement in the Balkans in the 1830–1945 period, see ch. 6.

and normal peace. In South America, in contrast, the evolution of normal peace proceeded slowly over a long period, encompassing almost the whole century. In the Middle East, however, due to the lengthy period of hot and cold wars and the severe problems of state-to-nation imbalances, intensive hegemonic involvement is essential to sustain a cold peace, thus possibly enabling the evolution of the conditions for a normal peace. Similarly, in the Balkans, there is a great need for sustained engagement of a concert of great powers led by the United States and the European Union to enable peaceful conflict resolution in Bosnia and Kosovo; this would also enable economic development and a successful transition to democracy (though some unmixing of ethnic groups following the wars of the 1990s might reduce the state-to-nation imbalance in some places in the Balkans and thus increase the prospects for peace).[5]

The dynamics in the Middle East and South America, in particular, were mirror-images. While the European migrants to South America were flexible in their national-territorial identities and could adopt those of the new countries to which they emigrated, the Zionists were committed to establishing a Jewish homeland in a certain territory – the Land of Israel – even if its boundaries were not completely specified (they are still disputed; they thus produce a major source of conflict between the Israelis and the Arabs). On the other hand, while the indigenous people were suppressed, if not destroyed, in the New World, the Zionist settlers were too weak (or too humane, at least partly because of norms of the later period in which they settled the land), and especially too dependent on the great powers, to destroy the local population in Palestine. The flexibility of national identities of immigrants versus the relatively fixed nature of the identity of indigenous population has also meant the relative weakness of preexisting pan-Hispanic identities in South America as compared to the new state identities. In contrast, the preexisting pan-Arab and pan-Islamic, let alone subnational and transborder ethnic and sectarian identities, proved to be more resistant to the emergence of the new state identities in the post-World War I Arab world. This is due to the long duration of unified political frameworks of Arabs and Muslims, and the persistence of ethnic identities, in the centuries before

[5] See Downes 2004; for example, before the Croat–Serb war of the early 1990s, some 600,000 Serbs lived in Croatia, making up 12 percent of the total population. According to the census of 2001, only just over 200,000 live there today (4.5 percent of the population) (*Economist*, July 30, 2005, 29–30).

the relatively recent creation of the new Arab state system imposed by the Western colonial powers only following World War I.

The outcome was a state-to-nation balance in South America (and indeed in most of the New World) and a state-to-nation imbalance in the Middle East, especially, though not only, in the Arab–Israeli sector. This variation provides a powerful explanation of the difference in the level of peace despite the similarity in the clash between European settlers and native peoples in the two regions: normal or high-level warm peace in South America and in the New World versus protracted conflict and at best cold peace in the Middle East.

Utility of the theory

The theory proposed in this book is able to explain empirical variations among different regions such as the high war proneness of the Middle East and the Balkans in contrast to the peacefulness of South America during most of the twentieth century and of post-1945 Western Europe. Indeed, in the Middle East and the Balkans, there is a high extent of state-to-nation imbalance. In contrast, there is a relatively high degree of a state-to-nation balance in South America and Western Europe.

The theory can also account for the transitions within regions such as the emergence of cold peace in the Middle East in the post-Cold War era and in the Balkans during the Cold War period (and later in the late 1990s following the great power intervention in Bosnia and Kosovo), as well as the evolution of normal peace in South America during the twentieth century and high-level warm peace in Western Europe during the post-World War II era.

The theory presented here is relevant for explaining different levels of conflict in different time periods and regions. Thus, the theory's purview is not limited to conflicts of the Cold War era (such as the Arab–Israeli wars or issues related to German reunification) or even of the post-Cold War period (such as the wars in the former Yugoslavia). It extends equally well to major earlier conflicts such as the wars of German unification in the nineteenth century and the Balkan wars that preceded World War I. Similarly, the theory is relevant for explaining the French–German nationalist rivalry over Alsace-Lorraine.

In addition to the conflicts addressed in the book in regions such as the Middle East and the Balkans, the theory is also able to explain some of the key contemporary crises, such as the East Asian conflicts between China and Taiwan and in Korea. Both of these cases involve demands for national unification based on the claim that there are "too many states" in relation to the number of nations, as was similarly the case with the Vietnam War. The India–Pakistan conflict is another case of state-to-nation conflict revolving around Pakistan's irredentist demands on India's Kashmir.

Finally, the present framework helps to overcome the divide between civil and international conflicts. Observers have underlined this divide, particularly in the post-Cold War era, with the claim that civil wars are replacing international wars as the key conflicts in global politics. This book shows the common sources of numerous conflicts of both types, which result from variations in the extent of the state-to-nation balance in different parts of the world (affecting the hot outcomes of hot war and warm peace). Nevertheless, the cold outcomes of these conflicts are affected by variations in the type of great power engagement in these regions.

Ethnonational conflict is a more important source of regional conflict and of violence than what both realism and liberalism (and the substantive-territorial school) would lead us to expect. More precisely, the state-to-nation balance in the region is the key for explaining variations in the level of regional violence. State weakness and national incongruence in a certain region lead to insecurity, transborder intervention and violence, regional wars, and instability, while regions populated by states that are both strong and congruent tend to be more stable and peaceful.

To demonstrate the utility of the theory with regard to a new phenomenon of organized violence, I show the relevance of the state-to-nation imbalance for accounting for the new global terrorism of Al Qaeda.

(1) The pan-Islamic identity of an Islamic *umma* (or "nation") which should have a political authority of its own – the Islamic caliphate – reviving the pre-World War I Islamic empire with its supposed past glory. Similarly to pan-national movements, Al Qaeda calls for transborder unification based both on present grievances against the current state system and on the glory of a past "golden age," whether real or imagined.

(2) One of the key grievances highlighted by Al Qaeda is what they see as the suppression by non-Muslims of Muslims fighting for national self-determination such as in Bosnia, Chechnya, Kashmir, Palestine,

and Iraq. These conflicts are also a major tool for mobilizing volunteers and raising funds.

(3) Weak or failed states serve as hosts for Al Qaeda, notably Afghanistan until 2001; to a lesser extent this is also the case in Yemen, Sudan, Somalia, and Pakistan. The great worry is that an American failure in Iraq will make it a new, and perhaps even more destabilizing, Afghanistan.

(4) A key demand of Al Qaeda is a classical nationalist demand – the call for the removal of foreign troops from Muslim lands, notably of the US-led coalition from Iraq and earlier US troops from the Arabian Peninsula (Pape 2005). The war against the Soviet occupation of Afghanistan in the 1980s was a formative experience for many of the leaders and activists of Al Qaeda, who went to Afghanistan from all over the Arab and Muslim worlds to fight the occupation. Thus, the war helped to mobilize a transborder pan-Islamic organization.

(5) Assistance (direct or indirect) to Al Qaeda and to Islamic radicals from states which suffer state-to-nation imbalances such as Pakistan (notably in Kashmir in addition to internal cleavages such as in Baluchistan), and Saudi Arabia, whose legitimacy is based on a strict interpretation of Sunni Islam, but has a sizable Shiite minority located in an oil-rich region of the country. Pakistan, in particular, needs radical Islamic fighters to combat the Indian rule of Kashmir; thus, Pakistani intelligence trained and financed the Taliban and related militant groups as part of its irredentist war against India. To divert attention from the legitimacy problems of its corrupt ruling family, which controls the state and, in fact, owns its vast resources exclusively, Saudi Arabia tries to show its pan-Islamic credentials. For example, it finances the establishment of *madrasas*, where many young Muslims get a radical Islamic and an anti-Western education in various places, notably in Pakistan, and then become easy recruits for militant Islamic organizations.

How to advance regional peace: lessons and suggestions

In chapter 3, I distinguished among four categories of states, and their war and peace orientations, based on the two key components of the state-to-nation balance: state strength and national congruence. The extent and type of war proneness in the region depend on the relative

Table 9.3 *Which regional peace strategy fits best which category of state as the first priority?*

	Congruent states (civic nationalism is strong)	**Incongruent states**
Strong states	Democratization/liberalization followed by regional integration	Defeat of revisionism followed by the decline of ethnic nationalism
	The French–German case in the 1950s	Germany in WWII; Egypt 1967; Serbia 1999; Iraq 1991; post-1973 Israel
Weak states	State-building followed by conflict resolution of territorial disputes	Security provision by great powers followed by revision (partition) or preservation
	South America in the twentieth century	Post-2003 Iraq; Israel–Palestine; Bosnia; Kosovo

prominence of each of these state categories in the region. Accordingly, the prevalent category of state also determines which type of peace strategy is the most relevant for addressing the state-to-nation imbalance in the region, at least as the first priority, as is shown in table 9.3. This first-priority strategy might be followed later by additional strategies if the appropriate conditions develop in the region. At the end of the section, I will provide a sequence of the stages to be implemented in regional peacemaking.

When states are *strong and incongruent*, coercive strategies (whether internally or externally directed) are more useful in addressing the state-to-nation imbalance and promoting peace. When these states are nationalist-revisionist, thus becoming aggressive (and they will have this tendency especially when they are externally incongruent), the highest priority for promoting peace is to defeat them militarily. Such a defeat might result in the decline of revisionist ethnic nationalism. When the incongruence is internal, illiberal states tend to adopt the strategy of control by the dominant group, while liberal states used to promote nation-building by assimilation, although in recent decades the element of coercion associated with it made the strategy less popular among them.

Weak and incongruent states are the most prone to state collapse and to civil wars. The highest priority here is international intervention to stop the killing and to provide a secure environment. Here the great powers can play the key role in the security, diplomatic, and economic arenas. Following the intervention, the key dilemma is whether to partition the state or to preserve its territorial integrity and pursue power-sharing. The challenge is to specify the conditions under which priority should be given to promote any one of these options.

For frontier states, which are *weak and congruent*, the best strategy is state-building followed by regional conflict resolution.

Strong and congruent states are the most ripe for peaceful democratization followed by regional integration, which helps to keep them status quo states. Defeat of strong and incongruent states may transform them to strong and congruent, ripe for liberalization and its stabilizing effects. Yet, they may also become weak and incongruent and thus prone to civil wars and not ripe for democratization. While post-World War II Germany reflects the potentially stabilizing effects of defeat, the Weimar Republic and post-Saddam Iraq represent the potentially destabilizing effects.

Strong and incongruent states: defeat of the revisionists and the coercive approach

If there are strong and incongruent states in the region, at least some of them may pose a powerful challenge to regional peace, especially if they are externally incongruent. This is because of their revisionist/irredentist tendencies. The best way to advance regional peace under these conditions is to defeat these powers militarily if they try to carry out their aggressive/revisionist plans despite serious efforts to contain and deter them. Here the logic of superior military power advanced by offensive realism is useful.[6] Superior military power can be accumulated

[6] On offensive realism, see chs. 1 and 3. The utility of military force in bringing about a certain level of peace, even if initially a cold one, is demonstrated by quantitative data which indicate that most civil wars end in military victory and not by negotiated settlements. This is especially true for ethnic wars. Negotiated settlements to ethnic wars are relatively scarce, occurring in only about 20 to 25 percent of cases. While this ratio is not much different from the likelihood of negotiated end of ideological civil wars, the key difference between ethnic and ideological civil wars is that settlements to ethnic wars much more often collapse into renewed war than do ethnic wars ended by military victory: 67 percent of negotiated settlements to ethnic wars eventually broke down into war, while this occurred only 21 percent of the time after a military victory by one of the sides. In

by regional actors or by a coalition thereof. Sometimes the only way to defeat the revisionist powers is by the intervention of great powers.

But mostly useful here is the logic of the state-to-nation balance, which suggests that a military defeat of revisionist ethnic nationalism has stabilizing effects because it decreases the regional imbalance. As proposed in chapter 2, the decline of revisionism is an important stage on the way to state- and nation-building, reinforcing the pragmatic status quo forces, thus leading eventually to regional peace. A key avenue for this decline is a military failure of revisionist ethnic nationalism, although major economic failure can also be helpful in this respect. Revisionist ethnic nationalism poses a challenge to the status quo in the region and inside the states, thus producing instability. A military defeat of revisionism discredits its cause and strengthens the status quo parties, who are willing to advance negotiated conflict resolution.

The crucial importance of military power and decisive military victories for bringing about greater state-to-nation balance and thus peaceful regional systems is shown by the military defeat of revisionist nationalism such as in the cases of Germany, Egypt, Iraq, Serbia, and to a considerably lesser extent Israel. What emerges from the historical record produces another avenue for a greater state-to-nation balance. The challenge posed by revisionist nationalism is resolved by a military defeat. A decisive military defeat of revisionist nationalism leads to a greater state-to-nation balance because the promise of revisionism is discredited as *failed aggression*. Both conditions – unprovoked aggression on the part of the revisionist power and its complete military failure – have to be present and perceived in the region. This results in strengthening of the status quo, maybe even leading to a greater acceptance of civic nationalism instead of the discredited revisionist ethnic nationalism. But the defeat has to be decisive. Otherwise, it will not be sufficient to bring about normal or high-level warm peace.

A key case is post-*World War II Germany*. The sharp decline of revisionist ethnic nationalism in postwar Germany and the inclination toward regional integration was derived first of all from the outcome of World War II: "The dream of a German nation-state during the nineteenth century had seemingly held out great promise for the future of the German people, but the reality had been overshadowed by defeat, collapse and criminality. The national hope of a Reich embracing the whole German

contrast, none of the ideological wars in that study reignited, whether settled by negotiations or victory. See Walter 2002, Appendix 1, Table A.1, pp. 169–170; Downes 2001, 72–73, citing also Walter 1997 and Licklider 1995. See also Downes 2004.

race had been realized only in the nightmare of Hitler's 'Great German Reich.' The path to unification had ended in oppression, persecution and the . . . atrocities of Auschwitz and Treblinka, and their outcome was the destruction of the German nation-state."[7]

The unconditional defeat of Germany was a crucial element in eventually creating the conditions for the high-level warm peace in post-1945 Europe. Such a decisive blow was necessary to discredit revisionist ethnic nationalism in Germany and in Europe as a whole. It also made possible the removal of millions of ethnic Germans from Eastern Europe in the aftermath of World War II, which contributed to a greater state-to-nation balance on the continent, and especially in a region which had been a source of instability and wars. Consider, for example, the nationalist tensions of interwar Poland with its ethnonational minorities in comparison to the homogeneous post-World War II Poland which, after its liberation from Soviet control, could liberalize peacefully and join European institutions.[8]

Similarly, the decisive defeat of Egypt in the 1967 war discredited the nationalist revisionism of pan-Arabism, thus eventually paving the way for more peaceful relations among the Arab states as well as to the emergence of the Camp David accords between Egypt and Israel (Ajami 1978/9; Sela 1998; Barnett 1998). The recent defeats of Saddam Hussein – self-styled Nasser's heir as the leading pan-Arabist – have further discredited revisionist nationalism in the Middle East. The first defeat – the 1991 Gulf War – made possible the Madrid/Oslo Arab–Israeli peace process of the 1990s (see chapter 5). On the other hand, since the defeat was incomplete, it did not remove some key obstacles to the peace process, and revisionist nationalism continued in Iraq and the Middle East. The defeat of Iraq in 2003 was much more decisive and removed the key remaining pan-Arabist from power. Yet, in this case a foreign superpower not only inflicted this blow, but has occupied the country; it has thus induced anti-imperialist nationalist resistance.

Germany compared to Iraq

A defeat can be stabilizing if the state becomes strong and congruent, notably like Germany after World War II.[9] A defeat might, however,

7 Schulze 1996, pp. 315–316.

8 Becoming more homogeneous in this case, however, came at a terrible price, notably to the Jews; thus, it is definitely **not** a recommended policy prescription by any means.

9 See below on the conduciveness of this type of state to the stabilizing effects of democracy, civic nationalism, and regional integration.

also be destabilizing if the state is transformed to weak and incongruent or stays strong and incongruent. Post-World War I Germany is a case of a state which became much weaker as a result of its defeat and the Versailles accords, but also more incongruent than before the war, with millions of ethnic Germans left outside Germany's boundaries – in Poland and Czechoslovakia, and with nationalist demands on Alsace-Lorraine, which had been transferred to France.[10] This situation made Germany likely to become unstable and potentially revisionist, which could be translated into aggression when it became stronger under the Nazis. Post-Saddam Iraq, on the other hand, became a weak state, held together by foreign forces, but it continues to be highly incongruent (see chapter 4). It is thus being transformed from a revisionist-aggressive state into one prone to civil wars and foreign intervention by the United States and its allies, by its own neighbors, and by jihadists from all over the Islamic world, similar to Afghanistan under and following the Soviet occupation in the 1980s.

In contrast to Iraq, post-World War II West Germany was an internally congruent state with a very homogeneous population. Moreover, even though Germany was divided after the war between the blocs, the external dimension of German incongruence was lessened by the expulsion of ethnic Germans from the east. Most important, as chapter 8 suggested, the dream of German reunification was completely impractical in the context of the division of Europe by the superpowers and, at any rate, revisionist nationalism by resort to military force lost any appeal following the outcome of the war. In addition, shortly after the war, initially with US help via the Marshall Plan, West Germany returned to being a strong and functioning state. Even though foreign troops remained on its soil for an extended period, they provided a security umbrella under which German citizens could develop their state and devote their resources to socioeconomic reconstruction. Being strong and congruent made it easier for West Germany under these conditions to become a peaceful and democratic state.

The Israeli case shows how a military victory by a state founded on ethnic nationalism, even though it is a democracy, can enhance nationalist revisionism, while military setbacks can moderate it. Thus, its overwhelming victory in the 1967 war increased the revisionist/nationalist tendencies in Israel manifested in the settlement enterprise in the occupied territories viewed as the historical homeland. At the same time,

10 See Ben-Israel 1991, Gutmann 1991, Reichman and Golan 1991, and Stoess 1991.

subsequent military difficulties and the growing costs of the occupation had moderating effects on decline in revisionist nationalism, increasing the prospects for regional peace. This applies to the Israeli experience in the post-1967 military confrontations: the initial setbacks in the 1973 war, the controversial Lebanon war of 1982 and the low-intensity warfare in its aftermath in South Lebanon until the Israeli unilateral withdrawal in 2000, and the two Palestinian intifadas of the late 1980s and early 2000s. One key recent outcome of these setbacks is the Israeli unilateral disengagement from Gaza in the summer of 2005 – the beginning of the end of the nationalist dream of establishing a "Greater Israel" in all the biblical lands occupied in the 1967 war. An important qualification, however, is that, since the Israeli military setbacks were limited and Israel maintains its overall military superiority, it can still deter potential Arab (and Iranian) aggression derived from their nationalist revisionism.

A final current example refers to the defeat of Milošević's Serbia by US-led NATO forces in the Kosovo war of 1999, and his subsequent removal from power by a popular revolt. As a result, a more moderate leadership came to power in Serbia; this had pacifying effects on the former Yugoslavia in the early 2000s. Still, nationalist revisionism remains a powerful force in Serbian politics; it might be partly related to the still unresolved state-to-nation conflicts in Bosnia and with the Muslims over Kosovo.

Nation-building: the "offensive liberal" way to reach internal congruence – France and the United States

For strong states that are internally incongruent, there is another coercive method to reach national congruence, which might be called an "offensive liberal" way when it is carried out by democratic states that espouse the idea of "a state of all its citizens." This strategy favors domestic integration by inclusive nation-building based on the assimilation of the various ethnic groups in the state into a single civic nation.[11] Such a "melting pot" has been relatively easier to accomplish on a voluntary basis in the immigrant societies of the New World.[12] Still, the white settlers in the New World used coercive means to marginalize the indigenous population in the Americas and Australia (see chapters 3 and 7).

[11] See Byman 2002, pp. 100–108, and p. 237, n. 3, for references to key works on assimilation and nation-building.
[12] On nation-building in the United States, see Yacobson and Rubinstein 2003, pp. 386–391, and the citations there.

These settlers could afford to use coercion because they had superior technology and were on the whole backed by the great powers of the day (Britain, Spain, France).

In the Old World during state formation, the state-builders in Western Europe imposed the new states on the local population while disarming those elements who opposed the state, and forcing assimilation on ethnic minorities through the education system.[13] A key example is France, which succeeded in producing near cultural homogenization at the expense of local identities as a result of a combination of state sanctions/coercion and incentives regarding language, dress, education, and military service.[14] France used a coercive policy to "Frenchify" the non-French speaking parts of the republic such as Brittany.[15]

Thus, it is somewhat ironic that some of the most successful and coherent states in the current international system, many of them liberal democracies advocating the supposedly tolerant civic nationalism, have been built, at least to some degree, on superior military power, intolerance, and coercive means.[16]

Drawbacks of offensive/coercive approaches to resolving state-to-nation conflicts

It is not acceptable in a modern liberal democracy to apply such severe pressures for the dissolution or modification of local identities, even in the cause of nation-building (Stepan 1998, pp. 220, 224–225; Yacobson and Rubinstein 2003, p. 377). Assimilation is less feasible today than it was in the nineteenth century because of the national-cultural resistance to assimilation of mobilized ethnic groups (Connor 1994). Specifically, assimilation might not be appealing to groups which are in ethnic conflict because conflict hardens ethnic identities (Kaufmann 1998).

Thus, nowadays the assimilation strategy is not only undesirable – it is considered an immoral approach that violates fundamental human rights and might lead even to genocide in extreme cases – but it is also

[13] See the work of Tilly 1975a, 1975b, 1985, on state formation in Europe; Ayoob 1995.

[14] E. Weber 1976, cited in Stepan 1998, p. 224; and Yacobson and Rubinstein 2003, pp. 375–386. Coercive assimilation was attempted also in Turkey, especially regarding the Kurds, and in Greece, especially regarding the Turks. On coercive attempts at nation-building in the Middle East, see Byman 2002, ch. 5.

[15] See E. Weber 1976.

[16] For an overview and citations of the limitations to the clear-cut distinction between liberal, tolerant civic nationalism and illiberal ethnic nationalism, see Yacobson and Rubinstein 2003, pp. 359–413. See also chapters in Paul et al. 2003, Part I.

much less likely to be effective. The use of coercive means could work in the New World and nineteenth-century Europe because of superiority in the balance of power and because of the norms of that era, but it is much less likely to work with today's emphasis on human rights (though notable cases of ethnic cleansing took place in the 1990s in Yugoslavia and Rwanda). Discrimination against subordinated ethnic groups also erodes the democratic rights of the dominant group (J. Snyder 2000, p. 324).

Such a coercive approach is also much less effective today because most of the countries that face state-to-nation challenges are weak states which lack the power to pursue a coercive strategy. These states also depend on the great powers; thus, the latter can pressure them to avoid coercive means, even if not always successfully, as the 1994 Rwanda genocide shows most clearly. At the same time, some powerful states, which face similar problems, might be freer to resort to coercive strategies, especially if the other great powers have shared interests at that time. Thus, post-9/11 Russia is more able to coerce Chechnya due to its supposedly shared interests with the United States in fighting Al Qaeda and its seemingly radical Islamist affiliates; Russia thus has greater freedom of action, allowing it to resort to coercion.

Nowadays offensive liberals would try to combine integration and democracy by focusing, for example, on majoritarian democracy. Although a recent successful case seems to be post-apartheid South Africa, majoritarian democracy is problematic in divided societies and might be destabilizing. Extremist outbidding by politicians on sensitive ethnic issues is very attractive in such situations; there is not much flexibility in the voting patterns of the members of the ethnic groups; and there is a potential for continuous exclusion of minority-based political parties, while the majority group governs exclusively (Sisk 1996, p. 32; Mansfield and Snyder 2005).

Instead, a modern variant of integration constitutes sophisticated institutional arrangements to encourage cross-ethnic political alliances (Sisk 1996, ch. 3; he cites the important work of Donald Horowitz), although critics argue that there is not much direct empirical evidence in support of Horowitz's claims (Sisk 1996, p. 44; J. Snyder 2000, p. 331; but see also below on building civic nationalism in a democratic framework).

Those strong and incongruent states that are not liberal democracies might pursue hegemonic policies toward their own ethnic subordinates and thus advance domestic peace under a "control" system based on one level or another of use of force.[17] Some of these regimes might try coercive assimilation, which could fail if they focus only on coercion without some positive incentives (Byman 2002). If the state is strong, the hegemonic/coercive strategy might help to keep domestic peace, but as soon as the state becomes weaker the underprivileged groups might facilitate its collapse and disintegration, as in the cases of the USSR and Yugoslavia. In Iraq, following its 1991 defeat, one oppressed group – the Kurds – achieved a de facto state (Byman 2002, pp. 164–169); in the post-Saddam era, the other previously discriminated-against group – the Shiites – demanded autonomy for their regions in the south of the country, which may yet result in the collapse of the Iraqi state.[18]

Occupation of a territory that could potentially provide security to the state because of its strategic importance becomes a burden rather than an asset if the territory is populated by a hostile nation that resists the occupation on nationalist grounds. An offensive/coercive strategy also causes resentment in the longer term, for example, by generating nationalist backlash and resistance. Such a strategy might also create stateless revisionist refugees, who provide ready recruits to join in asymmetric warfare such as terrorism and guerrilla movements. The fear of such aggressive behavior by neighbors increases the security dilemma in the region.

Even the liberal democracies of Western Europe, which do not face regional security dilemmas anymore, and have a good record in nation-building, have had to confront in recent years a certain variant of the incongruence problem: the challenge of the Muslim immigrants, some of whom resist integration, let alone assimilation, into European societies. While imposed assimilation is no longer politically correct and multiculturalism has flourished, especially in Britain and the Netherlands, recent tensions involving Muslims in these countries as well as in France have led to a greater emphasis on integration. While France forbids Muslim girls to wear headscarves to school, the British and the Dutch governments consider asking those seeking citizenship both to show some knowledge of the history and culture of their new countries and to take a pledge of allegiance.

[17] On such a system as a mechanism to produce domestic peace in deeply divided societies through various tools of coercion, see Byman 2002, ch. 3, and Sisk 1996, pp. 27–33.
[18] *Washington Post*, Aug. 15, 2005.

Incongruent and weak states: great power intervention followed by partition or power-sharing

Hegemony, concert, and regional cold peace

Great power involvement (in the form of either concert or hegemony) is conducive to the emergence of a cold regional peace in which the substantive issues in conflict and the problems of regional legitimacy have been moderated or reduced, but are still far from being fully resolved. The role of the great powers is critical in stopping civil wars in weak and incongruent states, as in US-led interventions in Bosnia and Kosovo in the 1990s (see chapter 6), although the great power role is also very important in generating a peace process between stronger states that are incongruent (the Arab–Israeli situation, discussed in chapter 5) or are suspicious of each other due to recent nationalist conflicts (France and Germany after World War II; see chapter 8).

Because of the great importance of a secure environment in enabling the development of peace, there is a crucial role for the great powers or other international forces as security providers, supplying guarantees and reassurance, playing the role of referee for the enforcement of peace accords, monitoring disarmament and ceasefires, and verifying compliance in general (Hampson 1996).[19] The great powers possess more resources than other actors to help them play these roles, especially under hegemony or concert (see chapters 5 and 6). On the other hand, it is especially advantageous if the great powers as the third parties are distant from the region and thus less likely to generate an intense security dilemma than more proximate states. On the whole, the great powers can reduce and manage, but do not resolve the regional conflict.

As this study makes clear, this kind of great power-induced peace amounts to no more than cold peace, as in the cases of post-1979 Egypt–Israel, the post-Cold War peace between Jordan and Israel, the Balkans during the Cold War (under Soviet hegemony) and after 1995 (following US-led interventions), and Western Europe from 1945 to 1955 (under the US security umbrella). Although these cases of peace were cold, it included an important element of conflict reduction. Indeed, the secure environment provided by the great powers is useful not only for

[19] Walter (2002, pp. 94–95) found that, unless augmented by a third-party guarantee, power-sharing failed to end civil wars in eight of ten cases. In contrast, almost every peace treaty that included both a power-sharing agreement and a third-party security guarantee was successful.

stopping the violence and separating the rival forces;[20] it is also conducive for enabling state-building, conflict resolution, and potentially democratization in later stages. This may result in higher levels of peace, as has been the case in Western Europe since the mid-1950s and might have begun in the Balkans in recent years.

When the great powers disengaged from regional conflicts, as they did in the Balkans in the early 1990s, or were not involved as guarantors, monitors, and referees, as in the Middle East before 1973, the regional state-to-nation imbalance became conducive to erupt to hot wars. Despite its encouragement of the Oslo process between the Palestinians and Israel in the 1990s, the United States was not intensely enough involved as a monitor and a referee with deployment on the ground. This had negative implications: contributing to the collapse of the Oslo process and the slide into violence after the failure of the Camp David summit in 2000, where the United States was also not forceful enough in inducing the parties to reach an accord (Ben Ami 2004; see also D. Ross 2004).

Conflict reduction – induced by the great powers – may strengthen the regional states at the expense of pan- and subnational forces because of two major developments. The first is that the aid provided by the great powers as an inducement for participation in the peace process increases the resources at the disposal of the local states, which can be used for state-building. The aid will also increase the states' ability and willingness to prevail over domestic secessionists and external pan-national challenges to their states using both sticks and carrots. The external aid will also increase the support of domestic constituencies in the regional peace process because of the economic benefits associated with it. Similarly, the growing stability in the region will also attract new investment and may bring about an economic boom, thus broadening the domestic coalitions supporting accommodation. The second development is the decline in the political power and popular appeal of revisionists/nationalists as the peace process progresses, various national problems (related to territorial claims) are reduced, and the sense of mutual security rises under the reassuring great power umbrella, which also contains or overwhelms the power of the revisionist states.

Indeed, for the initially crucial and difficult stages the parties might need the support of a hegemon or a concert of great powers as brokers and providers of economic aid and security guarantees. The resolution

[20] On outside military intervention in ethnic wars, see Byman 2002, ch. 8.

of the remaining territorial issues between France and Germany in the 1950s was helpful for the evolution of peace, but the US role in that period as guarantor and security provider was crucial. Similarly, this was the case in the Camp David accords, and will probably be the case in a future Palestinian–Israeli peace accord. Even though US intervention in Iraq generated anti-Americanism in the region, anyone who is interested in the promotion of regional peace understands that there is no real substitute for US leadership, even if it takes place in cooperation with the UN and the other great powers. Thus, observers have recently made some suggestions about security provision involving the United States with significant multilateral participation:

- deploy NATO troops in the occupied Palestinian territories.[21]
- establish a Kosovo-style international trusteeship over the Palestinian territories.[22]
- set up a US-led trusteeship – backed by American, British, and Australian special forces – that would oversee the building of a democratic Palestinian state while uprooting the terrorist infrastructure.[23]

The problem is, however, that it is not easy to find a credible and powerful actor(s) willing and able to play the role of guarantor, security provider, monitor, and referee. International institutions might be too ineffective in violent situations, as is shown by the record of the UN in the Balkans until the US-led NATO intervention in 1995. At the same time, the great powers might not have important enough interests to justify the costs involved in such interventions. In places where they have important interests, their intervention might threaten the interests of other great powers; cooperation among them is not easy to achieve and might be unlikely unless they face a common threat, such as Al Qaeda post-9/11. Even this threat, however, did not bring about a common position of the great powers regarding the US intervention in Iraq, despite one of its declared aims being to fight global terrorism.

Even if a successful great power intervention takes place, and a secure environment is created, a key question regarding weak and incongruent

[21] Friedman 2002. See also Hughes 2005. Hughes was the director-general of the Multinational Force and Observers, the US-led group that monitors the Egyptian–Israeli peace treaty. While commenting on the effectiveness of the force in verifying compliance and building confidence between Egypt and Israel, he suggests a similar deployment between Israel and the Palestinians.

[22] See *Jerusalem Report*, Dec. 2002.

[23] This was proposed by Martin Indyk, the former US ambassador to Israel. See also the recent book by the former Israeli foreign minister, Shlomo Ben Ami (2004) on lessons from the failure of the Oslo process in the 1990s. He calls for peace imposed by the great powers, due to the inability of the regional parties to reach peace by themselves.

Table 9.4 *Preservation of the status quo or ethnically based (territorial and demographic) revision?*

Revision	Preservation
Partition	Power-sharing
Unification	A state of all its citizens
Ethnic transfer without right of return	No ethnic transfers

states is whether to maintain the territorial integrity of the state(s) or to follow the path of partition.

Addressing the state-to-nation imbalance: revision vs. preservation

This section discusses briefly the advantages and shortcomings of major strategies to address the state-to-nation imbalance, whether by revision of current boundaries (notably, partition) or by their preservation (pursuing power-sharing or nation-building). Each of these strategies has major drawbacks. Still, partition has some utility under certain conditions to be defined below. In other situations, power-sharing or nation-building under democracy could be effective in addressing the state-to-nation problems, if they follow the stages in regional peacemaking addressed in this book and summarized below, especially state-building with international help.

A key dilemma in the resolution of state-to-nation conflicts is whether to preserve the current territorial and demographic status quo or to revise it in order to create a greater state-to-nation congruence. Obviously this applies only to conflicts in which ethnic nationalism is the dominant affiliation, as in the Middle East and the Balkans, rather than civic nationalism, as in South America. Ethnically based revisions of boundaries include:

(1) Partition into two or more ethnonation states: British India in 1947, Palestine in 1948–1949, Ireland in 1921, and Cyprus in 1974.
(2) Unification of states (or regions) that share the same ethnonational identification (Italy in 1860, Germany in 1870 and again in 1990, and Vietnam in 1975).
(3) Ethnic transfer, so as to make the relevant states more ethnically homogeneous.

The idea behind this kind of solution to state-to-nation conflicts is that each of these ethnonational groups prefers to exercise their right to national self-determination in their own ethnonational homeland. Especially when such groups engage in violent conflict, it shows that they cannot coexist peacefully in the same political entity. The violence further hardens their distinctive ethnonational identities and their aspiration to live independently of each other. Both partition and unification may arouse intense resistance from existing states, which first of all prefer to preserve themselves and their territorial integrity (Waltz 1979); thus, quests for unification and partition frequently lead to violence, as suggested in this book. Still, due to the great number of violent ethnic civil wars which took place in the 1990s, some realists forcefully advocate partition as a practical, security-based solution to ethnic civil wars irrespective of the ideological, moral, or legal aspects (Kaufmann 1998; Downes 2001).

When the state collapses, and there is no overall security provider, intermingling of different ethnic groups leads to the security dilemma and a sense of high threat, and thus to incentives to attack first and to preempt (Posen 1993b). In order to end the violence, realists argue that the competing national parties should be separated – each with its own autonomous region or state (Kaufmann 1998). In many other cases, the struggle is between the state and an ethnic group that aspires to its own independent state (Toft 2002/3, 2003; see also Laitin 2004). The solution should then be partition into fully independent states (Downes 2001, 61–62; Downes 2004). Such a separation or partition decreases the points of potential clash, thus reducing the likelihood of violence.

Realists further argue that separation, especially if it is enhanced by a balance of power, deterrence, and security arrangements, strengthens the defense at the expense of the offense, reducing the level of threat and making war less likely. Some of the measures to weaken the security dilemma and reinforce defensive/nonthreatening strategies, reducing the threat of surprise attack and preemptive strike, include the establishment of: defensible borders and demilitarized buffer zones; zones of reduced forces; security regimes that regulate the military behavior of the regional parties; outside forces for separation and peacekeeping forces; nonthreatening deterrence, which relies on mutually survivable second-strike capabilities in the case of powerful states with nuclear capabilities (India and Pakistan, India and China, etc.); and confidence-building measures such as the conduct of joint maneuvers, deployment of observers, and prenotification of military steps by each side.

In this view, the disputed land should be partitioned according to a demographic criterion; if the population is mixed, there should be mutual population transfer, even if a forcible one, to reduce the intermingling of the hostile populations (Kaufmann 1998).

Yet, the prescription of partition has some major shortcomings. For one thing, partition causes violence in the short term and makes the conflict permanent rather than solving it. The record in Palestine, India–Pakistan, and Northern Ireland are supposed to show the endurance of the conflict following the partition (Kumar 1997). Partition might also be unnecessary because of the supposed flexibility of ethnic identities, which can be manipulated so as to generate ethnic cooperation and nation-building (Byman 2002; see the citations in Downes 2001, 59, n. 5). Moreover, partition is opposed by neighbors, who are concerned that the new states will threaten their territorial integrity because of transborder ethnic ties. Partition is also opposed by the international community, which might worry about precedent-setting; this would challenge the norm of territorial integrity and cause the dismemberment of numerous states, resulting in economically unviable mini-states (Fearon 2004; see the citations in Downes 2001, 60, n. 8). Finally, unless the ethnonational groups live separately from each other, partition may require coercive separation of the groups, and thus violation of human rights and potentially violent resistance by the evacuated population (Stepan 1998, p. 224; Paris 2004). After a forced evacuation, the stateless refugees might be a source of irredentism and demand the right of return unless they are well integrated into their new societies.

In light of these major shortcomings, we should generate strict criteria under which partition might occasionally take place:

(1) Mutual consent – the ethnically based revisions should be agreed upon by all the parties concerned, although the international community could encourage it if all the other conditions for partition are present.
(2) A strong aspiration for independence by the ethnonational groups – measured by a long struggle for self-determination and a willingness to sacrifice.
(3) History of violence and high likelihood of repetition – indicated by mutual hostility and a lasting willingness to use violence to reach the nationalist goal. A related measurement is continued hostile rhetoric indicating malign intentions. A recent history of violence with the other ethnic groups reduces the trust that the other party will fulfill

its commitment to the peace accords and will not abuse the cooperation of the other to its unilateral advantage.

(4) Territorial concentration on ethnic basis – the disputed land should be partitioned according to demographic criteria. Partition is facilitated when there is a geographical concentration of the ethnonational population (Toft 2002/3; Stepan 1998, p. 224; Sisk 1996, pp. 28–29); this was the case in the Czech Republic and Slovakia, Slovenia in the former Yugoslavia, and Singapore's secession from Malaya.

If the population is mixed, mutual population unmixing could reduce the intermingling of hostile groups. So long as hostility remains, refugees should not be allowed to exercise the right of return to their previous homes if their land is now resettled with the majority group in that territory. At the same time, recent settlers, brought in by a dominant power for political reasons to change the demographics in a land populated by a rival ethnonational group, should return to their core homeland.

A key example of separation of ethnonational groups leading to peace is the "unmixing of peoples" following the two world wars in Eastern Europe (Brubaker 1996, ch. 6), including the expulsion of millions of ethnic Germans. Current cases which seem to meet the criteria for partition are Israel–Palestine, Kosovo, and perhaps Bosnia. Following partition, states are likely to be weak and congruent, and thus conducive to state-building.

In cases that do not meet the conditions cited here, liberal mechanisms might be appropriate in order to reduce the high costs associated with partition.

Liberal mechanisms to address the state-to-nation imbalance

If the conditions for partition are not met, current borders should be preserved and democratization should be combined either with power-sharing arrangements among the ethnic groups (including regional autonomy) if ethnic nationalism is strong, which is true in the overwhelming majority of these cases, or with nation-building along the lines of civic nationalism if ethnic nationalism is weaker.

The idea behind these mechanisms is that democracy is the best recipe for preventing war – both civil and international – and it can also address most successfully the state-to-nation imbalance in the region as well as within states. On the regional level, democracies do not fight each other, while domestically building democracy is the best way to promote nation-building, and identification of the people with their state and its territorial identity. Democracy provides useful mechanisms for reconciliation among the various ethnic groups. Democracy may also empower ethnic groups to struggle effectively against socioeconomic discrimination; thus, they might be less motivated to fight for secession. Liberal compatibility warms regional peace by facilitating integration and transcending nationalism.

What might be called "the defensive" version of liberalism calls for democratization by power-sharing.[24] This mechanism accommodates ethnicity and democracy, while maintaining the territorial integrity of the state, and avoids the pitfalls of partition and transfer. The most notable multiethnic power-sharing arrangements are consociationalism (Lijphart 1977; Belgium and Switzerland are examples, discussed in chapter 8), autonomy, and ethnofederalism.[25] Consociationalism is based on elite cooperation. These elites represent the various social groups in deeply divided societies. The basic principles of this approach are: "grand" coalition executive; minority veto; proportionality in the allocation of civil service positions and public funds; and group autonomy (Sisk 1996, pp. 36–38).

The effective use of this liberal strategy faces, however, a number of tough challenges in places where there is a state-to-nation imbalance, and where the empirical record of democratization's success is very problematic. Indeed, this provides more support for this book's argument that state-to-nation issues are a major cause of war and conflict. First, premature democratization in incongruent states with weak and ill-functioning institutions can be destabilizing through encouraging ethnonational extremism and violent conflicts. While authoritarian regimes may curtail ethnonational radicalism for the sake of stability, under democratizing systems, ethnic entrepreneurs might take advantage of the new freedoms to agitate against other groups to increase

[24] The distinction mentioned here between an "offensive" liberalism (which calls, as noted, for assimilation and for imposed democratization) and a "defensive" branch of liberalism parallels a foreign policy distinction inside liberalism between a defensive version which favors the spread of democracy by example and "soft power" vs. an offensive branch willing to consider the use of force to spread democracy to foreign countries. See Miller 2004.

[25] Examples of ethnofederalism include Nigeria, the USSR, Sudan, and India. On these examples, see Sisk 1996, pp. 51–52; see also Downes 2001, 59, n. 4, and 89–97. For a sophisticated discussion of nationalism and federalism, see O'Leary 2003.

their electoral appeal. The expected losers in the elections, such as ethnic minorities, might resort to violence to defend themselves against the ascendant groups, which they fear will abuse their newly gained powers. The elites of the old regime might use nationalist agitation or resort to force to hold on to their existing privileges, which would be lost in a democracy.[26]

More specifically, consociationalism can be criticized on two mutually contradictory grounds. One line of criticism is that it is not integrative enough, thus leading to ethnic conflict. Other analysts suggest that it is too integrative for ethnonational conflicts; thus, it is not effective enough in preventing such conflicts.

The first criticism suggests that consociationalism encourages ethnic conflict. Critics argue that reliance on elite accommodation is misplaced, because elites initiate secession and conflict, and consociationalism reinforces ethnic rigidity rather than mitigating ethnic conflicts. It creates barriers to an integrated civic nation while a political system should be creating incentives for national integration.[27]

The other kind of critique suggests that power-sharing was not originally developed to address ethnonational conflicts. It was applied successfully to cases of other cultural-ideological-religious cleavages (notably in West European states), which are easier to reconcile without dismembering the state than are ethnonational conflicts.[28] Moreover, severe ethnonational conflicts frequently have a crossborder dimension, which is not usually addressed by the power-sharing arrangement. Weak and incongruent states are a special target for intervention by neighbors. Thus, there is a need to address the regional dimension by creating balances of power, deterrence, and security arrangements, and by conflict resolution of transborder state-to-nation issues, to be brokered by the great powers.

A key realist critique is that even if the parties are able to sign a power-sharing accord (a very demanding challenge in an ethnonational conflict), until the power-sharing institutions start to function effectively, which might take some time, the transition period produces insecurity due to the lack of a credible security provider and the weakness

[26] On the difficulties of building a stable democracy in weak and incongruent societies, see Dahl 1989; Horowitz 1994; Linz and Stepan 1996, ch. 2; Lind 1994; Mansfield and Snyder 2005.

[27] See the citations in Sisk 1996, pp. 38–42, and esp. references to the work of Horowitz 1985.

[28] See McGarry 2005, discussed in chapter 8.

of enforcement mechanisms. This highly uncertain situation, and the resultant distrust among the antagonists, each of them afraid to disarm first, can lead to violence through the destabilizing effects of the security dilemma (J. Snyder and Jervis 1999, cited in Byman 2002, p. 129; Walter 2002; Downes 2001, 2004).

Indeed, on empirical grounds, the record of power-sharing arrangements in societies, where ethnic nationalism dominates, is very problematic. Notable failures, which collapsed in civil wars, include Lebanon (1958, 1976), Yugoslavia (1991), Rwanda (1993), Angola (1994), and Chad (1979).[29] Similarly to the critiques of consociationalism from the integrationists, the provision of autonomy to minorities may actually increase rather than decrease the likelihood of conflict.[30] Territorial autonomy, however, fits state-to-nation conflicts better than does non-territorial power-sharing (McGarry 2005). Ethnofederalism[31] also encourages ethnic nationalism (Brubaker 1996, ch. 2, cited in J. Snyder 2000, p. 327) and makes secession easier by preparing the structures of the ethnic state. It thus eventually results in the breakup of the federation along ethnic lines: Yugoslavia, the USSR, and Czechoslovakia are examples.[32] Most recently, some political (and military) elements in Spain worry that the increasing autonomy of Catalonia and the Basques might bring the eventual dismemberment of their country.[33]

"Offensive" liberalism and imposing democracy as the solution

Because of the expected pacifying effects of democracy, what I call "offensive liberals" (their current branch in the United States is commonly called neoconservatives) are willing under certain conditions to consider imposing it from the outside by sanctions and even in extreme cases by the use of force (Miller 2004). But such an imposition is likely to generate nationalist resistance and lead to instability. It might transform strong and incongruent states into weak and incongruent ones. The outcome might be violent, especially in a deeply divided society such as Iraq (see chapter 4).

[29] See Downes 2001, 89, 92; 2004; J. Snyder 2000, p. 330.

[30] Cornell 2002. There have been failures of agreements providing regional autonomy to rebellious ethnic groups in the cases of the Sri Lankan Tamils, the Moros in the Philippines, India's Kashmir, Palestinians in the occupied territories, and Russia's Chechens. See Downes 2004, 232, 245–247.

[31] For references that argue that federalism is a good solution for civil wars, see Walter 2002, p. 28, n. 16.

[32] On the failure of federalism, see also Downes 2001, 93.

[33] *Economist*, Jan. 14, 2006.

Thus, in the case of weak and incongruent states, there is a need to focus on partition or on state-building (helped by the international community), with some elements of power-sharing and regional conflict resolution before democratization can proceed very far.

Congruent and weak: state-building leading to regional conflict resolution

The South American case shows the importance of state-building as a key prerequisite for successful conflict resolution. A certain degree of state strength is necessary to avoid the pitfalls of incoherence/instability, but too much success might generate a surplus of power, which made possible the aggressive behavior of the European powers before World War I. Thus, the medium-level success of the South American states was useful for stabilizing the region.

State-building

Effective state institutions are a necessary, even if not sufficient, condition for a stable regional peace and for the implementation of peace accords. With the initiation of a conflict-reduction process, which is led, for example, by the great powers, the new states should strengthen themselves, first of all, by monopolizing the means of violence in their sovereign territory and establishing law and order. This will prevent the destabilizing manifestations of anarchy, where the lack of security provider produces security dilemmas and conflicts, including unintended ones, even by status quo actors. Weak or failed states are a major source not only of domestic civil wars but also of regional, and potentially global, instability. As 9/11 showed, the weakness of Afghanistan did not adversely affect regional security only in South Asia, but also US national security and international security in general. This insight is overlooked by offensive realism, which focuses only on the strong states as the source of security threats, instability, and wars. The strengthening of the states in South America at the end of the nineteenth century and in the Arab world since the 1970s – at the expense of pan-Arabism – brought about greater regional stability, though the level of stability has been lower in the Middle East due to much greater remaining state-to-nation imbalances.

On the other hand, this defensive realist focus on security also warns against moving too quickly to premature democratization without ensuring a secure environment, by some combination of the great powers and state strengthening, because it can aggravate national/ethnic conflicts.

Beyond the key component of the monopoly on the means of violence, institution-building should include building legitimate and professional law-and-order institutions, an effective and unbiased state bureaucracy, an independent court system, a professional military and police force, and free media. A key point is that the public institutions should be effective, functioning, and professional, so that they will be able to deliver key services to all the citizens of the state, irrespective of ethnicity, in the area of law and order, infrastructure (water, electricity, transportation, communications, mail delivery, etc.), socioeconomic services, and public education, thus preventing the capture of these services by radical religious or nationalist organizations.[34]

The strengthening of the state and its institutions at the expense of revisionist ethnic nationalism is stabilizing because states tend, in general, to be more rational and cautious than ultranationalists, although occasionally the state might be captured by these elements. This is most likely when the state is nationally incongruent – Germany in the 1930s was captured by the Nazis – and then the most stabilizing response is, as noted, a military defeat of these states if and when they become aggressive. The reason for the usual state caution is that states must first of all take care of their survival under anarchy (Waltz 1979), which means paying attention to the balance of power and to economic considerations. Regional states must worry about their dependence on the great powers, which is a restraining factor (see chapter 5). Ultranationalists, on the other hand, are much less pragmatic and are willing to pay a heavy price to fulfill ideological aspirations of unifying the whole nation in its historic homeland. Strong state institutions can be the basis for an acceptance of the status quo by making states reliable partners for negotiating and implementing peace agreements with other states. Strong states can also, over time, potentially create some extent of civic/territorial nationalism based on the acceptance of the existing territorial status quo even if it falls short of achieving the ultranationalist dreams of the "Greater state."

Thus, for example, the recent disengagement of Israel from the Gaza Strip might be the first step in the process of the pragmatic Israeli state (or

[34] For a useful advocacy of state- and institution-building, see Paris 2004 and Fukuyama 2004.

stateness) overcoming the ultranationalist "Greater Israel" aspirations of controlling all the biblical territories of the Promised Land.

Regional conflict resolution and the emergence of normal peace

The international society perspective, discussed in chapter 2, emphasizes the mutual recognition of sovereignty, the sanctity of boundaries, and noninterference in domestic affairs. This study suggests that the prerequisite for these norms – and for conflict resolution – to be effective is the emergence of strong and functioning states as took place in South America with the transition from the nineteenth century to the twentieth. Thus, the defensive realist logic of the stabilizing effects of the security provision by a strong state, which controls the means of violence in its sovereign territory, is a crucial condition for the working of the international society strategy of conflict resolution. Commitments made by strong states are more reliable than those made by weak states, which might not be able to carry them out, even if they want to, due to fragility of state institutions. While the role of international forces in the regional conflict resolution in South America was limited due to a relatively low extent of national incongruence, this is not the case in regions with a high state-to-nation imbalance. In these places, the role of international forces is, as noted, crucial. As the conflict resolution process develops, however, it can also help to mitigate the state-to-nation imbalance and weaken revisionist nationalism.

Thus, nationalist forces inside those states that participate in the regional peace process are marginalized, and their power to obstruct peace processes declines, because the external enemies are less threatening and the substantive components of the conflict are in the process of being reduced. For example, as refugees are resettled and integrated in areas in which they are part of the demographic majority (as the German expellees were after World War II), there is a decline in the support for nationalist revisionism. As a result there is also a decrease in the reservoir of volunteers for guerrilla or terrorist organizations, which have challenged state coherence in the region; allowing freedom of access to holy nationalist/religious sites, facilitated by neutral international forces, reduces the claim to control them exclusively. Growing segments of the public in those states see the issues in a more pragmatic light as security and economic state interests, rather than as emotionally laden indivisible nationalist symbols on which compromise is neither feasible nor desirable. This progress may encourage and allow local elites to show the necessary flexibility to proceed toward the resolution of the disputed state-to-nation issues and their territorial manifestations, and thus to allow the establishment of normal peace.

Congruent and strong: integration of democracies

The level of normal peace reached through conflict resolution by strong states is, in turn, conducive to domestic liberalization in the regional states. As a major comparative study shows, democratization in Scandinavia and North America was preceded by the achievement of normal peace, which quelled the rivalry among states for regional hegemony.[35] International threats reinforce the power of anti-democratic forces in the domestic politics of states involved in protracted conflict. The anti-democratic elements controlling the state use the external threats to justify the limits to political freedom inside the state supposedly in order not to undermine internal unity against the external enemy (as Arab state elites used the Arab–Israeli conflict; see chapter 4).[36] In contrast, a moderation in the level of external threats reduces both the necessity and the pretext for the repression of democratic opposition.[37] Thus, the South American peace evolving during most of the twentieth century made possible the democratization process in the 1980s, the post-World War II Pax Americana in Western Europe made possible the successful and durable democratization of Germany and Italy, and the post-Cold War peace in Eastern Europe enabled the democratization of former communist states in the region. The lack of peace in the Middle East, however, has prevented the advance of democracy in that region.

The presence of strong and congruent states will be most conducive to the promotion of democracy and regional integration; these two factors will further reduce the danger of war and warm the peace. Even for this group of states realist/systemic factors, such as a common threat and hegemony, might, however, be necessary in the initial stages to enable regional integration, as happened with the common Soviet threat and US hegemony in Western Europe in the years after World War II.

If democratization follows the creation of a great power security umbrella, effective state-building, and regional conflict resolution that has produced normal peace, it may go hand in hand with enhanced civic nationalism, thus producing greater internal congruence even in those states which are ethnically heterogeneous. These days nation-building

[35] See Thompson 1996.
[36] This is based on the logic of the scapegoat or diversionary theory discussed in ch. 3.
[37] See Gurr 1988.

by assimilation, as noted, is problematic and generates national-cultural opposition (Connor 1994; Byman 2002, pp. 100–108). An alternative avenue is to encourage civic nationalism by domestic integration and the construction of common unifying symbols for the various groups in the state (flag, anthem, national civic holidays, national heroes), even if each ethnic group maintains its unique cultural heritage. Under the common umbrella of civic nationalism, it would be helpful to teach the languages of the key ethnonational groups in school, even if there is one major language in the country; to advance common civic education, which exposes the wrongs of one's own group as well as those of the ethnic rivals; to promote media free of ethnic biases; to facilitate the political participation of all groups; to end socioeconomic discrimination based on ethnicity; and to strengthen civil society institutions independent of the state.[38] This last task should be undertaken only if state institutions are already functioning well and these civil society institutions do not come at their expense and erode their effectiveness.

Implementing such tasks is, of course, extremely difficult in a society which has experienced severe ethnic conflicts. Yet the point is that a reduction in the level of conflict, coming after the construction of a secure environment, and state-building followed by democratization, makes easier the reinforcement of civic nationalism, which itself might facilitate conflict resolution. For example, resolution of the Arab–Israel conflict would make it much easier to construct some components of civic identity for both Jews and Arabs in pre-1967 Israel. An example might be adding a few lines to the national Israeli anthem, which currently expresses only the old-time aspiration of the Jewish people to return to their ancient homeland in the Land of Israel. The new lines could refer to something in common to all Israelis or specifically also to the aspirations of the Arab minority. Such changes would be extremely problematic and generate strong opposition because both groups are not only suspicious of each other, but also would like to preserve their particular national-cultural heritage. The Jews in particular would like to have their national homeland in Israel as a Jewish state, after fulfilling their long-held national dream following ages of persecution and pogroms. The Israeli Arabs, for their part, would like to maintain their ethnonational affiliation with their Palestinian and Arab brethren. Therefore it is possible to imagine the formation of any civic nationalism in Israel only after the settlement of the Arab–Israeli conflict (and even then the

[38] Paris 2004; *Haaretz*, May 6, 2005.

likelihood is quite low – the entire legitimacy and raison d'état of Israel is as a Jewish state even if a democratic one). If this civic formation is successful, however, it will strengthen the peace and further warm it.

West Germany is a good example of successful democratization and the evolution of postethnic nationalism and elements of civic nationalism. There were, however, quite a number of conditions that were helpful for such evolution, as noted in chapter 8: the total defeat of revisionist nationalism and its moral bankruptcy, and the presence of the US security umbrella and economic aid, motivated by the Cold War. The economic aid, in turn, facilitated an economic boom. In addition, the major ethnic presence in the East ended, while conflict resolution occurred in the West linked to the emerging regional integration with France.

In contrast, post-Saddam Iraq shows the instability produced by premature democratization under the combination of a collapse of the state, following the US invasion, and the failure to form a civic identity common to all Iraqis during the preceding decades of Iraqi independence. This is both a domestic failure, among Kurds, Shiites, and Sunnis, and an external one, due to transborder ties between the Iraqi Shiites and the Shiite Iranians, Iraqi Kurds and Kurds in Turkey and Iran, Iraqi Sunnis and the Sunnis in Jordan and Saudi Arabia, Iraqi Arabs and Arab nationalists in the Arab world, and Iraqi Islamists and Islamists in the Muslim world.

Regional integration

A secure environment which is going through democratization by strong states with effective institutions and reduced ethnic nationalism is conducive to a growing trust among the regional states. It allows for the establishment of regional institutions and the development of transnational relations and thus the evolution of high-level warm peace.

The French–German case is the classic example of transition from hot war through all the stages to eventually high-level warm peace. Yet, the combination of facilitating conditions is uncommon and thus extremely difficult to recreate in other regions (notably the combination of the unconditional surrender of German nationalism in World War II, followed immediately by the emergence of the Cold War with the resultant US commitment to secure Europe and help it economically). Still, in light of the powerful nationalist rivalry between the two states until the 1940s, this development can be inspiring to other regions. At least some of the facilitating conditions noted in this section might be developed in other regions and thus make possible a transition from war to peace, even if not a smooth and perfect transition to high-level warm peace.

The conditions that make possible an effective regional integration and the warming effects of democracy are:

(1) strong and functioning states;
(2) a relatively ethnically homogeneous society or the dominance of civic nationalism over ethnic nationalism[39] (or at least ethnic issues emerging relatively late in the state-building game and in relation to other cleavages, so that party politics is not dominated by them);[40]
(3) the absence of major problems of external incongruence; and
(4) an agreement on boundaries, as contested ones reduce the prospects of successful democratization.

Conditions that are helpful also include the absence of a major refugee problem; if there are refugees, they should be well integrated into the local society. Similarly, the absence of a major over-the-frontier settler community will also be helpful.

Sequencing the stages in regional peacemaking: an integrated-gradual approach

While the three levels of peace have been described as analytically distinct, they may also be regarded as successive stages in a regional peace process, with the achievement of each stage conducive to the next. Thus, in order to enhance the likelihood of successful implementation of the liberal remedies, even if not guaranteeing it, certain conditions have to be met as described in the following stages of peacemaking derived from the analysis in the book. Due to the limitations of power-sharing arrangements and of imposing democracy, five mechanisms should be addressed: the role of the great powers as brokers and providers of security and economic aid; state-building; regional conflict resolution; civic nationalism; and regional integration, which can help to transcend ethnic nationalism and limit the ability of all the parties to act unilaterally. In some situations an additional process – defeat of the revisionist nationalist forces in the region – might have to take place in order to enable the utility of these mechanisms.

[39] See also Kupchan 1995a, p. 3. [40] See Horowitz 1994, p. 37.

Accordingly, one may suggest the following six stages in regional peacemaking:

(1) *Defeat of nationalist revisionists*, thus changing the state-to-nation balance in favor of the status quo forces in the region, as a prerequisite for regional peacemaking. If, in addition, an unmixing of ethnic populations took place during wartime and in its immediate aftermath, the state-to-nation imbalance is reduced, and states are more congruent and thus more ripe for conflict resolution following the next stages.
(2) *Third parties playing a key role*, especially the great powers, as security providers, brokers, and monitors – leading to cold peace.
(3) *State-building*, creating the conditions for normal peace by enhancing the capacity of institutions and provision of services by functioning states in the region.
(4) *Conflict resolution*, leading to normal peace among regional states manifested by the acceptance of permanent boundaries (resolving territorial and boundary disputes based as much as possible on enhancing state-to-nation congruence; no right of return for refugees and no over-the-frontier settlements; partition only if there is intense violence and territorial concentrations on ethnonational basis). The regional conflict resolution and the evolving normal peace can be conducive also to domestic developments, notably:
(5) *Democratization* and the encouragement of civic nationalism (or, if appropriate due to the strength of ethnic nationalism, power-sharing or federalism); and
(6) *Regional integration* of liberal democracies.

Thus, in more general terms, the causal chain between the key concepts of security, peace, and democracy is the following:

Security (cold peace guaranteed by defeat of revisionists, great power management, and/or strong status quo states)

↓

Peace (normal peace achieved by regional conflict resolution among strong states)

↓

Democracy (high-level warm peace including regional integration and cooperation).

I illustrate now how the idea of a gradual progress toward a warm peace can be implemented, for example, in the Middle East, using successively the three peacemaking strategies discussed in chapters 7 and 8. However, such an implementation will be a struggle because there are still strong forces that increase the state-to-nation imbalance in the region. These are irredentist/nationalist forces on both sides advancing competing claims over boundaries and territories but, in fact, each reinforcing the other's political appeal in its own camp: Jewish settlers in the occupied territories and their right-wing supporters inside Israel; Palestinian refugees claiming the right of return and the commitment of the Palestinian leadership to this claim; and a major nationalist-religious struggle over the future of Jerusalem.

Because of the great differences of opinion between Israel and the Palestinians and their mutual distrust, a negotiated accord does not seem very likely in the near future, especially after the coming to power of the militant Hamas in the Palestinian Authority. Most Israelis have lost the belief both in a negotiated peace in the framework of a "New Middle East" and in the expansionist "Greater Israel." Thus, Israeli unilateral steps such as disengagement from large parts of the West Bank and the construction of a security fence are most likely in the foreseeable future, though the willingness in Israel to implement such a disengagement declined drastically following the recent war with Hezbollah in summer 2006. These steps reduce the state-to-nation incongruence because they reduce, even if not completely terminating, foreign occupation and settlements; they are thus welcome. In order to reach a stable peace, however, both an agreement among the parties and an intense international engagement are essential.

At the first stage, the United States can help in resolving the Palestinian problem – a major source of instability in the whole Middle East region – by brokering a negotiated agreement on the establishment of a Palestinian state. This brokerage should offer economic and security carrots to those who are willing to cooperate as well as sticks to the obstructionists. The brokerage should also include multilateral components of cooperation with the other major powers, notably the Europeans, as well as others, such as the Russians and the UN, as reflected in the Quartet and its "road map" to peace. The international dimension should include tough diplomatic brokerage, NATO deployment to ensure a secure environment, and major economic aid for parties that show flexibility and moderation. Such a hegemonic – or, less likely, concert-brokered – settlement may produce only a cold peace.

A clear-cut political separation between the two parties (Israel and the Palestinians) is likely to reduce the points of potential clash among them. American security guarantees and reassurances to both sides can diminish their mutual fears and security dilemmas. Over time a normal peace may evolve to the extent that the demarcation of recognized boundaries and mutual recognition will confer legitimacy on each state by the public of the other side. Having a state of their own will increase the Palestinian stake in the status quo (due to fears of what they could lose if they behave aggressively) and will reduce the appeal of the revisionist/irredentist forces, leading, in turn, to a reciprocal decline in the power of the revisionists inside Israel. The fulfillment of the national aspirations of the Palestinians is likely also to diminish the power of radical pan-Arabism, since fighting for the stateless Palestinians has ostensibly been one of its main causes. It might also diminish the power of Al Qaeda, which thrives on the suffering of various Muslim groups in Kashmir, Chechnya, and Palestine.

The Palestinian state, for its part, will have to disarm the remaining revisionist forces, thus establishing a strong and coherent state, which has a monopoly on the means of violence inside its territory. Such a monopoly is essential and will reduce terrorist activities against Israelis; this will increase their support of the peace process. The Palestinian state will also have to build effective institutions and create the capacity to deliver social and economic services, instead of allowing other groups (such as the Islamic organizations related to Hamas) to do so; in this way, the state will increase its domestic legitimacy at the expense of the radicals. After the recent capture of power by Hamas, this looks like an impossible mission, but it is to be hoped that the state-building process will create impartial state institutions and the external donors should insist on it. Indeed, external powers will be able to play an important role in providing aid for these purposes: both financial and know-how. But the success of this institution-building will eventually depend on the political and economic system of the Palestinians. Such a success is likely to help to absorb many Palestinian refugees in their own state and thus moderate their claim for exercising the right of return to Israel. Addressing the refugee problem will remove a major revisionist source of regional instability. Resolution of the Palestinian refugee problem will diminish the reservoir of new recruits to militant armed groups and thus reduce Israeli security fears and increase Israel's willingness to make concessions. A comprehensive settlement of the Palestinian problem will reduce opposition in the Arab world to the establishment of normal peace with Israel. In its turn, Israel must address one of the key issues of the state-to-nation imbalance by removing most of the Jewish settlements in the occupied territories, especially those that prevent a contiguous Palestinian state; Israel has started to do this in Gaza with its unilateral disengagement.

In the early stages of state-building, an immediate full-blown democratization might be too premature and might even have destabilizing consequences (similar to what happened recently with the Hamas victory), although some political accountability, economic openness, and bureaucratic reforms will be helpful. However, as soon as institution-building reaches a certain level of maturity, liberalization, encouraged by the hegemon, may produce the conditions for a warm liberal peace, including some degree of economic integration.

Regional peacemaking: summary

This study, specifically in chapters 5–8, establishes linkages between three mechanisms for regional peacemaking and three types of peace. Not less important, these chapters specify the conditions necessary for the effectiveness of these strategies. One of the mechanisms is international (great power intervention in the form of either a great power concert or hegemony) and two are regional/domestic (regional conflict resolution and regional integration).

The regional/domestic strategies are more desirable because they can bring about higher levels of peace, namely, normal peace (by conflict resolution among strong and congruent states) or high-level warm peace (through integration, but only if it takes place among liberal democracies). The international strategy can produce, at best, only a relatively low level of peace, that is, cold peace. But the international mechanism – when available – can still be useful when regional strategies are not feasible; this may be the case in some important regions. For example, the Middle East is not yet ready for a West European style of regional integration leading to high-level warm peace, due to the weakness of all the liberal factors in the region (the absence especially of liberal democracies, but also of international institutions, economic interdependence, or transnational ties); thus, former Israeli prime minister Peres's idea of a "New Middle East" (Peres 1993) is premature. Moreover, in the short term, full-blown democratization under the state-to-nation imbalance in the Middle East may be destabilizing because it may weaken status quo elites and regimes and bring to power radical Islamic fundamentalist forces (as has indeed happened recently in some countries; see chapter 4). Thus, it might also be undesirable for the purpose of promoting regional peace.

At the same time, despite some considerable progress made in the Middle East peace process during the 1990s, the regional actors have had a hard time resolving the regional state-to-nation problems on their own. There are still powerful nationalist/irredentist forces in Israel, the Arab world, and Iran. There are also strong subnational forces with transborder ties in Lebanon, Syria, Jordan, and Iraq, which challenge the stability of these states and make them incoherent. In such states, the regimes face powerful nationalist and ethnic opposition, which constrains their ability to resolve conflicts fully and to establish normal peace with ex-enemies. Yet as long as US hegemony prevails over the region, there is a window of opportunity for the establishment of a regional cold peace, which may, in turn, facilitate progress toward normal peace, that is, settling the substantive issues in dispute between Israel and the Arabs – sovereignty, boundaries, settlements, refugees, Jerusalem, and other territorial questions. Such a resolution will enhance the level of regional legitimacy, strengthen local states, and markedly reduce the danger of war.

Playing a leading role in resolving the Arab–Israeli conflict will enhance US standing in the region and thus might reduce the hostility it faces in the Arab world since its intervention in Iraq. At the same time, to resolve the severe Iraqi crisis, the United States must strengthen the Iraqi state and its security forces while exercising pressures on and providing incentives to the rival groups to reach a power-sharing agreement that includes the Sunnis in addition to the Shiites and the Kurds in some kind of a federal Iraq. If that does not work, there will be no alternative but to consider partition, although that might be a very problematic and costly option, opposed by the Sunnis and the neighboring states.

In the longer term, the resolution of the Palestinian and Iraqi conflicts, and the establishment of effective and functioning states there, should allow for the enhancement of the legitimacy of the regional order. The normal peace that will follow will be favorable for the evolution, over time, of democratization and economic interdependence in the region; thus, a high-level warm peace in a "New Middle East" will gradually emerge, even if extremely slowly and with numerous ups and downs.

As in the Middle East, an active engagement of the great powers is crucial for stabilizing another region with acute state-to-nation problems – the Balkans. Such a stabilization started to take place under US hegemony in the late 1990s, with increasing elements of a concert, involving the heavy engagement of the Europeans and the United Nations in addition to the United States.

The French–German case shows the interrelationships between state strength and state-to-nation balance and conflict resolution of residual territorial issues. While state strength helped the conflict resolution of outstanding territorial issues, this enhanced the state-to-nation balance; it thus was stabilizing and made it easier to pursue more ambitious strategies such as regional integration by liberal democracies.

The case of South America demonstrates that a regional state-to-nation balance can lead to a more or less normal peace. The strong European states also needed an active US hegemony and democracy in order to reach a higher level of peace. Yet both the South American and the West European cases show that beyond a certain point it is up to the regional parties, rather than the global powers, to move the relations to higher levels of a normal, let alone a full-blown, warm peace.

The regional/domestic factors, by addressing the actors' motivations for war and resolving (or transcending) the state-to-nation imbalance, have the big advantage that they can establish warm peace, whereas the global factors on their own can at best bring about cold peace. Warm peace is also independent of the continuing stabilizing engagement of external powers in the region. Yet, the regional/domestic prerequisites for warm peace, especially successful state-building and nation-building or democratization leading to liberal compatibility, are very demanding and hard to reach in many regions. For this reason, great power hegemony or concert can be critical in advancing peaceful regional settlements, even if only cold ones, in regions in which there are intractable state-to-nation conflicts that the regional actors have a hard time resolving without external assistance.[41]

Agenda for future research

Future research could, for example, examine the theoretical pathways to regional peace presented here in other regional settings such as various parts of Africa, Asia, and the Caucasus. These studies should examine further both the distinctive effects of each of the factors addressed here and their combined effect. The studies should explore regions in

[41] For a related point, see Kolodziej and Zartman 1996.

different historical periods but should also do a comparative case study of a set of regions at the same point in time, for example, the post-1945 era, using the present framework to control for history, polarity, dominant technologies, and so forth. More specific studies could further investigate the effects of the key factors in the following ways.

Great power engagement

An examination of all post-1945 regions as well as earlier eras according to the type of great power engagement will make it possible to study whether regions under great power hegemony or cooperation have indeed been more peaceful than those under great power competition or disengagement. A key challenge is to try to identify whether there are *any conditions* under which hegemony or cooperation could produce higher levels of peace than what is defined here as cold peace. Will such conditions hold even in cases of state-to-nation imbalances and in the absence of democracy in all key states? On the other hand, under what conditions could regions reach cold peace in the absence of great power hegemony or cooperation?

The state-to-nation balance

An investigation of the relations between the state-to-nation balance and regional stability in all post-1945 regions could ask: is a certain level of state-to-nation balance a prerequisite for what is defined here as normal peace? Are weak and nationally incongruent states able to maintain stable peace over time or will they face major challenges of instability which, even if initially domestic (civil wars), will over time have transborder/regional effects? Does a state that succeeds in state-building and nation-building serve as a stabilizing force in the region? In this context, there is an important role for specialists in comparative politics to collaborate with students of IR in identifying which states and regions have been more successful in these tasks so we will be able to examine to what extent variations in state- and nation-building affect regional stability. It is necessary to control for economic factors and investigate the causal relations among economic prosperity, state-to-nation imbalance, and violence: is the real problem here the poverty of states, which results in violence, or is the state-to-nation imbalance the key problem? For example, will China and India become more satisfied as they get richer and thus be more amenable to peaceful resolution of the key state-to-nation conflicts of Taiwan and Kashmir? Or will the likelihood of war increase in the absence of resolution of these conflicts as these states get richer and thus accumulate more power? But if these conflicts are resolved, will the likelihood of the resort to violence by China and India decrease even if they have more power, as the current study expects?

Democratization

Is democratization able to overcome the destabilizing effects of the state-to-nation imbalance or will it only aggravate the problems associated with such imbalances? Another area of comparative–IR collaboration is to examine the effects of hegemonic or cooperative liberal great powers on democratization as a major mechanism for regional peace. Since the third wave of democratization started in the middle of the 1970s (Huntington 1991), we have a much richer record of states that have gone through democratization; thus, we have a fruitful field for research. An interesting region in which to continue to explore many of these questions, and the logic of the integrated-gradual approach, is the Balkans; the region was stabilized in the late 1990s by Western military intervention, leading to steps to resolve outstanding state-to-nation issues as well as toward democratization in recent years. Thus, it would be useful to continue to examine the effects of all of these changes on the degree and level of regional peace there as well as the causal relations between conflict resolution and democratization.

The evolving situation in Iraq also tests the relations among the key variables mentioned here: hegemonic intervention, state-building and nation-building, and democratization, and their effects on domestic and regional peace. Thus far, it seems that the Iraqi case shows some of the opportunities, but mostly the limits to the ability of a hegemon to democratize and pacify a state (and a region) with major internal and external state-to-nation imbalances.

This book has found that under a high state-to-nation balance, sometimes with the help of great powers, democratization, in contrast to the view of some skeptics, warms the regional peace and brings about a higher level of regional cooperation. Under a state-to-nation imbalance, however, democratization – disappointing its most optimistic enthusiasts – might result in regional hot wars. Future studies could further elaborate and specify how best to fine-tune the various stages of regional peacemaking suggested here. While peacemakers should consider a substantial number of important factors, this study suggests that the state-to-nation balance and the role of the great powers in the region will exercise key effects on the various steps in building regional security and peace, as well as on when and how it will be best to introduce democratization.

The first steps toward regional peace should focus, with the help of the great powers, on security provision and state-building, leading to conflict resolution of outstanding state-to-nation issues. However, following some degree of stabilization and reduction of these problems, democratization should be introduced, together with the construction of some extent of civic nationalism (and, in places with powerful ethnic nationalism, power-sharing and federalism as well). How, when, to what degree, and in what order these various steps should take place – in different regional situations – should be the subject of another study.

Thus, working on resolving the state-to-nation issues in the region, and enhancing security and peace, with the help of the great powers, should precede full-blown democratization. But if democratization takes place as these issues are seriously addressed, then it could be the best source of regional high-level peace and cooperation.

This book shows that rigorous synthesis of key variables at different levels of analysis and from different schools of thought in IR and comparative politics is a useful strategy to advance our understanding of complex phenomena in world politics such as variations and transitions in regional war and peace. Such a synthesis, one hopes, might also offer some sound policy-relevant advice for the advancement of peace in those regions which are in such great need of it. As the post-9/11 world shows all too clearly, regional peace is not only relevant for the war-torn regions and their inhabitants, but also for the world as a whole, including the generally peaceful and prosperous West.

Appendix A: Comparative dimensions of the state-to-nation imbalance in the Middle East, the Balkans, South America, and Western Europe in the post-1945 era

	Middle East	Balkans[1]	South America	Western Europe
No. of illegitimate states	**4** (Israel; Kuwait; Lebanon; Jordan)	**3** (Bosnia; Croatia; Macedonia)	**0**	**0**
Nations divided among some states	**4** (Arabs; Kurds; Palestinians; the Muslim *umma*)	**3** (Croats; Serbs; Albanians)	**0**	**2** (Irish; Germans)
Pan-national movements	**2** (pan-Arabism; pan-Islam)	**0**	**0**	**0**
The "Greater state"/ irredentism	**7** (Iraq; Syria; Israel; North Yemen (toward S. Yemen 1971–1990); intermittently Egypt (toward Sudan); Turkey (N. Iraq and N. Cyprus); Yemen (parts of Saudi Arabia))[2]	**3** (Croatia toward Bosnia; Serbia toward Bosnia and Croatia; Albanians (KLA etc.) toward Serbia (Kosovo, Montenegro) and Macedonia)[3]	**1** (Argentina toward the Falklands, though it was a war against an extraregional power)	**3** (UK and Ireland toward Northern Ireland; Spain toward Gibraltar (under UK sovereignty); Austria toward South Tyrol (Italy))
Stateless refugees	**1** (Palestinians spread in a number of Arab states and occupied territories)	**4** (Albanians (Kosovars); Serbs; Croats; Bosniaks (all spread across region))	**0**	**0**
Settlers	**2** (Israelis in occupied territories; Arabs in Kurdish parts of Iraq)	**0**	**0**	**1** (Scots and English (Protestants) in Northern Ireland)
Ethnically fragmented states[4]	**17 of 22** (77%)	**6 of 8** (75%)	**8 of 13** (62%)[5]	**8 of 18** (44%)
States without nations	**10 or so** (Lebanon; Iraq; Sudan; Syria?; Jordan?; Libya; Gulf States)	**1** (Bosnia)	**0**	**0**
Transborder secessionist movements	**2** (Palestinians; Kurds)	**3** (Serbs; Albanians; Croats)	**0**	**1** (Catholics in Northern Ireland)
Internal secessionist movements[6]	**7** (4 in Iran and 3 in Lebanon)	**1** (Montenegrins in Serbia and Montenegro)	**0** (a few indigenous groups request limited autonomy, mainly for economic reasons)	**9** (3 in France, 3 in Italy, 2 in Spain, and 1 in Switzerland)

[1] Due to the rapid changes happening in this region, this column mainly describes the situation as it was in the 1990s.
[2] See Halliday 2005, pp. 207–209.
[3] On "Greater Albania," see Hedges 1999.
[4] Defined as ethnic minorities being more than 5 percent of population (see definition in ch. 3 based on Welsh 1993, p. 45). Sources include Atlapedia (accessed in 2004); CIA World Factbook (accessed in 2004); and Nahari 2001.
[5] Due to the civic nature of South American nationalism, this ethnic fragmentation has little significance for state-to-nation issues except in Guyana and Suriname (see ch. 7).
[6] Gurr 1993, Appendix, and Minorities at Risk dataset.

Comments: The Middle East has more of the dimensions of the external incongruence; this explains the greater tendency toward interstate and transborder violence (see ch. 4).

In South America there is a good match between state and nation apart from a few cases of indigenous peoples. They, at least until recently, had limited political power in relation to the immigrants-settlers from Europe, in contrast to the much stronger power of the indigenous people in the Middle East in relation to the immigrants-settlers, the Zionists. This helped to maintain regional stability in South America, especially at the interstate and transborder levels, in contrast to the protracted conflict in the Middle East (see chs. 4 and 7).

In Western Europe there are a few cases of internal incongruence and some limited and specific cases of irredentism. They are not regionwide and transborder as in the Middle East. The combination of strong states and democracy was very helpful in transcending these problems in the framework of European integration (see ch. 8).

States included in each region

Middle East: Algeria, Bahrain, Cyprus**, Egypt, Iran, Iraq, Israel, Jordan, Kuwait, Lebanon, Libya, Morocco**, Oman, Palestinian Authority (after 1993), Qatar, Saudi Arabia, Sudan, Syria, Tunisia, Turkey**, United Arab Emirates, Yemen

Balkans: Albania, Bosnia, Bulgaria, Croatia, Greece, Macedonia, Serbia and Montenegro, Slovenia

South America: Argentina, Bolivia, Brazil, Chile, Colombia, Ecuador, French Guiana, Guyana, Paraguay, Peru, Suriname, Uruguay, Venezuela

Western Europe: Andorra*, Austria, Belgium, Denmark, Finland, France, Germany, Iceland, Ireland, Italy, Liechtenstein*, Luxembourg, Malta, Monaco*, Netherlands, Norway, Portugal, San Marino*, Spain, Sweden, Switzerland, UK, Vatican City*

* Micro states are not included for table calculations.

** Morocco is included because of its Arab affiliation; Turkey and Cyprus are included based on geography and their security interdependence with other states of the region.

Appendix B: Data-file: major armed conflicts/wars by region, type, and modes of great power regional involvement (1945–2004)

Cold War era: 1945–1991

Western Europe Type of great power regional involvement: **hegemony (US)**

Conflict/war	Major cause
Greece (1945–9) (UK, Yugoslavian, Bulgarian, and Albanian intervention)	Internal factional/ ideological
Spain (1968–93[1]) Spanish government vs. Basque opposition	**State to nation**
UK (Northern Ireland) (1969–98) Protestant paramilitary and UK government vs. Catholic opposition	**State to nation**

3 wars

No. of state-to-nation wars: 2

No. of non-state-to-nation wars: 1

No. of interstate wars: 0

No. of civil wars: 3, of which no. of civil wars with foreign intervention: 1

The basis of this data-file is Holsti's lists of major armed conflicts (1991, 1996) which was expanded to include conflicts which continued into or started since the end of the cold war era. Especialy useful were the yearly (since 1993) armed conflict reports in the *Journal of Peace Research* (esp. the 2004 report) and the Uppsala Armed Conflict Dataset which was created as a consequence. Also useful were Allcock et al. 1992; Huth 1996; Project Ploughshares Armed Conflict Report 2004; and SIPRI 2004.

[1] Has operated since 1993 at a very low level.

Eastern Europe Type of great power regional involvement: **hegemony (USSR)**

Conflict/war	Major cause
USSR–Hungary (1956)	Autonomy: Hungary; national security, preserve alliance unity, protect ideological confreres: USSR; government composition
USSR–Czechoslovakia (1968)	Government composition; preserve alliance unity, protect ideological confreres: USSR

2 wars

No. of state-to-nation wars: 0

No. of non-state-to-nation wars: 2

No. of interstate wars: 2

No. of civil wars: 0, of which no. of civil wars with foreign intervention: 0

South America Type of great power regional involvement: **partial US hegemony**

Conflict/war	Major cause
Colombia (1948–58)	Internal factional/ideological
Bolivia (1952)	Internal factional/ideological
Colombia (1965–2004)	Internal factional/ideological
Chile (1973) (US intervention)	Internal factional/ideological
Argentina (1976–83)	Internal factional/ideological
Peru (1981–99)	Internal factional/ideological
Argentina–UK (Falklands) (1982)	**State to nation** + (Territory; regime survival: Argentina; protect nationals/commercial interests abroad: UK)
Peru (1984–99)	Internal factional/ideological
Suriname (1986)	Internal factional/ideological

9 wars

No. of state-to-nation wars: 1

No. of non-state-to-nation wars: 8

No. of interstate wars: 1

No. of civil wars: 8, of which no. of civil wars with foreign intervention: 1

Central America and the Caribbean Type of great power regional involvement: **hegemony (US)**

Conflict/war	Major cause
Costa Rica (1948)	Internal factional/ideological
Guatemala (1954) (Honduran and Nicaraguan intervention)	Internal factional/ideological
Cuba (1956–9)	Internal factional/ideological
Nicaragua–Honduras (1957)	Territory; enforce treaty obligations (arbitral award): Honduras
Nicaragua (1960–79)	Internal factional/ideological
Cuba–United States (1961)	Government composition and ideological liberation: USA; regime survival: Cuba
Dominican Republic (1965) (US intervention)	Internal factional/ideological, government composition; protect nationals/ commercial interests abroad: US; population protection/peacekeeping: US
Guatemala (1966–95)	Internal factional/ideological
El Salvador–Honduras (1969)	Territory (border dispute); protect nationals abroad: El Salvador; prevent population movement/refugees and enforce domestic legislation: Honduras
El Salvador (1979–91) (US intervention)	Internal factional/ideological
Nicaragua (1981–90) (US intervention)	Internal factional/ideological
Grenada (1983) (US, Jamaican, Barbadian, and Organization of East Caribbean States intervention)	Internal factional/ideological
Panama (1989–90)	US invasion to arrest Panamanian leader Manuel Noriega for drug conspiracy

13 wars

No. of state-to-nation wars: 0

No. of non-state-to-nation wars: 13

No. of interstate wars: 4 (including Panama)

No. of civil wars: 9, of which no. of civil wars with foreign intervention: 5

Southeast Asia Type of great power regional involvement: **competition**

Conflict/war	Major cause
Indonesia (1945–9) Dutch colonial administration vs. nationalist opposition	**State to nation** (anti-colonial/national liberation)

(*cont.*)

Conflict/war	Major cause
North Vietnam (1946–54) French colonial administration vs. nationalist opposition	**State to nation** (anti-colonial liberation, national unification; ideological liberation: North Vietnam)
Malaysia (1948–60) (UK intervention)	Internal factional/ideological
Myanmar (1948–2004) (Chinese intervention) Myanmar government vs. Karen rebels	**State to nation**
Myanmar (1948–1994) Myanmar government vs. Araken rebels	**State to nation**
Myanmar (1949–2003?[2]) Myanmar government vs. Shan rebels	**State to nation**
Indonesia (1950) Indonesian government vs. South Moluccan rebels	**State to nation**
Philippines (1950–5)	Internal factional/ideological
Myanmar (1957–2004) Myanmar government vs. Karenni national progressive party (KNPP)	**State to nation**
South Vietnam–North Vietnam (1958–75) (US intervention)	**State to nation** (national unification and ideological liberation: North Vietnam; regime/state survival: South Vietnam)
Indonesia (1958–9) Indonesian government vs. West Sumatran rebels	**State to nation**
Laos (1960–74) (US and North Vietnamese intervention)	Internal factional/ideological
Myanmar (1961–95) Myanmar government vs. Kachin rebels	**State to nation**
Indonesia (1962–3) Dutch colonial administration in West Irian vs. Indonesia	**State to nation** (anti-colonial liberation)
Brunei (1962) (UK intervention) Brunei government vs. rebels in Sarawak and North Borneo opposed to entry of Brunei into Malaysian Federation	**State to nation**

[2] Continued fighting in 2003 uncertain.

Conflict/war	Major cause
Indonesia–Malaysia (1963–6) (UK, Australian, and New Zealand intervention)	**State to nation** (territory: West Irian; colonialism: Indonesia, a demand of self-determination for peoples of Sarawak and Sabah; maintain integrity of state: Malaysia)
Indonesia (1965–6) (UK intervention)	Internal factional/ideological
Indonesia (1965–2004) Indonesian government vs. OPM rebels in Irian Jaya	**State to nation**
Philippines (1968–2004) Philippine government vs. communist party of the Philippines (CPP/NPA)	Internal factional/ideological
Cambodia/Kampuchea (1970–5) (US and North Vietnamese intervention)	Internal factional/ideological
Philippines (1972–2004) (US intervention) Philippine government vs. MNLF, MILF (Moro) rebels, and Abu Sayyaf group	**State to nation**
East Timor–Indonesia (1975) Indonesian annexation of East Timor	**State to nation** (national liberation/state creation: East Timor; national consolidation: Indonesia)
Indonesia (1975–2000) Indonesian government and associated paramilitary and militia groups vs. FRETILIN (Timorese) rebels (UN and Australian intervention)	**State to nation**
Cambodia/Kampuchea (1977–9) (Vietnamese intervention)	Internal factional/ideological
Cambodia/Kampuchea–Vietnam (1978–9)	**State to nation** (In most of the areas in dispute Cambodia claimed Vietnamese territory populated by sizable Cambodian minorities) + government composition, humanitarian aid, maintain regional dominance: Vietnam; regime survival: Cambodia
China–Vietnam (1979)	Maintain regional dominance; territory (Spratly, Paracel)

(*cont.*)

Conflict/war	Major cause
Cambodia/Kampuchea (1980–99) (Vietnamese and Thai intervention)	Internal factional/ideological
Papua New Guinea (1988–97) Papua New Guinea government vs. BRA rebels	**State to nation**
Indonesia (1989–2004) Indonesian government vs. Aceh rebels	**State to nation**
Myanmar (1990) Myanmar government vs. new Mon state party (NMSP)	**State to nation**

30 wars

No. of state-to-nation wars (3 anti-colonial wars included): 21

No. of non-state-to-nation wars: 9

No. of interstate wars: 4

No. of civil wars: 23, of which no. of civil wars with foreign intervention: 10

East Asia Type of great power regional involvement: **competition**

Conflict/war	Major cause
China (1946–58) (US intervention)	Internal factional/ideological
North Korea–South Korea (1950–53) (Chinese, US, and UN intervention)	**State to nation** (national unification and ideological liberation: North Korea; state/regime survival: South Korea)
China–Tibet (1950–1) Chinese annexation of Tibet/Xizang province	**State to nation** (national consolidation and ideological liberation: China; state/regime survival: Tibet)
China (1958–95[3]) Chinese government vs. Tibetan rebels in Xizang province	**State to nation**
China (1966–83)	Internal factional/ideological
China–USSR (1969)	Territory

6 wars

No. of state-to-nation wars: 3

No. of non-state-to-nation wars: 3

[3] No new information found on conflict after 1995.

No. of interstate wars: 3
No. of civil wars: 3, of which no. of civil wars with foreign intervention: 1

South Asia Type of great power regional involvement: **competition**

Conflict/war	Major cause
India (1946–7)	Internal factional/ideological
India–Pakistan (1947–9)	**State to nation** (ethnic/religious unification: Pakistan; national consolidation: India) + territory
India–Hyderabad (1948) Indian annexation of Hyderabad	**State to nation** (national consolidation: India; state survival: Hyderabad)
India (1955–69) Indian government vs. Naga rebels	**State to nation**
India (1961) Indian government vs. Portuguese colonial administrations in Goa, Daman, and Diu	**State to nation** (anti-colonial liberation; national consolidation: India)
India–China (1962)	Territory (border dispute)
India–Pakistan (1965)	**State to nation** (ethnic/religious unity: Pakistan; national consolidation: India) + territory
India (1966–8) Indian government vs. Mizo rebels	**State to nation**
India (1968–2004) Indian government + Green Tigers vigilante group vs. Naxalites/PWG and various communist groups	Internal factional/ideological
Sri Lanka (1971)	Internal factional/ideological
Pakistan (1971) (Indian intervention) Pakistani government vs. Bangladeshi rebels in East Pakistan	**State to nation**
Mukti Bahini (India)–Pakistan (1971)	**State to nation** + (territory (Kashmir), prevent population movement/refugees: India; maintain integrity of state: Pakistan)
Pakistan (1973–7) (Afghan intervention) Pakistani government vs. Baluchi rebels	**State to nation**

(*cont.*)

Conflict/war	Major cause
Bangladesh (1974–1992) Bangladeshi government vs. Chittagong tribal people	**State to nation**
Afghanistan (1975–91) (USSR intervention) Afghan government vs. mujahideen rebels	Internal factional/ideological
India (1977–97) Indian government vs. Naga NSCN rebels (Burmese intervention)	**State to nation**
India (1981–95) Indian government vs. Sikh rebels	**State to nation**
India (1982–2004) Indian government vs. UNLF rebels in Manipur	**State to nation**
India (1982–2004) Indian government vs. Kashmiri rebels	**State to nation**
Sri Lanka (1984–2004) (Indian intervention) Sri Lankan government vs. LTTE (Tamilese) rebels	**State to nation**
India (1988–2003?[4]) Indian government vs. Bodo rebels in Assam (Burmese intervention)	**State to nation**
India (1988–2004) Indian government vs. Assamese rebels (mostly ULFA) in Assam (Burmese, Bhutanese intervention)	**State to nation**

22 wars

No. of state-to-nation wars: 17 (1 anti-colonial war included)

No. of non-state-to-nation wars: 5

No. of interstate wars: 5

No. of civil wars: 16, of which no. of civil wars with foreign intervention: 5

[4] Conflict may be over with peace agreement with main faction in December 2003 and subsequent laying down of arms.

Africa Type of great power regional involvement: **competition**

Conflict/war	Major cause
Madagascar (1947–8) French colonial administration vs. nationalist opposition	**State to nation** (anti-colonial liberation)
Kenya (1952–63) UK colonial administration vs. nationalist opposition	**State to nation** (anti-colonial liberation)
Cameroon (1955–60) UK and French colonial administrations vs. nationalist opposition	**State to nation** (anti-colonial liberation)
Rwanda (1956–65) Hutu government vs. Tutsi rebels	**State to nation**
Zaire (Democratic Republic of Congo) (1960–5) (Belgian and UN intervention) Zairean government vs. FNLC rebels in Shaba	**State to nation**
South Africa (1960–94)	Internal factional/ideological
Angola (1961–74) (USSR and South African intervention) Portuguese colonial administration vs. nationalist opposition	**State to nation** (anti-colonial liberation)
Guinea-Bissau (1962–74) Portuguese colonial administration vs. nationalist opposition	**State to nation** (anti-colonial liberation)
Somalia–Ethiopia (1963–4)	**State to nation** (irredentist claims toward Ogaden area, inhabited by nomadic pastoral peoples belonging ethnically to the Somali nation: Somalia; protect integrity of state: Ethiopia)
Somalia–Kenya (1963–7)	**State to nation** (Somali irredentism: unification of the Somali nation or demand for self-determination for Somalis within Kenya)
Mozambique (1965–75) Portuguese colonial administration vs. nationalist opposition	**State to nation** (anti-colonial liberation) + ideological liberation
Chad (1966–78) (Libyan intervention)	Internal factional/ideological

Conflict/war	Major cause
Uganda (1966) Ugandan government vs. Bugandan rebels	**State to nation**
Namibia (1966–89) South African government vs. nationalist opposition	**State to nation** (anti-colonial liberation)
Biafra–Nigeria (1967–70) Nigerian government vs. Ibo rebels in Biafra	**State to nation** (secession/independence, ethnic/religious unification: Biafra; maintain integrity of state: Nigeria) + commerce/resources
Rhodesia (1967–80) Rhodesian government vs. nationalist opposition	**State to nation** (anti-colonial liberation)
Ethiopia (1971–92) Ethiopian government vs. EPLF (Eritrean) rebels	**State to nation**
Burundi (1972) Tutsi-led government vs. Hutu rebels	**State to nation**
Angola (1974–2002) (South African, Cuban intervention)	Internal factional/ideological, government composition; commerce/resources
Ethiopia (1975–92) Ethiopian government vs. ALF rebels	**State to nation**
Ethiopia (1975–92) Ethiopian government vs. EPRP rebels	**State to nation**
Mozambique (1975–94)	Internal factional/ideological
Ethiopia (1976–92) Ethiopian government vs. TPLF rebels	**State to nation**
Ethiopia (1977–92) Ethiopian government vs. OLF rebels	**State to nation**
Zaire (Democratic Republic of Congo) (1977–8) (French and Belgian intervention) Zairean government vs. FNLC rebels	**State to nation**
Somalia–Ethiopia (1977–80)	**State to nation** (ethnic unification: Somalia; protect integrity of state: Ethiopia) + strategic territory
Uganda–Tanzania (1978–9)	Territory (border dispute), government composition: Tanzania
Chad (1979–82)	Internal factional/ideological

Conflict/war	Major cause
Nigeria (1980–4)	Internal factional/ideological
Ghana (1981) Tribal fighting (Nanumbas vs. Konkombas)	**State to nation**
Uganda (1981–5)	Internal factional/ideological
Somalia (1981–91) Somali government vs. SNM rebels	**State to nation**
Chad (1982–7) (Libyan, French, and Organization of African Unity intervention)	Internal factional/ideological, government composition; commerce/resources, territory: Chad and Libya
Senegal (1983–2004) Senegalese government vs. Casamance rebels	**State to nation**
Mali–Burkina Faso (1985)	**State to nation** (Malian irredentist claims toward Beli region, inhabited by Malians, based on geographic and historical grounds)
Uganda (1985–6)	Internal factional/ideological
Uganda (1986–2004)	Internal factional/ideological
Burundi (1988–92) Tutsi government massacre of Hutu civilians	**State to nation**
Mauritania–Senegal (1989–91)	Territory (border dispute)
Chad (1989–2003) Chadian government vs. MDJT	Internal factional/ideological
Somalia (1989–91) Somali government vs. SPM rebels	**State to nation**
Somalia (1990–4) (US and UN intervention) Somali government vs. USC and SNA rebels	**State to nation**
Chad (1990–1)	Internal factional/ideological
Mali (1990–4) Mali government vs. Tuareg rebels	**State to nation**
Niger (1990–7) Niger government vs. Tuareg rebels	**State to nation**

45 wars

No. of state-to-nation wars: 31 (8 anti-colonial wars included).

No. of non-state-to-nation wars: 14

No. of interstate wars: 6

No. of civil wars: 31, of which no. of civil wars with foreign intervention: 7

Middle East Type of great power regional involvement: **competition**

Conflict/war	Major cause
Syria (1945–6) French colonial administration vs. nationalist opposition	**State to nation** (anti-colonial liberation)
Israel (1946–8) UK colonial administration vs. nationalist Jewish opposition	**State to nation** (anti-colonial liberation)
Israel–Arab League states (1948–9)	**State to nation** (national liberation/state creation: Israel; nation survival, protect ethnic/religious confreres: Arab League states)
Tunisia (1952–6) French colonial administration vs. nationalist opposition	**State to nation** (anti-colonial liberation)
Morocco (1953–6) (Spanish intervention) French colonial administration vs. nationalist opposition	**State to nation** (anti-colonial liberation)
Algeria (1954–62) French colonial administration vs. nationalist opposition	**State to nation** (anti-colonial liberation)
Sudan (1955–2004) Sudanese government vs. insurgent southern provinces	**State to nation**
Cyprus (1955–60) UK colonial administration vs. nationalist opposition	**State to nation** (anti-colonial liberation)
Israel (UK, France)–Egypt (1956)	**State to nation** + strategic territory: Israel, UK; autonomy: Egypt; prevent regional hegemony: UK; commerce/navigation
Oman (1957) (UK intervention)	Internal factional/ideological
Lebanon (1958) (US and Syrian intervention)	Internal factional/ideological
Iraq (1959) Iraqi government vs. Shammar rebels	**State to nation**
Iraq (1961–2003) (Iranian intervention) Iraqi government vs. Kurdish rebels	**State to nation**

Conflict/war	Major cause
Yemen (1962–7) (Egyptian and Saudi Arabian intervention)	Internal factional/ideological
Algeria–Morocco (1962)	**State to nation** (Morocco laid claim to western sections of southern Algeria based on historical argument that these territories had been part of Morocco in precolonial times)
Cyprus (1963–4) (UN and UK intervention) Cypriot government vs. rebel Turks	**State to nation**
South Yemen (1963–7) UK colonial administration vs. nationalist opposition	**State to nation**
Israel (1964–2004) Israeli government vs. PLO and non-PLO rebels	**State to nation**
Israel–Egypt, Syria, Jordan (1967)	**State to nation** + national survival: Israel; strategic territory; commerce/navigation: Egypt
Oman (1968–76) (UK, Iranian, and South Yemeni intervention) Omani government vs. Dhofari rebels	**State to nation**
Jordan (1970) Jordanian army vs. PLO rebels	**State to nation**
Israel–Egypt (1969–70) (USSR intervention)	**State to nation**
Yemen–South Yemen (1971–90) (Saudi Arabian intervention)	**State to nation** (North Yemen's desire to incorporate South Yemen into a Greater Yemen state)
Egypt, Syria–Israel (1973)	**State to nation** + territory; strategic territory; national survival: Israel
Cyprus (1974) (Turkish intervention) Cypriot government vs. rebel Turks	**State to nation** (protect ethnic confreres: Turkey; ethnic unification: Cyprus; autonomy: Turkish Cypriots) + government composition

(*cont.*)

Conflict/war	Major cause
Morocco, Mauritania/Western Sahara (1975–93[5]) Morocco, Mauritania (to 1979) governments vs. Polisario rebels	**State to nation** (national liberation/state creation: Polisario; ethnic/language unification: Mauritania) + territory; commerce/resources: Morocco, Mauritania
Lebanon (1975–91) (Syrian, Israeli, and UN intervention)	**State to nation** + internal factional/ideological Syria–Lebanon: government composition; strategic territory, protect population/peacekeeping: Syria Israel–PLO; strategic territory, protect domestic population: Israel; national liberation/state creation: PLO
Syria (1976–87) Syrian government vs. Sunni Muslim Brotherhood rebels	Internal factional/ideological
Libya–Egypt (1977)	Territory (border dispute)
Iran (1978–9) Iranian (Shah) government vs. fundamental Islamic (Khomeini) rebels	Internal factional/ideological **Also state to nation because of pan-Islamic ideology?**
Iran–Iraq (1979–89)	**State to nation** + strategic territory; territory: Iran, Iraq
South Yemen–North Yemen (1979)	**State to nation** (national unification: South Yemen)
Iran (1979–94) (Iraqi intervention) Iranian government vs. Kurdish rebels	**State to nation**
Iran (1979–2003) (Iraqi intervention) Iranian government vs. mujahedeen Khalq	Internal factional/ideological
Iraq (1980–2003) (Iranian intervention) Iraqi government vs. Supreme Assembly for the Islamic Revolution in Iraq rebels	Internal factional/ideological
Turkey (1984–2004) Turkish government vs. Pesh Merga (PKK) rebels	**State to nation**
South Yemen (1986–7)	Internal factional/ideological

[5] No new information about significant armed conflict found after 1993.

37 wars
No. of state-to-nation wars: 28 (7 anti-colonial wars included)
No. of non-state-to-nation wars: 9 (including Iran 1978–9)
No. of interstate wars: 10
No. of civil wars: 20, of which no. of civil wars with foreign intervention: 10

Post-Cold War era: 1991–2004[6]

Southeast Asia

Conflict/war	Major cause
Laos (1992)	Internal factional/ideological
Myanmar (1991–2) Myanmar government vs. ABSDF (All Burma Students' Democratic Front)	Internal factional/ideological

2 wars
No. of state-to-nation wars: 0
No. of non-state-to-nation wars: 2
No. of interstate wars: 0
No. of civil wars: 2, of which no. of civil wars with foreign intervention: 0

South Asia

Conflict/war	Major cause
India (1992–2004) Indian government vs. Tripura tribal rebels	**State to nation**
Afghanistan (1992–2001) (Pakistani intervention)	**State to nation – civil wars in incoherent states** + internal factional/ideological
Pakistan (1992–9) Pakistani government vs. MQM rebels (Mohajirs) vs. QMG rebels (Sindah nationalists)	**State to nation**

[6] I have followed Eriksson and Wallensteen (2004) in leaving out armed conflicts in which Al Qaeda is the exclusive anti-government protagonist due to the unique nature of this type of conflict. If this type of conflict were included, there would be at least two more armed conflicts: the United States vs. Al Qaeda (2001–4) and Saudi Arabia vs. Al Qaeda (2003–4). The Al Qaeda cases might, however, also be related to state-to-nation imbalances, as discussed in ch. 9.

India (1993) Indian government vs. Jharkand Mukti Morcha	**State to nation**
Nepal (1996–2004) Nepalese government vs. Communist Party of Nepal–Maoist (CPN)	Internal factional/ideological
Pakistan (1999–2004) Pakistani government vs. Sunni Muslim militant groups vs. Shiite Muslim militant groups	Internal factional/ideological
Afghanistan (2001–4) Afghani government (US, US-led coalition, Pakistan) vs. Taliban + Islamic party + Al Qaeda (?)	**State to nation – civil wars in incoherent states** + internal factional/ideological

7 wars

No. of state-to-nation wars: 5

No. of non-state-to-nation wars: 2

No. of interstate wars: 0

No. of civil wars: 7, of which no. of civil wars with foreign intervention: 2

Balkans

Conflict/war	Major cause
Slovenia–Serbia (1991)	**State to nation**
Croatia–Serbia (1991)	**State to nation**
Croatia (1990–5) (UN intervention) Croatian government vs. Serbian rebels in Krajina	**State to nation**
Bosnia-Herzegovina (1992–5) (UN intervention) Bosnian (Muslim) government vs. Serb irregulars vs. Croat irregulars	**State to nation**
Serbia (1998–9) Serbian government vs. Albanian rebels (UCK) (NATO intervention)	**State to nation**
Serbia (2000–3) Serbia + Nato KFOR (Kosovo Force Peace Keeping Mission) vs. Albanian irregulars (area under UN administration)	**State to nation**
Macedonia (2001) Macedonian government vs. Albanian rebels (UCK)	**State to nation**

7 wars
No. of state-to-nation wars: 7
No. of non-state-to-nation wars: 0
No. of interstate wars: 2
No. of civil wars: 5, of which no. of civil wars with foreign intervention: 4

Middle East

Conflict/war	Major cause
Iraq–Kuwait (1990)	**State to nation** (Iraqi invasion of Kuwait in pursuit of "Greater Iraq" territorial designs)
Turkey (1991–2) Turkish government vs. Devirimci Sol (revolutionary left)	Internal factional/ideological
Iraq–Gulf Allies (1991) (UN intervention)	**State to nation**
Egypt (1992–5) Egyptian government vs. fundamentalist Islamic rebels	Internal factional/ideological
Algeria (1992–2004) Algerian government vs. fundamentalist Islamic rebels	Internal factional/ideological
Lebanon (1992–2004[7])	**State to nation** + Israeli intervention in southern Lebanon/self-declared security zone against Lebanese-based Amal, Hezbollah, and Hamas guerrillas
Yemen (1994) Northern forces loyal to President Saleh vs. southern forces loyal to Vice President Al-Baid	**State to nation**
Sudan (2003–4) Sudanese government + Janjaweed and various Arab militias vs. insurgent western provinces (Darfur)	**State to nation**
Iraq–US (UK, Australia, and others) (2003)	Enforce Security Council resolutions, stop proliferation, use of WMD, democratization: US; regime survival: Iraq
Iraq (2003–4) US-led coalition and Iraqi provisional government vs. various insurgent groups (Sunni, Shiite, foreign)	**State to nation**

[7] In summer 2006, a major clash erupted between Israel and Hezbollah.

10 wars
No. of state-to-nation wars: 6
No. of non-state-to-nation wars: 4
No. of interstate wars: 4
No. of civil wars: 6, of which no. of civil wars with foreign intervention: 0

Africa

Conflict/war	Major cause
Djibouti (1991–4) (French intervention)	Internal factional/ideological
Liberia (1991–6) (Economic Community of West African States Monitoring Group and Burkina Faso intervention)	Internal factional/ideological
Sierra Leone (1991–2002)	Internal factional/ideological
Rwanda (1991–3) (UN intervention) Rwandan (Hutu-led) government vs. Tutsi-dominated RPF rebels	**State to nation**
Chad (1991–3)	Internal factional/ideological
Zaire (Democratic Republic of Congo) (1993)	Internal factional/ideological
Zaire (Democratic Republic of Congo) (1993–4) Government-sanctioned ethnic "cleansing" in Shaba	**State to nation**
Burundi (1993–2004) Burundian government vs. Hutu rebels (African Union intervention)	**State to nation**
Angola (1994–2004) Angolan government vs. Cabindan rebels	**State to nation**
Rwanda (1994–2001) RPF (Tutsi-led) government vs. Hutu rebels	**State to nation**
Democratic Republic of Congo (Zaire) (1996–2004) Democratic Republic of Congo, Zimbabwe, Angola, Namibia, and various militias vs. RCD, UPC, MCL (and various split factions and militias), Uganda, Rwanda, Burundi (UN intervention)	**State to nation**
Cameroon–Nigeria (1996)	Border dispute (commerce/economic)

Conflict/war	Major cause
Niger (1996–7) Niger government vs. Toubou rebels	**State to nation**
Ethiopia (1996–9) Ethiopian government vs. Somali rebels	**State to nation**
Ethiopia (1996) government vs. Afar rebels	**State to nation**
Guinea-Bissau (1998–9) (Senegalese and Guinean intervention)	Internal factional/ideological
Eritrea (1997–2003) Eritrean government vs. Eritrea Islamic Jihad	Internal factional/ideological
Somalia (1997–2004) interclan fighting	**State to nation**
Comoros (1997) Comoros government vs. MPA rebels (Anjouan)	**State to nation**
Congo-Brazzaville (1997–9) Congo-Brazzaville government and Cobra militia vs. Cocoye and Ninja militias (Angolan intervention)	Internal factional/ideological
Ethiopia–Eritrea (1998–2000)	**State to nation**[8]
Ethiopia (1999–2004) Ethiopian government vs. OLF (Oromiya) rebels	**State to nation**
Guinea (2000–1) Guinean government vs. RDFG	Internal factional/ideological
Liberia (2000–4) Liberian government vs. LURD and MODEL insurgents (Economic Community of West African States Monitoring Group and US, UN, Guinea?, Cote D'Ivoire?, Sierra Leone? intervention)	Internal factional/ideological
Central African Republic (2002–3)	Internal factional/ideological
Côte d'Ivoire (2002–4) Côte d'Ivoire government vs. MJP, MPIGO rebels (French, Liberian, and Economic Community of West African States intervention)	Internal factional/ideological

26 wars
No. of state-to-nation wars: 13
No. of non-state-to-nation wars: 13
No. of interstate wars: 3 (1 war combination civil and interstate)

[8] See SIPRI 1999, pp. 18–21, and Gilkes and Plaut 1999.

No. of civil wars: 23, of which no. of civil wars with foreign intervention: 8

Central America and the Caribbean

Conflict/war	Major cause
Haiti (1991–4) (US and UN intervention)	Internal factional/ideological

1 war
No. of state-to-nation wars: 0
No. of non-state-to-nation wars: 1
No. of interstate wars: 0
No. of civil wars: 1, of which no. of civil wars with foreign intervention: 0

Former USSR

Conflict/war	Major cause
Azerbaijan (1989–95) (Armenian intervention) Azerbaijan government vs. rebel forces in Nagorno-Karabakh	**State to nation**
Moldova (1992) Moldovan government vs. Slav rebels in Transdnestr region	**State to nation**
Georgia (1992–4) Georgian government vs. rebels in South Ossetia	**State to nation**
Georgia (1992–4) Georgian government vs. rebels in Abkhazia	**State to nation**
Georgia (1992–4)	Internal factional/ideological
Tajikistan (1992–2000) (Uzbek and Russian intervention)	Internal factional/ideological
Russia (1995–6) Russian government vs. rebel Chechen separatists	**State to nation**
Russia (1999) Russian government vs Dagestan	**State to nation**
Russia (1999–2004) Russian government vs. rebel Chechen separatists	**State to nation**
Uzbekistan (1999–2000) (Kyrgyz intervention)	Internal factional/ideological

10 wars
No. of state-to-nation wars: 7
No. of non-state-to-nation wars: 3
No. of interstate wars: 0
No. of civil wars: 10, of which no. of civil wars with foreign intervention: 3

Summary tables:

Cold War era: 1945–1991

	Western Europe	Eastern Europe	South America	Central America and Caribbean	Southeast Asia	East Asia	South Asia	Africa	Middle East	Total
No. of wars	3	2	9	13	30	6	22	45	37	167
No. and % of state-to-nation wars	2 66.6%	0 0%	1 11%	0 0%	21 70%	3 50%	17 77%	31 69%	28 76%	103 62%
No. and % of civil wars	3 100%	0 0%	8 89%	9 69%	23 77%	3 50%	16 73%	31 69%	20 54%	113 69%
No. and % of civil wars with external intervention (of total civil wars)	1 33.3%	0 0%	1 12.5%	5 55.5%	10 43%	1 33%	5 31%	7 23%	10 50%	40 35%

Post-Cold War era: 1991–2004 *(includes only those conflicts beginning or recommencing since start of era)*

	Balkans	Former USSR	Central America and Caribbean	Southeast Asia	South Asia	Africa	Middle East	Total
No. of wars	7	10	1	2	7	26	10	63
No. and % of state-to-nation wars	7	7	0	0	5	13	6	38
	100%	70%	0%	0%	71%	50%	60%	60%
No. and % of civil wars	5	10	1	2	7	23	6	54
	71%	100%	100%	100%	100%	88%	60%	86%
No. and % of civil wars with external intervention (of total civil wars)	4	3	1	0	2	8	0	18
	80%	30%	100%	0%	29%	35%	0%	33%

Bibliography

9/11 Commission, 2004. *The 9//11 Commission Report: Final Report of the National Commission on Terrorist Attacks Upon the United States*. New York: W. W. Norton.

Adenauer, Konrad 1965. *Erinnerungen* [*Memories*], vol. I. Hamburg: Fischer-Bucherei.

Adler, Emanuel 1991. "Seasons of Peace: Progress in Postwar International Security," in Adler, Emanuel and Crawford, Beverley (eds.) 1991. *Progress in International Relations*. New York: Columbia University Press, pp. 128–173.

Adler, Emanuel and Barnett, Michael (eds.) 1998. *Pluralistic Security Communities*. Cambridge: Cambridge University Press.

Ajami, Fouad 1978/9. "The End of Pan-Arabism," *Foreign Affairs* 57(2): 355–373.

1981. *The Arab Predicament*. Cambridge: Cambridge University Press.

1982. "The Arab Road," *Foreign Policy* 47: 3–25.

Allcock, John B. et al. 1992. *Border and Territorial Disputes*, rev. 3rd edn. London: Longman.

Alpher, Joseph and Shikaki, Khalil et al. 1999. "Concept Paper: The Palestinian Refugee Problem and the Right of Return," *Middle East Policy* 6: 167–189.

Alter, Peter 1992. "Nationalism and German Politics After 1945," in Breuilly, John (ed.) 1992. *The State of Germany: The National Idea in the Making, Unmaking and Remaking of a Modern Nation-State*. New York: Longman, pp. 154–176.

Anderson, Benedict 1991. *Imagined Communities: Reflections on the Origins and Spread of Nationalism*, 2nd edn. London: Verso.

Anderson, Matthew 1966. *The Eastern Question, 1774–1923: A Study in International Relations*. New York: St. Martin's Press.

Andreski, Stanislav 1992. *Wars, Revolutions, Dictatorships: Studies of Historical and Contemporary Problems from a Comparative Viewpoint*. London: Frank Cass.

Arens, Moshe 1995. *Broken Covenant: American Foreign Policy and the Crisis Between the US and Israel*. New York: Simon & Schuster.

Arreguin-Toft, Ivan 2005. *How the Weak Win Wars*. Cambridge: Cambridge University Press.

Art, Robert J. 1992. "A Defensible Defense: America's Grand Strategy After the Cold War," in Lynn-Jones, Sean M. and Miller, Steven E. (eds.) 1992. *America's Strategy in a Changing World*. Cambridge, MA: MIT Press, pp. 68–118.

1996. "Why Western Europe Needs the United States and NATO," *Political Science Quarterly* 111(1): 1–39.

Atherton, Alfred 1994. "The US and the Suez Crisis: The Diplomacy and Its Limitations," in Shemsh, Moshe and Troen, Ilan (eds.) 1994. *The Suez–Sinai Crisis 1956: Retrospective and Reappraisal*. Beer-Sheva: Ben-Gurion University Press (Hebrew).

Atlapedia Online Atlas and factbook, www.atlapedia.com.

Auty, Phyllis 1965. *Yugoslavia*. New York: Walker & Company.

Avi-Ran, Rueven 1986. *The Syrian Involvement in Lebanon*. Tel Aviv: Maarchot (Hebrew).

Avineri, Shlomo 1994. "Comments on Nationalism and Democracy," in L. Diamond and Plattner 1994, pp. 28–31.

Axelrod, Robert 1984. *The Evolution of Cooperation*. New York: Basic Books.

Ayoob, Mohammed 1993. "Unraveling the Concept: 'National Security' in the Third World," in Korany, Noble, and Brynen 1993, pp. 31–56.

1995. *The Third World Security Predicament*. Boulder: Lynne Rienner.

1996. "State Making, State Breaking, and State Failure," in Crocker, Hampson, and Aall 1996, pp. 37–52.

Bahbah, Bishara A. 1991. "The Crisis in the Gulf – Why Iraq Invaded Kuwait," in Bennis, Phillis and Moushabeck, Michel (eds.) 1991. *Beyond the Storm: A Gulf Crisis Reader*. New York: Olive Branch Press, pp. 50–54.

Baker, James and DeFrank, T. 1995. *The Politics of Diplomacy*. New York: Putnam.

Baldwin, David A. (ed.) 1993. *Neorealism and Neoliberalism: The Contemporary Debate*. New York: Columbia University Press.

Banac, Ivo 1984. *The National Question in Yugoslavia: Origins, History, Politics*. Ithaca: Cornell University Press.

1992. "The Fearful Asymmetry of War: The Causes and Consequences of Yugoslavia's Demise," *Daedalus* 121(2): 141–175.

Baram, Amatzia 1993. "The Iraqi Invasion of Kuwait: Decision-Making in Baghdad," in Baram and Rubin 1993b, pp. 5–36.

Baram, Amatzia and Rubin, Barry 1993a. "Introduction," in Baram and Rubin 1993b, pp. ix–xx.

(eds.) 1993b. *Iraq's Road to War*. New York: St. Martin's Press.

Bar-Joseph, Uri 2001. *The Watchman Fell Asleep: The Surprise of Yom-Kippur and Its Sources*. Lod: Zmora-Bitan (Hebrew).

Bar-On, Mordechai 1992. *The Gates of Gaza: Israel's Security Policy and Foreign Policy, 1955–1957*. Tel Aviv: Am Oved (Hebrew).

Bar Siman-Tov, Yaacov 1980. *The Israeli–Egyptian War of Attrition, 1969–1970*. New York: Columbia University Press.

1983. *Linkage Politics in the Middle East: Syria Between Domestic and External Conflict, 1961–1970*. Boulder: Westview Press.

1984. "The Strategy of War by Proxy," *Cooperation and Conflict* 19: 263–273.
1987. *Israel, the Superpowers and the War in the Middle East*. New York: Praeger.
Barkin, Samuel and Cronin, Bruce 1994. "The State and the Nation: Changing Norms and the Rules of Sovereignty in International Relations," *International Organization* 48(1): 107–130.
Barman, Roderick J. 1988. *Brazil, the Forging of a Nation (1798–1852)*. Stanford: Stanford University Press.
Barnett, Michael 1992. *Confronting the Costs of War: Military Power, State, and Society in Egypt and Israel*. Princeton: Princeton University Press.
1995. "Sovereignty and Nationalism in the Arab World," *International Organization* 49(3): 479–510.
1996/7. "Regional Security After the Gulf War," *Political Science Quarterly* 111(4): 597–618.
1998. *Dialogues in Arab Politics: Negotiations in Regional Order*. New York: Columbia University Press.
Barrington, Lowell W. 1997. "'Nation' and 'Nationalism': The Misuse of Key Concepts in Political Science," *PS: Political Science & Politics* 30(4): 712–716.
Bartlett, C. J. 1996. *Peace, War and the European Powers, 1814–1914*. London: Macmillan.
Beinart, Peter 2002. "Understate." *New Republic* 4 (563) (July 1): 6.
Beloff, Max 1963. *The United States and the Unity of Europe*. London: Faber & Faber.
Ben Ami, Shlomo 2004. *A Battlefront Without a Home-Front: A Journey to the Borders of the Peace Process*. Tel Aviv: Yediot Aharonot (Hebrew).
Ben-Dor, Gabriel 1982. "Conflict Reduction Through Negative Peace: Exploring the Future of the Arab–Israeli Conflict," in N. Oren 1982, pp. 196–225.
1983. *State and Conflict in the Middle East: Emergence of the Post-Colonial State*. New York: Praeger.
Ben-Israel, Hedva 1991. "Irredentism: Nationalism Reexamined," in Chazan 1991, pp. 23–36.
Ben-Porat, Joel 1985. "The Yom-Kippur War: Error in May and Surprise in October," *Maarachot* 299 (July–August): 2–9 (Hebrew).
Ben-Yehuda, Hemda and Sandler, Samuel 2002. *The Arab–Israeli Conflict Transformed*. New York: SUNY Press.
Ben-Zvi, Abraham 1993. *The United States and Israel: The Limits of the Special Relationship*. New York: Columbia University Press.
Bengio, Ofra 1999. "Nation Building in Multiethnic Societies: The Case of Iraq," in Bengio and Ben-Dor 1999, pp. 149–170.
Bengio, Ofra and Ben-Dor, Gabriel (eds.) 1999. *Minorities and the State in the Arab World*. Boulder: Lynne Rienner.
Bethell, Leslie (ed.) 1989. *Brazil: Empire and Republic, 1822–1930*. New York: Cambridge University Press.
(ed.) 1993. *Chile Since Independence*. New York: Cambridge University Press.
Bethell, Leslie and Carvalho, Jose 1989. "1822–1850," in Bethell 1989, pp. 45–112.

Betts, Richard 1999. "Must War Find a Way? A Review Essay," *International Security* 24(2): 166–198.
Birch, Roy 1966. *Britain and Europe, 1871–1939*. Oxford: Pergamon Press.
Blakemore, Harold 1993. "From the War of the Pacific to 1930," in Bethell 1993, pp. 33–86.
Boulding, Kenneth A. 1962. *Conflict and Defense: A General Theory*. New York: Harper Torchbooks.
1978. *Stable Peace*. Austin: University of Texas Press.
Bremer, Stuart A. 1992. "Dangerous Dyads: Conditions Affecting the Likelihood of Interstate War, 1816–1965," *Journal of Conflict Resolution* 36(2): 309–341.
Breslauer, George 1983. "Soviet Policy in the Middle East, 1967–1972: Unalterable Antagonism or Collaborative Competition?," in George et al. 1983, pp. 65–105.
(ed.) 1990. *Soviet Strategy in the Middle East*. Winchester: Unwin Hyman.
Breuilly, John 1993. *Nationalism and the State*, 2nd edn. Manchester: Manchester University Press.
Bridge, Roy and Bullen, Roger 1980. *The Great Powers and the European States System 1815–1914*. London: Longman.
Bronson, Rachel 2005. "Where Credit Is Due: The Provenance of Middle East Reform," *National Interest* 80: 107–112.
Brooks, Stephen G. 1997. "Dueling Realisms," *International Organization* 51(3): 445–477.
Brown, L. Carl 1984. *International Politics and the Middle East: Old Rules, Dangerous Game*. Princeton: Princeton University Press.
Brown, Michael (ed.) 1993. *Ethnic Conflict and International Security*. Princeton: Princeton University Press.
(ed.) 1996. *The International Dimensions of Internal Conflict*. Cambridge, MA: MIT Press.
Brown, Michael, Lynn-Jones, Sean M. and Miller, Steven E. (eds.) 1995. *The Perils of Anarchy: Contemporary Realism and International Security*. Cambridge, MA: MIT Press.
(eds.) 1996a. *Debating the Democratic Peace*. Cambridge, MA: MIT Press.
(eds.) 1996b. *East Asian Security*. Cambridge, MA: MIT Press.
Brubaker, Rogers 1992. *Citizenship and Nationhood in France and Germany*. Cambridge, MA: Harvard University Press.
1996. *Nationalism Reframed: Nationhood and the National Question in the New Europe*. Cambridge: Cambridge University Press.
1998. "Myths and Misconceptions in the Study of Nationalism," in Hall 1998, pp. 272–306.
Brynen, Rex 1991. "Palestine and the Arab State System: Permeability, State Consolidation, and the Intifada," *Canadian Journal of Political Science* 24(3): 595–621.
Buchheit, Lee C. 1978. *Secession: The Legitimacy of Self-Determination*. New Haven: Yale University Press.
Bueno de Mesquita, Bruce 1981. *The War Trap*. New Haven: Yale University Press.

Bull, Hedley 1977. *The Anarchical Society: A Study of Order in World Politics*. New York: Columbia University Press.

Burr, Robert 1965. *By Reason or Force: Chile and the Balancing of Power in South America, 1830–1905*. Berkeley: University of California Press.

Bushnell, David and Macaulay, Neill 1994. *The Emergence of Latin America in the Nineteenth Century*, 2nd edn. New York: Oxford University Press.

Butenschon, Nils A. 1992. "Israel as a Regional Great Power: Paradoxes of Regional Alienation," in I. Neumann 1992.

Butfoy, Andrew 1997. "Offense–Defense Theory: The Problem with Marginalizing the Context," *Contemporary Security Policy* 18(3): 38–58.

Butterfield, Herbert and Wight, Martin (eds.) 1966. *Diplomatic Investigations: Essays in the Theory of International Politics*. London: George Allen & Unwin.

Buzan, Barry 1983. *People, States and Fear: The National Security Problem in International Relations*, 1st edn. Chapel Hill: University of North Carolina Press.

1984. "Peace, Power and Security: Contending Concepts in the Study of International Relations," *Journal of Peace Research* 21(2): 109–125.

1991. *People, States and Fear: An Agenda for International Security Studies in the Post-Cold War Era, 2nd edn*. Boulder: Lynne Rienner.

1993. "From International System to International Society: Structural Realism and Regime Theory Meet the English School," *International Organization* 47(3): 327–352.

1995. "The Level of Analysis Problem in International Relations Reconsidered," in Booth, Ken and Smith, Steve (eds.), *International Relations Theory Today*. University Park, PA: Penn State University Press, pp. 198–216.

2004. *From International to World Society: English School Theory and the Social Structure of Globalization*. Cambridge: Cambridge University Press.

Buzan, Barry and Waever, Ole 2003. *Regions and Powers: The Structure of International Security*. Cambridge: Cambridge University Press.

Buzan, Barry et al. 1990. *The European Security Order Recast: Scenarios for the Post-Cold War Era*. London: Pinter.

Byman, Daniel 2002. *Keeping the Peace: Lasting Solutions to Ethnic Conflicts*. Baltimore: Johns Hopkins University Press.

2003. "Constructing a Democratic Iraq: Challenges and Opportunities," *International Security* 28(1): 47–78.

Byman, Daniel and Van Evera, Stephen 1998. "Why They Fight: Hypotheses on the Causes of Contemporary Deadly Conflict," *Security Studies* 7(3): 1–50.

Calvert, Peter 1969. *Latin America: Internal Conflict and International Peace*. New York: St. Martin's Press.

Caratan, Branko 1995. "The Breakup of Former Yugoslavia and the Serbian War," *Politicka Misao – Croatian Political Science Review* (English edn.) 32(5): 130–146.

Carment, David 1993. "The International Dimension of Ethnic Conflict," *Journal of Peace Research* 30(2): 137–150.

Carment, David and Patrick, James (eds.) 1997. *Wars in the Midst of Peace: The International Politics of Ethnic Conflict*. Pittsburgh: University of Pittsburgh Press.

Carr, E. H. 1946. *The Twenty Years' Crisis, 1919–1939*, 2nd edn. New York: Harper & Row.

Cederman, Lars-Erik 1997. *Emergent Actors in World Politics: How States and Nations Develop and Dissolve*. Princeton: Princeton University Press.

Centeno, Miguel Angel 2002. *Blood and Debt: War and the Nation-State in Latin America*. University Park, PA: Penn State University Press.

Chan, Steve 1997. "In Search of Democratic Peace: Problems and Promise," *Mershon International Studies Review* 41 (supplement 1): 59–92.

Chazan, Naomi (ed.) 1991. *Irredentism and International Politics*. Boulder: Lynne Rienner.

Child, Jack 1985. *Geopolitics and Conflict Within South America: Quarrels Among Neighbors*. New York: Praeger.

Chipman, John 1993. "Managing the Politics of Parochialism," in M. Brown 1993, pp. 237–264.

Christopher, Warren 1998. *In the Stream of History*. Stanford: Stanford University Press.

Chubin, Shahram and Tripp, Charles 1988. *Iran and Iraq at War*. Boulder: Westview Press.

CIA World Factbook, www.cia.gov/cia/publications/factbook.

Clark, Ian 1989. *The Hierarchy of States: Reform and Resistance in the International Order*. Cambridge: Cambridge University Press.

1997. *Globalization and Fragmentation: International Relations in the Twentieth Century*. Oxford: Oxford University Press.

Clayton, Gerald D. 1971. *Britain and the Eastern Question: Missolonghi to Gallipoli*. London: University of London Press.

Clogg, Richard 1979. *A Short History of Modern Greece*. Cambridge: Cambridge University Press.

Cohen, Youssef et al. 1981. "The Paradoxical Nature of State Making: The Violent Creation of Order," *American Political Science Review* 75(4): 901–910.

Collier, Simon 1993. "From Independence to the War of the Pacific," in Bethell 1993, pp. 1–32.

Congressional Quarterly 1991. *The Middle East*, 7th edn. Washington, DC: Congressional Quarterly Press.

Connor, Walker 1972. "Nation-Building or Nation-Destroying," *World Politics* 24: 319–355.

1994. *Ethnonationalism: The Quest for Understanding*. Princeton: Princeton University Press.

Cooper, Robert 2003. *The Breaking of Nations: Order and Chaos in the Twenty-First Century*. New York: Atlantic Monthly Press.

Copeland, Dale C. 1996. "Economic Interdependence and War: A Theory of Trade Expectations," *International Security* 20(4): 5–41.

2000. *The Origins of Major War*. Ithaca: Cornell University Press.
Cordesman, Anthony and Wagner, Abraham 1990. *The Lessons of Modern War*, vol. II, *The Iran–Iraq War*. London: Mansell.
Cornell, Svante E. 2002. "Autonomy as a Source of Conflict: Caucasian Conflicts in Theoretical Perspective," *World Politics* 54: 145–183.
Craig, Gordon and George, Alexander 1995. *Force and Statecraft*, 3rd edn. New York: Oxford University Press.
Crocker, C., Hampson, F. and Aall, P. (eds.) 1996. *Managing Global Chaos*. Washington, DC: USIPE.
Cronin, Bruce 2002. "Creating Stability in the New Europe: The OSCE High Commissioner on National Minorities and the Socialization of Risky States," *Security Studies* 12(1): 132–163.
Csergo, Zsuzsa and Goldgeier, James 2004. "Nationalist Strategies and European Integration," *Perspectives on Politics* 2: 21–37.
Cutler, Claire 1991. "The 'Grotian Tradition' in International Relations," *Review of International Studies* 17: 41–65.
Cvijić, Jovan 1918a. "The Geographical Distribution of the Balkan Peoples," *Geographical Review* 5(5): 345–361.
1918b. "The Zones of Civilization of the Balkan Peninsula," *Geographical Review* 5(6): 470–482.
D'Agostino, Thomas J. 1997. "Latin American Politics," in Hillman 1997, pp. 51–94.
Dahl, Robert A. 1971. *Polyarchy: Participation and Opposition*. New Haven: Yale University Press.
1989. *Democracy and Its Critics*. New Haven: Yale University Press.
David, Charles-Philippe 1994. "Procrastinating into the New World Order: American Policy Towards the Yugoslav Crisis," paper presented at the annual meeting of the International Studies Association, Washington, DC, March 28 – April 1.
David, Steven R. 1991a. *Choosing Sides: Alignment and Realignment in the Third World*. Baltimore: Johns Hopkins University Press.
1991b. "Explaining Third World Alignment," *World Politics* 43: 233–256.
1992/3. "Why the Third World Still Matters," *International Security* 17: 127–159.
1998. "The Primacy of Internal Wars," in Neuman, Stephanie G. (ed.) 1998. *International Relations Theory and the Third World*. New York: St. Martin's Press, pp. 77–102.
Davis, David, Jaggers, Keith and Moore, Will H. 1997. "Ethnicity, Minorities, and International Conflict," in Carment and Patrick 1997, pp. 148–163.
Dawisha, Added 2002a. "Footprints in the Sand: The Definition and Redefinition of Identity in Iraq's Foreign Policy," in Telhami and Barnett 2002a, pp. 117–136.
2002b. "Nation and Nationalism: Historical Antecedents to Contemporary Debates," *International Studies Review* 4: 3–22.
Dayan, Moshe 1977. *Story of My Life*. London: Sphere Books.

De Nevers, Renee 1993. "Democratization and Ethnic Conflict," in M. Brown 1993, pp. 61–78.

Dean, Warren 1989. "Economy," in Bethell 1989, pp. 217–257.

Desch, Michael 1993. *When the Third World Matters: Latin America and United States Grand Strategy.* Baltimore: Johns Hopkins University Press.

Dessouki, Ali E. Hillal 1991. "The Primacy of Economics: The Foreign Policy of Egypt," in Korany and Dessouki 1991a, pp. 156–185.

Deutsch, Karl et al. 1957. *Political Community and the North Atlantic Area: International Organization in the Light of Historical Experience.* Princeton: Princeton University Press.

Devlen, Balkan, James, Patrick and Ozdamar, Ozgur 2005. "The English School, International Relations, and Progress," *International Studies Review* 7(2): 171–198.

Dewar, Michael 1993. "Intervention in Bosnia: The Case Against," *World Today* 49(2): 32–33.

Di Palma, Giuseppe 1991. "Legitimation from the Top to Civil Society: Political–Cultural Change in Eastern Europe," *World Politics* 44(1): 49–80.

Diamond, Jared 1999. *Guns, Germs and Steel.* New York: W. W. Norton.

Diamond, Larry 2005. *Squandering Victory: The American Occupation and the Bungled Effort to Bring Democracy to Iraq.* New York: Times Books.

Diamond, Larry and Plattner, Marc F. (eds.) 1994. *Nationalism, Ethnic Conflict and Democracy.* Baltimore: Johns Hopkins University Press.

DiCicco, Jonathan M. and Levy, Jack S. 2003. "The Power Transition Research Program: A Lakatosian Analysis," in Elman, Colin and Elman, Miriam F. (eds.) 2003. *Progress in International Relations Theory.* Cambridge, MA: MIT Press, pp. 109–158.

Diehl, Paul F. (ed.) 1999. *A Road Map to War.* Nashville: Vanderbilt University Press.

Diehl, Paul F. and Goertz, Gary 2000. *War and Peace in International Rivalry.* Ann Arbor: University of Michigan Press.

Diehl, Paul F. and Lepgold, Joseph (eds.) 2003. *Regional Conflict Management.* Boulder: Rowman & Littlefield.

Dixon, William J. 1996. "Third-Party Techniques for Preventing Conflict Escalation and Promoting Peaceful Settlement," *International Organization* 50(4): 653–682.

Djilas, Aleksa 1995. "Fear Thy Neighbor: The Breakup of Yugoslavia," in Kupchan 1995b, pp. 85–106.

Djordjevic, Dimitrije and Galati, Stephen Fischer 1981. *The Balkan Revolutionary Tradition.* New York: Columbia University Press.

Doder, Dusko 1993. "Yugoslavia: New War, Old Hatreds," *Foreign Policy* 91: 3–23.

Dominguez, Jorge I. et al. 2003. "Boundary Disputes on Latin America," *Peaceworks*, No. 50. Washington, DC: USIPE.

Donnelly, Jack 2000. *Realism and International Relations.* Cambridge: Cambridge University Press.

Doran, Charles F. 1992. "The Globalist–Regionalist Debate," in Schrader, Peter (ed.) 1992. *Intervention into the 1990s: US Foreign Policy in the Third World*. Boulder: Lynne Rienner.

Dowek, Ephraim 1998. *Israeli–Egyptian Relations, 1980–2000*. London: Frank Cass.

Downes, Alexander B. 2001. "The Holy Land Divided: Defending Partition as a Solution to Ethnic Wars," *Security Studies* 10(4): 58–116.

2004. "The Problem with Negotiated Settlements to Ethnic Civil Wars," *Security Studies* 13(4): 230–279.

Doyle, Michael W. 1986. "Liberalism and World Politics," *American Political Science Review* 80(4): 1151–1169.

1997. *Ways of War and Peace*. New York: W. W. Norton.

Dragnich, Alex N. 1954. *Tito's Promised Land: Yugoslavia*. New Brunswick: Rutgers University Press.

Dyadic MID Dataset (Version 2.0), psfaculty.ucdavis.edu/zmaoz/dyadmid.html.

Eban, Abba S. 1977. *An Autobiography*. New York: Random House.

Eckstein, Harry 1975. "Case Study and Theory in Political Science," in Greenstein, Fred and Polsby, Nelson (eds.) 1975. *Handbook of Political Science*, vol. VII, *Strategies of Inquiry*. Reading, MA: Addison-Wesley, pp. 79–138.

Eisenberg, Laura Z. and Caplan, Neil 1998. *Negotiating Arab–Israeli Peace*. Bloomington: Indiana University Press.

El-Nawawy, Mohammed and Iskandar, Adel 2002. *Al-Jazera: How the Free Arab Network Scooped the World and Changed the Middle East*. New York: Westview.

Elrod, Richard 1976. "The Concert of Europe: A Fresh Look at an International System," *World Politics* 28: 159–174.

Eriksson, Mikael and Wallensteen, Peter 2004. "Armed Conflict, 1989–2003," *Journal of Peace Research* 41(5): 625–636.

Escude, Carlos 1988. "Argentine Territorial Nationalism," *Journal of Latin American Studies* 20(1): 139–165.

Estman, Milton and Rabinovich, Itamar (eds.) 1988. *Ethnicity, Pluralism and the State in the Middle East*. Ithaca: Cornell University Press.

Evans, Peter 1997. "The Eclipse of the State? Reflections on Stateness in an Era of Globalization," *World Politics* 50(1): 68–82.

Evron, Yair 1973. *The Middle East: Nations, Superpowers, and Wars*. London: Elek.

1987. *War and Intervention in Lebanon: The Israeli–Syrian Deterrence Dialogue*. Baltimore: Johns Hopkins University Press.

1994. "Gulf Crisis and War: Regional Rules of the Game and Policy and Theoretical Explanation," *Security Studies* 4(1): 115–154.

Eytan, Walter 1958. *The First Ten Years: Israel Between East and West*. London: Weidenfeld & Nicolson.

Faour, Muhammad 1993. *The Arab World After Desert Storm*. Washington, DC: USIPE.

Fawcett, Louise and Hurrell, Andrew (eds.) 1995. *Regionalism in World Politics*. Oxford: Oxford University Press.

Fearon, James D. 1995. "Rationalist Explanations for War," *International Organization* 49(3): 379–414.
2004. "Separatist Wars, Partition, and World Order," *Security Studies* 13(4): 394–415.
Fearon, James D. and Laitin, David D. 2003. "Ethnicity, Insurgency, and Civil Wars," *American Political Science Review* 97(1): 75–90.
Feldman, Shai 1996. *The Future of US–Israel Strategic Cooperation*. Washington, DC: Washington Institute for Near East Policy.
Foreign Policy 2005. "The Failed States Index," 149: 56–65.
Frankel, Benjamin (ed.) 1996. *Realism: Restatement and Renewal*. London: Frank Cass.
Fraser, Cleveland 1997. "International Relations," in Hillman 1997, pp. 151–176.
Freedman, Lawrence 1994/5. "Why the West Failed," *Foreign Policy* 97: 53–69.
(ed.) 1998. *Strategic Coercion: Concepts and Cases*. Oxford: Oxford University Press.
Freedman, Robert O. 1991. *Moscow and the Middle East: Soviet Policy Since the Invasion of Afghanistan*. New York: Cambridge University Press.
Freymond, Jacques 1960. *The Saar Conflict 1945–1955*. Westport: Greenwood Press.
Friedberg, Aaron L. 1993/4. "Ripe for Rivalry: Prospects for Peace in a Multipolar Asia," *International Security* 18(3): 5–33.
Friedman, Thomas 2002. "Israel, Palestine and NATO," *International Herald Tribune* December (12): 8 (originally published in *New York Times*).
Friend, Julius W. 1991. *The Linchpin: French–German Relations 1950–1990*. New York: Praeger.
Frisch, Hillel 2002a. "Explaining Third World Security Structures," *Journal of Strategic Studies* 25(3): 161–190.
2002b. "Fuzzy Nationalism: The Case of Jordan," *Nationalism and Ethnic Politics* 8(4): 86–103.
Fritsch–Bournazel, Renata 1989. "The French View," in Moreton, E. (ed.) 1989. *Germany Between East and West*. Cambridge: Cambridge University Press, pp. 64–82.
Fromkin, David 1989. *A Peace to End All Peace: Creating the Modern Middle East, 1914–1922*. New York: Henry Holt.
Fukuyama, Francis 2004. *State-Building: Governance and World Order in the Twenty-First Century*. Ithaca: Cornell University Press.
Fuller, Graham E. 2000. "Longing for a 'Reasonable' Arab World," *Middle East Quarterly* 7(4): 23–24.
Fund for Peace 2005 Failed States Index, www.fundforpeace.org/programs/fsi/fsindex.
Gaddis, John Lewis 1992. "The Cold War, the Long Peace, and the Future," in Hogan, Michael J. (ed.) 1992. *The End of the Cold War: Its Meaning and Implications*. Cambridge: Cambridge University Press, pp. 21–38.

Gagnon, V. P. 1994/5. "Ethnic Nationalism and International Conflict: The Case of Serbia," *International Security* 19(3): 130–166.

Gallo, Ezequiel 1993. "Society and Politics, 1880–1916," in Bethell 1993, pp. 79–111.

Garnham, David and Tessler, Mark (eds.) 1995. *Democracy, War and Peace in the Middle East*. Bloomington: Indiana University Press.

Gati, Charles 1992. "From Sarajevo to Sarajevo," *Foreign Affairs* 71(4): 64–79.

Gause, Gregory F. 1992. "Sovereignty, Statecraft, and Stability in the Middle East," *Journal of International Affairs* 45: 441–469.

1999. "Systemic Approaches to Middle East International Relations," *International Studies Review* 1(1): 11–31.

Geller, Daniel S. and Singer, David J. 1998. *Nations at War: A Scientific Study of International Conflict*. Cambridge: Cambridge University Press.

Gellner, Ernest 1983. *Nations and Nationalism*. Ithaca: Cornell University Press.

1994. *Conditions of Liberty: Civil Society and Its Rivals*. London: Penguin Books.

George, Alexander (ed.) 1991. *Avoiding War: Problems of Crisis Management*. Boulder: Westview Press.

George, Alexander, Farley, Philip and Dallin, Alexander (eds.) 1988. *US–Soviet Security Cooperation: Achievements, Failures, Lessons*. New York: Oxford University Press.

George, Alexander and Simons, William (eds.) 1994. *The Limits of Coercive Diplomacy*, 2nd edn. Boulder: Westview Press.

George, Alexander et al. (eds.) 1983. *Managing US–Soviet Rivalry: Problems of Crisis Prevention*. Boulder: Westview Press.

Geraud, Andre 1947. "Can France Again be a Great Power?," *Foreign Affairs* 26(1): 24–35.

Gerbet, Pierre 1996. "European Integration as an Instrument of French Foreign Policy," in Heller, Francis H. and Gillingham, John R. (eds.) 1996. *The United States and the Integration of Europe*. New York: St. Martin's Press, pp. 57–79.

Gerges, Fawaz 1994. *The Superpowers and the Middle East: Regional and International Politics, 1955–1967*. Boulder: Westview.

1995. "Egyptian–Israeli Relations Turn Sour," *Foreign Affairs* 74(3): 69–78.

Ghareeb, Edmund 1990. "The Roots of Crisis: Iraq and Iran," in Joyner, Christopher C. (ed.) 1990. *The Persian Gulf War: Lessons for Strategy, Law, and Diplomacy*. New York: Greenwood Press, pp. 21–38.

Gholz, Eugene, Press, Daryl G. and Sapolsky, Harvey M. 1997. "Come Home, America: The Strategy of Restraint in the Face of Temptation," *International Security* 21(4): 5–48.

Gilkes, P. and Plaut, M. 1999. "Conflict in the Horn: Why Eritrea and Ethiopia Are at War," Royal Institute of International Affairs, Briefing Paper new series no. 1 (March).

Gillingham, John R. 1991. *Coal, Steel and the Rebirth of Europe, 1945–1955*. Cambridge: Cambridge University Press.

Gilpin, Robert 1981. *War and Change in World Politics*. Cambridge: Cambridge University Press.

Glaser, Charles L. 1994/5. "Realists as Optimists: Cooperation as Self-Help," *International Security* 19(3): 50–90.

1997. "The Security Dilemma Revisited," *World Politics* 50(1): 171–201.

Glaser, Charles L. and Kaufmann, Chaim 1998. "What Is the Offense–Defense Balance and How Can We Measure It?," *International Security* 22(4): 44–82.

Gleditsch, Kristian Skrede 2002. *All International Politics Is Local: The Diffusion of Conflict, Integration and Democratization*. Ann Arbor: University of Michigan Press.

Gleditsch, N. P. 1995. "Democracy and the Future of European Peace," *European Journal of International Relations* 1(4): 539–571.

Glenny, Misha 1999. *The Balkans: Nationalism, War and the Great Powers, 1804–1999*. New York: Penguin.

Globe, Paul 1996. "Dangerous Liaisons: Moscow, the Former Yugoslavia, and the West," in Ullman 1996b, pp. 182–197.

Gochman, Charles S. 1990. "The Geography of Conflict: Militarized Interstate Disputes Since 1816," paper presented at the 31st Annual Convention of the International Studies Association, Washington, DC, April 10–14.

Gochman, Charles S. and Maoz, Zeev 1984. "Militarized Interstate Disputes, 1816–1976: Procedures, Patterns, Insights," *Journal of Conflict Resolution* 29(4): 585–615.

Gochman, Charles S. et al. 1996/7. "Correspondence: Democracy and Peace," *International Security* 21(3): 177–187.

Goemans, Hein E. 2000. *War and Punishment: The Causes of War Termination and the First World War*. Princeton: Princeton University Press.

Goertz, Gary and Diehl, Paul F. 1992a. "The Empirical Importance of Enduring Rivalries," *International Interactions* 18: 151–163.

1992b. *Territorial Changes and International Conflict*. London: Routledge.

1994. "International Norms and Power Politics," in Wayman, Frank W. and Diehl, Paul F. (eds.) 1994. *Reconstructing Realpolitik*. Ann Arbor: University of Michigan Press, pp. 101–122.

Golan, Galia 1977. *Yom Kippur and After: The Soviet Union and the Arab–Israeli Crisis*. Cambridge: Cambridge University Press.

1990. *Soviet Policies in the Middle East from World War Two to Gorbachev*. Cambridge: Cambridge University Press.

Goldgeier, James and McFaul, Michael 1992. "A Tale of Two Worlds: Core and Periphery in the Post-Cold War Era," *International Organization* 46(2): 467–491.

Gompert, David C. 1994. "How to Defeat Serbia," *Foreign Affairs* 73(4): 30–49.

1996. "The United States and Yugoslavia's Wars," in Ullman 1996b, pp. 122–144.

Gottlieb, Gidon 1993. *Nation Against State*. New York: Council on Foreign Relations.

Gow, James 1997. *Triumph of the Lack of Will: International Diplomacy and the Yugoslav War*. London: Hurst.
Gowa, Joanne 1995. "Democratic States and International Disputes," *International Organization* 49(3): 511–522.
Graham, Richard 1989. "1850–1870," in Bethell 1989, pp. 113–160.
Greenfeld, Liah 1992. *Nationalism: Five Roads to Modernity*. Cambridge: Harvard University Press.
Grieco, Joseph M. 1988. "Anarchy and the Limits of Cooperation: A Realist Critique of the Newest Liberal Institutionalism," *International Organization* 42(3): 485–507.
1990. *Cooperation Among Nations: Europe, America, and Non-Tariff Barriers to Trade*. Ithaca: Cornell University Press.
Grosser, Alfred 1963. "France and Germany in the Atlantic Community," *International Organization* 17(3): 550–569.
1971. *Germany in Our Time*. London: Pall Mall Press.
Guazzone, Laura (ed.) 1997. *The Middle East in Global Change*. London: Macmillan.
Gurr, Ted Robert 1988. "War, Revolution, and the Growth of the Coercive State," *Comparative Political Studies* 21: 45–65.
1993. *Minorities at Risk: A Global View of Ethnopolitical Conflicts*. Washington, DC: USIPE.
2000. *Peoples Versus States*. Washington, DC: USIPE.
Gurr, Ted Robert and Harff, Barbara 1994. *Ethnic Conflict in World Politics*. Boulder: Westview Press.
Gutmann, Emanuel 1991. "Concealed or Conjured Irredentism: The Case of Alsace," in Chazan 1991, pp. 37–50.
Haas, Ernst B. 1958. *The Uniting of Europe: Political, Social and Economic Forces*. Stanford: Stanford University Press.
1964. *Beyond the Nation State*. Stanford: Stanford University Press.
Hall, John (ed.) 1998. *The State of the Nation: Ernest Gellner and the Theory of Nationalism*. Cambridge: Cambridge University Press.
Halliday, Fred 1991a. "The Crisis of the Arab World," in Sifry, Micah and Cerf, Christopher (eds.) 1991. *The Gulf War Reader*. New York: Random House, pp. 395–401.
1991b. "The Gulf War and Its Aftermath: First Reflections," *International Affairs* 67: 223–234.
2005. *The Middle East in International Relations*. Cambridge: Cambridge University Press.
Halperin, Morton H. and Scheffer, David J. et al. 1992. *Self-Determination in the New World Order*. Washington, DC: Carnegie.
Hampson, Fen Olser 1996. *Nurturing Peace*. Washington, DC: USIPE.
Handel, Michael 1981. *Weak States in the International System*. London: Frank Cass.
Hannum, Hurst 1990. *Autonomy, Sovereignty and Self-Determination*. Philadelphia: University of Pennsylvania Press.

Harff, Barbara 1993. "Minorities, Rebellion, and Repression in North Africa and the Middle East," in Gurr 1993, pp. 217–251.

Harik, Iliya 1990. "The Origins of the Arab State System," in Luciani 1990, pp. 1–28.

Harkabi, Yehoshafat 1977. *Arab Strategies and Israel's Response*. New York: Free Press.

1990. *War and Strategy*. Tel Aviv: Ministry of Defense (Hebrew).

Hedges, Chris 1999. "Kosovo's Next Masters?," *Foreign Affairs* 78(3): 24–42.

Heikal, Mohamed 1975. *The Road to Ramadan*. New York: Quadrangle.

1978. *The Sphinx and the Commissar*. New York: Harper & Row.

Hellmann, Gunther 2003. "Are Dialogue and Synthesis Possible in International Relations?," *International Studies Review* 5: 123–153.

Helman, Gerald B. and Ratner, Steven R. 1992/3. "Saving Failed States," *Foreign Policy* 89: 3–20.

Hensel, Paul R. 2001. "Contentious Issues and World Politics: The Management of Territorial Claims in the Americas, 1816–1992," *International Studies Quarterly* 45(1): 81–109.

Heppell, Muriel and Singleton, Fred 1961. *Yugoslavia*. New York: Praeger.

Herbst, Jeffrey 1989. "The Creation and Maintenance of National Boundaries in Africa," *International Organization* 43(4): 673–692.

Herrmann, Richard 1994. "Coercive Diplomacy and the Crisis over Kuwait 1990–1991," in George and Simons 1994, pp. 229–266.

Herz, John H. 1950. "Idealist Internationalism and the Security Dilemma," *World Politics* 2: 157–180.

Hillman, Richard (ed.) 1997. *Understanding Contemporary Latin America*. Boulder: Lynne Rienner.

Hinnebusch, Raymond 1991. "Revisionist Dreams, Realist Strategies: The Foreign Policy of Syria," in Korany and Dessouki 1991a, pp. 374–409.

2002a. "Introduction: The Analytical Framework," in Hinnebusch, Raymond and Ehteshami, Anoushiravan (eds.) 2002. *Foreign Policies of Middle East States*. London: Lynne Rienner, pp. 1–28.

2002b. "The Middle East Regional System," in Hinnebusch, Raymond and Ehtashami, Anoushivaran (eds.) 2002. *Foreign Policies of Middle East States*. London: Lynne Rienner, pp. 29–54.

2002c. "The Foreign Policy of Egypt," in Hinnebusch, Raymond and Ehtashami, Anoushivaran (eds.) 2002. *Foreign Policies of Middle East States*. London: Lynne Rienner, pp. 91–114.

2003. *The International Politics of the Middle East* Manchester: Manchester University Press.

Hinsley, Francis H. 1963. *Power and the Pursuit of Peace: Theory and Practice in the History of Relations Between States*. Cambridge: Cambridge University Press.

Hirst, David 1984. *The Gun and the Branch: The Roots of Violence in the Middle East*. London: Faber & Faber.

Hitchens, Marilyn G. 1983. *Germany, Russia and the Balkans: Prelude to the Nazi–Soviet Non-Aggression Pact*. Boulder: East European Monographs.

Hobsbawm, Eric J. 1990. *Nations and Nationalism Since 1780: Programme, Myth, Reality*. Cambridge: Cambridge University Press.

Hoffmann, Stanley 1990/1. "The Case for Leadership," *Foreign Policy* 81 (Winter).

1998. *World Disorders: Troubled Peace in the Post-Cold War Era.* Lanham: Rowman & Littlefield.

Hollis, Martin and Smith, Steve 1991. *Explaining and Understanding International Relations.* Oxford: Clarendon.

Holm, Hans Henrik and Sorensen, George (eds.) 1995. *Whose World Order? Uneven Globalization and the End of the Cold War*. Boulder: Westview Press.

Holsti, K. J. 1991. *Peace and War: Armed Conflicts and International Order 1648–1989*. Cambridge: Cambridge University Press.

1992. "International Theory and War in the Third World," in Job 1992, pp. 37–62.

1996. *War, the State, and the State of War*. Cambridge: Cambridge University Press.

Hopmann, Terrence P. 1994. *Resolving International Conflicts: The Negotiation Process*. Columbia: University of South Carolina Press.

Horowitz, Donald L. 1985. *Ethnic Groups in Conflict*. Berkeley: University of California Press.

1991. "Irredentas and Secessions: Adjacent Phenomena, Neglected Connections," in Chazan 1991, pp. 9–22.

1994. "Democracy in Divided Societies," in L. Diamond and Plattner 1994, pp. 35–55.

Hudson, Michael C. 1968. *The Precarious Republic: Political Modernization in Lebanon.* New York: Random House.

1977. *Arab Politics: The Search for Legitimacy*. New Haven: Yale University Press.

1995. "Democracy and Foreign Policy in the Arab World," in Garnham and Tessler 1995, pp. 195–220.

1996. "To Play the Hegemon: Fifty Years of US Policy Toward the Middle East," *Middle East Journal* 50(3): 329–343.

Hughes, Arthur 2005. "Bring in the Peacekeepers, Post-Pullout," *Haaretz* (July 8), B5.

Huntington, Samuel P. 1968. *Political Order in Changing Societies.* New Haven: Yale University Press.

1991. *The Third Wave: Democratization in the Late Twentieth Century*. Norman: University of Oklahoma Press.

1993. "The Clash of Civilizations," *Foreign Affairs* 72(3): 22–49.

1996. *The Clash of Civilizations and the Remaking of World Order*. New York: Simon & Schuster.

1999. "The Lonely Superpower," *Foreign Affairs* 78(2): 35–49.

Hupchick, Dennis P. 1995. *Conflict and Chaos in Eastern Europe.* New York: St. Martin's Press.

Hurrell, Andrew 1995. "Regionalism in Theoretical Perspective," in Fawcett and Hurrell 1995, pp. 37–73.

1998. "An Emerging Security Community in South America?," in Adler and Barnett 1998, pp. 228–264.
Hussein, H. M. 1969. *My War with Israel*. New York: William Morrow.
Huth, Paul K. 1996. *Standing Your Ground: Territorial Disputes and International Conflict*. Ann Arbor: University of Michigan Press.
1999. "Enduring Rivalries and Territorial Disputes, 1950–1990," in Diehl 1999, pp. 37–72.
Huth, Paul K. and Allee, Todd L. 2002. *The Democratic Peace and Territorial Conflict in the Twentieth Century*. Cambridge: Cambridge University Press.
Ibrahim, Saad Eddin 1995. "Ethnic Conflict and State Building in the Arab world," in Kemp and Stein 1995, pp. 45–64.
Ikenberry, G. John 1989. "Rethinking the Origins of American Hegemony," *Political Science Quarterly* 104: 375–400.
2001. *After Victory: Institutions, Strategic Restraint, and the Rebuilding of Order After Major Wars*. Princeton: Princeton University Press.
(ed.) 2002. *America Unrivaled: The Future of the Balance of Power*. Ithaca: Cornell University Press.
Ikenberry, John G. and Kupchan, Charles A. 1990. "The Legitimation of Hegemonic Power," in Rapkin, David (ed.) 1990. *World Leadership and Hegemony*. Boulder: Lynne Rienner, pp. 49–70.
Inbar, Efraim (ed.) 1995. *Regional Security Regimes: Israel and Its Neighbors*. Albany: SUNY Press.
1999. *Yitzhak Rabin and Israel's National Security*. Baltimore: Johns Hopkins University Press.
Indyk, Martin 1992. "The Postwar Balance of Power in the Middle East," in Nye, Joseph S. and Smith, Roger K. (eds.) 1992. *After the Storm: Lessons from the Gulf War*. Lanham: Madison, pp. 83–112.
Ireland, Gordon 1938. *Boundaries, Possessions, and Conflicts in South America*. Cambridge: Harvard University Press.
Israelyan, Victor 1995. *Inside the Kremlin During the Yom Kippur War*. University Park, PA: Penn State University Press.
Jackman, Robert W. 1993. *Power Without Force: The Political Capacity of Nation States*. Ann Arbor: University of Michigan Press.
Jackson, Robert H. 1990. *Quasi-States: Sovereignty, International Relations and the Third World*. Cambridge: Cambridge University Press.
Jackson, Robert H. and Rosberg, Carl G. 1982. "Why Africa's Weak States Persist: The Empirical and the Juridical in Statehood," *World Politics* 35(1): 1–24.
Jaggers, Keith 1992. "War and the Three Faces of Power: War Making and State Making in Europe and the Americas," *Comparative Political Studies* 25(1): 26–62.
Jakobsen, Peter V. 1997. *Western Use of Coercive Diplomacy After the Cold War: A Challenge for Theory and Practice*. London: Macmillan.
Jelavich, Barbara 1973. *The Ottoman Empire, the Great Powers and the Straits Question: 1870–1887*. London: Indiana University Press.

1983. *History of the Balkans: Eighteenth and Nineteenth Centuries*. Cambridge: Cambridge University Press.

Jelavich, Barbara and Jelavich, Charles 1965. *The Balkans*. Englewood Cliffs: Prentice-Hall.

Jenkins, Brian and Sofos, Spyros A. (eds.) 1996. *Nation and Identity in Contemporary Europe*. New York: Routledge.

Jervis, Robert 1976. *Perception and Misperception in International Politics*. Princeton: Princeton University Press.

1978. "Cooperation Under the Security Dilemma," *World Politics* 30(2): 167–214.

1979. "Systems Theories and Diplomatic History," in Lauren, Paul G. (ed.) 1979. *Diplomacy: New Approaches in History, Theory and Policy*. New York: Free Press, pp. 212–244.

1986. "From Balance to Concert: A Study of International Security Cooperation," in Oye, Kenneth A. (ed.) 1986. *Cooperation Under Anarchy*. Princeton: Princeton University Press, pp. 58–79.

1997. *System Effects: Complexity in Political and Social Life*. Princeton: Princeton University Press.

Jervis, Robert, Lebow, R. N. and Stein, J. G. 1985. *Psychology and Deterrence*. Baltimore: Johns Hopkins University Press.

Job, Brian (ed.) 1992. *The Insecurity Dilemma: National Security of Third World States*. Boulder: Lynne Rienner.

1997. "Matters of Multilateralism: Implications for Regional Conflict Management," in Lake and Morgan 1997, pp. 165–194.

Joffe, George H. 1997. "Disputes Over State Boundaries in the Middle East and North Africa," in Guazzone 1997, pp. 58–94.

Joffe, Josef 1984. "Europe's American Pacifier," *Foreign Policy* 50: 64–82.

1987. *The Limited Partnership: Europe, the United States, and the Burdens of Alliance*. Cambridge: Ballinger.

1992. "Collective Security and the Future of Europe," *Survival* 34: 36–50.

1999. "Three Unwritten Rules That Undermined NATO's War," *International Herald Tribune*, July (28): 8.

Johnson, Lyndon B. 1971. *The Vantage Point: Perspectives on the Presidency 1963–1969*. New York: Holt, Rinehart & Winston.

Kacowicz, Arie M. 1994. *Peaceful Territorial Change*. Columbia: University of South Carolina Press.

1995. "Explaining Zones of Peace: Democracies as Satisfied Powers?," *Journal of Peace Research* 32(3): 265–276.

1996. "The South American Zone of Peace, 1883–1996," *Peace Papers* 7, Harry S Truman Research Institute, Hebrew University of Jerusalem.

1998. *Zones of Peace in the Third World: South America and West Africa in a Comparative Perspective*. Albany: SUNY Press.

Kacowicz, Arie, Bar Siman-Tov, Yaacov, Elgstrom, Ole and Jerneck, Magnus (eds.) 2000. *Stable Peace Among Nations*. New York: Rowman & Littlefield.

Kagan, Korina 1997/8. "The Myth of the European Concert: The Realist–Institutionalist Debate and Great Power Behavior in the Eastern Question, 1821–1841," *Security Studies* 7(2): 1–57.

2000. "Great Power Spheres of Influence." Ph.D dissertation, Hebrew University of Jerusalem.

Kanet, Roger and Kolodziej, Edward (eds.) 1991. *The Cold War as Cooperation*. Baltimore: Johns Hopkins University Press.

Kaplan, Morton. 1957. *System and Process in International Politics*. New York: Wiley.

Kaplan, Robert 1993. *Balkan Ghosts: A Journey Through History*. New York: St. Martin's Press.

1998. "Iraq: Anyone Have a Post-Saddam Recipe?," *International Herald Tribune*, December (22): 8.

2000. *The Coming Anarchy*. New York: Random House.

Karsh, Efraim 1997. "Cold War, Post-Cold War: Does It Make a Difference in the Middle East?," *Review of International Studies* 23: 271–291.

2000. *Empires of Sand*. Cambridge: Harvard University Press.

Karsh, Efraim and Karsh, Inari 1996. "Reflections on Arab Nationalism," *Middle Eastern Studies* 32(4): 367–392.

Katz, Mark N. 1996. "Collapsed Empires," in Crocker, Hampson, and Aall 1996, pp. 25–36.

Katzenstein, Peter (ed.) 1996a. *The Culture of National Security: Norms and Identity in World Politics*. New York: Columbia University Press.

1996b. "Regionalism in Comparative Perspective," *Cooperation and Conflict* 31(2): 123–159.

2005. *A World of Regions*. Ithaca: Cornell University Press.

Katzenstein, Peter J. and Okawara, Nobuo 2001/2. "Japan, Asian-Pacific Security, and the Case for Analytical Eclecticism," *International Security* 26(3): 153–185.

Kaufman, Stuart J. 2001. *Modern Hatreds: The Symbolic Politics of Ethnic War*. Ithaca: Cornell University Press.

Kaufmann, Chaim D. 1998. "When All Else Fails: Ethnic Population Transfers and Partitions in the Twentieth Century," *International Security* 23(2): 120–156.

2005. "Rational Choice and Progress in the Study of Ethnic Conflict: A Review Essay," *Security Studies* 14(1): 167–194.

Kaye, Dalia 2001. *Beyond the Handshake: Multilateral Cooperation in the Arab–Israeli Peace Process, 1991–1996*. New York: Columbia University Press.

Keal, Paul 1983. *Unspoken Rules and Superpower Dominance*. London: Macmillan.

Kedourie, Elie 1987. "The Nation-State in the Middle East," *Jerusalem Journal of International Relations* 9: 1–9.

Kegley, Charles (ed.) 1995. *Controversies in International Relations Theory: Realism and the Neoliberal Challenge*. New York: St. Martin's Press.

Kemp, Geoffrey and Pressman, Jeremy 1997. *Point of No Return: The Deadly Struggle for Middle East Peace*. Washington, DC: Carnegie.

Kemp, Geoffrey and Stein, Janice Gross (eds.) 1995. *Powder Keg in the Middle East*. Washington, DC: AAAS.

Keohane, Robert O. 1984. *After Hegemony: Cooperation and Discord in the World Political Economy*. Princeton: Princeton University Press.

(ed.) 1986. *Neorealism and Its Critics*. New York: Columbia University Press.

1989. *International Institutions and State Power: Essays in International Relations Theory*. Boulder: Westview Press.

Keohane, Robert O. and Hoffmann, Stanley 1990. "Conclusions: Community Politics and Institutional Change," in Wallace, William (ed.) 1990. *The Dynamics of European Integration*. London: Pinter, pp. 276–300.

(eds.) 1991. *The New European Community*. Boulder: Westview Press.

Keohane, Robert O. and Martin, Lisa L. 1995. "The Promise of Institutionalist Theory," *International Security* 20(1): 39–51.

Keohane, Robert O. and Nye, Joseph S. (eds.) 1972. *Transnational Relations and World Politics*. Cambridge: Harvard University Press.

1977. *Power and Interdependence: World Politics in Transition*. Boston: Little, Brown.

Kerr, Malcolm 1971. *The Arab Cold War 1958–1967: A Study of Ideology in Politics*, 2nd edn. Oxford: Oxford University Press.

Khalidi, Rashid 2004. *Resurrecting Empire: Western Footprints and America's Perilous Path in the Middle East*. Boston: Beacon Press.

Khong, Yuen Foong 1997. "ASEAN and the Southeast Asian Security Complex," in Lake and Morgan 1997, pp. 318–342.

Khoury, Philip and Kostiner, Joseph (eds.) 1990. *Tribes and State Formation in the Middle East*. Berkeley: University of California Press.

Kimche, David and Bavly, Dan 1968. *The Fire Storm: The Six-Day War, Its Sources and Consequences*. Tel Aviv: AM-Acefer (Hebrew).

Kimmerling, Baruch 1982. *Zionism and Territory*. Berkeley: Institute of International Studies.

King, Gary, Keohane, Robert O. and Verba, Sidney 1994. *Designing Social Inquiry: Scientific Inference in Qualitative Research*. Princeton: Princeton University Press.

Kinsella, David 1994. "Conflict in Context: Arms Transfers and Third World Rivalries During the Cold War," *American Journal of Political Science* 38(3): 557–581.

Kissinger, Henry A. 1979. *White House Years*. Boston: Little, Brown.

1982. *Years of Upheaval*. Boston: Little, Brown.

Klein, Robert A. 1974. *Sovereign Equality Among States: The History of an Idea*. Toronto: University of Toronto Press.

Knischewski, Gerd 1996. "Post-War National Identity in Germany," in Jenkins and Sofos 1996, pp. 125–151.

Kocs, Stephen A. 1995. "Territorial Disputes and Interstate War, 1945–1987," *Journal of Politics* 57(1): 159–175.

Kohn, Hans 1967. *The Idea of Nationalism: A Study in Its Origins and Background*, 3rd edn. New York: Macmillan.

Kolodziej, Edward A. and Zartman, I. William 1996. "Coping with Conflict: A Global Approach," in Kolodziej, Edward A. and Kanet, Roger E. (eds.) 1996. *Coping with Conflict After the Cold War*. Baltimore: Johns Hopkins University Press, pp. 3–34.

Korany, Bahgat 1987. "Alien and Besieged, Yet Here to Stay: The Contradictions of the Arab Territorial State," in Salame, Ghassan (ed.) 1987. *The Foundations of the Arab State*. London: Croom Helm, pp. 47–74.

1997. "The Old/New Middle East," in Guazzone 1997, pp. 135–152.

Korany, Bahgat and Dessouki, Ali E. Hillal (eds.) 1991a. *The Foreign Policies of Arab States: The Challenge of Change*. Boulder: Westview Press.

1991b. "The Global System and Arab Foreign Policies," in Korany and Dessouki 1991a, pp. 25–48.

Korany, Bahgat, Noble, Paul and Brynen, Rex (eds.) 1993. *The Many Faces of National Security in the Arab World*. London: Macmillan.

Kosev, Dimitur 1976. "Vasil Levski and the Bucharest Bulgarian Revolutionary Central Committee," in Butler, Thomas (ed.) 1976. *Bulgaria Past and Present: Studies in History, Literature, Economics, Music, Sociology, Folklore and Linguistics*. Columbus: American Association for the Advancement of Slavic Studies, pp. 54–64.

Krasner, Stephen D. (ed.) 1983. *International Regimes*. New York: Cornell University Press.

1985. *Structural Conflict: The Third World Against Global Liberalism*. Berkeley: University of California Press.

1997. "The Middle East and the End of the Cold War," in Guazzone 1997, pp. 201–215.

Krause, Keith 1992. "Arms Imports, Arms Production, and the Quest for Security in the Third World," in Job 1992, pp. 121–142.

1996. "Insecurity and State Formation in the Global Military Order," *European Journal of International Relations* 2(3): 319–354.

Kriesberg, Louis 1992. *International Conflict Resolution*. New Haven: Yale University Press.

Kumar, Radha 1997. "The Troubled History of Partition," *Foreign Affairs* 76(1): 22–34.

Kumaraswamy, P. R. 2006. "Who Am I? The Identity Crisis in the Middle East," *Middle East Review of International Affairs* 10(1): 63–73.

Kunz, Diane 1997. "The Marshall Plan Reconsidered: A Complex of Motives," *Foreign Affairs* 76(3): 162–170.

Kupchan, Charles A. 1995a. "Introduction: Nationalism Resurgent," in Kupchan 1995b, pp. 1–14.

(ed.) 1995b. *Nationalism and Nationalities in the New Europe*. Ithaca: Cornell University Press.

1998. "After Pax Americana: Benign Power, Regional Integration, and the Sources of a Stable Multipolarity," *International Security* 23(2): 40–79.

2002. *The End of the American Era*. New York: Knopf.

Kupchan, Charles A. and Kupchan, Clifford A. 1991. "Concerts, Collective Security, and the Future of Europe," *International Security* 16: 114–161.
Kurtenbach, Sabine 2002. "The Central American Conflict System: External Players and Changing Violence," in Debiel, Tobias and Klein, Axel (eds.) 2002. *Fragile Peace: State Failure, Violence and Development in Crisis Regions*. London: Zed Books, pp. 129–145.
Kuttab, Daoud 1990. "The Arabs, the West, and the Gulf Crisis," *New Outlook* 33(9): 18–19.
Labs, Eric J. 1997. "Beyond Victory: Offensive Realism and the Expansion of War Aims," *Security Studies* 6(4): 1–49.
Laitin, David 2004. "Ethnic Unmixing and Civil War," *Security Studies* 13(4): 350–365.
Lake, David A. 1997. "Regional Security Complexes: A Systems Approach," in Lake and Morgan 1997, pp 45–67.
Lake, David A. and Morgan, Patrick M. (eds.) 1997. *Regional Orders: Building Security in a New World*. University Park, PA: Penn State University Press.
Lake, David and Rothchild, Donald (eds.) 1998a. *The International Spread of Ethnic Conflict*. Princeton: Princeton University Press.
1998b. "Spreading Fear: The Genesis of Transnational Ethnic Conflict," in Lake and Rothchild 1998a, pp. 3–32.
Lampe, John R. 1996. *Yugoslavia as History*. Cambridge: Cambridge University Press.
Lang, David 1976. *The Bulgarians from Pagan Times to the Ottoman Conquest*. Southampton: Thames & Hudson.
Larrabee, S. F. 1992. "Instability and Change in the Balkans," *Survival* 34: 31–49.
Larson, Deborah 1985. *Origins of Containment: A Psychological Explanation*. Princeton: Princeton University Press.
Lauren, Paul G. 1983. "Crisis Prevention in Nineteenth-Century Diplomacy," in George et al. 1983, pp. 31–64.
1994. "Coercive Diplomacy and Ultimata: Theory and Practice in History," in George and Simons 1994, pp. 23–52.
Lawson, Fred. H. 1996. *Why Syria Goes to War: Thirty Years of Confrontation*. Ithaca: Cornell University Press.
Layne, Christopher 1993. "The Unipolar Illusion: Why New Great Powers Will Rise," *International Security* 17(4): 5–51.
Lebow, Richard Ned 1981. *Between Peace and War: The Nature of International Crisis*. Baltimore: Johns Hopkins University Press.
Lebow, Richard Ned and Risse-Kappen, Thomas (eds.) 1995. *International Relations Theory and the End of the Cold War*. New York: Columbia University Press.
Legro, Jeffrey and Moravcsik, Andrew 1999. "Is Anybody Still a Realist?," *International Security* 24: 5–55.
Lemke, Douglas 2002. *Regions of War and Peace*. Cambridge: Cambridge University Press.

Lepsius, Ranier 1985. "The Nation and Nationalism in Germany," *Social Research* 52(1): 43–64.

Levite, A., Jentleson, B. and Berman, L. (eds.) 1992. *Foreign Military Intervention: The Dynamics of Protracted Conflict*. New York: Columbia University Press.

Levy, Jack S. 1987. "Declining Power and the Preventive Motivation for War," *World Politics* 40(1): 82–107.

1989a. "The Causes of War: A Review of Theories and Evidence," in Tetlock, Philip et al. (eds.) 1989. *Behavior, Society and Nuclear War*, vol. I. New York: Oxford University Press, pp. 271–298.

1989b. "The Diversionary Theory of War: A Critique," in Midlarsky, Manus I. (ed.) 1989. *Handbook of War Studies*. Ann Arbor: University of Michigan Press, pp. 259–288.

1989c. "Domestic Politics and War," in Rotberg, Robert I. and Rabb, Theodore K. (eds.) 1989. *The Origin and Prevention of Major Wars*. Cambridge: Cambridge University Press, pp. 79–100.

1991. "Long Cycles, Hegemonic Transitions, and the Long Peace," in Kegley, Charles (ed.) 1991. *The Long Postwar Peace*. New York: HarperCollins, pp. 147–176.

1996. "Contending Theories of International Conflict: A Levels-of-Analysis Approach," in Crocker, Hampson, and Aall 1996, pp. 3–25.

1998. "The Causes of War and the Conditions of Peace," *Annual Review of Political Science* 1(1): 139–165.

2001. "Theories of Interstate and Intrastate War: A Levels of Analysis Approach to International Conflict," in Crocker, Chester A., Hampson, Fen Osler and Aall, Pamela (eds.) 2001. *Turbulent Peace: The Challenges of Managing International Conflict*. Washington, DC: USIPE, pp. 3–27.

Levy, Jack S. and Gochal, Joseph R. 2001. "Democracy and Preventive War: Israel and the 1956 Sinai Campaign," *Security Studies* 11(2): 1–49.

Levy, Marc 1995. "Is the Environment a National Security Issue?," *International Security* 20(2): 35–62.

Lewis, Bernard 1995. *The Middle East: 2000 Years of History from the Rise of Christianity to the Present Day*. London: Phoenix Giant.

1998a. *The Multiple Identities of the Middle East*. New York: Schocken.

1998b. "There Was No Genocide," *Haaretz* January (23): 66.

Lewy, Guenter 2004. "Were American Indians the Victims of Genocide?," *Commentary* 18(2): 55–63.

Liberman, Peter 1993. "The Spoils of Conquest," in M. Brown, Lynn-Jones, and Miller 1993, pp. 179–207.

Licklider, Roy E. 1976/7. "Soviet Control of Eastern Europe: Morality Versus American National Interests," *Political Science Quarterly* 91(4): 619–624.

1995. "The Consequences of Negotiated Settlements in Civil Wars, 1945–1993," *American Political Science Review* 89(3): 681–690.

Lieber, Robert J. 1995. "The American Role in a Regional Security Regime," in Inbar 1995, pp. 59–80.

Lijphart, Arend 1977. *Democracy in Plural Societies*. New Haven: Yale University Press.

Lind, Michael 1994. "In Defence of Liberal Nationalism," *Foreign Affairs* 73(3): 87–99.

Lindberg, Leon N. 1963. *The Political Dynamics of European Economic Integration*. Stanford: Stanford University Press.

Lindberg, Leon N. and Scheingold, Stuart (eds.) 1971. *Regional Integration: Theory and Research*. Cambridge: Harvard University Press.

Linden, Ronald 2000. "Putting on Their Sunday Best: Romania, Hungary, and the Puzzle of Peace," *International Studies Quarterly* 44: 119–151.

Linz, Juan J. and Stepan, Alfred 1996. *Problems of Democratic Transition and Consolidation*. Baltimore: Johns Hopkins University Press.

Lipset, Seymour Martin 1981. *Political Man: The Social Bases of Politics*, expanded edn. Baltimore: Johns Hopkins University Press.

Lobell, Steven E. and Mauceri, Philip (eds.) 2004. *Ethnic Conflict and International Politics*. New York: Palgrave.

Logoreci, Anton 1977. *The Albanians: Europe's Forgotten Survivors*. Boulder: Westview Press.

Luard, Evan 1986. *War in International Society*. New Haven: Yale University Press.

Luciani, Giacomo (ed.) 1990. *The Arab State*. London: Routledge.

Lundestad, Geir 1990. *The American "Empire" and Other Studies of US Foreign Policy in a Comparative Perspective*. Oxford: Oxford University Press.

1992. "The End of the Cold War, the New Role for Europe, and the Decline of the United States," in Hogan, Michael (ed.) 1992. *The End of the Cold War: Its Meanings and Implications*. Cambridge: Cambridge University Press, pp. 195–206.

Lustick, Ian S. 1997. "The Absence of Middle Eastern Great Powers: Political 'Backwardness' in Historical Perspective," *International Organization* 51(4): 653–683.

Luttwak, Edward N. 1995. "Toward Post-Heroic Warfare," *Foreign Affairs* 74(3): 109–122.

Lynch, John 1993. "From Independence to National Organization," in Bethell 1993, pp. 1–47.

Lynn-Jones, Sean M. 1995. "Offense–Defense Theory and Its Critics," *Security Studies* 4: 660–694.

Lynn-Jones, Sean M. and Miller, Steven E. (eds.) 1993. *The Cold War and After: Prospects for Peace*. Cambridge, MA: MIT Press.

Macdermott, Mercia 1962. *A History of Bulgaria: 1393–1885*. London: George Allen & Unwin.

MacFarlane, Neil 1992. "The Superpowers and Third World Security," in Job 1992, pp. 209–229.

MacFarlane, Neil and Weiss, Thomas G. 1992. "Regional Organizations and Regional Security," *Security Studies* 2(1): 6–37.

Mackenzie, David 1967. *The Serbs and Russian Pan-Slavism 1875–1878*. Ithaca: Cornell University Press.

Makovsky, David 1996. *Making Peace with the PLO: The Rabin Government's Road to the Oslo Accord*. Boulder: Westview Press.

Malley, Robert 2004. "Israel and the Arafat Question," *New York Review of Books* October (7): 19–23.

Mandel, Robert 1980. "Roots of the Modern Interstate Border Dispute," *Journal of Conflict Resolution* 24(3): 427–454.

Mandelbaum, Michael 1988. *The Fate of Nations*. New York: Cambridge University Press.

1996. *The Dawn of Peace in Europe*. New York: Twentieth Century Fund Press.

Mandell, Brian S. 1990. "Anatomy of a Confidence Building Regime: Egyptian–Israeli Security Co-operation, 1973–1979," *International Journal* 45(2): 202–223.

Mandell, Brian S. and Tomlin, Brian W. 1991. "Mediation in the Development of Norms to Manage Conflict: Kissinger in the Middle East," *Journal of Peace Research* 28(1): 43–56.

Mann, Michael 1993. *The Sources of Social Power*, vol. II, *The Rise of Classes and Nation-States, 1760–1914*. Cambridge: Cambridge University Press.

Mansfield, Edward D. and Snyder, Jack 1996. "Democratization and the Danger of War," in M. Brown, Lynn-Jones, and Miller 1996a, pp. 301–336.

2002. "Democratic Transitions, Institutional Strength and War," *International Organization* 56: 297–337.

2005. *Electing to Fight: Why Emerging Democracies Go to War*. Cambridge, MA: MIT Press.

Maoz, Zeev 1995. "Domestic Norms, Structural Constraints, and Enduring Rivalries in the Middle East, 1948–1988," in Garnham and Tessler 1995, pp. 170–194.

1996. *Domestic Sources of Global Change*. Ann Arbor: University of Michigan Press.

(ed.) 1997. *Regional Security in the Middle East: Past, Present and Future*. London: Frank Cass.

2001. "Democratic Networks: Connecting National, Dyadic, and Systemic Levels of Analysis in the Study of Democracy and War," in Maoz, Zeev and Gat, Azar (eds.) 2001. *War in a Changing World*. Ann Arbor: University of Michigan Press, pp. 143–182.

Maoz, Zeev and Mor, Ben 2002. *Bound by Struggle: The Strategic Evolution of Enduring International Rivalries*. Ann Arbor: University of Michigan Press.

Mares, David 1997. "Regional Conflict Management in Latin America: Power Complemented by Diplomacy," in Lake and Morgan 1997, pp. 195–218.

2001. *Latin America's Violent Peace*. New York: Columbia University Press.

Marriott, Sir John A. 1917. *The Eastern Question*. Oxford: Clarendon Press.

Marshall, Monty G. 1997. "Systems at Risk: Violence, Diffusion, and Disintegration in the Middle East," in Carment and Patrick 1997, pp. 82–115.

Massad, Joseph A. 2001. *Colonial Effects: The Making of National Identity in Jordan*. New York: Columbia University Press.
Mastanduno, Michael 1997. "Preserving the Unipolar Moment: Realist Theories and US Grand Strategy After the Cold War," *International Security* 21(4): 49–88.
Mayall, James 1990. *Nationalism and International Society*. Cambridge: Cambridge University Press.
Maynes, Charles W. 1995. "Relearning Intervention," *Foreign Policy* 98: 96–113.
McFaul, Michael 2002. "An Alliance That Really Works," *New York Times, Internet Edition*, nytimes.com, November 24.
McGarry, John 2005. "Consociationalism and Pluri-National States: Northern Ireland and Other Cases," Jerusalem: Van Leer Workshop.
McIntyre, David 1993. "'La Paz Larga': Why Are There So Few Interstate Wars in South America?," University of Chicago typescript.
McMillan, Susan 1997. "Interdependence and Conflict," *Mershon International Studies Review* 41 (supplement 1): 33–58.
Mearsheimer, John J. 1983. *Conventional Deterrence*. Ithaca: Cornell University Press.
1990. "Back to the Future: Instability in Europe After the Cold War," *International Security* 15(1): 5–56.
1994/5. "The False Promise of International Institutions," *International Security* 19(3): 5–49.
2001. *The Tragedy of Great Power Politics*. New York: W. W. Norton.
Mearsheimer, John J. and Pape, Robert 1993. "The Answer – A Partition Plan for Bosnia," *New Republic* June (14): 22–28.
Merquior, Jose G. 1987. "Patterns of State Building in Brazil and Argentina," in Hall, John (ed.) 1987. *States in History*. Oxford: Basil Blackwell, pp. 264–288.
Migdal, Joel S. 1988. *Strong Societies and Weak States: State–Society Relations and State Capabilities in the Third World*. Princeton: Princeton University Press.
Mill, John Stuart 1861. *Considerations on Representative Government*. London.
Miller, Benjamin 1981. "The Linkage Between Domestic Politics and Foreign Policy: The Case of Israel, 1953–1956," MA thesis, Hebrew University, Jerusalem.
1992a. "Explaining Great Power Cooperation in Conflict Management," *World Politics* 45: 1–46.
1992b. "A 'New World Order': From Balancing to Hegemony, Concert or Collective Security?," *International Interactions* 18: 1–33.
1994a. "Explaining the Emergence of Great Power Concerts," *Review of International Studies* 20: 327–348.
1994b. "Polarity, Nuclear Weapons, and Major War," *Security Studies* 4(3): 598–649.
1995. "International Systems and Regional Security: From Competition to Cooperation, Dominance or Disengagement?," *Journal of Strategic Studies* 18(2): 52–100.

1996. "Competing Realist Perspectives on Great Power Crisis Behavior," *Security Studies* 5(3): 309–357.
1997. "The Great Powers and Regional Peacemaking: Patterns in the Middle East and Beyond," *Journal of Strategic Studies* 20(1): 103–142.
1998. "The Logic of US Military Intervention in the Post-Cold War Era," *Contemporary Security Policy* 19(3): 72–109.
2002. *When Opponents Cooperate: Great Power Conflict and Collaboration in World Politics*, 2nd edn. Ann Arbor: University of Michigan Press.
2004. "The Rise (and Decline?) of Offensive Liberalism," paper presented at the annual meeting of the American Political Science Association, Chicago, Sep.
Miller, Benjamin and Kagan, Korina 1997. "The Great Powers and Regional Conflicts: Eastern Europe and the Balkans from the Post-Napoleonic Era to the Post-Cold War Era," *International Studies Quarterly* 41(1): 51–85.
Millington, Thomas 1996. *Colombia's Military and Brazil's Monarchy: Undermining the Republican Foundations of South American Independence*. Westport: Greenwood Press.
Milner, Helen 1993. "The Assumption of Anarchy in International Relations Theory: A Critique," in Baldwin 1993, pp. 144–169.
Minorities at Risk (MAR) Dataset 1945–2003 (stage 4), www.cidcm.umd.edu/inscr/mar/data.asp.
Mitchell, Brian R. 1999. *International Historical Statistics: The Americas, 1750–1993*. London: Palgrave Macmillan.
Mitchell, Christopher R. 1981. *The Structure of International Conflict*. New York: St. Martin's Press.
Moore, Will H. and Davis, David R. 1998. "Transnational Ethnic Ties and Foreign Policy," in Lake and Rothchild 1998a, pp. 89–103.
Moravcsik, Andrew 1997. "Taking Preferences Seriously: A Liberal Theory of International Politics," *International Organization* 51(4): 513–554.
1998. *The Choice for Europe: Social Purpose and State Power from Messina to Maastricht*. Ithaca: Cornell University Press.
2003. "Theory Synthesis in International Relations: Real Not Metaphysical," *International Studies Review* 5(1): 131–136.
Morgan, Patrick M. 1997. "Regional Security Complexes and Regional Orders," in Lake and Morgan 1997, pp. 20–44.
Morgenthau, Hans J. 1978. *Politics Among Nations*, 5th edn. New York: Knopf.
Morris, Benny 1988. *The Birth of the Palestinian Refugee Problem*. Cambridge: Cambridge University Press.
1996. *Israel's Border Wars, 1949–1956*. Tel Aviv: Am Oved (Hebrew).
2001. *Righteous Victims: A History of the Zionist–Arab Conflict, 1881–2001*. New York: Vintage Books.
Morris, Bernard S. 1994. "The End of Ideology, the End of Utopia and the End of History – On the Occasion of the End of the USSR," *History of European Ideas* 19(4): 699–708.
Mosse, George L. 1964. *The Crisis of German Ideology: The Origins of the Third Reich*. New York: Grosset & Dunlop.

Mueller, John 1989. *Retreat from Doomsday: The Obsolescence of Major War*. New York: Basic Books.

Mufti, Malik 1996. *Sovereign Creations: Pan-Arabism and Political Order in Syria and Iraq*. Ithaca: Cornell University Press.

Mychajlyszyn, Natalie and Ripsman, Norrin M. 2001. "What Ever Happened to the Bloody Post-Cold War Era?," paper presented at International Studies Association conference, Chicago, Feb.

Myers, David (ed.) 1991. *Regional Hegemons*. Boulder: Westview Press.

Nafaa, Hassan 1987. "Arab Nationalism: A Response to Ajami's Thesis on the End of Pan-Arabism," in Farah, Tawfic E. (ed.) 1987. *Pan-Arabism and Arab Nationalism*. Boulder: Westview Press, pp. 133–151.

Nahari, Oren (ed.) 2001. *Atlas of the World*. Tel Aviv: MAP – Mapping & Publishing (Hebrew).

Naimark, Norman M. 2002. *Fires of Hatred: Ethnic Cleansing in Twentieth-Century Europe*. Cambridge: Harvard University Press.

Nerlich, Uwe 1979. "Western Europe's Relations with the United States," *Daedalus* 108(1): 87–113.

Nettl, J. P. 1968. "The State as a Conceptual Variable," *World Politics* 20: 559–592.

Neuberger, Benjamin 1991. "Irredentism and Politics in Africa," in Chazan 1991, pp. 97–110.

Neuman, Stephanie 1986. *Military Assistance in Recent Wars: The Dominance of the Superpowers*. New York: Praeger.

Neumann, Iver B. (ed.) 1992. *Regional Great Powers in International Politics*. New York: St. Martin's Press.

1994. "A Region-Building Approach to Northern Europe," *Review of International Studies* 20(1): 53–74.

Nevo, Joseph 1979. "The Attitude of the Palestinian Arabs to the Jewish Community in Palestine and to the Zionist Movement," in *Zionism and the Arab Question: Collected Historical Studies*. Jerusalem: Zalman Shazar Center, pp. 163–172 (Hebrew).

Noble, Paul C. 1991. "The Arab System: Pressures, Constraints, and Opportunities," in Korany and Dessouki 1991a, pp. 49–103.

Nordlinger, Eric 1995. *Isolationism Reconfigured: American Foreign Policy for a New Century*. Princeton: Princeton University Press.

Nye, Joseph S. 1971. *Peace in Parts: Integration and Conflict in Regional Organization*. Boston: Little, Brown.

1990. *Bound to Lead: The Changing Nature of American Power*. New York: Basic Books.

1993. *Understanding International Conflicts: An Introduction to Theory and History*. New York: HarperCollins.

1996. "Conflicts After the Cold War," *Washington Quarterly* 19(1): 5–24.

2002. *The Paradox of American Power: Why the World's Only Superpower Can't Go It Alone*. New York: Oxford University Press.

O'Leary, Brendan 2003. "What States Can Do with Nation: An Iron Law of Nationalism and Federation?," in Paul, Ikenberry, and Hall 2003, pp. 51–78.

Oren, Michael 2002. *Six Days of War: June 1967 and the Making of the Modern Middle East*. New York: Oxford University Press.

Oren, Nissan (ed.) 1982. *Termination of Wars*. Jerusalem: Magnes.

Organski, A. F. K. and Kugler, Jacek 1980. *The War Ledger*. Chicago: University of Chicago Press.

Ovendale, Ritchie 1992. *The Origins of the Arab–Israeli Wars*. London: Longman.

Owen, John M. 1997. *Liberal Peace, Liberal War: American Politics and International Security*. New York: Cornell University Press.

Owen, Roger 1992. *State, Power and Politics in the Making of the Modern Middle East*. New York: Routledge.

Oye, Kenneth A. 1986. "Explaining Co-operation Under Anarchy," in Oye, Kenneth A. (ed.) 1986. *Cooperation Under Anarchy*. Princeton: Princeton University Press, pp. 1–24.

Palmer, Alan 1970. *The Lands Between: A History of East-Central Europe Since the Congress of Vienna*. London: Weidenfeld & Nicolson.

Papayoanou, Paul A. 1997. "Great Powers and Regional Orders: Possibilities and Prospects After the Cold War," in Lake and Morgan 1997, pp. 125–139.

Pape, Robert 2005. *Dying to Win: The Strategic Logic of Suicide Terrorism*. New York: Random House.

Pappe, Ilan 2004. *A History of Modern Palestine*. Cambridge: Cambridge University Press.

Paris, Roland 1997. "Peacebuilding and the Limits of Liberal Internationalism," *International Security* 22(2): 54–89.

2004. *At War's End: Building Peace After Civil Conflict*. Cambridge: Cambridge University Press.

Pastor, Robert 1992. *Whirlpool: US Foreign Policy Toward Latin America and the Caribbean*. Princeton: Princeton University Press.

Patchen, Martin 1988. *Resolving Disputes Between Nations: Coercion or Conciliation?* Durham: Duke University Press.

Paul, T. V. 1994. *Asymmetric Conflicts: War Initiation by Weaker Powers*. New York: Cambridge University Press.

Paul, T. V., Ikenberry, G. John and Hall, John A. (eds.) 2003. *The Nation-State in Question*. Princeton: Princeton University Press.

Paul, T. V., Wirtz, Jim and Fortmann, Michel (eds.) 2004. *Balance of Power: Theory and Practice in the Twenty-First Century*. Stanford: Stanford University Press

Pavlowitch, Stevan 1971. *Yugoslavia*. New York: Praeger.

Pearson, Frederic, Baumann, Robert and Pickering, Jeffrey 1994. "Military Intervention and Realpolitik," in Wayman, Frank and Diehl, Paul F. (eds.) 1994. *Reconstructing Realpolitik*. Ann Arbor: University of Michigan Press, pp. 205–226.

Peres, Shimon with Aori, Naori 1993. *The New Middle East*. New York: Henry Holt.

Perthes, Volker 1995. *The Political Economy of Syria Under Asad*. London: I. B. Tauris.

Pervin, David J. 1997. "Building Order in Arab–Israeli Relations: From Balance to Concert?," in Lake and Morgan 1997, pp. 271–295.

1998. "Global Effects on Regional Relations: Differences Between Preventive and Promoting Action," paper presented at the annual meeting of the American Political Science Association, Boston, September 3–6.

Peterson, Roger D. 2002. *Understanding Ethnic Violence: Fear, Hatred, and Resentment in Twentieth-Century Eastern Europe*. Cambridge: Cambridge University Press.

Petrowich, Michael 1956. *The Emergence of Russian Pan-Slavism, 1856–1870*. New York: Columbia University Press.

Pillar, Paul 1983. *Negotiating Peace: War Termination as a Bargaining Process*. Princeton: Princeton University Press.

Pinson, Mark 1975. "Ottoman Bulgaria in the First Tanzimat Period: The Revolts in Nish (1841) and Vidin (1850)," *Middle Eastern Studies* 11(2): 103–146.

Pipes, Daniel 1990. *Greater Syria*. New York: Oxford University Press.

1996. "Just Kidding," *New Republic* January (6): 18–19.

Podeh, Elie 1995. *The Quest for Hegemony in the Arab World: The Struggle over the Baghdad Pact*. Leiden: Brill.

2003. "From Fahd to 'Abdallah: The Origins of the Saudi Peace Initiatives and Their Impact on the Arab System and Israel," Gitelson Peace Publication no. 24. Jerusalem: Harry S Truman Research Institute for the Advancement of Peace.

Pollo, Stefanaq and Puto, Arben 1981. *The History of Albania from Its Origins to the Present Day*. London: Routledge & Kegan Paul.

Porath, Yehoshua 1974. *The Emergence of the Palestinian–Arab National Movement, 1918–1929*. London: Frank Cass.

1977. *The Palestinian Arab National Movement: From Riots to Rebellion 1929–1939*. London: Frank Cass.

1986. *In Search of Arab Unity, 1930–1945*. London: Frank Cass.

Porter, Bruce D. 1984. *The USSR in Third World Conflicts*. Cambridge: Cambridge University Press.

Posen, Barry R. 1984. *The Sources of Military Doctrine: France, Britain, and Germany Between the World Wars*. Ithaca: Cornell University Press.

1993a. "Nationalism, the Mass Army, and Military Power," *International Security* 18(2): 80–124.

1993b. "The Security Dilemma and Ethnic Conflict," in M. Brown 1993, pp. 103–124.

1996. "Military Responses to Refugee Disasters," *International Security* 21(1): 72–111.

Posen, Barry R. and Ross, Andrew L. 1996/7. "Competing Visions for US Grand Strategy," *International Security* 21(3): 5–53.

Poulton, Hugh 1995. *Who Are the Macedonians?* London: Hurst & Company.

Powell, Robert 1994. "Anarchy in International Relations Theory: The Neorealist–Neoliberal Debate," *International Organization* 48(2): 313–344.

Project Ploughshares Armed Conflicts Report 2004, www.ploughshares.ca.

PRIO/Uppsala Armed Conflict Dataset (Version 2.1) – Armed Conflict List 1946–2001 by Gleditsch, Nils Petter, Wallensteen, Peter Eriksson, Mikael, Sollenberg, Margareta and Strand, Håvard www.prio.no/page/Project_detail//9244/45926.html.

Puchala, Donald J. 1970. "Integration and Disintegration in Franco-German Relations, 1954–1965," *International Organization* 24(2): 183–208.

Puig, Juan Carlos 1983. "Controlling Latin American Conflicts: Current Juridical Trends and Perspectives for the Future," in Morris, Michael A. and Millan, Victor (eds.) 1983. *Controlling Latin American Conflicts*. Boulder: Westview Press, pp. 11–39.

Pundeff, Marin V. 1969. "Bulgarian Nationalism," in Sugar, Peter F. and Lederer, Ivo J. (eds.) 1969. *Nationalism in Eastern Europe*. Seattle: University of Washington Press, pp. 93–165.

Quandt, William 1986. *Camp David: Peacemaking and Politics*. Washington, DC: Brookings Institution Press.

1993. *Peace Process: American Diplomacy and the Arab–Israeli Conflict Since 1967*. Berkeley: University of California Press.

2001. *Peace Process: American Diplomacy and the Arab–Israeli Conflict Since 1967*, revised edn. Berkeley: University of California Press.

Rabi, Uzi and Kostiner, Joseph 1999. "The Shiis in Bahrain: Class and Religious Protest," in Bengio and Ben-Dor 1999, pp. 171–190.

Rabinovich, Itamar 1985. *The War for Lebanon, 1970–1985*. Ithaca: Cornell University Press.

1998. *The Brink of Peace: The Israeli–Syrian Negotiations*. Princeton: Princeton University Press.

Rachum, Ilan 1990. *Brazil Past and Present: The Elite and the People*. Tel Aviv: Papyris (Hebrew).

Reichman, Shalom and Golan, Arnon 1991. "Irredentism and Boundary Adjustments in Post-World War I Europe," in Chazan 1991, pp. 51–68.

Report of the International Commission to Inquire into the Causes and Conduct of the Balkan Wars, 1914. Washington, DC: Carnegie Endowment for International Peace, Division of Intercourse and Education, Publication no. 4.

Riad, Mahmoud 1981. *The Struggle for Peace in the Middle East*. London: Quartet Books.

Richardson, Louise 1999. "The Concert of Europe and Security Management in the Nineteenth Century," in Haftendorn, Helga, Keohane, Robert O. and Wallander, Celeste A. (eds.) 1999. *Imperfect Unions: Security Institutions over Time and Space*. Oxford: Oxford University Press, pp. 162–194.

Rieber, Alfred 2000. "Repressive Population Transfers in Central, Eastern and South-Eastern Europe: A Historical Overview," *Journal of Communist Studies and Transition Politics* 16: 1–27.

Ripsman, Norrin M. 2002. *Peacemaking by Democracies: The Effect of State Autonomy on the Post-World War Settlements*. University Park, PA: Penn State University Press.

2005. "Two Stages of Transition from a Region of War to a Region of Peace: Realist Transition and Liberal Endurance," *International Studies Quarterly* 49(4): 669–694

Ripsman, Norrin M. and Blanchard, Jean 1996/7. "Commercial Liberalism Under Fire: Evidence from 1914 and 1936," *Security Studies* 6(2): 5–50.

Robinson, Glenn E. 1997. *Building a Palestinian State: The Incomplete Revolution*. Bloomington: Indiana University Press.

Rock, Stephen R. 1989. *Why Peace Breaks Out: Great Power Rapprochement in Historical Perspective*. Chapel Hill: University of North Carolina Press.

Rodman, Peter W. 1994. *More Precious than Peace: The Cold War and the Struggle for the Third World*. New York: Scribner's.

Rogel, Carole 1977. *The Slovenes and Yugoslavism, 1890–1914*. Boulder: East European Quarterly.

Rose, Gideon 1998. "Neoclassical Realism and Theories of Foreign Policy," *World Politics* 51(1): 144–172.

Rosecrance, Richard N. 1986. *The Rise of the Trading State: Commerce and Conquest in the Modern World*. New York: Basic Books.

1991. "Regionalism and the Post-Cold War Era," *International Journal* 46: 373–393.

Rosecrance, Richard N. and Schott, Peter 1997. "Concerts and Regional Intervention," in Lake and Morgan 1997, pp. 140–164.

Ross, Dennis B. 1990. "The Soviet Union and the Lebanon War, 1982–1984," in Breslauer 1990, pp. 99–123.

2004. *The Missing Peace*. New York: Farrar, Straus & Giroux.

Ross, Robert (ed.) 1995. *East Asia in Transition: Toward a New Regional Order*. Armonk: M. E. Sharp.

Rotberg, Robert I. (ed.) 2003. *State Failure and State Weakness in a Time of Terror*. Washington, DC: Brookings Institution Press.

Rothstein, Robert L. 1992. "Weak Democracy and the Prospect for Peace and Prosperity in the Third World," in Brown, Sheryl J. and Schraub, Kimber M. (eds.) 1992. *Resolving Third World Conflicts: Challenges for a New Era*. Washington, DC: USIPE, pp. 15–50.

Rubin, Barry 1988. "The US, USSR, and the Conduct of Middle East Wars," in Spiegel, Steven, Heller, Mark A. and Goldberg, Jacob (eds.) 1988. *The Soviet–American Competition in the Middle East*. Lexington: Lexington Books, pp. 241–253.

2002. *The Tragedy of the Middle East*. Cambridge: Cambridge University Press.

2006. "Getting to Arab Democracy: Dealing with Communism," *Journal of Democracy* 17(1): 51–62.

Rudolph, Christopher 2003. "Globalization and Security: Migration and Evolving Conceptions of Security in Statecraft and Scholarship," *Security Studies* 13(1): 1–32.

Russett, Bruce M. 1967. *International Regions and the International System*. Chicago: Rand McNally.

1993. *Grasping the Democratic Peace: Principles for a Post-Cold War World*. Princeton: Princeton University Press.

Russett, Bruce and Oneal, John R. 2001. *Triangulating Peace: Democracy, Interdependence, and International Organizations*. New York: W. W. Norton.

Russett, Bruce M. and Starr, Harvey 1992. *World Politics: The Menu for Choice*. New York: Freeman.

Rustow, Dankwart A. 1970. "Transitions to Democracy," *Comparative Politics* 2(3): 337–363.

Rynhold, Jonathan 2005. "Why Did Oslo Fail to Reproduce the European Model of Peace: An Integrated Theoretical Explanation," paper presented at the annual meeting of Israeli Association for International Studies, April.

Sadat, Anwar 1977. *In Search of Identity*. New York: Harper & Row.

Sadowski, Yahya 2002. "The Evolution of Political Identity in Syria," in Telhami and Barnett 2002a, pp. 137–154.

Safran, Nadav 1969. *From War to War: The Arab–Israeli Confrontation, 1948–1967*. New York: Pegasus.

Saideman, Stephen M. 1997. "Explaining the International Relations of Secessionist Conflicts: Vulnerability Versus Ethnic Ties," *International Organization* 51(4): 721–753.

2001. *The Ties That Divide: Ethnic Politics, Foreign Policy, and International Conflict*. New York: Columbia University Press.

2002. "Conclusions: Thinking Theoretically About Identity and Foreign Policy," in Telhami and Barnett 2002a, pp. 169–200.

Salame, Ghassan 1988. "Inter-Arab Politics: The Return of Geography," in Quandt, William B. (ed.) 1988. *The Middle East: Ten Years After Camp David*. Washington, DC: Brookings Institution Press, pp. 344–353.

1990. "Strong and Weak States: A Qualified Return to the Muqaddimah," in Luciani 1990, pp. 29–64.

Sater, William 1986. *Chile and the War of the Pacific*. Lincoln: University of Nebraska Press.

Sayigh, Yezid 1997. *Armed Struggle and the Search for State: The Palestinian National Movement, 1949–1993*. Oxford: Oxford University Press.

Schelling, Thomas C. 1960. *The Strategy of Conflict*. Cambridge: Harvard University Press.

1966. *Arms and Influence*. New Haven: Yale University Press.

Schiff, Zeev and Yaari, Ehud 1984. *Israel's Lebanon War*. New York: Simon & Schuster.

1990. *Intifada: The Palestinian Uprising – Israel's Third Front*. New York: Simon & Schuster.

Schmitter, Philippe C. 1969. "Three Neo-Functional Hypotheses About Regional Integration," *International Organization* 23(1): 161–166.
1991. "Change in Regime Type and Progress in International Relations," in Adler, Emanuel and Crawford, Beverly (eds.) 1991. *Progress in Postwar International Relations*. New York: Columbia University Press, pp. 89–127.
Schneider, Ben Ross 1991. *Politics Within the State: Elite Bureaucrats and Industrial Policy in Authoritarian Brazil*. Pittsburgh: University of Pittsburgh Press.
Schofield, Richard N. 1991. *Kuwait and Iraq: Historical Claims and Territorial Dispute*. London: Royal Institute of International Affairs.
Schoultz, Lars 1998. *Beneath the United States: A History of US Policy Toward Latin America*. Cambridge, MA: Harvard University Press.
Schroeder, Paul 1986. "The Nineteenth-Century International System: Changes in the Structure," *World Politics* 34: 1–26.
1994. "Historical Reality vs. Neo-Realist Theory," *International Security* 19(1): 108–148.
Schulze, Hagen 1996. *States, Nations and Nationalism*. Oxford: Blackwell.
Schweller, Randall 1994. "Bandwagoning for Profit: Bringing the Revisionist State Back In," *International Security* 19: 72–107.
1996. "Neorealism's Status Quo Bias: What Security Dilemma?," *Security Studies* 5(3): 90–121.
1998. *Deadly Imbalances: Tripolarity and Hitler's Strategy of World Conquest*. New York: Columbia University Press.
Seale, Patrick 1986 [1965]. *The Struggle for Syria*. New Haven: Yale University Press.
1988. *Asad of Syria: The Struggle for the Middle East*. London: I. B. Tauris.
Seaman, Lewis 1963. *From Vienna to Versailles*. New York: Harper & Row.
Seckinger, Ron 1984. *The Brazilian Monarchy and the South American Republics, 1822–1831*. Baton Rouge: Louisiana State University Press.
Sela, Avraham 1998. *The Decline of the Arab–Israeli Conflict: Middle East Politics and the Quest for Regional Order.* Albany: SUNY Press.
Seton-Watson, Hugh 1962. *Eastern Europe Between the Wars, 1918–1941*. Hamden: Archon Books.
1977. *Nations and States: An Enquiry into the Origins of Nations and the Politics of Nationalism*. Boulder: Westview Press.
Seton-Watson, Robert W. 1969 [1911]. *The Southern Slav Question and the Habsburg Monarchy*. New York: Howard Fertig.
Shamir, Shimon 1980. "Egypt's Reorientation Towards the United States: Factors and Conditions of Decision Making," in Shaked, Haim and Rabinovich, Itamar (eds.) 1980. *The Middle East and the United States: Perceptions and Policies*. New Brunswick: Transaction, pp. 275–300.
Sharett, Moshe 1978. *A Personal Diary*, 8 vols. Tel Aviv: Maariv (Hebrew).
Sheetz, Mark 1996. "Is 'Security Cooperation' an Oxymoron? The Case of France and Germany," paper presented at meeting of the International Studies Association, San Diego, April 16–20.

Sherman, Martin and Doron, Gideon 1997. "War and Peace as Rational Choice in the Middle East," in Maoz 1997, pp. 72–102.
Shils, Edward 1975. *Center and Periphery: Essays in Macrosociology*. Chicago: University of Chicago Press.
Shin, Doh Chull 1994. "On the Third Wave of Democratization: A Synthesis and Evaluation of Recent Theory and Research," *World Politics* 47(1): 135–170.
Shlaim, Avi 1995. *War and Peace in the Middle East: A Concise History*. New York: Penguin.
2000. *The Iron Wall: Israel and the Arab World*. New York: W. W. Norton.
Shumway, Nicolas 1991. *The Invention of Argentina*. Berkeley: University of California Press.
Simmons, Beth 1999. "See You in 'Court'? The Appeal to Quasi-Judicial Legal Process in the Settlement of Territorial Disputes," in Diehl 1999, pp. 205–237.
Singer, David J. 1961. "The Level of Analysis Problem," *World Politics* 14(1): 77–92.
1997. *Cultural Composition of Interstate System Members*. Ann Arbor: University of Michigan.
Singleton, Fred 1985. *A Short History of the Yugoslav Peoples*. Cambridge: Cambridge University Press.
SIPRI 1999. Yearbook of World Armaments and Disarmament. Stockholm: Stockholm International Peace Research Institute, www.sipri.org.
2004. Yearbook of World Armaments and Disarmament. Stockholm: Stockholm International Peace Research Institute, www.sipri.org.
Sisk, Timothy D. 1996. *Power Sharing and International Mediation in Ethnic Conflicts*. Washington, DC: USIPE.
Sivan, Emmanuel 2005. *The Crush Within Islam*. Tel Aviv: Am Oved (Hebrew).
Skendi, Stavro 1967. *The Albanian National Awakening, 1878–1912*. Princeton: Princeton University Press.
Slater, Jerome 1990/1. "The Superpowers and an Arab–Israeli Political Settlement: The Cold War Years," *Political Science Quarterly* 105(4): 557–578.
Small, Melvin and Singer, J. David 1982. *Resort to Arms: International and Civil Wars, 1816–1980*. Beverly Hills: Sage.
Smith, Anthony D. 1986a. *The Ethnic Origin of Nations*. Oxford: Basil Blackwell.
1986b. "State-Making and Nation-Building," in Hall, John A. (ed.) 1986. *States in History*. Oxford: Basil Blackwell, pp. 228–263.
1991. *National Identity*. London: Penguin Books.
1993. "The Ethnic Sources of Nationalism" in M. Brown 1993, pp. 27–42.
1998. *Nationalism and Modernism*. London: Routledge.
1999. *Myths and Memories of the Nation*. Oxford: Oxford University Press.
2000. *The Nation in History*. Hanover: University Press of New England.
Smith, Tony 1994. *America's Mission: The United States and the World-Wide Struggle for Democracy in the Twentieth Century*. Princeton: Princeton University Press.

Snidal, Duncan 1985. "The Limits of Hegemonic Stability," *International Organization* 39(4): 579–614.

Snyder, Glenn H. 2002. "Mearsheimer's World-Offensive Realism and the Struggle for Security: A Review Essay," *International Security* 27(1): 149–173.

Snyder, Glenn H. and Deising, Paul 1977. *Conflict Among Nations*. Princeton: Princeton University Press.

Snyder, Jack 1990. "Averting Anarchy in the New Europe," *International Security* 14(4): 5–41.

1991. *Myths of Empire: Domestic Politics and International Ambition*. Ithaca: Cornell University Press.

2000. *From Voting to Violence: Democratization and Nationalist Conflict*. New York: W. W. Norton.

Snyder, Jack and Ballentine, Karen 1996. "Nationalism and the Marketplace of Ideas," *International Security* 21(2): 5–40.

Snyder, Jack and Jervis, Robert 1999. "Civil War and the Security Dilemma," in Walter, Barbara F. and Snyder, Jack (eds.) 1999. *Civil Wars, Insecurity, and Intervention*. New York: Columbia University Press, pp. 15–37.

Solingen, Etel 1998. *Regional Orders at Century's Dawn*. Princeton: Princeton University Press.

Spiegel, Steven 1972. *Dominance and Diversity*. Boston: Little, Brown.

1985. *The Other Arab–Israeli Conflict: Making America's Middle East Policy, from Truman to Reagan*. Chicago: University of Chicago Press.

1988. "American Middle East Policy Since the Six Day War," in Lukacs, Yehuda and Battah, Abdalla M. (eds.) 1988. *The Arab–Israeli Conflict: Two Decades of Change*. Boulder: Westview Press, pp. 199–216.

1992. "Arab–Israeli Crises, 1945–1990: The Soviet–American Dimension," in Spiegel, Steven (ed.) 1992. *Conflict Management in the Middle East*. Boulder: Westview Press, pp. 149–174.

1997. "Eagle in the Middle East," in Lieber, Robert J. (ed.) 1997. *Eagle Adrift: American Foreign Policy at the End of the Century*. New York: Longman, pp. 295–317.

Stannard, David E. 1992. *American Holocaust: The Conquest of the New World*. New York: Oxford University Press.

Starr, Harvey and Most, Benjamin A. 1976. "The Substance and Study of Borders in International Relations Research," *International Studies Quarterly* 20(4): 581–620.

Stavrianos, Leften S. 1958. *The Balkans Since 1453*. New York: Holt, Rinehart & Winston.

Stein, Arthur 1983. "Coordination and Collaboration: Regimes in an Anarchic World," in Krasner 1983, pp. 115–140.

1991. *Why Nations Cooperate: Circumstance and Choice in International Relations*. Ithaca: Cornell University Press.

Stein, Arthur and Lobell, Steven E. 1997. "Geostructuralism and International Politics," in Lake and Morgan 1997, pp. 101–124.

Stein, Janice G. 1975. "War Termination and Conflict Reduction, or How Wars Should End," *Jerusalem Journal of International Relations* 1(1): 1–27.

1985. "Calculation, Miscalculation, and Conventional Deterrence I: The View from Cairo," in Jervis, Lebow, and Stein 1985, pp. 34–59.

1987. "A Common Aversion to War: Regime Creation by Egypt and Israel as a Strategy of Conflict Management," in Ben-Dor, Gabriel and Dewitt, David B. (eds.) 1987. *Conflict Management in the Middle East*. Lexington: Lexington Books, pp. 59–78.

1988. "The Managed and the Managers: Crisis Prevention in the Middle East," in Winham, Gilbert R. (ed.) 1988. *New Issues in International Crisis Management*. Boulder: Westview Press, pp. 171–198.

1991a. "The Arab–Israeli War of 1967: Inadvertent War Through Miscalculated Escalation," in George 1991, pp. 126–159.

1991b, "Deterrence and Reassurance," in Tetlock, Philip et al. (eds.) 1991. *Behavior, Society and International Conflict*. Oxford: Oxford University Press, pp. 8–27.

1993. "The Security Dilemma in the Middle East: A Prognosis for the Decade Ahead," in Korany, Noble, and Brynen 1993, pp. 36–75.

Stepan, Alfred 1998. "Modern Multinational Democracies: Transcending a Gellnerian Oxymoron," in Hall 1998, pp. 219–242.

Stoess, Richard 1991. "Irredentism in Germany Since 1945," in Chazan 1991, pp. 69–79.

Stojanović, M. D. 1939. *The Great Powers and the Balkans, 1875–1878*. Cambridge: Cambridge University Press.

Susser, Asher 1999. "The Palestinians in Jordan," in Bengio and Ben-Dor 1999, pp. 91–110.

Sylvia, Haim G. 1976 [1962]. *Arab Nationalism: An Anthology*. Berkeley: University of California Press.

Taliaferro, Jeffrey W. 2000/1. "Security Seeking Under Anarchy: Defensive Realism Revisited," *International Security* 25(3): 128–161.

2004. *Balancing Risks: Great Power Intervention in the Periphery*. Ithaca: Cornell University Press.

Taylor, A. J. P. 1961. *The Origins of the Second World War*. New York: Atheneum.

Telhami, Shibley 1990. *Power and Leadership in International Bargaining: The Path to the Camp David Accords*. New York: Columbia University Press.

2001 "Sympathy for the Palestinians," *Washington Post* July 25.

2002. *The Stakes: America and the Middle East*. Boulder: Westview Press.

Telhami, Shibley and Barnett, Michael (eds.) 2002a. *Identity and Foreign Policy in the Middle East*. Ithaca: Cornell University Press.

2002b. "Introduction: Identity and Foreign Policy in the Middle East," in Telhami and Barnett 2002a, pp. 1–25.

Tessler, Mark and Grobschmidt, Marilyn 1995. "Democracy in the Arab World and the Arab–Israeli Conflict," in Garnham and Tessler 1995, pp. 135–169.

Ther, Philipp and Siljak, Ana (eds.) 2001. *Redrawing Nations: Ethnic Cleansing in East-Central Europe, 1944–1948*. Lanham: Rowman & Littlefield.

Thompson, William R. 1973. "The Regional Subsystem: A Conceptual Explication and a Propositional Inventory," *International Studies Quarterly* 17: 89–117.

1996. "Democracy and Peace: Putting the Cart Before the Horse?," *International Organization* 50(1): 141–174.

Thomson, David 1990. *Europe Since Napoleon*, 3rd edn. London: Penguin Books.

Thucydides [trans. by Richard Crawley] 1950. *The History of the Peloponnesian War*. New York: E. P. Dutton.

Tibi, Bassam 1998. *The Challenge of Fundamentalism: Political Islam and the New World Disorder*. Berkeley: University of California Press.

Tilly, Charles 1975a. "Reflections on the History of European State-Making," in Tilly, Charles (ed.) 1975. *The Formation of National States in Western Europe.* Princeton: Princeton University Press, pp. 3–83.

1975b. "Western State-Making," in Tilly, Charles (ed.) 1975. *The Formation of National States in Western Europe.* Princeton: Princeton University Press, pp. 601–638.

1985. "War Making and State Making as Organized Crime," in Evans, Peter B. et al. (eds.) 1985. *Bringing the State Back In.* New York: Cambridge University Press, pp. 169–191.

1990. *Coercion, Capital, and European States, AD 990–1990.* Cambridge: Basil Blackwell.

Toft, Monica Duffy 2002/3. "Indivisible Territory, Geographic Concentration, and Ethnic War," *Security Studies* 12(2): 82–119.

2003. *Geography of Ethnic Violence: Identity, Interests, and the Indivisibility of Territory.* Princeton: Princeton University Press.

Tomaszewski, Jerzy 1993. "Regional Conflicts in East and Central Europe," in Lundestad, Geir and Westad, Odd (eds.) 1993. *Beyond the Cold War: New Dimensions in International Relations*. Oslo: Scandinavian Press, pp. 145–156.

Touval, Saadia 1982. *The Peace Brokers: Mediators in the Arab–Israeli Conflict, 1948–1979*. Princeton: Princeton University Press.

1992. "The Superpowers as Mediators," in Bercovitch, Jacob and Rubin, Jeffrey Z. (eds.) 1992. *Mediation in International Relations: Multiple Approaches to Conflict Management*. New York: St. Martin's Press, pp. 232–248.

Trachtenberg, Marc 1999. *A Constructed Peace: The Making of the European Settlement, 1945–1963*. Princeton: Princeton University Press.

Treverton, Gregory 1992. *America, Germany, and the Future of Europe*. Princeton: Princeton University Press.

Tripp, Charles 2000. *A History of Iraq*. Cambridge: Cambridge University Press.

2002. "The Foreign Policy of Iraq," in Hinnebusch, Raymond and Ehteshami, Anoushiravan (eds.) 2002. *The Foreign Policies of Middle East States*. Boulder: Lynne Rienner, pp. 167–192.

Trumbore, Peter F. 2003. "Victims or Aggressors? Ethno-Political Rebellion and Use of Force in Militarized Interstate Disputes," *International Studies Quarterly* 47(2): 183–202.

Ullman, Richard 1990. "Enlarging the Zone of Peace," *Foreign Policy* 80: 102–120.

1996a. "Introduction: The World and Yugoslavia's Wars," in Ullman 1996b, pp. 1–41.

(ed.) 1996b. *The World and Yugoslavia's Wars*. New York: Council on Foreign Relations.

Uricoechea, Fernando 1980. *The Patrimonial Foundations of the Brazilian Bureaucratic State*. Berkeley: University of California Press.

Vachudova, Milada Anna 1996. "Peaceful Transformations in East-Central Europe," in M. Brown 1996, pp. 69–105.

Van den Berghe, Pierre 1983. "Class, Race, and Ethnicity in Africa," *Ethnic and Racial Studies* 6: 221–236.

Van Evera, Stephen 1990. "Why Europe Matters, Why the Third World Doesn't: American Grand Strategy After the Cold War," *Journal of Strategic Studies* 13(2): 1–51.

1993. "Primed for Peace: Europe After the Cold War," in Lynn-Jones and Miller 1993, pp. 193–243.

1994. "Hypotheses on Nationalism and War," *International Security* 18(4): 5–39.

1997. *Guide to Methods for Students of Political Science*. Ithaca: Cornell University Press.

1998. "Offense, Defense, and the Causes of War," *International Security* 22(4): 5–43.

1999. *Causes of War: Power and the Roots of Conflict*. Ithaca: Cornell University Press.

Vasquez, John A. 1993. *The War Puzzle*. Cambridge: Cambridge University Press.

1995. "Why Do Neighbors Fight? Proximity, Interaction or Territoriality," *Journal of Peace Research* 32(3): 277–293.

Vatikiotis, P. J. 1976. *The Modern History of Egypt*. Baltimore: Johns Hopkins University Press

Vayrynen, Raimo 1984. "Regional Conflict Formations: An Intractable Problem of International Relations?," *Journal of Peace Research* 21(4): 337–359.

Verheyen, Dirk 1991. *The German Question: A Cultural, Historical, and Geopolitical Exploration*. Oxford: Westview Press.

Viotti da Costa, Emilia 1989. "1879–1889," in Bethell 1989, pp. 161–216.

Vital, David 1971. *The Survival of Small States: Studies in Small Power/Great Power Conflict*. London: Oxford University Press.

Wallace, William 1995. "Regionalism in Europe: Model or Exception?," in Fawcett and Hurrell 1995, pp. 201–227.

Walt, Stephen M. 1987. *The Origins of Alliances*. Ithaca: Cornell University Press.

1989. "The Case for Finite Containment: Analyzing US Grand Strategy," *International Security* 14(1): 5–49.

1996. *Revolution and War*. Ithaca: Cornell University Press.
Walter, Barbara F. 1997. "The Critical Barrier to Civil War Settlement," *International Organization* 51(3): 335–364.
2002. *Committing to Peace: The Successful Settlement of Civil Wars*. Princeton: Princeton University Press.
2003. "Explaining the Intractability of Territorial Conflict," *International Studies Review* 5(4): 137–153.
Waltz, Kenneth N. 1959. *Man, the State and War*. New York: Columbia University Press.
1979. *Theory of International Politics*. Reading, MA: Addison-Wesley.
Walzer, Michael 1977. *Just and Unjust Wars*. New York: Basic Books.
1997. *On Toleration*. New Haven: Yale University Press.
Wang, Jianwei 2000. "Democratization and China's Nation Building," in Friedman, Edward and McCormick, Barrett L. (eds.) 2000. *What If China Doesn't Democratize? Implications for War and Peace*. New York: M. E. Sharpe, pp. 49–73.
Webb, Michael C. and Krasner, Stephen D. 1989. "Hegemonic Stability Theory: An Empirical Assessment," *Review of International Studies* 15: 183–198.
Weber, Eugene 1976. *Peasants into Frenchmen: The Modernization of Rural France*. Stanford: Stanford University Press.
Weber, Max [Roth, Guenther and Wittich, Claus (eds.)] 1978. *Economy and Society: An Outline of Interpretive Sociology*. Berkeley: University of California Press.
Weiner, Myron 1971. "The Macedonian Syndrome: A Historical Model of International Relations and Political Development," *World Politics* 23: 665–683.
1987. "Political Change: Asia, Africa and the Middle East," in Weiner, Myron and Huntington, Samuel P. (eds.) 1987. *Understanding Political Development*. Boston: Little, Brown, pp. 33–64.
1995. "Security, Stability, and International Migration," in Lynn-Jones, Sean M. and Miller, Steven E. (eds.) 1995. *Global Dangers*. Cambridge, MA: MIT Press, pp. 183–218.
Welsh, David 1993. "Domestic Politics and Ethnic Conflict," in M. Brown 1993, pp. 43–60.
Wendt, Alexander 1987. "The Agent–Structure Problem in International Relations," *International Organization* 41(3): 335–370.
1992. "Anarchy Is What States Make of It: The Social Construction of Power Politics," *International Organization* 46(2): 391–425.
1999. *Social Theory of International Relations*. New York: Cambridge University Press.
Whetten, Lawrence L. 1981. "The Arab–Israeli Dispute: Great Power Behavior," in Treverton, Gregory (ed.) 1981. *Crisis Management and the Superpowers in the Middle East*. Farnborough: Gower, pp. 44–88.
White, George W. 2000. *Nationalism and Territory*. Lanham: Rowman & Littlefield.
Wiarda, Howard and Kline, Harvey 1979. *Latin American Politics and Development*. Boulder: Westview Press.

Wight, Martin 1973. "The Balance of Power and International Order," in Alan, James (ed.) 1973. *The Bases of International Order*. London: Oxford University Press, pp. 85–115.

Williams, Kristen P. 2001. *Despite Nationalist Conflicts: Theory and Practice of Maintaining World Peace*. Westport: Praeger.

Willis, Roy 1968. *France, Germany, and the New Europe, 1945–1967*. Stanford: Stanford University Press.

Wilson, Duncan 1979. *Tito's Yugoslavia*. Cambridge: Cambridge University Press.

Wiskemann, Elizabeth 1956. "The Saar Moves Toward Germany," *Foreign Affairs* 34(2): 287–297.

Wohlforth, William C. 1993. *Elusive Balance: Power and Perceptions During the Cold War*. Ithaca: Cornell University Press.

1999. "The Stability of a Unipolar World," *International Security* 24(1): 5–41.

Wolfers, Arnold 1962. *Discord and Collaboration*. Baltimore: Johns Hopkins University Press.

Wolff, Robert Lee 1956. *The Balkans in Our Time*. Cambridge: Harvard University Press.

Woodward, Susan L. 1995. *Balkan Tragedy: Chaos and Dissolution After the Cold War*. Washington, DC: Brookings Institution Press.

Woodwell, Douglas 2004. "Unwelcome Neighbors: Shared Ethnicity and International Conflict During the Cold War," *International Studies Quarterly* 48(1): 197–223.

Wriggins, William Howard (ed.) 1992. *Dynamics of Regional Politics*. New York: Columbia University Press.

Wurmser, David 2000. "A Richer Pedigree," *Middle Eastern Quarterly* 7(4): 27–29.

Wyatt-Walter, Holly 1997. *The European Community and the Security Dilemma 1979–1992*. New York: St. Martin's Press.

Yaari, Ehud 1987. *Peace by Piece: A Decade of Egyptian Policy Toward Israel*. Washington, DC: Washington Institute for Near East Policy.

Yacobson, Alexander and Rubinstein, Amnon 2003. *Israel and the Family of Nations*. Tel Aviv: Schocken (Hebrew).

Yaniv, Avner 1987. *Dilemmas of Security: Politics, Strategy, and the Israeli Experience in Lebanon*. Oxford: Oxford University Press.

Yariv, Aaron (ed.) 1985. *War by Choice*. Tel Aviv: Hakibbutz Hameuchad Publishing House (Hebrew).

Young, Oran 1983. "Regime Dynamics: The Rise and Fall of International Regimes," in Krasner 1983, pp. 93–114.

1986. "International Regimes: Toward a New Theory of Institutions," *World Politics* 34(1): 104–122.

Zacher, Mark W. 2001. "The Territorial Integrity Norm: International Boundaries and the Use of Force," *International Organization* 55(2): 215–250.

Zacher, Mark W. and Matthew, Richard A. 1995. "Liberal International Theory: Common Threads, Divergent Strands," in Kegley 1995, pp. 107–150.

Zakaria, Fareed 1992. "Realism and Domestic Politics: A Review Essay," *International Security* 17(1): 177–198.

1997. "The Rise of Illiberal Democracy," *Foreign Affairs* 76(6): 22–43.
1998. *From Wealth to Power: The Unusual Origins of America's World Role*. Princeton: Princeton University Press.
2002. *The Future of Freedom: Illiberal Democracy at Home and Abroad*. New York: W. W. Norton.
Zamir, Meir 1999. "From Hegemony to Marginalism: The Maronites of Lebanon," in Bengio and Ben-Dor 1999, pp. 111–128.
Zartman, William I. 1995a. *Collapsed States: The Disintegration and Restoration of Legitimate Authority*. Boulder: Lynne Rienner.
1995b. "Systems of World Order and Regional Conflict Reduction," in Zartman, William I. and Kremenyuk, Victor A. (eds.) 1995. *Cooperative Security: Reducing Third World Wars*. Syracuse: Syracuse University Press, pp. 3–24.
Zartman, William I. and Rasmussen, Lewis (eds.) 1997. *Peacemaking in International Conflict*. Washington, DC: USIPE.
Zelikow, Philip 1992. "The New Concert of Europe," *Survival* 34(2): 12–30.
Zertal, Judith and Eldar, Akiva 2004. *The Lords of the Land: The Settlers and the State of Israel 1967–2004*. Or Yehuda: Kinnert, Zmora-Bitan & Dvir (Hebrew).
Zisser, Eyal 1999. "The Alawis, Lords of Syria: From Ethnic Minority to Ruling Sect," in Bengio and Ben-Dor 1999, pp. 129–148.

Index

CAMBRIDGE STUDIES IN INTERNATIONAL RELATIONS

92 *Paul Keal*
European conquest and the rights of indigenous peoples
The moral backwardness of international society

91 *Barry Buzan and Ole Waever*
Regions and powers
The structure of international security

90 *A. Claire Cutler*
Private power and global authority
Transnational merchant law in the global political economy

89 *Patrick M. Morgan*
Deterrence now

88 *Susan Sell*
Private power, public law
The globalization of intellectual property rights

87 *Nina Tannenwald*
The nuclear taboo
The United States and the non-use of nuclear weapons since 1945

86 *Linda Weiss*
States in the global economy
Bringing domestic institutions back in

85 *Rodney Bruce Hall and Thomas J. Biersteker (eds.)*
The emergence of private authority in global governance

84 *Heather Rae*
State identities and the homogenisation of peoples

83 *Maja Zehfuss*
Constructivism in international relations
The politics of reality

82 *Paul K. Ruth and Todd Allee*
The democratic peace and territorial conflict in the twentieth century

81 *Neta C. Crawford*
Argument and change in world politics
Ethics, decolonization and humanitarian intervention

80 *Douglas Lemke*
Regions of war and peace

79 *Richard Shapcott*
Justice, community and dialogue in international relations

78 *Phil Steinberg*
The social construction of the ocean

77 *Christine Sylvester*
Feminist international relations
An unfinished journey

76 *Kenneth A. Schultz*
Democracy and coercive diplomacy

75 *David Houghton*
US foreign policy and the Iran hostage crisis

74 *Cecilia Albin*
Justice and fairness in international negotiation

73 *Martin Shaw*
Theory of the global state
Globality as an unfinished revolution

72 *Frank C. Zagare and D. Marc Kilgour*
Perfect deterrence

71 *Robert O'Brien, Anne Marie Goetz, Jan Aart Scholte and Marc Williams*
Contesting global governance
Multilateral economic institutions and global social movements

70 *Roland Bleiker*
Popular dissent, human agency and global politics

69 *Bill McSweeney*
Security, identity and interests
A sociology of international relations

68 *Molly Cochran*
Normative theory in international relations
A pragmatic approach

67 *Alexander Wendt*
Social theory of international politics

66 *Thomas Risse, Stephen C. Ropp and Kathryn Sikkink (eds.)*
The power of human rights
International norms and domestic change

65 *Daniel W. Drezner*
The sanctions paradox
Economic statecraft and international relations

64 *Viva Ona Bartkus*
The dynamic of secession

63 *John A. Vasquez*
The power of power politics
From classical realism to neotraditionalism

62 *Emanuel Adler and Michael Barnett (eds.)*
Security communities

61 *Charles Jones*
E. H. Carr and international relations
A duty to lie

60 *Jeffrey W. Knopf*
Domestic society and international cooperation
The impact of protest on US arms control policy

59 *Nicholas Greenwood Onuf*
The republican legacy in international thought

58 *Daniel S. Geller and J. David Singer*
Nations at war
A scientific study of international conflict

57 *Randall D. Germain*
The international organization of credit
States and global finance in the world economy

56 *N. Piers Ludlow*
Dealing with Britain
The Six and the first UK application to the EEC

55 *Andreas Hasenclever, Peter Mayer and Volker Rittberger*
Theories of international regimes

54 *Miranda A. Schreurs and Elizabeth C. Economy (eds.)*
The internationalization of environmental protection

53 *James N. Rosenau*
Along the domestic–foreign frontier
Exploring governance in a turbulent world

52 *John M. Hobson*
The wealth of states
A comparative sociology of international economic and political change

51 *Kalevi J. Holsti*
The state, war, and the state of war

50 *Christopher Clapham*
Africa and the international system
The politics of state survival

49 *Susan Strange*
The retreat of the state
The diffusion of power in the world economy

48 *William I. Robinson*
Promoting polyarchy
Globalization, US intervention, and hegemony

47 *Roger Spegele*
Political realism in international theory

46 *Thomas J. Biersteker and Cynthia Weber (eds.)*
State sovereignty as social construct

45 *Mervyn Frost*
Ethics in international relations
A constitutive theory

44 *Mark W. Zacher with Brent A. Sutton*
Governing global networks
International regimes for transportation and communications

43 *Mark Neufeld*
The restructuring of international relations theory

42 *Thomas Risse-Kappen (ed.)*
Bringing transnational relations back in
Non-state actors, domestic structures and international institutions

41 *Hayward R. Alker*
Rediscoveries and reformulations
Humanistic methodologies for international studies

40 *Robert W. Cox with Timothy J. Sinclair*
Approaches to world order

39 *Jens Bartelson*
A genealogy of sovereignty

38 *Mark Rupert*
Producing hegemony
The politics of mass production and American global power

37 *Cynthia Weber*
Simulating sovereignty
Intervention, the state and symbolic exchange

36 *Gary Goertz*
Contexts of international politics

35 *James L. Richardson*
Crisis diplomacy
The Great Powers since the mid-nineteenth century

34 *Bradley S. Klein*
Strategic studies and world order
The global politics of deterrence

33 *T. V. Paul*
Asymmetric conflicts: war initiation by weaker powers

32 *Christine Sylvester*
Feminist theory and international relations in a postmodern era

31 *Peter J. Schraeder*
US foreign policy toward Africa
Incrementalism, crisis and change

30 *Graham Spinardi*
From Polaris to Trident: the development of US Fleet Ballistic Missile technology

29 *David A. Welch*
Justice and the genesis of war

28 *Russell J. Leng*
Interstate crisis behavior, 1816–1980: realism versus reciprocity

27 *John A. Vasquez*
The war puzzle

26 *Stephen Gill (ed.)*
Gramsci, historical materialism and international relations

25 *Mike Bowker and Robin Brown (eds.)*
From cold war to collapse: theory and world politics in the 1980s

24 *R. B. J. Walker*
Inside/outside: international relations as political theory

23 *Edward Reiss*
The strategic defense initiative

22 *Keith Krause*
Arms and the state: patterns of military production and trade

21 *Roger Buckley*
US–Japan alliance diplomacy 1945–1990

20 *James N. Rosenau and Ernst-Otto Czempiel (eds.)*
Governance without government: order and change in world politics

19 *Michael Nicholson*
Rationality and the analysis of international conflict

18 *John Stopford and Susan Strange*
Rival states, rival firms
Competition for world market shares

17 *Terry Nardin and David R. Mapel (eds.)*
Traditions of international ethics

16 *Charles F. Doran*
Systems in crisis
New imperatives of high politics at century's end

15 *Deon Geldenhuys*
Isolated states: a comparative analysis

14 *Kalevi J. Holsti*
Peace and war: armed conflicts and international order 1648–1989

13 *Saki Dockrill*
Britain's policy for West German rearmament 1950–1955

12 *Robert H. Jackson*
Quasi-states: sovereignty, international relations and the Third World

11 *James Barber and John Barratt*
South Africa's foreign policy
The search for status and security 1945–1988

10 *James Mayall*
Nationalism and international society

9 *William Bloom*
Personal identity, national identity and international relations

8 *Zeev Maoz*
National choices and international processes

7 *Ian Clark*
The hierarchy of states
Reform and resistance in the international order

6 *Hidemi Suganami*
The domestic analogy and world order proposals

5 *Stephen Gill*
American hegemony and the Trilateral Commission

4 *Michael C. Pugh*
The ANZUS crisis, nuclear visiting and deterrence

3 *Michael Nicholson*
Formal theories in international relations

2 *Friedrich V. Kratochwil*
Rules, norms, and decisions
On the conditions of practical and legal reasoning in international relations and domestic affairs

1 *Myles L. C. Robertson*
Soviet policy towards Japan
An analysis of trends in the 1970s and 1980s